INSTRUCTOR'S MANUAL
WITH TEST BANK

for Murrin, Johnson, McPherson,
Gerstle, Rosenberg, & Rosenberg's

Liberty, Equality, Power

VOLUME I: TO 1877

INSTRUCTOR'S MANUAL
WITH TEST BANK

for Murrin, Johnson, McPherson, Gerstle, Rosenberg, *&* Rosenberg's

Liberty, Equality, Power
A History of the American People

VOLUME I: TO 1877

FOURTH EDITION

Pat Ledbetter
North Central Texas College

THOMSON
WADSWORTH

Australia • Canada • Mexico • Singapore • Spain • United Kingdom • United States

Printed in the United States of America
2 3 4 5 6 7 08 07 06 05

Printer: West Group

ISBN 0-534-62751-X

For more information about our products, contact us at:
Thomson Learning Academic Resource Center
1-800-423-0563
For permission to use material from this text or product, submit a request online at
http://www.thomsonrights.com
Any additional questions about permissions can be submitted by email to thomsonrights@thomson.com

Thomson Wadsworth
10 Davis Drive
Belmont, CA 94002-3098
USA

Asia
Thomson Learning
5 Shenton Way #01-01
UIC Building
Singapore 068808

Australia/New Zealand
Thomson Learning
102 Dodds Street
Southbank, Victoria 3006
Australia

Canada
Nelson
1120 Birchmount Road
Toronto, Ontario M1K 5G4
Canada

Europe/Middle East/South Africa
Thomson Learning
High Holborn House
50/51 Bedford Row
London WC1R 4LR
United Kingdom

Latin America
Thomson Learning
Seneca, 53
Colonia Polanco
11560 Mexico D.F.
Mexico

Spain/Portugal
Paraninfo
Calle/Magallanes, 25
28015 Madrid, Spain

PREFACE

This combined Instructor's Manual and Test Bank is intended as a teaching supplement and as a guide for assembling exams that evaluate the reading level, analytical skills, and specific knowledge of American history students. It is designed to be used in conjunction with Murrin, Johnson, McPherson, Gerstle, Rosenberg and Rosenberg's *Liberty Equality Power: A History of the American People,* Fourth Edition.

The Test Bank contains Multiple Choice, True/False, Fill-Ins, Identifications, Short Essays, and Long Essay questions for each chapter. The answer key immediately follows each objective question and contains the following information: **TYPE** references the question type; **KEY 1** references the type of learning objective; **KEY 2** references the level of difficulty; and **PAGE** references the text page or pages on which the correct answer is located.

TYPE	KEY 1	KEY 2	PAGE
M Multiple Choice	A Analytical	1 Least difficult	Page number(s)
T True/False	F Factual	2 Average	
F Fill-Ins		3 Most difficult	

In addition to the test questions, each chapter contains the following sections:

- Chapter Outline—outline of key chapter topics
- Chronology—timeline of events or movements during the period covered by that chapter
- Thematic Topics for Enrichment—suggested topics for classroom discussion
- Suggested Essay Topics—ideas for written essay assignments or exams
- Lecture Outline—outline of the chapter's content, including references to the Wadsworth U.S. History Overhead Transparencies to aid in lecture planning and preparation
- Teaching Resources—listing of video resources to augment classroom lectures

These materials are intended as teaching aids that will help the instructor organize materials for courses using this textbook

TABLE OF CONTENTS

CHAPTER 1
WHEN OLD WORLDS COLLIDE: CONTACT, CONQUEST, CATASTROPHE

CHAPTER OUTLINE

I.   Peoples in Motion
    A.   From Beringia to the Americas
    B.   The Great Extinction and the Rise of Agriculture
    C.   The Polynesians and Hawaii
    D.   The Norsemen

II. Europe and the World in the 15th Century
    A.   China: The Rejection of Overseas Expansion
    B.   Europe versus Islam
    C.   The Legacy of the Crusades
    D.   The Unlikely Pioneer: Portugal
    E.   Africa, Colonies, and the Slave Trade
    F.   Portugal's Asian Empire
    G.   Early Lessons

III. Spain, Columbus, and the Americas
    A.   Columbus
    B.   Spain and the Caribbean

IV. The Emergence of Complex Societies in the Americas
    A.   The Rise of Sedentary Culture
    B.   The Andes: Cycles of Complex Cultures
    C.   Inca Civilization
    D.   Mesoamerica: Cycles of Complex Cultures
    E.   The Aztecs and Tenochtitlán
    F.   North American Mound Builders
    G.   Urban Cultures of the Southwest

V.   Contact and Cultural Misunderstanding
    A.   Religious Dilemmas
    B.   War as Cultural Misunderstanding
    C.   Gender and Cultural Misunderstanding

VI. Conquest and Catastrophe
    A.   The Conquest of Mexico and Peru
    B.   North American *Conquistadores* and Missionaries
    C.   The Spanish Empire and Demographic Catastrophe
    D.   Brazil
    E.   Global Colossus, Global Economy

VII. Explanations: Patterns of Conquest, Submission, and Resistance

VIII. Conclusion

CHRONOLOGY

50,000-10,000 B.C.	Migrations over Beringia into the Americas.
9000-8000 B.C.	Clovis-tip hunter-gatherer culture spreads throughout North America.
5000 B.C.–700 B.C.	Louisiana moundbuilders' culture extends through southeastern North America.
500 B.C–A.D. 400	Adena–Hopewell moundbuilders flourish in the Ohio Valley.
A.D. 874	Norsemen reach Iceland.
A.D. 982	Norse settle Greenland.
A.D. 900–1200	Anasazi culture expands through southwest North America.
1001–1014	Leif Erikson leads three voyages to North America.
	Norse found Newfoundland

1347–1351	Bubonic plague, the "Black Death," decimates one-third of the European population.
1400–1450	Aztec and Incan conquests of, respectively, Mesoamerica and Andean South America.
1404–1434	Cheng Ho makes voyages of exploration for China.
1434	Gil Eannes rounds Cape Bojador and returns safely to Portugal.
1430s	Johann Gutenberg invents movable-type printing press.
1440s	Portuguese enter the African slave trade.
1492	Spanish victory at Granada results in overthrow of last outpost of Islam in Iberia.
	Christopher Columbus's first voyage to the Western Hemisphere.
1494	Treaty of Tordesillas divides non-Christian world between Spanish and Portuguese.
1497–1499	Vasco da Gama sails to India and back.
1500	Portuguese discover Brazil.
1501	First slaves carried from Africa to the Americas.
1513	Vasco Núñez de Balboa crosses Isthmus of Panama to Pacific
1519	Ferdinand Magellan sets sail from Seville, Spain, beginning the first circumnavigation of the globe.
	Hernán Cortés begins conquest of Aztecs.
1528–1536	Cabeza de Vaca travels overland from Florida to Mexico.
1531–1532	Francisco Pizarro leads expedition against the Inca.
1539–1543	Hernando de Soto's expedition through the southeastern part of North America.
1540–1542	Francisco de Coronado's expedition through the southwestern part of North America.
1540s	Spanish assume control over the silver mines at Potosí.
1570–1571	First Spanish Jesuit mission in Chesapeake Bay.
1580	Philip II unites the Spanish and Portuguese empires.

THEMATIC TOPICS FOR ENRICHMENT

1. What elements of world geography did Columbus possess knowledge of right before setting out in 1492? What elements did he have wrong?

2. Give examples of the biological, environmental, and cultural consequences of the Columbian Exchange.

3. Discuss the use of the word *catastrophe* to describe the results of "Old Worlds Colliding" in the fifteenth and sixteenth centuries.

4. List the merits and detractions of the following terms used to identify the peoples of the Americas: Indians, Americans, Amerindians, Natives, Native Americans.

5. Contrast the various peoples who came to the Americas before 1600. Why did some stay, but others did not?

6. Explain the statement: "In 1400, Europe stood at the edge, not the center, of world commerce."

7. Discuss the rise of Portugal as a seaborne empire in the fifteenth century. Why does the text call it an "unlikely pioneer"?

8. What were Columbus's motives in 1492, and what were those of the Spaniards who followed him to the Americas?

9. How did the Spanish conquistadors manage to subdue the great Amerindian civilizations of the Aztecs and the Inca?

10. Contrast the idealism and chauvinism of the missionary efforts in the Western Hemisphere.

SUGGESTED ESSAY TOPICS

1. After 500 years, how has our evaluation of Columbus's voyages changed?

2. What advantages did Europeans have over other civilizations in 1500? What disadvantages did they turn to their ultimate benefit?

3. Create your own accounts of the conquest of the Aztec civilization from the contrasting points of view of Moctezuma and Cortés. In what ways can the conflict be described as a "cultural misunderstanding"?

4. What were the basic mechanisms of the slave trade? Assess the relationship of slavery and the conquest of the Western Hemisphere.

LECTURE OUTLINE

1. The story of the settlement of the Americas is only one part of a larger epic of **peoples in motion,** of which the Western Hemisphere was only one destination.

   a. The first immigrants traveled from **Beringia to the Americas** over the land bridge created during the last Ice Age.

   (SHOW TRANSPARENCY 1: NORTH AMERICAN MIGRATION AND SETTLEMENT)

   b. Advanced weaponry coupled with climatic changes led to the **great extinction** of the large mammals upon which the bands of hunters depended; extinction led to the **rise of agriculture** in the aftermath of the last Ice Age.

   c. Peoples from the north, **Norsemen,** traveled from the upper reaches of Europe to North America long before Columbus's voyages.

2. **Europe in the fifteenth century** was just one part of a world that encompassed myriad complex and competing societies.

   a. For reasons that are not entirely clear, **China,** the world's most populous country and in many ways its most advanced, rejected any organized plan of **overseas expansion.**

   b. One key theme of fifteenth-century expansion was the persistent competition of **Europe versus Islam,** which included the cultural **legacy of the Crusades** and bitter enmity.

   c. Portugal was the **unlikely pioneer** of European expansion, as the nation of only several hundred thousand established a remarkable empire in Africa, India, and Asia; its experiences and instigation of the **slave trade** provided the rest of Europe with important early lessons.

   (SHOW TRANSPARENCY 2: AFRICAN TRADE ROUTES, 15TH CENTURY)

   d. Much larger and more populous than its neighbor, **Spain** followed closely on Portugal's heels and soon eclipsed it in the race for an Atlantic empire.

i.   Sailing under the Spanish flag, **Christopher Columbus** accidentally found the Americas.

(SHOW TRANSPARENCY 3: COLUMBUS'S FIRST VOYAGE, 1492)

ii.   Spain quickly established an empire in the **Caribbean** in the aftermath of Columbus's expeditions.

3.   The centuries before Columbus witnessed the **emergence of complex societies in the Americas.**

a.   The rise of **sedentary cultures** occurred throughout the Americas.

i.   The **Andes** contained a number of **cycles of complex cultures,** culminating in the **Inca civilization,** which thrived on its ingenious methods of terrace agriculture.

ii.   **Mesoamerica** also featured successive cycles of complex cultures, including the **Aztecs and Tenochtitlán, North American moundbuilders,** and **urban cultures of southwest North America.**

(SHOW TRANSPARENCY 4: INCA EMPIRE AND PRINCIPAL EARLIER CULTURES; AND TRANSPARENCY 6: NATIVE AMERICAN REGIONS, 1492)

4.   1492 marked the first permanent contact; shortly thereafter, **cultural misunderstandings,** particularly over issues of religion and gender, resulted in conflict and open warfare.

5.   By the turn of the century, cultural misunderstandings resulted in **conquest and catastrophe.**

a.   Hernán Cortés led a band of less than a thousand men in the **conquest of Mexico,** while little more than a decade later the **Pizarro brothers** brutally subdued the Incas in Peru.

(SHOW TRANSPARENCY 5: MEXICO UNDER THE AZTECS)

b.   **North American conquistadors and missionaries** soon spread out from the Caribbean, simultaneously spreading Christianity and establishing Spanish dominion.

(SHOW TRANSPARENCY 7: PRINCIPAL SPANISH EXPLORATIONS OF NORTH AMERICA)

6.   Through the sixteenth century, the Spaniards erected a remarkable **Empire** while unleashing a **demographic catastrophe** on the Indians.

7.   Spanish and other European seamen copied Portuguese activities in **Brazil,** creating the beginnings of a **global economy** based largely upon slave labor and staple crop production.

(SHOW TRANSPARENCY 8: SPANISH EMPIRE AND GLOBAL LABOR SYSTEM)

8.   Historians have suggested many conflicting explanations for the various **patterns of conquest, submission, and resistance** in the century following Columbus's voyages.

American Album: Global Empire: The Aesthetics of Power

Conclusion: By accident, on October 12, 1492, Christopher Columbus found America. From then on, and for the next several hundred years, Europeans contested for domination of the Western Hemisphere. The costs were high, and the consequences for the peoples of Europe, Africa, and the Americas proved immeasurable. For the indigenous peoples of the Western Hemisphere, the consequences of contact proved catastrophic.

TEACHING RESOURCES

Vikings! is a nine-part series "through the legendary world" of the Norsemen, narrated by Magnus Magnusson. PBS Video (running time is about 60 minutes per tape).

Vikings in North America offers a briefer account of the early expeditions. A&E (50 minutes).

Surviving Columbus: The Story of the Pueblo People, tells "the other side of history-as viewed by America's Pueblo people." PBS Home Video (52 minutes).

The First Americans reviews likely migration across Beringia into the Americas and is based on meteorological and archeological evidence. Filmic Archives (53 minutes).

Mesa Verde National Park is an archeological exploration through this Colorado national park, featuring Robert H. Lister, one of the United States' foremost anthropologists of the Anasazi civilization. Holiday Video Library (60 minutes).

Ferdinand and Isabella tells the story of the Spanish monarchy in the age of Columbus. Filmic Archives (30 minutes).

Central America: The Burden of Time explores the ways the Aztecs and Mayans developed civilization isolated from the rest of the world. Filmic Archives (60 minutes).

The Search for Ancient Americans attempts to unlock the secrets of the American past through the examination of five archeological landmarks. Filmic Archives (58 minutes).

Cannibals! examines missionary tales of human sacrifice and consumption in light of European bias and the historical record. Were the tales of cannibalism fantasy or fact? Films for the Humanities (28 minutes).

The Shape of the World: Staking a Claim details the Spanish conquistadors as they wreaked havoc upon the Mesoamerican and South American civilizations. Filmic Archives (55 minutes).

Ten Who Dared: Francisco Pizarro recreates this Spaniard's dramatic expedition of discovery and conquest. BBC/Time-Life Video (52 minutes).

Mysteries of Peru: Enigma of the Ruins explores in detail the remarkable and sophisticated Inca civilization of the Andes. Filmic Archives (50 minutes).

MULTIPLE CHOICE

1. Human habitation of the Americas began approximately
    a. 500,000 years ago.
    b. 100,000 years ago.
    c. 14,000 years ago.
    d. 5,000 years ago.
    e. 500 years ago.

ANS: C   **TYPE: M**   **KEY 1: F**   **KEY 2: 2**   **PAGE: 4**

2. The Americas were first settled by
   a. Asians.
   b. western Europeans.
   c. eastern Europeans.
   d. Africans.
   e. Europeans.

ANS: A   TYPE: M   KEY 1: F   KEY 2: 1   PAGE: 4

3. The leader of the Norsemen who settled in Greenland was
   a. King Harold.
   b. Erik the Red.
   c. Prester John.
   d. Leif Eriksson.
   e. Columbus.

ANS: B   TYPE: M   KEY 1: F   KEY 2: 2   PAGE: 7

4. The nation that led the way for European expansion into the Americas was
   a. France.
   b. England.
   c. China.
   d. Portugal.
   e. Spain

ANS: E   TYPE: M   KEY 1: F   KEY 2: 2   PAGE: 9

5. The early civilizations of America were basically _____ age cultures.
   a. bronze
   b. stone
   c. wood
   d. iron
   e. agricultural

ANS: B   TYPE: M   KEY 1: A   KEY 2: 2   PAGE: 18

6. The earliest Native American civilization to leave detailed written records of their activities were the
   a. Aztec.
   b. Texaca.
   c. Cherokee
   d. Olmec.
   e. Maya.

ANS: E   TYPE: M   KEY 1: F   KEY 2: 2   PAGE: 23

7. The leading practitioners of human sacrifice in the Americas were the
   a. Maya.
   b. Incas.
   c. Aztec.
   d. Olmec.
   e. Spaniards.

ANS: C   TYPE: M   KEY 1: F   KEY 2: 2   PAGE: 25

8. The leader of the Aztecs at the time of their defeat was
    a. Atahualpa.
    b. Moctezuma.
    c. Tenochtitlan.
    d. Texcoco.
    e. Geronimo.

ANS: B   TYPE: M   KEY 1: F   KEY 2: 2   PAGE: 31

9. The major source of wealth exploited by the Spaniards in the Americas was
    a. gold.
    b. silver.
    c. tobacco.
    d. cotton.
    e. iron

ANS: B   TYPE: M   KEY 1: F   KEY 2: 2   PAGE: 34

10. The European discoverer of the Grand Canyon was
    a. Francisco de Coronado.
    b. Amerigo Vespucci.
    c. Francisco Pizarro.
    d. Hernan Cortés.
    e. Prince Henry

ANS: A   TYPE: M   KEY 1: F   KEY 2: 2   PAGE: 34

11. The system of labor control that allowed a person to exploit the labor force for a certain period of time was called
    a. *hacienda.*
    b. *encomienda.*
    c. *bandeirante.*
    d. *requerimiento.*
    e. *casa grande*

ANS: B   TYPE: M   KEY 1: F   KEY 2: 2   PAGE: 38

12. The most devastating weapon brought to the Americas by the Europeans was
    a. the horse
    b. gunpowder.
    c. cannon.
    d. bronze weaponry.
    e. disease.

ANS: E   TYPE: M   KEY 1: F   KEY 2: 2   PAGE: 38

13. In the period 1530 to 1630, the population of Mexico and Peru decreased by approximately
    a. 10 percent.
    b. 25 percent.
    c. 50 percent.
    d. 90 percent.
    e. 100 percent

ANS: D   TYPE: M   KEY 1: A   KEY 2: 2   PAGE: 38

14. Unlike the Spanish in America, Portugal did not attempt to rule the Indian population directly, but attempted to
    a. use it as labor.
    b. remove it to Portugal.
    c. enslave and eventually replace it.
    d. Christianize it
    e. exterminate it.

ANS: C   **TYPE: M**   **KEY 1: F**   **KEY 2: 2**   **PAGE: 38**

15. The most likely reason for European success in conquering the American Indian population is
    a. the prolonged isolation of the Americas from the rest of the world.
    b. the superiority of European civilizations.
    c. the warlike savagery of the Europeans.
    d. the passivity of Native Americans.
    e. the success of the priests in converting them to Christianity.

ANS: A   **TYPE: M**   **KEY 1: A**   **KEY 2: 2**   **PAGE: 40**

16. Who of the following was the conqueror of the Inca empire?
    a. Francisco Pizarro
    b. Hernán Cortés
    c. Francisco de Coronado
    d. Vasco da Gama
    e. Bishop de las Casas.

ANS: A   **TYPE: M**   **KEY 1: F**   **KEY 2: 2**   **PAGE: 32**

17. Each of the following could be referred to as a *conquistador* except
    a. Hernán Cortés.
    b. Francisco Pizarro.
    c. Vasco da Gama.
    d. Francisco de Coronado.
    e. Hernando de Soto

ANS: C   **TYPE: M**   **KEY 1: F**   **KEY 2: 2**   **PAGE: 13**

18. By the mid-sixteenth century, the most powerful nation in Europe was
    a. England.
    b. France.
    c. Spain.
    d. Portugal.
    e. Germany

ANS: C   **TYPE: M**   **KEY 1: F**   **KEY 2: 2**   **PAGE: 38**

19. The Chinese developed all of the following except
    a. movable type.
    b. gunpowder.
    c. paper money.
    d. the compass.
    e. a complex political system.

ANS: A   **TYPE: M**   **KEY 1: F**   **KEY 2: 1**   **PAGE: 8**

20. The major reason that western Europe engaged in explorations in the fifteenth century was
    a. the desire to spread Christianity.
    b. to control the oceans.
    c. to expand trade with the non-Christian world.
    d. to export domestic products.
    e. to escape the Black Death.

ANS: C   TYPE: M   KEY 1: A   KEY 2: 2   PAGE: 9-10

21. Most of the native languages of North and South America were
    a. derived from the Amerind language.
    b. completely eradicated by the introduction of European languages.
    c. a combination of Germanic and Asian linguistics.
    d. already developed as written languages before the arrival of the Europeans.
    e. understandable to the Europeans.

ANS: A   TYPE: M   KEY 1: F   KEY 2: 2   PAGE: 4

22. All of the following were food crops grown in the Americas during the late Stone Age (Neolithic) except
    a. maize.
    b. white potatoes.
    c. tomatoes.
    d. oranges.
    e. squash.

ANS: D   TYPE: M   KEY 1: F   KEY 2: 2   PAGE: 6

23. By 1400, western European society was
    a. self-sufficient and had no interest in trading with Asia.
    b. primarily interested in importing gold and silver from Russia.
    c. backward and isolated when compared with Chinese and Islamic societies.
    d. scientifically and mathematically the most advanced culture in the world.
    e. not influenced by religion.

ANS: C   TYPE: M   KEY 1: A   KEY 2: 3   PAGE: 8

24. The crusades influenced European expansion by
    a. establishing permanent Christian control of the holy city of Jerusalem.
    b. demonstrating that the Arab nations of the East were weak and easily defeated.
    c. developing a colonial economic system based on the production of staple crops by slave labor.
    d. discouraging trade with Asian and African nations.
    e. providing slaves for the plantations in the Caribbean.

ANS: C   TYPE: M   KEY 1: A   KEY 2: 3   PAGE: 9

25. Which of the following is true of the Atlantic slave trade in the late fifteenth century and thereafter?
    a. Most slaves were taken by Europeans who raided coastal villages and enslaved the inhabitants.
    b. Slavery did not exist in Africa until the Europeans introduced it.
    c. Most slaves were first enslaved by other Africans and then were sold to European traders.
    d. The Portuguese opposed slavery and tried to prevent its extension to the New World.
    e. Most slaves were Native Americans.

ANS: C   TYPE: M   KEY 1: F   KEY 2: 3   PAGE: 11

26. Which of the following was true of Christopher Columbus?
    a. He was the first person to believe that the Earth is round.
    b. He was an Italian navigator whose four voyages to the West were financed by the Spanish.
    c. He accurately calculated the circumference of the Earth to be 26,000 miles.
    d. He received land, titles, and wealth from his discoveries and died the richest commoner in Europe.
    e. He rejected offers from England and Portugal to finance his voyages.

ANS: B   TYPE: M   KEY 1: F   KEY 2: 3   PAGE: 14-15

27. Before the arrival of the Europeans, the Indian societies of the Americas
    a. were all primitive, nomadic hunters and gatherers.
    b. were democratic cultures in which all members, including women, could vote.
    c. used bronze and iron for tools and weapons.
    d. had all developed a written language.
    e. were Stone Age cultures

ANS: E   TYPE: M   KEY 1: A   KEY 2: 2   PAGE: 18

28. The mound builders and the Anasazi were similar in that both
    a. were complex societies that developed north of Mexico.
    b. depended on the horse as the major beast of burden.
    c. were primarily hunter-warrior societies.
    d. were the ancestors of the Mayans and the Aztecs.
    e. had developed a written language.

ANS: A   TYPE: M   KEY 1: A   KEY 2: 3   PAGE: 29

29. Most European Christians viewed the Indians as
    a. innocent, childlike people who should be treated kindly.
    b. descendants of the ancient survivors of the lost continent of Atlantis.
    c. subhuman, soulless devil worshippers.
    d. sophisticated people who were morally and ethically superior to the inhabitants of Asia and Europe.
    e. one of the lost tribes of Israel.

ANS: C   TYPE: M   KEY 1: A   KEY 2: 3   PAGE: 29

30. Which of the following is not true of the Spanish *conquistadores*?
    a. They succeeded in part because smallpox decimated the Indian population.
    b. They led huge armies of 50,000 to 100,000 well-trained Europeans.
    c. They searched unsuccessfully for fabulous golden cities in North America.
    d. They conquered two major empires in the Americas and greatly increased the wealth and power of Spain.
    e. They destroyed religious items of the native people.

ANS: B   TYPE: M   KEY 1: F   KEY 2: 2   PAGE: 31-34

31. The sixteenth century Catholic missions in North America
    a. were most successful in Virginia and the Carolinas.
    b. trained Indians as soldiers to protect the settlements from English and French attacks.
    c. were administered by unarmed Franciscan priests.
    d. failed to convert any Indians to Christianity.
    e. all of the above

ANS: C   TYPE: M   KEY 1: F   KEY 2: 2   PAGE: 35

32. Which of the following was true of serfdom?
    a. By 1500, serfdom had virtually disappeared and had been replaced by free labor in western Europe.
    b. Serfs were similar to slaves in that both could be bought and sold individually.
    c. In North America, serfdom was more widespread and more profitable than was slavery.
    d. Russia was the only European country that relied entirely on a free labor system.
    e. Serfs were forcibly resettled in the Americas.

ANS: A　　　**TYPE: M**　　　**KEY 1: F**　　　**KEY 2: 2**　　　**PAGE: 39**

33. During the reign of Philip II,
    a. the Moors were driven off of the Iberian Peninsula.
    b. toleration of Jews and Moslems was established throughout the Spanish Empire.
    c. the first global economic system was created by the union of Spain and Portugal.
    d. the Spanish peacefully mediated between competing European and Asian nations.
    e. France merged with Spain.

ANS: C　　　**TYPE: M**　　　**KEY 1: F**　　　**KEY 2: 2**　　　**PAGE: 38**

34. The era of exploration contributed to world progress by
    a. bringing previously isolated societies into contact with other nations and cultures.
    b. promoting peaceful and friendly relations between different ethnic groups.
    c. promoting religious toleration and ending the persecution of non-Christians around the globe.
    d. spreading technology.
    e. all of the above.

ANS: A　　　**TYPE: M**　　　**KEY 1: A**　　　**KEY 2: 2**　　　**PAGE: 38-41**

35. All except which of the following were negative results of the exploration and discovery era?
    a. Millions of Africans were enslaved and transported to other parts of the world.
    b. Warfare, slavery, and disease killed millions of Indians.
    c. Many plants native to the Americas were displaced by European imports.
    d. The Asian nations of China, India, and Japan became the wealthiest and most powerful countries in the world.
    e. European animals overran American rivals.

ANS: D　　　**TYPE: M**　　　**KEY 1: A**　　　**KEY 2: 3**　　　**PAGE: 38-41**

36. Amerind was the forerunner of all of the following languages except
    a. Algonquian.
    b. Navajo.
    c. Muskogean.
    d. Iroquoian.
    e. Siouan.

ANS: B　　　**TYPE: M**　　　**KEY 1: F**　　　**KEY 2: 3**　　　**PAGE: 5**

37. Amaranth was a type of
    a. spear point.
    b. animal.
    c. cereal.
    d. disease.
    e. liquor.

ANS: C　　　**TYPE: M**　　　**KEY 1: F**　　　**KEY 2: 2**　　　**PAGE: 6**

38. As of 1400, _____ mariners were the world's best.
   a. English
   b. Spanish
   c. Portuguese
   d. Chinese
   e. Arab

ANS: E   TYPE: M   KEY 1: F   KEY 2: 3   PAGE: 8

39. The Black Death reduced Europe's population by
   a. one-quarter.
   b. two-thirds.
   c. one-third.
   d. half.
   e. none.

ANS: C   TYPE: M   KEY 1:FA   KEY 2: 2   PAGE: 8

40. Europe's pioneer in the area of exploration was
   a. Spain.
   b. Germany.
   c. Italy.
   d. France.
   e. Portugal

ANS: E   TYPE: M   KEY 1: F   KEY 2: 2   PAGE: 9

41. Which of the following did Portugal acquire first?
   a. São Tomé
   b. the Madeira Islands
   c. the Cape Verde group
   d. the Azores
   e. Spain

ANS: D   TYPE: M   KEY 1: F   KEY 2: 3   PAGE: 11

42. The center of the Portuguese empire in Asia was
   a. Japan.
   b. the Moluccas.
   c. Goa.
   d. China.
   e. Indonesia.

ANS: B   TYPE: M   KEY 1: F   KEY 2: 3   PAGE: 13

43. Before the nineteenth century, about _____ of the people who sailed across the Atlantic were slaves.
   a. one-half
   b. one-third
   c. one-quarter
   d. two-thirds
   e. one-tenth

ANS: D   TYPE: M   KEY 1: F   KEY 2: 3   PAGE: 14

44. The Olmec people of Mesoamerica were known for all of the following except
    a. building the first pyramids.
    b. constructing ballparks.
    c. using terrace agriculture.
    d. developing a writing system and a calendar.
    e. building colossal stone heads.

ANS: C   **TYPE: M**   **KEY 1: A**   **KEY 2: 3**   **PAGE: 22**

45. One factor that distinguished the Americas from Eurasia in the pre-Columbian era is that
    a. no large animals were domesticated in the Americas except the llama in South America.
    b. agriculture had not developed in the Americas.
    c. no society in the Americas had developed a written language.
    d. no maritime cultures had developed in the Americas.
    e. no laarge cities existed in the Americas.

ANS: A   **TYPE: M**   **KEY 1: A**   **KEY 2: 2**   **PAGE: 6**

46. The Norse settlements founded in the 1000s on the coast of Newfoundland
    a. left a lasting legacy in that region.
    b. endured until after Columbus's voyages.
    c. met no resistance from native Americans.
    d. brought African slavery to the Americas.
    e. died out before Columbus's voyages, leaving no lasting impact.

ANS: E   **TYPE: M**   **KEY 1: A**   **KEY 2: 2**   **PAGE: 7**

47. In spite of being the most complex culture in the world, China did not expand outward because
    a. the Chinese religion forbade overseas ventures.
    b. it was conquered by the Europeans.
    c. it produced little that the outside world wanted.
    d. it was a self-contained system that needed little from the rest of the world.
    e. it was defeated by Europe in the 1400s.

ANS: D   **TYPE: M**   **KEY 1: A**   **KEY 2: 3**   **PAGE: 8**

48. After the 1430s information was able to circulate more freely in Europe than anywhere else in the world because
    a. of the political unity achieved by the monarchs.
    b. of the invention of the printing press.
    c. of the rapid development of sailing vessels.
    d. of the social mobility that came with the break down of feudalism.
    e. of the invention of the telephone.

ANS: B   **TYPE: M**   **KEY 1: A**   **KEY 2: 2**   **PAGE: 8**

49. Under slavery as it existed in Africa
    a. the slaves were forced to work long hours in commercial agriculture.
    b. slaves' descendents were often assimilated into the captor's society.
    c. only Christians were enslaved.
    d. slaves were isolated as a separate caste.
    e. slaves were executed after serving five years.

ANS: B   **TYPE: M**   **KEY 1: A**   **KEY 2: 3**   **PAGE: 11**

50. Prior to Columbus's voyages Spain had conquered
    a. the Canary Islands.
    b. the Holy Land.
    c. Ireland.
    d. Portugal.
    e. England.

ANS: A   TYPE: M   KEY 1: F   KEY 2: 3   PAGE: 14

TRUE/FALSE

_____ 1.   Generally, the Spanish were very generous when dealing with Native American civilizations.

ANS: F   TYPE: T   KEY 1: A   KEY 2: 1   PAGE: 40

_____ 2.   One of the major advantages Portugal had in the race for exploration was its leader, Henry the Navigator.

ANS: T   TYPE: T   KEY 1: F   KEY 2: 2   PAGE: 10

_____ 3.   Unlike Spain, Portugal refused to enslave Africans.

ANS: F   TYPE: T   KEY 1: F   KEY 2: 2   PAGE: 11

_____ 4.   The greatest loss of life among the Indian population came from warfare with the European invaders.

ANS: F   TYPE: T   KEY 1: F   KEY 2: 1   PAGE: 38

_____ 5.   Most Indian societies engaged in clan or family ownership of landholdings.

ANS: T   TYPE: T   KEY 1: A   KEY 2: 3   PAGE: 18

_____ 6.   Vasco da Gama was the first European to reach India via an eastward water route.

ANS: T   TYPE: T   KEY 1: F   KEY 2: 2   PAGE: 13

_____ 7.   The most sophisticated civilization in the world at the time of European exploration was in China.

ANS: T   TYPE: T   KEY 1: F   KEY 2: 3   PAGE: 7

_____ 8.   Most Native American Indian populations were "hunters and gatherers."

ANS: F   TYPE: T   KEY 1: A   KEY 2: 2   PAGE: 18

_____ 9.   The rise of slavery in the New World was closely related to the demands of the capitalist market in Europe.

ANS: T   TYPE: T   KEY 1: A   KEY 2: 2   PAGE: 39

_____ 10.   The Indian peoples of the Americas had only domesticated one animal species, the dog, before the arrival of the Europeans.

ANS: F   TYPE: T   KEY 1: F   KEY 2: 1   PAGE: 6

_____ 11.   The Norsemen's lasting contributions to the development of American society included architectural designs and coined money.

ANS: F   TYPE: T   KEY 1: A   KEY 2: 2   PAGE: 7

_____ 12.   Johann Gutenberg invented paper and block printing.

ANS: F   TYPE: T   KEY 1: F   KEY 2: 2   PAGE: 8

_____ 13.   The Portuguese ocean-going ship that combined lateen sails with square rigging was called a caravel.

ANS: T   TYPE: T   KEY 1: F   KEY 2: 1   PAGE: 10

_____ 14.   Christians during the fifteenth and sixteenth centuries did not believe in executing people for violating religious doctrines.

ANS: F   TYPE: T   KEY 1: A   KEY 2: 2   PAGE: 30

_____ 15.   Beringia proved a hospitable place for plant and animal life.

ANS: F   TYPE: T   KEY 1: A   KEY 2: 1   PAGE: 4

_____ 16.   Humans did not actually live on Beringia; it was used only as a means of travel between Siberia and Alaska.

ANS: F   TYPE: T   KEY 1: A   KEY 2: 1   PAGE: 4

_____ 17.   The Indians of the Pacific northwest divided tasks along gender lines.

ANS: T   TYPE: T   KEY 1: F   KEY 2: 1   PAGE: 6

_____ 18.   Women were probably the first in Indian society to actually plant and harvest crops.

ANS: T   TYPE: T   KEY 1: F   KEY 2: 2   PAGE: 6

_____ 19.   In the Americas as in Africa, the rise of farming was closely linked to the domestication of animals.

ANS: F   TYPE: T   KEY 1: A   KEY 2: 3   PAGE: 6

_____ 20.   The Norse exerted a significant impact on American history well into the 1500s.

ANS: F   TYPE: T   KEY 1: A   KEY 2: 2   PAGE: 7

_____ 21.   The first European slaves were black Africans.

ANS: F   TYPE: T   KEY 1: F   KEY 2: 1   PAGE: 9

_____ 22.   In 1400, Europe was clearly posed for dramatic expansion.

ANS: F   **TYPE: T**   **KEY 1: A**   **KEY 2: 1**   **PAGE: 8**

_____ 23.   Portuguese mariners borrowed heavily from Arab ship designs and used Arab navigational tools.

ANS: T   **TYPE: T**   **KEY 1: F**   **KEY 2: 2**   **PAGE: 9-10**

_____ 24.   During the long history of the Atlantic slave trade, nearly every African shipped overseas had first been enslaved by other Africans.

ANS: T   **TYPE: T**   **KEY 1: F**   **KEY 2: 1**   **PAGE: 11**

_____ 25.   Portuguese explorers never penetrated Japan.

ANS: F   **TYPE: T**   **KEY 1: F**   **KEY 2: 2**   **PAGE: 13**

_____ 26.   Europe's most fiercely Catholic society as the sixteenth century began was Spain.

ANS: T   **TYPE: T**   **KEY 1: F**   **KEY 2: 2**   **PAGE: 14**

_____ 27.   Christopher Columbus's first voyage across the Atlantic was controversial because of his belief that the world was round.

ANS: F   **TYPE: T**   **KEY 1: A**   **KEY 2: 2**   **PAGE: 15**

_____ 28.   The Aztec capital of Tenochtitlán was much more populated than any city in western Europe.

ANS: T   **TYPE: T**   **KEY 1: F**   **KEY 2: 2**   **PAGE: 17**

_____ 29.   Among Indian societies, tobacco was grown exclusively by women.

ANS: F   **TYPE: T**   **KEY 1: F**   **KEY 2: 1**   **PAGE: 17**

_____ 30.   The Toltecs were a peaceful people.

ANS: F   **TYPE: T**   **KEY 1: F**   **KEY 2: 1**   **PAGE: 24**

_____ 31.   Many Mesoamerican artifacts have been found in the southeastern United States.

ANS: F   **TYPE: T**   **KEY 1: F**   **KEY 2: 2**   **PAGE: 22**

_____ 32.   Women in semi sedentary Indian societies did most of the farming.

ANS: T   **TYPE: T**   **KEY 1: A**   **KEY 2: 2**   **PAGE: 17-18**

_____ 33.   Spanish *conquistadores* led large armies of around 5,000 men.

ANS: F   **TYPE: T**   **KEY 1: F**   **KEY 2: 3**   **PAGE: 31**

_____ 34.   The Franciscans were the first Catholic missionaries to the North American Indians.

ANS: F   **TYPE: T**   **KEY 1: F**   **KEY 2: 3**   **PAGE: 35**

_____ 35. In 1573, the Spanish King disavowed the enslavement of Indians or even attacks against them.

ANS: T   **TYPE: T**   **KEY 1: A**   **KEY 2: 2**   **PAGE: 35**

_____ 36. Franciscan missionaries systematically tortured their Mayan converts when they caught them worshipping their old gods.

ANS: T   **TYPE: T**   **KEY 1: F**   **KEY 2: 2**   **PAGE: 38**

_____ 37. American silver made the king of Spain the most powerful monarch in Christendom.

ANS: T   **TYPE: T**   **KEY 1: F**   **KEY 2: 2**   **PAGE: 38**

_____ 38. In the fifteenth century, the Chinese government ruled 100 million people.

ANS: T   **TYPE: T**   **KEY 1: F**   **KEY 2: 3**   **PAGE: 7**

_____ 39. Aside from Marco Polo, the Chinese had no contact whatsoever with the rest of the world.

ANS: F   **TYPE: T**   **KEY 1: A**   **KEY 2: 2**   **PAGE: 8**

_____ 40. For the Western Hemisphere as a whole, any given region probably lost at least 90 percent of its population within a year of sustained contact with Europeans.

ANS: T   **TYPE: T**   **KEY 1: F**   **KEY 2: 1**   **PAGE: 38**

FILL-INS

1. In 1580, the _____ Empire was the greatest empire the world had ever known.

ANS: Spanish   **TYPE: F**   **KEY 1: F**   **KEY 2: 2**   **PAGE: 38**

2. The conqueror of the Aztecs was _____.

ANS: Hernán Cortés   **TYPE: F**   **KEY 1: F**   **KEY 2: 3**   **PAGE: 31-32**

3. Pedro Alvares Cabral discovered _____ in South America accidentally.

ANS: Brazil   **TYPE: F**   **KEY 1: F**   **KEY 2: 3**   **PAGE: 14**

4. The marriage of Queen Isabella of Castile and King _____ of Aragon formed the foundation for modern Spain.

ANS: Ferdinand   **TYPE: F**   **KEY 1: F**   **KEY 2: 3**   **PAGE: 14**

5. The papal decree that divided the Americas between Portugal and Spain was called the

_____.

ANS: Inter Caeteras   **TYPE: F**   **KEY 1: F**   **KEY 2: 3**   **PAGE: 16**

6. The _____ was a type of spear point that originated in the New Mexico–Texas area, spread rapidly across the Americas, and contributed to the elimination of large game animals.

ANS: Clovis point   **TYPE: F**   **KEY 1: F**   **KEY 2: 2**   **PAGE: 6**

7. _____ was the eleventh-century Norse explorer who established Vinland, the first European colony in North America.

ANS: Leif Eriksson   **TYPE: F**   **KEY 1: F**   **KEY 2: 1**   **PAGE: 7**

8. In the fourteenth century an outbreak of the _____ wiped out one third of Europe's population.

ANS: Black Death (or bubonic plague)   **TYPE: F**   **KEY 1: F**   **KEY 2: 2**   **PAGE: 8**

9. Humans definitely were living in western Alaska about _____ years ago.

ANS: 12,000   **TYPE: F**   **KEY 1: F**   **KEY 2: 2**   **PAGE: 4**

10. The primary crop of the first American farmers in Peru, Mexico, and the southwestern United States was _____.

ANS: maize (or Indian corn)   **TYPE: F**   **KEY 1: F**   **KEY 2: 2**   **PAGE: 6**

11. The world's largest and grandest city in the 1200s was in _____.

ANS: China   **TYPE: F**   **KEY 1: F**   **KEY 2: 2**   **PAGE: 8**

12. By 1300, more than _____ million people were living in Europe.

ANS: 100   **TYPE: F**   **KEY 1: F**   **KEY 2: 2**   **PAGE: 8**

13. The Aztec capital, _____, was more populated than any western European city.

ANS: Tenochtitlán   **TYPE: F**   **KEY 1: F**   **KEY 2: 2**   **PAGE: 17**

14. Almost _____ million people lived in the Western Hemisphere in 1492.

ANS: 50   **TYPE: F**   **KEY 1: F**   **KEY 2: 2**   **PAGE: 18**

15. _____ was the Inca capital.

ANS: Cuzco   **TYPE: F**   **KEY 1: F**   **KEY 2: 2**   **PAGE: 21**

16. The _____ practiced human sacrifice on a scale that had no parallel anywhere else in the world.

ANS: Aztecs   **TYPE: F**   **KEY 1: F**   **KEY 2: 1**   **PAGE: 25**

17. The world's largest earthen work was constructed by the Mississippian mound building people at _____.

ANS: Cahokia   **TYPE: F**   **KEY 1: F**   **KEY 2: 2**   **PAGE: 27**

18. The _____ helped the Spanish conquer the Aztecs.

ANS: Tlaxcalans   **TYPE: F**   **KEY 1: F**   **KEY 2: 3**   **PAGE: 32**

19. By the mid-1600s, there were _____ Spanish missions in Florida containing about 26,000 converted Indians.

ANS: 30   **TYPE: F**   **KEY 1: F**   **KEY 2: 2**   **PAGE: 36**

20. By _____, the Pueblo, Apache, and Navajo Indians of New Mexico had accepted baptism.

ANS: 1630   **TYPE: F**   **KEY 1: F**   **KEY 2: 2**   **PAGE: 36**

21. The first crop produced by African slave labor in the Caribbean was _____.

ANS: Sugar   **TYPE: F**   **KEY 1: F**   **KEY 2: 3**   **PAGE: 39**

22. More than any other technological advantage, _____ made European military conquest possible.

ANS: steel   **TYPE: F**   **KEY 1: A**   **KEY 2: 2**   **PAGE: 40**

23. The _____ established their first African fort at Cape Blanco in 1448.

ANS: Portuguese   **TYPE: F**   **KEY 1: F**   **KEY 2: 3**   **PAGE: 11**

24. The Spanish kingdom of _____ sent its first settlers to the Canary Islands just after 1400.

ANS: Castile   **TYPE: F**   **KEY 1: F**   **KEY 2: 2**   **PAGE: 14**

25. _____ entered the sixteenth century as Europe's most fiercely Catholic society.

ANS: Spain   **TYPE: F**   **KEY 1: F**   **KEY 2: 2**   **PAGE: 14**

26. In 1492, Spain took control of _____, the last outpost of Islam on the Iberian peninsula.

ANS: Granada   **TYPE: F**   **KEY 1: F**   **KEY 2: 2**   **PAGE: 14**

27. The first mariner to sail around the world was _____.

ANS: Ferdinand Magellan   **TYPE: F**   **KEY 1: F**   **KEY 2: 1**   **PAGE: 17**

28. The Inca Empire stretched _____ miles north to south.

ANS: 2,000   **TYPE: F**   **KEY 1: F**   **KEY 2: 2**   **PAGE: 21**

29. The _____ Empire was the largest non-literate empire in history.

ANS: Inca   **TYPE: F**   **KEY 1: F**   **KEY 2: 3**   **PAGE: 21**

30. Some estimates claim that the Aztecs sacrificed _____ people at the dedication of the Great Pyramid of the Sun in 1487.

ANS: 14,000   TYPE: F   KEY 1: F   KEY 2: 3   PAGE: 25

31. The _____ were cliff-dwelling people in the American southwest.

ANS: Anasazi   TYPE: F   KEY 1: F   KEY 2: 1   PAGE: 29

IDENTIFICATIONS

1. **Maya:** complex and advanced pre-Columbian Indian society. Chichen Itza was a leading city. Constructed canals for irrigation, developed an accurate calendar and a writing system, and practiced human sacrifice.

2. **conquistadores**: Spanish warriors who conquered the native people of the Americas.

3. **Christopher Columbus**: Italian mariner. "Admiral of the Ocean Sea." First modern European to make contact with the Americas. Made four voyages to the New World searching for sea route to Asia. Never actually realized he had discovered a new land.

4. *encomienda:* system of labor tribute implemented by the Spanish in the Americas that demanded Indians work for the local lord.

5. **Atahualapa:** leader of the Incas; captured and killed by Pizarro.

6. **Beringia:** a name given by geographers to the 600-mile-wide land bridge that linked Siberia and Alaska for over ten thousand years. Plants, animals and people probably lived there.

7. **Vinland:** the first European colony in North America; founded by the Norse explorer Leif Eriksson in the eleventh century A.D. Located near L'Anse aux meadows on the northern coast of Newfoundland. Internal struggles and Indian troubles led to abandonment of the colony.

8. **Marco Polo**: thirteenth-century Italian merchant who spent twenty years at the court of Chinese Emperor Kublai Khan. Wrote about the riches of the East in *The Travels of Marco Polo*.

9. *Inter Caeteras*: papal bull issued in 1493 by Pope Alexander VI (a Spaniard). Divided the non-Christian world between Portugal and Spain. Revised a year later by the Treaty of Tordesillas, which gave Spain most of the Western Hemisphere, along with the Philippine Islands, and awarded to Portugal most of the Eastern Hemisphere, including the African coast, and Brazil. Effectively ended Spain's direct access to the African slave trade.

10. **"slash and burn"** agriculture: practiced by semisedentary Indian societies. Involved cutting down or girdling trees, burning away the underbrush, and using the resulting ash as fertilizer. Eventually depleted the soil and forced tribes to move every 10 to 15 years.

11. **Royal Orders for New Discoveries**: issued by Spanish King Philip II in 1573. Made it illegal to enslave
Indians or even to attack them. Instead, unarmed priests were to bring them to together in missions and convert them into peaceful Catholic subjects of Spain.

1.   Examine the reasons why Portugal rose to the forefront during the early period of European exploration.

Answer: Portugal's rise to leadership of European expansion seemed improbable in 1400. A small country of fewer than one million people, it had been united as a nation for less than a century. Portugal had a small middle class and credit system, making investment in commercial enterprises unlikely. Its leading city, Lisbon, had less than forty thousand people and its educational system was wholly inadequate.

Portugal's advantages, however, lay in an efficient government and internal peace. Its greatest advantage lay in Prince Henry the Navigator. Henry joined together scholars and navigators, studied geography, and designed sleek new ocean-going vessels (caravels). These advantages allowed Portugal to explore the African coast and, later, South America. In addition, with liberal credit from Italian bankers, Portugal was able to finance its voyages and turn a profit.

2.   Explain the victory of Hernán Cortés over the large and powerful Aztec Empire.

Answer: The conquistador Hernán Cortés arrived at Tenochtitlán, the capital city of the Aztec Empire, in 1519, with some four hundred soldiers. Although the Aztec ruler Moctezuma attempted to dissuade the Spaniards through expensive gifts, this actually increased their greed for the gold and silver they saw bestowed liberally throughout the capital city. Cortés took Moctezuma prisoner and began replacing Aztec idols with Christian ones. The people rose against the Spanish and they were driven out of the city with heavy losses. But they left smallpox behind, with which the Aztecs had never had contact—killing tens of thousands.

The next year, Cortés returned with cannon and thousands of Indian allies hostile to the Aztecs. After building warships, Cortés conquered the city, but only after heavy losses to the population and the destruction of much of the city. After Cortés gained control, he looted gold and silver, put into place a new imperial government, and began to build Mexico City.

3.   Describe European society in the fifteenth and sixteenth centuries.

Answer: Europe, in the years before 1400, was a relatively backward place. In no way a self-contained economy, the various rising monarchies in Europe were in constant competition with each other. Little manufacturing, very limited access to liquid capital, constant internal warfare and strife all worked together to create a politically unstable and dangerous place. Over a third of the population perished because of the Black Death in the mid-fourteenth century.

But Europe was poised for growth and expansion in ways that other places were not. While China, far more advanced technologically, politically, and militarily than Europe, looked inward and shut off contact with the outside world, Europe was attempting to increase contacts with the East. Attracted by Asian spices and luxuries, plus the desire among merchants for large profits, Europeans embarked headlong, led by the Portuguese, into the exploration of the oceans for quick routes to the East. Even such apparent adversities as the Black Death worked to their advantage since it built immunities to diseases that the Europeans would contact around the world. On balance, an unlikely place, small provincial Europe was on the verge of unequaled exploration and colonization because of several of its disadvantages.

4.   Examine Mayan society at its peak from the sixth to the tenth centuries.

Answer: Mayan society, perhaps the most advanced in the Americas, grew out of Olmec civilization. Located in the southern lowlands of Central America, the Maya were an urbanized but decentralized civilization. Mayan political structure was constructed around a series of competing city-states that shared a similar culture. Mayan society was very sophisticated, resting on an extensive system of canals and waterways to the cities and surrounding agricultural regions. During the fourth century A.D., the Mayans began to record and leave detailed accounts of their civilization.

Mayan society began to decline around the ninth century for a variety of reasons. The aristocracy had outgrown the ability of the common population to support them; ecological decay and wars all exerted their influence on the declining population. Mayan civilization underwent a renaissance in the city of Chichen Itza, but this was clearly a post classic era. The Maya now were strongly influenced by the warrior Toltec.

5.   Describe the successes and failures of Christopher Columbus's voyages at the end of the fifteenth century.

Answer: Christopher Columbus's voyages bore mixed results. Columbus, a Genoese mariner sailing for Spain, ultimately made four voyages for the crown, of which the first is certainly the most famous and successful. Appointed "Admiral of the Ocean Sea," by Ferdinand and Isabella, Columbus set sail in 1492 for the Far East. Convinced that a short western journey would get him there, Columbus hoped to establish a short trade route to Asia, opening up that region to commerce.

Of course, Columbus's great feat was in exploring the Americas for Spain, a significant and momentous accomplishment. Within the confines of what he had hoped to do, however, his success was limited. Although he was certain he had reached the East Indies, he was, in fact, in the Bahamas. He made three more journeys, each in search of China, but was unsuccessful. Indeed, after his third voyage, he was shipped back to Spain in chains. He spent much of his life vainly attempting to gain great wealth that he believed was his.

6.   Describe the origin and expansion of the European slave trade.

Answer: The economic base of the European slave trade was a legacy of the Crusades. During the period in which Christians controlled the kingdom of Jerusalem, the Europeans profited from sugar plantations, which used both slave and free laborers. This system was extended to the Mediterranean islands of Cyprus, Malta, Crete, and Rhodes. After losing their foothold in the Middle East, the European Christians continued to enslave captured non-Christian Moslems and Slavs. They also purchased black African slaves from Arab traders. Thus the model for the forced-labor plantation system used extensively in the Americas was created before the discovery of the New World.

During the fifteenth century, the Portuguese, under the leadership of Prince Henry, began the systematic exploration of the Atlantic Ocean and the African coastline. Portugal established colonies and transplanted the sugar plantation economy to the islands of Madeira, the Azores, Cape Verde, and São Tomé. They acquired African slaves by raiding coastal villages and kidnapping the inhabitants. The raids, however, interfered with the ivory and gold trade and created hostile relations with African leaders. Eventually the Portuguese built fortified slave "factories" on the coast and on offshore islands and purchased slaves from African traders. Slavery was an ancient and accepted tradition in Africa. Since slaves were usually prisoners captured during wars, the development of the European trade instigated an increase in military activity among African tribes. Participation in the trade became a matter not only of profit but also of survival for the Africans. Those tribes that attempted to stop the slave trade were often enslaved by others. The slave system that developed in the fifteenth century continued to operate for four hundred years. When the New World was discovered and the Indian population of the Americas was decimated by warfare and disease, the Portuguese system was transported across the Atlantic. Its most brutal expression was in the Portuguese colony of Brazil, where thousands of Indians and Africans were worked to death. Eventually the slave labor force in South America and the Caribbean was predominantly African rather than Indian.

7.   Describe the most significant plant, animal, and bacterial aspects of the exchanges between Europe and the Americas.

Answer: Whenever peoples from different parts of the world come into contact with each other there is always an exchange of goods, diseases, ideas, and cultural traits. This was especially true when the Old World and New World made first contact. The European explorers and colonists brought with them to the Americas cereal crops, sugar cane, horses, cows, sheep, goats, pigs, and even sparrows. They introduced the practical use of the wheel and metallurgy to the Stone Age "Indians" who had used the wheel only for toys and who did not know how to produce bronze or to work iron. European diseases such as smallpox, mumps, and measles were also new to the Americas, and in the first years of contact these microbes killed millions of Indians.

Clearly the European conquerors of the Americas benefited the most from the Columbian exchange. The diets and health of people all over the world were improved by the introduction of New World agricultural products such as cotton, potatoes, tomatoes, corn, and rubber. Tobacco was also a New World product that changed European health and social habits, but not necessarily for the better. European economies prospered from the influx of gold, silver, and precious gems from Central and South America and from slave-labor-produced products such as sugar, rice, and coffee. The Americas served as an outlet for disgruntled and dispossessed members of European society and offered opportunities for social and economic advancement unavailable at home. In the exchange of diseases, the Indians gave the Europeans syphilis.

LONG ESSAYS

1.   Examine the variety of Native American societies in the period before European conquest.

Answer: Essay should address several key points:

A.   Mayan civilization
  1.   Urbanization
    a.   Complex canal and irrigation system
    b.   Consequences
  2.   Competing city-states
  3.   Literate people
    a.   Recorded history
    b.   Implications
B.   Aztec society
  1.   Warrior people
  2.   Urban/Tenochtitlán (200,000 people)
  3.   Sophistication
    a.   Metallurgy
    b.   Medicine
  4.   Religious beliefs
    a.   Human sacrifice/ritual cannibalism
    b.   Conquest by Cortés
C.   Inca civilization
  1.   Technologically advanced
    a.   Roads and suspension bridges
    b.   Sophisticated agricultural methods
  2.   Sprawling empire
    a.   Eight to twelve million people
    b.   Internal strife/defeat by Pizarro

2.   What explains the European desire for exploration and settlement in the fifteenth century?

Answer: Essay should address several key points:

A.   Trade and commerce routes
  1.   Desire for Asian goods
  2.   Expensive overland routes
  3.   Preeminence of Portugal
B.   Desire for wealth
  1.   Africa
    a.   Gold and ivory
    b.   Slave trade

2. Asia
    a. Spices
    b. Silk
3. Americas
    a. Precious metals
    b. Tobacco and spices
C. Religion
    1. Spread of the faith
        a. Portugal and Catholicism
        b. Columbus and millennialism

3. Describe and analyze the consequences of the exchange of goods, technology, and bacteria between the Old and New Worlds.

Answer: Essay should address several key points:

A. "Old" and "New" Worlds meet
    1. Fifteenth- and sixteenth-century contacts
        a. Christopher Columbus and "discovery"
        b. Hernán Cortés, conquest, and silver
    2. African contacts
        a. Vasco da Gama and trade
        b. European desires for spices and gold
B. Effects on Europe
    1. New trade and commercial exchange
        a. Silver
        b. Tobacco
        c. Spices
    2. Colonization
        a. Europe settles the Americas
        b. European exploitation
    3. Rise of European nation-states
C. Effects on the Americas and Africa
    1. Disease and destruction
        a. Conquered peoples
        b. Mass depopulation
    2. New institutions
        a. Catholic Church
        b. *Encomienda* and *hacienda*
        c. Forced labor
    3. Slavery
        a. African peoples enslaved
        b. Millions "emigrated" through middle passage
        c. Millions die/death and transport

4. Discuss the role of religion in the era of exploration and discovery.

Answer: Essay should address several key points.

A. The Crusades
    1. Freeing the Holy Land from Moslem control
    2. Expansion of sugar plantations to Mediterranean Islands
    3. Enslaving non-Christians/Moslems, Slavs, Africans
    4. Search for Prester John

B.   Prince Henry and the Order of Christ
        1.   Voyages of exploration
        2.   African trade/gold, ivory and slaves
        3.   Island colonies/Madiera, Azores, Cape Verde Islands
        4.   Vasco da Gama sails to India
C.   Ferdinand and Isabella of Spain
        1.   Expelling the Moors and Jews
        2.   Exterminating the Guanches of the Canary islands
        3.   Christopher (Christ-bearer) Columbus
        4.   Treaty of Tordesillas/Pope Alexander VI
D.   Dilemmas in the New World
        1.   Questions of origin of the Indians
        2.   Theory of St. Thomas the Doubter
        3.   Human sacrifice versus the Spanish Inquisition
        4.   Christian versus pagan military objectives
E.   The conquistadors and missionaries
        1.   Cortez destroys the Aztec gods
        2.   Pizarro conquers the Incas
        3.   Searching for golden cities
        4.   The Jesuits
                a.   Mission in Virginia
                b.   Don Luis (Openchancanough)
        5.   The Franciscans
                a.   Goals and policies
                b.   The mission system
                c.   Brutal treatment of Mayan lapsed converts

CHAPTER 2
THE CHALLENGE TO SPAIN AND THE SETTLEMENT OF NORTH AMERICA

CHAPTER OUTLINE

I. The Protestant Reformation and the Challenge to Spain
II. New France
    A. Early French Explorers
    B. Missions and Furs
    C. New France Under Louis XIV
III. The Dutch and Swedish Settlements
    A. The East and West India Companies
    B. The New Netherlands as a Pluralistic Society
    C. Swedish and English Encroachments
IV. The Challenge from Elizabethan England
    A. The English Reformation
    B. Hawkins and Drake
    C. Gilbert, Ireland, and America
    D. Ralegh, Roanoke, and War with Spain
V. The Swarming of the English
VI. The Chesapeake and West Indian Colonies
    A. The Jamestown Disaster
    B. Reorganization, Reform, and Crisis
    C. Tobacco, Servants, and Survival
    D. Maryland
    E. Chesapeake Family Life
    F. The West Indies and the Transition to Slavery
    G. The Rise of Slavery in North America
VII. The New England Colonies
    A. The Pilgrims and Plymouth
    B. Covenant Theology
    C. Massachusetts Bay
    D. Puritan Family Life
    E. Conversion, Dissent, and Expansion
    F. Congregations, Towns, and Colony Governments
    G. Infant Baptism and New Dissent
VIII. The English Civil Wars
IX. The First Restoration Colonies
    A. Carolina, Harrington, and the Aristocratic Ideal
    B. New York: An Experiment in Absolutism
X. Brotherly Love: The Quakers and America
    A. Quaker Beliefs
    B. Quaker Families
    C. West New Jersey
    D. Pennsylvania
XI. Conclusion

CHRONOLOGY

1497	John Cabot reaches North America.
1517	Martin Luther posts Ninety-Five Theses on Wittenburg Church, inaugurating the Protestant Reformation.
1524	Giovanni Verrazano explores the coast of North America.

1534–1543	Jacques Cartier explores the St. Lawrence valley.
1558	Accession of Queen Elizabeth I.
1560–1590s	English conquest of Ireland.
1577–1580	Sir Francis Drake circumnavigates the globe.
1583	Humphrey Gilbert claims Newfoundland for England.
1585–1590	Walter Ralegh's three failed attempts to launch a colony off Virginia.
1588	Defeat of the Spanish Armada.
1602	Dutch East India Company chartered.
1603	James I becomes King of England.
1607	Virginia Company founds Jamestown.
1608	Samuel de Champlain founds Quebec.
1609	Henry Hudson sails into Hudson River valley.
	Virginia receives sea-to-sea charter.
1613–1614	John Rolfe grows tobacco, marries Pocahontas.
1618–1648	Thirty Years' War.
1619	Virginia House of Burgesses and Headright System created.
	First African slaves sold in British North America.
1620	Pilgrims adopt Mayflower Compact and found Plymouth Colony.
1621	Dutch West India Company chartered.
1622	Opechancanough attacks Virginia.
1624	King assumes direct control of Virginia.
1626	Pierre Minuit buys Manhattan Island, establishing New Netherland colony.
1630	Puritans found Massachusetts Bay Colony.
1632	George Calvert founds Maryland.
1636	Harvard College founded.
1636–1638	Roger Williams founds Rhode Island.
	Thomas Hooker founds Hartford.
1637	New England settlers slaughter Pequot Indians.
1638	Anne Hutchinson banished to Rhode Island.
	Pierre Minuit founds New Sweden.
1640–1649	First English civil war.
1641	Massachusetts General Court issues Body of Liberties.
1643	New Netherland carries out the Pavonia massacre.
1649	Maryland Act of Toleration.
1640s	The sugar revolution and the rise of slavery in Barbados.
1655	New Netherland conquers New Sweden.
	Quakers invade New England.
1660–1688	Restoration era.
1660	Charles II becomes King of England.
1660s	Royal African Company established.
1662	Half-Way Covenant.
1663	Louis XIV assumes direct control over New France.
1663–1665	Carolina colony established by Ashley-Cooper.
1664	Duke of York granted charter for New York colony.
1665	New Jersey charter.
1670	First permanent English settlement established in South Carolina.
1680	Charleston founded.
1680–1681	William Penn founds Pennsylvania colony.
1705	Virginia adopts comprehensive slave code.

THEMATIC TOPICS FOR ENRICHMENT

1. Define the various "spiritual frontiers" in the Americas. How important was missionary work in the European settlements?

2. Assess the statement of King Francis I of France that only by occupying a distant land could one acquire a valid claim to it. In what ways was New France a successful colony, and in what ways was it a failure?

3. Describe life in the early Chesapeake Bay area.

4. Discuss the special problems of the New Netherland colony and its attempts to overcome them. Were they successful?

5. Evaluate the Dutch conviction that "frank acceptance of religious diversity might stimulate trade."

6. Compare the demographics of the several New World colonies. Why was the mortality rate in New England so much lower than in the Chesapeake?

7. What was the Massachusetts 1641 "Body of Liberties," and what precedents did it set?

8. What was the relationship between toleration and suppression of dissent in Puritan Massachusetts?

9. What were the chief differences between class and caste in the American colonies?

10. What was the Puritan Revolution of the 1640s, and what were its effects upon colonial development?

11. Explain the quote: "England discovered its colonies and their importance around 1650."

12. Give a brief overview of the founding of the Restoration colonies. What do the authors mean by "Far more than New England or Virginia, the Restoration colonies foreshadowed what the United States became in later centuries"?

13. Which British colonies were proprietorships? Who were the proprietors, and what did they hope to accomplish?

14. Discuss the significance of the Dutch roots of the New York colony.

15. Enumerate and discuss the unique social features of the Pennsylvania colony.

16. What were the causes and the consequences of Bacon's Rebellion in Virginia?

SUGGESTED ESSAY TOPICS

1. In what ways did the societies that Europeans created in America differ from one another? In what ways were they similar?

2. Explain the major differences between Catholicism and Protestantism (Calvinism, in particular).

3. How successful were colonists at duplicating the society of their parent cultures?

4. Assess the following statement: "New England proved an ideal model for how to build a colony, while Virginia proved an example of how not to establish one."

5. Discuss the role of religion in the founding of the European colonies in the Americas.

LECTURE OUTLINE

1. The **Protestant Reformation** in Europe provided one **challenge to Spain** and set the tenor of European conflict, based on religious differences.

2.   **New France** comprised sparsely settled trading entrepôts primarily along the Saint Lawrence River, where the inhabitants suffered through the frigid winter in order to trade in furs.

         a.   **Early French** explorers included Verrazzano and Cartier; they were sent abroad at the behest of King Francis I in an attempt to claim some of the Western Hemisphere for France.

         b.   **New France under Louis XIV** remained an under populated outpost characterized by **missions and the fur trade**, but little else.

3.   The **Dutch and Swedish settlements** of North America in the Hudson River and Delaware Bay were primarily trading outposts characterized by reasonably good relations with the Indian peoples.

         a.   Sparsely populated **New Netherland** was essentially the dominion of the East and West India Companies, as the government of the Netherlands had few resources to devote to full-scale colonization of North America.

         b.   New Netherland proved one of the first **pluralistic societies**, by necessity containing ethnic and religious diversity.

         c.   **Swedish and English encroachments** on the Dutch led to conflict in the 1640s.

(SHOW TRANSPARENCY 13: NORTH AMERICA IN THE EARLY 17TH CENTURY)

4.   Increasing numbers of settlers, relative stability, and a growing economy helped to spark a **challenge to all empires from Elizabethan England.**

         a.   When the strife of the **English Reformation** finally subsided with the accession of Queen Elizabeth and the permanent establishment of the Anglican Church, England could direct more of its resources to colonization.

         b.   England benefited from its several **rehearsals for colonization** of North America.

                 i.   Before any full-scale colonization, the pirates **Hawkins and Drake** plundered the Spanish Main in search of gold and glory.

                 ii.   **Sir Humphrey Gilbert,** having brutally colonized Ireland, set his sights on establishing settlements in America.

                 iii.   **Walter Raleigh** attempted three successive settlements in the Chesapeake, including **Roanoke**, but was refused by the queen to lead his expeditions in person.

(SHOW TRANSPARENCY 10: ROANOKE COLONY, 1584-1590)

         c.   The seventeenth century marked the **swarming of the English** in successive waves onto the North American shores in numbers unmatched by any other European nation.

(SHOW TRANSPARENCY 11: THE ENGLISH IN AMERICA, 1583-1607)

         d.   The first permanent English migrations went to the **Chesapeake and the West Indian Colonies,** where they suffered greatly from disease and Indian attacks.

i.   The first Chesapeake settlement turned into the **Jamestown Disaster** of 1607, when the colony ran out of food, and the settlers suffered from devastating illnesses.

ii. More attention by the Crown led to **reorganization, reform, and crisis** in the first decades of Virginia's history, culminating in the replacement of the Virginia Company's charter with royal control.

iii. The survival and economic viability of the fledgling colony depended overwhelmingly on tobacco and the importation of white indentured **servants**.

iv. Charles I granted Lord Baltimore the charter to **Maryland** in 1632.

v.   A disproportion of men, short life expectancy, high rates of illegitimacy, and frequent remarriage among women characterized **Chesapeake family life**.

vi. The **West Indies** produced labor-intensive staple crops that virtually guaranteed the transition to slavery.

(SHOW TRANSPARENCY 14: PRINCIPAL WEST INDIAN COLONIES IN THE 17TH CENTURY)

vii. The **rise of slavery in North America** proved gradual, with few laws distinguishing between white and black until the eighteenth century.

e.   Seeking relief from religious persecution, dissenters of all stripes dominated the settlement of the **New England colonies**.

i.   The **Pilgrims** fled Europe to establish **Plymouth** in 1620.

ii. Protestants articulated their relationship with God by means of a **covenant theology** articulated by a learned ministry and a devout laity.

iii. Puritans settled **Massachusetts Bay** with thirteen thousand people in what has been called the Great Migration between 1629 and 1639.

iv. Close ties of extended families, corporate communities, and church life characterized **Puritan family life** in the seventeenth century.

v.   **Conversion, dissent, and expansion** marked the inevitable movement away from the closed corporate communities of the early years of settlement.

vi. Puritans established forms of self-government through **congregations, towns, and colony governments.**

vii. Controversy over **infant baptism and new dissent** caused repeated crises in New England's Congregational churches, the most important of which resulted in the articulation of the **Half-Way Covenant.**

f.   **The English civil wars** temporarily halted the progress of North American colonization between 1640 and 1660.

g.   The **first Restoration colonies** followed closely on the heels of the restoration of Charles II in 1660.

i. **James Harrington and the Aristocratic Ideal** of a self-governed land of enlightened landholders figured prominently in the foundation of the Carolinas.

ii. The colony of **New York** proved a failed experiment in absolutism but thrived as a diverse colony of traders and landowners.

iii. William Penn founded Pennsylvania as a colony of brotherly love dominated by the **Quakers**, whose religious and familial beliefs made the colony unique and attractive for immigrants.

(SHOW TRANSPARENCY 15: FRENCH, ENGLISH, DUTCH, AND SWEDISH COLONIES IN EASTERN NORTH AMERICA, 1650)

Conclusion: It took the nations of northwest Europe some time to plant colonies in the Western Hemisphere, but by 1600 they had begun to expand in earnest. Within a century, the French, Dutch, and English had effectively challenged Spanish domination of the Atlantic frontier and had firmly established colonies throughout the Atlantic coast of North America.

TEACHING RESOURCES

The Magna Carta is an examination of the origins and historical significance of one of the most important documents of Anglo-American political culture. Films for the Humanities (22 minutes).

America: The Newfound Land, narrated by Alistair Cooke, discusses how the British decimated the Indians and out-dueled the Spanish and French for North America. BBC/Time–Life Video (52 minutes).

Colonizing North America: Early Settlements depicts the lives of early settlers, from Jamestown through the turn of the eighteenth century. Filmic Archives (18 minutes).

The Enterprise of England offers an analysis of the reign of Elizabeth I. BBC Video (58 minutes).

America: Home Away from Home examines the Puritan, Pilgrim, and Quaker settlements of the east coast. Narrated by Alistair Cooke. BBC/Time–Life Video (52 minutes).

Plimoth Plantation reveals the life of Plymouth colony in the year 1627 as told by its "residents." VideoTours History Collection (30 minutes).

MULTIPLE CHOICE

1. The Protestant Reformation argued that
   a. a person could find salvation through faith alone.
   b. a person could find salvation through good works alone.
   c. a papal hierarchy was necessary for good order.
   d. the seven sacraments were necessary for salvation.
   e. the world was about to end.

ANS: A   **TYPE: M**   **KEY 1: F**   **KEY 2: 1**   **PAGE: 44**

2. The man most responsible for the French colonization of North America was
    a. King Louis XIV
    b. Samuel de Champlain.
    c. François Quebec.
    d. Cardinal Richelieu.
    e. Cabeza de Vaca.

ANS: B   **TYPE: M**   **KEY 1: A**   **KEY 2: 2**   **PAGE: 46**

3. The coureurs de bois were
    a. French Jesuits.
    b. French fur traders.
    c. French tax collectors.
    d. French craftsmen.
    e. French hair stylists.

ANS: B   **TYPE: M**   **KEY 1: F**   **KEY 2: 1**   **PAGE: 47**

4. By the mid-eighteenth century, the most important French colony was
    a. Martinique.
    b. St. Dominque (Haiti).
    c. Guadeloupe.
    d. Canada.
    e. Florida.

ANS: B   **TYPE: M**   **KEY 1: A**   **KEY 2: 3**   **PAGE: 49**

5. A Dutch patroonship was
    a. a high government office in North America.
    b. about $100.
    c. a large estate.
    d. a fur trader.
    e. an improved sailing vessel.

ANS: C   **TYPE: M**   **KEY 1: F**   **KEY 2: 2**   **PAGE: 50**

6. The English monarch most responsible for defining the Protestant Reformation in England was
    a. Mary of Scotland.
    b. James II.
    c. Charles I.
    d. Elizabeth I.
    e. Philip II.

ANS: D   **TYPE: M**   **KEY 1: F**   **KEY 2: 1**   **PAGE: 52**

7. The model for England's conquest and colonization of North America was
    a. New Spain.
    b. Brazil.
    c. Greenland.
    d. Wales.
    e. Ireland.

ANS: E   **TYPE: M**   **KEY 1: A**   **KEY 2: 2**   **PAGE: 53**

8. Which of the following statements about early Jamestown is most correct?
   a. It was a great success.
   b. Its success or failure was unclear.
   c. It was saved by the discovery of silver.
   d. It was a deathtrap.
   e. It was a profitable venture for the London Company.

ANS: D   **TYPE: M**   **KEY 1: A**   **KEY 2: 1**   **PAGE: 55-56**

9. The primary export of the Virginia Colony was
   a. cotton.
   b. wheat.
   c. tobacco.
   d. flax.
   e. sugar.

ANS: C   **TYPE: M**   **KEY 1: F**   **KEY 2: 2**   **PAGE: 57**

10. The colony that was established as a Catholic refuge was
    a. Massachusetts.
    b. New Jersey.
    c. Delaware.
    d. Maryland.
    e. Pennsylvania.

ANS: D   **TYPE: M**   **KEY 1: F**   **KEY 2: 3**   **PAGE: 59**

11. The colony of Massachusetts Bay was settled by
    a. Catholics.
    b. Puritans.
    c. Quakers.
    d. Anglicans.
    e. Jews.

ANS: B   **TYPE: M**   **KEY 1: F**   **KEY 2: 1**   **PAGE: 66**

12. One of the primary founders of the colony of Rhode Island was
    a. Thomas Hooker.
    b. John Winthrop.
    c. Roger Williams.
    d. William Bradstreet.
    e. John Smith.

ANS: C   **TYPE: M**   **KEY 1: F**   **KEY 2: 2**   **PAGE: 69**

13. The popular religious leader who was banned from Massachusetts in the 1630s was
    a. John Cotton.
    b. Increase Mather.
    c. Anne Hutchinson.
    d. Cotton Mather.
    e. Squanto.

ANS: C   **TYPE: M**   **KEY 1: F**   **KEY 2: 2**   **PAGE: 69**

14. The Half-way Covenant refers to
    a. religious concessions made to those who had not had the salvation experience.
    b. the responsibilities a person had to the community in which they lived.
    c. the status of a couple between engagement and marriage.
    d. contractual landholding responsibilities.
    e. the labor contract that bound servants to work in return for their passage to the New World.

ANS: A   **TYPE: M**   **KEY 1: F**   **KEY 2: 1**   **PAGE: 71**

15. The "jeremiad" was
    a. a sermon that lamented religious shortcomings.
    b. the rite practiced at Indian powwows.
    c. the good works individuals engaged in for salvation.
    d. indulgences sold by the church for salvation.
    e. the campaign against the Indians in New England.

ANS: A   **TYPE: M**   **KEY 1: F**   **KEY 2: 2**   **PAGE: 71**

16. Puritans believed that a person's salvation depended on
    a. good works.
    b. following the teachings of the church.
    c. God's covenant of grace.
    d. chance.
    e. intercession by the

ANS: C   **TYPE: M**   **KEY 1: A**   **KEY 2: 2**   **PAGE: 65**

17. Jamestown was established and settled by
    a. Elizabeth I.
    b. coastal fishermen from New England.
    c. a joint-stock company.
    d. Puritans.
    e. Quakers.

ANS: C   **TYPE: M**   **KEY 1: F**   **KEY 2: 2**   **PAGE: 55**

18. The Indian warrior who led the massacre of 1622 against the Virginia settlers was
    a. Powhatan.
    b. Massasoit.
    c. Opechancanough.
    d. Squanto.
    e. Tonto.

ANS: C   **TYPE: M**   **KEY 1: F**   **KEY 2: 2**   **PAGE: 57**

19. The monarch who sat on the English throne during early seventeenth-century colonization in North America was
    a. Elizabeth I.
    b. James I.
    c. James II.
    d. Charles II.
    e. Philip II.

ANS: B   **TYPE: M**   **KEY 1: F**   **KEY 2: 2**   **PAGE: 55**

20. All of the following religious groups followed Calvinist principles except
    a. Lutherans.
    b. Presbyterians.
    c. Puritans.
    d. Huguenots.
    e. Dutch Reformed Church.

ANS: A   TYPE: M   KEY 1: F   KEY 2: 2   PAGE: 45

21. Calvinists believe that
    a. Christians should give away all their material possessions.
    b. women were spiritually inferior and could not be saved.
    c. a person's salvation or damnation was predestined by God.
    d. the elect earned their salvation through acts of penitence.
    e. all human beings were saved.

ANS: C   TYPE: M   KEY 1: A   KEY 2: 2   PAGE: 45

22. Which of the following is true of Samuel de Champlain?
    a. He was a devout Catholic who enslaved the Indians who would not convert to Christianity.
    b. He explored the St. Lawrence River and founded the French colony of Quebec.
    c. He was the French king who offered religious toleration to the Huguenots.
    d. He was so harsh and autocratic that his own soldiers murdered him.
    e. He sailed for the English.

ANS: B   TYPE: M   KEY 1: F   KEY 2: 2   PAGE: 46

23. In the colony of New France,
    a. high ranking government officials were elected by the local land owners.
    b. fur trading and wheat farming provided the basis for a prosperous economy.
    c. slavery was outlawed.
    d. the population was two times larger than that of France itself.
    e. Indians were all killed.

ANS: B   TYPE: M   KEY 1: F   KEY 2: 2   PAGE: 48

24. The Dutch Republic and its North American colonies
    a. were primarily motivated by a desire to spread Christianity around the world.
    b. were ruled by centralized monarchial governments.
    c. promoted free trade, religious toleration, and local political control.
    d. were the smallest and poorest of the European empires.
    e. had the largest number of African slaves in the world.

ANS: C   TYPE: M   KEY 1: F   KEY 2: 2   PAGE: 53

25. In the English Reformation,
    a. the monastic orders expanded their landholdings and increased church taxes.
    b. thousands of Catholics were burned as witches.
    c. Henry VIII proclaimed himself the "only Supreme Head" of the Church of England.
    d. the Pope appointed Henry VIII his agent in England.
    e. all of the above

ANS: C   TYPE: M   KEY 1: F   KEY 2: 3   PAGE: 52

26. Sir Francis Drake was
    a. the leader of the English Reformation.
    b. an English explorer who led an expedition to locate the "Northwest Passage."
    c. the Italian mapmaker for whom the continents of the Western Hemisphere were named.
    d. the founder of the colony of Jamestown.
    e. an English slave trader and pirate who raided Spanish possessions in South America.

ANS: E   TYPE: M   KEY 1: F   KEY 2: 1   PAGE: 52

27. English colonization efforts in Ireland and North America were similar in that in both places
    a. the Protestants comprised an overwhelming majority of the population.
    b. the English used harsh tactics, including massacring of women and children, to subdue the native peoples.
    c. the English liberated the oppressed natives and introduced democratic self-government.
    d. the English admired and copied many of the traditions and beliefs of the natives.
    e. the conquest was accomplished without bloodshed.

ANS: B   TYPE: M   KEY 1: A   KEY 2: 3   PAGE: 52-3

28. Richard Nicolls was
    a. the first English governor of New York.
    b. the founder of the Baptist Church.
    c. a prosperous New England shipbuilder.
    d. hanged for religious heresy in Massachusetts.
    e. the founder of the Massachusetts Bay Colony.

ANS: A   TYPE: M   KEY 1: F   KEY 2: 3   PAGE: 74

29. All of the following were problems faced by the early settlers of Jamestown except that
    a. there were not enough gentlemen and specialized craftsmen to provide leadership for the colony.
    b. the colony was located in a malaria- and typhoid-infested area.
    c. the colonists often faced starvation due to lack of supplies and lack of farming skills.
    d. local Indians were unpredictable and often hostile toward the colonists.
    e. After Smith returned to England, the colonly lacked firm leadership.

ANS: A   TYPE: M   KEY 1: A   KEY 2: 3   PAGE: 55

30. John Smith is noted for
    a. encouraging the London Company to forget about colonization.
    b. saving the Jamestown Colony by forcing the colonists to work.
    c. marrying the beautiful Indian princess Pocahontas.
    d. leading several successful English attacks on Panama.
    e. introducing the production of tobacco in Virginia.

ANS: B   TYPE: M   KEY 1: F   KEY 2: 2   PAGE: 55

31. Under the headright system,
    a. a colonist received fifty acres of free land for every person for whom he paid passage to Virginia.
    b. a head tax was levied on every adult man and woman in the colonies.
    c. serious crimes were punished by decapitation.
    d. the wealthiest males in the colony were allowed to go first (at the head) of community processions.
    e. a tax was levied for each slave brought into the colony.

ANS: A   TYPE: M   KEY 1: F   KEY 2: 2   PAGE: 57

32. Early colonial population statistics for Virginia and Maryland reveal that
    a. women outnumbered men by a ratio of five to one.
    b. most men outlived their first wives and immediately remarried.
    c. most men lived to age 45, while most women died before the age of 40.
    d. colonials were healthier and lived longer than people in England.
    e. their colonists lived longer than those in the northern colonies.

ANS: C   **TYPE: M**   **KEY 1: F**   **KEY 2: 2**   **PAGE: 61**

33. Which of the following is true of the Massachusetts Bay Colony?
    a. Its original colonists were mostly educated, prosperous property owners.
    b. It was founded by English Puritans who created their own joint-stock company.
    c. Its colonists were healthier and lived longer than the Virginia Colonists.
    d. New England towns formed tight communities.
    e. all of the above

ANS: D   **TYPE: M**   **KEY 1: F**   **KEY 2: 2**   **PAGE: 66-68**

34. Roger Williams was banished from Massachusetts because he believed that
    a. the king lacked the authority to grant title to Indian lands.
    b. only adult male Puritans should be allowed to vote and hold office.
    c. no Jews or atheists should be allowed in the colony.
    d. all colonial churches should be under the authority of the Anglican Archbishop of Canterbury.
    e. the king ruled by divine right.

ANS: A   **TYPE: M**   **KEY 1: F**   **KEY 2: 2**   **PAGE: 69**

35. Anne Hutchinson was
    a. one of the hysterical girls who participated in the Salem witchcraft trials.
    b. a Puritan woman who was expelled from Massachusetts for claiming that she communicated directly with God.
    c. the wife of the first royal governor of Massachusetts.
    d. the first English woman brought to Virginia as an indentured servant.
    e. a famous poet.

ANS: B   **TYPE: M**   **KEY 1: F**   **KEY 2: 2**   **PAGE: 69**

36. The Restoration colonies were
    a. the smallest and least profitable colonies in New England.
    b. founded by political exiles who were driven out of the Puritan colonies.
    c. Rhode Island, Connecticut, Maine, and Vermont.
    d. founded by the Catholics.
    e. proprietary colonies founded by cavalier supporters of Charles II and James II.

ANS: E   **TYPE: M**   **KEY 1: F**   **KEY 2: 3**   **PAGE: 72**

37. The colony of New York
    a. attracted thousands of English colonists because of its democratic government and elected assembly.
    b. was established by a charter written by John Locke.
    c. remained predominately Dutch in population and culture throughout the seventeenth century.
    d. was founded by Quakers escaping from religious persecution in England.
    e. was founded as a have for debtors.

ANS: C   **TYPE: M**   **KEY 1: F**   **KEY 2: 3**   **PAGE: 76**

38. Quakers were persecuted for all except which of the following reasons?
    a. They believed in the absolute authority of a trained minister over the congregation.
    b. They were pacifists.
    c. They believed that God dwelt within each individual in the form of an Inner Light.
    d. They granted women almost complete social and spiritual equality.
    e. They denounced oath-taking as sinful.

ANS: A   TYPE: M   KEY 1: A   KEY 2: 3   PAGE: 76

39. Which of the following is true of slavery in the English colonies?
    a. By the time of the American Revolution, most colonies had outlawed slavery.
    b. Most of the slaves in North America lived in the New England colonies.
    c. The Dutch first introduced slavery to the Virginia colony before 1619.
    d. Since slavery was common in England, it also was a basic feature of all the colonies.
    e. Only South Carolina had established slavery at the time of the American Revolution.

ANS: C   TYPE: M   KEY 1: F   KEY 2: 2   PAGE: 62

40. The "lord protector" who led England following the beheading of Charles I was
    a. James Harrington.
    b. Oliver Cromwell
    c. William of Orange.
    d. John Locke.
    e. James II.

ANS: B   TYPE: M   KEY 1: F   KEY 2: 1   PAGE: 71

41. The author of *Oceana* was
    a. James Harrington.
    b. John Milton.
    c. Niccolo Machiavelli.
    d. King James II.
    e. Bishop de las Casas.

ANS: A   TYPE: M   KEY 1: F   KEY 2: 3   PAGE: 72

42. The staple export of South Carolina by the early eighteenth century was
    a. tobacco.
    b. wheat.
    c. cotton.
    d. rice.
    e. tomatoes.

ANS: D   TYPE: M   KEY 1: F   KEY 2: 2   PAGE: 73-4

43. The founder of the Society of Friends, or Quakers, was
    a. John Milton.
    b. John Calvin.
    c. John Winthrop.
    d. George Fox.
    e. William Penn.

ANS: D   TYPE: M   KEY 1: F   KEY 2: 2   PAGE: 76

44. Quakers believed that each individual could be saved by
    a. attendance in church on Sundays.
    b. the active involvement of church ministers.
    c. the covenant.
    d. the "Inner Light."
    e. priests.

ANS: D   **TYPE: M**   **KEY 1: F**   **KEY 2: 3**   **PAGE: 76**

45. Early Pennsylvania also was referred to as
    a. the "city upon a hill."
    b. the "holy experiment."
    c. the "city of God."
    d. the "holy commune."
    e. the "hotbed of sin."

ANS: B   **TYPE: M**   **KEY 1: F**   **KEY 2: 2**   **PAGE: 77**

46. Settlers were attracted to Pennsylvania in large numbers because of
    a. liberal land grants.
    b. religious toleration.
    c. the democratically elected assembly.
    d. liberal legal code and protection of rights
    e. all of the above.

ANS: E   **TYPE: M**   **KEY 1: A**   **KEY 2: 1**   **PAGE: 77-9**

47. Which of the following is not true of the society envisioned in the Fundamental Constitutions of
    Carolina?
    a. Religious toleration was guaranteed.
    b. Slavery was prohibited.
    c. Nobles would control 40 percent of the land.
    d. Citizenship depended on church membership.
    e. a class of lowly whites would live on small tracts of land and serve their landlords.

ANS: B   **TYPE: M**   **KEY 1: A**   **KEY 2: 3**   **PAGE: 73**

48. Which of the following had established a permanent settlement in North America before 1600?
    a. France
    b. Spain
    c. England
    d. the Netherlands
    e. Portugal

ANS: B   **TYPE: M**   **KEY 1: F**   **KEY 2: 1**   **PAGE: 44**

49. By 1700, the largest city in New France was
    a. Quebec.
    b. Three Rivers.
    c. Montreal.
    d. Toronto.
    e. Cincinati

ANS: C   **TYPE: M**   **KEY 1: F**   **KEY 2: 3**   **PAGE: 48**

50. Henry Hudson sailed for
    a. the Nethelands.
    b. France.
    c. England.
    d. Portugal.
    e. Italy.

ANS: A   TYPE: M   KEY 1: F   KEY 2: 2   PAGE: 50

51. The Toleration Act applied to
    a. Virginia.
    b. Maryland.
    c. Rhode Island.
    d. Massachusetts.
    e. New Spain.

ANS: B   TYPE: M   KEY 1: F   KEY 2: 2   PAGE: 60

52. The Puritan idea that God would not punish the whole community for misdeeds of individuals stemmed from the
    a. covenant of works.
    b. covenant of grace.
    c. church covenant.
    d. national covenant.
    e. Bible.

ANS: D   TYPE: M   KEY 1: A   KEY 2: 3   PAGE: 66

53. Of the 13,000 settlers who went to New England by 1641, _____ were families.
    a. few
    b. most
    c. none
    d. all
    e. twelve

ANS: B   TYPE: M   KEY 1: A   KEY 2: 3   PAGE: 66

54. Roger Williams and a handful of disciples founded
    a. Newport.
    b. Portsmouth.
    c. Providence.
    d. New Haven.
    e. Canada.

ANS: C   TYPE: M   KEY 1: F   KEY 2: 2   PAGE: 69

55. William Penn's constitution for Pennsylvania was called the
    a. Plan of Government.
    b. Fundamental Governing Law.
    c. First Frame of Government.
    d. Governmental Outline.
    e. Bill of Rights.

ANS: C   TYPE: M   KEY 1: F   KEY 2: 3   PAGE: 78

56. By 1620, _____ foreign trade probably exceeded that of the rest of Europe combined.
    a. German
    b. Spanish
    c. Portuguese
    d. English
    e. Dutch

ANS: E   TYPE: M   KEY 1: F   KEY 2: 2   PAGE: 50

57. By 1645, the primary crop of Barbados was
    a. cotton.
    b. sugar.
    c. tobacco.
    d. hemp.
    e. rice.

ANS: B   TYPE: M   KEY 1: F   KEY 2: 2   PAGE: 62

58. Among the Quakers hanged by Massachusetts was
    a. Mary Dyer.
    b. Anne Hutchinson.
    c. Samuel Gorton.
    d. Henry Dinster.
    e. John Winthrop.

ANS: A   TYPE: M   KEY 1: F   KEY 2: 3   PAGE: 71

59. Before becoming Lord Protector of England, Oliver Cromwell gained fame as a
    a. member of the House of Lords.
    b. member of the House of Commons.
    c. military commander.
    d. religious leader.
    e. popular singer.

ANS: C   TYPE: M   KEY 1: F   KEY 2: 3   PAGE: 71

60. The last of the original thirteen colonies to be founded was
    a. North Carolina.
    b. South Carolina.
    c. New Hampshire.
    d. Georgia.
    e. New York.

ANS: D   TYPE: M   KEY 1: F   KEY 2: 2   PAGE: 72

TRUE/FALSE

_____ 1.   Women far outnumbered men in early Virginia.

ANS: F   TYPE: T   KEY 1: F   KEY 2: 1   PAGE: 60

_____ 2.   The Puritans attempted to "purify" the Catholic Church.

ANS: F   TYPE: T   KEY 1: A   KEY 2: 3   PAGE: 52

_____ 3.   The person most responsible for the development of tobacco as a cash crop in Virginia was John Rolfe.

ANS: T   **TYPE: T**   **KEY 1: F**   **KEY 2: 2**   **PAGE: 57**

_____ 4.   Most of the colonists who sailed to England's North American colonies were young, unmarried men.

ANS: T   **TYPE: T**   **KEY 1: A**   **KEY 2: 1**   **PAGE: 59**

_____ 5.   Quakers saw children as tiny sinners and practiced harsh discipline.

ANS: F   **TYPE: T**   **KEY 1: A**   **KEY 2: 2**   **PAGE: 77**

_____ 6.   Early Virginia was a paradise compared to seventeenth-century England.

ANS: F   **TYPE: T**   **KEY 1: A**   **KEY 2: 1**   **PAGE: 55**

_____ 7.   Anne Hutchinson was banished from Massachusetts Bay because of her religious beliefs.

ANS: T   **TYPE: T**   **KEY 1: F**   **KEY 2: 1**   **PAGE: 69**

_____ 8.   The Protestants in the New World treated the Indians more humanely than did the Catholics.

ANS: F   **TYPE: T**   **KEY 1: A**   **KEY 2: 2**   **PAGE: 47**

_____ 9.   The French Jesuit missionaries were unique in that they believed in converting the Indians to Christianity without interfering with tribal customs.

ANS: T   **TYPE: T**   **KEY 1: A**   **KEY 2: 2**   **PAGE: 47**

_____ 10.   New Netherland was the most religiously and ethnically diverse of the seventeenth-century North American colonies.

ANS: T   **TYPE: T**   **KEY 1: F**   **KEY 2: 2**   **PAGE: 51**

_____ 11.   The term Yankee is derived from an Indian word meaning foreigner.

ANS: F   **TYPE: T**   **KEY 1: F**   **KEY 2: 2**   **PAGE: 51**

_____ 12.   William Penn received his Pennsylvania grant in payment of a debt owed by Charles II to his father.

ANS: T   **TYPE: T**   **KEY 1: F**   **KEY 2: 2**   **PAGE: 78**

_____ 13.   Calvinism gave special emphasis to predestination.

ANS: T   **TYPE: T**   **KEY 1: A**   **KEY 2: 2**   **PAGE: 44**

_____ 14.   The New York Charter of Liberties imposed Dutch law on the English parts of the province.

ANS: F   **TYPE: T**   **KEY 1: A**   **KEY 2: 3**   **PAGE: 76**

_____ 15.   Samuel de Champlain succeeded in uniting Catholics and Protestants in New France in mutual harmony.

ANS: F   **TYPE: T**   **KEY 1: F**   **KEY 2: 1**   **PAGE: 46**

_____ 16.   Jesuits did not believe that Indians had to be Europeanized before they could be Christianized.

ANS: T   **TYPE: T**   **KEY 1: A**   **KEY 2: 2**   **PAGE: 47-8**

_____ 17.   The church tithe in New France was higher than in France itself.

ANS: F   **TYPE: T**   **KEY 1: F**   **KEY 2: 3**   **PAGE: 48**

_____ 18.   For most of the seventeenth century, the Dutch were more active overseas than the French.

ANS: T   **TYPE: T**   **KEY 1: F**   **KEY 2: 2**   **PAGE: 50-1**

_____ 19.   The Church of England became Catholic in doctrine and theology but remained largely Calvinist in structure, liturgy, and ritual.

ANS: F   **TYPE: T**   **KEY 1: A**   **KEY 2: 3**   **PAGE: 52**

_____ 20.   The bicameral legislature that Lord Baltimore instituted in Maryland was likely to see Protestants dominate the elective assembly and Catholics control the appointive council.

ANS: T   **TYPE: T**   **KEY 1: A**   **KEY 2: 3**   **PAGE: 60**

_____ 21.   Before 1700, far more Englishmen went to the West Indies than the Chesapeake.

ANS: T   **TYPE: T**   **KEY 1: A**   **KEY 2: 2**   **PAGE: 62**

_____ 22.   At first, men outnumbered women in Virginia and Maryland.

ANS: T   **TYPE: T**   **KEY 1: A**   **KEY 2: 1**   **PAGE: 60**

_____ 23.   By the early 1700s, racial caste was replacing opportunity as the organizing principle of Chesapeake society.

ANS: T   **TYPE: T**   **KEY 1: A**   **KEY 2: 2**   **PAGE: 63-4**

_____ 24.   In New England, Puritan orthodoxy was mostly an urban phenomenon.

ANS: F   **TYPE: T**   **KEY 1: F**   **KEY 2: 2**   **PAGE: 57**

_____ 25.   The founders of Connecticut feared that Massachusetts was too lenient in certifying church members.

ANS: F   **TYPE: T**   **KEY 1: A**   **KEY 2: 2**   **PAGE: 68-9**

_____ 26.   Early Pennsylvanians fought often with their Indian neighbors.

ANS: F   **TYPE: T**   **KEY 1: A**   **KEY 2: 2**   **PAGE: 68**

_____ 27.   The Baptists posed the greatest alarm for the Puritan establishment.

ANS: F   **TYPE: T**   **KEY 1: A**   **KEY 2: 2**   **PAGE: 71**

_____ 28.   The Fundamental Constitutions of Carolina sought to create an ideal aristocratic society.

ANS: T   **TYPE: T**   **KEY 1: A**   **KEY 2: 2**   **PAGE: 73**

_____ 29.   Pennsylvanians organized a militia shortly after the founding of their colony.

ANS: F   **TYPE: T**   **KEY 1: A**   **KEY 2: 3**   **PAGE: 78**

_____ 30.   From the start, wealth in Pennsylvania rested on trade with other colonies, especially the West Indies.

ANS: T   **TYPE: T**   **KEY 1: A**   **KEY 2: 2**   **PAGE: 80**

_____ 31.   The only Catholic sacrament accepted by Calvinists was baptism.

ANS: F   **TYPE: T**   **KEY 1: A**   **KEY 2: 2**   **PAGE: 44**

_____ 32.   The Jesuits focused their missionary efforts on the Iroquois Five Tribes.

ANS: F   **TYPE: T**   **KEY 1: F**   **KEY 2: 3**   **PAGE: 47-8**

_____ 33.   During the seventeenth century, Spain was the most populated part of Europe.

ANS: F   **TYPE: T**   **KEY 1: A**   **KEY 2: 2**   **PAGE: 49**

_____ 34.   The Dutch Republic was religiously homogeneous.

ANS: F   **TYPE: T**   **KEY 1: F**   **KEY 2: 2**   **PAGE: 50**

_____ 35.   By 1620, Dutch foreign trade probably exceeded that of the rest of Europe combined.

ANS: T   **TYPE: T**   **KEY 1: F**   **KEY 2: 2**   **PAGE: 50**

_____ 36.   The Dutch East India Company was chartered before the Dutch West India Company.

ANS: T   **TYPE: T**   **KEY 1: F**   **KEY 2: 3**   **PAGE: 50**

_____ 37.   The Dutch and the French both ventured deep into the woods of their respective territorial holdings.

ANS: F   **TYPE: T**   **KEY 1: A**   **KEY 2: 2**   **PAGE: 50**

_____ 38.   The Dutch patroonship system thrived in New Netherland.

ANS: F   **TYPE: T**   **KEY 1: F**   **KEY 2: 2**   **PAGE: 50**

_____ 39.   The London Company performed abysmally in Virginia, spending an extravagant sum for very little return.

ANS: T   **TYPE: T**   **KEY 1: A**   **KEY 2: 2**   **PAGE: 58**

_____ 40.   Like Virginia, Maryland had established churches and vestries.

ANS: F   TYPE: T   KEY 1: A   KEY 2: 2   PAGE: 60

FILL-INS

1.   The Englishman who explored the North River was _____.

ANS: Henry Hudson   TYPE: F   KEY 1: F   KEY 2: 1   PAGE: 50

2.   The colony of Maryland was founded by the _____ family.

ANS: Calvert   TYPE: F   KEY 1: F   KEY 2: 3   PAGE: 59

3.   The man most responsible for increasing immigration to Virginia and for implementing a series of major reforms after 1618 was _____.

ANS: Edmund Sandys   TYPE: F   KEY 1: F   KEY 2: 3   PAGE: 57

4.   For Puritans, the agreement between God and man under which all humans deserve damnation was the _____.

ANS: Covenant of Works   TYPE: F   KEY 1: F   KEY 2: 2   PAGE: 65

5.   More thought went into the planning of _____ than into the creation of any other colony.

ANS: Pennsylvania   TYPE: F   KEY 1: F   KEY 2: 2   PAGE: 78

6.   The German monk who launched the Protestant Reformation by nailing his 95 Theses to the door of Wittenberg Cathedral was _____.

ANS: Martin Luther   TYPE: F   KEY 1: F   KEY 2: 1   PAGE: 44

7.   _____ was the first Englishman to circumnavigate (sail around) the Earth.

ANS: Francis Drake   TYPE: F   KEY 1: F   KEY 2: 2   PAGE: 52

8.   The Puritans wanted to push the Church of England in a more _____ direction.

ANS: Calvinist   TYPE: F   KEY 1: A   KEY 2: 2   PAGE: 45

9.   Henry IV granted limited toleration to _____ through the Edict of Nantes in 1598.

ANS: Huguenots   TYPE: F   KEY 1: F   KEY 2: 2   PAGE: 46

10.   Samuel de Champlain founded _____.

ANS: Quebec   TYPE: F   KEY 1: F   KEY 2: 1   PAGE: 46

11.   After 1750, _____ became the world's richest colony.

ANS: Saint-Domingue   TYPE: F   KEY 1: F   KEY 2: 2   PAGE: 49

12. _____ became North America's first experiment in ethnic and religious pluralism.

ANS: New Netherland   TYPE: F   KEY 1: F   KEY 2: 3   PAGE: 51

13. By 1700, _____ was the first largest city in western Europe.

ANS: London   TYPE: F   KEY 1: F   KEY 2: 2   PAGE: 52

14. After victory in the Irish wars of the 1560s, Sir _____ sought to colonize Newfoundland for England.

ANS: Humphrey Gilbert   TYPE: F   KEY 1: F   KEY 2: 3   PAGE: 52

15. _____ was responsible for introducing tobacco to Virginia.

ANS: John Rolfe   TYPE: F   KEY 1: F   KEY 2: 2   PAGE: 57

16. _____ was the first royal colony.

ANS: Virginia   TYPE: F   KEY 1: F   KEY 2: 2   PAGE: 58

17. The population of Virginia and Maryland became self-sustaining about _____, when live births finally began to outnumber deaths.

ANS: 1680   TYPE: F   KEY 1: F   KEY 2: 3   PAGE: 60

18. The founders of _____ believed that Massachusetts was much too lenient in certifying church members.

ANS: New Haven Colony   TYPE: F   KEY 1: A   KEY 2: 2   PAGE: 68

19. The Cambridge Platform defined _____ worship and church organization.

ANS: Congregationalist   TYPE: F   KEY 1: F   KEY 2: 3   PAGE: 69

20. England had founded _____ of the original thirteen colonies before 1640.

ANS: six   TYPE: F   KEY 1: F   KEY 2: 2   PAGE: 72

21. _____, located at the confluence of the Ashley and Cooper rivers, was the first genuine city in the American South.

ANS: Charleston   TYPE: F   KEY 1: F   KEY 2: 2   PAGE: 73

22. _____ founded the Society of Friends, or Quakers.

ANS: George Fox   TYPE: F   KEY 1: F   KEY 2: 3   PAGE: 76

23. By 1700, about _____ of the Quakers in England and Wales had moved to America.

ANS: half   TYPE: F   KEY 1: F   KEY 2: 3   PAGE: 77

24. Henry IV of France was _____, which meant that he insisted that the survival of the state took precedence over religious differences.

ANS: *politique*   **TYPE: F**   **KEY 1: F**   **KEY 2: 3**   **PAGE: 46**

25. By 1560, England's chief export was _____.

ANS: woolen cloth   **TYPE: F**   **KEY 1: F**   **KEY 2: 2**   **PAGE: 52**

26. _____ was governor of Plymouth almost continuously from 1620 to his death in 1656.

ANS: William Bradford   **TYPE: F**   **KEY 1: F**   **KEY 2: 3**   **PAGE: 64**

27. _____ formulated the idea that New England would be a "city upon a hill."

ANS: John Winthrop   **TYPE: F**   **KEY 1: F**   **KEY 2: 1**   **PAGE: 66**

28. The Body of Liberties, formulated in _____ in 1641, may be history's first bill of rights.

ANS: Massachusetts   **TYPE: F**   **KEY 1: F**   **KEY 2: 2**   **PAGE: 70**

29. The most fascinating social experiment of the Restoration era was the founding and spread of the _____.

ANS: Quakers (or Society of Friends)   **TYPE: F**   **KEY 1: A**   **KEY 2: 2**   **PAGE: 76**

30. _____ drafted the West Jersey governmental plan known as the Concessions and Agreements.

ANS: Edmund Byllinge   **TYPE: F**   **KEY 1: F**   **KEY 2: 3**   **PAGE: 77**

IDENTIFICATIONS

1. **John Smith**: adventurer often credited with saving the early Chesapeake settlement of Jamestown by forcing the colonists to work. His real impact is hard to assess because of his habit of exaggerating his exploits.

2. **joint-stock company**: precursor of the modern corporation. Acted as an organizing force in the settlement of North America. Each stockholder had one vote regardless of how many shares he owned. The stockholders met quarterly but entrusted everyday management to the company's treasurer.

3. **patroonship**: large grant of land from the Dutch West India Company to a few individual landholders in New Netherland. Meant to act as a spur to settlement, it actually retarded New Netherland's growth.

4. **Anne Hutchinson**: powerful, religious woman in early Massachusetts Bay whose attack on the clergy in the colony threatened the male power structure and led to her banishment.

5. *coureurs de bois*: French fur traders who lived among the Native Americans with whom they traded in the forests.

6. **John Calvin**: French Protestant leader who wrote *The Institutes of the Christian Religion*. His emphasis on predestination and hard work influenced the English Puritans, French Huguenots, Scots Presbyterians, and Dutch Reformed churches.

7. **Sir Walter Raleigh**: half-brother of Sir Humphrey Gilbert. Made two unsuccessful attempts to colonize in North America. The inhabitants of his lost colony of Roanoke disappeared between 1587 and 1590.

8. **James Harrington**: author of *Oceana* (1656). Greatly influenced colonial political thought by advocating a republic based on widespread land ownership, with term limits for officeholders, secret balloting, and a two-house legislature.

9. **predestination**: religious doctrine that asserted that God had already decreed who would be saved and who would be damned. Engendered in Calvinists a compelling inner need to find out whether they had been saved. Forced them to struggle to recognize in themselves a conversion experience--the process by which God's elect discovered that they had been saved.

10. **Pavonia Massacre**: 1643 massacre of Indian refugees led by New Netherland governor Willem Kieft. Against Indians who had been granted asylum from other Indians on Manhattan. Set off a war with the nearby Algonquian nations that nearly destroyed New Netherland.

11. **covenant theology**: religious system embraced by the Puritans of Massachusetts Bay. Held that God had made two biblical covenants with humans, the covenant of works and the covenant of grace. The covenant of works, which grew out of Adam's fall, saw humans as evil and incapable of obeying God's laws. The covenant of grace promised eternal salvation to those whom God had chosen. Puritans added communal counterparts to these individual covenants. The church covenant called for the organization of a church body, most of the members of which were presumed to be saved. The national covenant ensured that if the community as a whole adhered to God's laws, it wold not be punished for the misdeeds of individuals.

SHORT ESSAYS

1.   Examine the Puritans. Describe their religious beliefs as well as the reasons they left England for North America.

Answer: The Puritans left England for two reasons, both relating to religious circumstances. On one hand, the unfavorable and, at times, persecutory conditions under which they lived in pre-civil war England made emigration popular. In addition, the strict religious beliefs of these seventeenth-century Puritans were so at odds with the Church of England that many felt emigration, though not separation was their only alternative. On the other hand, some, though not most, came to North America for economic reasons. It should be clear, however, that many Puritans, such as John Winthrop, gave up great estates to venture to New England.

Once here, the Puritans were able to institutionalize their own beliefs in an environment they could control. The central and most characteristic Puritan institution was the covenant. The covenant worked on several levels: individual, religious, and social. Only the elect, or saved, were part of the Covenant of Grace. The other covenants worked more or less to enforce a communitarian ethic. The Church Covenant connected all church members, and the Social Covenant connected members of a town or community. Indeed, although inherent in Puritanism was an individualistic strain, in early seventeenth-century New England, the prevailing trend was toward community.

2.   Describe the French colonization of Canada.

Answer: The French colonization of North America was unique, whether compared to other European nations or to other French strategies in the Atlantic islands. The French began colonizing much later than the Spanish and Portuguese and were delayed further (until after 1600) because of a lack of interest and capital. Samuel de Champlain was the major instigator of French colonization of Canada. Canadian colonization was characterized by two groups: fur traders and missionaries. Fur traders, or coureurs de bois, lived among the Indians, sometimes intermarried with them, and carried on a vigorous trade for furs and beaver. But they never numbered more than a few hundred, few women came until after 1660, and no real large-scale attempts to build settlements were begun until after the French crown took over the colony in the 1660s.

The second major goal of colonization, and the one that often overshadowed the first, was the missionary goal. The Society of Jesus, or the Jesuits, made a major effort to convert the local Indian population. At times, this effort was very successful, especially with the Huron and Algonquin. At other times, this effort ran into roadblocks from Native Americans and even the coureurs de bois. Never as successful as other French colonies, the central import of France's adventure in Canada remained fur.

3.   Who were Anne Hutchinson and Roger Williams? Why were they banished from Massachusetts Bay?

Answer: Anne Hutchinson and Roger Williams were both religious nonconformists whose banishment from Massachusetts reveals the limits of free expression in a society that was most interested in order and conformity. Hutchinson questioned many of the sermons of Boston's clergy, arguing that they were supporting the Covenant of Works, not the Covenant of Grace. In essence, by questioning the ideals of the Puritan church, she also was questioning and threatening the hierarchy of Puritan society. After making the fatal admission that she received direct messages from God (blasphemy according to Puritans), she was banished. Central to her banishment, and revealing of Puritan attitudes, was that she was a strong woman who seemed to threaten established gender roles.

Roger Williams was banished as well, both for his nonconformity and for the threat he represented to the official congregational churches. Williams was an extreme separatist who demanded that Puritan New England move further away from the Church of England, something most Puritans were not ready or willing to do. Williams demanded an almost complete separation of church and state (to protect the purity of the church from the government) as well as proper payment to local Indian tribes for land used by Massachusetts Bay. The Massachusetts government demanded his banishment. The central theme to both incidents is that the Puritans were suspicious of, and resistant to, those who challenged their beliefs or power.

4.   Examine the early Jamestown settlement. What were the problems and successes there?

Answer: The problems of Virginia's early settlement in Jamestown seem to outweigh its successes. The colony was settled in 1607 by the Virginia Company of London, a joint-stock company committed to turning a profit for its investors. Over one hundred young men, many unsuited for farming or survival, were sent. The first winter proved devastating, as indeed, did the first several years. About 80 percent of the settlers died because of disease (Jamestown was located in a malaria-infested swamp), starvation, or warfare with the Indians. Starvation was a problem because so few settlers came properly supplied or prepared for farming. Most came with the idea of finding some cash crop and returning home rich.

Problems with the Indians persisted through the first several decades, as the Indians became resentful about white encroachment, theft, and diseases. These problems culminated in the massacre of 1622, when over three hundred settlers perished. During the early lean years, however, Virginia finally did discover a profitable crop: tobacco. Although this made very little noticeable difference for most early settlers, it did promise future success for the colony.

5.   Analyze relations between Native Americans and European colonizers in North America.

Answer: Relations between Native Americans and Europeans were generally poor. Occasionally, as with the people of Plymouth and local Indian tribes, these relations began in a friendly manner, but soon deteriorated. The English and Dutch more or less followed the Spanish and Portuguese in South America, if not in policies, in general results. Relations that would begin amiably, or at least peacefully, soon became strained, aggressive, and violent.

The French, however, were far more successful than the other Europeans at establishing friendly relations with most Indians. Although the French had disastrous initial relations with the Iroquois, they went much further in missionary work, living among the Indians and marrying into Indian tribes. The

Dutch, under Willem Kieft, began a war with an Algonquian nation that nearly led to the destruction of the colony. The English, particularly in the Chesapeake, began their relationship with local Indians poorly, and this led to some thirty years of virtual guerrilla warfare. The one theme that emerges from these various contacts was that most European settlers tended to see Native Americans as less than fully human and as a hindrance to their (European) settlement efforts.

6.   Examine the origin and theology of the Quakers and explain the reasons they were persecuted.

Answer: In the 1640s, George Fox founded The Society of Friends in England. From the very beginning members of this religious group, commonly known as Quakers, were persecuted by every society in which they established themselves. Despite their peaceful and orderly behavior the Quakers were considered dangerous radicals. In a world of public and private violence, they were pacifists. The Quakers felt that killing was a violation of the Ten Commandments and of Jesus' philosophy of turning the other cheek. Thus, Quakers would not participate in war and often spoke out in protest. They believed that all human beings possessed an "Inner Light" that, if followed, would guide them and help them perfect themselves. They also refused to "swear" even though assuming public office and participating in court proceedings required oath taking.

The Quakers also disapproved of slavery and eventually spearheaded the abolitionist movement in North America. Their belief in the spiritual equality of all people led them to defy social traditions that elevated one person above another. Therefore, Quakers would not doff their hats or use titles in deference to members of the upper classes. They referred to everyone with the polite and egalitarian "Thee" and "Thou." Their concept of equality extended to women, who fully participated in decision making, preaching, and even martyrdom when necessary. Quaker families reared their children with gentleness instead of harsh discipline. Marrying a non-Quaker was, however, a violation that would cause expulsion from the Society of Friends.

Other Protestants were shocked by Quaker theology as well as by Quaker social and political views. The concept of the "Inner Light" supplanted Calvinist predestination and original sin. Quaker religious services were unstructured and they had no use for either an established clergy or even the sacraments. Men and women spoke openly in religious meetings whenever they felt compelled by the Light to do so. In almost every way, these calm and gentle people challenged the power structure of the government, institutionalized religion, and society in general.

7.   Examine the Protestant and English reformations. What was the most significant difference between the two?

Answer: The Protestant Reformation was started by Martin Luther in 1517. Luther was a German Roman Catholic monk who disputed with high church authorities over doctrinal issues. Contrary to accepted Catholic doctrine, Luther asserted that good works could not warrant salvation. Instead he insisted that salvation came through the grace of God who bestowed eternal life upon those who recognized their unworthiness and yet who demonstrated their faith by struggling to live according to Christian principles. Luther founded the Lutheran Church, which spread throughout Germany and Scandinavia.

Probably the most influential sixteenth-century leader was John Calvin. Calvin was a French Catholic who was converted to Protestantism through Luther's writings. He moved to Geneva, Switzerland, where he developed his own brand of militant Christianity. Calvin adopted Luther's "faith alone" theory and rejected Roman Catholic traditions such as veneration of saints, celibacy of clergy, papal supremacy, and good works. Calvin emphasized that God separated the elect, who were saved, from the non elect, who were condemned to hell, before the creation of the Earth. All were predestined either to eternal salvation or damnation. Calvin's ideas influenced the French Huguenots, Dutch Reformed Church, Scots Presbyterian Church, and Anglican Puritans.

While the continental Protestant reform movements of Luther and Calvin stemmed from serious theological disagreements, the English Reformation was the result of economic concerns. King Henry VIII of England launched the Protestant movement in his realm because the Pope would not give him a divorce from his first wife. Henry VIII broke with the Roman Church, divorced his wife, made himself the "Only Supreme Head" of the Anglican Church, and enriched his treasury by confiscating monastic property. His youngest daughter, Elizabeth I, solidified the Protestant movement in England through a compromise between Calvinist religious precepts and Catholic organization and ceremony. The Book of Common

Prayer became the basis of Anglican rituals. Within the Church of England, reformers continued to push for changes that would eliminate the vestiges of Roman Catholicism and thereby "purify" the church. Eventually many of the Puritans and Separatists came to the New World to establish Protestant colonies.

LONG ESSAYS

1. Compare and contrast the colonies of Virginia and Massachusetts Bay. Describe the similarities and differences as well as the objectives of settlement.

Answer: Essay should address several key points:

A. Reasons for settlement
   1. Virginia
      a. Profit-oriented
      b. Founding
   2. Massachusetts
      a. Religious
      b. Social
B. New World experience
   1. Virginia
      a. Difficult early years
      b. Starvation/death and disease
      c. Failure
   2. Massachusetts
      a. Winthrop
      b. Puritan ideal
      c. A covenanted society
C. Economic and social development
   1. Virginia
      a. Tobacco
      b. Economic stability
   2. Massachusetts
      a. Communitarian ethos
      b. A "New England"/mixed economy

2. Compare and contrast the Dutch colonization of North America with that of the English.

Answer: Essay should address several key points:

A. Reasons for colonization
   1. English
      a. Economic/financial
      b. Religious/Puritans
      c. Entrepreneurial/corporation
   2. Dutch
      a. Economic/trade (Dutch West India Co.)
      b. Little religious imperative (more than Virginia, less than New England)
B. Settlement patterns
   1. English
      a. Virginia
      b. Communitarian towns (Massachusetts)
      c. Individual freeholders
   2. Dutch
      a. Patroonships
      b. Trading centers/Albany

C.   Long-term commitment
        1.   English
                a.   Large-scale immigration
                b.   Imperial ties
        2.   Dutch
                a.   Small population
                b.   Weak imperial support

3.   Compare and contrast the settlers' relations with Indians in early Virginia and New England.

Answer: Essay should address several key points:

A.   Early contact
        1.   Jamestown
                a.   English and Powhatan
                b.   Settlers dependent upon Indians for survival
                c.   John Rolfe, tobacco and Indian trade
                d.   English encroachment and violence
        2.   New England
                a.   Amicable early relations with local tribes
                b.   Squanto, Massasoit, and Wampanoags
                c.   Mutual trade
B.   Developing relations
        1.   Jamestown
                a.   Strained food supply and strained relations
                b.   Opechancanough
                c.   Massacre of 1622
                d.   Increased European immigration and westward push of Indians
        2.   New England
                a.   Land pressures lead to encroachment on Indian land
                b.   Pequot War (1637)
                c.   Roger Williams and the spectrum of Indian relations

4.   Examine the role of religion in stimulating seventeenth-century English colonization efforts in North America.

Answer: Essay should address several key points:

A.   The English Reformation
        1.   Henry VIII
                a.   Reasons for creating Church of England
                b.   Policies
        2.   Mary I
                a.   Struggle between Catholics and Protestants
                b.   Consequences
        3.   Elizabeth I
                a.   Characteristics of Church of England
                b.   Origin of Puritans and Separatists
                c.   Defeat of Spanish Armada
B.   Maryland
        1.   Catholic Calverts
                a.   Organization of the colony
                b.   Consequences
        2.   Impact of English Civil War
                a.   Toleration Act of 1649
                b.   Conditions in 1660

C.   The New England Colonies
1.   Plymouth
      a.   Pilgrims or Separatists
      b.   Surviving the first year
2.   Massachusetts Bay Colony
      a.   Puritans
      b.   Organizing the colony
3.   Basic beliefs
      a.   Covenant theology
      b.   Halfway covenant
4.   Founding of Connecticut and Rhode Island
      a.   Disputes over theology
      b.   Consequences
D.   Pennsylvania and West New Jersey
1.   Origin of Quakers
      a.   Basic beliefs
      b.   Expansion of faith
2.   William Penn
      a.   Organizing the colony
      b.   Dealing with disputes

CHAPTER 3
ENGLAND DISCOVERS ITS COLONIES: EMPIRE, LIBERTY, AND EXPANSION

CHAPTER OUTLINE

I.   The Atlantic Prism and the Spectrum of Settlement
    A.   Demographic Differences
    B.   Race, Ethnicity, and Economy
    C.   Religion and Education
    D.   Local and Provincial Governments
    E.   Unifying Trends: Language, War, Law, and Inheritance

II.   The Beginnings of Empire
    A.   Upheaval in America: The Critical 1640s
    B.   Mercantilism as a Moral Revolution
    C.   The First Navigation Act
    D.   Restoration Navigation Acts

III.   Indians, Settlers, Upheaval
    A.   Indian Strategies of Survival
    B.   Puritan Indian Missions
    C.   Metacom's (or King Phillip's) War
    D.   Virginia's Indian War
    E.   Bacon's Rebellion

IV.   Crisis in England and the Redefinition of Empire
    A.   The Popish Plot, the Exclusion Crisis, and the Rise of Party
    B.   The Lords of Trade and Imperial Reform
    C.   The Dominion of New England

V.   The Glorious Revolution
    A.   The Glorious Revolution in America
    B.   The English Response
    C.   The Salem Witch Trials
    D.   The Completion of Empire
    E.   Imperial Federalism
    F.   The Mixed and Balanced Constitution

VI.   Contrasting Empires: Spain and France in North America
    A.   The Pueblo Revolt
    B.   New France and the Middle Ground
    C.   French Louisiana and Spanish Texas

VII.   An Empire of Settlement: The British Colonies
    A.   The Engine of British Expansion: The Colonial Household
    B.   The Voluntaristic Ethic and Public Life
    C.   Three Warring Empires, 1689-1716

VIII. Conclusion

CHRONOLOGY

1649	England becomes a Commonwealth.
1651	First of the Navigation Acts.
1660	Parliament passes new Navigation Act.
1663	Staple Act passed.
1675	Metacom's (King Philip's) War begins in New England. Lords of Trade created.
1673	Jacques Marquette and Louis Joliet explore the Mississippi. Plantation Duty Act passed.

1676	Bacon's Rebellion in Virginia.
1680	Pueblo Indian revolt.
1683	New York Charter of Liberties.
1685	James II becomes king of England.
	Louis XIV revokes Edict of Nantes.
1686–1689	Dominion of New England.
1688	Glorious Revolution in England.
1689	Leisler's Rebellion in New York.
	William and Mary ascend to English throne.
	Andros is overthrown in Boston.
	Catholic government is overthrown in Maryland.
1689–1697	King William's War.
1692	Salem witch trials.
1696	Creation of the Board of Trade.
	Parliament passes comprehensive Navigation Act.
1699	First permanent French settlement in Louisiana.
1702–1713	War of Spanish Succession (Queen Anne's War).
1707	Act of Union joins England and Scotland.
1721–1742	Robert Walpole ministry.

THEMATIC TOPICS FOR ENRICHMENT

1. What were the differences between Whigs and Tories in seventeenth-century England? What contributions did each faction make to the creation of British political culture?

2. How did the Glorious Revolution in England destroy absolutism and guarantee representative government in British North America?

3. In what ways did the Spanish, French, and English empires develop differently from one another?

4. Discuss the ways in which Indian tribes took advantage of—and, in turn, were taken advantage of by—the imperial conflicts among Spain, France, and England.

5. What factors led to a remarkable increase in the population of the British colonies of North America after 1660?

6. In what ways were colonial households similar to their English counterparts, and in what ways were they different?

7. Explain the consequences for both Indians and European settlers of the numerous Indian wars between 1690 and 1716.

SUGGESTED ESSAY TOPICS

1. Discuss the relationship between England's commerce and its colonies.

2. Evaluate the various Indian strategies of survival in North America in the years after European colonization.

3. Define the term *mercantilism* and explain its significance for British colonial policy. In what ways did the Navigation Acts express mercantilistic ideas?

4. What do you think the authors mean by the metaphor "spectrum of settlement" to describe England's colonial possessions (3-2)?

5. Discuss the development of the colonies in terms of demography, race, religion, and economy.

LECTURE OUTLINE

1. In many ways the Atlantic Ocean functioned as a prism refracting English aims into the spectrum of **settlement** of North America.

    (SHOW TRANSPARENCY 20: NORTH AMERICA IN 1700)

    a. The colonies featured profound **demographic differences** from one region to the next with New England's salubrious climate at one extreme and the sugar islands of the Caribbean at the other.

    b. The English colonies also featured profound differences from one another in **race, ethnicity, and economy;** the colonies comprised four distinct regions: New England, the Middle Colonies, the Chesapeake, and the Deep South.

    c. Although most colonists were Protestant, **religious** differences within, and among, colonies stood out as one of North America's unique social features.

    d. **Local and provincial government** also varied throughout the colonies, from proprietorships to royal colonies; some colonies boasted rather open, democratic governments, while others proved more autocratic.

    e. The colonies did boast some **unifying trends,** including those of **language, war** (common enemies), **law,** and **inheritance.**

2. The **beginnings of empire** stemmed from England's growing realization that the colonies served vital needs both economically and politically.

    a. The **critical 1640s** were a time of **upheaval in America,** characterized by Indian warfare, instability, and a general lack of direction from England.

    b. The most important imperial innovation proved to be the advent of the **mercantilist** system, which historians have called part of a **moral revolution.**

        i. Following the Thirty Years' War, Parliament passed the **First Navigation Act** banning foreign ships in the colonies.

        ii. The **Restoration Navigation Acts** were a crucial series of measures that sought to oversee virtually all aspects of colonial trade, "enumerating" commodities, as well as regulating goods going to and from England's outposts.

3. Growing conflicts between **Indians and settlers** led to a number of conflagrations as both parties sought to master their new relationships.

    a. **Indian strategies of survival** varied greatly, from outright warfare to conversion and alliance.

    b. Among the most promising, if ultimately unsuccessful, attempts to attain a modus vivendi between settlers and the local inhabitants were the **Puritan Indian missions,** which sought to bring Indians into the fold of European civilization and thereby end the strife between the two peoples.

c. Cultural differences and colonists' insatiable appetite for land led to **Metacom's (or King Philip's) War** in 1675, a bloody conflagration in which some eight hundred settlers and an unknown number of Indians perished.

(SHOW TRANSPARENCY 16: NEW ENGLAND AT THE TIME OF KING PHILLIP'S WAR, 1675-1676)

d. **Virginia's Indian War** during the governorship of Sir William Berkeley caused great insecurity on the frontier for several years.

e. Led by the recent immigrant Nathaniel Bacon, **Bacon's Rebellion** of 1675-1676 resulted in the devastation of much of Virginia and the temporary collapse of royal government.

(SHOW TRANSPARENCY 17: BACON'S REBELLION IN VIRGINIA, 1676)

4. Bacon's Rebellion helped to trigger a **crisis in England and the redefinition of empire** in hopes of improving imperial oversight and control.

a. **The Popish Plot, the Exclusion crisis, and the rise of party** combined to undermine the Stuart monarchy and bring about the Glorious Revolution of 1688.

b. Indian wars and domestic considerations compelled the Crown to create the **Lords of Trade** and undertake wholesale **imperial reform** in the latter half of the seventeenth century.

c. In 1685, James II disallowed the New York Charter of Liberties of 1683 and forced New York to join with its northern neighbors to form the **Dominion of New England.**

d. In overthrowing the Stuart monarchy, the **Glorious Revolution** of 1688 had significant consequences for colonial affairs, leading to what historians call the **Glorious Revolution in America.**

(SHOW TRANSPARENCY 18: GOVERNMENT AND RELIGION IN THE BRITISH COLONIES, 1720)

i. Virtually every colony underwent some form of **political crisis from 1688 to 1689,** including New York and Maryland.

ii. The **English response** to the Glorious Revolution in America proved remarkably lenient and sympathetic for the most part, as William and Mary sought reconciliation, not conflict.

iii. At the time when Massachusetts had virtually no central government, the **Salem witch trials** convulsed eastern Massachusetts, resulting in the capital punishment of twenty accused persons.

e. The Glorious Revolution dispatched absolutism in the colonies and helped to guarantee that the Completion of Empire would put **representative government** in the colonies on far more sure footing.

i. **Imperial federalism** is the term used to describe the division of power between the center and the periphery of the empire.

ii. English people on both sides of the Atlantic viewed with pride their unwritten **mixed and balanced Constitution**, which included institutional authority along the Aristotelian model of one, few, and many.

5.   The tenuous coexistence of the **contrasting empires** of England, France, and Spain erupted into war after the Glorious Revolution.

    a.   In 1680, a San Juan Pueblo medicine man led a revolt against the Spaniards known as the **Taos Pueblo revolt**.

    b.   Relying more on intelligence than force, **New France** maintained a strong colonial presence in the Saint Lawrence and Mississippi valleys in a region called the **Middle Ground**.

(SHOW TRANSPARENCY 21: FRENCH MIDDLE GROUND, CIRCA 1700)

    c.   France and Spain were considerably less successful at maintaining peace in their imperial possessions in **French Louisiana and Spanish Texas.**

6.   With a population of at least 250,000 settlers by 1700 and an explosive growth rate, the **British colonies** could fairly be called an empire of settlement.

    a.   The key institution of the engine of British expansion proved to be the **colonial household**, the center of economic production and reproduction.

    b.   Householders carried their quest for independence outside the home, embracing a **voluntaristic ethic** as the personal codes of both private life and **public life**.

    c.   France, Spain, and England devolved into **three warring empires** from **1689** through **1716.**

(SHOW TRANSPARENCY 22: NORTHEASTERN THEATER OF WAR, 1689-1713; AND TRANSPARENCY 23: SOUTHEASTERN THEATER OF WAR 1702-1713)

Conclusion: In the course of the seventeenth century, England became a global giant in large measure on the basis of its American colonies and the important economic role they played in the empire. Fitting perfectly into the mercantilist scheme, colonies served as markets for finished goods and supplied vital raw materials to the mother country.

TEACHING RESOURCES

Three Sovereigns for Sarah is the portrayal of the Salem Witch Trials through the experiences of the three Towne sisters. Originally a PBS miniseries (2 hours, 46 minutes).

Where America Began explores the life and culture of seventeenth-century Jamestown. VideoTours History Collection (60 minutes).

Colonial America recalls America's earliest days, when empires were competing for the continent. Mastervision Humanities Series (52 minutes).

Black Robe is a stunning portrait of the challenges facing Jesuit missionaries. Vidmark Films (80 minutes).

Unearthing the Slave Trade shows how archaeologists attempt to reconstruct the lives of African Americans in the colonies. Films for the Humanities (60 minutes).

Indians among Us describes the upheaval resulting from the clash of cultures between Indians and European settlers. Re-Discovering America (60 minutes).

1. Sir William Berkeley
    a. was the Virginia governor at the time of Metacom's War.
    b. was noted for putting down Bacon's Rebellion and hanging twenty-three rebels.
    c. died in disgrace in England before he could defend his policies.
    d. favored a defensive strategy against the Indians.
    e all of the above

ANS: E   TYPE: M   KEY 1: F   KEY 2: 3   PAGE: 97-100

2. By 1700, the population of England's mainland colonies was doubling every _____ years.
    a. 10
    b. 15
    c. 20
    d. 25
    e. 2

ANS: D   TYPE: M   KEY 1: F   KEY 2: 3   PAGE: 112

3. The policy of mercantilism entails all of the following except that
    a. colonies exist for the benefit of the mother country.
    b. colonies should act as a source of raw materials for the mother country.
    c. colonies should act as markets for the mother country.
    d. colonies should develop manufacturing to export products to the mother country.
    e. trade would increase overall wealth.

ANS: D   TYPE: M   KEY 1: A   KEY 2: 2   PAGE: 89-90

4. Which of the following was not stated in the Navigation Act of 1651?
    a. Non-European goods could be imported into the colonies only in English-owned ships.
    b. English coastal trade was forbidden to foreigners.
    c. The crews of ships trading with the colonies had to be at least half English.
    d. Goods from Asia and the East could be imported to America only after passing through England.
    e. Foreigners could not trade between one English port and another.

ANS: D   TYPE: M   KEY 1: F   KEY 2: 2   PAGE: 91

5. For the most part, England's North American colonies responded to the Navigation Acts.
    a. with little interest.
    b. very unfavorably.
    c. by ignoring them.
    d. very enthusiastically.
    e. by openly rebelling.

ANS: B   TYPE: M   KEY 1: A   KEY 2: 2   PAGE: 91

6. The Staple Act of 1663 regulated goods
    a. going to America.
    b. coming from America.
    c. involved in the coastal trade.
    d. between England and India.
    e. all of the above

ANS: A   TYPE: M   KEY 1: F   KEY 2: 3   PAGE: 91

7. The autocratic governor of New York and the Dominion of New England was
    a. Sir Edmund Andros.
    b. Jacob Leisler.
    c. Increase Mather.
    d. Sir Robert Walpole.
    e. William Berkeley

ANS: A   TYPE: M   KEY 1: F   KEY: 2: 2   PAGE: 101

8. Colonists in New York were angry with James, Duke of York, because
    a. he governed without an elected assembly.
    b. he granted religious freedom to all.
    c. he restricted trade opportunities.
    d. he gave liberal land grants.
    e. he prohibited the sale of alcohol.

ANS: A   TYPE: M   KEY 1: A   KEY 2: 3   PAGE: 101

9. The large-scale warfare between European settlers and the Indians of New England in 1675 and 1676 was called
    a. King James's War.
    b. Metacom's War.
    c. Bacon's Rebellion.
    d. Leisler's Rebellion.
    e. Stono's Rebellion.

ANS: B   TYPE: M   KEY 1: F   KEY 2: 1   PAGE: 95-97

10. The leader of the 1676 Virginia rebellion was
    a. Thomas Berkeley.
    b. Nathaniel Bacon.
    c. Jacob Leisler.
    d. Edward Randolph.
    e. William Berkeley.

ANS: B   TYPE: M   KEY 1: F   KEY 2: 2   PAGE: 98-99

11. The Catholic successor to Charles II of England who was overthrown in the Revolution of 1689 was
    a. William of Orange.
    b. Mary of Scotland.
    c. James II.
    d. Charles I.
    e. Philip II.

ANS: C   TYPE: M   KEY 1: F   KEY 2: 1   PAGE: 101

12. The Glorious Revolution in England led to the elevation of _____ as king of England.
    a. William III
    b. James II
    c. Edward VI
    d. Charles I
    e. Henry VIII.

ANS: A   TYPE: M   KEY 1: F   KEY 2: 3   PAGE: 101

13. Colonists in North America reacted to the Glorious Revolution
    a. with indifference.
    b. by overthrowing the governors of the Dominion of New England and Maryland.
    c. with public protests against the new king.
    d. by attacking Dutch settlements in Delaware.
    e. by launching Indian wars.

ANS: B   TYPE: M   KEY 1: F   KEY 2: 2   PAGE: 102-103

14. The leader of the large-scale rebellion in New York in 1689 was
    a. Thomas Berkeley.
    b. Jacob Leisler.
    c. Edward Randolph.
    d. Francis Nicholson.
    e. William Bradford.

ANS: B   TYPE: M   KEY 1: F   KEY 2: 1   PAGE: 102

15. The extended life expectancy and healthiness of the New England population
    a. produced a feeling of public optimism and cheerfulness.
    b. led to an increase in procrastination and laziness among the working class.
    c. created a large number of elderly dependents and caused economic stagnation.
    d. enhanced the power of women in society.
    e. limited opportunities for young men who wanted to hold political office.

ANS: E   TYPE: M   KEY 1: A   KEY 2: 3   PAGE: 85

16. In North America, educational opportunities
    a. were very limited in areas where slavery was the dominant labor system.
    b. existed only in the French colony of Quebec.
    c. were denied to women and working-class men in all the Puritan colonies.
    d. were nonexistent.
    e. were more widespread in the South than elsewhere.

ANS: A   TYPE: M   KEY 1: F   KEY 2: 3   PAGE: 87

17. The English colonies in North America were united by all but which of the following?
    a. a uniform language based on the London English dialect
    b. traditional English inheritance laws
    c. an uncomplicated legal system with few professional lawyers
    d. military concepts based on volunteer militia and the use of terror tactics
    e. widespread ownership of land

ANS: B   TYPE: M   KEY 1: A   KEY 2: 3   PAGE: 88

18. According to the theory of mercantilism,
    a. the wealth of a nation depended upon the size of its population.
    b. development of rigorous trade and control of colonial commerce were essential for national power.
    c. colonies were an economic drain on national resources and thus should be given independence.
    d. only merchants should be eligible for election to the House of Commons.
    e. merchants were God's elect.

ANS: B   TYPE: M   KEY 1: F   KEY 2: 3   PAGE: 89-90

19. Seventeenth-century philosophers believed that
    a. the government must prevent commercial competition and trade wars.
    b. all human beings were basically uncivilized barbarians.
    c. positive legislation could change human behavior and assure the continued progress of modern society.
    d. God was going to destroy the earth at the beginning of the next millennium.
    e. Native Americans were superior to Europeans.

ANS: C   TYPE: M   KEY 1: A   KEY 2: 3   PAGE: 90

20. The Navigation Acts required that
    a. all goods imported into the colonies be carried by English-owned ships.
    b. only Dutch ships be allowed to carry goods directly from one colony to another.
    c. the colonies export only manufactured goods and import only agricultural goods.
    d. Native Americans sell their goods only to English merchants.
    e. all of the above

ANS: A   TYPE: M   KEY 1: F   KEY 2: 2   PAGE: 91

21. The "Five Nations" of the colonial period were
    a. England, Spain, France, Holland, and Sweden.
    b. a European mutual defense league dedicated to reducing the power of Spain.
    c. the first South American countries to win independence from European colonial powers.
    d. the lost tribes of Israel.
    e. an Iroquois confederation that usually maintained friendly relations with the English.

ANS: D   TYPE: M   KEY 1: F   KEY 2: 2   PAGE: 93

22. Which of the following is not true of Metacom's (King Philip's) War?
    a. It was started by non-Christian Indians who feared that their culture was being destroyed by contact with whites.
    b. The Puritan army either massacred or sold into slavery hundreds of Christian and non-Christian Indians.
    c. The Indians proved to be better shots than the whites and virtually destroyed a dozen settlements.
    d. It involved only the Wampanoags.
    e. The war divided the New England colonies internally.

ANS: D   TYPE: M   KEY 1: F   KEY 2: 3   PAGE: 96-96

23. Nathaniel Bacon was
    a. the governor of Virginia who successfully opened up the tidewater area for settlement.
    b. the only congregational minister to openly protest against the slave trade.
    c. a rebellious Virginia planter who murdered peaceful Indians and burned Jamestown.
    d. a businessman who organized the first slaughterhouse and sausage factory in Massachusetts.
    e. a minister of the Great Awakening.

ANS: C   TYPE: M   KEY 1: F   KEY 2: 2   PAGE: 98-99

24. Which of the following accurately distinguishes between the original Whigs and Tories?
    a. The Whigs wore hairpieces; the Tories did not wear hairpieces.
    b. The Whigs were Irish and Scots politicians; the Tories were English and Welsh politicians.
    c. The Whigs were a country party that favored limiting the king's power; the Tories were a court party that favored legitimate royal succession.
    d. The Whigs were Catholics; the Tories were Anglicans.
    e. The Whigs sought peaceful relations with the Indians; the Tories advocated war against the Indians.

ANS: C   **TYPE: M**   **KEY 1: F**   **KEY 2: 3**   **PAGE: 100**

25. Colonists objected to the Dominion of New England because
    a. it established an autocratic government without an elected assembly.
    b. the royal governor was not given enough authority to enforce the Navigation Acts effectively.
    c. it forced both Puritans and non-Puritans to pay taxes to support the Congregational Church.
    d. it forced Native Americans on to reservations.
    e. all of the above

ANS: A   **TYPE: M**   **KEY 1: F**   **KEY 2: 2**   **PAGE: 101**

26. When William III and Mary II became the monarchs of England, Parliament
    a. executed Charles I and his entire family.
    b. offered toleration to all Protestants and guaranteed that the royal succession would remain Protestant in the future.
    c. expelled the Quakers, Jews, and other dissidents from England.
    d. revoked the charters of all the proprietary colonies in North America.
    e. abolished the monarchy.

ANS: B   **TYPE: M**   **KEY 1: F**   **KEY 2: 2**   **PAGE: 102**

27. As a result of the witchcraft trials in Salem,
    a. the Puritans lost control of the government of Massachusetts.
    b. a majority of colonial citizens became convinced that witchcraft was being practiced in every colony.
    c. dozens of people were burned at the stake in New England.
    d. twenty people were executed either by hanging or by crushing.
    e. the settlement became better united against its enemies.

ANS: D   **TYPE: M**   **KEY 1: F**   **KEY 2: 2**   **PAGE: 105**

28. The Salem Witchcraft Trials ended when
    a. the girls admitted that they were lying.
    b. all the real witches had been tried and executed.
    c. the girls started accusing prominent people, such as the governor's wife, of witchcraft.
    d. the court rejected the use of "spectral" evidence.
    e. the king sent troops to arrest the judges responsible for this outrage.

ANS: C   **TYPE: M**   **KEY 1: F**   **KEY 2: 2**   **PAGE: 105**

29. By the mid–1700s, most of the English colonies in North America were
    a. proprietary colonies with tax-supported established churches.
    b. royal colonies with appointed governors and elected assemblies.
    c. united in their support of the Board of Trade's reorganization of colonial governments.
    d. heavily dependent upon slave labor for agricultural production.
    e. paying high taxes to the British treasury.

ANS: B   TYPE: M   KEY 1: F   KEY 2: 3   PAGE: 105

30. The Pueblo Revolt in Spanish New Mexico
    a. permanently freed the Navajos and Apaches from Spanish authority.
    b. virtually destroyed the Hopi tribe.
    c. was more successful than any other Indian rebellion in American history.
    d. was staged by Mexican peasants who wanted a more democratic government.
    e. threatened the British settlements.

ANS: C   TYPE: M   KEY 1: F   KEY 2: 2   PAGE: 110

31. The French in the Great Lakes and Ohio River areas
    a. launched a war of extermination against all Indians.
    b. supplied their Algonquian allies with weapons and alcohol in order to halt the expansion of the Iroquois and the British.
    c. were forced to withdraw by the depletion of fur-bearing animals and the decline of trade.
    d. exchanged their claims to the territory for access to English fishing sites on the Atlantic coast.
    e. sold their claims to the Spanish.

ANS: B   TYPE: M   KEY 1: F   KEY 2: 3   PAGE: 110-111

32. Titus Oakes earned fame by
    a. leading attacks against Indians in Maryland.
    b. fabricating a supposed "Popish Plot" against King Charles III.
    c. founding trading settlements in western Virginia.
    d. serving as Nathaniel Bacon's top assistant.
    e. planting oak trees across America.

ANS: B   TYPE: M   KEY 1: F   KEY 2: 3   PAGE: 100

33. Colonists viewed military service as
    a. a temporary, voluntaristic experience.
    b. a lifelong commitment and career choice.
    c. the public duty of each young man when he reached the age of 18.
    d. the responsibility of men who actually lived in England rather than in the colonies.
    e. the highest honor that the empire could offer them.

ANS: A   TYPE: M   KEY 1: F   KEY 2: 2   PAGE: 114

34. By 1675, perhaps _____ of all those Indians living in southeastern New England were in various stages of conversion to Christianity.
    a. half
    b. one-third
    c. one-quarter
    d. two-thirds
    e. three-fourths

ANS: C   TYPE: M   KEY 1: F   KEY 2: 2   PAGE: 94

35. The lowest minister-to-resident ratio among the English colonies was found in
    a. the sugar islands.
    b. the Chesapeake.
    c. New York.
    d. New England.
    e. Georgia.

ANS: D　　　**TYPE: M**　　　**KEY 1: F**　　　**KEY 2: 1**　　　**PAGE: 87**

36. Only _____ avoided war with the Indians during the 1640s.
    a. the Chesapeake.
    b. New England.
    c. New Netherland.
    d. New France.
    e. New Spain.

ANS: B　　　**TYPE: M**　　　**KEY 1: F**　　　**KEY 2: 2**　　　**PAGE: 89**

37. The Great Swamp Fight was a conflict between Puritans and
    a. Iroquois.
    b. Wampanoags.
    c. Narragansetts.
    d. Hurons.
    e. Apache.

ANS: C　　　**TYPE: M**　　　**KEY 1: F**　　　**KEY 2: 2**　　　**PAGE: 95**

38. Which of the following events occurred first?
    a. creation of the Board of Trade
    b. creation of the Bank of England
    c. passage of the Act of Union
    d. the Salem Witch Trials
    e. Queen Anne's War

ANS: D　　　**TYPE: M**　　　**KEY 1: F**　　　**KEY 2: 3**　　　**PAGE: 103-107**

39. All of the following were critics of Britain's central government except
    a. John Trenchard.
    b. Robert Walpole.
    c. Henry St. John.
    d. Alexander Pope.
    e. Thomas Gordon.

ANS: B　　　**TYPE: M**　　　**KEY 1: F**　　　**KEY 2: 3**　　　**PAGE: 109**

40. All of the following explored the Mississippi River except
    a. Pierre le Moyne d'Iberville.
    b. Father Jacques Marquette.
    c. Louis Joliet.
    d. René-Robert Cavelier.
    e. Father Hennepin.

ANS: A　　　**TYPE: M**　　　**KEY 1: A**　　　**KEY 2: 3**　　　**PAGE: 111**

41. African slaves comprised _____ percent of Virginia's population by the 1730s.
    a. 30
    b. 35
    c. 40
    d. 45
    e. 10

ANS: C   TYPE: M   KEY 1: F   KEY 2: 3   PAGE: 86

42. The only important local institution in the sugar islands and in South Carolina was the
    a. parish.
    b. town.
    c. county.
    d. burrough.
    e. assembly

ANS: A   TYPE: M   KEY 1: F   KEY 2: 2   PAGE: 87

43. Women stood the best chance of inheriting property in
    a. New England.
    b. the sugar islands.
    c. the Middle Atlantic colonies.
    d. the Chesapeake.
    e. New York

ANS: D   TYPE: M   KEY 1: F   KEY 2: 2   PAGE: 88

44. In the British colonies life expectancy was longest in
    a. the Caribbean
    b. the Chesapeake region
    c. South Carolina
    d. Canada
    e. New England

ANS: E   TYPE: M   KEY 1: F   KEY 2: 2   PAGE: 85

45. Thomas Mayhew, Sr., Thomas Mayhew, Jr. and John Elliot
    a. led vicious raids against the Indians in New England.
    b. attempted to convert Indians to Protestantism.
    c. encouraged intermarriage between Indians and Englishmen.
    d. recognized and respected the power of Indian religious leaders.
    e. became governors of Massachusetts.

ANS: B   TYPE: M   KEY 1: F   KEY 2: 2   PAGE: 93

46. When Nathaniel Bacon was elected to the Virginia assembly, Gov. Berkeley
    a. had him arrested.
    b. welcomed him as a hero.
    c. had him killed.
    d. refused to allow him to take his seat.
    e. ignored him.

ANS: A   TYPE: M   KEY 1: F   KEY 2: 3   PAGE: 98

47. The 1691 charter for the colony of Massachusetts
    a. established religious requirements for voting.
    b. granted toleration to all Protestants.
    c. granted religious toleration to Catholics.
    d. recognized Indian land rights.
    e. denied the authority of the King.

ANS: B　　　**TYPE: M**　　　**KEY 1: F**　　　**KEY 2: 2**　　　**PAGE: 103**

48. In the Salem witch trials
    a. only those who confessed to being witches were hanged.
    b. no one who confessed guilt was hanged.
    c. the convicted witches were burned at stake.
    d. no one was actually convicted of being a witch.
    e. those who were convicted were exiled from the colony.

ANS: B　　　**TYPE: M**　　　**KEY 1: F**　　　**KEY 2: 2**　　　**PAGE: 105**

49. After the Glorious Revolution, colonists assumed that their governments would be
    a. dictatorships.
    b. direct democracies.
    c. representative governments.
    d. proprietary governments.
    e. abolished.

ANS: C　　　**TYPE: M**　　　**KEY 1: A**　　　**KEY 2: 2**　　　**PAGE: 105**

50. England's "mixed and balanced" constitution meant that
    a. government by King, Lords, and Commons balanced power.
    b. Parliament governed America.
    c. liberty for all Englishmen was assured.
    d. an absolute monarchy ruled the empire.
    e. power was concentrated in the aristocracy.

ANS: A　　　**TYPE: M**　　　**KEY 1: A**　　　**KEY 2: 3**　　　**PAGE: 107**

TRUE/FALSE

_____ 1.　　Mercantilists assumed that the colonies only existed to enrich the mother country.

ANS: T　　　**TYPE: T**　　　**KEY 1: A**　　　**KEY 2: 1**　　　**PAGE: 90**

_____ 2.　　Most of the New England colonies had proprietary governments.

ANS: F　　　**TYPE: T**　　　**KEY 1: F**　　　**KEY 2: 2**　　　**PAGE: 105**

_____ 3.　　The governmental body charged with overseeing the Navigation Acts in the colonies was the Lords of Trade.

ANS: T　　　**TYPE: T**　　　**KEY 1: F**　　　**KEY 2: 3**　　　**PAGE: 100**

_____ 4.　　The Toleration Act of 1689 allowed Catholics to worship publicly.

ANS: F　　　**TYPE: T**　　　**KEY 1: F**　　　**KEY 2: 2**　　　**PAGE: 102**

_____ 5.   The Glorious Revolution led to the ascension of Oliver Cromwell as leader of England.

ANS: F   TYPE: T   KEY 1: F   KEY 2: 2   PAGE: 102

_____ 6.   The Navigation Acts were attempts to give England sole control over the trade of its
             North American colonies.

ANS: T   TYPE: T   KEY 1: A   KEY 2: 3   PAGE: 91-92

_____ 7.   Seventeenth-century philosophers believed that the government should encourage its
             peoples' greed and pursuit of self-interest.

ANS: T   TYPE: T   KEY 1: A   KEY 2: 3   PAGE: 90

_____ 8.   Sir Edmund Andros was a Protestant missionary who set up a model mission community
             in Massachusetts.

ANS: F   TYPE: T   KEY 1: F   KEY 2: 1   PAGE: 101

_____ 9.   All of the proprietary colonies eventually became royal colonies.

ANS: F   TYPE: T   KEY 1: A   KEY 2: 2   PAGE: 105

_____ 10.   The French explorer Sieur de la Salle sailed down the Mississippi River to the Gulf of
             Mexico and named the area Louisiana.

ANS: T   TYPE: T   KEY 1: F   KEY 2: 1   PAGE: 111

_____ 11.   King William's War occurred before Queen Anne's War.

ANS: T   TYPE: T   KEY 1: A   KEY 2: 1   PAGE: 114

_____ 12.   In 1603, England was a weak power on the fringes of Europe.

ANS: T   TYPE: T   KEY 1: A   KEY 2: 2   PAGE: 83

_____ 13.   Young men dominated New England society.

ANS: F   TYPE: T   KEY 1: A   KEY 2: 2   PAGE: 85

_____ 14.   Uncertainty in the sugar and tobacco colonies led to widespread despondency among the
             population.

ANS: F   TYPE: T   KEY 1: A   KEY 2: 2   PAGE: 85

_____ 15.   The French were much more skilled--and successful--in dealing with Native Americans
             than the British.

ANS: T   TYPE: T   KEY 1: A   KEY 2: 3   PAGE: 111

_____ 16.   The farther south one went in the English colonies in North America, the more diverse
             the population.

ANS: T   TYPE: T   KEY 1: A   KEY 2: 2   PAGE: 87

_____ 17.   High literacy prevailed wherever slavery predominated.

ANS: F   TYPE: T   KEY 1: A   KEY 2: 2   PAGE: 87

_____ 18.   Public support for the clergy was much stronger in the North than in the South.

ANS: T   TYPE: T   KEY 1: F   KEY 2: 1   PAGE: 87

_____ 19.   The English people during the 1640s were very interested in what happened in the colonies.

ANS: F   TYPE: T   KEY 1: A   KEY 2: 2   PAGE: 89

_____20.   The Navigation Act of 1660 dealt primarily with products going into the colonies.

ANS: F   TYPE: T   KEY 1: A   KEY 2: 3   PAGE: 91

_____ 21.   The Navigation Acts were tremendously successful and accomplished just what they were designed to do.

ANS: T   TYPE: T   KEY 1: A   KEY 2: 2   PAGE: 92

_____ 22.   Spain and France were more concerned with religious missionary activity in their colonies than England was.

ANS: T   TYPE: T   KEY 1: F   KEY 2: 1   PAGE: 109

_____ 23.   John Eliot was the most successful of the early Protestant missionaries to the Native Americans.

ANS: F   TYPE: T   KEY 1: F   KEY 2: 3   PAGE: 93

_____ 24.   After the Lords of Trade began enforcing the Navigation Acts in 1675, the West Indies became the first object of most of the new policies.

ANS: T   TYPE: T   KEY 1: A   KEY 2: 2   PAGE: 100

_____ 25.   The Lords of Trade had numerous instruments for punishing violators of the Navigation Acts.

ANS: F   TYPE: T   KEY 1: A   KEY 2: 2   PAGE: 101

_____ 26.   Merchants were consistent in their support for the government of the Dominion of New England.

ANS: F   TYPE: T   KEY 1: A   KEY 2: 2   PAGE: 101

_____ 27.   The Glorious revolution had no effect on Europe.

ANS: F   TYPE: T   KEY 1: A   KEY 2: 3   PAGE: 101

_____ 28.   The Glorious Revolution reaffirmed absolutism in English America.

ANS: F   TYPE: T   KEY 1: A   KEY 2: 2   PAGE: 105

_____ 29. The Board of Trade, which replaced the Lords of Trade in 1696, had extensive powers to enforce the Navigation Acts.

ANS: F   **TYPE: T**   **KEY 1: A**   **KEY 2: 2**   **PAGE: 107**

_____ 30. The Hat Act prohibited the manufacture of hats in the colonies.

ANS: F   **TYPE: T**   **KEY 1: F**   **KEY 2: 1**   **PAGE: 107**

_____ 31. The Dominion of New England had no elective assembly.

ANS: T   **TYPE: T**   **KEY 1: F**   **KEY 2: 1**   **PAGE: 101**

_____ 32. The greatest challenge to the Spanish position in North America came in New Mexico.

ANS: T   **TYPE: T**   **KEY 1: F**   **KEY 2: 2**   **PAGE: 110**

_____ 33. The French used European rules when conducting diplomacy with the Indians.

ANS: F   **TYPE: T**   **KEY 1: A**   **KEY 2: 2**   **PAGE: 111**

_____ 34. The French established Pensacola in 1698 to protect their position on the Gulf of Mexico.

ANS: F   **TYPE: T**   **KEY 1: A**   **KEY 2: 1**   **PAGE: 112**

_____ 35. The growing population of its North American empire was Great Britain's greatest advantage.

ANS: T   **TYPE: T**   **KEY 1: A**   **KEY 2: 1**   **PAGE: 112**

_____ 36. Several English colonies replicated the complexity of England itself.

ANS: F   **TYPE: T**   **KEY 1: A**   **KEY 2: 1**   **PAGE: 84**

_____ 37. After 1680, natural increase replaced immigration as the main source of population growth in Virginia.

ANS: T   **TYPE: T**   **KEY 1: A**   **KEY 2: 2**   **PAGE: 85**

_____ 38. Life expectancy was pretty uniform throughout the colonies.

ANS: F   **TYPE: T**   **KEY 1: A**   **KEY 2: 2**   **PAGE: 85**

_____ 39. Charles II and James II were brothers.

ANS: T   **TYPE: T**   **KEY 1: F**   **KEY 2: 1**   **PAGE: 100**

_____ 40. English settlers were probably always a minority in the Middle Atlantic region.

ANS: T   **TYPE: T**   **KEY 1: A**   **KEY 2: 1**   **PAGE: 87**

1. In the 1680s, the colonies of New York, Massachusetts, and Connecticut were joined together in one colony, known as the _____.

ANS: Dominion of New England   **TYPE: F**   **KEY 1: F**   **KEY 2: 3**   **PAGE: 101**

2. The English Navigation Acts were implemented to hurt the power of the _____ in North America.

ANS: Dutch   **TYPE: F**   **KEY 1: F**   **KEY 2: 2**   **PAGE: 91**

3. The Dutch merchant who rose to power during the "Glorious Revolution" in New York was _____.

ANS: Jacob Leisler   **TYPE: F**   **KEY 1: F**   **KEY 2: 2**   **PAGE: 102**

4. The _____ Act (1663) regulated goods going to North America from around the world.

ANS: Staple   **TYPE: F**   **KEY 1: F**   **KEY 2: 2**   **PAGE: 91**

5. The _____ was a hoax by Titus Oates who claimed that Catholics were planning to murder King Charles II.

ANS: Popish Plot   **TYPE: F**   **KEY 1: F**   **KEY 2: 2**   **PAGE: 100**

6. _____ was the first English colony to require each community to create a public school.

ANS: Massachusetts   **TYPE: F**   **KEY 1: F**   **KEY 2: 2**   **PAGE: 87**

7. In 1720, South Carolina had fewer than _____ settlers.

ANS: 6,000   **TYPE: F**   **KEY 1: F**   **KEY 2: 3**   **PAGE: 116**

8. Prior to the beginning of the American Revolution, the largest revolt in the English colonies was _____.

ANS: Bacon's Rebellion   **TYPE: F**   **KEY 1: F**   **KEY 2: 2**   **PAGE: 99**

9. By 1700, England possessed _____ colonies in North America and the Caribbean.

ANS: twenty   **TYPE: F**   **KEY 1: F**   **KEY 2: 2**   **PAGE: 83**

10. African slaves became a majority in the colony of _____ around 1710.

ANS: South Carolina   **TYPE: F**   **KEY 1: F**   **KEY 2: 2**   **PAGE: 86**

11. By 1700, the predominant crop of the Middle Atlantic colonies was _____.

ANS: wheat   **TYPE: F**   **KEY 1: F**   **KEY 2: 2**   **PAGE: 87**

12. By 1650, most sugar and tobacco exports were going to _____, not London.

ANS: Amsterdam   TYPE: F   KEY 1: F   KEY 2: 3   PAGE: 88

13. England discovered the importance of its colonies around _____.

ANS: 1650   TYPE: F   KEY 1: A   KEY 2: 2   PAGE: 88

14. The only New England staple desired in Europe was _____.

ANS: fish   TYPE: F   KEY 1: F   KEY 2: 1   PAGE: 91

15. In 1670, _____ was the largest city north of Mexico.

ANS: Boston   TYPE: F   KEY 1: F   KEY 2: 2   PAGE: 93

16. Massasoit's son _____ was also known as King Philip.

ANS: Metacom   TYPE: F   KEY 1: F   KEY 2: 2   PAGE: 94

17. Bacon's Rebellion exposed weaknesses in the leadership of Virginia governor _____.

ANS: William Berkeley   TYPE: F   KEY 1: F   KEY 2: 2   PAGE: 99

18. _____, an aggressive British customs officer sent to Massachusetts in 1676, recommended that the colony's charter be revoked.

ANS: Edward Randolph   TYPE: F   KEY 1: F   KEY 2: 3   PAGE: 101

19. As late as 1678, _____ remained the only royal colony on the mainland.

ANS: Virginia   TYPE: F   KEY 1: F   KEY 2: 2   PAGE: 101

20. Sir _____ headed the government of the Dominion of New England.

ANS: Edmund Andros   TYPE: F   KEY 1: F   KEY 2: 3   PAGE: 101

21. The most successful Indian revolt in American history was led by _____, a San Pueblo medicine man, in 1680.

ANS: Popé   TYPE: F   KEY 1: F   KEY 2: 3   PAGE: 110

22. Miantonomo was sachem of the _____.

ANS: Narragansetts   TYPE: F   KEY 1: F   KEY 2: 2   PAGE: 89

23. Parliament's 1650 decision to ban foreign ships from English colonies was designed to stifle _____ competition.

ANS: Dutch   TYPE: F   KEY 1: F   KEY 2: 2   PAGE: 91

24. The 1651 Navigation Act decreed that all ship masters and _____ of each ship's crew entering American waters had to be Englishmen.

ANS: half   **TYPE: F**   **KEY 1: F**   **KEY 2: 2**   **PAGE: 91**

25. By 1700, _____ had become the largest city in western Europe.

ANS: London   **TYPE: F**   **KEY 1: F**   **KEY 2: 2**   **PAGE: 92**

26. _____ translated the Bible and other religious works into the Wampanoag language.

ANS: John Eliot   **TYPE: F**   **KEY 1: F**   **KEY 2: 2**   **PAGE: 94**

27. The ascension of William of Orange brought England closer to _____.

ANS: the Netherlands   **TYPE: F**   **KEY 1: A**   **KEY 2: 2**   **PAGE: 102**

28. _____ was the last colony to accept William and Mary as England's rulers.

ANS: Maryland   **TYPE: F**   **KEY 1: F**   **KEY 2: 2**   **PAGE: 102**

29. The Pueblo Uprising of 1680 killed _____ of the 2,300 Spaniards in New Mexico.

ANS: 400   **TYPE: F**   **KEY 1: F**   **KEY 2: 3**   **PAGE: 110**

30. After capturing Acadia in 1710, the British renamed it _____.

ANS: Nova Scotia   **TYPE: F**   **KEY 1: F**   **KEY 2: 2**   **PAGE: 114**

IDENTIFICATIONS

1. **Salem Witch Trials**: gripped the town of Salem, Massachusetts in the spring and summer of 1692. Began when a group of young women accused many neighbors of witchcraft. (Significantly, many of the accused had been critical of the town's religious establishment.) About 150 were eventually accused. Nineteen people were hanged, one was pressed to death, and several others died in jail. Fifty others confessed. The trials were only halted when the wife of the governor was accused.

2. **Metacom's War**: large-scale military action fought in New England in the 1670s between European settlers and Native Americans. Often called King Philip's War. Initiated by sachem of the Wampanoags. Eventually involved the Narragansetts and the Mohawks. Ended with major Indian defeat, as hundreds of Indians were killed and hundreds more were sold into slavery in the West Indies.

3. **Toleration Act:** act of Parliament following Glorious Revolution. Granted toleration to Protestants. Significantly did not include Catholics.

4. **Sir William Berkeley**: governor of Virginia. Favored defensive strategy against Indians. Tried to distinguish between neutral and friendly Indians and hostile ones. Put down Bacon's Rebellion. Died in disgrace in England.

5. **Mercantilism:** economic theory that a nation's power and wealth depended on maintaining a favorable balance of trade and controlling colonial commerce. Colonies were to provide the mother country with raw materials and serve as markets for the mother country's finished goods. The Navigation Acts were passed to implement this theory.

6. **Glorious Revolution**: peaceful revolution in 1688-89 in which the Catholic King James II was overthrown and replaced by the Protestant King William III and Queen Mary II. Resulted in the destruction of the Dominion of New England in the colonies. Parliament passed legislation that officially established the policy that the English monarch *must* be Protestant.

7. **Mourning wars**: engaged in by Native American tribes, most often the Iroquois. Often initiated by female relatives of a deceased loved one who insisted that their male kin repair the loss. Her warrior relatives would then launch a raid and bring back captives. Male prisoners would usually be killed, but women and children would be adopted and assimilated. Adoptees became full Iroquois, and as early as the 1660s, a majority of the Indians of the Five Nations were adoptees, not native-born Iroquois.

8. **Dominion of New England**: created in 1686 by James II. Joined Massachusetts, New Hampshire, Rhode Island, Connecticut, New York, and both Jerseys. Governor Edmund Andros governed through an appointive council and a superior court that rode circuit. There was no elective assembly. Religious toleration was forced upon the Puritans. Dismantled after the Glorious Revolution.

9. **"Mixed and balanced" constitution**: English philosophy of government that emerged from the Glorious Revolution. Liberty was maintained because power was balanced among the monarchy, aristocracy and commonality.

10. **Pope:** Pueblo medicine man who organized the most successful Indian uprising against the Spanish.

SHORT ESSAYS

1.   Examine Bacon's Rebellion. What were its causes, course, and results?

Answer: Bacon's Rebellion grew out of a number of circumstances, the primary ones being a growing class of indentured servants and a decreasing amount of available land for use by those servants when their term of indenture was complete. Nathaniel Bacon was a recently wealthy emigrant to the Virginia backcountry who rallied the landless, former servants of the area around the idea of gaining access to Indian lands by enslaving them or expelling them. The governor, Sir William Berkeley, was opposed to this idea for several reasons, one being to limit warfare on the frontier. Bacon ignored the governor's order not to attack, did so in 1676, and was labeled a traitor.

Although not very successful in moving the Indians, Bacon was far more successful in raising the largest rebellion in colonial American history. After several months of fighting between Bacon and Berkeley, Jamestown, the capital, was put under siege and then burned. The rebellion, which had become a class struggle, came to an abrupt halt with the death of Bacon from dysentery. Berkeley hanged several Bacon supporters, but the Virginia elite began to limit the number of indentured servants allowed into Virginia to prevent this type of occurrence in the future.

2.   What was Metacom's War? Describe and detail the causes and results.

Answer: The causes of Metacom's War, named after the Wampanoag sachem Metacom, were an outgrowth of the continual stresses and pressures that existed between European settlers and the native tribes. Although the immediate reason for the outbreak of hostilities included attempts to Christianize the Indian population, the larger reasons were increased European-settler demand for Indian land. The war itself began on the frontier when settlers killed a Wampanoag they found looting a house they had abandoned.

The white settlers had a difficult time defeating the Wampanoags, who were armed with guns and were excellent marksmen. The war spread to the Narragansetts and resulted in the deaths of approximately 800 settlers and the near destruction of 24 communities. Both whites and Indians committed atrocities. In the end, the New Englanders won the war, slaughtered hundreds of Indians, and sent others to the Caribbean as slaves.

3.   Examine the causes and course of the Glorious Revolution.

Answer: The Glorious Revolution (1688–1689) grew out of the Protestant Parliament's mounting fear that King James II of England was certain to raise his son and future king of England as a Catholic. James had proclaimed toleration for Protestants and Catholics and began naming Catholics to high office. Both Whigs and Tories joined together to remove the king, but not by the violent means by which his father (Charles I) had been removed. These leaders invited William of Orange, husband of James's Protestant daughter, Mary, to be the new leader of England.

William landed in England in late 1688 and, within a few weeks, gained the support of the English army. James fled to France, where he received the protection of the monarch there. Parliament declared that James had abdicated the throne and named William and Mary in his place. In addition, it passed a Toleration Act that gave Protestants the right to worship publicly. Also, it passed a Bill of Rights that guaranteed Protestant succession to the throne.

4.   Examine the theory of mercantilism. How did this policy shape the British imperial system (of which the colonies were a part)?

Answer: The theory and policy of mercantilism began to be developed during the seventeenth century. Mercantilism, in essence, asserts that colonies can serve the economic and social interests of the mother country if the mother country maintains complete control over their trade. In addition, mercantilism argued that a strengthened imperial system, closely regulated through acts of trade and commerce, would best supply the economic needs of the mother country. Fueling this belief, of course, was the idea that this type of protective system was essential for the security of nations in perpetual warfare with each other.

The basic precepts of mercantilism were simple. Colonies were to send raw materials (tobacco, cotton, sugar) to the mother country for processing there. Also, colonies were to act as markets for the manufactured products of the mother country. In traditional mercantilist theory, colonies were not supposed to compete with the mother country, because their role actually was to promote the economic health and wealth of the empire as a whole.

5.   Discuss the impact of European colonization on the Indian societies of North America. How did the Native Americans react to the dangers inherent in contact with the whites?

Answer: The spread of European diseases such as smallpox decimated the tribes along the Atlantic Seaboard and precipitated intertribal warfare. "Mourning Wars" in which bereaved families replaced lost members through battle and with kidnapping and adoption of tribal enemies became more common. Captured females and children were assimilated into the captor's tribe, while male prisoners were killed. Among the Five Nations, adoption accounted for more than half of the tribal members during the 1660s.

Besides diseases, American Indians also acquired guns, cloth, axes, knives, pots, and alcohol from the Europeans. These items transformed Indian society and resulted in tribal dependence on European trade. Traditional skills and social patterns were eroded as Indians competed for and relied on European goods. Alcohol was especially destructive and spread violence and disharmony throughout the Indian communities. In areas where whites and Indians were interdependent, alliances were formed. The fur traders in New France, the Dutch in New Netherlands, and the English in New York and Virginia made peace and mutual defense agreements with local tribes. Some Protestants in New England established "praying towns" where they converted Indians to Christianity. These efforts undermined the traditional power and gender structure of Indian society and caused some young warrior-hunters to fear that their lifestyle was being destroyed. In times of war, whites usually attacked indiscriminately and killed friendly Christian Indians as well as unfriendly non-Christian ones.

6.   Discuss the evolution of the English concept of constitutional government during the late seventeenth and early eighteenth centuries.

Answer: The Glorious Revolution of 1688–89 ended a period of upheaval and instability in English politics. The absolutist dreams of the Stuart kings were replaced by a "mixed and balanced" constitutional process where Parliament, the monarchy, and the nobility each retained and exercised influence and power. Ministers were public officials whose actions were subject to examination and whose positions were based upon support from below and above. The government that emerged under the constitutional limitations was actually more centralized and powerful than the pre-Revolutionary system. Englishmen celebrated their creation of a monarchial structure in which republican liberties were protected and corrupt aristocratic self interest was contained. In theory, each segment of the government acted in the best interest of the public.

The political debates of the period centered on establishing the extent to which power would be controlled within the system. The dangers of corruption inherent in the appointment and taxing powers of the crown caused concern. "Court" advocates encouraged greater consolidation of England's war-making capacity through military expansion, revenue enhancement, and patronage. "Country" advocates, on the other hand, favored frequent elections and dual office holding and opposed standing armies and financial innovations. Both the Whig and Tory parties contained court and country factions. The disputes between these groups eventually spread to the colonies in North America where the northern colonies embraced the court position and the southern colonies admired the country position.

7.   Examine the common bonds that united the colonies and contributed to their homogeneity in the seventeenth century.

Answer: While there was great diversity in colonial America, the English colonies were also similar in language, law, warfare, and inheritance patterns. Although certain regions of colonial America were settled by peoples from specific areas of England who spoke local dialects, each colony included large numbers of landowners. Thus London English was influential in shaping the speech patterns of every colony and in lessening the regional differences.

The colonists also developed a common approach to waging war that was different from the English traditions. Most European nations had professional armies with fulltime soldiers who were expected to adhere to established rules concerning the treatment of noncombatants. The colonists, on the other hand, favored volunteer militia who signed up for short-term, temporary enlistments and who routinely slaughtered Indian women and children.

The legal system that developed in the colonies was simple and more localized than that of England. The legal profession was not institutionalized until the eighteenth century, and colonists were accustomed to receiving quick and uncomplicated justice. The rigid English inheritance regulations did not gain acceptance in the New World. In England, primogeniture rules gave all inheritance rights to the eldest son, while in the colonies younger sons and even daughters could inherit property. Only the New England colonies gave preference to the eldest son by doubling his portion of the inheritance.

LONG ESSAYS

1.   Compare and contrast Bacon's Rebellion with Leisler's Rebellion in the late seventeenth century. Were there any common causes or patterns that link these rebellions together?

Answer: Essay should address several key points:

A.   Bacon's Rebellion (1676)
    1.   Causes
        a.   Land shortage
        b.   Growing number of indentured servants
        c.   Frontier clashes with Indians
    2.   Course and results
        a.   Large-scale rebellion
        b.   Property damage and casualties
        c.   Jamestown burned/governor forced to flee
        d.   Bacon dies/slaves increasingly replace indentured servants
B.   Leisler's Rebellion
    1.   Causes
        a.   English-Dutch rivalry
        b.   Disenchantment with Dominion of New England
        c.   Growing gap between rich and poor
        d.   News of Glorious Revolution

	2.	Course and results
		a. Takeover by Jacob Leisler and non-English followers
		b. Refusal to respect rights of political opponents
		c. Driven from power by English New Yorkers
		d. Executed for treason

2. Explore the Acts of Trade and Navigation in the mid-seventeenth century. What were their goals, and how successful were they?

Answer: Essay should address several key points:

A. Goal of British imperial system
    1. Removal of Dutch
        a. Major trade rival in North America
        b. Consequences
    2. Increased colonial economic development
        a. Need to make colonies more lucrative
        b. Consequences
    3. Implemented during leadership of Cromwell
B. Provisions of Navigation Acts
    1. Act of Trade and Navigation (1651)
        a. Non-European goods must be shipped on English ships
        b. Crews must be half English
    2. Enumerated Commodities Act (1660)
        a. Certain products could be shipped only to England or to other English colonies
        b. Consequences
    3. Staple Act (1663)
        a. Regulated goods going to America
        b. African, Asian, and European goods first had to pass through English ports
C. Outcome
    1. Properly enforced, Navigation Acts would establish English hegemony over North American trade
    2. Actual results

3. Examine the French and Spanish Empires in North America and discuss their struggles with the English in the colonial wars of 1699-1716.

Answer: Essay should address several key points:

A. Spanish colonies
    1. New Mexico
        a. Changes in mission system
        b. Pueblo Revolt (1680)
        c. Return of the Spanish (1690s)
    2. Texas
        a. Early settlements
        b. Temporary withdrawal
B. French colonies
    1. New France
        a. Iroquois wars
        b. Establishment of the "middle ground"
        c. French negotiation strategies
    2. Louisiana
        a. Explorers
        b. Early settlements
        c. Relations with Indians

C.   Colonial wars
        1.   General goals
                    a.   King William's War
                    b.   Queen Anne's War
                    c.   Attacks on Spanish Florida
        2.   Overall results

4.   Discuss the differences and similarities among the English colonies in the early 1700s. What aspects of colonial life united them?

Answer: Essay should address several key points.

A.   Caribbean islands
        1.   Demographics
                    a.   Life expectancy
                    b.   Gender ratio
                    c.   Family structure
                    d.   Race and ethnicity
        2.   Economics
                    a.   Wealthy elite
                    b.   Slavery and cash crops
        3.   Political system
                    a.   Royal government
                    b.   The parish
        4.   Religion and education
B.   Southern colonies
        1.   Demographics
                    a.   Life expectancy
                    b.   Gender ratio
                    c.   Family structure
                    d.   Race and ethnicity
        2.   Economics
                    a.   Wealthy elite
                    b.   Slavery and cash crops
        3.   Political system
                    a.   Proprietary government
                    b.   The parish
        4.   Religion and education
C.   Middle Atlantic and New England colonies
        1.   Demographics
                    a.   Life expectancy
                    b.   Gender ratio
                    c.   Family structure
                    d.   Race and ethnicity
        2.   Economics
                    a.   The wheat belt
                    b.   Subsistence farming
                    c.   Fishing
        3.   Political system
                    a.   Townships
                    b.   Counties
                    c.   Corporate government
        4.   Religion and education
D.   Common bonds
        1.   Colonial similarities
                    a.   Language, war, law and inheritance

2. English differences
   a. Language, war, law and inheritance

CHAPTER 4
PROVINCIAL AMERICA AND THE STRUGGLE FOR A CONTINENT

CHAPTER OUTLINE

I.   Expansion versus Anglicization
    A.   Threats to Householder Authority
    B.   Anglicizing the Role of Women
II.   Expansion, Immigration, and Regional Differentiation
    A.   The Emergence of the Old South
    B.   The Mid-Atlantic Colonies: The "Best Poor Man's Country"
    C.   The Backcountry
    D.   New England: A Faltering Economy and Paper Money
III.   Anglicizing Provincial America
    A.   The World of Print
    B.   The Enlightenment in America
    C.   Lawyers and Doctors
    D.   Georgia: The Failure of an Enlightenment Utopia
IV.   The Great Awakening
    A.   Origins of the Revivals
    B.   Whitefield Launches the Transatlantic Revival
    C.   Disruptions
    D.   Long-Term Consequences of the Revivals
    E.   New Colleges
    F.   The Denominational Realignment
V.   Political Culture in the Colonies
    A.   The Rise of the Assembly and the Governor
    B.   "Country" Constitutions: The Southern Colonies
    C.   "Court" Constitutions: The Northern Colonies
VI.   The Renewal of Imperial Conflict
    A.   Challenges to French Power
    B.   The Danger of Slave Revolts and War with Spain
    C.   France versus Britain: King George's War
    D.   The Impending Storm
VII.   The War for North America
    A.   The Albany Congress and the Onset of War
    B.   Britain's Years of Defeat
    C.   A World War
    D.   Imperial Tensions: From Loudoun to Pitt
    E.   The Years of British Victory
    F.   The Cherokee War and Spanish Intervention
    G.   The Peace of Paris
VIII.   Conclusion

CHRONOLOGY

1704	*Boston News-Letter* becomes first newspaper in British colonies.
1714	George I brings the Hanoverian dynasty to the British throne.
1715–1716	Yamassee War in South Carolina.
1721	Zabdiel Boylston introduces smallpox inoculation in Boston.
1722	New Orleans founded.
1727	George II succeeds George I.
1730s–1740s	Great Awakening.

1732–1733	Founding of Georgia.
1733	Molasses Act.
1734	Jonathan Edwards launches religious revival in Connecticut Valley.
1735	John Peter Zenger trial.
1739	George Whitefield's second trip to British colonies launches Great Awakening. Stono Rebellion.
1739–1742	War of Jenkins' Ear.
1741	New York slave conspiracy trials.
1744–1748	King George's War.
1748	Treaty of Aix-la-Chapelle.
1754	Washington surrenders at Great Meadows. Albany Congress.
1755	Edward Braddock defeated. Acadians expelled from Nova Scotia.
1756–1763	Seven Years' War (French and Indian War).
1757	William Pitt becomes war minister.
1759	Wolfe defeats Montcalm on Plains of Abraham.
1760	Accession of George III as king of Great Britain. Cherokee War devastates Carolina backcountry.
1763	Peace of Paris.

THEMATIC TOPICS FOR ENRICHMENT

1. How did the massive influx of African slaves between 1700 and 1740 transform the social structure of the southern colonies?

2. What was "householder autonomy" and what factors threatened to undermine it?

3. How did life in the backcountry differ from that on the coast?

4. Discuss the changing role of women throughout the eighteenth century.

5. Why was the utopian experiment in Georgia such a failure?

6. What were the unique features of South Carolina? Contrast gang labor with the task system.

7. Why were the Mid-Atlantic colonies considered to be the "best poor man's country"?

8. What were the key features of denomination realignment in the Great Awakening?

9. List the colonial colleges of the eighteenth century and the dates they were founded.

10. Compare the power of the colonial governors with that of the colonial assemblies.

11. Detail the main features of British opposition ideology.

12. Assess the military aspects of the French and Indian War. In what ways did the conflict lead to misunderstandings between colonists and the mother country?

SUGGESTED ESSAY TOPICS

1. Discuss the process of Anglicization in the colonies to 1750. How did the colonists seek "to emulate their homeland"?

2. What was the role of religion in the settlement and growth of the North American colonies?

3. Define the term *Enlightenment*. In what ways did colonial development reflect Enlightenment ideas?

4. Detail the basic features of government in the American colonies. What were the major similarities and differences between the government of the mother country and that of the colonies?

LECTURE OUTLINE

1. Competing social and economic pressures compelled colonists to attempt to reconcile provincial desire for uncontrolled expansion with England's attempts toward **Anglicization.**

    a. Economic inequality in a number of circumstances led directly to a **threat to householder autonomy,** as the economy of colonial America became more complex and differentiated.

    b. Changes from settlement to a stratified society led colonists toward **Anglicizing the role of women,** a change that had both advantages and disadvantages for women.

2. The eighteenth century witnessed dramatic changes in North America as territorial expansion and growing numbers of immigrants brought about **regional differentiation** within the empire.

    a. Immigration and the advent of plantation slavery on a large scale signaled the emergence of the **Old South,** characterized by the production of staple crops for export.

(SHOW TRANSPARENCY 26: AFRICAN-AMERICAN POPULATION IN COLONIAL BRITISH AMERICA, C. 1760)

    b. With the phenomenal growth of Pennsylvania and New Jersey, the Mid-Atlantic colonies, came to be known as the **"best poor man's country."**

(SHOW TRANSPARENCY 27: GERMAN AND SCOTS-IRISH SETTLEMENTS IN COLONIAL BRITISH AMERICA, C. 1760)

    c. The growth and social differentiation of the coast ensured that the **backcountry** would be a distinct region, sparsely settled, relatively dangerous, and politically underrepresented.

    d. In the course of the eighteenth century, New England suffered from a faltering economy and currency problems related in part to the circulation of **paper money.**

3. What made these diverse regions more alike was their slow process of **Anglicization,** or the slow development of more English characteristics.

    a. Although few colonists owned books or engaged in intellectual debate the **world of print** was spreading its way through the colonies.

    b. The **Enlightenment in America,** in both its religious and secular forms, transformed colonists' assumptions and modes of thinking.

    c. As in England, **lawyers and doctors** began to emerge as part of a coterie of professionals with growing prestige and power.

    d. Founded in 1732–1733, **Georgia** failed as Enlightenment utopia imagined by its founders; it became just another southern colony dominated by slavery and local exigencies.

4.   The **Great Awakening** convulsed religious institutions and virtually all of society in provincial America.

   a.   The **origins of the revivals** remain obscure but may be tied to the rise of a new generation of ministers with decidedly novel ideas.

   b.   Many historians date the beginning of religious enthusiasm in America to **George Whitefield** launching the transatlantic revivals, particularly in his second trip to the colonies in 1739.

   c.   The revivals caused **disruptions** in virtually every colony that took years to die down.

   d.   Historians have debated the exact **long-term consequences of the revivals,** but they agree that the Great Awakening affected almost every colonial community.

      i.   Religious schisms from the revivals resulted in the establishment of a number of **new colleges.**

      ii.   The **denominational realignment** that ensued from the awakenings is a unique feature of American religion.

5.   A mixture of local and English traditions, the **political culture in the colonies** developed rapidly in the eighteenth century.

   a.   The two key institutional developments were the **rise of the assembly** and the governor's growing responsibilities.

   b.   The southern colonies had **"Country Constitutions;"** that emphasized the importance of restricting corruption and central power.

   c.   **"Court Constitutions"** were characteristic of the northern colonies where powerful councils closely advised imperial governors.

6.   Contention with France and Spain led to a **renewal of imperial** conflict by mid-century.

   a.   The colonists were eager to offer **challenges to French power** in the interior regions of North America.

(SHOW TRANSPARENCY 29: FRENCH LOUISIANA AND SPANISH TEXAS, C. 1730)

   b.   The danger of **slave revolts and war with Spain** grew in the first decades of the century, ultimately culminating in the Stono Rebellion and the War of Jenkins' Ear in 1739.

(SHOW TRANSPARENCY 30: CARIBBEAN THEATER OF WAR, 1739–1742)

   c.   In 1744, France joined Spain to fight Britain in **King George's War,** in which untrained Yankee volunteers subdued the great French fortress of Louisbourg on June 16, 1745.

(SHOW TRANSPARENCY 31: SOUTHEASTERN THEATER OF WAR, 1739–1742)

   d.   All of these conflicts merely foreshadowed the **impending storm** that would take place after mid-century.

7.   The **war for North America** occurred between 1755 and 1763.

(SHOW TRANSPARENCY 33: SEVEN YEARS' WAR IN NORTH AMERICA)

a. Ben Franklin's 1754 plan for the **Albany Congress** to discuss mutual defense proved an utter failure at the onset of war.

b. The first years of the French and Indian War, especially with the death of **General Edward Braddock,** proved to be bitter years filled with British defeats.

c. Years of war and uncertainty led to grave imperial tensions as successive administrations from **Loudoun to Pitt** failed to satisfy the Crown.

d. The years from 1760 to 1763 can be termed the years of **British victory,** as the war finally became clearly winnable.

(SHOW TRANSPARENCY 34: GROWTH OF POPULATION TO 1760)

e. In an effort to take advantage of the great burden of England's war with France, southern Indians commenced the **Cherokee War,** while the Spanish intervened in the South.

f. The **Peace of Paris** of 1763 marked the pinnacle of the first British Empire.

Conclusion: As the colonists of provincial America struggled to secure more land and greater security, they created a socially stratified society of richer and poorer, ins and outs that increasingly resembled England through the eighteenth century. The costs and consequences of a succession of imperial struggles set the stage for the demise of the empire.

TEACHING RESOURCES

Multicultural Peoples of North America video series. This collection celebrates the varied cultural heritage of different cultural groups. Includes videos on African Americans and the Amish. Filmic Archives (30 minutes each).

Working for the Lord depicts American religious development into the nineteenth century. Republic Pictures Home Video (52 minutes).

The Inventory examines the life of a typical middle-class family in the eighteenth century through an examination of its possessions and values. Films for the Humanities (28 minutes).

Old Salem and *Cavaliers and Craftsmen-Williamsburg* depict life in two of America's oldest communities through both a social and historical approach. VideoTours History Collection (30 minutes each).

Colonial America: Life in the Maturing Colonies focuses on the colonies between the turn of the eighteenth century and the French and Indian War. Filmic Archives (17 minutes).

From Waalstraat to Wall Street explores the development of English New York from its Dutch roots as New Amsterdam. Films for the Humanities (50 minutes).

The Battle of Quebec: 1759, the End of the French and Indian War describes the Battle of Quebec while analyzing the causes of the French and Indian War from a Canadian perspective. Films for the Humanities (32 minutes).

In Search of the Dream: Unearthing the Slave Trade examines slavery in New York City through a close review of the archaeological records unearthed in lower Manhattan. Films for the Humanities (28 minutes).

The Last of the Mohicans is a feature film, starring Daniel Day Lewis that gives a strong dramatization of the James Fennimore Cooper tale about the French and Indian War. (1 hour, 57 minutes).

1. The Great Awakening of the 1740s refers to
    a. a massive religious revival.
    b. the beginning of colonial strains with Great Britain.
    c. the British attempt to implement imperial controls.
    d. the spread of enlightenment ideals.
    e. the rapid spread of disease in America.

ANS: A　　　**TYPE: M**　　　**KEY 1: F**　　　**KEY 2: 1**　　　**PAGE: 134**

2. By 1750, the richest men in British North America were
    a. South Carolina rice planters.
    b. New England merchants.
    c. Virginia tobacco planters.
    d. New York landlords.
    e. the King's tax collectors.

ANS: A　　　**TYPE: M**　　　**KEY 1: F**　　　**KEY 2: 2**　　　**PAGE: 122**

3. Only _____ percent of the volunteers in the War of Jenkins's Ear returned home.
    a. 25
    b. 20
    c. 15
    d. 10
    e. 2

ANS: D　　　**TYPE: M**　　　**KEY 1: F**　　　**KEY 2: 2**　　　**PAGE: 142**

4. The Molasses Act (1733)
    a. forbade the importation of molasses into the colonies.
    b. placed a prohibitive duty on foreign molasses.
    c. forbade the production of molasses in the colonies.
    d. decreed that all molasses must go to the mother country.
    e. attempted to abolish the manufacture of rum.

ANS: B　　　**TYPE: M**　　　**KEY 1: F**　　　**KEY 2: 1**　　　**PAGE: 127**

5. Most money issued in eighteenth-century America was backed by
    a. gold.
    b. silver.
    c. hard specie.
    d. government bonds.
    e. the government's promise to accept it in payment of taxes.

ANS: E　　　**TYPE: M**　　　**KEY 1: F**　　　**KEY 2: 1**　　　**PAGE: 127**

6. The region of least economic growth during the eighteenth century was
    a. the mid-Atlantic colonies.
    b. New England.
    c. Chesapeake.
    d. the Deep South.
    e. New York.

ANS: B　　　**TYPE: M**　　　**KEY 1: A**　　　**KEY 2: 2**　　　**PAGE: 127**

7. Georgia was founded originally as
    a. a refuge for Catholics.
    b. a refuge for Quakers.
    c. a refuge for the poor.
    d. a refuge for the "criminally insane."
    e. a profitable business venture.

ANS: C　　　**TYPE: M**　　　**KEY 1: F**　　　**KEY 2: 1**　　　**PAGE: 127**

8. The author of *A Faithful Narrative of the Surprising Work of God* was
    a. Solomon Stoddard.
    b. John Locke.
    c. Benjamin Franklin.
    d. Jonathan Edwards.
    e. Squanto.

ANS: D　　　**TYPE: M**　　　**KEY 1: F**　　　**KEY 2: 2**　　　**PAGE: 132**

9. The most popular revivalist of the Great Awakening was
    a. Gilbert Tennent.
    b. George Whitefield.
    c. James Davenport.
    d. Hugh Bryan.
    e. John Winthrop.

ANS: B　　　**TYPE: M**　　　**KEY 1: F**　　　**KEY 2: 1**　　　**PAGE: 134**

10. The right to vote among white males in colonial America was
    a. unrestricted.
    b. limited by property requirements.
    c. severely restricted.
    d. determined by one's religion.
    e. based on nationality.

ANS: B　　　**TYPE: M**　　　**KEY 1: F**　　　**KEY 2: 1**　　　**PAGE: 138**

11. The religious message of the Great Awakening can best be described as
    a. the rejection of predestination.
    b. a belief that good works were the key to salvation.
    c. the idea that a conversion experience was essential to salvation.
    d. the conviction that the clergy was most responsible for a person's salvation.
    e. the belief in the essential goodness of man.

ANS: C　　　**TYPE: M**　　　**KEY 1: A**　　　**KEY 2: 2**　　　**PAGE: 134**

12. Benjamin Franklin's profession was as a
    a. lawyer.
    b. doctor.
    c. printer.
    d. farmer.
    e. baker.

ANS: C   TYPE: M   KEY 1: A   KEY 2: 2   PAGE: 130

13. When the British fought the Spanish and French in the era 1740 to 1763, most slaves and eastern land Indians
    a. had no opinion.
    b. sympathized with Spain and France.
    c. allied with the English.
    d. were taken as hostages by the English.
    e. united against all whites.

ANS: B   TYPE: M   KEY 1: A   KEY 2: 1   PAGE: 140-44

14. Political factions were most likely to develop in the
    a. northern colonies.
    b. Mid-Atlantic colonies.
    c. upper South colonies.
    d. lower South colonies.
    e. Caribbean colonies.

ANS: A   TYPE: M   KEY 1: A   KEY 2: 2   PAGE: 139

15. Which of the following is an example of the Anglicanization of the colonies?
    a. Wealthy colonials copied London styles of clothing and architecture.
    b. Clergymen educated at Oxford and Cambridge were offered parishes in the colonies.
    c. Colonial gentlemen who avoided manual labor dominated local politics.
    d. The import of British goods grew rapidly.
    e. all of the above

ANS: E   TYPE: M   KEY 1: F   KEY 2: 2   PAGE: 120-121

16. The Anglicanization of the role of colonial women was exemplified by
    a. an expansion of women's property rights.
    b. the use of the judicial theory that a wife could make legal contracts without the consent of her husband.
    c. a double standard that punished women but not men for sexual indiscretions.
    d. the dowry tradition which endowed women with land when they married.
    e. reduction in the work load of most women.

ANS: C   TYPE: M   KEY 1: F   KEY 2: 2   PAGE: 121

17. Under the task system, slaves were
    a. organized into work gangs supervised by white slave drivers.
    b. "taken to task" or beaten for the slightest infraction of the rules.
    c. allowed to choose the work they would do and to switch tasks when they became bored.
    d. given specific jobs to do and allowed free time when the tasks were completed.
    e. allowed to change masters if the work load became too heavy.

ANS: D   TYPE: M   KEY 1: F   KEY 2: 3   PAGE: 124

18. Which of the following was not a major southern cash crop in the early 1700s?
    a. cotton
    b. tobacco
    c. indigo
    d. wheat
    e. rice

ANS: A   **TYPE: M**   **KEY 1: F**   **KEY 2: 2**   **PAGE: 125**

19. Which of the following was true of the Scots-Irish?
    a. They were Catholic Irishmen who moved to Scotland and then to North America.
    b. They were clannish, violent, heavy-drinking Indian-haters who dominated the back country of Virginia and South Carolina.
    c. They were Quakers who set up Protestant missions to Christianize the Indians.
    d. They were the best educated and most dignified of the Anglican immigrants in the Middle Colonics.
    e. They were the governing elite in Virginia.

ANS: B   **TYPE: M**   **KEY 1: A**   **KEY 2: 3**   **PAGE: 126**

20. The economy of the New England colonies
    a. attracted the largest number immigrants of any region.
    b. was based on agriculture and trade with the Indians.
    c. depended on shipbuilding, whaling, and trade with the French West Indies.
    d. depended on slave labor to produce exportable products.
    e. exported manufactured goods to England.

ANS: C   **TYPE: M**   **KEY 1: F**   **KEY 2: 2**   **PAGE: 127**

21. Which of the following is true of Benjamin Franklin?
    a. During his lifetime, Franklin was virtually unknown outside of Boston.
    b. He was most famous for his electrical experiments for which he received honorary degrees from Harvard, Yale, and other colleges.
    c. He was the first president of Harvard University.
    d. He was sent to prison for writing libelous articles about the governor of New York.
    e. He did not become well known until the American Revolution.

ANS: B   **TYPE: M**   **KEY 1: F**   **KEY 2: 2**   **PAGE: 130**

22. The Enlightenment
    a. was a religious movement emphasizing strict adherence to biblical teachings.
    b. was a rational philosophy that rejected religious fanaticism and asserted that human knowledge would improve society.
    c. excluded the writings of Thomas Jefferson and Benjamin Franklin because they were "too idealistic."
    d. was an organization of scientists who experimented with electricity.
    e. had no impact on England.

ANS: B   **TYPE: M**   **KEY 1: A**   **KEY 2: 3**   **PAGE: 130-31**

23. Which of the following was true of George Whitefield?
    a. He claimed he could divide the waters of the Savannah River and set the slaves free.
    b. He was an English Anglican minister whose dramatic sermons attracted crowds of thousands.
    c. He wrote the *Book of Common Prayer.*
    d. He led major religious dissenting factions in the Middle Colonies.
    e. He led a major slave rebellion.

ANS: B   TYPE: M   KEY 1: F   KEY 2: 3   PAGE: 135

24. The religious revivals of the 1740s through 1770s
    a. led to a decline in the number of female church members.
    b. almost destroyed the Freemasons.
    c. united all the major colonial churches into one interdenominational organization.
    d. increased the size and strength of the Baptist, Methodist, and Presbyterian churches.
    e. converted most of the Indians in the colonies.

ANS: D   TYPE: M   KEY 1: A   KEY 2: 3   PAGE: 136

25. By the 1720s, most colonial governments
    a. included an appointed governor, a council, and an elected assembly.
    b. had a hereditary governor's office.
    c. had lost legislative independence and were virtually powerless.
    d. were corrupt, inefficient, and undemocratic.
    e. had declared their independence of the King.

ANS: A   TYPE: M   KEY 1: F   KEY 2:   PAGE: 137

26. Colonial governors dealt with the assemblies by
    a. using the army to enforce royal prerogatives.
    b. appealing to church leaders to mediate disputes.
    c. using the courts to control their power.
    d. ignoring their complaints.
    e. relying on flattery, patronage, and persuasion.

ANS: C   TYPE: M   KEY 1: F   KEY 2: 2   PAGE: 138

27. Colonists usually viewed men who held positions of power as
    a. trustworthy, honest civil servants.
    b. lazy bums who wouldn't work at respectable jobs.
    c. God's chosen representatives.
    d. potentially corrupt officials who, if given the opportunity, would undermine the liberty of the people.
    e. having no significance to their lives.

ANS: D   TYPE: M   KEY 1: A   KEY 2: 3   PAGE: 139

28. In regard to slavery, the government of Spanish Florida
    a. participated in and profited from the international slave trade.
    b. prohibited Africans, free or slave, from entering the colony.
    c. offered freedom and protection to runaway slaves from the English colonies.
    d. never established an official policy.
    e. executed any slave found in its territory.

ANS: C   TYPE: M   KEY 1: F   KEY 2: 3   PAGE: 141

29. In the 1759 siege of Quebec, British General _____ was killed along with his French counterpart, General Montcalm.
    a. Braddock
    b. Wolfe
    c. Amherst
    d. Abercrombie
    e. Winthrop

ANS: B   **TYPE: M**   **KEY 1: F**   **KEY 2: 2**   **PAGE: 156**

30. The largest slave revolt in the history of the thirteen colonies was
    a. the Stono Rebellion.
    b. Bacon's Rebellion.
    c. Leisler's Rebellion.
    d. the War of Jenkins's Ear.
    e. Turner's Rebellion.

ANS: A   **TYPE: M**   **KEY 1: F**   **KEY 2: 1**   **PAGE: 141**

31. The War of Jenkins's Ear was fought between
    a. the British and the Prussians.
    b. the British and the Spanish.
    c. the Spanish and the French.
    d. the British and the Indians.
    e. the Dutch and the Indians.

ANS: B   **TYPE: M**   **KEY 1: F**   **KEY 2: 2**   **PAGE: 141**

32. Which of the following was not a result of the French and Indian War?
    a. France surrendered New Orleans to Britain.
    b. Spain ceded Florida to Britain.
    c. France gave all of Louisiana west of the Mississippi to Spain.
    d. Britain returned Martinique to France.
    e. France surrendered Canada to Britain.

ANS: A   **TYPE: M**   **KEY 1: A**   **KEY 2: 3**   **PAGE: 156**

33. The largest concentration of slaves in North America, outside of Charleston, was in
    a. Richmond.
    b. Baltimore.
    c. New Orleans.
    d. New York City.
    e. Florida.

ANS: D   **TYPE: M**   **KEY 1: F**   **KEY 2: 2**   **PAGE: 142**

34. The Albany Congress refers to
    a. the drafting of New York's colonial government.
    b. the extra-legal group opposed to British policy.
    c. the attempt to unite the British mainland colonies into a federation.
    d. the proclamation drafted against France.
    e. an organization to defend Canada against the British.

ANS: C   **TYPE: M**   **KEY 1: F**   **KEY 2: 2**   **PAGE: 146-47**

35. Colonial politics in the eighteenth century were characterized by
    a. the rise of the assembly and the decline of royal governors.
    b. the growing effectiveness of royal governors and the decline of the assembly.
    c. the growing effectiveness of both the assembly and the royal governor.
    d. the concentration of British troops in the port cities.
    e. none of the above.

ANS: C   TYPE: M   KEY 1: F   KEY 2: 3   PAGE: 137-38

36. During the French and Indian War, British and American troops differed in that
    a. the British were disciplined professionals; the Americans were undisciplined volunteers.
    b. the British followed orders without question; the Americans only obeyed orders they considered reasonable.
    c. the British enlisted for long terms of service; the Americans enlisted for one campaign.
    d. the British subjected soldiers to harsh discipline; the Americans thought that harsh discipline violated the terms of their enlistment.
    e. all of the above

ANS: E   TYPE: M   KEY 1: A   KEY 2: 3   PAGE: 152

37. In the Peace of Paris (1763) that ended the French and Indian War, Britain
    a. lost Florida to France.
    b. acquired all of North America east of the Mississippi except for New Orleans.
    c. gave Martinique, Guadalupe, and Cuba to Spain.
    d. withdrew from Canada.
    e. surrendered Georgia to Spain.

ANS: B   TYPE: M   KEY 1: F   KEY 2: 2   PAGE: 156

38. In 1745, an ill-equipped colonial army successfully captured the Canadian fortress city of
    a. Quebec.
    b. Toronto.
    c. Montreal.
    d. Louisbourg.
    e. Great Lakes.

ANS: D   TYPE: M   KEY 1: F   KEY 2: 1   PAGE: 144

39. King George's War ended with the Treaty of
    a. Paris.
    b. Amsterdam.
    c. Aix-la-Chapelle.
    d. London.
    e. New York.

ANS: C   TYPE: M   KEY 1: F   KEY 2: 2   PAGE: 144

40. The African slave trade in North American reached its peak between
    a. 1710 and 1750.
    b. 1730 and 1775.
    c. 1750 and 1760.
    d. 1700 and 1770.
    e. 1800 and 1850.

ANS: B   TYPE: M   KEY 1: A   KEY 2: 3   PAGE: 122

41. Eliza Lucas Pinckney was
    a. a religious leader.
    b. responsible for introducing indigo to South Carolina.
    c. adopted by Native Americans.
    d. killed by Native Americans.
    e. the inventor of the cotton gin.

ANS: B   TYPE: M   KEY 1: F   KEY 2: 2   PAGE: 125

42. Zabdiel Boylston
    a. was a famous Indian fighter.
    b. discovered that Africans were immune to malaria.
    c. saved Boston from a smallpox epidemic.
    d. gained fame as a preacher during the Great Awakening.
    e. the leader of a slave rebellion.

ANS: C   TYPE: M   KEY 1: F   KEY 2: 3   PAGE: 127

43. The Shepherd's Tent in New London to train awakened preachers was founded by
    a. George Whitefield.
    b. James Davenport.
    c. Gilbert Tennent.
    d. Hugh Bryan.
    e. John Winthrop.

ANS: B   TYPE: M   KEY 1: F   KEY 2: 3   PAGE: 135

44. All of the following colleges were founded before 1740 except
    a. Harvard.
    b. the College of New Jersey.
    c. William and Mary.
    d. Yale.
    e. none of the above

ANS: B   TYPE: M   KEY 1: F   KEY 2: 3   PAGE: 136

45. By the 1720s, every colony had an appointive governor except
    a. Connecticut and Rhode Island.
    b. Pennsylvania.
    c. Massachusetts and Rhode Island.
    d. Massachusetts and Connecticut.
    e. South Carolina.

ANS: A   TYPE: M   KEY 1: F   KEY 2: 3   PAGE: 137

46. George Whitefield was embraced by all of the following except
    a. Congregationalists.
    b. Baptists.
    c. Presbyterians.
    d. Anglicans.
    e. none of the above

ANS: D   TYPE: M   KEY 1: F   KEY 2: 2   PAGE: 135

47. For most of the Seven Years' War, Spain
    a. sided with England.
    b. sided with France.
    c. alternated between England and France.
    d. remained completely neutral and uninvolved.
    e. sided with the Indians.

ANS: D   **TYPE: M**   **KEY 1: F**   **KEY 2: 3**   **PAGE: 151**

48. All of the following British officers remained in America after the Seven Years' War and became generals in the American army during the Revolution except
    a. Hugh Mercer.
    b. Horatio Gates.
    c. Arthur St. Clair.
    d. Richard Montgomery.
    e. James Wolfe.

ANS: E   **TYPE: M**   **KEY 1: F**   **KEY 2: 3**   **PAGE: 156**

49. Before the Revolution, _____ colonial physicians embraced radical politics.
    a. many
    b. few
    c. no
    d. all
    e. 57

ANS: A   **TYPE: M**   **KEY 1: F**   **KEY 2: 2**   **PAGE: 132**

50. The most prosperous family farms in America were found in
    a. the Chesapeake.
    b. the Mid-Atlantic colonies.
    c. New England.
    d. the lower South.
    e. the area west of the mountains.

ANS: B   **TYPE: M**   **KEY 1: A**   **KEY 2: 3**   **PAGE: 125**

51. The immigrants saw _____ as their favored destination because the region's expanding economies offered many opportunities.
    a. the Chesapeake.
    b. New England.
    c. the lower South.
    d. the Mid-Atlantic colonies.
    e. the area west of the mountains.

ANS: D   **TYPE: M**   **KEY 1: A**   **KEY 2: 2**   **PAGE: 125**

52. Until independence, the printing capital of North America was
    a. New York.
    b. Princeton
    c. Philadelphia.
    d. Charleston.
    e. Boston

ANS: E   **TYPE: M**   **KEY 1: F**   **KEY 2: 2**   **PAGE: 128**

_____ 1.   Legally, in colonial America, women were considered equal to men.

ANS: F   **TYPE: T**   **KEY 1: F**   **KEY 2: 1**   **PAGE: 121**

_____ 2.   During the course of the eighteenth century, those who held high political office came from the lower social status.

ANS: F   **TYPE: T**   **KEY 1: A**   **KEY 2: 1**   **PAGE: 121**

_____ 3.   The founder of the Georgia colony was John Locke.

ANS: F   **TYPE: T**   **KEY 1: F**   **KEY 2: 2**   **PAGE: 132**

_____ 4.   William Pitt, who became Britain's war minister in 1757, believed that coercion was the only way to deal with the colonies.

ANS: F   **TYPE: T**   **KEY 1: A**   **KEY 2: 2**   **PAGE: 152**

_____ 5.   The settlers of Georgia shared the proprietors' dislike of slavery and alcohol.

ANS: F   **TYPE: T**   **KEY 1: F**   **KEY 2: 3**   **PAGE: 133**

_____ 6.   Benjamin Franklin founded the first newspaper in British America.

ANS: F   **TYPE: T**   **KEY 1: F**   **KEY 2: 2**   **PAGE: 128**

_____ 7.   Africans and African Americans who genetically inherit sickle cell anemia have some immunity to malaria.

ANS: T   **TYPE: T**   **KEY 1: F**   **KEY 2: 2**   **PAGE: 123**

_____ 8.   In the 1770s, Boston was the largest city in the colonies.

ANS: F   **TYPE: T**   **KEY 1: F**   **KEY 2: 2**   **PAGE: 126**

_____ 9.   By 1720, only Connecticut and Rhode Island had elected governors.

ANS: T   **TYPE: T**   **KEY 1: A**   **KEY 2: 3**   **PAGE: 137**

_____ 10.   The French constructed Fort Duquesne at present-day Erie, Pennsylvania.

ANS: F   **TYPE: T**   **KEY 1: A**   **KEY 2: 2**   **PAGE: 147**

_____ 11.   George Washington commanded the Virginia contingent during the defeat of General Braddock's forces in western Pennsylvania.

ANS: T   **TYPE: T**   **KEY 1: A**   **KEY 2: 3**   **PAGE: 148**

_____ 12.   The "country" constitutions of the southern colonies relied on elaborate royal patronage to achieve political stability.

ANS: F   **TYPE: T**   **KEY 1: F**   **KEY 2: 2**   **PAGE: 138-39**

_____ 13.   The "court" constitutions of the northern colonies cultivated a politic of harmony to achieve political stability.

ANS: F   **TYPE: T**   **KEY 1: A**   **KEY 2: 2**   **PAGE: 139**

_____ 14.   George Washington ordered the attack that started the French and Indian War.

ANS: T   **TYPE: T**   **KEY 1: F**   **KEY 2: 1**   **PAGE: 147**

_____ 15.   After 1740, the import of British goods increased dramatically.

ANS: T   **TYPE: T**   **KEY 1: F**   **KEY 2: 2**   **PAGE: 120**

_____ 16.   A woman's dowry usually included cash and goods.

ANS: T   **TYPE: T**   **KEY 1: F**   **KEY 2: 2**   **PAGE: 121**

_____ 17.   Most of the 230,000 voluntary immigrants to British North America between 1730 and 1775 settled in New England.

ANS: F   **TYPE: T**   **KEY 1: A**   **KEY 2: 2**   **PAGE: 122**

_____ 18.   The task system was employed by Carolina rice planters.

ANS: T   **TYPE: T**   **KEY 1: F**   **KEY 2: 2**   **PAGE: 123**

_____ 19.   Many Chesapeake planters turned to wheat as a second crop.

ANS: T   **TYPE: T**   **KEY 1: F**   **KEY 2: 2**   **PAGE: 125**

_____ 20.   The Mid-Atlantic colonies were pluralistic societies from the start.

ANS: T   **TYPE: T**   **KEY 1: F**   **KEY 2: 1**   **PAGE: 125**

_____ 21.   As late as 1750, New Jersey had as many settlers as New York, but fewer slaves.

ANS: T   **TYPE: T**   **KEY 1: F**   **KEY 2: 2**   **PAGE: 125**

_____ 22.   The majority of Irish immigrants after 1720 came from Ulster.

ANS: T   **TYPE: T**   **KEY 1: F**   **KEY 2: 2**   **PAGE: 125**

_____ 23.   After 1720, Ireland and Germany replaced England as the source of most free immigrants.

ANS: T   **TYPE: T**   **KEY 1: F**   **KEY 2: 2**   **PAGE: 125**

_____ 24.   The Molasses Act of 1733 virtually ended New England's molasses trade with the French West Indies.

ANS: F   **TYPE: T**   **KEY 1: F**   **KEY 2: 2**   **PAGE: 127**

_____ 25.   New Englanders constructed more ships than all of the other colonies combined.

ANS: T   **TYPE: T**   **KEY 1: F**   **KEY 2: 1**   **PAGE: 127**

_____ 26.	In seventeenth-century America, many settlers owned books.

ANS: F	TYPE: T	KEY 1: F	KEY 2: 2	PAGE: 128

_____ 27.	Benjamin Franklin's greatest fame came from his work in founding the Library Company of Philadelphia.

ANS: F	TYPE: T	KEY 1: A	KEY 2: 2	PAGE: 130

_____ 28.	Land prices in Georgia were among the lowest in North America.

ANS: F	TYPE: T	KEY 1: A	KEY 2: 3	PAGE: 133

_____ 29.	Baptists and Methodists expected their ministers to attend college.

ANS: F	TYPE: T	KEY 1: F	KEY 2: 2	PAGE: 137

_____ 30.	Of the four wars fought between Britain and France from 1689 to 1763, only the last began in America.

ANS: T	TYPE: T	KEY 1: F	KEY 2: 1	PAGE: 147

_____ 31.	Virginia and New Jersey were not invited to attend the 1754 Albany Congress.

ANS: F	TYPE: T	KEY 1: F	KEY 2: 3	PAGE: 146

_____ 32.	Connecticut and Rhode Island declined to attend the 1754 Albany Congress.

ANS: F	TYPE: T	KEY 1: F	KEY 2: 2	PAGE: 146

_____ 33.	British colonists considered themselves the freest people on earth.

ANS: F	TYPE: T	KEY 1: F	KEY 2: 2	PAGE: 119

_____ 34.	In the eastern woodlands, most Indians identified with France, not England, as the only ally committed to their survival and independence.

ANS: T	TYPE: T	KEY 1: F	KEY 2: 1	PAGE: 119

_____ 35.	The Treaty of Aix-la-Chapelle forced Britain to return Louisbourg to France.

ANS: T	TYPE: T	KEY 1: F	KEY 2: 2	PAGE: 144

_____ 36.	After 1750, Oxford and Cambridge Universities continued to meet the colonies' need for Anglican churchmen.

ANS: F	TYPE: T	KEY 1: A	KEY 2: 2	PAGE: 120

_____ 37.	Even the poorest colonial families refused to revert to English social norms.

ANS: F	TYPE: T	KEY 1: A	KEY 2: 2	PAGE: 121

_____ 38.	By 1750, tobacco and rice planters had many contacts with each other and thought of themselves as "southerners."

ANS: F	TYPE: T	KEY 1: A	KEY 2: 3	PAGE: 122

_____39. Until 1700, many Chesapeake widows inherited all of their husbands' property and administered their own estates.

ANS: T   **TYPE: T**   **KEY 1: F**   **KEY 2: 2**   **PAGE: 121**

_____40. After 1700, the European double standard that punished women for their sexual indiscretions while tolerating male infractions became the norm in New England.

ANS: T   **TYPE: T**   **KEY 1: A**   **KEY 2: 2**   **PAGE: 121**

FILL-INS

1. The possession of a _____ granted Africans real protection against malaria.

ANS: sickle cell   **TYPE: F**   **KEY 1: F**   **KEY 2: 2**   **PAGE: 123**

2. The leading industry of New England was _____.

ANS: shipbuilding   **TYPE: F**   **KEY 1: F**   **KEY 2: 2**   **PAGE: 127**

3. The person who most fully represented the enlightenment in America was _____.

ANS: Benjamin Franklin   **TYPE: F**   **KEY 1: A**   **KEY 2: 1**   **PAGE: 130**

4. One of the leading families of the Great Awakening, and the founders of the Log College in Neshaminy, Pennsylvania, was the _____ family.

ANS: Tennent   **TYPE: F**   **KEY 1: F**   **KEY 2: 3**   **PAGE: 134**

5. The concept that a wife's legal existence was "covered" by her husband and that he alone could make binding choices was called _____.

ANS: coverture   **TYPE: F**   **KEY 1: F**   **KEY 2: 2**   **PAGE: 121**

6. _____ was the pidgin African language that is the basis of modern black English.

ANS: Gullah   **TYPE: F**   **KEY 1: F**   **KEY 2: 3**   **PAGE: 125**

7. To celebrate _____ Day, violent Boston mobs burned effigies of the Pope, Satan, and the Stuart pretender.

ANS: Guy Fawkes's   **TYPE: F**   **KEY 1: F**   **KEY 2: 2**   **PAGE: 139**

8. The descendants of the Acadians who migrated to Louisiana after they were expelled from Nova Scotia by the British are called _____.

ANS: Cajuns   **TYPE: F**   **KEY 1: F**   **KEY 2: 2**   **PAGE: 149**

9. Slaves considered _____ a beacon of liberty.

ANS: Spain   **TYPE: F**   **KEY 1: F**   **KEY 2: 2**   **PAGE: 119**

10. In _____, about 630,000 settlers and slaves lived in the mainland colonies.

ANS: 1730   TYPE: F   KEY 1: F   KEY 2: 3   PAGE: 127

11. Almost _____ percent of African slaves arriving in the American colonies between 1730 and 1775 arrived on British-owned ships.

ANS: 80   TYPE: F   KEY 1: F   KEY 2: 2   PAGE: 122

12. Chesapeake tobacco planters employed the _____ labor system.

ANS: gang   TYPE: F   KEY 1: F   KEY 2: 2   PAGE: 123

13. By the 1720s, slaves in _____ were beginning to achieve a rate of reproduction that almost equaled that of the settlers.

ANS: the Chesapeake   TYPE: F   KEY 1: F   KEY 2: 2   PAGE: 123

14. Indigo became a second staple crop in _____.

ANS: South Carolina   TYPE: F   KEY 1: F   KEY 2: 2   PAGE: 125

15. Irish immigrants from Ulster were members of the _____ Church.

ANS: Presbyterian   TYPE: F   KEY 1: F   KEY 2: 3   PAGE: 125

16. By 1775, _____ was the largest city in British North America.

ANS: Philadelphia   TYPE: F   KEY 1: F   KEY 2: 2   PAGE: 126

17. Before the 1680s, the only North American colony with printing presses was _____.

ANS: Massachusetts   TYPE: F   KEY 1: F   KEY 2: 2   PAGE: 128

18. The colonies' first newspaper was established in the city of _____.

ANS: Boston   TYPE: F   KEY 1: F   KEY 2: 2   PAGE: 130

19. John Trenchard and Thomas Gordon jointly used the pen name _____ when writing about religious bigotry and political and financial corruption.

ANS: Cato   TYPE: F   KEY 1: F   KEY 2: 3   PAGE: 130

20. After taking over the _____ in 1729, Benjamin Franklin turned it into the best-edited and most widely read newspaper in America.

ANS: *Pennsylvania Gazette*   TYPE: F   KEY 1: F   KEY 2: 2   PAGE: 130

21. The *New York Weekly Journal* 's _____ won a major victory for freedom of the press in 1735.

ANS: John Peter Zenger   TYPE: F   KEY 1: F   KEY 2: 1   PAGE: 130

22. Georgia became a royal colony in _____.

ANS: 1752   **TYPE: F**   **KEY 1: F**   **KEY 2: 2**   **PAGE: 133**

23. _____ attempted to part the waters of the Savannah River and lead the slaves to freedom in Georgia.

ANS: Hugh Bryan   **TYPE: F**   **KEY 1: F**   **KEY 2: 3**   **PAGE: 135**

24. Of the mainland colonies, only the governor of _____ emerged weaker by 1760 than he had been in 1720.

ANS: New York   **TYPE: F**   **KEY 1: F**   **KEY 2: 2**   **PAGE: 139**

25. _____ led the unsuccessful 1758 British assault on Fort Ticonderoga.

ANS: James Abercrombie   **TYPE: F**   **KEY 1: F**   **KEY 2: 3**   **PAGE: 155**

26. Dower rights provided a widow with about _____ of her husband's estate if he preceded her in death.

ANS: one-third   **TYPE: F**   **KEY 1: F**   **KEY 2: 2**   **PAGE: 121**

27. Almost _____ percent of the African slaves to arrive in America between 1730 and 1775 went to the southern colonies.

ANS: 90   **TYPE: F**   **KEY 1: A**   **KEY 2: 2**   **PAGE: 122**

28. After _____, the typical member of Virginia's House of Burgesses was a great planter who owned at least twenty slaves.

ANS: 1730   **TYPE: F**   **KEY 1: F**   **KEY 2: 3**   **PAGE: 122**

29. By the mid-eighteenth century, _____ had become the leading tobacco port of the Atlantic.

ANS: Glasgow   **TYPE: F**   **KEY 1: F**   **KEY 2: 2**   **PAGE: 125**

30. Anglican minister _____ attracted thousands to his lively, theatrical sermons.

ANS: George Whitefield   **TYPE: F**   **KEY 1: F**   **KEY 2: 2**   **PAGE: 135**

31. _____ organized a book burning of works by Increase Mather and other New England dignitaries.

ANS: James Davenport   **TYPE: F**   **KEY 1: F**   **KEY 2: 3**   **PAGE: 135**

32. _____ was the last really powerful governor of New York.

ANS: Robert Hunter   **TYPE: F**   **KEY 1: F**   **KEY 2: 3**   **PAGE: 139**

33. North America's most formidable fortress was erected by the _____ at Louisbourg on Cape Breton Island.

ANS: French   **TYPE: F**   **KEY 1: F**   **KEY 2: 1**   **PAGE: 140**

34. _____, north of St. Augustine, Florida, was the first community of free blacks in what is now the United States.

ANS: Mose TYPE: F KEY 1: F KEY 2: 3 PAGE: 141

35. The Mohawks' Chief _____ declared the Covenant Chain between New York and the Iroquois League broken due to the blatant encroachments of New Yorkers on Mohawk lands.

ANS: Hendrik TYPE: F KEY 1: F KEY 2: 3 PAGE: 144

36. King George's War ended in _____.

ANS: 1748 TYPE: F KEY 1: F KEY 2: 2 PAGE: 144

37. _____ formulated a plan for colonial union that was considered at the Albany Congress in 1754.

ANS: Benjamin Franklin TYPE: F KEY 1: F KEY 2: 2 PAGE: 146

38. The Battle of Quebec in 1759 was a _____ victory.

ANS: British TYPE: F KEY 1: F KEY 2: 2 PAGE: 156

IDENTIFICATIONS

1. **Jonathan Edwards:** intellectual religious leader of Great Awakening; pastor of Northampton Church. Author of *A Faithful Narrative of the Surprising Work of God* (1737), which explained what a revival was. Also wrote *A Treatise Concerning Religious Affections* (1745), which provided a rational defense of emotion.

2. **George Whitefield:** Anglican minister. Follower of John Wesley, foremost evangelical leader of the Great Awakening. Toured American colonies twice in mid-eighteenth century drawing crowds (and converts) of thousands.

3. **General James Oglethorpe**: founder of Georgia colony. Set up nonprofit organization to fund and administer Georgia. Gave free passage and free land to immigrants.

4. **John Wesley:** founder of Methodist church. Missionary to Georgia in 1735. Returned to England and dedicated his life to saving souls through conversion.

5. **John Witherspoon**: Scottish evangelist who became president of Princeton College. Changed curriculum to include Scottish enlightenment.

6. **Francisco Menendez:** escaped slave who fled to Florida, learned Spanish, was re-enslaved, became a militia captain, won freedom, and was appointed to govern the first free black community, Mose.

7. **Stono Rebellion**: large slave revolt that rocked South Carolina in the mid-eighteenth century (1739). Twenty slaves stole weapons from a store, murdered twenty-five whites, tried to escape to Florida. Most caught and killed by South Carolina militia.

8. **Albany Congress**: meeting of colonies and Iroquois in 1754 called by governor of New York to discuss problems and keep Indians from allying with France. Governor of Massachusetts invited Rhode Island and Connecticut and encouraged plans for intercolonial union. Benjamin Franklin's Albany Plan adopted by the Congress but rejected by the colonies.

9. **Task system:** system of slave labor organization employed in South Carolina because of high death rates from malaria. After a slave completed all assigned daily tasks, any time left in the day could be devoted to activities at the slave's discretion.

10. **Redemptioners:** form of indentured service attractive to married couples. Allowed them to find and bind themselves to their own masters. Popular among German immigrants after 1720. After completing their service, most redemptioners went to the interior of Pennsylvania or the southern backcountry.

SHORT ESSAYS

1.   Examine the founding of the Georgia colony. What were the goals of the founders and the successes of the colonists?

Answer: Georgia was an enlightened utopian colony, the only one of its kind in colonial America. Set aside as a refuge for the "deserving poor," the idea behind the colony was to establish a planned community for the indigent of England (imprisoned there) to begin new lives in America. A second important feature of the colony was the plan to protect the colony's Spanish border by populating the province with armed freemen. Additionally, the sponsor of the project hoped to strengthen the imperial economy by producing products not grown anywhere else in the empire (silk and wine). Two requirements were made of the project, however: slavery and hard alcohol were to be forbidden.

Several problems arose in Georgia. First, little attention was given to the desires and needs of the settlers themselves. No elective assembly was established and no real legal recourse on the part of the colonists was allowed. Second, economic conditions for farming, winemaking, and silk production were poor, virtually removing them as a real possibility for settlers. In the 1750s, the trustees simply gave up control of the colony when the population fell even lower than it had been in the 1730s. With this move, Georgia turned primarily toward rice production (like South Carolina) and also began the importation of slaves.

2.   Describe and analyze family relations in colonial America.

Answer: Family relations in colonial America were much like what they had been in Europe—patriarchal and undemocratic. At the head of the household, both sexually and legally, was the father and husband. As in Europe, he had virtually complete legal authority over the entire household—voting rights, legal responsibility, and control over land distribution and inheritance. Wives, although superior in social rank to children, were clearly secondary in status and subordinate to their husbands. Indeed, through the process of coverture, a wife's property and legal power was subsumed to that of her husband.

Central to a society based on land possession and use was the power over land distribution and division. Two important practices, primogeniture and entail, were practiced among English households, but they never acquired the power to structure social relations that they had in England. Primogeniture was a legal device that required a landowner to bequeath all of his property to his eldest son. Entail prohibited the owner from dividing up the estate during his lifetime. But these practices were not universal. Through the eighteenth century, Dutch farmers continued to practice Dutch inheritance and family values. These practices did not employ entail and primogeniture, and they granted far more power and autonomy to wives and daughters than did traditional English common law.

3.   Explore the values and beliefs of the family and their relationship to the larger community in colonial America.

Answer: Early America, although not a communitarian society, was far from the individualistic, capitalist world of modern America. In terms of understanding the orientation of the family household to the larger community of which these people were a part, it is important to remember that, in many ways, colonial Americans had more in common with the traditional pre-modern world of the fifteenth and sixteenth centuries than with the nineteenth and twentieth centuries. European Americans re-created the villages and communities they had left behind across the Atlantic. Patriarchal families were the norm: Each household was, on a smaller scale, a re-creation of the hierarchical society in which people lived. Some ruled, others were ruled. This was an understood and, to a significant degree, accepted part of the social system, though far less pervasive than in England.

Although independent from each other (dependency on others was viewed as a form of subservience or slavery), these families were mutually dependent in a variety of areas: exchange of labor, animals, farm equipment, and the like. This type of cooperation was absolutely essential not only for the individual family to survive, but for the community to survive as well. Farm households were likely to produce an agricultural surplus of some kind (in New York, wheat or rye) that was traded or sold to merchants, who then sent their goods into larger markets. However, the purpose of this production was rarely to make a great profit, but was more to protect the lineal family unit—in case of drought, flood, or some other natural disaster.

4.   Compare and contrast the development of the "old South" and the middle-Atlantic region during the eighteenth century.

Answer: From its beginning, the middle-Atlantic region had been settled by a variety of ethnic and religious groups. Dutch, English, Germans, and African Americans all had lived throughout the colonies of Pennsylvania, New York, and New Jersey. This variety led to an ethnic pluralism that was not nearly as pronounced in any other part of North America. Over the course of the eighteenth century, this region became a staple crop-producing area (particularly in wheat, grain, and other foodstuffs), dominated primarily by small freehold farms. Except for the manorial system in New York and certain tenanted holdings in Jersey and Pennsylvania, independent farming tended to be the norm.

The "old South" developed along distinctly different lines during the eighteenth century. Never as heterogeneous as the middle colonies, the Europeans who settled in this region tended to share much in their ethnic and religious backgrounds. Indeed, where differences among Europeans were pronounced in the North, the southern colonies distinguished between classes based almost solely on race. The South also witnessed far fewer independent land holdings, with large plantations (primarily tobacco and rice) dominating. The most prominent difference was, however, the importance of slavery. Never vital to the middle colonies, slavery was, from the beginning, central to the South.

5.   Describe the outbreak of the French and Indian War.

Answer: The French and Indian War was the only war between France and England that began in America. Indeed, it was George Washington's attempt to build a fort along the Ohio River in 1753–54 (in order to intimidate the French there), that ultimately led to the outbreak of hostilities. Neither New France nor Virginia anticipated the global struggle that would follow.

In addition, the home governments of France and England also had little desire to engage in a world war, and their hope was to limit the confrontation to the North American frontier. New Englanders, however, saw the contest as a struggle between the French and the English, Catholics and Protestants, the unfree and the free. For this group, a millenarian vision prevailed.

The British government sent General Edward Braddock with two regiments to Virginia in an attempt to gain control of the upper Ohio Valley. Braddock did not receive much aid from the middle colonies (several of which had just unsuccessfully attempted to hammer out agreements at the Albany Congress), except for Virginia itself. Braddock's plans were ambitious—not only did he want to take control of the Ohio River, but he implemented a four-pronged attack on New France as well. Braddock's defeat in Pennsylvania and other setbacks for the British provincial forces were to turn this North American struggle into a world war.

6.   Examine the political culture of eighteenth-century America.

Answer: During the founding of the colonies, North American politics tended to move further away from the British model. Indeed, many of the early colonies were conscious attempts to move away from the British political system. The eighteenth century, however, witnessed a different movement, as American political culture tended to replicate Britain's. There was one significant difference, however, which was the high rate of political participation in most North American colonies. The assemblies in each colony were elected, and the franchise was fairly high among white males.

The most striking characteristic of American political culture was the competition between the governor (appointed in most colonies by the king of England) and the assembly (which was popularly elected in each colony). Indeed, this competition was the pronounced political struggle in early America, as the governor attempted to implement the policies and practices of the empire, policies that often were opposed to the desires and needs of the residents of the colonies. The other characteristic feature of North American politics was the emphasis on "opposition" political ideology, the attempt on the part of political minorities to battle the governor or majority faction in the assembly. Indeed, this emphasis on opposition ideology was even greater in the colonies than in Britain, because of the larger proportion of voters in the colonies as well as because of the divergent interests of the empire and its colonies.

7.   Explore the significance of the imperial wars of 1689–1716 for colonial Americans.

Answer: As colonies of the British empire, the North American colonies participated in the larger imperial struggles with France and Spain. Although sometimes this participation occurred under duress (there was often little support for these wars in the southernmost middle colonies and in the upper South), often the colonies participated willingly, since their foe was not necessarily imperial France, but French Canada and its Indian allies. For New England, these struggles often took the shape of a "holy war" against the "papists," besides having the obvious advantages of pushing into new territory to the north and west.

King William's War (1689–1697) and Queen Anne's War (1702–1713) offered both attractions described above (a religious war and territorial aggrandizement). Unfortunately for the North American colonists, neither was achieved. In King William's War, a massive New England naval and overland invasion of Quebec failed amidst poor planning and intercolonial bickering, opening up the western frontier for French and Indian incursions that devastated coastal Maine and destroyed the Mohawk town of Schenectady. Queen Anne's War saw much of the same, when a mixed French-Indian invasion destroyed Deerfield, Massachusetts, and carried several hundred villagers into captivity. A major invasion of Quebec once again fell apart in the treacherous St. Lawrence. The result of both of these wars was to contain New England expansion, as well as hem in the Deep South.

LONG ESSAYS

1.   Examine the Great Awakening. What were its results?

Answer: Essay should address several key points:

A.   Origins of revivals
    1.   Circumstances of particular communities
    2.   George Whitefield
        a.   American tour
        b.   Idea of rebirth
    3.   Gilbert Tennent and James Davenport
        a.   Insistence on personal conversion
        b.   Critical of recognized clergy
B.   Immediate consequences of revivals
    1.   Shattered unity of the Congregational Church in New England
    2.   Strengthened denominational loyalties in mid-Atlantic
    3.   Breakdown of localism
    4.   Jonathan Edwards's rational defense of emotional religion
C.   Long-term consequences of revivals
    1.   Three new major denominations
        a.   Methodists
        b.   Baptists
        c.   Presbyterians
    2.   Founding of new denominational colleges
    3.   Impact on American Revolution

2.   Compare and contrast economic development in eighteenth-century America among the three major regions: New England, the mid-Atlantic, and the South.

Answer: Essay should address several key points:

A.   New England
        1.   Major industries
                a.   Fishing
                b.   Shipbuilding
        2.   Mercantile activity
                a.   Traders for other colonies
                b.   Peculiar role in imperial economy
                c.   Commercial economy/paper money
        3.   Weakest productive economy in North America
                a.   Region with the least economic growth
                b.   Consequences
B.   Mid-Atlantic
        1.   Major industries
                a.   Agricultural production
                b.   Grain
        2.   Mercantile activity
                a.   Central role in imperial economy
                b.   Importance
        3.   Land organization
                a.   Small freehold farms
                b.   Large manors (New York)
        4.   Steady economic and population growth
C.   South
        1.   Major products
                a.   Chesapeake
                        i)   Tobacco
                        ii)   Grain
                b.   Deep South
                        i)   Rice
                        ii)   Indigo
                        iii)   Large plantation as primary unit of production
        2.   Primary role in imperial economy
        3.   Sustained economic growth

3.   Describe the Enlightenment and its impact and reception in North America.

Answer: Essay should address several key points:

A.   Origins in England
        1.   Political ideas of Trenchard and Gordon
        2.   Enlightened religious ideas of John Tillotson
                a.   Impact of Tillotson in North America
                b.   Role of newspapers in disseminating enlightened ideas
B.   Enlightenment in America
        1.   Religious influences
                a.   Conversion of Yale faculty to Anglicanism
                b.   Consequences
        2.   Founding of legal profession
                a.   Professionalization of law
                b.   Consequences
        3.   Enlightened influences on medicine

<ol start="4">
<li>Benjamin Franklin
<ol type="a">
<li>One-man enlightenment
<ol type="i">
<li>Library Company of Philadelphia</li>
<li>Union Fire Company</li>
<li>Philadelphia Hospital</li>
<li>Philadelphia Academy (later, University of Pennsylvania)</li>
</ol>
</li>
<li>Scientific experimentation</li>
</ol>
</li>
</ol>

4. Examine the course and consequence of the French and Indian War.

Answer: Essay should address several key points:

A. Competition between New France and North America
  1. Virginia and Ohio River
      a. Washington and Fort Duquesne
      b. Consequences
  2. New England and anti-Catholicism
  3. Middle colonies and Indian tensions
B. Years of British defeat
  1. Braddock and disaster on the Monongahela
  2. William Johnson and New York
  3. Disunity between British and colonists
C. Years of British victory/conquest of New France
  1. Wolfe, Montcalm, and Quebec
      a. Deaths of Wolfe and Montcalm on the Plains of Abraham
      b. Consequences
  2. Fall of Louisbourg, Quebec, and Montreal
  3. Treaty of Paris (1763)

5. Examine the course of King George's War (1739–1748).

Answer: Essay should address several key points:

A. War of Jenkins's Ear (1739–1744)
  1. Origins with English sea captain
      a. Failed invasion of Cartagena
      b. Ninety percent of colonial volunteers killed or missing
  2. Spanish invasion of Georgia
      a. Plans to plunder and liberate slaves
      b. Oglethorpe fools Spanish into withdrawing
B. King George's War (1744–1748)
  1. France joins Spain in war against Britain
      a. French lay siege to Port Royal
      b. Consequences
  2. Successful colonial assault on Louisbourg fortress
      a. Untrained Massachusetts militia defeat French regulars
      b. Failed assaults on Quebec
  3. Treaty of Aix-la-Chapelle
      a. Louisbourg returned to France
      b. New Englanders upset by this apparent slight

CHAPTER 5
REFORM, RESISTANCE, REVOLUTION

CHAPTER OUTLINE

I.   Imperial Reform
    A.   From Pitt to Grenville
    B.   Indian Policy and Pontiac's War
    C.   The Sugar Act
    D.   The Currency Act and the Quartering Act
    E.   The Stamp Act
II. The Stamp Act Crisis
    A.   Nullification
    B.   Repeal
III. The Townshend Crisis
    A.   The Townshend Program
    B.   Resistance: The Politics of Escalation
    C.   An Experiment in Military Coercion
    D.   The Second Wilkes Crisis
    E.   The Boston Massacre
    F.   Partial Repeal
    G.   Disaffection
IV. Internal Cleavages: The Contagion of Liberty
    A.   The Feudal Revival and Rural Discontent
    B.   The Regulator Movements in the Carolinas
    C.   Slaves and Women
V.   The Last Imperial Crisis
    A.   The Tea Crisis
    B.   Britain's Response: The Coercive Acts
    C.   The Radical Explosion
    D.   First Continental Congress
    E.   Toward War
VI. The Improvised War
    A.   The Second Continental Congress
    B.   War and Legitimacy, 1775-1776
    C.   Independence
VII. Conclusion

CHRONOLOGY

1760	George III becomes King of Great Britain.
1763	Peace of Paris.
	George Grenville administration begins.
	Pontiac's War begins.
	Proclamation of 1763.
1764	Sugar and Currency Acts passed by Parliament.
1765	Stamp and Quartering Acts passed.
	Rockingham replaces Grenville.
1765–1766	First imperial crisis.
1766	Parliament repeals Stamp Act.
	Pitt replaces Rockingham.
	Declaratory Act and Revenue Act passed.
1767	Townshend Duties passed by Parliament.
	Grafton replaces Pitt.

	John Dickinson publishes *Letters.*
1767–1770	Second imperial crisis.
1768	Massachusetts assembly dispatches Circular Letter.
	John Hancock's sloop *Liberty* seized, sparking Boston riots.
1770	North becomes Prime Minister.
	Boston Massacre.
1771	Regulators defeated at Alamance Creek, North Carolina.
1772	British customs vessel *Gaspée* burned.
	Colonies create committees of correspondence.
1773	Tea Act passed by Parliament.
	Boston Tea Party.
1773–1776	Third imperial crisis.
1774	Quebec Act.
	Coercive Acts imposed.
	First Continental Congress.
1775	Battles of Lexington and Concord.
	Second Continental Congress creates Continental Army.
	Battle of Bunker Hill.
	Lord Dunmore's Proclamation.
	Olive Branch Petition sent to King George III.
1776	Thomas Paine publishes *Common Sense.*
	Battle of Dorchester Heights.
	Battle of Moore's Creek Bridge.
	Declaration of Independence.

THEMATIC TOPICS FOR ENRICHMENT

1. What was "virtual representation"? Explain why the colonies so vigorously rejected the idea. Why did they similarly decline actual representation in Parliament?

2. Why did Parliament repeal the Stamp Act? What was the point of repealing the Stamp Act, yet passing the Declaratory Act?

3. Was the colonial distinction between regulation and taxation a legitimate one? Was there any precedent for such a distinction in English history?

4. What was the "feudal revival"? Assess its significance for revolutionary America.

5. Discuss the meaning of liberty to women and slaves. How was it distinct from the liberty of white males?

6. How did the government of George III change its tactics for punishing the colonies after the Boston Massacre, the *Gaspée* affair, and the Boston Tea Party? By the third imperial crisis, was the empire held together solely by force?

SUGGESTED ESSAY TOPICS

1. The historian Lawrence Henry Gipson once argued that if there had been no French and Indian War, the American Revolution would not have occurred, at least not when it did. Make a case both for and against Gipson's claim.

2. Some historians have claimed that the era of the American Revolution was characterized by paranoia. Does this description make sense? What underlying fears drove Britain into its imperial reforms? What aspects of these reforms made the colonies fear for their liberties? Were these fears justified on either side? On both sides?

3. How did thirteen disparate colonies that had failed all attempts at collective actions before 1763 manage to unite and declare their independence by 1776?

LECTURE OUTLINE

1. King and Parliament began a large-scale process of **imperial reform** in response to waging a costly war in North America.

    a. The **Bute ministry,** led by the king's principal advisor, John Stuart, began the first steps toward reducing Britain's foreign financial obligations.

    b. The **Grenville minist**ry inaugurated an ambitious program intended to effect better administration of the colonies, augmenting revenues in particular.

        i. Tailored to meet treaty obligations, Grenville's Indian policy rested on the **Proclamation Line of 1763,** which sought to restrict colonists' encroachment onto Indian lands.

        ii. **Pontiac's War** of 1763 caught many frontier folk by surprise, but the Ottawa chief's (and the other tribes') aggression failed to halt—or even slow down— European penetration into the interior of the continent.

(SHOW TRANSPARENCY 35: PONTIAC'S WAR AND THE PROCLAMATION LINE OF 1763)

    c. The **Sugar Act** sought to increase revenue and inhibit smuggling by simultaneously lowering duties on molasses and making it more profitable for customs officers to prosecute violators of the Navigation Acts.

    d. Following closely on the heels of the Sugar Act, the **Currency Act and the Quartering Act** respectively constituted bold new regulation of colonial "paper" currency and restated the colonists' obligations to quarter his majesty's troops.

    e. The **Stamp Act** sought to raise revenue in the colonies by means of a tax on all official documents.

2. Colonial dismay at the **Stamp Act** and the other parliamentary initiatives since 1763 climaxed in the Stamp Act crisis, as colonists gathered in a Stamp Act Congress to fight Parliament.

    a. By means of the nonimportation agreement of the Stamp Act Congress and the extralegal initiatives of the **Sons of Liberty,** the colonies sought nullification of the Stamp Act.

    b. Colonial vigilance and pressure from London's suffering merchant community forced Parliament to repeal the dreaded stamp tax, while simultaneously passing the **Declaratory Act.**

3. Relative quiet returned to imperial relations until the eruption of the **Townshend crisis** in 1767.

    a. Named for the Chancellor of the Exchequer, the **Townshend program** was an ill-fated attempt to raise revenue through "external" taxation on colonial imports such as lead, china, and tea.

    b. Parliament's 1768 experiment in **military coercion** accomplished little more than to convince many colonists that the British government was openly seeking to undermine their liberty.

c.   As colonials saw parallels between their situation and that of John Wilkes, the **second Wilkes crisis** in England reinforced colonial convictions that the king and Parliament were corrupt and power hungry.

d.   The **Boston Massacre** of March 5, 1770, marked the failure of Britain's first attempts at military coercion and served to galvanize anti-imperial sentiment throughout North America.

e.   Rather than bringing about renewed affection, disaffection set in between colonies and mother country despite the **repeal of the Townshend taxes.**

4.   After the second imperial crisis, the **contagion of liberty** grew slowly as colonists faced many internal cleavages.

     a.   Although the colonies were moving away from British political domination, many regions witnessed what historians call a **feudal revival,** especially in New York's Hudson Valley, as well as in Maryland and Pennsylvania.

     b.   The **regulator movements in the Carolinas** resulted from the remarkable under-representation of rural folk in the low-country-dominated houses of assembly.

     c.   From the death of **Crispus Attacks** in the Boston Massacre to wives offering their willing support to nonimportation, **slaves and women** responded in a number of meaningful ways to colonial discussions of freedom and liberty.

5.   The **last imperial crisis** broke the relative calm of the period 1770–1773, as colonists and mother country failed to resolve amicably their simmering differences.

     a.   The **tea crisis** resulted from the Boston Tea Party of December 16, 1773, when angry Bostonians threw India Tea Company tea into Boston Harbor.

     b.   Britain's response to the Tea Party was a set of **Coercive Acts,** which shut down Boston's port with the intent to force colonial submission.

     c.   Instead of restoring order, the Intolerable Acts, as the colonists styled them, resulted in a **radical explosion,** which cowed those who had cautioned against rash actions against England.

     d.   The **First Continental Congress** met in Philadelphia in September 1774 to act as the voice of the united colonies.

     e.   England's intransigence and colonial unity precipitated the Battles of Lexington and Concord, which inevitably moved the empire **toward war.**

(SHOW TRANSPARENCY 36: BATTLES IN EASTERN MASSACHUSETTS)

6.   The **improvised war** of colonies and mother country, centering primarily in Massachusetts, lasted until the declaration of American independence in the summer of 1776.

     a.   The **Second Continental Congress,** which met in Philadelphia in May 1775, organized national defense and acted as the executive for the fledgling United States.

     b.   Independence came with the signing of the Declaration of Independence in July 1776.

American Album: American Artists and the Revolution in Painting

Conclusion: In the aftermath of the Peace of Paris, three successive imperial crises convinced England that the colonies desired nothing short of independence and convinced the colonists that king and Parliament sought to destroy their liberties through an overarching imperial power. The result of this almost paranoid view was the disintegration of the empire.

TEACHING RESOURCES

Liberty: The American Revolution, volumes I–III, tells the story of the coming of the American war for independence by means of actors reading contemporary writings. PBS Video (60 minutes each).

Private Yankee Doodle views the life and suffering of the average American soldier in the Revolutionary War through the re-creation of a Continental army encampment. Films for the Humanities (28 minutes).

To Keep Our Liberty: Minutemen of the American Revolution traces the growing movement toward independence through the eyes of one American patriot. National Park Service Video (35 minutes).

Meet George Washington is a humanizing portrait of Washington as a Virginia planter and colonial businessman who reluctantly assumes a leadership role in the politics of a new nation. Filmic Archives (60 minutes).

Samuel Adams portrays the life and significance of the man who helped create the Sons of Liberty, led the Boston Tea Party, and served in the Continental Congress. Filmic Archives (10 minutes).

Independence, as directed by John Huston, details the dramatic events that led to America's declaration of independence in 1776. MPI Home Video (30 minutes).

America: Making a Revolution details the blunders of the imperial government, the increasing colonial agitation for reform, and, ultimately, independence. BBC/Time—Life Video (52 minutes).

MULTIPLE CHOICE

1. Britain's new imperial policy after 1763 can best be described as
    a. one of increased centralized control over the colonies.
    b. one of relaxed control over the colonies.
    c. unchanged from before 1763.
    d. one that sought to get rid of the colonies.
    e. one that sought to exterminate the Indians.

ANS: A   TYPE: M   KEY 1: A   KEY 2: 2   PAGE: 161

2. During Pontiac's War,
    a. combined Indian tribal forces seized ten British forts and besieged two others.
    b. the English introduced germ warfare by giving the Indians smallpox-infested blankets.
    c. the Paxton Boys murdered unarmed Christian Indian men, women, and children.
    d. the Indians were united as never before.
    e. all of the above

ANS: E   TYPE: M   KEY 1: F   KEY 2: 3   PAGE: 161-63

3. The Sugar Act (1764) placed a duty, or tax, on
   a. imported French molasses.
   b. domestic refined sugar.
   c. British molasses.
   d. Canadian rum.
   e. all agricultural products.

ANS: A   TYPE: M   KEY 1: F   KEY 2: 1   PAGE: 163

4. The group most angered by the passage of the Sugar Act (1764) was
   a. Virginia planters.
   b. New England merchants.
   c. Pennsylvania farmers.
   d. New York manorial lords.
   e. newspaper editors.

ANS: B   TYPE: M   KEY 1: A   KEY 2: 1   PAGE: 163

5. The Proclamation of 1763
   a. called for an intercolonial government.
   b. prohibited American settlements west of the Appalachian mountains.
   c. attempted to raise a revenue in the colonies.
   d. attempted to grant the colonists representatives in Parliament.
   e. declared colonial resistance to imperial rule.

ANS: B   TYPE: M   KEY 1: F   KEY 2: 1   PAGE: 161

6. Which of the following was not part of Britain's new imperial system after 1763?
   a. the Sugar Act
   b. the Molasses Act
   c. the Stamp Act
   d. the Currency Act
   e. the Quartering Act

ANS: B   TYPE: M   KEY 1: F   KEY 2: 3   PAGE: 163

7. The reason most Americans took up arms in 1775 was
   a. to establish a republican regime.
   b. to avoid paying taxes.
   c. to restore the empire to what it had been before 1763.
   d. to establish a radically new vision of the future.
   e. to fight the Indians.

ANS: C   TYPE: M   KEY 1: A   KEY 2: 2   PAGE: 187

8. George Washington was named commander of the Continental Army primarily because
   a. of his victory at Fort Duquesne in 1755.
   b. he was from the South.
   c. he was respected as a powerful leader.
   d. he had amassed a large fighting force loyal only to him.
   e. he was sympathetic to the British position.

ANS: B   TYPE: M   KEY 1: A   KEY 2: 2   PAGE: 186

9. The so-called Olive Branch Petition to the king in 1775
    a. more or less declared that a state of war existed in North America.
    b. called for increased trade between the colonies and the mother country.
    c. attacked George III.
    d. belligerently affirmed colonial rights.
    e. affirmed the loyalty of the colonists to the crown

ANS: E   **TYPE: M**   **KEY 1: F**   **KEY 2: 2**   **PAGE: 187**

10. The main argument of Thomas Paine's *Common Sense*
    a. moderated the system of taxation employed by the British.
    b. demanded representation in the British Parliament.
    c. denounced the monarchy as a degenerate institution.
    d. called for George Washington to be named king.
    e. demanded that France enter the war.

ANS: C   **TYPE: M**   **KEY 1: A**   **KEY 2: 1**   **PAGE: 188**

11. Britain's hiring soldiers from _____ to fight the colonists infuriated North Americans.
    a. Russia
    b. Germany
    c. France
    d. Spain
    e. Portugal

ANS: B   **TYPE: M**   **KEY 1: F**   **KEY 2: 1**   **PAGE: 189**

12. The English responded to colonial complaints against "taxation without representation" by asserting that
    a. colonial lobbyists in London represented local interests there.
    b. the assemblies provided adequate protection for colonial rights.
    c. each member of Parliament virtually represented all the citizens of the empire.
    d. each colony could send a representative to the House of Commons.
    e. representation was not necessary for a government to tax.

ANS: C   **TYPE: M**   **KEY 1: A**   **KEY 2: 3**   **PAGE: 165**

13. _____ drafted the Virginia Resolutions in 1765, which stated that colonists could be taxed only by their own assemblies.
    a. George Washington
    b. John Dickinson
    c. Patrick Henry
    d. Thomas Jefferson
    e. James Madison

ANS: C   **TYPE: M**   **KEY 1: F**   **KEY 2: 2**   **PAGE: 164-65**

14. The Declaratory Act
    a. repealed the Stamp Act.
    b. declared that the colonies were in a state of insurrection.
    c. asserted Parliament's absolute right to legislate for the colonies.
    d. nullified the charters of Massachusetts and Rhode Island.
    e. established new taxes on the colonists.

ANS: C   **TYPE: M**   **KEY 1: F**   **KEY 2: 2**   **PAGE: 166**

15. The principal reform envisioned by the Townshend Revenue Act was
    a. to raise revenue.
    b. to unload tea from the East India Company.
    c. to establish the power of the King to tax.
    d. to hurt colonial trade.
    e. to pay the salaries of colonial governors and judges.

ANS: E   TYPE: M   KEY 1: F   KEY 2: 1   PAGE: 169

16. In response to the *Gaspée* affair of 1772–73, colonial assemblies formed
    a. militia units.
    b. committees of correspondence.
    c. provisional governments.
    d. a national army.
    e. a delegation to Parliament.

ANS: B   TYPE: M   KEY 1: F   KEY 2: 2   PAGE: 174-75

17. The "regulators" in the Carolinas were
    a. committees that opposed British policy.
    b. committees that attempted to regulate the backcountry economy.
    c. settlers that attempted to impose order in the absence of an organized government or to reform abuses in existing local governments.
    d. tax collectors who visited residents regularly.
    e. farmers who made illegal liquor.

ANS: C   TYPE: M   KEY 1: F   KEY 2: 1   PAGE: 176-78

18. Reasons for the colonists' anger over the Tea Act included
    a. the monopolization rights given to certain merchants.
    b. the attempt to tax the colonists with cheaper tea.
    c. many tea merchants would be hurt by the act.
    d. fear that it would lead to further destruction of liberty.
    e. all of the above.

ANS: E   TYPE: M   KEY 1: A   KEY 2: 1   PAGE: 180

19. The Coercive Acts
    a. attempted to impose new taxes on the colonies.
    b. closed the port of Boston.
    c. reorganized the government of Massachusetts.
    d. extended the power of the governor of New York.
    e. both b and c

ANS: E   TYPE: M   KEY 1: F   KEY 2: 2   PAGE: 181

20. The British government measure that established French civil law and the Roman Catholic Church in the province of Quebec was known as the
    a. Toleration Act.
    b. Quebec Act.
    c. Proclamation of 1763.
    d. Coercive Act.
    e. the Stamp Act.

ANS: B   TYPE: M   KEY 1: F   KEY 2: 1   PAGE: 181-82

21. The colonial response to the Coercive Acts (1774) was the calling of
    a. the Confederation Congress.
    b. the First Continental Congress.
    c. the Second Continental Congress.
    d. the Albany Congress.
    e. a constitutional convention.

ANS: B   TYPE: M   KEY 1: F   KEY 2: 2   PAGE: 184

22. The goal of the British troops sent to Lexington and Concord in April 1775 was
    a. to destroy the military equipment stored there.
    b. to arrest John Hancock.
    c. to arrest Samuel Adams.
    d. to demonstrate the authority to use force against the delinquents.
    e. all of the above.

ANS: E   TYPE: M   KEY 1: F   KEY 2: 1   PAGE: 184

23. The Tea Act (1773)
    a. attempted to save the British East India Company from financial disaster.
    b. removed the tax on colonists' tea.
    c. increased the price of colonists' tea.
    d. placed a high new tax on the colonists' tea.
    e. was welcomed by the Americans.

ANS: A   TYPE: M   KEY 1: F   KEY 2: 2   PAGE: 180

24. In 1770, British Parliament repealed each of the Townshend Duties except for the one on
    a. glass.
    b. lead.
    c. tea.
    d. paper.
    e. painters' colors.

ANS: C   TYPE: M   KEY 1: F   KEY 2: 1   PAGE: 173

25. The group most responsible for overt resistance to acts of Parliament was the
    a. Paxton Boys.
    b. Sons of Liberty.
    c. colonial assemblies.
    d. Regulators.
    e. slaves.

ANS: B   TYPE: M   KEY 1: F   KEY 2: 2   PAGE: 165

26. The Revenue Act of 1766 amended the _____ Act by reducing the duty on molasses from three pence per gallon to one penny.
    a. Sugar
    b. Stamp
    c. Quartering
    d. Townshend
    e. Declaratory

ANS: A   TYPE: M   KEY 1: F   KEY 2: 2   PAGE: 166

27. In 1772, Rhode Islanders boarded the British customs vessel _____ and burned it.
   a. *Liberty*
   b. *Hispaniola*
   c. *Gaspée*
   d. *Constitution*
   e. *Maine*

ANS: C   **TYPE: M**   **KEY 1: F**   **KEY 2: 1**   **PAGE: 174**

28. The religious group in North America that led the attack on slavery was the
   a. Catholics.
   b. Presbyterians.
   c. Baptists.
   d. Quakers.
   e. Jews.

ANS: D   **TYPE: M**   **KEY 1: F**   **KEY 2: 2**   **PAGE: 178**

29. The colonial response to the Stamp Act included
   a. street violence and riots.
   b. economic boycotts.
   c. petitions to Parliament.
   d. resolutions passed by colonial assemblies
   e. all of the above.

ANS: E   **TYPE: M**   **KEY 1: F**   **KEY 2: 2**   **PAGE: 164-66**

30. The colonists opposed the Stamp Tax because it
   a. was the first direct internal tax passed by Parliament for the North American colonies.
   b. was an indirect external tax on goods imported into the colonies.
   c. was too expensive to enforce.
   d. gave too much authority to colonial common law courts.
   e. required a large number of tax collectors to be sent from England.

ANS: A   **TYPE: M**   **KEY 1: F**   **KEY 2: 2**   **PAGE: 164-66**

31. The Declaration of Independence was written primarily by
   a. John Adams.
   b. Benjamin Franklin.
   c. Thomas Jefferson.
   d. James Madison.
   e. Patrick Henry.

ANS: C   **TYPE: M**   **KEY 1: F**   **KEY 2: 1**   **PAGE: 190**

32. The purpose of George Grenville's revenue policies was to
   a. force the colonies to pay the entire British debt.
   b. reward the colonies for their cooperation during the Seven Years' War.
   c. centralize and increase British control over the colonies.
   d. encourage voluntaristic participation of the colonies in determining their own tax burden.
   e. encourage the colonies to declare independence.

ANS: C   **TYPE: M**   **KEY 1: F**   **KEY 2: 3**   **PAGE: 161**

33. The Sons of Liberty was
    a. the committee that wrote the Declaration of Independence.
    b. a group of English customs officials who refused to take bribes from colonial merchants.
    c. a division of the Continental Army.
    d. a group of Indians that united to resist white settlement in the West.
    e. a vigilante group that organized violent protests against English tax laws.

ANS: E   TYPE: M   KEY 1: F   KEY 2: 2   PAGE: 165

34. Which of the following was not part of the Townshend program?
    a. a tax on tea, paper, paint, lead, and glass imported into the colonies
    b. recognition of colonial authority in providing supplies and housing for British troops
    c. the use of tax revenues to pay the salaries of colonial governors and judges
    d. relocation of British troops from the frontier to the major seaport cities
    e. creation of a separate American Board of Customs Commissioners in Boston

ANS: B   TYPE: M   KEY 1: F   KEY 2: 3   PAGE: 168-70

35. Colonial assemblies set up committees of correspondence to
    a. coordinate intercolonial communication and organize efforts to defend American liberties.
    b. send letters and petitions expressing colonial views to England.
    c. organize the first postal system in North America.
    d. promote friendly relations by encouraging colonials to write to English pen pals.
    e. deal with Indian uprisings.

ANS: A   TYPE: M   KEY 1: F   KEY 2: 3   PAGE: 174-75

36. The Boston Massacre trials and the *Gaspee* Affair
    a. convinced the English that they should punish and "make an example of" individual political activists.
    b. led to improved relations between the colonies and England.
    c. increased colonial fear and distrust of English motives and policies.
    d. effectively established Parliament's right to tax the colonies.
    e. had no lasting impact on relations between the colonies and England.

ANS: C   TYPE: M   KEY 1: A   KEY 2: 3   PAGE: 174-75

37. One of the consequences of colonial rhetoric about liberty and rights was
    a. the ordination of women as lay preachers in the Anglican church.
    b. an end to the use of indentured servants.
    c. an increase in the number of declared skeptics and atheists.
    d. extending the right to vote to women.
    e. agitation for the extension of equality and freedom to all people including slaves.

ANS: E   TYPE: M   KEY 1: A   KEY 2: 3   PAGE: 178

38. Sarah Osborn was noted as
    a. the first black college student in American history.
    b. one of the victims of the Boston Massacre.
    c. the founder of an innovative Newport School for women and Africans.
    d. a vocal opponent of the nonimportation policy.
    e. a delegate to the Second Continental Congress.

ANS: C   TYPE: M   KEY 1: F   KEY 2: 2   PAGE: 179

39. Colonists objected to the Quebec Act because it
    a. nullified colonial property rights in Ohio.
    b. extended French civil law to—and protected the Roman Catholic Church in—the area between the Great Lakes and the Ohio River.
    c. established French as the official language of Canada.
    d. blocked chances for their own expansion.
    e. raised their taxes.

ANS: B **TYPE: M** **KEY 1: F** **KEY 2: 2** **PAGE: 181-82**

40. The Boston Massacre
    a. occurred when a group of British soldiers illegally fired into a crowd that was harassing them.
    b. was followed by a murder trial in which John Adams and Josiah Quincy, Jr. acted as defense attorneys.
    c. resulted in a change of quarters for British soldiers from the city of Boston to Castle William in Boston Harbor.
    d. marked the failure of Britain's attempt at military coercion.
    e. all of the above.

ANS: E **TYPE: M** **KEY 1: F** **KEY 2: 3** **PAGE: 172-75**

41. By early 1776, delegates within the Second Continental Congress from all of the following colonies except _____ favored independence.
    a. New England.
    b. Georgia.
    c. New York.
    d. Virginia.
    e. Massachusetts

ANS: C **TYPE: M** **KEY 1: F** **KEY 2: 2** **PAGE: 190**

42. The Stamp Act
    a. was at first accepted grudgingly by most colonial leaders.
    b. was an external tax.
    c. was the last in a series of direct taxes on the colonies.
    d. exempted newspapers and pamphlets.
    e. lowered taxes in the colonies.

ANS: A **TYPE: M** **KEY 1: A** **KEY 2: 3** **PAGE: 164**

43. All of the following are true about the Revenue Act of 1766 except that
    a. it reduced the duty on molasses.
    b. it was clearly a revenue measure.
    c. it generated more income for the empire than any other colonial tax.
    d. it applied only to foreign molasses imported into the mainland.
    e. few colonists attacked it for violating the principle of no taxation without representation.

ANS: D **TYPE: M** **KEY 1: A** **KEY 2: 3** **PAGE: 166**

44. The 1767 confrontation over implementation of the Quartering Act occurred in
    a. Massachusetts.
    b. New York.
    c. Pennsylvania.
    d. Virginia.
    e. Georgia.

ANS: B　　　**TYPE: M**　　　**KEY 1: F**　　　**KEY 2: 2**　　　**PAGE: 168**

45. Revenues raised by the Townshend Revenue Act of 1767 were to be used for
    a. paying off Britain's national debt.
    b. supporting the British Treasury.
    c. paying the salaries of governors and judges in the colonies.
    d. paying for British soldiers stationed in the colonies.
    e. payments to corrupt customs collectors.

ANS: C　　　**TYPE: M**　　　**KEY 1: A**　　　**KEY 2: 3**　　　**PAGE: 169**

46. Which of the following statements about the Tea Act of 1773 is not true?
    a. It repealed import duties on tea in England.
    b. It mandated that tea to the colonies arrive only on special East India Company ships.
    c. It restricted tea sales to only a few distributors in each colonial port.
    d. The East India Company's tea would sell cheaper than smuggled tea.
    e. It was designed to provide the British government with much-needed revenue.

ANS: E　　　**TYPE: M**　　　**KEY 1: A**　　　**KEY 2: 3**　　　**PAGE: 180**

47. The only colony not to send a delegation to the First Continental Congress was
    a. Georgia.
    b. Vermont.
    c. Rhode Island.
    d. South Carolina.
    e. Massachusetts.

ANS: A　　　**TYPE: M**　　　**KEY 1: F**　　　**KEY 2: 2**　　　**PAGE: 184**

48. The greatest revenues to come in from the Sugar Act were likely the result from the tax on
    a. refined sugar.
    b. molasses.
    c. Madeira wine.
    d. coffee.
    e. tea.

ANS: B　　　**TYPE: M**　　　**KEY 1: F**　　　**KEY 2: 3**　　　**PAGE: 163**

49. The Cherokee War
    a. lasted from 1750-1770.
    b. occurred in South Carolina.
    c. began when Cherokee warriors attacked Charleston.
    d. demonstrated the strength of British troops in America.
    e. was fought against the Spanish in Florida.

ANS: B　　　**TYPE: M**　　　**KEY 1: F**　　　**KEY 2: 2**　　　**PAGE: 176**

50. Which of the following was not a consequence of the Boston Tea Party?
    a. British soldiers could now be housed among civilians if necessary.
    b. Town meetings in Massachusetts were prohibited.
    c. The port of Boston was closed until Bostonians had made restitution for the tea.
    d. British soldiers or officials charged with a crime while carrying out duties in Massachusetts would be tried either in another colony or in England.
    e. the Massachusetts council was to be appointed.

ANS: B   **TYPE: M**   **KEY 1: A**   **KEY 2: 3**   **PAGE: 181**

51. The First Continental Congress met in
    a. New York.
    b. Boston.
    c. Philadelphia.
    d. Charleston.
    e. Washington.

ANS: C   **TYPE: M**   **KEY 1: F**   **KEY 2: 1**   **PAGE: 184**

52. Which of the following statements is not true concerning the New England Restraining Act?
    a. It barred New Englanders from the Atlantic fisheries.
    b. It allowed New England to trade with England.
    c. It was introduced to Parliament in January 1775.
    d. It prohibited commerce between New England and any place except Britain and the British West Indies.
    e. It banned New England's commerce with the British West Indies.

ANS: E   **TYPE: M**   **KEY 1: F**   **KEY 2: 3**   **PAGE: 184**

TRUE/FALSE

_____ 1.   The Quartering Act (1765) stated that one-fourth of the revenue from the Stamp Act was to be given back to the colonies.

ANS: F   **TYPE: T**   **KEY 1: F**   **KEY 2: 2**   **PAGE: 164-65**

_____ 2.   The Proclamation of 1763 was followed earnestly by North American colonists.

ANS: F   **TYPE: T**   **KEY 1: F**   **KEY 2: 3**   **PAGE: 161**

_____ 3.   The unpopular lieutenant governor of Massachusetts, whose home was destroyed by a 1765 crowd, was John Hancock.

ANS: F   **TYPE: T**   **KEY 1: F**   **KEY 2: 3**   **PAGE: 165**

_____ 4.   John Wilkes was the advisor to the king most criticized by North American colonists.

ANS: F   **TYPE: T**   **KEY 1: F**   **KEY 2: 2**   **PAGE: 172**

_____ 5.   The Proclamation of 1763 attempted to stop white colonization at the Appalachian watershed.

ANS: T   **TYPE: T**   **KEY 1: F**   **KEY 2: 2**   **PAGE: 161**

_____ 6.   The Currency Act of 1764 forbade the colonies to issue any paper money as legal tender.

ANS: T   TYPE: T   KEY 1: F   KEY 2: 1   PAGE: 163

_____ 7.   The Quartering Act of 1765 resolved once and for all the vexing problem of how to house British troops in the Americas.

ANS: F   TYPE: T   KEY 1: A   KEY 2: 2   PAGE: 163-64

_____ 8.   George Washington was named military commander of the Continental Army because he was a man with military experience and was from a region outside of the northeast.

ANS: T   TYPE: T   KEY 1: A   KEY 2: 2   PAGE: 186

_____ 9.   All thirteen colonial assemblies objected to a stamp tax as unconstitutional.

ANS: T   TYPE: T   KEY 1: F   KEY 2: 2   PAGE: 165

_____ 10.   The Coercive Acts were implemented in response to the Boston Massacre.

ANS: F   TYPE: T   KEY 1: F   KEY 2: 1   PAGE: 181

_____ 11.   The idea that the British Parliament represented the needs and interests of all the empire's subjects was known as virtual representation.

ANS: T   TYPE: T   KEY 1: A   KEY 2: 1   PAGE: 164-65

_____ 12.   In response to the Coercive Acts, the American colonies called the First Continental Congress.

ANS: T   TYPE: T   KEY 1: F   KEY 2: 1   PAGE: 184

_____ 13.   The author of *Letters from a Farmer in Pennsylvania* was Thomas Jefferson.

ANS: F   TYPE: T   KEY 1: F   KEY 2: 2   PAGE: 170

_____ 14.   The Quebec Act (1774) established French civil law and the Roman Catholic Church in Quebec.

ANS: T   TYPE: T   KEY 1: F   KEY 2: 1   PAGE: 181-82

_____ 15.   A common colonial complaint against the Sugar and Stamp Acts was that they were implemented to regulate trade and not to raise a revenue.

ANS: F   TYPE: T   KEY 1: A   KEY 2: 1   PAGE: 168

_____ 16.   During the 1760s, the Hudson River Valley was the scene of widespread tenant unrest.

ANS: T   TYPE: T   KEY 1: F   KEY 2: 1   PAGE: 175

_____ 17.   The goal of George Grenville's revenue plan was to force the colonies to pay Britain's national debt.

ANS: F   TYPE: T   KEY 1: F   KEY 2: 1   PAGE: 161

_____ 18.	By the summer of 1776, patriot forces had won control of the territory in all thirteen colonies.

ANS: T	TYPE: T	KEY 1: F	KEY 2: 2	PAGE: 187

_____ 19.	The skirmish between British troops and Bostonians that led to the death of five colonists was the Boston Massacre.

ANS: T	TYPE: T	KEY 1: F	KEY 2: 2	PAGE: 172-73

_____ 20.	The first colonial crisis to develop after 1763 was over the Tea Act.

ANS: F	TYPE: T	KEY 1: F	KEY 2: 1	PAGE: 159

_____ 21.	Throughout the fighting during the spring and summer of 1775, the colonial objective was to restore government by consent of the Crown.

ANS: T	TYPE: T	KEY 1: A	KEY 2: 2	PAGE: 187

_____ 22.	At first, Britain's George Grenville employed voluntary measures to get the colonists to pay for British troops stationed in North America.

ANS: F	TYPE: T	KEY 1: A	KEY 2: 3	PAGE: 161

_____ 23.	Pontiac's War was named for a Seneca chief.

ANS: F	TYPE: T	KEY 1: F	KEY 2: 3	PAGE: 161

_____ 24.	The Paxton Boys were all eventually convicted of murder.

ANS: F	TYPE: T	KEY 1: F	KEY 2: 2	PAGE: 163

_____ 25.	The 1773 Molasses Act had been very successful in keeping French molasses out of the British colonies in North America.

ANS: F	TYPE: T	KEY 1: F	KEY 2: 3	PAGE: 163

_____ 26.	The motive behind the American invasion of Canada in June 1775 was territorial acquisition.

ANS: F	TYPE: T	KEY 1: A	KEY 2: 3	PAGE: 186-87

_____ 27.	The Quartering Act of 1765 required the army to quarter its soldiers in public buildings rather than private homes.

ANS: T	TYPE: T	KEY 1: A	KEY 2: 2	PAGE: 164

_____ 28.	The Stamp Act was the last in a series of direct taxes on the colonies.

ANS: F	TYPE: T	KEY 1: A	KEY 2: 3	PAGE: 165

_____ 29.	The turmoil in the colonies over the Stamp Act cost George Grenville his job.

ANS: F	TYPE: T	KEY 1: F	KEY 2: 3	PAGE: 166

_____ 30.   Parliament repealed the Stamp Act primarily because of pressure from British merchants and manufacturers.

ANS: T   **TYPE: T**   **KEY 1: F**   **KEY 2: 2**   **PAGE: 166**

_____ 31.   The Declaratory Act was acceptable to the colonists because they interpreted it as prohibiting Parliament from levying taxes on the colonists.

ANS: T   **TYPE: T**   **KEY 1: A**   **KEY 2: 3**   **PAGE: 166**

_____ 32.   The Townshend Revenue Act was designed primarily to generate revenue.

ANS: F   **TYPE: T**   **KEY 1: F**   **KEY 2: 2**   **PAGE: 169**

_____ 33.   Tea provided three-quarters of the revenue raised under the Townshend Revenue Act.

ANS: T   **TYPE: T**   **KEY 1: F**   **KEY 2: 2**   **PAGE: 174**

_____ 34.   As the various unpopular parliamentary restrictions on the colonists' activities were repealed in the early 1770s, the colonists' confidence in the justice and decency of the British government was restored.

ANS: F   **TYPE: T**   **KEY 1: A**   **KEY 2: 3**   **PAGE: 174-75**

_____ 35.   Many colonists blamed one another for failing to win complete repeal of all of the Townshend duties.

ANS: T   **TYPE: T**   **KEY 1: A**   **KEY 2: 2**   **PAGE: 174**

_____ 36   No one in Boston considered paying restitution for the tea destroyed during the Boston Tea Party.

ANS: F   **TYPE: T**   **KEY 1: F**   **KEY 2: 2**   **PAGE: 181**

_____ 37.   The threat of colonial nonexportation was much more radical than nonimportation.

ANS: T   **TYPE: T**   **KEY 1: A**   **KEY 2: 2**   **PAGE: 184**

_____ 38.   The Second Continental Congress came to see itself as an American equivalent of Parliament.

ANS: F   **TYPE: T**   **KEY 1: A**   **KEY 2: 2**   **PAGE: 187**

_____ 39.   Thomas Paine's _Common Sense_ was particularly effective in nudging the Mid-Atlantic colonies toward independence.

ANS: T   **TYPE: T**   **KEY 1: A**   **KEY 2: 2**   **PAGE: 188**

_____ 40.   The Paxton Boys went after Indians who refused to convert to Christianity.

ANS: F   **TYPE: T**   **KEY 1: A**   **KEY 2: 2**   **PAGE: 162-63**

1. The _____ Act (1764) forbade the colonies from issuing any paper money as legal tender.

    ANS: Currency   **TYPE: F**   **KEY 1: F**   **KEY 2: 2**   **PAGE: 163**

2. Pennsylvania vigilantes that attempted to destroy Christian Indians on the western frontier were known as the _____.

    ANS: Paxton Boys   **TYPE: F**   **KEY 1: F**   **KEY 2: 2**   **PAGE: 162-63**

3. _____ Rising in 1763 had as its goal the removal of British colonists from the area between the Ohio River and the Great Lakes.

    ANS: Pontiac's   **TYPE: F**   **KEY 1: F**   **KEY 2: 2**   **PAGE: 161**

4. The principal advisor to King George III was John Stuart, more commonly known as the earl of _____.

    ANS: Bute   **TYPE: F**   **KEY 1: F**   **KEY 2: 3**   **PAGE: 160**

5. In response to the Boston Port Act, the colonists summoned the First _____.

    ANS: Continental Congress   **TYPE: F**   **KEY 1: F**   **KEY 2: 2**   **PAGE: 184**

6. The British commander who took over as governor of Massachusetts and closed the Port of Boston was General _____.

    ANS: Thomas Gage   **TYPE: F**   **KEY 1: F**   **KEY 2: 3**   **PAGE: 183**

7. The colonists named the Coercive Acts and the Quebec Act the _____.

    ANS: Intolerable Acts   **TYPE: F**   **KEY 1: F**   **KEY 2: 1**   **PAGE: 182**

8. The Boston slave whose poetry deplored the institution of slavery was _____.

    ANS: Phillis Wheatley   **TYPE: F**   **KEY 1: A**   **KEY 2: 1**   **PAGE: 179**

9. Volunteer colonial militia who were ready to defend their communities at a moment's notice were called _____.

    ANS: minutemen   **TYPE: F**   **KEY 1: F**   **KEY 2: 2**   **PAGE: 183**

10. German mercenary soldiers hired by the English during the American Revolution were called _____.

    ANS: Hessians   **TYPE: F**   **KEY 1: F**   **KEY 2: 1**   **PAGE: 189**

11. Sir _____, British commander in the colonies, requested the Quartering Act in 1765.

    ANS: Thomas Gage   **TYPE: F**   **KEY 1: F**   **KEY 2: 2**   **PAGE: 164**

12. The _____ Act launched the first post-1763 colonial crisis.

ANS: Stamp   **TYPE: F**   **KEY 1: F**   **KEY 2: 1**   **PAGE: 164**

13. During the Seven Years' War, _____ was Britain's only major ally in Europe.

ANS:Prussia   **TYPE: F**   **KEY 1: F**   **KEY 2: 2**   **PAGE: 160**

14. _____ led the first wave of opposition to the Stamp Act in the Virginia House of Burgesses.

ANS: Patrick Henry   **TYPE: F**   **KEY 1: F**   **KEY 2: 2**   **PAGE: 164-65**

15. _____ colonies sent delegates to the Stamp Act Congress.

ANS: Nine   **TYPE: F**   **KEY 1: F**   **KEY 2: 3**   **PAGE: 168**

16. The greatest Indian opposition to the Proclamation of 1763 came from the _____.

ANS: Iroquois   **TYPE: F**   **KEY 1: F**   **KEY 2: 2**   **PAGE: 161**

17. The stamp masters in every colony except _____ were forced to resign even before the Stamp Act was scheduled to go into effect.

ANS: Georgia   **TYPE: F**   **KEY 1: F**   **KEY 2: 3**   **PAGE: 165**

18. _____, a Philadelphia lawyer, authored *Letters from a Farmer in Pennsylvania* in which he argued that all parliamentary taxation for revenue violated individual rights.

ANS: John Dickinson   **TYPE: F**   **KEY 1: F**   **KEY 2: 3**   **PAGE: 170**

19. _____ led colonial opposition to the Townshend Revenue Act.

ANS: Massachusetts   **TYPE: F**   **KEY 1: F**   **KEY 2: 2**   **PAGE: 170**

20. "The Declaration of the Causes and Necessities of Taking Up Arms" was written mostly by _____.

ANS: Thomas Jefferson   **TYPE: F**   **KEY 1: F**   **KEY 2: 2**   **PAGE: 187**

21. The state of _____ abstained in the vote to approve the Declaration of Independence.

ANS: New York   **TYPE: F**   **KEY 1: F**   **KEY 2: 2**   **PAGE: 190**

22. The western Delaware who had a vision in 1761 that God wanted Indians to resume their ancestral ways was _____.

ANS: Neolin   **TYPE: F**   **KEY 1: F**   **KEY 2: 3**   **PAGE: 161**

23. The first Sons of Liberty were organized in the city of _____.

ANS: Boston   **TYPE: F**   **KEY 1: F**   **KEY 2: 2**   **PAGE: 165**

24. Britain's first effort at military coercion of the colonies resulted in the _____ and failed.

ANS: Boston Massacre   **TYPE: F**   **KEY 1: F**   **KEY 2: 2**   **PAGE: 172-73**

25. _____ was a radical member of Parliament who defended English liberties and openly sympathized with North American protestors. American colonists held him up as representative of freedom.

ANS: John Wilkes   **TYPE: F**   **KEY 1: A**   **KEY 2: 2**   **PAGE: 161, 172**

26. The first direct tax that Parliament levied on the colonists was the _____ tax.

ANS: Stamp   **TYPE: F**   **KEY 1: F**   **KEY 2: 1**   **PAGE: 164**

27. An act, passed after the failure of the Stamp Act that affirmed Parliament's sovereignty over the colonies was the _____ Act.

ANS: Declaratory   **TYPE: F**   **KEY 1: F**   **KEY 2: 2**   **PAGE: 166**

28. The minister in charge of colonial policy under William Pitt was _____.

ANS: Charles Townshend   **TYPE: F**   **KEY 1: F**   **KEY 2: 2**   **PAGE: 168**

29. The Massachusetts assembly urged other assemblies to resist new taxes in the _____ Letter. This letter led to a crisis when colonial assemblies refused to rescind it and governors dissolved the assemblies.

ANS: Circular   **TYPE: F**   **KEY 1: F**   **KEY 2: 2**   **PAGE: 170**

30. Riots broke out in Boston when John Hancock's sloop, the _____, was seized.

ANS: *Liberty*   **TYPE: F**   **KEY 1: F**   **KEY 2:2**   **PAGE: 170**

IDENTIFICATIONS

1. **Stamp Act:** Passed by George Grenville in 1765, angering much of the colonial population because it taxed newspapers, pamphlets, and most legal procedures. Led to colonial resistance. Eventually repealed.

2. **Sugar Act**: important part of Britain's attempt to reorganize its imperial system in 1764 and to raise revenue. Called for duties to be placed on a variety of products, the most important of which was molasses.

3. **John Wilkes**: popular British oppositionist writer. Author of the *North Britain.* Accused of seditious libel against King George III in 1763. Was jailed, freed, but forced to flee to France. Later elected to, expelled from, and re-elected to the House of Commons. Became increasingly popular in the colonies, where he was considered a champion of individual rights.

4. **John Dickinson**: colonial pamphlet writer opposed to British imperial policy. In his *Letters from a Pennsylvania Farmer,* he questioned the distinction between internal and external taxes, opposed all revenue-raising Parliamentary taxes, and examined the motives behind the Townshend Acts.

5. **First Continental Congress**: intercolonial body organized in 1774 by North American colonies to voice protest over recent Coercive Acts.

6. **John Hancock**: Boston merchant who was active within the Sons of Liberty.

7. **Phillis Wheatley**: former slave from Boston whose poetry deplored the institution of slavery. Raised as a daughter by owners. Educated, then freed when of age.

8. **Sons of Liberty**: patriotic group dedicated to resisting British imperial reforms in the American colonies. Although central to Boston's revolutionary movement, a variation on this group could be found in many colonial cities and towns.

9. **Virtual representation**: British political concept. Maintained that all Englishmen were represented by all members of Parliament regardless of an individual MP's constituency. Designed to counter colonial cries against taxation without representation. British thinking maintained that the colonies were indeed represented--in the same way that the large, nonvoting majority in Great Britain was.

10. **Nonimportation agreements**: agreements among colonial merchants not to import British goods. Economic measures used in an effort to force concessions from Parliament.

SHORT ESSAYS

1.   What was the purpose of the Stamp Act?

Answer: The Stamp Act was part of the new British imperial policy following the French and Indian War. With the acquisition of Canada, Britain determined that the colonies would have to pay for some portion of their own military protection along the frontier. Following the Sugar Act, George Grenville made it clear that a second revenue-raising measure would be required to increase revenue from the colonies and help to pay the cost of the defensive military force. In 1765, Grenville proposed, and Parliament passed, the Stamp Act.
The Stamp Act mandated that a tax stamp be placed on a variety of goods sold in the colonies (ranging from playing cards to newspapers). This tax (along with the Sugar Act) was the first time Parliament had attempted to tax the colonies directly for the purpose of raising a revenue. It met with quick and stiff resistance in the colonies.

2.   Describe the state of British politics in the critical decade of the 1760s.

Answer: If British policy in the years between 1763 and 1775 seems a unified system of reorganizing the empire and integrating the colonies into the larger imperial system, the politicians who were implementing this system were anything but unified. Indeed, British politics during these years were among the most factious and crisis-ridden of the eighteenth century. A series of alliances, shifting often, attempted to establish policy, rarely with the support of the opposition, sometimes without the support of George III and his leading advisor, Lord Bute. William Pitt, Earl of Chatham, had been forced to resign from the prime minister's position before the end of the Seven Years' War because of his desire to attack Spain, which was seen by Bute and the king as too extravagant and expensive. In addition, Bute forced the powerful Lord Newcastle, First Lord of the Treasury, to resign, in order to economize.
This resignation helped to set the stage for the new imperial system of the 1760s—attempts to reorganize imperial power, control, and raise revenue in the colonies. George Grenville became prime minister in 1763 and began to promote a series of measures designed to raise a revenue in the colonies to pay for a British military presence there. Factious British politics continued, however, with Pitt denouncing Grenville's (Pitt's brother-in-law) policies. This internal squabbling continued through the passage of the Stamp Act and eventually, forced the resignation of Grenville, who was spending much of his time dealing with the constitutional issues raised by the Wilkes Affair, and not with matters involving the American colonies. All in all, although colonial commentators believed British politicians to be involved in a conspiratorial attempt to erode their liberties, this threat to colonial liberties was far more likely to come from royal governors. British politicians were more often in cutthroat competition with each other. Grenville outmaneuvered and defeated Wilkes, then passed his American reforms by large majorities but was ultimately dismissed by George III.

3.   Describe the regulator movements.

Answer: Following the Cherokee War, South Carolina's backcountry faced serious crime problems as huge bands of outlaws roamed the countryside. In the mid-1760s, settlers organized themselves as vigilantes and called themselves "regulators." In North Carolina, the problem was not the absence of government, but its corruption. The court system was under the control of established wealthy families in the eastern part of the colony, as was the legislature. North Carolina regulators decided to take matters into their own hands by organizing militia units, refusing to pay taxes, and agitating for political reform.

In 1771, Governor William Tryon responded to this challenge to traditional authority by organizing militia units and marching west to meet the regulators. At Alamance Creek, one thousand militia men engaged a larger force of regulators and defeated them in battle. Several regulator leaders were hanged, further inflaming a volatile situation. Although the regulator movement was temporarily defeated, the seed of discord and division had been planted in the Carolinas and this would reveal itself regularly throughout the Revolutionary period.

4.   Examine the colonial response to the Coercive Acts of 1774.

Answer: Following the Boston Tea Party and the destruction of East India tea by Boston citizens, Parliament responded with a variety of restrictions—referred to as the Coercive Acts—aimed at punishing and disciplining the colony of Massachusetts Bay. The Coercive Acts included the closing of the Port of Boston and the restructuring of the Massachusetts government. Immediate reactions in Massachusetts included the formation of extralegal governments to counterbalance military rule in Boston as well as the formation of militia units.

The general response throughout the colonies was equally strong. Each of the colonies enacted nonimportation agreements and sent aid to Boston. Far more important was the calling of the First Continental Congress, which, for the first time, attempted to bring about intercolonial unity. The Continental Congress demanded the repeal of the Coercive Acts and all taxes for revenue. It also tried to define colonial rights while conceding to Parliament the power to regulate trade. In addition, Congress called for a general nonimportation agreement, constructed a militia system, and made the radical move of planning to meet a second time should the crown's answer prove unsatisfactory.

5.   Describe the causes and significance of the Boston Massacre in 1770.

Answer: Problems between British troops stationed in Boston and the citizens of the town had developed immediately upon the troops' arrival in the city. Constant confrontations between the town's watch and British sentries, as well as stiff competition for limited jobs in a depressed economy between off-duty British troops and city workmen increased the intense animosity between Bostonians and their "army of occupation." Problems grew worse, though, in late February 1770 after the killing of Christopher Seider (killed by a Bostonian supporter of the British troops), which erupted into a full-fledged riot between British soldiers (looking for work at a local wharf) and workmen in early March. These various preliminaries led to the confrontation between frightened British sentries and a snowball-throwing crowd outside the customs office on the night of March 5, 1770. In the confusion of the moment, the soldiers fired on the crowd, killing five civilians and wounding six more.

Although each of the soldiers was acquitted of murder charges with the help of defense attorney John Adams, two were found guilty of manslaughter—but none received any jail sentence. The significance of the "massacre," as it came to be called by the Sons of Liberty, cannot be overlooked. Not only does it represent the failure of Britain's attempt to coerce the colonists with military force, it also became a symbol for the emerging resistance movement. Each year, the people of Boston, under the orchestration of the Sons of Liberty, celebrated the day with the solemnity of a religious event and the symbolism was not lost on the Bostonians or the British.

6.   Describe the beginnings of the antislavery movement in pre-revolutionary America.

Answer: During the mid-1700s, the institution of slavery in America came under sustained attack for the first time in its history. The antislavery movement arose on both sides of the Atlantic at roughly the same time, but the movement in North America received an added incentive from the revolutionary movement. Quakers were the first significant abolitionists in America, arguing that the institution was incompatible with the teachings of the Bible and the "Inner Light." New Englanders, unsympathetic to Quakers, also began to challenge the institution on both moral and economic grounds.

The most interesting arguments for the abolition of slavery came from the slaves themselves. They paraded through the streets of Charleston in 1765 chanting for liberty (shortly after a Sons of Liberty parade of the same theme—albeit from a different oppressor). This made a lasting impression on the people of the town. Equally impressive were the writings of Boston slave Phillis Wheatley, who, in 1772 at the age of 20, published a book of poetry in London. The extent of the antislavery fervor (small, but growing) is revealed by the fact that the first defenses of the institution of slavery began to appear in the 1760s and 1770s. These defenses gave testament to the ways that many Americans dealt with the obvious moral contradictions between their own demands for liberty and their continuing enslavement of Africans.

7.   What was the "Feudal Revival" and in what ways did it help generate rural participation in the revolutionary movement?

Answer: Between 1730 and 1750, a series of interrelated trends increased social tensions in rural America and led many into armed rebellion. Known as the "Feudal Revival," these trends included the revival of old proprietary charters, widespread immigration, and increasing settlement in the backcountry. The revival of charters was most pronounced in the middle colonies, particularly areas like the mid-Hudson Valley. There, manor lords foresaw the possibility for making profits for the first time and began to demand more restrictive leases and commercial payments from their tenants. These demands, occurring at the same time that widespread immigration from New England was taking place, set off a series of manorial rebellions throughout the valley.

Similar occurrences took place in New Jersey, Pennsylvania, Virginia, North Carolina, and Maryland. In those places, landed proprietors began to rationalize and commercialize their practices, as well as to challenge the land titles of small landholders. These practices, much like those of the Hudson Valley, led to discontent among the small farming population and to outright rebellion in some areas. British troops had to be called in to suppress the Hudson Valley revolts, but riots in other areas never reached the same proportion. All of these events, however, added to the feeling of frustration and agitation in the countryside and helped to bring the rural population into the political turmoil that was engulfing the eastern towns. Although their frustration had little to do with British policy, it was related to an antiestablishment, antiauthoritarian attitude developing in mid-eighteenth-century North America.

LONG ESSAYS

1.   Explain the development of British imperial policy following the French and Indian War.

Answer: Essay should address several key points:

A.   New goals of empire
     1.   Acquisition of Canada and support for troops
         a.   Proclamation of 1763
         b.   Quartering Act
     2.   Revenue generation
         a.   Sugar Act (1764)
         b.   Stamp Act (1765)
B.   Colonial response
     1.   All thirteen colonies object to Stamp Act
     2.   Many mainland colonies attack revenue clause of Sugar Act
     3.   Colonists reject distinction between "internal" and "external" taxation

2.   Describe the response of the colonists to the British policy from 1763 to 1773.

Answer: Essay should address several key points:

A.   Intellectual and constitutional arguments
      1.   Debate over Sugar Act
            a.   Limited primarily to merchants
            b.   Implications
      2.   Opposition to Stamp Act
            a.   Daniel Dulany's attack on "virtual" representation
            b.   Benjamin Franklin and "external" taxation
B.   Popular response to new taxes
      1.   Crowd actions and Stamp Act
            a.   Home of Thomas Hutchinson destroyed
            b.   Riots in New York City
      2.   Townshend Duties and boycotts
C.   Renewed constitutional and popular arguments
      1.   Daniel Dulany and "virtual" representation
      2.   New colonial limitations on British power
      3.   Opposition to Tea Act
            a.   Opposition to right to tax
            b.   Boston Tea Party

3.   Outline the final imperial crisis of 1773–1775 that led to the outbreak of the Revolutionary War.

Answer: Essay should address several key points:

A.   Tea Act and response (1773)
      1.   Terms and purpose of Tea Act
      2.   Refusal to accept shipped tea
      3.   Boston radicals "dump" tea
B.   British response/Coercive Acts
      1.   Massachusetts Government Act
            a.   Restructured power of town meetings and upper house
            b.   Implications
      2.   Boston Port Act
            a.   Port of Boston closed
            b.   Implications
      3.   Administration of Justice Act
      4.   Quartering Act
            a.   British troops could be quartered in colonial homes
            b.   Implications
      5.   Quebec Act (not a Coercive Act, but considered "intolerable" by the colonists)
            a.   French law and Catholic Church established in Quebec
            b.   Quebec Act unrelated to Coercive Acts
            c.   Implications
C.   Radical explosion
      1.   Colonists implement nonimportation
      2.   Massachusetts Government Act nullified by colonists
      3.   Committee movement spreads throughout Northeast
D.   First Continental Congress
      1.   Meets in Philadelphia to discuss British measures
            a.   Twelve colonies represented
            b.   Implications
      2.   Congress repudiates Parliamentary right to legislate, except to regulate trade

      a.   Congress deals directly with the king

      b.   Creation of the Association
            i)   Enforces trade sanctions against Britain
            ii)   Implications

4.   Describe the intellectual movement toward independence in 1776.

Answer: Essay should address several key points:

A.   War of rebellion becomes a war for revolution
    1.   King's refusal of Olive Branch Petition
    2.   Thomas Paine's *Common Sense*
        a.   Denounces idea of monarchical government
        b.   Criticizes imperial system
            i)   "No island should govern a continent"
            ii)   Implications
        c.   Calls for a republic

B.   Declaration of Independence
    1.   Public opinion shifted toward independence
        a.   Many colonists recognized reunification with Britain was untenable
        b.   Implications
    2.   Continental Congress and the Declaration of Independence
        a.   Congress approves Richard Lee's call for "independent states"
        b.   Jefferson drafts and Congress amends the Declaration of Independence
            i)   Twelve states (with one abstention) unanimously approve the Declaration
            ii)   Implications

CHAPTER 6
THE REVOLUTIONARY REPUBLIC

CHAPTER OUTLINE

I. Hearts and Minds: The Northern War, 1776-1777
    A. The British Offensive
    B. The Trenton-Princeton Campaign

II. The Campaigns of 1777 and Foreign Intervention
    A. The Loss of Philadelphia
    B. Saratoga
    C. French Intervention
    D. Spanish Expansion and Intervention

III. The Reconstitution of Authority
    A. John Adams and the Separation of Powers
    B. The Virginia Constitution
    C. The Pennsylvania Constitution
    D. Massachusetts Redefines Constitutionalism
    E. Confederation

IV. The Crisis of Revolution, 1779-1783
    A. The Loyalists
    B. Loyalist Refugees, Black and White
    C. The Indian Struggle for Unity and Survival
    D. Attrition

V. The British Offensive in the South
    A. The Partisan War
    B. Mutiny and Reform
    C. From the Ravaging of Virginia to Yorktown and Peace

VI. A Revolutionary Society
    A. Religious Transformations
    B. The First Emancipation
    C. The Challenge to Patriarchy
    D. Western Expansion, Discontent, and Conflict with Indians
    E. The Northwest Ordinance

VII. A More Perfect Union
    A. Commerce, Debt, and Shays's Rebellion
    B. Cosmopolitans versus Localists
    C. The Philadelphia Convention
    D. Ratification

VIII. Conclusion

CHRONOLOGY

1775	Daniel Boone leads first settlers to Kentucky.
1776	Virginia Constitution and Bill of Rights.
	Declaration of Independence.
	Battles of Long Island and Trenton.
1777	Congress completes the Articles of Confederation.
	Battles of Princeton, Bennington, and Bemis Heights.
	The Howes take Philadelphia, and Congress flees.
	Burgoyne surrenders at Saratoga.
1778	Franco–American treaties signed.
	Battle of Monmouth Court House.
1779	Spain declares war on Britain.

1778–1781	British offensive in the South.
1780	Massachusetts Constitution.
	Benedict Arnold's treason.
1781	Articles of Confederation ratified.
	Lord Cornwallis surrenders at Yorktown, Virginia.
1782	Resignation of Lord North as prime minister.
1783	Treaty of Paris.
1786	Virginia enacts Jefferson's Statute for Religious Freedom.
	Shays's Rebellion in western Massachusetts.
1787	Northwest Ordinance passed by Congress.
	Constitutional Convention meets in Philadelphia.
1787–1788	*The Federalist* published in New York.
1788	New Hampshire is ninth state to ratify Constitution.
1789	First federal Congress sends Bill of Rights to the states.

THEMATIC TOPICS FOR ENRICHMENT

1. Assess the authors' statement that the Revolution "was a civil war in its own right."

2. Define the terms *republicanism* and *popular sovereignty.* How were they manifested in the years of the American Revolution?

3. Why did Americans begin to think increasingly in terms of race in the era of the American Revolution? What was the "first emancipation"?

4. Explain the weaknesses of the Articles of Confederation. Why did the Second Continental Congress create such a weak body?

5. What mistakes did the British make in their attempt to win over the hearts and minds of the Americans during the early stages of the war?

6. Discuss the similarities and differences among some of the state constitutions written during the Revolutionary War. In what ways did Massachusetts redefine constitutionalism?

7. Who was a loyalist and who was a patriot in the American Revolution? Did many people change sides during the war?

8. How did the Continental Congress finance the war?

9. What were the main differences between a "cosmopolitan" and a "loyalist"?

SUGGESTED ESSAY TOPICS

1. On what basis did Americans reconstruct authority during the American Revolution? What replaced the power and authority of the monarchy? What new institutions were devised to secure authority?

2. Contrast the Articles of Confederation and the Constitution in terms of liberty and power. Was the Constitution a fulfillment of the Revolution or a reaction to its excesses?

3. In what ways did the movement toward independence transform American life? Be sure to discuss politics, economics, and social issues in your answer.

4. After the middle of the eighteenth century, what options did Indians still have in responding to the encroachment of settlers? How had Indian behavior changed since the Iroquois mourning wars of the seventeenth century?

1. The Revolutionary War was as much a struggle for hearts and minds as it was one of competing armies, as the conflict turned on social issues as well as political ones, especially early on in the northern war of 1776–1777.

   a. The British offensive of 1776 succeeded in gaining ground and wreaking havoc in New York and New Jersey, but it failed to achieve any decisive advantage.

   (SHOW TRANSPARENCY 37: NORTHERN CAMPAIGNS, 1776-1778)

   b. The Trenton–Princeton campaign proved to be crucial successes for Washington's army, predominantly insofar as it helped keep alive the "spirit of '76."

2. The campaigns of 1777 and foreign intervention, particularly of the French after Saratoga, proved to be the turning points of the war.

   a. Despite the loss of Philadelphia, the Continental Army continued to fight, even as it could not defend the nominal capital of the nation and as the Continental Congress virtually disbanded.

   b. John Burgoyne's army of 7,800 surrendered to American forces under the command of Horatio Gates at Saratoga on October 17, 1777.

   c. French intervention, which proved critical to ultimate triumph, came almost immediately after the signal victory at Saratoga.

   d. Spanish expansion and intervention, also in the aftermath of Saratoga, greatly assisted the American war efforts, particularly insofar as the Spanish forced the British to spread their forces even more thinly.

3. With the Declaration of Independence and the withdrawal of many Tories, Americans faced the uncertain challenge of the **reconstitution of authority**.

   a. A first attempt to reconstitute legitimate authority came from John Adams and his theories in *Thoughts on Government* on the separation of powers.

   b. The Virginia Constitution, which contained a declaration of rights drafted by George Mason, served as a model for other states to follow.

   c. More radical than that of Virginia, the Pennsylvania Constitution and its unicameral legislature and plural executive never really worked as its framers had envisioned.

   d. John Adams and his colleagues in Massachusetts redefined constitutionalism, incorporating a unique system of checks and balances, and submitting its drafted constitution to a town meeting for ratification.

   e. A palpable lack of power and a visceral mistrust of central authority plagued the confederation of the states throughout the revolutionary period.

4. The crisis of the Revolution in the years 1779–1783 resulted from the fact that the war dragged on at great social and personal cost for more than six years.

   a. The loyalists were many in number and often struggled with the fact that they supported British liberty and simultaneously opposed the war.

b.   The lot of loyalist refugees, black and white, proved harsh as many thousands emigrated under duress to Nova Scotia and England.

c.   The Indian struggle for unity and survival during the war ran the gamut from bitter opposition to England to awesome frontier violence against American troops.

5.   Perhaps the most gruesome events of the Revolutionary War took place during the British offensive in the South, which included Clinton's virtual destruction of Charleston, South Carolina.

(SHOW TRANSPARENCY 38: SOUTHERN CAMPAIGNS, 1778-1781)

a.   The partisan war frequently pitted native-born Tories against patriots in vicious confrontations.

b.   The British offensive and the partisan warfare that ensued led to mutiny and reform in the ranks of the Continental Army as well as in the militias.

c.   The final stages of the war in 1781 included Cornwallis's ravaging of Virginia, his surrender at Yorktown, and subsequent peace negotiations.

(SHOW TRANSPARENCY 39: VIRGINIA AND THE YORKTOWN CAMPAIGN; AND TRANSPARENCY 40: NORTH AMERICA IN 1783)

6.   Years of warfare and independence from Britain inevitably led to a revolutionary society that few had imagined a decade earlier.

a.   Several of the most profound changes in society were the religious transformations which included increasing religious toleration and the growth of denominationalism.

b.   The fervor of revolutionary sentiment convinced virtually all of the North, and much of the upper South as well, to free its slaves in what historians call the first emancipation.

c.   The logic of revolutionary ideology also led to some changes in the life of women that constituted the challenge to patriarchy.

d.   Simultaneous with the defeat of the British there occurred a renewed thrust of western expansion and conflict with Indians that would take several decades to resolve.

e.   One of Congress's last acts was the passage of the Northwest Ordinance, which would ultimately bring Ohio, Indiana, Illinois, and Michigan into the Union on equal footing with the original thirteen states.

(SHOW TRANSPARENCY 41: WESTERN LAND CESSIONS, 1782-1802; AND TRANSPARENCY 42: THE NORTHWEST TERRITORY AND THE RECTANGULAR SURVEY)

7.   Out of the strains and trials of the decade of revolution, many Americans called for the wholesale revision of the Articles of Confederation and the creation of a more perfect union.

a.   There was no one precipitate of the Constitutional Convention; rather, a combination of problems with commerce, debt, currency, and Shays's Rebellion contributed to the growing discontent with the Articles.

b.   The struggle over the government of the Union took the form of a fight between cosmopolitans versus localists.

c.   In the course of the summer of 1787, participants at the Philadelphia Convention drafted the Constitution, scrapping the Articles altogether.

d.   Ratification was confirmed when New Hampshire, the ninth state, voted in favor of the Constitution on June 21, 1788.

(SHOW TRANSPARENCY 43: RATIFICATION OF THE CONSTITUTION)

American Album: Toward Equality: The Affectionate Family

Conclusion: Despite daunting odds and the dangers of what amounted to a civil war, the Americans managed to persevere through years of warfare, economic tribulations, and weak leadership to defeat the British. Imperial ineptitude greatly enhanced the Americans' chances for victory. Victory did not come without significant social upheaval that caused grave problems under the Articles of Confederation.

TEACHING RESOURCES

Abigail Adams discusses the life of this important American in light of the changing attitudes toward women in the era of the American Revolution. Filmic Archives (30 minutes).

Liberty: The American Revolution, volumes IV–VI, offers abroad, well-narrated portrait of the Revolutionary War, with particular emphasis on the military campaigns. PBS Video (55 minutes each).

Valley Forge: The Battle for Survival portrays the events of the fateful winter of 1778 and its larger implications for American independence. Films for the Humanities (23 minutes).

The Battle of Yorktown: 1781 examines the origins of the Revolution, culminating in the British surrender at Yorktown, from a long-term perspective. Films for the Humanities (30 minutes).

Christmas 1783 celebrates America's victory over the British from the perspective of Annapolis, Maryland, where George Washington went to resign as commander in chief before the Confederation Congress. Films for the Humanities (28 minutes).

Fighting for Independence: The Revolutionary War reenacts the major events of the war, political and military, from a number of perspectives. Filmic Archives (20 minutes).

George Mason and the Bill of Rights focuses on the Virginia Ratifying Convention and the debates over the federal Constitution. ETV Video through Social Studies School Service (50 minutes).

Breaking Colonial Ties: Declaration of Independence explains the patriot and Tory viewpoints in Revolutionary America and examines the position of women, slaves, and Native Americans in the debate. Filmic Archives (20 minutes).

1. Those who remained loyal to the British crown made up about _____ of the white population in North America.
   a. one-half
   b. one-third
   c. one-sixth
   d. one-tenth
   e. none of the above

   ANS: C   **TYPE: M**   **KEY 1: F**   **KEY 2: 1**   **PAGE: 205**

2. During the Revolutionary War, about _____ slaves fled their masters.
   a. 5,000
   b. 15,000
   c. 25,000
   d. 50,000
   e. none of the above

   ANS: D   **TYPE: M**   **KEY 1: F**   **KEY 2: 1**   **PAGE: 205**

3. The Ohio Company was organized by veterans from
   a. New York.
   b. Pennsylvania.
   c. Connecticut.
   d. Massachusetts.
   e. Georgia.

   ANS: D   **TYPE: M**   **KEY 1: F**   **KEY 2: 2**   **PAGE: 220**

4. George Washington's forces were not permanently defeated or captured by the British in the Battle for New York because
   a. of Washington's skilled troop movements.
   b. the British commanders were inept.
   c. the British commanders chose not to capture them.
   d. the British were woefully outnumbered.
   e. of the skilled fighting of the French troops.

   ANS: C   **TYPE: M**   **KEY 1: A**   **KEY 2: 2**   **PAGE: 195**

5. Washington's victory at _____ over the Hessians on Christmas night was a dramatic morale booster to the American cause.
   a. Brooklyn Heights
   b. Trenton
   c. Valley Forge
   d. Westchester
   e. Yorktown

   ANS: B   **TYPE: M**   **KEY 1: F**   **KEY 2: 1**   **PAGE: 196**

6. British policy regarding the loyalists was
   a. well planned and executed.
   b. very important to the British war effort.
   c. poorly planned and implemented.
   d. nonexistent.
   e. based on the assumption that they were all spying for the Americans.

ANS: C   **TYPE: M**   **KEY 1: A**   **KEY 2: 2**   **PAGE: 205**

7. The most important outcome of the Battle of Saratoga was
   a. that the French entered the war on the side of the colonies.
   b. that it ended the war in North America.
   c. that it led to Washington's election as commander in chief.
   d. that it brought an end to the British ministry that was waging the war.
   e. that the Spanish entered the war on the side of the colonies.

ANS: A   **TYPE: M**   **KEY 1: F**   **KEY 2: 1**   **PAGE: 198-99**

8. One of the major problems of the Confederation Congress was that
   a. it did not have the power to raise an army.
   b. it did not have the power to regulate trade.
   c. it did not have the power to borrow money.
   d. it did not have the power to make foreign treaties.
   e. most of the states never ratified it.

ANS: B   **TYPE: M**   **KEY 1: A**   **KEY 2: 1**   **PAGE: 204**

9. During the Revolutionary War, most Indian tribes
   a. remained neutral.
   b. sided with the revolutionaries.
   c. sided with the British.
   d. split down the middle.
   e. sided with the Spanish.

ANS: C   **TYPE: M**   **KEY 1: F**   **KEY 2: 2**   **PAGE: 206**

10. After 1779, most fighting took place in
    a. the western frontier.
    b. the middle states.
    c. New England.
    d. the South.
    e. Canada.

ANS: D   **TYPE: M**   **KEY 1: F**   **KEY 2: 1**   **PAGE: 210**

11. Loyalist forces in the South were under the command of
    a. Banastre Tarleton.
    b. Ben Butler.
    c. Francis Marion.
    d. Thomas Sumter.
    e. Nathaniel Green.

ANS: A   **TYPE: M**   **KEY 1: F**   **KEY 2: 2**   **PAGE: 210**

12. The final major battle in the Revolutionary War was fought at
    a. Yorktown.
    b. Jamestown.
    c. Saratoga.
    d. Charleston.
    e. Concord.

ANS: A   TYPE: M   KEY 1: F   KEY 2: 1   PAGE: 214

13. The peace treaty ending the war between Britain and America was the
    a. Treaty of London.
    b. Treaty of Paris.
    c. Treaty of Lisbon.
    d. Versailles Treaty.
    e. Treaty of Ghent.

ANS: B   TYPE: M   KEY 1: F   KEY 2: 1   PAGE: 215

14. The church that suffered most from the revolutionary conflict was
    a. the Congregational Church.
    b. the Methodist Church.
    c. the Catholic Church.
    d. the Baptist Church.
    e. the Anglican Church.

ANS: E   TYPE: M   KEY 1: F   KEY 2: 2   PAGE: 217

15. The first state to end the institution of slavery through a gradual abolition law was
    a. Massachusetts.
    b. New York.
    c. Delaware.
    d. Pennsylvania.
    e. Georgia.

ANS: D   TYPE: M   KEY 1: F   KEY 2: 1   PAGE: 218

16. All except which one of the following were important gains in women's rights in the post-revolutionary era?
    a. Female academies educated most of the native-born women of the Northeast.
    b. The common law rule of coverture was abolished.
    c. New Jersey briefly gave voting rights to female tax-paying heads of household.
    d. Popular novels centered on female main characters who were often portrayed as morally superior to men.
    e. The ideal of "Republican" wife and mother gave women an expanded role within the family.

ANS: B   TYPE: M   KEY 1: F   KEY 2: 3   PAGE: 218

17. The Northwest Ordinance included all of the following except
    a. a prohibition on slavery.
    b. a division of the territory into three to five future states.
    c. the prohibition of African Americans moving into the territory.
    d. provisions for the territories to enter the confederation on equal footing with those already in existence.
    e. protection for civil liberties.

ANS: C   **TYPE: M**   **KEY 1: F**   **KEY 2: 3**   **PAGE: 220-21**

18. Spain chose to enter the war for independence because
    a. it was deeply committed to American independence.
    b. it was hoping to get back at France for losses in the last war.
    c. it hoped to retake Gibraltar and Florida.
    d. it desired to take control of Canada.
    e. it hoped to gain new island possessions in the Caribbean.

ANS: C   **TYPE: M**   **KEY 1: F**   **KEY 2: 2**   **PAGE: 200-01**

19. Cornwallis and the British army were pinned down at Yorktown Port by a French navy under the command of
    a. Marquis de LaFayette.
    b. Pierre de Beaumarchais.
    c. Charles DeGaulle.
    d. Marquis de LaFitte
    e. François de Grasse.

ANS: E   **TYPE: M**   **KEY 1: F**   **KEY 2: 2**   **PAGE: 214**

20. Many slaves earned their freedom during the Revolutionary War
    a. by fighting for the British.
    b. by running away.
    c. by fighting for the Americans.
    d. through court decisions and legislative actions.
    e. all of the above.

ANS: E   **TYPE: M**   **KEY 1: F**   **KEY 2: 2**   **PAGE: 205, 217**

21. The idea of the republican mother argued that women were
    a. equal to men in the fight for liberty.
    b. the true educators of patriotism for their children.
    c. guaranteed the same property rights as men in American society.
    d. subordinate to men in all ways.
    e. required to fight in the military.

ANS: B   **TYPE: M**   **KEY 1: F**   **KEY 2: 1**   **PAGE: 218**

22. The only state to meet the original deadline for ratifying the Articles of Confederation was
    a. New York.
    b. Virginia.
    c. Rhode Island.
    d. Massachusetts.
    e. Georgia.

ANS: B   **TYPE: M**   **KEY 1: F**   **KEY 2: 3**   **PAGE: 204**

23. Admiral Richard Howe and General William Howe
    a. were French commanders who assisted General Washington at Yorktown.
    b. had the same last name but were not related.
    c. forced General Washington and the Continental Army out of New York City in the fall of 1776.
    d. had the smallest army in North America but still managed to hold on to Boston throughout the Revolutionary War.
    e. were spies for the British in the American army.

ANS: C   TYPE: M   KEY 1: F   KEY 2: 2   PAGE: 195

24. After the Battles of Trent and Princeton, the Continental Army was improved by
    a. increasing the term of enlistment to three years.
    b. instituting strict discipline and increasing the severity of punishment for misdeeds.
    c. introducing Prussian drill techniques and standards.
    d. offering cash bonuses and land bounties for those who reenlisted.
    e. all of the above.

ANS: E   TYPE: M   KEY 1: F   KEY 2: 2   PAGE: 197

25. During the American Revolution, Benjamin Franklin impressed the French by
    a. arguing loudly with anyone who opposed the American Revolution.
    b. wearing plain clothes and a fur hat and pretending to be a simple frontiersman.
    c. referring to his French ancestry.
    d. carefully following the strict rules of French etiquette.
    e. setting up a newspaper.

ANS: B   TYPE: M   KEY 1: A   KEY 2: 2   PAGE: 200

26. The state governments set up during the Revolution reflected the American belief in
    a. the British tradition of unwritten political precedents and customs.
    b. the necessity for a written constitution to define citizens' rights and to limit the government's power.
    c. the importance of a strong executive with compulsory powers.
    d. the division of political power between separate economic classes.
    e. the importance of strong courts to interpret the laws.

ANS: B   TYPE: M   KEY 1: A   KEY 2: 3   PAGE: 201

27. The central government under the Articles of Confederation raised money by
    a. enacting a national sales tax.
    b. passing import/export tariffs.
    c. attacking British merchant ships.
    d. imposing an income tax.
    e. requisitioning funds and printing currency.

ANS: E   TYPE: M   KEY 1: F   KEY 2: 2   PAGE: 204

28. The Articles of Confederation
    a. gave the central government complete and compulsive power over the states and the citizens.
    b. included an independent executive branch.
    c. never went into effect because it was never ratified.
    d. created a strong court system.
    e. created a central government that was weaker than the individual states.

ANS: E   TYPE: M   KEY 1: A   KEY 2: 3   PAGE: 204

29. Most loyalists
    a. strongly rejected the American ideals of liberty and self-government.
    b. remained neutral during the American Revolution.
    c. sided with England because it seemed less risky than supporting an untried American union.
    d. patriotically participated in the fight for American independence.
    e. joined the Indian tribes.

ANS: C   TYPE: M   KEY 1: A   KEY 2: 3   PAGE: 205

30. George Washington is best described as
    a. a dignified, determined leader who was often in despair because of his disorganized, under equipped army.
    b. the greatest field commander in U.S. history, who almost single-handedly won the American Revolution, wrote the Constitution, and created the United States.
    c. an inept military strategist who constantly had to rely on more-competent subordinate officers to plan battles and save troops from defeat.
    d. a devout Calvinist who led his men into battle with the cry "God is an American."
    e. a consistent supporter of the Revolutionary ideals of liberty and equality for all.

ANS: A   TYPE: M   KEY 1: F   KEY 2: 3   PAGE: 195-97

31. In the peace treaty that ended the American Revolution,
    a. New Englanders lost fishing rights off the Coast of Newfoundland.
    b. the English retained their forts in the Ohio territory.
    c. France acquired Florida.
    d. the Mississippi River was recognized as the western boundary of the United States.
    e. the Appalachian Mountains were recognized as the western boundary of the United States.

ANS: D   TYPE: M   KEY 1: F   KEY 2: 2   PAGE: 215

32. In the years after the end of the American Revolution, slavery
    a. was abolished in all the Northern states.
    b. became less important in the South because of the decline of the cotton culture.
    c. almost disappeared in the upper South.
    d. was strengthened in the Northern cities.
    e. remained the same as before the war.

ANS: A   TYPE: M   KEY 1: F   KEY 2: 3   PAGE: 217-18

33. One ongoing source of trouble between England and the United States after the revolution was
    a. the breakdown of trade between the two countries.
    b. England's support of Barbary Coast pirate attacks on U.S. shipping.
    c. disputes over fishing rights off the coast of Maine.
    d. England's occupation of forts in the U.S.-owned territory bordering the Great Lakes.
    e. The Americans' continuing efforts to take over Canada.

ANS: D   TYPE: M   KEY 1: F   KEY 2: 2   PAGE: 219-20

34. Shays's rebellion was significant because it
    a. convinced many conservatives that a stronger central government was necessary.
    b. led to state laws exempting farmland from foreclosure.
    c. was the only debtors' rebellion in U.S. history.
    d. destroyed the power of the "cosmopolitan" group in Massachusetts politics.
    e. marked the beginning of the labor movement in American history.

ANS: A   **TYPE: M**   **KEY 1: A**   **KEY 2: 3**   **PAGE: 223**

35. In the Virginia Plan, James Madison proposed
    a. that the president and senators serve lifetime terms of office.
    b. a two-house legislature with representation based on population.
    c. that all public officials be elected by popular vote.
    d. a one house legislature based on the principle of one state, one vote.
    e. separation of church and state.

ANS: B   **TYPE: M**   **KEY 1: F**   **KEY 2: 2**   **PAGE: 225-26**

36. The Connecticut or Great Compromise of the Constitution
    a. established the status of slaves for both taxation and representation purposes.
    b. was proposed by Alexander Hamilton.
    c. created the Bill of Rights.
    d. established a legislature with one house based on population and one house based on state equality.
    e. determined how slaves were to be counted.

ANS: D   **TYPE: M**   **KEY 1: F**   **KEY 2: 2**   **PAGE: 205**

37. The Constitution of 1787 provided that the president and vice president
    a. would be elected by popular vote.
    b. would be chosen by state legislatures.
    c. would be chosen by an electoral college.
    d. would be limited to two terms of office.
    e. would be elected by the House and Senate.

ANS: C   **TYPE: M**   **KEY 1: F**   **KEY 2: 1**   **PAGE: 226**

38. The central government created by the Constitution of 1787 had the power to
    a. tax.
    b. control foreign trade.
    c. pass and enforce laws.
    d. regulate interstate trade
    e. all of the above

ANS: E   **TYPE: M**   **KEY 1: F**   **KEY 2: 3**   **PAGE: 226**

39. The Constitution of 1787 was ratified by
    a. the unanimous consent of the state legislatures.
    b. a public referendum of adult white males.
    c. its acceptance by at least nine states in special conventions.
    d. the governors of three-fourths of the states.
    e. the Confederation Congress.

ANS: C   **TYPE: M**   **KEY 1: F**   **KEY 2: 2**   **PAGE: 226**

40. The most serious criticism of the Constitution during ratification was the
    a. establishment of a standing army.
    b. lack of a specific list of citizens' rights.
    c. absence of references to God.
    d. failure to designate a national capital.
    e. undemocratic nature of the electoral college.

ANS: B   TYPE: M   KEY 1: F   KEY 2: 2   PAGE: 227

41. The protection of state sovereignty included in the Articles of Confederation was the brainchild of
    a. North Carolina.
    b. South Carolina.
    c. Virginia.
    d. Georgia.
    e. Rhode Island.

ANS: A   TYPE: M   KEY 1: F   KEY 2: 3   PAGE: 204

42. When the British withdrew after the Revolution, _____ blacks went with them.
    a. 10,000
    b. 15,000
    c. 20,000
    d. 25,000
    e. none of the above

ANS: C   TYPE: M   KEY 1: F   KEY 2: 3   PAGE: 205

43. After the Revolution, _____ colonists left the states for other parts of the British Empire.
    a. 15,000 to 25,000
    b. 80,000 to 90,000
    c. 60,000 to 70,000
    d. 35,000 to 45,000
    e. none of the above

ANS: C   TYPE: M   KEY 1: F   KEY 2: 3   PAGE: 205

44. The first state to ratify the Constitution was
    a. Virginia.
    b. Delaware.
    c. Connecticut.
    d. Pennsylvania.
    e. Rhode Island.

ANS: B   TYPE: M   KEY 1: F   KEY 2: 2   PAGE: 227

45. British ally Joseph Brant was a
    a. Shawnee.
    b. Mohawk.
    c. Oneida.
    d. Cherokee.
    e. Apache

ANS: B   TYPE: M   KEY 1: F   KEY 2: 3   PAGE: 207

46. Shawnee and Delaware leaders who pursued friendly relations with the Americans but refused to fight other Indians included all of the following except
    a. Joseph Brant.
    b. White Eyes.
    c. Killbuck.
    d. Corn planter.
    e. none of the above

ANS: A   **TYPE: M**   **KEY 1: F**   **KEY 2: 3**   **PAGE: 206**

47. During the Revolution, Congress passed all of the following except
    a. "resolves."
    b. "orders."
    c. "laws."
    d. "ordinances."
    e. none of the above

ANS: C   **TYPE: M**   **KEY 1: F**   **KEY 2: 3**   **PAGE: 214**

48. The idea of proportional representation in one house and state equality in the other was proposed by
    a. New Hampshire.
    b. Rhode Island.
    c. Maryland.
    d. Connecticut.
    e. New York.

ANS: D   **TYPE: M**   **KEY 1: F**   **KEY 2: 2**   **PAGE: 226**

49. In contrast with those who enlisted in the Continental Army, militia troops tended to be
    a. loyal to the British.
    b. willing to sign up for longer periods of time.
    c. less likely to attend church.
    d. from the more economically secure ranks of their communities.
    e. those who could not find work anywhere else.

ANS: D   **TYPE: M**   **KEY: A**   **KEY 2: 3**   **PAGE: 197**

50. In his efforts to persuade the French to ally with the Americans, Benjamin Franklin
    a. threatened the use of military force against them.
    b. identified strongly with the aristocratic elements of French society.
    c. played the role of a innocent common man of nature.
    d. alienated most Frenchmen.
    e. learned to speak French.

ANS: C   **TYPE: M**   **KEY: A**   **KEY 2: 2**   **PAGE: 200**

TRUE/FALSE

_____ 1.   The French secretly aided the American rebellion through a fictitious corporation.

ANS: T   **TYPE: T**   **KEY 1: F**   **KEY 2: 2**   **PAGE: 199**

_____ 2.   Philadelphia's "Fort Wilson" riot was a violent confrontation between supporters and opponents of price controls.

ANS: T   **TYPE: T**   **KEY 1: F**   **KEY 2: 2**   **PAGE: 213**

_____ 3.   The Revolutionary War officially came to a close with the Treaty of Paris (1783).

ANS: T   **TYPE: T**   **KEY 1: F**   **KEY 2: 1**   **PAGE: 215**

_____ 4.   An attempted *coup d'etat* of Continental Army officers was averted by George Washington at Yorktown.

ANS: F   **TYPE: T**   **KEY 1: F**   **KEY 2: 3**   **PAGE: 216**

_____ 5.   The Northwest Ordinance (1787) prohibited slavery in the Northwest (Ohio) Territory.

ANS: T   **TYPE: T**   **KEY 1: F**   **KEY 2: 3**   **PAGE: 220-21**

_____ 6.   Ratification of the Constitution was a relatively easy and quick affair once the document had been written.

ANS: F   **TYPE: T**   **KEY 1: A**   **KEY 2: 2**   **PAGE: 227**

_____ 7.   In *Federalist #10*, James Madison argued for the greater stability of a large republic over a small one.

ANS: T   **TYPE: T**   **KEY 1: F**   **KEY 2: 1**   **PAGE: 227**

_____ 8.   The British victory at Saratoga convinced France to stay out of the American war for independence.

ANS: F   **TYPE: T**   **KEY 1: F**   **KEY 2: 1**   **PAGE: 200**

_____ 9.   The greatest opposition to the Northwest Ordinance of 1787 came from the South over the institution of slavery.

ANS: F   **TYPE: T**   **KEY 1: F**   **KEY 2: 2**   **PAGE: 220**

_____ 10.   Before 1787, most of the land in the Northwest Territory was purchased by independent settlers.

ANS: F   **TYPE: T**   **KEY 1: F**   **KEY 2: 2**   **PAGE: 220-21**

_____ 11.   Benedict Arnold attempted to undermine the revolutionary cause by betraying New York City to the British.

ANS: F   **TYPE: T**   **KEY 1: F**   **KEY 2: 2**   **PAGE: 211**

_____ 12.   Most Indians and slaves hoped that the colonies would be victorious in the Revolutionary War.

ANS: F   **TYPE: T**   **KEY 1: F**   **KEY 2: 2**   **PAGE: 205-07**

_____ 13.   American exports to Britain in 1784 were less than half the level of 1774.

ANS: T   **TYPE: T**   **KEY 1: T**   **KEY 2: 2**   **PAGE: 223**

_____ 14.   The Massachusetts constitution that was ratified in 1780 is still in effect and is the oldest constitution in the world.

ANS: T   **TYPE: T**   **KEY 1: F**   **KEY 2: 2**   **PAGE: 204**

_____ 15.   Loyalists were colonial patriots who loyally supported the Continental Army in the American Revolution.

ANS: F   **TYPE: T**   **KEY 1: F**   **KEY 1: 1**   **PAGE: 205**

_____ 16.   Southern delegates to Congress all opposed the Northwest Ordinance.

ANS: F   **TYPE: T**   **KEY 1: A**   **KEY 1: 2**   **PAGE: 220**

_____ 17.   The British never really had a chance to win a decisive military victory during the Revolution.

ANS: F   **TYPE: T**   **KEY 1: A**   **KEY 2: 2**   **PAGE: 195**

_____ 18.   The Revolutionary War demonstrated the weakness of Congress.

ANS: T   **TYPE: T**   **KEY 1: F**   **KEY 2: 1**   **PAGE: 195**

_____ 19.   George Washington's attack on Trenton resulted in substantial patriot losses.

ANS: F   **TYPE: T**   **KEY 1: F**   **KEY 2: 2**   **PAGE: 195**

_____ 20.   The Land Ordinance of 1785 required purchasers to buy an entire 6 mile square township.

ANS: F   **TYPE: T**   **KEY 1: A**   **KEY 2: 3**   **PAGE: 220**

_____ 21.   After the Battles of Trenton and Princeton, Congress promised a cash bonus to all soldiers who served for the duration of the conflict.

ANS: F   **TYPE: T**   **KEY 1: A**   **KEY 1: 2**   **PAGE: 197**

_____ 22.   French aid to the Americans during the Revolution was insignificant.

ANS: F   **TYPE: T**   **KEY 1: A**   **KEY 2: 1**   **PAGE: 200**

_____ 23.   In 1779, Spain signed a direct treaty of alliance with the United States.

ANS: F   **TYPE: T**   **KEY 1: F**   **KEY 2: 2**   **PAGE: 200-01**

_____ 24.   John Adams was horrified by the idea of a unicameral legislature.

ANS: T   **TYPE: T**   **KEY 1: F**   **KEY 2: 2**   **PAGE: 205**

_____ 25.   Most slaves who reached British units during the Revolution won their freedom.

ANS: T   TYPE: T   KEY 1: F   KEY 2: 2   PAGE: 205

_____ 26.   Massachusetts slave Elizabeth Freeman sued her master in 1781 and won her liberty.

ANS: T   TYPE: T   KEY 1: F   KEY 2: 2   PAGE: 217

_____ 27.   After 1778, political opposition in England to the war in America was nonexistent.

ANS: F   TYPE: T   KEY 1: F   KEY 1: 2   PAGE: 214-15

_____ 28.   By 1780, military leaders on both sides believed that events in Virginia would decide the war.

ANS: T   TYPE: T   KEY 1: F   KEY 2: 2   PAGE: 214

_____ 29.   Kentucky was heavily populated by Native Americans.

ANS: F   TYPE: T   KEY 1: F   KEY 2: 2   PAGE: 219

_____ 30.   The 1790 Federal Census reported that the population of Kentucky was about half of the population of Tennessee.

ANS: F   TYPE: T   KEY 1: F   KEY 2: 2   PAGE: 219

_____ 31.   Indians who had supported the Americans during the Revolution suffered the most from land seizures after 1783.

ANS: T   TYPE: T   KEY 1: A   KEY 2: 2   PAGE: 220

_____ 32.   When the first townships in Ohio were offered for sale in late 1787, there were few buyers.

ANS: T   TYPE: T   KEY 1: F   KEY 2: 2   PAGE: 221

_____ 33.   No southern state supported the 1786 treaty that John Jay negotiated with Spain.

ANS: T   TYPE: T   KEY 1: F   KEY 1: 1   PAGE: 225

_____ 34.   The Annapolis Conference was called to discuss revisions to the Articles of Confederation.

ANS: F   TYPE: T   KEY 1: A   KEY 2: 2   PAGE: 225

_____ 35.   Most Indians and slaves hoped that Britain would win the Revolution.

ANS: T   TYPE: T   KEY 1: F   KEY 2: 1   PAGE: 193

_____ 36.   During their winter at Valley Forge, George Washington's troops became much more soldierly.

ANS: T   TYPE: T   KEY 1: F   KEY 2: 3   PAGE: 198

_____ 37.   Little went right for the British after their victory at Fort Ticonderoga in June 1777.

ANS: T   TYPE: T   KEY 1: A   KEY 2: 2   PAGE: 197

_____ 38.   France declared war on England after the treaties with the United States were signed in early 1778.

ANS: F   TYPE: T   KEY 1: A   KEY 2: 3   PAGE: 200

_____ 39.   All Anglican churchmen supported the Revolution.

ANS: F   TYPE: T   KEY 1: F   KEY 2: 2   PAGE: 217

_____ 40.   Thomas Jefferson wrote _Thoughts on Government_ in 1776.

ANS: F   TYPE: T   KEY 1: F   KEY 2: 2   PAGE: 201

FILL-INS

1.   The commander of British troops at the Battle of Saratoga was John _____.

ANS: Burgoyne   TYPE: F   KEY 1: F   KEY 2: 2   PAGE: 198

2.   The _____ linked the American states together before the Constitution of 1787 was written.

ANS: Articles of Confederation   TYPE: F   KEY 1: F   KEY 2: 1   PAGE: 213

3.   _____ headed the Ohio Company.

ANS: Manassah Cutler   TYPE: F   KEY 1: F   KEY 2: 3   PAGE: 220

4.   The war for American independence was ended with the Treaty of _____.

ANS: Paris   TYPE: F   KEY 1: F   KEY 2: 2   PAGE: 215

5.   The last state to ratify the Articles of Confederation was _____.

ANS: Maryland   TYPE: F   KEY 1: F   KEY 2: 2   PAGE: 204

6.   _____ closed the Mississippi River to travel in 1784.

ANS: Spain   TYPE: F   KEY 1: F   KEY 2: 2   PAGE: 220

7.   The only state that refused to send delegates to the Constitutional Convention of 1787 was _____.

ANS: Rhode Island   TYPE: F   KEY 1: F   KEY 2: 1   PAGE: 225

8.   The _____ compromise of the Constitution established the ratio for counting slaves for the purposes of taxation and representation.

ANS: three–fifths   TYPE: F   KEY 1: F   KEY 2: 2   PAGE: 226

9. The supporters of the Constitution of 1787 during the ratification process were called
    _____.

ANS: Federalists   **TYPE: F**   **KEY 1: F**   **KEY 2: 2**   **PAGE: 227**

10. George Washington refused to accept a letter from brothers William and Richard Howe about
    discussing peace terms in the summer of 1776 because it did not address him as _____.

ANS: general   **TYPE: F**   **KEY 1: F**   **KEY 2: 3**   **PAGE: 195**

11. Congress never came close to raising the _____ men it had hoped for.

ANS: 75,000   **TYPE: F**   **KEY 1: F**   **KEY 2: 2**   **PAGE: 197**

12. _____ headed the series of Spanish missions in California.

ANS: Junípero Serra   **TYPE: F**   **KEY 1: F**   **KEY 2: 2**   **PAGE: 200**

13. In June 1776, _____ became the first state to adopt a permanent, republican constitution.

ANS: Virginia   **TYPE: F**   **KEY 1: F**   **KEY 2: 2**   **PAGE: 197**

14. The only Indians in the Deep South to fight on the American side during the Revolution were the
    _____.

ANS: Catawbas   **TYPE: F**   **KEY 1: F**   **KEY 2: 3**   **PAGE: 206**

15. Philadelphia merchant _____ helped to organize the Bank of North America.

ANS: Robert Morris   **TYPE: F**   **KEY 1: F**   **KEY 2: 2**   **PAGE: 213**

16. The American victory at _____ brought down the British government.

ANS: Yorktown   **TYPE: F**   **KEY 1: F**   **KEY 2: 2**   **PAGE: 214**

17. _____ authored Virginia's Statute on Religious Freedom.

ANS: Thomas Jefferson **TYPE: F**   **KEY 1: F**   **KEY 2: 2**   **PAGE: 217**

18. _____ of Maryland was the first Roman Catholic bishop in the United States.

ANS: John Carroll   **TYPE: F**   **KEY 1: F**   **KEY 2: 2**   **PAGE: 217**

19. In the 1780s, the Church of England in the United States reorganized itself as the Protestant
    _____ Church.

ANS: Episcopal   **TYPE: F**   **KEY 1: F**   **KEY 2: 2**   **PAGE: 217**

20. _____ presided over the Constitutional Convention.

ANS: George Washington   **TYPE: F**   **KEY 1: F**   **KEY 2: 2**   **PAGE: 225**

21. The Tennessee settlers who seceded from North Carolina called their separate state
_____.

ANS: Franklin　　　**TYPE: F**　　　**KEY 1: F**　　　**KEY 2: 3**　　　**PAGE: 220**

22. _____ drafted the large state plan discussed at the Constitutional Convention.

ANS: James Madison　　**TYPE: F**　　**KEY 1: F**　　**KEY 2: 2**　　**PAGE: 225-26**

23. _____ drafted the state of Virginia's declaration of rights.

ANS: George Mason　　**TYPE: F**　　**KEY 1: F**　　**KEY 2: 3**　　**PAGE: 202**

24. The British believed that the _____ was the most likely recruiting ground for armed
loyalists.

ANS: Deep South　　**TYPE: F**　　**KEY 1: A**　　**KEY 2: 3**　　**PAGE: 205**

25. During the Revolution, about _____ percent of slaves fled their owners.

ANS: 10　　　**TYPE: F**　　　**KEY 1: F**　　　**KEY 2: 1**　　　**PAGE: 205**

26. Virginia's _____ thwarted an attempted all-out Indian offensive along the frontier with
his capture of Vincennes.

ANS: George Rogers Clark　　**TYPE: F**　　**KEY 1: F**　　**KEY 2: 2**　　**PAGE: 207**

27. _____ enacted the modern world's first gradual emancipation statute in 1780.

ANS: Pennsylvania　　**TYPE: F**　　**KEY 1: F**　　**KEY 2: 3**　　**PAGE: 218**

28. The _____ state constitution of 1776 allowed women to vote if they headed a household
and paid taxes.

ANS: New Jersey　　**TYPE: F**　　**KEY 1: F**　　**KEY 2: 3**　　**PAGE: 218**

29. By _____, nearly all native-born women in the northeast had become literate.

ANS: 1830　　　**TYPE: F**　　　**KEY 1: F**　　　**KEY 2: 3**　　　**PAGE: 218**

30. After their defeat in 1776, _____ ceded a large tract of land in Tennessee.

ANS: Cherokees　　**TYPE: F**　　**KEY 1: F**　　**KEY 2: 2**　　**PAGE: 219**

IDENTIFICATIONS

1. Charles Lord Cornwallis: British commander of the 1780–81 southern campaign that ended in defeat
at Yorktown.

2. Statute for Religious Freedom (1786): written by Thomas Jefferson. Argued for the disestablishment
of the Anglican Church as the official church of Virginia and affirmed religious liberty for all citizens.

3. Daniel Boone: North Carolina hunter who led the settlement of Kentucky. Created the Wilderness
Road through the Appalachian Mountains.

4. **Shays's Rebellion**: large-scale, unsuccessful rural revolt in early 1787 in western Massachusetts. Led by debtor farmers against commercial forces located in the eastern part of the state. Convinced many gentlemen and artisans of the need for a strong central government.

5. **New Jersey Plan**: proposed by William Paterson at the Constitutional Convention. Called for equal representation among all the states in Congress.

6. **Benedict Arnold**: Revolutionary War hero of battles of Quebec and Saratoga. Disgruntled because he felt his bravery was not rewarded. Plotted to turn over West Point to the English in return for money. When his plot was exposed, he escaped and became a British general.

7. **Robert Morris**: merchant from Philadelphia. Appointed as the first secretary of finance under the Articles of Confederation. Set up the first Bank of North America. Helped equip the Continental Army.

8. *The Federalist:* a series of eighty-five newspaper articles, later published in pamphlet form, written by Alexander Hamilton, James Madison, and John Jay. Explained each provision of the Constitution. Helped convince people to support ratification.

9. **Gnadenhutten massacre**: 1782 slaughter of 100 Moravian mission Indians in Ohio by Americans. Nearly all were women and children who knelt in prayer as they were murdered. Led Indians to resume selective ritual torture of prisoners. When known leaders of the massacre were captured, they were burned alive.

10. **Land Ordinance of 1785**: authorized the survey of the Northwest Territory into townships 6 miles square. Land would be sold at auction, with bids starting at one dollar an acre.

SHORT ESSAYS

1. Describe the role of loyalists in the American Revolution.

Answer: Loyalists occupied a confused and, at times, contradictory role in British strategy during the American Revolution. Always overestimated in size by British policymakers, loyalists never made up more than one-sixth of the white population. At the beginning of the war, loyalists enjoyed little or no role in British strategy. They felt safe pledging their allegiance to the king in those areas not controlled by rebel leaders. Throughout 1775 and 1776, with little or no support from the crown, many loyalists were forced to relocate (from the Mohawk Valley and western New Jersey, for example). In 1776, with the large British force under Sir William Howe in possession of New York City, loyalists in the middle states were persuaded by the British to express their loyalty to the crown openly. Loyalists were left to their own devices, however, when British forces left New Jersey.

   Not until 1777 and 1778 did the British realize that loyalists could be valuable in the military arena. Indeed, in the final stage of the war in the South, loyalists were an integral part of the British military machine. About 1,900 loyalists took up arms during the war, and many of these saw fighting in the South. The British believed that a majority of southerners were loyalists, and this would help the crown in its attempt to "win the hearts and minds" of the southern population. The loyalists were not that powerful, however, and still were left exposed at crucial points by the British government. Ultimately, British policymakers never fully constructed an effective role for the "loyal Americans," certainly a factor in their final defeat.

2. Compare and contrast the Virginia and New Jersey Plans that were debated at the Constitutional Convention.

Answer: Both the Virginia and New Jersey Plans were attempts at governmental organization and were promoted by various supporters at the Philadelphia convention. Both plans were attempts to restructure the old Confederation government that, most agreed, was ineffective. The Virginia Plan put forward by Edmund Randolph proposed a bicameral legislature, with both houses apportioned according to population, which would choose the national executive and the national judiciary. Several of the smaller states, alarmed at the power being granted to the larger states, responded with the New Jersey Plan.

The work of William Paterson, the New Jersey Plan proposed to strengthen the existing Congress with the power to regulate trade and impose some taxes. Unlike Randolph's plan, the New Jersey Plan retained state equality in Congress. The small states claimed they would bolt the convention before they would approve a document based on the Virginia model. Ultimately, the "Connecticut Compromise" called for state equality in the upper house and proportional representation in the lower, and was agreed to by both factions.

3.   Explore the implications of the American Revolution for black Americans.

Answer: The war had mixed results for African Americans. Although many thousands achieved emancipation from the institution of slavery, nowhere did African Americans achieve equality of opportunity. Many slaves were offered their freedom by invading British armies. Thousands of others fought for the Continental Army in order to achieve emancipation. Ultimately, the northern states, following the lead of Pennsylvania, put into motion the framework for the abolition of slavery in the North.

The South, however, did not end the institution of slavery. Although certain religious groups advocated abolition, as a rule, southern states supported the strengthening of slavery. Indeed, on balance, although the ideology of the Revolution promoted the idea of abolition, there was little room for equal opportunity. The policy of gradual emancipation guaranteed that black men, when they became adults, could not possess the same economic resources that most white men enjoyed.

4.   Describe the failure of the British military strategy in the war for American independence.

Answer: Part of the problem with British military strategy lay, of course, in the great distance between Britain and its colonies. Attempts to devise tactics and strategy several thousand miles and two months' journey from the battlefield took its toll. In addition, those controlling the war effort knew too little about the political atmosphere of the colonies and were often under the false assumption that many loyalists were ready to spring into action to assist British armies.

Equally important to the British failure was the inability of the armies and their commanders to coordinate their activities effectively. The best example of this, of course, was William Howe's failure to come to the aid of General John Burgoyne at Saratoga. Finally, even under the best of circumstances, British victory may have been impossible. Even if the British had been successful militarily, it was overly ambitious of the British to expect to fully pacify the North American continent and make the colonists loyal subjects once again.

5.   Describe the internal civil war that commenced with the beginning of hostilities in 1775.

Answer: Although in popular imagery and memory the Revolutionary War is seen as a battle between George Washington's Continental Army and British "redcoats," a far deeper internal struggle often manifested itself during the fighting. New England, the site of the war's beginning, had relatively few vocal Tories, but the middle and southern colonies had many more men and women (from all social strata) who maintained their loyalty to the crown. Loyalists, poorly employed by the British at the beginning of the war, were increasingly important in the western campaigns (most notably the Mohawk Valley) and in the South.

One of the most vicious of the "civil wars" took place in New York's Mohawk River Valley. There, loyalists who had fled the region at the war's beginning invaded the valley in 1777 and engaged in brutal warfare with their own former neighbors. The siege of Fort Stanwix and the Battle of Oriskany were fought primarily between Americans. The same was true of the civil war in the Carolina backcountry, where loyalists under Banastre Tarleton regularly engaged in vicious combat with rebel troops led by Thomas Sumter and Francis Marion. Atrocities abounded in these campaigns, far worse than those between regular army units.

6.   Examine the provisions and significance of the Northwest Ordinance of 1787.

Answer: The Confederation Congress did not have the authority to pass and enforce laws that were binding on the states but it could legislate for the territories. In order to convince Maryland to ratify the Articles, Virginia and other states ceded their western land claims to the central government. In 1784, Thomas Jefferson drew up a resolution that would have organized and prepared the territories for eventual statehood, but his ideas were not accepted by the original states. The following year, Congress passed a land ordinance that established a process for surveying the territories, establishing townships, and auctioning land in the Northwest.

In 1787, the issue of western land claims was revisited by members of both Congress and the Constitutional Convention. Revolutionary War veterans from Massachusetts organized the Ohio Company, and New York land speculators set up the Scioto Company to develop the Northwest. Both groups appealed to Congress for grants of millions of acres of land. The Confederation Congress responded by passing the Northwest Ordinance of 1787. The Northwest Ordinance established a three-step process through which the territories would be organized, gradually introduced to self-government, and eventually admitted to the union as full and equal members of the body politic. The area would be divided into from three to five territories in which slavery was prohibited. Inhabitants of the new territories would have civil rights and public schools. When the population of the territory was below 5,000 the governor and council would be chosen by Congress; in the next stage the inhabitants would elect a legislature; and finally, when the population grew to 60,000, the territory could draw up a constitution and request admission as a state. This policy established a coherent system that was followed as the United States continued to expand its borders westward. The ordinance also outlawed slavery in the Northwest Territory and provided for education in the various localities that would be carved from it.

7.   Describe John Adams's ideas regarding the separation of powers.

Answer: John Adams disagreed with Thomas Paine's assertion that a one-house assembly was the best repository of the sovereignty of the people. He also questioned the British view of the superiority of a "mixed and balanced" constitution that reflected the nation's economic and social stratification. Adams wrote *Thoughts on Government* in which he examined the concept of separation of powers. Adams advocated a three-branch government with provisions that checked the possible abuse of power by any one branch. He suggested an executive with the power to veto legislation, a two-house legislature, and an independent judiciary. Each branch would balance and counteract the excesses of the others.

In Adams's opinion, the government was responsible for promoting the happiness of the citizens. He believed that patriotism and public/private virtue were the foundations of a republican system. The British policy of separating the social orders into a House of Lords and a House of Commons was impossible and undemocratic in a nation of commoners such as the United States. Instead, Adams believed, a more complex system that mirrored the diversity of American society was needed. The discussion of these ideas provided the impetus for state constitutional conventions that established strong state legislatures during the American Revolution.

LONG ESSAYS

1.   Examine the British strategy of 1776 and 1777 that attempted to bring the war to a close. Why did this strategy fail?

Answer: Essay should address several key points:

A.   Howe brothers (William and Richard) and large British armada arrive in New York City
      1.   Attempt to wear down Washington's army
            a.   Best chance for British to win the war
            b.   Size and capabilities of British forces
      2.   Peace offerings to Continental Congress
            a.   Attempt to convince Congress to surrender
            b.   Full pardons offered
B.   Campaign for New York City
      1.   Battles for Long Island, Manhattan, White Plains, and Brooklyn

2.   Washington defeated, but escapes
3.   Washington's Trenton-Princeton campaign leads to evacuation of New Jersey
C.   Burgoyne and Saratoga campaign
1.   Failure of Howe to reinforce Burgoyne
2.   Communications problems inherent in the war
3.   Defeat of Burgoyne at Saratoga
D.   Reasons for British failure
1.   Sympathetic leanings of Howes
a.   Howe brothers both suspected of some sympathy toward American cause (why they were given command)
b.   Results
2.   Jealousies among commanding officers
3.   Logistical problems
a.   Conflicting strategy
b.   Consequences

2.   Describe the major debates and points of tension at the Constitutional Convention in 1787.

Answer: Essay should address several key points:

A.   Desires and goal of large states' representatives
1.   Edmund Randolph and Virginia Plan
a.   Bicameral legislature apportioned by population
b.   No mention of taxation and trade regulation
2.   William Paterson and New Jersey Plan
a.   Continuance of the existing Congress by granting it the power to levy imposts
b.   Regulate trade and commerce
c.   Retain state equality in Congress
3.   Connecticut Compromise
a.   State equality in one house
b.   Proportional representation in the second

3.   Explore the implications of the American Revolution for both women and black Americans.

Answer: Essay should address several key points:

A.   Implications for women
1.   Women gain added authority
a.   Gain control of household while males are away at war
b.   Few changes in practices of coverture and divorce
c.   Literacy
2.   Republican motherhood
a.   Women given expanded educational role within the household
b.   Women became the inculcators of virtue and patriotism of their husbands and sons
B.   Implications for black Americans
1.   British offer freedom to blacks who fight for the crown
a.   Many blacks use the war to emancipate themselves
b.   Consequences
2.   Ideology of the Revolution encourages abolition
a.   Pennsylvania and northern states lead path to emancipation
b.   Debates begin in southern states, but planters resistant to abolition
c.   On balance, Revolution ended slavery in the North, and in the South, reforms to humanize the institution were encouraged.

4.   Discuss the Confederation era and analyze the state constitutions and the government created by
        the Articles of Confederation. How did the central government deal with the major issues of the
        period?

Answer: Essay should address certain key points:

A.   State constitutions
        1.   Areas of agreement
                a.   Importance of written constitution
                b.   Reliance on popular sovereignty
        2.   Models for state governments
                a.   Virginia constitution
                b.   Pennsylvania constitution
                c.   Massachusetts constitution
B.   Articles of Confederation
        1.   Basic provisions
                a.   Representation
                b.   Taxes and trade
                c.   Monetary policy
                d.   State powers

        2.   Ratification
                a.   Land claims and disputes
                b.   Maryland and Virginia compromise
C.   Major problems
        1.   Discontent in the army
                a.   Mutiny in Pennsylvania
                b.   "Fort Wilson" riot
                c.   Congressional reforms
        2.   Legislative issues
                a.   Amendments require unanimous state approval
                b.   No power to pass or enforce laws
        3.   Western land policies
                a.   Expansion into Kentucky and Tennessee
                b.   Conflict with Indians and Spanish
                c.   Northwest Ordinance of 1787
        4.   Monetary problems
                a.   Trade imbalance with England
                b.   Paying the nation's debts
                c.   Shays's Rebellion

CHAPTER 7
THE DEMOCRATIC REPUBLIC, 1790–1820

CHAPTER OUTLINE

I.   The Farmer's Republic
   A.   Households
   B.   Rural Industry
   C.   Neighbors
   D.   Inheritance
   E.   Standards of Living

II. From Backcountry to Frontier
   A.   The Destruction of the Woodlands Indians
   B.   The Failure of Cultural Renewal
   C.   The Backcountry, 1790-1815

III. The Plantation South, 1790-1820
   A.   Slavery and the Republic
   B.   The Recommitment to Slavery
   C.   Race, Gender, and Chesapeake Labor
   D.   The Lowland Task System

IV. The Seaport Cities, 1790-1815
   A.   Commerce
   B.   Poverty
   C.   The Status of Labor

V.   The Withering of Patriarchal Authority
   A.   Paternal Power in Decline
   B.   The Alcoholic Republic
   C.   The Democratization of Print
   D.   Citizenship

VI. Republican Religion
   A.   The Decline of the Established Church
   B.   The Rise of the Democratic Sects
   C.   The Christianization of the White South
   D.   Evangelicals and Slavery
   E.   The Beginnings of African American Christianity
   F.   Black Republicanism: Gabriel's Rebellion

VII. Conclusion

CHRONOLOGY

1782	Crevecoeur publishes his *Letters of an American Farmer*.
1789	National government commences under the Constitution.
1791	Vermont becomes the fourteenth state.
1792	Kentucky becomes the fifteenth state.
1793	Eli Whitney invents the cotton gin.
	Anglo–French War begins.
1794	Anthony Wayne's Third Army is victorious at Fallen Timbers.
1795	Treaty of Greenville signed.
1796	Tennessee becomes the sixteenth state.
1799	Successful slave revolution in Saint Dominique.
1800	Gabriel's Rebellion in Virginia.
1801	First camp meeting at Cane Ridge, Kentucky.
1803	Jefferson purchases Louisiana from France.
	Ohio becomes the seventeenth state of the Union.

1805	Tenskwatawa's first vision.
1811	Battle of Tippecanoe.
1812	War of 1812 commences.

THEMATIC TOPICS FOR ENRICHMENT

1. Define the term *competence*. Explain how the goal of competence was distinct from the more contemporary goal of "getting rich."

2. What were the basic beliefs of "agrarian republicanism"? Why was the ownership of property so important in the republican theory?

3. How did the rise of markets change the lives of various Americans from farmers and artisans to frontiersmen and slaves?

4. What were the major factors in the destruction of the Woodlands Indians? Why did "many Indian societies sink into despair"?

5. What was meant by the epithet "our white savages"? Who might call a frontiersman by such a name?

6. In what ways did slaves' lives change in the years after American independence?

7. Why might the first decades of the nineteenth century be called the "alcoholic republic"?

8. In what ways did the admission of new states change the meaning of citizenship and suffrage?

SUGGESTED ESSAY TOPICS

1. In what ways did the American economy diversify during the first decades of the early republic? Discuss the impact of diversification on the economy of the different regions of the nation.

2. Explain the importance of gender roles in a patriarchal society. How did the role of women and men change in the course of the early republic? How did paternal authority decline? How did it retain or increase its strength?

3. In the years after the American Revolution, the country seemed to go in two opposite directions on the issue of slavery. Why did some sections of the country "recommit to slavery," while other regions gradually terminated the institution altogether? Why did Methodists fail in their attempts to spread John Wesley's message that slavery transgressed "all the laws of Justice, Mercy and Truth"?

LECTURE OUTLINE

1. The United States at the turn of the nineteenth century was a farmer's republic, composed of a rural people whose lives revolved around community and family. Few Americans lived in metropolitan areas or regularly engaged in market relations.

    a. **Households** were more than just the primary social unit, as most production, even that for overseas markets was done within the household economy with a gender division of labor.

    b. Most manufacturing was part of what was called the **rural industry,** such as shoe making, quilting, and carpentry, and served as part-time work that supported traditional paternal authority.

    c. **Neighbors** proved especially important as sources of information, exchange, and assistance, as people might not travel much beyond their village in their entire lifetime.

d.   Children still gained the wealth of their parents through **inheritance,** but the institution underwent dramatic changes in the early years of the new republic.

e.   Rising **standards of living** materially improved the lives of many Americans, while also parity between rich and poor.

2.   Americans flooded out of the East, continuing a constant emigration from backcountry to frontier that would last at least a century.

a.   The eventual eviction of the British from the continent, combined with Americans' insatiable appetite for western lands, virtually guaranteed the **destruction of the Woodlands Indians** in only a few decades at the end of the eighteenth and beginning of the nineteenth century.

(SHOW TRANSPARENCY 44: NATIVE AMERICA, 1783–1819)

b.   Despite the efforts of the likes of Alexander McGillivray, Tecumseh, and the Prophet to articulate some form of Indian **cultural renewal,** Indians could secure no real modus vivendi with the American nation.

c.   While remaining an area largely beyond effective government and organized institutions, the **backcountry** was transformed by the flood of western settlers from 1790 to 1815.

(SHOW TRANSPARENCY 45: POPULATION DENSITY, 1790–1820)

3.   The plantation South underwent a similar transformation as new settlers and new crops—cotton in particular—changed the character of much of the region from 1790 to 1820.

a.   Despite the first emancipation, **slavery** became increasingly enmeshed in the life of the nation south of the Mason–Dixon Line in the first decades of the nineteenth century.

b.   The upper and lower South made a particularly strong, if unpremeditated, **recommitment to slavery,** particularly after the development of the cotton gin.

(SHOW TRANSPARENCY 46: DISTRIBUTION OF SLAVE POPULATION, 1790–1820)

c.   Nowhere were the issues of **race, gender, and labor** more contested than in the Chesapeake, where the economic transition from tobacco to grain altered many social institutions.

d.   The areas of the Deep South where rice and indigo were the primary staples developed a **lowland task system** of slave labor in which slaves gained a significant amount of autonomy as well as separation from white masters.

4.   Seaport cities grew incredibly swiftly in the years 1790–1815, at the beginning of which only six percent of Americans lived in areas with a population over twenty-five hundred.

a.   **Commerce,** particularly the trafficking in foodstuffs, fueled the steady growth of the urban centers of the Atlantic seaboard.

b.   **Poverty** was more visible in cities, where slums emerged as the self-contained neighborhood of a growing indigent population.

c.   The **status of labor** changed with the decline of the unique position of artisans, some of whom became owners, but far more joined the growing pool of unskilled laborers, further undermining the idea of an independent patriarchy.

5. The assault on authority and the concomitant decline of deference were the characteristic features of the rise of a democratic society, as well as the result of the stratification of the American social structure.

   a. Many contemporaries believed they were witnessing the declension of **paternal** power; relied less on parents for inheritance or marriage choices, and the entire country seemed to celebrate youth.

   b. Americans drank such a high volume of intoxicating beverages that some have called the period the **alcoholic republic.**

   c. Continuing a trend that had commenced in the eighteenth century, the **democratization of print** in the early republic was unmistakable, particularly the rise of literacy and the proliferation of newspapers.

   d. **Citizenship** remained the province of white males but expanded greatly to include virtually all white men, especially in the new western states.

6. Americans embraced a form of republican religion that in many ways reflected the democratization of the polity.

   a. The most important feature of republican religion was the decline of tax-supported **established churches,** with only Massachusetts holding out until 1833.

   b. The **rise of the democratic sects,** Baptists and Methodists especially, reflected Americans' desire to have as much choice and freedom in religion as in other walks of life.

   (SHOW TRANSPARENCY 47: GROWTH OF AMERICAN METHODISM, 1775–1850)

   c. The **Christianization of the white South** featured great camp revivals and the simultaneous growth of black and white denominations of Baptists, Methodists, and others.

   d. **Evangelicals and slavery** maintained a tenuous relationship, with evangelicals ultimately remaining subservient to the economic interests of the plantation South.

   e. The first decades of the nineteenth century witnessed the beginnings of **African-American Christianity** and religious institutions in which blacks maintained autonomy from the dominant white society.

   f. **Gabriel's Rebellion** was brutally subdued in the summer of 1800, but nonetheless expressed a unique version of **black republicanism.**

Conclusion: The Americans who celebrated the beginning of national government in the 1790s were overwhelmingly a rural people. Yet, these same folks comprised a nation in the midst of many changes that would usher in a more individualistic, acquisitive republic in the years to come. Transformations in the cultural life of the country clearly reflected the economic ferment of the period.

TEACHING RESOURCES

Lewis and Clark: The Journey of the Corps of Discovery is Ken Burns's rendition of the most famous American expedition of the nineteenth century. PBS Video (120 minutes each).

A Few Men Well-Conducted: The George Rogers Clark Story tells the epic story of courage on the frontier and the trek into the Kentucky and Illinois backcountry in the era of the American Revolution. Filmic Archives (23 minutes).

Settling the Old Northwest details the dynamics of settlement and socialization in the lands between the Ohio and Mississippi Rivers. Filmic Archives (18 minutes).

Thomas Jefferson: The Pursuit of Liberty attempts to give a balanced portrait of the man and his ideas. It explores the complex life of the man who simultaneously held slaves and authored the Declaration of Independence. Thomas Jefferson Memorial Foundation Video (38 minutes).

Awakening Land, based on the Conrad Richter trilogy, details the story of life on the Ohio frontier. PBS Video (108 minutes).

A Midwife's Tale, based on the Pulitzer Prize winning book by historian Laurel Thatcher Ulrich, documents the life of Maine farm woman and midwife Martha Ballard during the late eighteenth and early nineteenth century. PBS Video (88 minutes).

MULTIPLE CHOICE

1. The U.S. Army general who defeated the Indians at the Battle of Fallen Timbers was
   a. George Washington.
   b. Josiah Harmar.
   c. Anthony Wayne.
   d. Arthur St. Clair.
   e. Nathaniel Greene.

ANS: C   **TYPE: M**   **KEY l: F**   **KEY 2: 1**   **PAGE: 238**

2. The Indian leader whose forces were badly beaten at the Battle of Tippecanoe was
   a. Tenskwatawa.
   b. John Ross.
   c. Geronimo.
   d. Alexander McGillivray.
   e. Joseph Brant.

ANS: A   **TYPE: M**   **KEY 1: F**   **KEY 2: 1**   **PAGE: 240**

3. In 1790, the future of slavery in the Chesapeake seemed to be
   a. very bright.
   b. uncertain.
   c. very poor.
   d. unchanged from the time prior to the war.
   e. none of the above.

ANS: B   **TYPE: M**   **KEY 1: A**   **KEY 2: 1**   **PAGE: 243**

4. The inventor of the cotton gin was
   a. Eli Whitney.
   b. Samuel Slater.
   c. Richard Arkwright.
   d. Benjamin Franklin.
   e. Thomas Edison

ANS: A   **TYPE: M**   **KEY 1: F**   **KEY 2: 1**   **PAGE: 244**

5. The cotton gin resulted in
   a. the death of slavery.
   b. a slight increase in slavery.
   c. the rejuvenation of slavery.
   d. no noticeable increase in slavery.
   e. the extension of slavery to the North.

ANS: C   TYPE: M   KEY 1: A   KEY 2: 2   PAGE: 244

6. During the period from 1790 to 1840, artisans were losing their independent status; most became
   a. master craftsmen.
   b. wage laborers.
   c. merchants.
   d. farmers.
   e. soldiers.

ANS: B   TYPE: M   KEY 1: F   KEY 2: 1   PAGE: 249

7. In the late eighteenth century, _____ percent of first-child births occurred within eight months of marriage.
   a. 10
   b. 25
   c. 40
   d. 50
   e. none of the above

ANS: B   TYPE: M   KEY 1: F   KEY 2: 2   PAGE: 251

8. All of the following are true statements about the relationship between slaves and the southern religious revival except
   a. the revivalists welcomed slaves and free blacks into their meetings.
   b. slaves and free blacks were never recruited to serve as preachers.
   c. some itinerant preachers met with slaves in their quarters.
   d. slaves and free blacks were most likely to join the Methodist or Baptist denominations.
   e. Methodists threatened to excommunicate slaveholders who failed to emancipate their slaves.

ANS: B   TYPE: M   KEY 1: F   KEY 2: 2   PAGE: 257-58

9. The "national drink" of the early republic was
   a. cider.
   b. whiskey.
   c. rum.
   d. milk.
   e. lemonade.

ANS: B   TYPE: M   KEY 1: F   KEY 2: 1   PAGE: 251

10. The first best-selling novel in the United States was
    a. *The Grapes of Wrath*.
    b. *The Power of Sympathy*.
    c. *Uncle Tom's Cabin*.
    d. *A New Home*.
    e. *Lassie Come Home*.

ANS: B   TYPE: M   KEY 1: F   KEY 2: 2   PAGE: 253

11. The most widely distributed publications in early nineteenth-century America were
    a. books.
    b. magazines.
    c. newspapers.
    d. religious tracts.
    e. children's stories.

ANS: C   TYPE: M   KEY 1: F   KEY 2: 2   PAGE: 253

12. During the early nineteenth century, the franchise
    a. broadened.
    b. remained the same.
    c. decreased.
    d. was extended to blacks and women.
    e. none of the above

ANS: A   TYPE: M   KEY 1: F   KEY 2: 2   PAGE: 253

13. The state that first gave the franchise to women was
    a. New York.
    b. Massachusetts.
    c. New Jersey.
    d. New Hampshire.
    e. Maine.

ANS: C   TYPE: M   KEY 1: F   KEY 2: 2   PAGE: 254

14. Which of the following churches would be most likely to employ camp-meeting revivalism?
    a. Episcopal
    b. Methodist
    c. Congregational
    d. Roman Catholic
    e. Jewish

ANS: B   TYPE: M   KEY 1: A   KEY 2: 1   PAGE: 255

15. The fastest-growing churches during the early nineteenth century were
    a. Roman Catholic and Lutheran.
    b. Episcopal and Presbyterian.
    c. Baptist and Methodist.
    d. Congregational and Dutch Reformed.
    e. Lutheran and Episcopal.

ANS: C   TYPE: M   KEY 1: F   KEY 2: 1   PAGE: 255

16. The dominant religion of the white South was
    a. conservative Congregationalism.
    b. restrained Protestantism.
    c. evangelical Protestantism.
    d. conservative Anglicanism.
    e. none of the above.

ANS: C   TYPE: M   KEY 1: F   KEY 2: 2   PAGE: 256

17. After 1820, _____ southern evangelists demanded the end of slavery.
    a. few
    b. many
    c. most
    d. leading
    e. no

ANS: A   TYPE: M   KEY 1: F   KEY 2: 2   PAGE: 258

18. Thousands of slaves embraced Christianity for the first time in the years
    a. 1660–1700.
    b. 1700–1740.
    c. 1740–1780.
    d. 1780–1820.
    e. none of the above

ANS: D   TYPE: M   KEY 1: F   KEY 2: 2   PAGE: 258

19. Which of the following is not true concerning alcohol consumption in the early republic?
    a. Men drank more than women.
    b. Farmers drank more than city dwellers.
    c. Southerners drank more than northerners.
    d. Westerners drank more than easterners.
    e. Alcohol consumption was the highest that it has ever been.

ANS: B   TYPE: M   KEY 1: F   KEY 2: 2   PAGE: 251

20. Which of the following is not true of the religious changes that engulfed the United States between 1790 and 1820?
    a. There was a vast increase in the variety of churches on the American landscape.
    b. The Bible was still relied upon as the one source of religious knowledge.
    c. Crisis conversion came to be viewed as a necessary credential for preachers.
    d. There was a general acceptance of the need for a formally authorized clergy.
    e. The fastest growing sects shared a democratic style.

ANS: D   TYPE: M   KEY 1: A   KEY 2: 2   PAGE: 255

21. The rebel leader Gabriel hoped that his rebellion against Virginia merchants would become primarily
    a. a slave revolt.
    b. a republican revolt.
    c. a religious uprising
    d. an Indian war
    e. all of the above.

ANS: B   TYPE: M   KEY 1: F   KEY 2: 2   PAGE: 259

22. The first of the Caribbean islands to defeat Napoleon's armies and achieve its independence was
    a. Saint Dominque.
    b. the Dominican Republic.
    c. Costa Rica.
    d. Trinidad.
    e. Cuba.

ANS: A   TYPE: M   KEY 1: F   KEY 2: 2   PAGE: 259

23. When the Constitution went into effect in 1789, most Americans
    a. lived west of the Appalachian Mountains.
    b. were still loyal to the British.
    c. were employed as sailors, fishermen, or industrial workers.
    d. were high school graduates.
    e. were rural farmers and property owners.

    ANS: E   TYPE: M   KEY 1: F   KEY 2: 2   PAGE: 231

24. Which of the following was true of industrial development in the early constitutional era?
    a. There was none.
    b. A majority of northern men were industrial workers.
    c. Poor women and children did outwork on a part-time basis.
    d. In families where women worked, the authority of the husband or father was undermined.
    e. most workers belonged to a labor union.

    ANS: C   TYPE: M   KEY 1: F   KEY 2: 2   PAGE: 235

25. In the 1790s, the woodland Indians' culture was threatened by
    a. epidemics of smallpox, influenza, and measles.
    b. an increase in depression, suicide, and drunkenness.
    c. the disappearance of wildlife and despoliation of traditional hunting grounds.
    d. internal frictions.
    e. all of the above.

    ANS: E   TYPE: M   KEY 1: F   KEY 2: 2   PAGE: 238

26. Easterners described frontiersmen as
    a. violent, drunken, filthy "white savages."
    b. hard-working, productive yeomen farmers.
    c. simple, innocent, childlike primitives.
    d. honest, public-minded, democratic citizens.
    e. traitors who had joined forces with the French and Indians.

    ANS: A   TYPE: M   KEY 1: A   KEY 2: 2   PAGE: 241

27. Which of the following best describes Thomas Jefferson's actions in regard to slavery?
    a. In his writings, Jefferson defended slavery as a necessary evil.
    b. He owned, sold, and profited from slaves all his adult life.
    c. He freed his slaves and encouraged others to do likewise.
    d. Jefferson never personally owned slaves, but other members of his family were slave owners.
    e. He never owned more than five slaves.

    ANS: B   TYPE: M   KEY 1: A   KEY 2: 2   PAGE: 243

28. Which of the following was not characteristics of the task system?
    a. White overseers and owners supervised workers in the fields.
    b. Slaves set their own pace and received free time when they completed their assigned tasks.
    c. Slaves cultivated "private fields" and could sell what they produced.
    d. Slaves cooperated and helped each other complete the work.
    e. In the lowland, cotton and rice plantations used the task system.

    ANS: A   TYPE: M   KEY 1: F   KEY 2: 3   PAGE: 246

29. Which of the following was true of American cities in the period 1790–1815?
    a. There were fifty cities with populations exceeding 10,000.
    b. The largest cities were all seaports.
    c. Prosperity led to a decline in poverty in urban areas.
    d. Urban dwellers were healthier and lived longer than people in rural areas.
    e. From 1800 to 1810 the rural population grew at a faster rate than the urban population.

ANS: B   TYPE: M   KEY 1: F   KEY 2: 2   PAGE: 246-47

30. American society in the early nineteenth century
    a. became more democratic and individualistic.
    b. was authoritarian and paternalistic.
    c. witnessed a significant decline in alcohol consumption.
    d. slavishly copied European styles and manners.
    e. suffered a decline in population.

ANS: A   TYPE: M   KEY 1: A   KEY 2: 3   PAGE: 253

31. The "universal suffrage" characteristic of early nineteenth-century American politics
    a. eliminated property qualifications and extended voting rights to all white adult men.
    b. offered citizenship to Indians and blacks.
    c. allowed women property owners to vote.
    d. relaxed property restrictions but did not eliminate them completely.
    e. tied the right to vote to church membership.

ANS: A   TYPE: M   KEY 1: F   KEY 2: 3   PAGE: 253-54

32. Which of the following is not true of nineteenth-century Methodist preachers?
    a. They reached rural areas that lacked their own churches through a process called circuit-riding.
    b. They rejected predestination and emphasized a personal emotional conversion experience.
    c. They were professional, well educated, and formally ordained.
    d. They attracted converts by telling stories, singing simple hymns, and speaking plainly.
    e. They emphasized the conversion experience.

ANS: C   TYPE: M   KEY 1: F   KEY 2: 3   PAGE: 255

33. All except which of the following were true of farmers after 1790?
    a. They ate most of what they grew.
    b. They traded with their neighbors.
    c. They sent surplus products to outside markets.
    d. They generally raised only one variety of animal or plant.
    e. They profited from world markets without becoming dependent on them.

ANS: D   TYPE: M   KEY 1: F   KEY 2: 2   PAGE: 233

34. Urban artisans during the years of the early republic
    a. experienced no change in their social or economic status.
    b. faced difficulty maintaining their independence.
    c. lived in a pristine environment free from filth and disease.
    d. were able to support their families on their own.
    e. joined labor unions.

ANS: B   TYPE: M   KEY 1: A   KEY 2: 2   PAGE: 249

35. Slaves made up _____ percent of the population in South Carolina and Georgia during the early constitutional period.
    a. 70
    b. 50
    c. 80
    d. 40
    e. none of the above

ANS: C   TYPE: M   KEY 1: F   KEY 2: 2   PAGE: 246

36. Backcountry whites adopted all of the following practices except
    a. girdling tress so that they would fall down naturally.
    b. depending on game for food and animal skins for trade.
    c. leaving their women behind to tend the farms when they hunted.
    d. engaging in drunken brawls.
    e. cooperating economically with local Indians.

ANS: E   TYPE: M   KEY 1: A   KEY 2: 2   PAGE: 241-42

37. In 1790, there were _____ black churches in the United States.
    a. 10
    b. 0
    c. 25
    d. 5
    e. none of the above

ANS: B   TYPE: M   KEY 1: F   KEY 2: 2   PAGE: 259

38. The first frontier state to enter the Union was
    a. Tennessee.
    b. Vermont.
    c. Ohio.
    d. Kentucky.
    e. Louisiana

ANS: B   TYPE: M   KEY 1: F   KEY 2: 3   PAGE: 242

39. By 1820, evangelicals were _____ slavery.
    a. unalterably opposed to
    b. indifferent to
    c. coming to terms with
    d. supporters of
    e. active participants in

ANS: C   TYPE: M   KEY 1: F   KEY 2: 2   PAGE: 257-58

40. All of the following were problems faced by Native Americans during the early republic except
    a. shrinking territorial holdings.
    b. opposition from the British for Native help to the Americans during the Revolution.
    c. the disappearance of wildlife.
    d. epidemics of European diseases.
    e. internal divisions.

ANS: B   TYPE: M   KEY 1: F   KEY 2: 2   PAGE: 238-41

41. During the early constitutional period, planters in coastal South Carolina and Georgia adopted
_____ as their secondary crop.
   a. rice
   b. tobacco
   c. indigo
   d. cotton
   e. potatoes

ANS: D   TYPE: M   KEY 1: F   KEY 2: 2   PAGE: 244

42. Which of the following statements is not true concerning slavery during the period of the early
republic?
   a. Slaves moved into the Chesapeake during that period.
   b. Cotton was profitable regardless of whether it was grown in large quantities by many slaves or on
      small farms that had few or no slaves.
   c. Most of the slaves that came to the United States directly from Africa during this period went to
      Charleston and Savannah.
   d. The interstate slave trade brought many slaves to the plantations of Georgia, Alabama, and
      Mississippi.
   e. As the tobacco market declined, slave labor became less necessary in the Chesapeake area.

ANS: A   TYPE: M   KEY 1: A   KEY 2: 3   PAGE: 242-43

43. By 1840, fully _____ percent of blacks in the North lived in states that either banned or severely
restricted their right to vote.
   a. 63
   b. 73
   c. 83
   d. 93
   e. none of the above

ANS: D   TYPE: M   KEY 1: F   KEY 2: 2   PAGE: 254

44. In the South Carolina and Georgia low-country, there were _____ slave Christians before 1830.
   a. many
   b. no
   c. few
   d. some
   e. twelve

ANS: C   TYPE: M   KEY 1: F   KEY 2: 2   PAGE: 258

45. Taken together, Indian peoples controlled _____ of the land that treaties and maps showed as
the interior of the United States in 1790.
   a. most
   b. none
   c. all
   d. some
   e. one-half

ANS: A   TYPE: M   KEY 1: F   KEY 2: 2   PAGE: 238

46. In the early republic, the economy of rural neighborhoods depended largely on
    a. wives typically working in the field with their husbands.
    b. paper money issued by the national government.
    c. loans from foreign banks.
    d. loans from the national bank.
    e. neighborly exchanges of goods and services.

ANS: E   TYPE: M   KEY 1: A   KEY 2: 2   PAGE: 236

47. Tenskwatawa's message to the Western Indians insisted that they must
    a. return to their traditional ways.
    b. surrender to the whites
    c. ally with the British.
    d. live in peace with the whites.
    e. move beyond the Mississippi.

ANS: A   TYPE: M   KEY 1: A   KEY 2: 2   PAGE: 240

48. In the years following the Revolution, many farmers in Maryland and Delaware
    a. advocated re-opening the African slave trade.
    b. freed their slaves.
    c. supported complete equality for all blacks.
    d. converted to cotton production, thus increasing their reliance on slavery.
    e. sent their slaves to Africa.

ANS: B   TYPE: M   KEY 1: F   KEY 2: 2   PAGE: 243

49. The task system for organizing slave labor
    a. encouraged teaching slaves to read and write so that they could perform more complicated tasks.
    b. ended when cotton became the South's primary crop.
    c. gave slaves some autonomy and control over their labor.
    d. proved inefficient and expensive for the owners.
    e. was the most oppressive labor system adopted under slavery.

ANS: C   TYPE: M   KEY 1: A   KEY 2: 3   PAGE: 246

50. In the years following the Revolution, young people tended to
    a. rely more and more on parental approval for marriage.
    b. stay single.
    c. court and marry without parental approval.
    d. use marriage as a means of increasing their families' wealth.
    e. refuse to marry in the church.

ANS: C   TYPE: M   KEY 1: A   KEY 2: 2   PAGE: 250-51

TRUE/FALSE

_____ 1.   J. Hector St. John de Crèvecoeur led a doomed slave revolt in Haiti.

ANS: F   TYPE: T   KEY 1: F   KEY 2: 3   PAGE: 232

_____ 2.   Most farmers before the 1790s thought of farming as a business.

ANS: F   TYPE: T   KEY 1: A   KEY 2: 2   PAGE: 233

_____ 3.   "Mad" Anthony Wayne defeated the Indians at the Battle of Fallen Timbers.

ANS: T   TYPE: T   KEY 1: F   KEY 2: 2   PAGE: 238

_____ 4.   Tenskwatawa (The Prophet) and Tecumseh were not only both Delawares, but they were brothers as well.

ANS: F   TYPE: T   KEY 1: F   KEY 2: 2   PAGE: 240

_____ 5.   During the early national period, many in the upper South thought that slavery was on the decline.

ANS: T   TYPE: T   KEY 1: A   KEY 2: 2   PAGE: 242-43

_____ 6.   Eli Whitney, the inventor of the cotton gin, was a southerner.

ANS: F   TYPE: T   KEY 1: F   KEY 2: 3   PAGE: 244

_____ 7.   The first federal census in 1790 revealed that 94 percent of Americans lived on farms and in rural villages.

ANS: T   TYPE: T   KEY 1: F   KEY 2: 1   PAGE: 246

_____ 8   .Northeastern cities during the great commercial boom between 1790 and 1820 witnessed great poverty.

ANS: T   TYPE: T   KEY 1: A   KEY 2: 1   PAGE: 249

_____ 9.   The period from 1790 to 1820 witnessed a substantial religious revival in the South.

ANS: T   TYPE: T   KEY 1: F   KEY 2: 1   PAGE: 256

_____ 10.   The transition to grain and livestock raising in the Chesapeake and the rise of the cotton belt in the Lower South meant a greater reliance on slave women to work in agriculture.

ANS: F   TYPE: T   KEY 1: A   KEY 2: 2   PAGE: 245

_____ 11.   In the 1780s and 1790s, Americans believed that individual dignity and citizenship were derived from property ownership.

ANS: T   TYPE: T   KEY 1: A   KEY 2: 2   PAGE: 253

_____ 12.   In the late eighteenth century, only wealthy families could afford to light their homes at night.

ANS: T   TYPE: T   KEY 1: F   KEY 2: 2   PAGE: 237

_____ 13.   Plantation slaves were an integral part of Gabriel's Rebellion from the beginning.

ANS: F   TYPE: T   KEY 1: F   KEY 2: 2   PAGE: 259

_____ 14.   After 1790, the populations of the old farming communities became younger and more male, while the populations of the rising frontier settlements and seaport cities became older and more female.

ANS: F   TYPE: T   KEY 1: F   KEY 2: 3   PAGE: 237

_____ 15.   Neighborly cooperation was nonexistent during the early republic.

ANS: F   TYPE: T   KEY 1: A   KEY 2: 2   PAGE: 236

_____ 16.   The success of a slave rebellion that created the black republic of Haiti inspired American slaves' dreams of liberty and equality.

ANS: T   TYPE: T   KEY 1: F   KEY 2: 3   PAGE: 259

_____ 17.   Between 1793 and 1815, American farmers became dependent on world markets for their survival.

ANS: F   TYPE: T   KEY 1: A   KEY 2: 2   PAGE: 233

_____ 18.   Maintaining one's status as a propertied white male was relatively easy between 1790 and 1820.

ANS: F   TYPE: T   KEY 1: F   KEY 2: 2   PAGE: 237

_____ 19.   Few farmers after 1790 possessed the tools, the labor, and the food they would have needed to be truly independent.

ANS: T   TYPE: T   KEY 1: F   KEY 2: 2   PAGE: 236

_____ 20.   By 1790, 2 million Americans were westerners.

ANS: F   TYPE: T   KEY 1: F   KEY 2: 2   PAGE: 241

_____ 21.   It was the hopefulness and simplicity of Methodism that attracted ordinary Americans.

ANS: T   TYPE: T   KEY 1: F   KEY 2: 1   PAGE: 255

_____ 22.   The primary goal of farmers during the early republic was to achieve long-term security and the ability to pass their farm on to their sons.

ANS: F   TYPE: T   KEY 1: F   KEY 2: 2   PAGE: 236

_____ 23.   Many poor white people joined Gabriel's Rebellion.

ANS: F   TYPE: T   KEY 1: F   KEY 2: 2   PAGE: 259

_____ 24.   During the early years of the republic, young people could depend on inheriting sufficient land from their fathers to maintain their independence.

ANS: F   TYPE: T   KEY 1: A   KEY 2: 1   PAGE: 236-37

_____ 25.   In the early years of the republic, farm tenancy increased.

ANS: T   TYPE: T   KEY 1: F   KEY 2: 2   PAGE: 237

_____26.   The treaty that ended the American Revolution protected Indian rights to their lands.

ANS: F   TYPE: T   KEY 1: A   KEY 2: 3   PAGE: 238

_____27.   The task system encouraged slaves to work together.

ANS: T   TYPE: T   KEY 1: F   KEY 2: 2   PAGE: 246

_____28.   By 1830 alcohol consumption was the highest that it has ever been.

ANS: T   TYPE: T   KEY 1: T   KEY2: 3   PAGE: 251

_____29.   The literacy rate in early America was higher in the South than in the North.

ANS: F   TYPE: T   KEY 1: F   KEY 2: 3   PAGE: 253

_____30.   By the 1830s most states had adopted universal suffrage.

ANS: F   TYPE: T   KEY 1: A   KEY 2: 2   PAGE: 254

_____31.   In post revolutionary America, men and women performed essentially the same tasks on their farms.

ANS: F   TYPE: T   KEY 1: A   KEY 2: 2   PAGE: 233-34

_____32.   Industrial outwork performed by rural families gave women and children greater independence.

ANS: F   TYPE: T   KEY 1: A   KEY 2: 2   PAGE: 235

_____33.   Most economic transactions in rural America involved the exchange of cash for goods and services.

ANS: F   TYPE: T   KEY 1: F   KEY 2: 1   PAGE: 236

_____34.   In the early years of the republic, farm tenancy was on the increase.

ANS: T   TYPE: T   KEY 1: F   KEY 2: 3   PAGE: 237

_____35.   The Cherokee lost their land even though they fought for the Americans in the Revolution.

ANS: F   TYPE: T   KEY 1: A   KEY 2: 3   PAGE: 238

_____36.   In the Treaty of Greenville, Native Americans ceded the area that is now Tennessee and Kentucky to the United States.

ANS: F   TYPE: T   KEY 1: F   KEY 2: 3   PAGE: 238

_____37.   A revolt among the Cherokee was sparked by the selling of their lands.

ANS: T   TYPE: T   KEY 1: A   KEY 2: 3   PAGE: 240

_____38.   Tecumseh's confederacy posed a real threat to the United States.

ANS: T   TYPE: T   KEY 1: F   KEY 2: 1   PAGE: 240

_____39.   Between 1790 and 1820 the percentage of Americans living in the West decreased.

ANS: F   TYPE: T   KEY 1: A   KEY 2: 2   PAGE: 241

_____40.   By 1790 the tobacco economy of the Chesapeake was booming.

ANS: F   TYPE: T   KEY 1: F   KEY 2: 2   PAGE: 242

FILL-INS

1.   The leader of the failed 1800 slave revolt in Virginia was _____.

ANS: Gabriel   TYPE: F   KEY 1: F   KEY 2: 3   PAGE: 259

2.   The invention of the _____ helped to rejuvenate slavery in the United States.

ANS: cotton gin   TYPE: F   KEY 1: F   KEY 2: 1   PAGE: 243-44

3.   The primary crop grown in the new southern states to the west of the Chesapeake was
_____.

ANS: cotton   TYPE: F   KEY 1: F   KEY 2: 1   PAGE: 244

4.   As late as 1790, the only state that granted the franchise to all free men was _____.

ANS: Vermont   TYPE: F   KEY 1: F   KEY 2: 2   PAGE: 253

5.   The Southern and Western tradition of neighbors trading goods and services and informally recording debts was called a _____ system.

ANS: changing   TYPE: F   KEY 1: F   KEY 2: 2   PAGE: 236

6.   By 1815, _____ was the largest city in the United States.

ANS: New York City   TYPE: F   KEY 1: F   KEY 2: 1   PAGE: 247

7.   By _____, individual place settings with knives and forks and china plates, along with chairs instead of benches, had become common in rural America.

ANS: 1800   TYPE: F   KEY 1: F   KEY 2: 2   PAGE: 237

8.   Between 1788 and 1808, some _____ slaves were brought directly from Africa to the United States.

ANS: 250,000   TYPE: F   KEY 1: F   KEY 2: 1   PAGE: 245

9.   By 1820, there were roughly _____ independent black churches in the United States.

ANS: 700   TYPE: F   KEY 1: F   KEY 2: 2   PAGE: 259

10.   After 1789, backcountry residents demanded federal help in combating the Indians and in ensuring navigation on the Ohio and _____ rivers.

ANS: Mississippi   TYPE: F   KEY 1: F   KEY 2: 2   PAGE: 241

11. In 1790, planters in Virginia and Maryland owned _____ percent of American slaves.

ANS: 56   **TYPE: F**   **KEY 1: F**   **KEY 2: 2**   **PAGE: 245**

12. All five of the U.S. communities with populations of more than 10,000 in 1790 were _____.

ANS: seaport cities   **TYPE: F**   **KEY 1: F**   **KEY 2: 2**   **PAGE: 246-47**

13. Alexander McGillivray tried unsuccessfully to unite the _____ under a national council.

ANS: Creeks   **TYPE: F**   **KEY 1: F**   **KEY 2: 1**   **PAGE: 240**

14. The dominant religion of the white South was _____.

ANS: Evangelical Protestantism **TYPE: F**   **KEY 1: F**   **KEY 2: 2**   **PAGE: 256**

15. The essence of Southern evangelism was the _____ experience.

ANS: Conversion   **TYPE: F**   **KEY 1: F**   **KEY 2: 2**   **PAGE: 256-57**

16. Methodist preachers who traveled throughout the country to spread their message were called _____.

ANS: circuit riders   **TYPE: F**   **KEY 1: F**   **KEY 2: 3**   **PAGE: 255**

17. In the years following the Revolution, without state support, the _____ church declined in membership and support in Virginia.

ANS: Episcopal   **TYPE: F**   **KEY 1: F**   **KEY 2: 3**   **PAGE: 254**

18. Some women were permitted to vote in the state of _____.

ANS: New Jersey   **TYPE: F**   **KEY 1: F**   **KEY 2: 3**   **PAGE: 254**

19. A method of organizing slave labor that allowed slaves to work without direct supervision was called _____.

ANS: task system   **TYPE: F**   **KEY 1: F**   **KEY 2: 2**   **PAGE: 246**

20. When Jefferson wrote that Virginians held a "wolf by the ears," he referred to _____.

ANS: slavery   **TYPE: F**   **KEY 1: A**   **KEY 2: 3**   **PAGE: 243**

21. A slave state where most blacks were freed by 1861 was _____.

ANS: Delaware   **TYPE: F**   **KEY 1: F**   **KEY 2: 3**   **PAGE: 243**

22. The expansion of slavery in the South and Southwest was directly related to the success of producing _____.

ANS: cotton   **TYPE: F**   **KEY 1: A**   **KEY 2: 1**   **PAGE: 244**

23. The treaty that forced Native Americans to relinquish claim to two-thirds of Ohio and southeastern Indiana was the Treaty of _____.

ANS: Greenville   **TYPE: F**   **KEY 1: F**   **KEY 2: 3**   **PAGE: 238**

24. The process whereby merchants provided raw materials for rural families to produce finished products was known as _____.

ANS: outwork   **TYPE: F**   **KEY 1: F**   **KEY 2: 2**   **PAGE: 234**

25. The Cherokees, Creeks, Choctaws, Chickasaws, and Seminoles were referred to as the

_____.

ANS: Five Civilized Tribes   **TYPE: F**   **KEY 1: F**   **KEY 2: 3**   **PAGE: 238**

26. The Indian military leader who united the Indians of the Northwest against white encroachment on their lands was _____.

ANS: Tecumseh   **TYPE: F**   **KEY 1: F**   **KEY 2: 2**   **PAGE: 240**

27. After 1790, Chesapeake planters shifted to the production of _____.

ANS: grain and livestock   **TYPE: F**   **KEY 1: F**   **KEY 2: 2**   **PAGE: 243**

28. Inventor of the cotton gin was _____.

ANS: Eli Whitney   **TYPE: F**   **KEY 1: F**   **KEY 2: 1**   **PAGE: 244**

29. The fastest growing church denominations in the early republic were _____.

ANS: Baptists and Methodists   **TYPE: F**   **KEY 1: F**   **KEY 2: 2**   **PAGE: 255**

30. The states that permitted blacks to vote were all located in the _____.

ANS: Northeast   **TYPE: F**   **KEY 1: F**   **KEY 2: 2**   **PAGE: 254**

IDENTIFICATIONS

1. **Gabriel's Rebellion:** failed slave uprising in Virginia in 1800, led by republican blacksmith/slave Gabriel. He hoped poor whites and republicans would join him. He and twenty-six others were tried and hanged when the plan was revealed to authorities by a coconspirator.

2. **cotton gin:** engine that revolutionized the southern economy by allowing easier removal of cotton seeds. Invented by Eli Whitney in 1793, it reinvigorated slavery.

3. **the Prophet:** Indian visionary, brother of Tecumseh. Urged Indians to push whites back to the east. Defeated (but not completely) at Battle of Tippecanoe.

4. **J. Hector St. John de Crèvecoeur:** French immigrant to the United States. Wrote about the opportunity afforded by northeastern farming.

5. **backcountry:** refers to the wilderness and the settlement that took place there. Term was replaced in the early nineteenth century with *frontier*.

6. **Cane Ridge Camp Meeting**: Three-day annual Scots-Irish Presbyterian "Holy Feast" that was expanded in 1801 to include Methodists and Baptists. Hundreds converted. Ten to twenty thousand attended. Many fainted and experienced intense religious ecstasy.

7. **competence:** term used to refer to rural folks' ability to live up to neighborhood standards of material decency while protecting the long-term independence of their household--and thus the dignity and political rights of its head.

8. **Alexander McGillivray**: mixed-blood Creek who had sided with the British during the Revolution. Between 1783 and 1793, he tried to unite the Creeks under a national council and to form alliances with other tribes and with Spanish Florida. His death in 1793 prevented the realization of his vision.

9. **task system**: developed in the Chesapeake. Involved assigning each slave a certain job or task for the day. Once that job was finished, the rest of the day belonged to the slave. Was an effort to deal with the deadly heat and disease that kept white masters and overseers out of the fields. Allowed slaves to manage their own time and develop mutual-assistance networks.

10. **patriarchy**: refers to a social and economic system dominated by males.

SHORT ESSAYS

1. Examine the roots and implications of Gabriel's Rebellion.

Answer: The Age of Revolutions (1775–1815) had profound implications for Western society. The growth of the ideas of liberty and equality were not welcome ones in the South. There especially, news of the great slave revolt in Saint Dominque (a rebellion that ultimately defeated the armies of Napoleon), stirred thoughts of revolt and liberty for many slaves. One of the earliest of the major slave revolts (albeit unsuccessful) was the so-called Gabriel's Rebellion, named after the Virginia slave and blacksmith.

News of successful revolts abroad spurred Gabriel and others who planned a massive slave revolt to occur in August 1800. Gabriel had hopes that his revolt would be more than a slave uprising. He hoped it would be a "republican revolt" in which free, poor whites would participate. In any case, Gabriel believed that power would be shared with workers throughout Virginia. For him, the enemy was the colony's merchants, the captains of the commercial economy. Gabriel's Rebellion failed miserably because an informant spread news of the revolt to the authorities, who were then ready for Gabriel. Twenty-seven conspirators were executed, and new measures were taken in Virginia to control the large enslaved population.

2. Describe the recommitment to southern slavery in the period from 1790 to 1820.

Answer: In the years following the American Revolution, slavery in the upper South, particularly in the Chesapeake, was on the decline. Three major factors help to explain this decline. First, the political rhetoric of the American Revolution (the condemnation of slavery) led many slaveholders to reconsider their stance on the institution and manumit their slaves. Second, religious factors, specifically the evangelical revolt, witnessed the growing Protestant denominations' call for the abolition of the institution. Finally, and most important, were economic considerations. Quite simply, the exhaustion of Virginia soil pushed many planters to free their slaves because it was no longer economically feasible to keep them.

In 1793, Eli Whitney invented the cotton "gin," which reduced the time and effort it had previously taken to comb the seeds from the cotton fiber. Before the invention of Whitney's machine, it took a slave a full day to comb one pound of cotton. The "gin" allowed a slave to comb fifty pounds in one day. The implications for the institution of slavery were profound. In 1800, the United States produced 73,000 bales of cotton; that figure increased to 334,000 in 1820. Moreover, because cotton could grow in a variety of climates that were unsuited to other types of production, previously worthless land could be made profitable by planting it with cotton. The "slave crisis" (from the slave owner's viewpoint) ended where Whitney's invention began.

3.   Explore the growth of the franchise in the early nineteenth century.

Answer: Colonial America was not, by most indications, a democratic place. In this hierarchical, deferential society, few attempts were made to share political power or promote equality. Besides the institution of slavery and the general disenfranchisement of women, a majority of free whites most probably were disenfranchised in the years before the Revolution. The Revolution brought significant changes, however. The ideological argument for equality led many states to implement democratic reforms, such as abolishing slavery, and led many other states to implement voting reform. In 1790, only Vermont allowed universal white male suffrage, but by 1840, only Rhode Island still maintained a propertied electorate.

Major change came in the new western states. As these states entered the union, they tended to do so with no restrictions on white male voting. Kentucky led the way in 1792 with no property qualifications, and other western states, in attempts to increase their population, followed their example. Most interesting here is the fact that many northeastern states, in their revolutionary constitutions, allowed free African Americans to vote. This trend continued through the 1840s, when developing racist sentiment put a halt to it. Some states, particularly New Jersey, gave the franchise to some women, although this also was rescinded in the early nineteenth century.

4.   Examine the social and economic life of northern households in the early nineteenth century.

Answer: The early nineteenth century, despite its transportation and industrial revolutions, was not so far removed from the colonial period of American history. It is important to remember that, for farm families in the early nineteenth century, life continued much as it had earlier. Most farm families in the northeast lived in small communities that emphasized reciprocity of obligations and duties and a sharing of work, responsibilities, and tools. Very little of the goods these farms produced were market oriented, and little of the work was market directed. For the most part, these families grew enough food for themselves and some extra to trade with neighbors or to sell on the market.

These households were part of a patriarchal system of hierarchical control that dominated society at the time. The father figure, though not omnipotent, was extremely powerful and served as the final decision maker. Almost every aspect of life was divided and oriented based on gender. Increasingly, however, the growing shortage of land in the northeast was eroding the traditional avenues of authority. Farm fathers were no longer able to guarantee land to young sons or dowries to daughters. This often led to challenges within the family—young sons who moved away and daughters who became pregnant before marriage (challenging the authority of parents to choose spouses for their children as well as when to allocate land). All of these interfamily challenges, however, were primarily symptoms of larger changes in northeastern society in the nineteenth century.

5.   Explore the social ills that challenged the "republican experiment" in the years between 1790 and 1820.

Answer: The Revolutionary generation hoped to foster a new society that would strengthen the republican experiment they had launched. The will of this new society was put to the test by tremendous social forces, previously unknown, that threatened the experiment. The most important of these forces, of course, were the transportation and industrial revolutions, both of which challenged traditional forms of commerce and increased the dependence on commercial markets. These forces increased the pressures on the average American to conform to dramatic changes in society.

One social ill that grew dramatically during this period was alcohol abuse. In the eighteenth century, drinking was seen as a social custom with few proscriptions against it—its abuse was rare. In the early nineteenth century, however, with the great desire to compete, whether on the farm or in the shop, the abuse of alcohol increased as a safety valve of sorts. Many farmers and laborers, alienated by the breakdown of traditional relationships in society, turned to alcohol for release from the stress. The abuse of alcohol rose to such great heights that, by the 1820s, physicians were devoting increasing time and energy to its treatment.

6. Describe the U.S. standard of living during the period from 1790 to 1820.

Answer: During the period from 1790 to 1820, the market economy raised the standard of living for certain Americans but not for others. Subsistence farmers, especially in the South, seemed poorer in contrast to the more successful Northern farmers. Southern and western farm houses were cramped single-story dwellings with rundown fences and bare yards. Livestock foraged in garbage piled close to the houses. Every room served as a bedroom and most people shared sleeping facilities. Few poor families owned more than two candlesticks; thus, most homes were lighted primarily by fireplaces that also provided warmth. In many lower-class households, people ate from a common serving bowl either with their fingers or with spoons. More affluent home owners whitewashed their homes and took pride in improving the outward appearance of their property. China dishes and place settings of knives and forks were available for rural families who could afford them. Manufactured chairs, upholstered furniture, and mass-produced clocks were common in prosperous households.

7. Examine the role of the print media in promoting democracy in the early nineteenth century.

Answer: During the early nineteenth century, the literacy rate in the United States increased dramatically. This increase was accompanied by a corresponding rise in the variety and number of printed materials available for public consumption. New England set the standard for literacy: 85 percent of New England's adult males and 45 percent of its females could read and write in 1790. Overall, by 1820 most Americans were literate. The literacy rate was lower in the South than in the North and lower among women than men. One manifestation of the increase in literacy was the number and frequency of letters written and received by the average citizen. Friends and family members communicated over long distances with intimate personal letters. As the volume of mail expanded, so did the size of the postal department. For example, the number of U.S. post offices grew from 75 in 1790 to 903 in 1800. Most of the correspondence was conducted by women.

Novels also emerged as a popular literary form during the period. Women were the major readers of novels, and many writers catered to the new market by creating female heroines and by addressing women's issues. The most successful novel of the era, *The Power of Sympathy,* was a morality tale that depicted men as hypocrites who seduced and betrayed vulnerable women. Many men disapproved of women's literature because it seemed frivolous and possibly even subversive from a male perspective. Fathers and husbands were suspicious of the effect novels would have on their impressionable wives and daughters.

Newspapers were the most widely read literary form. Few families bought subscriptions but most people had access to the news through public readings and private loans. The number of newspapers in the United States increased from only 90 in 1790 to 370 in 1830. Thus, most nineteenth-century Americans kept up with the activities of their friends, neighbors, government, and society through letters, newspapers, and popular novels. Earlier generations had depended on male authority figures to report the news and to read aloud from a limited number of printed sources. During the years from 1780 to 1820, an ever growing number of literate men and women experienced the solitary liberating influence of the written word.

Explore the changes in women's roles within the family during the period 1790-1820.

Answer: One change that American women during the period 1790-1820 experienced took place on the farms. Some changes took women out of actual agricultural chores; others gave them increased responsibility in other areas. The switch from the sickle to the long-handled scythe meant that men took over the job of harvesting in the grain fields. Increasing reliance on the plow instead of the hoe also removed women from field work. At the same time, women were becoming more involved in creating a more varied and nutritious rural diet, working to keep butter and cheese on the table throughout the year (at least for the most prosperous farm families) and increasing the planting of crops like turnips, potatoes, and other vegetables that could be stored for long periods.

Another change for women during this period was the increasing practice of taking on small manufacturing tasks for city merchants. The merchants would provide farm families with the raw materials to produce hats, shoes, brooms, and other products and pay on the basis of each piece produced. Most often, the work was completed by the women of the family, but the accounts were kept in the name of the male family head. If the entire family contributed to the enterprise, the men would complete the skilled portion of the task while the women did the more menial steps. In this way, the patriarchal structure of the family remained intact.

9.   Describe the transformation of the American backcountry between 1790 and 1820.

Answer: During the period from 1790 to 1820, the American backcountry changed dramatically. At the time of the ratification of the Constitution, only 10,000 settlers lived west of the Appalachians--about 1 American in 40. Life for these Americans was hard, as they faced hostile Indians all around them, as well as threats to continued access to the Ohio and Mississippi rivers, the lifeblood of commerce. Backcountry farmers often adopted or modified Indian techniques for farming, prompting unfavorable comparisons between them and Native Americans. Easterners were shocked by the poverty, lice, and filth of the frontiersmen, as well as their violence and drunkenness. One New Englander, in fact, described them as "white savages."

By 1820, though, the backcountry had evolved into the frontier. Now 2 million Americans were westerners, which amounted to 1 American in 5. By 1820, 11 frontier states had entered the Union, and their residents had built frame houses surrounded by cleared fields, planted marketable crops, and were settling into the struggle to make farms out of the wilderness. The settlements they founded were no longer the backwash of civilization. They had become its cutting edge.

LONG ESSAYS

1.   Describe U.S. relations with the Indians from 1790 to 1820.

Answer: Essay should address several key points:

A.   Background: Impact of Revolutionary War
      1.   Woodland Indians relegated to small territory
      2.   White settlers pouring into Indian territory
      3.   Continued British presence
B.   Destruction of the Woodlands Indians: 1790–1820
      1.   "Mad" Anthony Wayne and U.S. victory at Fallen Timbers (1794)
            a.   Departure of British
            b.   Decimation of Native peoples through disease
            c.   Rise of Creeks and Cherokees
      2.   The rise of Indian visionaries
            a.   Tenskwatawa (The Prophet) vision
            b.   Settlement at Tippecanoe and Tecumseh's confederacy
            c.   Defeat at Battle of Tippecanoe (1811)
      3. Creek Red Sticks defeated by Andrew Jackson
C.   Repercussions of military engagements
      1.   Military power of the Woodland Indians destroyed
            a.   Creeks forced to cede millions of acres in Georgia and Alabama
            b.   Northern Indians lost hunting lands
      2.   Many Indians moved west; others remained and tried to farm
      3.   Most whites assumed Indians would be forced west of the Mississippi

2.   Examine the changes in religion that occurred between 1790 and 1820.

Answer: Essay should address several key points:

A.   Religion before 1790
      1.   Power of traditional churches in decline
            a.   Problems of Congregationalism in Northeast
            b.   Decline of Anglicanism in South
B.   Rise of new religions
      1.   Growth of Evangelical Christianity in South

    a. Rise of Baptists
    b. Growth of Methodists
  2. Rise of religious revivals
    a. New emotionalism in religion
    b. Supplanting of more restrained, logical religions
 3. Factors accounting for appeal of new denominations
C. African Americans and Christianity
  1. Appeal of Methodists and Baptists
  2. Evangelists call for abolition of slavery
  3. First large-scale movement toward Christianity on part of slaves
  4. Role of blacks in northern churches and in creating their own

3. Describe changes in the institution of slavery between 1790 and 1820.

Answer: Essay should address several key points.

A. Slavery and the cotton gin
  1. Slavery on the decline through Chesapeake
    a. Questions of profitability
    b. Religious argument against slavery
  2. Eli Whitney and the cotton gin
    a. Institution of slavery changed overnight
    b. Slavery takes real form in new western states
B. Slavery and religion
  1. Rise of Methodists and Baptists
    a. Evangelical appeal
    b. Revivals and slave life
  2. First large-scale conversion of slaves
    a. Many biracial churches
    b. Founding of exclusively black churches
C. Increase in slave resistance
  1. Influence of revolutionary thought
  2. Gabriel's Rebellion

4. Describe the characteristics of the seaport cities during the period 1790 to 1815.

Answer: Essay should address several key points:

A. Census statistics
  1. Most Americans were rural farmers
  2. Only 6 percent were town dwellers
  3. Seaports are largest cities
B. Trade
  1. Impact of war between Britain and France
    a. Seizures and bans
    b. Nonimportation and embargo
    c. Influence on seaports
  2. Growth of financial institutions
    a. Increase in private wealth
    b. New bookkeeping and accounting
    c. Signs of prosperity
C. Poverty
  1. Lifestyle of poor
    a. Characteristics of slums
    b. Epidemics and life expectancy
  2. Distribution of wealth

         a.   Rise of per-capita wealth

         b.   4 percent own more than half the wealth

         c.   Insecurities of bulk of population

D.   Labor

     1.   Artisans and skilled workers

         a.   Valuable and respected

         b.   Independence

         c.   Erosion of republican virtues

     2.   Semiskilled workers

         a.   Cheap labor and "slop work" increase

         b.   Rise of lifetime wage earners

         c.   Reliance on women's and children's earnings

         d.   Loss of independence

CHAPTER 8
COMPLETING THE REVOLUTION, 1789–1815

CHAPTER OUTLINE

CHRONOLOGY

1789	Washington inaugurated as first president of the United States in New York City.
	Judiciary Act establishes a Supreme Court and federal circuit courts.
1790	Report on Public Credit delivered to Congress.
	Bill of Rights drafted by Congress.
1792	French Republic proclaimed.
1793	Anglo–French War begins.
1794	Federalists' excise tax triggers Whiskey Rebellion.

1796	Jay's Treaty and Pinckney's Treaty ratified.
	John Adams elected second president.
	Washington delivers his farewell address.
1798	XYZ Affair.
	Undeclared war between the United States and France.
	Alien and Sedition Acts passed by Congress.
1799	Slave revolution in Haiti.
1800	Washington, D.C. becomes American capital.
	Republican Jefferson defeats Federalist.
1803	Louisiana Territory purchased from France.
	Marbury v. Madison case establishes doctrine of judicial review.
1804	Twelfth Amendment to the Constitution.
1806	Non-Importation Act.
1807	*Chesapeake–Leopard* affair.
	Congress passes Jefferson's Embargo Act.
1810	Macon's Bill No. 2.
1811	Henry Clay elected Speaker of the House.
1812–1814	War of 1812.
1814	Hartford Convention.
	Treaty of Ghent.
1815	American victory at the Battle of New Orleans.

THEMATIC TOPICS FOR ENRICHMENT

1. What were the different titles suggested for the American president? Why did the debate prove so vitriolic?

2. Who was likely to be a Federalist? A Democratic-Republican?

3. List the specific liberties guaranteed in the Bill of Rights.

4. Explain the main points of Hamilton's economic plans.

5. Who were the members of Washington's first cabinet? What were their home states?

6. Assess Hamilton's and Jefferson's views on the constitutionality of the Bank of the United States.

7. Explain why the Jeffersonians sympathized with France and the Federalists sided with England in the 1790s.

8. What were the warnings Washington delivered in his farewell address?

9. What were the Virginia and Kentucky Resolves written in response to? What was the basic principle behind them?

10. What was so important about New Orleans that Jefferson insisted that the United States gain control of the city?

11. Why did virtually all Federalists in the Twelfth Congress vote against going to war with England in 1812? Assess the Federalist claim that the conflict was solely a "war of territorial aggression."

SUGGESTED ESSAY TOPICS

1. In what ways did the fight between the Federalists and the Democratic-Republicans echo the Revolutionary contest between liberty and power?

2. What did Jefferson mean in his inaugural address of 1801 when he claimed that "we are all Republicans, we are all Federalists"? Assess the importance of the "peaceful transit of power" after the election of 1800.

3. Did Thomas Jefferson live up to his own political ideals of less government and "strict constructionism" during his two terms in the presidency?

4. Compare the foreign policies of the Federalists with those of the Republicans. Which were more effective?

5. Read "Federalist #10" by James Madison and answer the following questions: What is it about? Has the Constitution succeeded in checking the danger of majority factions as the author believed it would?

LECTURE OUTLINE

1. **Establishing the government** with the ability to tackle the economic and political problems was the first priority of Washington, his administration, and the First Congress.

   a. The Washington administration had to struggle with the irony of appearing to create a **"republican court"** of powerful appointed officials in a democratic society.

   b. Leadership in the **First Congress** fell to James Madison, under whose guidance the Congress pursued a course to strengthen central authority, as well as guarantee individual liberties with the Bill of Rights.

   c. The cornerstone of the first Washington administration was the system of **Hamiltonian economics** that would come to grips with the national debt, begin to regulate the currency, and foster economic expansion.

   d. Several aspects of the plan of Hamiltonian economics came under fire, particularly the proposals for the **bank and the excise.**

   e. The **rise of opposition** was inevitable, as southerners especially felt that Hamilton's plans favored the mercantile interests of the North.

   f. The beginnings of party politics stemmed from the growing rift between Washington's two principal advisors in the cabinet, **Jefferson and Hamilton.**

2. Foreign policy concerns often cast a shadow over domestic concerns as the nation's political leaders differed greatly in their views on the **Franco–English War** from 1793 to 1800.

   a. Most Americans initially considered the **French Revolution** to be a significant step toward a republican world, but Federalists soon came to view the events in France with skepticism, fear, and dismay.

   b. **Citizen Genêt,** as French minister to the United States in 1793, conspicuously intervened in American internal affairs.

   c. The Washington administration faced acute **western troubles,** the Whiskey rebels in particular, in the course of 1794, ultimately sending an army of twelve thousand men to quell the so-called rebellion.

(SHOW TRANSPARENCY 48: CONFLICT IN THE NORTHWEST TERRITORY, 1790-1796)

d.   Vehemently opposed by many, the **Jay Treaty** helped the United States avert war with England while settling many issues left unresolved in the Revolutionary War settlement.

e.   In September 1796, newspapers printed **Washington's farewell,** in which the chief executive announced his retirement and offered several admonitions about politics and foreign policy.

f.   John Adams, the heir apparent, narrowly defeated Jefferson in the **election of 1796,** winning New England and several of the middle states.

g.   **Troubles with France** plagued Adams's entire administration, overshadowing virtually all of Adams's domestic initiatives.

h.   The struggle with France and England turned into a **crisis at home from 1798 to 1800,** especially when the Federalist Congress passed the Alien and Sedition Acts and the Kentucky and Virginia legislatures sought to nullify them within their state boundaries.

i.   Politicians fought heatedly over the nature of the appropriations for, future size of, and leadership of the **United States Army.**

j.   Styled the "revolution of 1800" by the victorious Jefferson, the **election of 1800** marked the first defeat of an incumbent administration as well as the peaceful transit of power.

(SHOW TRANSPARENCY 50: THE ELECTION OF 1800)

3.   Making good on their campaign pledges, the **Jeffersonians in power** immediately sought to curtail the pomp and ceremony that was so prominent in the previous administration.

    a.   While it continued many of the features of its predecessors, the **Republican program**, articulated by Jefferson, Madison, and Albert Gallatin, sought to shrink the activities of the central government and to eliminate altogether the national debt.

    b.   **Cleansing the government** meant for Jefferson the removal of his partisan opponents while shrinking the size and scope of government.

    c.   The greatest disputes of the administration proved to be between the **Jeffersonians and the courts.**

        i.   Jefferson personally sought the **impeachments of Pickering and Chase** for a combination of partisanship and gross dereliction of duty.

        ii.   **Justice Marshall's court**—and Chief Justice John Marshall himself—proved to be Jefferson's greatest challenge, particularly after Marshall's Solomon-like decision in the case of *Marbury v Madison* in 1803.

    d.   Jefferson secured his legacy and his reelection with the remarkable purchase of **Louisiana** from the French in 1803 for the paltry sum of fifteen million dollars.

(SHOW TRANSPARENCY 51: THE LOUISIANA PURCHASE)

4.   Republican attention for many years remained riveted on the emerging crisis between the Republic and its involvement in the **Napoleonic Wars** between 1804 and 1815.

    a.   Jefferson and Madison understood the daunting **dilemmas of neutrality** in a world at war but had a great deal of difficulty convincing New Englanders that neutrality should be maintained at all costs.

b.	The Republicans desperately tried to steer clear of the **trouble on the high seas** created by both British and French naval depredations and the British practice of impressing American sailors into service on his majesty's ships.

c.	Jefferson sought to avoid war in the last years of his presidency by the passage of the **embargo** which proved extremely unpopular in New England.

d.	Jefferson's retirement and the failure of the embargo seemed to send the country inevitably down **the road to war** with Great Britain.

e.	Led by Henry Clay of Kentucky, the **Warhawk Congress of 1811–1812** wanted war with England in order to eliminate Britain's Indian allies in the West.

f.	Despite Washington's earlier warning and Jefferson's attempts at economic coercion, the United States all but backed into the **War of 1812.**

(SHOW TRANSPARENCY 52: WAR OF 1812)

i.	Early skirmishes included a failed northern invasion as part of the bloody **War with Canada from 1812 to 1813** that included depredations on both sides.

ii.	**Tecumseh** made his last stand at the Thames River on October 5, 1813, where Richard M. Johnson claimed to have fatally wounded the warrior.

iii.	The **British offensive of 1814** concluded with the humiliating sacking of the nation's capital.

iv.	A group of disgruntled Federalists gathered at the ill-fated **Hartford Convention** in order to publicly protest against "Mr. Madison's War."

v.	The war officially ended with the signing of the **Treaty of Ghent** on December 23, 1814, although news did not arrive in New Orleans until after Andrew Jackson's smashing victory over General Packenham's army.

American Album: The Capital of the Republic

Conclusion: Almost all of the founding generation agreed that the stronger national government ushered in by the Constitution was essential to American prosperity and security; nonetheless, fissures shortly developed between those who advocated an activist government and those who contended, with Jefferson, that "he who governs best, governs least."

TEACHING RESOURCES

Thomas Jefferson is Ken Burns's fine two-part examination of the third president, with Sam Waterston reading Jefferson's words. PBS Video (180 minutes total).

United States vs. Aaron Burr recreates the trial of Burr, the one-time vice president of the United States. Educational Video (60 minutes).

The Life of George Washington features Bill Bradley narrating a detailed portrait of the first president of the United States. Filmic Archives (32 minutes).

City out of the Wilderness: Washington details the founding of the American capital at the end of the eighteenth century. Filmic Archives (30 minutes).

Virginia Plantations focuses on two of Virginia's most famous homes, Monticello and Mount Vernon. Filmic Archives (30 minutes).

"Marbury v. Madison," one tape in the *Equal Justice Under Law* series, explains this 1803 Supreme Court case and its significance for American jurisprudence. PBS Video (30 minutes).

Mr. Jefferson and His University examines the originality of Jefferson's vision through an examination of the University of Virginia and several of his other achievements. Films for the Humanities (52 minutes).

MULTIPLE CHOICE

1. The principal author of the Bill of Rights was
   a. James Madison.
   b. Thomas Jefferson.
   c. Ben Franklin.
   d. Alexander Hamilton.
   e. George Washington

ANS: A　　　**TYPE: M**　　　**KEY 1: F**　　　**KEY 2: 1**　　　**PAGE: 265**

2. In Alexander Hamilton's Report on _____, the treasury secretary urged Congress to assume state debts and combine them with the government's foreign debt.
   a. Manufactures
   b. Public Credit
   c. Tariffs
   d. State Debts
   e. National Debt

ANS: B　　　**TYPE: M**　　　**KEY 1: F**　　　**KEY 2: 1**　　　**PAGE: 267**

3. Each of the following was a part of the Hamiltonian Plan except
   a. a national bank.
   b. a tariff.
   c. funding of the debt.
   d. building a turnpike.
   e. assuming state debts.

ANS: D　　　**TYPE: M**　　　**KEY 1: F**　　　**KEY 2:2**　　　**PAGE: 266-67**

4. "Mad" Anthony Wayne defeated the northwestern Indian tribes at the Battle of
   a. Tippecanoe.
   b. Thames.
   c. Fallen Timbers.
   d. Fort Mims.
   e. New Orleans.

ANS: C　　　**TYPE: M**　　　**KEY 1: F**　　　**KEY 2: 1**　　　**PAGE: 271**

5. The first contested presidential election in the United States was in
   a. 1788.
   b. 1792.
   c. 1796.
   d. 1800.
   e. 1804

ANS: C　　　**TYPE: M**　　　**KEY 1: F**　　　**KEY 2: 1**　　　**PAGE: 272**

6. The Alien and Sedition Acts contained each of the following except
    a. an extension of the naturalization period for immigrants.
    b. a provision that allowed the president to deport aliens deemed dangerous to the United States.
    c. a provision allowing the states to nullify federal laws.
    d. a provision setting jail terms for those who spoke "maliciously" against the president.
    e. a provision setting jail terms and fines for those who advocated disobedience to federal law.

ANS: C   TYPE: M   KEY 1: F   KEY 2: 2   PAGE: 274

7. The Virginia and Kentucky Resolves
    a. were written by Thomas Jefferson and James Madison.
    b. declared that the Alien and Sedition Acts gave the national government powers not mentioned in the Constitution.
    c. asserted that states could invalidate or nullify federal laws.
    d. interpreted the constitution as a compact between states.
    e. all of the above

ANS: E   TYPE: M   KEY 1: F   KEY 2: 3   PAGE: 274-75

8. Which of the following best describes John Adams's term in office?
    a. It was successful.
    b. It was embattled.
    c. It was uneventful.
    d. It was successful domestically but unsuccessful in foreign affairs.
    e. It united the Federalist Party but led to intense opposition from the Republicans.

ANS: B   TYPE: M   KEY 1: A   KEY 2: 2   PAGE: 273-75

9. The winner of the presidential election of 1800 was
    a. James Madison.
    b. John Adams.
    c. Thomas Jefferson.
    d. James Monroe.
    e. Aaron Burr.

ANS: C   TYPE: M   KEY 1: F   KEY 2: 1   PAGE: 275

10. In the court case _____, the Supreme Court ruled that only the Supreme Court itself could declare acts of Congress to be unconstitutional.
    a. *Gibbons v. Ogden*
    b. *Dartmouth v. Woodward*
    c. *Brown v. Board of Education*
    d. *McCullogh v. Maryland*
    e. *Marbury v. Madison*

ANS: E   TYPE: M   KEY 1: F   KEY 2: 2   PAGE: 280

11. The Louisiana Territory was purchased from
    a. Spain.
    b. Great Britain.
    c. Portugal.
    d. France.
    e. Native Americans.

ANS: D   TYPE: M   KEY 1: F   KEY 2: 1   PAGE: 280

12. The British Orders in Council (1806) attempted to stop world shipping with which nation?
    a. France
    b. United States
    c. Spain
    d. Russia
    e. Brazil.

ANS: A   TYPE: M   KEY 1: F   KEY 2:2   PAGE: 283

13. The Embargo Act (1807) cut off U.S. shipping with
    a. England.
    b. France.
    c. France and England.
    d. Spain and Portugal.
    e. all foreign countries.

ANS: E   TYPE: M   KEY 1: F   KEY 2: 1   PAGE: 284

14. The congressional group that most forcefully advocated war with Great Britain in 1812 was known as
    a. the Red Sticks.
    b. the War Hawks.
    c. the War Doves.
    d. the Red Coats.
    e. the Minutemen.

ANS: B   TYPE: M   KEY 1: F   KEY 2: 1   PAGE: 286

15. James Madison's war message listed all except which of the following as reasons for the War of 1812?
    a. U.S. interest in acquiring Canada
    b. attacks on U.S. shipping
    c. impressment of U.S. seamen
    d. use of foreign spies and provocations in the United States
    e. British influence over western Indians.

ANS: A   TYPE: M   KEY 1: A   KEY 2: 3   PAGE: 285

16. Tecumseh was killed at the Battle of
    a. the Thames.
    b. Detroit.
    c. Lake Erie.
    d. New Orleans.
    e. Baltimore.

ANS: A   TYPE: M   KEY 1: F   KEY 2: 1   PAGE: 289

17. Which of the following was not a resolution of the Hartford Convention?
    a. to remove the "three-fifths clause" from the Constitution
    b. to deny the right of naturalized citizens to hold office
    c. to end the War of 1812 immediately
    d. to make it increasingly difficult for a new state to enter the union
    e. to require two-thirds majority of both houses to declare war.

ANS: C   TYPE: M   KEY 1: F   KEY 2: 2   PAGE: 290-91

18. The Treaty of Ghent (1814), ending the War of 1812, can be best described as
    a. a British victory.
    b. an American victory.
    c. a draw.
    d. all of the above.
    e. an Indian victory.

ANS: C   **TYPE: M**   **KEY 1: A**   **KEY 2: 1**   **PAGE: 292**

19. One of the most peculiar aspects of the Battle of New Orleans was that
    a. American casualties were all the result of disease.
    b. Native Americans were responsible for the U.S. victory.
    c. the city was not captured even though it was a British victory.
    d. it was unclear who won.
    e. it occurred after the war had ended.

ANS: E   **TYPE: M**   **KEY 1: F**   **KEY 2: 1**   **PAGE: 289-90**

20. The hero of the Battle of New Orleans was
    a. William Henry Harrison.
    b. James Monroe.
    c. Andrew Jackson.
    d. Ulysses S. Grant.
    e. Tecumseh.

ANS: C   **TYPE: M**   **KEY 1: F**   **KEY 2: 1**   **PAGE: 290**

21. The man most responsible for the establishment of the system of government finance was
    a. James Madison.
    b. George Washington.
    c. Alexander Hamilton.
    d. Thomas Jefferson.
    e. Henry Knox.

ANS: C   **TYPE: M**   **KEY 1: A**   **KEY 2: 2**   **PAGE: 266-67**

22. Which of the following is not true about the Whiskey Rebellion?
    a. It was fought over the tax on whiskey.
    b. It was quelled by Washington and twelve thousand militia men.
    c. It was centered in rural New York.
    d. It was seen as a challenge to the power of the federal government.
    e. President Washington pardoned the rebels.

ANS: C   **TYPE: M**   **KEY 1: F**   **KEY 2: 2**   **PAGE: 267, 270-71**

23. The political party that formed around Washington and Hamilton in the 1790s was the
    _____ party.
    a. Federalist
    b. Democratic Republican
    c. National Republican
    d. Anti-Federalist
    e. Whig.

ANS: A   **TYPE: M**   **KEY 1: F**   **KEY 2: 1**   **PAGE: 263**

24. The authors of the Virginia and Kentucky Resolves were
    a. Ben Franklin and John Adams.
    b. George Washington and Alexander Hamilton.
    c. Thomas Jefferson and James Madison.
    d. Henry Clay and John C. Calhoun.
    e. Patrick Henry and Sam Adams.

ANS: C   **TYPE: M**   **KEY 1: F**   **KEY 2: 2**   **PAGE: 274**

25. George Washington's and the Federalists' goals included
    a. creating a sound economy and stimulating commercial activities.
    b. establishing respect for the United States at home and abroad.
    c. counteracting the excesses of the Revolution and restoring public order.
    d. defeating the Western Indian tribes.
    e. all of the above.

ANS: E   **TYPE: M**   **KEY 1: A**   **KEY 2: 3**   **PAGE: 263**

26. Thomas Jefferson and the Democratic-Republicans favored
    a. promoting the revolutionary concepts of limited government.
    b. establishing stronger ties with England instead of France.
    c. the economic interests of merchants, bankers, and businessmen.
    d. expanding the power of the national government.
    e. all of the above.

ANS: A   **TYPE: M**   **KEY 1: A**   **KEY 2: 2**   **PAGE: 263**

27. The argument over the president's title was
    a. a foolish waste of time.
    b. settled by the Constitution, which outlawed titles of all kinds.
    c. part of the process that determined whether the new government would be republican or courtly in style.
    d. started by Jefferson who wanted a lofty title as secretary of state.
    e. settled by popular ballot.

ANS: C   **TYPE: M**   **KEY 1: A**   **KEY 2: 2**   **PAGE: 264**

28. The First Amendment to the Constitution
    a. established the executive departments and the cabinet.
    b. guaranteed voting rights for all white adult men.
    c. guaranteed freedom of speech, press, and religion.
    d. was written by George Washington.
    e. guaranteed the right to trial by jury.

ANS: C   **TYPE: M**   **KEY 1: F**   **KEY 2: 2**   **PAGE: 265**

29. The Judiciary Act of 1789
    a. provided that all Supreme Court cases must originate in federal circuit courts.
    b. gave Congress the power to remove federal judges from office.
    c. established a six-member Supreme Court and set up the federal district and circuit court system.
    d. was the most important piece of legislation passed during Washington's presidency.
    e. gave Congress the power to appoint Supreme Court justices.

ANS: C   **TYPE: M**   **KEY 1: F**   **KEY 2: 2**   **PAGE: 265**

30. Which of the following best describes Alexander Hamilton?
    a. He was a modest, mild-mannered man who shied away from confrontations and arguments.
    b. He was a brilliant, ambitious, aggressive, arrogant economist.
    c. He was the least influential of Washington's cabinet members.
    d. He was so unpopular that Washington limited his public appearances and social activities.
    e. He supported Jefferson's political ideology.

ANS: B   **TYPE: M**   **KEY 1: A**   **KEY 2: 3**   **PAGE: 266**

31. Many states opposed federal assumption of state debts because
    a. most northern states had already paid their debts and saw the assumption plan as a southern plot to increase their power.
    b. the debt was so high that paying it would bankrupt the nation.
    c. most of the money would go to western states that had not been fiscally responsible during the war.
    d. it would be easier to repudiate the entire debt and start with "a clean slate."
    e. most southern states had already paid their debts and did not want to pay off the debts of others

ANS: E   **TYPE: M**   **KEY 1: A**   **KEY 2: 3**   **PAGE: 266**

32. The purpose of the excise tax on whiskey was to
    a. provoke an uprising in the west.
    b. cut down on alcohol consumption in the United States.
    c. establish the federal government's right to pass and collect internal taxes.
    d. drive the small independent whiskey producers out of business.
    e. solidify support for the Republican party.

ANS: C   **TYPE: M**   **KEY 1: A**   **KEY 2: 2**   **PAGE: 267**

33. Which of the following accurately contrasts the views of Hamilton and Jefferson?
    a. Hamilton wanted to expand federal power; Jefferson wanted to limit it.
    b. Hamilton protected the interests of working-class citizens; Jefferson protected the wealthy planters and merchants.
    c. Hamilton's support came from the South and West; Jefferson's from the Northeast.
    d. Hamilton patterned his program after the French model; Jefferson copied the English system.
    e. Hamilton upheld the ideals of the Revolution; Jefferson emphasized the need for law and order.

ANS: A   **TYPE: M**   **KEY 1: A**   **KEY 2: 3**   **PAGE: 267-68**

34. Citizen Edmond Genêt caused trouble during Washington's presidency by
    a. sending privateers to attack English ships and threatening to attack Spanish New Orleans.
    b. refusing to sell New Orleans to the United States.
    c. openly flirting with Martha Washington at state parties.
    d. offering bribes to congressmen in return for state secrets.
    e. threatening to assassinate President Washington.

ANS: A   **TYPE: M**   **KEY 1: F**   **KEY 2: 2**   **PAGE: 270**

35. In Pinckney's Treaty, the Spanish
    a. reasserted claims to Kentucky and Tennessee.
    b. offered military assistance in fighting the Indian confederation in the Northwest Territory.
    c. gave the United States free navigation of the Mississippi River.
    d. closed the port of New Orleans to U.S. commerce.
    e. surrendered Florida to the U. S.

ANS: C   **TYPE: M**   **KEY 1: F**   **KEY 2: 3**   **PAGE: 272**

36. In his Farewell Address, George Washington
    a. encouraged healthy sectional rivalry.
    b. denounced the actions of the French Republic.
    c. obligated the United States to support antimonarchical revolutions in the Western Hemisphere.
    d. encouraged the development of political parties.
    e. warned against entangling foreign alliances and partisan domestic politics.

ANS: E   TYPE: M   KEY 1: F   KEY 2: 2   PAGE: 272

37. The XYZ Affair
    a. took place during the presidency of Thomas Jefferson.
    b. was a failed attempt by Treasury officials to embezzle public education funds.
    c. was a demand by three French officials for a bribe in return for improving relations with the United States.
    d. was a scandal involving John Adams's secretary of war and the wife of the French ambassador.
    e. involved the British practice of impressment.

ANS: C   TYPE: M   KEY 1: F   KEY 2: 2   PAGE: 274

38. Which of the following best describes John Adams during his presidency?
    a. He had an optimistic faith in the goodness and support of the American people.
    b. He helped pass legislation that strengthened constitutional protection of the freedoms of speech and press.
    c. He had an embattled mentality and feared he was surrounded by enemies.
    d. He was bored with dull public life and decided not to run for a second term.
    e. He united his political party and proved to be an effective leader.

ANS: C   TYPE: M   KEY 1: F   KEY 2: 3   PAGE: 274-75

39. As president, Thomas Jefferson
    a. increased the size and expense of the government.
    b. used the Sedition Act to arrest outspoken Federalist opponents.
    c. reduced the size of the army and navy and cut back on military spending.
    d. spent thousands of dollars on extravagant balls and dinner parties.
    e. rejected the opportunity to expand the territory of the U.S.

ANS: C   TYPE: M   KEY 1: F   KEY 2: 3   PAGE: 277-78

40. The first judge to be removed from office as a result of impeachment proceedings was
    a. John Marshall.
    b. John Randolph.
    c. Samuel Chase.
    d. John Pickering.
    e. Aaron Burr.

ANS: D   TYPE: M   KEY 1: F   KEY 2: 2   PAGE: 279

41. John Marshall was
    a. a sinister man who was determined to destroy the Republican party at all costs.
    b. primarily interested in establishing the independence and interpretative powers of the federal judiciary.
    c. a strong supporter of Adams's war with France and use of the Alien and Sedition Acts.
    d. the first Republican appointed to the Supreme Court.
    e. an opponent of the expansion of the power of the national government.

ANS: B   **TYPE: M**   **KEY 1: F**   **KEY 2: 3**   **PAGE: 280**

42. The Louisiana Purchase
    a. occurred during the War of 1812.
    b. was acquired from Spain.
    c. was strongly supported by the Federalist party.
    d. was opposed by a majority of Americans who feared it would result in a decline in the U.S. population east of the Mississippi.
    e. was prompted by an impending war between England and France and by a slave rebellion in Saint Dominique (Haiti).

ANS: E   **TYPE: M**   **KEY 1: F**   **KEY 2: 2**   **PAGE: 280-81**

43. The undeclared naval war between France and the United States was focused in the
    a. North Atlantic.
    b. Caribbean.
    c. South Atlantic.
    d. Great Lakes.
    e. Pacific.

ANS: B   **TYPE: M**   **KEY 1: F**   **KEY 2: 2**   **PAGE: 274**

44. The first controversy of the Washington administration involved
    a. the dignity to attach to the president's office.
    b. the location of the nation's capital.
    c. the role of the cabinet in formulating policy.
    d. the name of the new country.
    e. the President's affair with an office worker.

ANS: A   **TYPE: M**   **KEY 1: F**   **KEY 2: 2**   **PAGE: 264**

45. The First Congress's first action was to
    a. approve the Bill of Rights.
    b. create a federal court system.
    c. create the executive departments of War, State, and Treasury.
    d. declare war on France.
    e. pass a tariff on imports.

ANS: E   **TYPE: M**   **KEY 1: F**   **KEY 2: 2**   **PAGE: 265**

46. Militiamen from all of the following except _____ helped to quell the Whiskey Rebellion.
    a. Maryland
    b. Virginia
    c. New York
    d. New Jersey
    e. Pennsylvania.

ANS: A   TYPE: M   KEY 1: F   KEY 2: 1   PAGE: 271-72

47. Which of the following is not true about the election of 1796?
    a. The major candidates campaigned in person.
    b. It resulted in the president and vice president being from different parties.
    c. Newspaper editors and foreign governments were very involved in shaping the outcome.
    d. It was decided in the states of Pennsylvania and New York.
    e. John Adams won.

ANS: A   TYPE: M   KEY 1: F   KEY 2: 2   PAGE: 273

48. Federal assumption of the state debts would funnel money out of all of the following sections of the country except
    a. the southern states.
    b. the middle states.
    c. the northeastern states.
    d. the western states.
    e. Canada.

ANS: C   TYPE: M   KEY 1: F   KEY 2: 2   PAGE: 266

49. Which of the following is true concerning the Alien and Sedition Acts?
    a. Many states joined Kentucky and Virginia in opposing them.
    b. The Sedition Act led to the prosecution of fourteen Federalists.
    c. They were passed by Congress at the instigation of John Adams.
    d. President Adams never used the powers granted under the Alien Act.
    e. none of the above.

ANS: D   TYPE: M   KEY 1: F   KEY 2: 3   PAGE: 274

50. All of the following served at one time as secretary of state except
    a. James Madison.
    b. Thomas Jefferson.
    c. John Marshall.
    d. Alexander Hamilton.
    e. James Monroe.

ANS: D   TYPE: M   KEY 1: F   KEY 2: 2   PAGE: 265, 280

51. As Thomas Jefferson stood for reelection in 1804, he could look back on _____ first term.
    a. an astonishingly successful
    b. a very unsuccessful
    c. a disappointing
    d. a moderately successful
    e. a violent

ANS: A   **TYPE: M**   **KEY 1: F**   **KEY 2: 1**   **PAGE: 281**

52. The Embargo Act hurt _____ the worst.
    a. western farmers
    b. southern plantation owners
    c. northern manufacturers
    d. Native Americans
    e. the seaport cities of the northeast

ANS: E   **TYPE: M**   **KEY 1: F**   **KEY 2: 2**   **PAGE: 284**

53. Washington and his closest advisers came to be called
    a. Washingtonians.
    b. Republicans.
    c. Federalists.
    d. Constitutionalists.
    e. Democrats.

ANS: C   **TYPE: M**   **KEY 1: F**   **KEY 2: 1**   **PAGE: 263**

54. The Constitution was designed to do all of the following except
    a. counter democratic excesses.
    b. make the government more democratic.
    c. improve the nation's standing vis-à-vis other nations.
    d. create a government that could impose order at home.
    e. enable the government to collect taxes.

ANS: B   **TYPE: M**   **KEY 1: A**   **KEY 2: 2**   **PAGE: 263**

55. The new government's chief source of income was to be
    a. a tariff on imports.
    b. an income tax.
    c. harbor and customs duties.
    d. excise taxes on domestic manufactures.
    e. interest on loans.

ANS: A   **TYPE: M**   **KEY 1: F**   **KEY 2: 2**   **PAGE: 265**

TRUE/FALSE

_____ 1.   Citizen Edmond Genêt was a French government official who commissioned American privateers to harass British shipping.

ANS: T   **TYPE: T**   **KEY 1: F**   **KEY 2: 2**   **PAGE: 270**

_____ 2.   Thomas Jefferson was less critical of the French Revolution than the Federalists.

ANS: T   TYPE: T   KEY 1: F   KEY 2: 2   PAGE: 270

_____ 3.   Jay's Treaty was unanimously praised in the United States.

ANS: F   TYPE: T   KEY 1: F   KEY 2: 2   PAGE: 272

_____ 4.   The "undeclared war with France" was fought because France was seizing American ships that were trading with Great Britain.

ANS: F   TYPE: T   KEY 1: A   KEY 2: 2   PAGE: 274

_____ 5.   The 1807 Embargo Act was a motivating force for American commerce.

ANS: F   TYPE: T   KEY 1: F   KEY 2: 1   PAGE: 284

_____ 6.   The Capitol and president's home were burned by the British during the War of 1812.

ANS: T   TYPE: T   KEY 1: F   KEY 2: 1   PAGE: 289

_____ 7.   The Whiskey Rebellion was waged because of the desire to acquire cheaper alcoholic spirits for urban laborers.

ANS: F   TYPE: T   KEY 1: F   KEY 2: 1   PAGE: 270

_____ 8.   Not one Federalist supported Madison's declaration of war in 1812.

ANS: T   TYPE: T   KEY 1: F   KEY 2: 1   PAGE: 286

_____ 9.   John Adams's vice president during his one term in office was his archenemy, Alexander Hamilton.

ANS: F   TYPE: T   KEY 1: F   KEY 2: 2   PAGE: 273

_____ 10.   John Adams chose the title "His Elective Highness" for the president and it is still used today.

ANS: F   TYPE: T   KEY 1: F   KEY 2: 1   PAGE: 264

_____ 11.   The choice of the site for Washington, D.C. was determined by a deal among Hamilton, Madison, and Jefferson.

ANS: T   TYPE: T   KEY 1: F   KEY 2: 2   PAGE: 268

_____ 12.   Although Federalists opposed the embargo in principle, once it went into operation they complied without exception.

ANS: F   TYPE: T   KEY 1: A   KEY 2: 2   PAGE: 284

_____ 13.   Federal judges receive lifetime appointments and can be removed from office by impeachment only.

ANS: T   TYPE: T   KEY 1: F   KEY 2: 2   PAGE: 279

_____ 14.   The "War Hawks" were northeastern Federalists who opposed the War of 1812.

ANS: F   TYPE: T   KEY 1: F   KEY 2: 1   PAGE: 286

_____ 15.   "The Star-Spangled Banner" was written by William Henry Harrison during the War of 1812.

ANS: F   TYPE: T   KEY 1: F   KEY 2: 1   PAGE: 289

_____ 16.   The excise tax that sparked the Whiskey Rebellion had not applied to any other commodity.

ANS: F   TYPE: T   KEY 1: F   KEY 2: 1   PAGE: 267

_____ 17.   Charles Cotesworth Pinckney was John Adams's running mate in the election of 1796.

ANS: F   TYPE: T   KEY 1: F   KEY 2: 3   PAGE: 273

_____ 18.   After taking office, Thomas Jefferson increased the number of federal governmental balls and dinners.

ANS: F   TYPE: T   KEY 1: F   KEY 2: 1   PAGE: 277

_____ 19.   In 1811-12, a united Democratic-Republican party controlled both houses of Congress.

ANS: F   TYPE: T   KEY 1: F   KEY 2: 3   PAGE: 286

_____ 20.   Purchasing Louisiana necessitated an increase in the size of the military to protect the new territory.

ANS: F   TYPE: T   KEY 1: A   KEY 2: 3   PAGE: 281

_____ 21.   The War of 1812 was ended by the Treaty of Paris.

ANS: F   TYPE: T   KEY 1: F   KEY 2: 1   PAGE: 292

_____ 22.   At first, Republicans dominated the federal court system.

ANS: F   TYPE: T   KEY 1: A   KEY 2: 2   PAGE: 279

_____ 23.   Congress gave itself the power to appoint the heads of the executive department.

ANS: F   TYPE: T   KEY 1: F   KEY 2: 1   PAGE: 265

_____ 24.   The debate over the national bank was the first to raise the question of "necessary and proper" laws and actions.

ANS: T   TYPE: T   KEY 1: A   KEY 2: 3   PAGE: 268

_____ 25.   The Washington administration sided with Britain in its war against France only because it wanted to protect Anglo-American trade.

ANS: F   TYPE: T   KEY 1: A   KEY 2: 3   PAGE: 270

_____ 26.   The crisis with France allowed the High Federalists to push their domestic agenda despite the opposition of President Adams.

ANS: T   **TYPE: T**   **KEY 1: A**   **KEY 2: 2**   **PAGE: 274-75**

_____ 27.   As President Jefferson insisted on giving an increasingly powerful role to the military in domestic affairs.

ANS: F   **TYPE: T**   **KEY 1: A**   **KEY 2: 2**   **PAGE: 278**

_____ 28.   With the Battle of New Orleans, the United States won the War of 1812.

ANS: F   **TYPE: T**   **KEY 1: A**   **KEY 2: 2**   **PAGE: 290**

_____ 29.   The Hartford Convention declared the secession of the New England states.

ANS: F   **TYPE: T**   **KEY 1: F**   **KEY 2: 2**   **PAGE: 290**

_____ 30.   The Treaty of Ghent merely returned the status quo prior to the war.

ANS: T   **TYPE: T**   **KEY 1: A**   **KEY 2: 2**   **PAGE: 292**

_____ 31.   The national debt was significantly reduced during Jefferson's administration.

ANS: T   **TYPE: T**   **KEY 1: F**   **KEY 2: 3**   **PAGE: 281**

_____ 32.   Jefferson believed that federal judges should be elected by popular ballot.

ANS: F   **TYPE: T**   **KEY 1: A**   **KEY 2: 3`**   **PAGE: 279**

_____ 33.   The Republicans impeached Chief Justice Samuel Chase and removed him from office.

ANS: F   **TYPE: T**   **KEY 1: F**   **KEY 2: 2**   **PAGE: 279**

_____ 34.   _Marbury vs. Madison_ set the precedence for judicial review.

ANS: T   **TYPE: T**   **KEY 1: A**   **KEY 2: 2**   **PAGE: 280**

_____ 35.   Aaron Burr was convicted of treason.

ANS: F   **TYPE: T**   **KEY 1: F**   **KEY 2: 3**   **PAGE: 280**

_____ 36.   The Embargo Act hurt the American economy more than it did the British.

ANS: T   **TYPE: T**   **KEY 1: F**   **KEY 2: 2**   **PAGE: 284**

_____ 37.   Federalists enthusiastically supported the Embargo Act.

ANS: F   **TYPE: T**   **KEY 1: F**   **KEY 2: 2**   **PAGE: 284**

_____ 38.   James Madison was President of the United States during the War of 1812.

ANS: T   **TYPE: T**   **KEY 1: F**   **KEY 2: 1**   **PAGE: 285**

_____ 39.   Strongest support for the War of 1812 came from New England.

ANS: F   **TYPE: T**   **KEY 1: A**   **KEY 2: 2**   **PAGE: 286**

_____ 40.   The congressmen known as War Hawks came from the South and West.

ANS: T   **TYPE: T**   **KEY 1: F**   **KEY 2: 2**   **PAGE: 286**

FILL-INS

1.   The chief justice of the Supreme Court during Thomas Jefferson's tenure as president was
_____.

ANS: John Marshall   **TYPE: F**   **KEY 1: F**   **KEY 2: 2**   **PAGE: 280**

2.   Andrew Jackson decisively defeated a British invasion force at _____.

ANS: New Orleans   **TYPE: F**   **KEY 1: F**   **KEY 2: 1**   **PAGE: 290**

3.   In return for agreeing to Hamilton's proposals for the debt, Jefferson and Madison won acceptance for a plan to locate the capital of the United States be moved from New York to _____.

ANS: Site on the Potomac   **TYPE: F**   **KEY 1: F**   **KEY 2: 2**   **PAGE: 268**

4.   The War of 1812 was fought between the United States and _____.

ANS: Great Britain   **TYPE: F**   **KEY 1: F**   **KEY 2: 1**   **PAGE: 285**

5.   When the Constitution went into effect in 1789, the capital of the United States was
_____.

ANS: New York City   **TYPE: F**   **KEY 1: F**   **KEY 2: 1**   **PAGE: 264**

6.   The first ten amendments to the Constitution are called _____.

ANS: The Bill Of Rights   **TYPE: F**   **KEY 1: F**   **KEY 2: 1**   **PAGE: 265**

7.   _____ was an insane, alcoholic federal judge who was tried by the Senate and removed from office.

ANS: John Pickering   **TYPE: F**   **KEY 1: F**   **KEY 2: 1**   **PAGE: 279**

8.   French displeasure at the election of John Adams resulted in the determination to seize without compensation all American ships carrying "so much as a _____ made in England."

ANS: handkerchief   **TYPE: F**   **KEY 1: F**   **KEY 2: 2**   **PAGE: 273-74**

9.   Republicans saw _____ as the best hope for the survival of the republic.

ANS: westward expansion   **TYPE: F**   **KEY 1: A**   **KEY 2: 2**   **PAGE: 281**

10. In 1804, Jefferson won the electoral votes of every state except Delaware and _____.

ANS: Connecticut   **TYPE: F**   **KEY 1: F**   **KEY 2: F**   **PAGE: 282**

11. An estimated _____ American citizens were impressed into the Royal Navy between 1803 and 1812.

ANS: 6,000 **TYPE: F** **KEY 1: F** **KEY 2: 2** **PAGE: 283**

12. "The Star Spangled Banner" was written during the battle over _____ in Baltimore.

ANS: Fort McHenry **TYPE: F** **KEY 1: F** **KEY 2: 1** **PAGE: 289**

13. The largest portion of the foreign public debt was owed to _____.

ANS: France **TYPE: F** **KEY 1: F** **KEY 2: 2** **PAGE: 266**

14. The _____ was at the center of Alexander Hamilton's plan for a powerful national state.

ANS: national debt **TYPE: F** **KEY 1: F** **KEY 2: 2** **PAGE: 267**

15. Alexander Hamilton modeled the Bank of the United States on the Bank of _____.

ANS: England **TYPE: F** **KEY 1: F** **KEY 2: 2** **PAGE: 267**

16. John Jay held the post of _____ when Washington commissioned him to negotiate an end to U.S. conflicts with Great Britain.

ANS: Chief Justice of the Supreme Court **TYPE: F** **KEY 1: F** **KEY 2: 2** **PAGE: 272**

17. In response to the election of John Adams, in 1797 _____ expelled the American minister.

ANS: France **TYPE: F** **KEY 1: A** **KEY 2: 2** **PAGE: 274**

18. The _____ perpetrated the Massacre at Fort Mims.

ANS: Red Sticks **TYPE: F** **KEY 1: F** **KEY 2: 2** **PAGE: 288**

19. _____, a Kentucky congressman, killed Tecumseh in the spring of 1814.

ANS: Richard M. Johnson **TYPE: F** **KEY 1: F** **KEY 2: 2** **PAGE: 289**

20. The Red Sticks were defeated at the Battle of Horseshoe Bend in _____.

ANS: Alabama **TYPE: F** **KEY 1: F** **KEY 2: 2** **PAGE: 289**

21. The first Congress decided to address the President as _____.

ANS: Mr. President **TYPE: F** **KEY 1: F** **KEY 2: 2** **PAGE: 264**

22. In Washington's administration Alexander Hamilton served as _____.

ANS: Secretary of Treasury **TYPE: F** **KEY 1: F** **KEY 2: 1** **PAGE: 266**

23. Leader of the first Congress was _____.

ANS: James Madison **TYPE: F** **KEY 1: F** **KEY 2: 2** **PAGE: 265**

24. Full payment of the national debt would benefit _____.

ANS: Speculators   **TYPE: A**   **KEY 1: F**   **KEY 2: 2**   **PAGE: 267**

25. In the European wars, the Federalists sympathized with the _____.

ANS: British   **TYPE: F**   **KEY 1: F**   **KEY 2: 2**   **PAGE: 273-74**

26. The general who defeated the northwestern tribes at Fallen Timbers was _____.

ANS: Anthony Wayne   **TYPE: F**   **KEY 1: F**   **KEY 2: 2**   **PAGE: 271**

27. The British agreed to remove troops from American territory in the _____ Treaty.

ANS: Jay   **TYPE: F**   **KEY 1: F**   **KEY 2: 2**   **PAGE: 272**

28. Spain gave the United States the right to navigate the Mississippi River in _____.

ANS: Pinckney's Treaty   **TYPE: F**   **KEY 1: F**   **KEY 2: 2**   **PAGE: 272**

29. _____ was elected John Adams's Vice President in 1796.

ANS: Jefferson   **TYPE: F**   **KEY 1: F**   **KEY 2: 3**   **PAGE: 273**

30. A Supreme Court Justice impeached by the Republicans but acquitted was _____.

ANS: Samuel Chase   **TYPE: F**   **KEY 1: F**   **KEY 2: 2**   **PAGE: 279**

IDENTIFICATIONS

1. **Virginia and Kentucky Resolves**: political tracts written by Thomas Jefferson and James Madison in response to the Federalist Alien and Sedition Acts. These resolves argued that a state legislature had the right to nullify a federal law that it deemed unconstitutional. One of the most important expositions of the states' rights position.

2. **Alexander Hamilton**: economic nationalist, treasurer to George Washington, and creator of the treasury debt-driven system of the Federalist state that has dominated American capitalist development. His proposals called for a large national debt, a national bank, and a system of tariffs to pay off interest owed on the debt. Hamilton's plan organized the government, not the market.

3. *Marbury v. Madison*: significant court case in which John Marshall first argued that the Supreme Court was the final arbiter on the constitutionality of an act of Congress.

4. **Louisiana Purchase**: large territorial purchase from France made by Jefferson in 1803 that virtually doubled the size of the United States. Caused an uproar among Federalists who doubted the constitutionality of the purchase.

5. **Aaron Burr**: Thomas Jefferson's vice president. Responsible for organizing the political coalition in New York that ultimately gave that state to Jefferson. Attempted to "steal" the presidency, however, when he and Jefferson tied in the electoral college.

6. **Bill of Rights**: the first ten amendments to the Constitution. Fulfillment of Federalists' promise made during ratification that the new government would protect the liberties of the people. James Madison as member of House of Representatives proposed nineteen amendments, which were reduced to ten.

7. **Citizen Edmond Genêt**: French minister to the United States during Washington's presidency. Tried to get the United States into war by hiring privateers to attack English merchant ships and by organizing an attack on Spanish New Orleans. Feared he would be executed if he returned to France. Remained in the United States and married George Clinton's daughter. Lived comfortably as country gentleman thereafter.

8. **William Hull**: governor of Michigan Territory who commanded a group of militiamen and volunteers in a planned invasion of Canada during the War of 1812. Surrendered his entire force of 2,000 men to a much smaller British force for fear he was about to be attacked by Indians allied with Britain. Later court-martialed for cowardice.

9. *Chesapeake*: U.S. frigate that became involved in a confrontation with the British warship *Leopard* off the coast of Virginia in the summer of 1807. The confrontation, which resulted in the deaths of 3 Americans and injuries to 18 others, stemmed from the presence of several British deserters among the *Chesapeake*'s crew. It also generated widespread public condemnations of Britain and even some calls for war.

10. **War Hawks**: group of young congressmen who took control of the House of Representatives in 1811-12. Mostly Republicans from the South or the West, they were ardent nationalists who were more than willing to declare war on England in order to protect U.S. rights. Their leader, Henry Clay, who became Speaker of the House.

11. **Henry Clay:** War Hawk who was elected Speaker of the House at the age of 34. Vigorously approached his position and worked hard to control floor debate, pack key committees with his allies, direct House affairs behind the scenes, and generally impose order on his fellow congressmen.

12. **Hartford Convention**: called by moderate Federalists in December 1814 in order to head off calls for secession among more radical party members. The convention proposed a number of amendments to the Constitution: elimination of the three-fifths compromise; denial of the right to hold office to naturalized citizens; making it harder for new states to enter the union; and requiring a two-thirds majority of both houses of Congress for a declaration of war. None of the amendments was acted upon, and the convention discredited the Federalists and led to their rapid demise.

SHORT ESSAYS

1. Describe Alexander Hamilton's proposal for funding the debt.

Answer: The idea of "funding," not conceived by Hamilton but by the British in the early eighteenth century, was based on the idea of using the large national debt that had accrued during the Revolutionary War years as a support for the expanding commercial system. At the time of Washington's inauguration, the United States owed (in combined federal and state debts to domestic and foreign debt holders) about $75 million. There was little possibility that the United States could pay these debts (all the while accruing interest) with the little income the government had. In addition, there was great debate about whether the entire debt had to be paid off at all. Everyone agreed that the foreign debt was sacred, but there was less agreement about the domestic debt.

Hamilton argued that the entire debt (domestic as well as foreign) had to be repaid. Only by guaranteeing those who had lent money to the government (the wealthiest citizens) that the debt owed them would be repaid, could the government hope to be seen as a worthwhile investment in the future. Hamilton's plan then, was to transform the old, depreciated certificates of indebtedness into new, interest-bearing bond issues at full face value. But the principal of the domestic debt would not be repaid—only the interest due on it would be. In this way, Hamilton reasoned, the richest men in America would have a stake in seeing the new debt-ridden government survive.

2.   What was the Whiskey Rebellion? What were its causes, course, and repercussions?

Answer: The Whiskey Rebellion was, on its face, a simple response by western farmers to (what they considered to be) an unfair tax on the distillation of alcoholic beverages. For Alexander Hamilton and the new government, however, it became a test of strength over whether the federal government had the power to enforce its will. The tax was placed on whiskey distillers by Hamilton for the purpose of raising money to pay the national debt. The tax fell disproportionately on western farmers, however, who had long transformed their grain into whiskey in order to move it more easily and cheaply to market. These farmers from western Pennsylvania, Virginia, and Kentucky refused to pay the tax. They employed Revolutionary forms of organization (committees and republican rhetoric) in order to voice their opposition.

Following several crowd uprisings and small skirmishes, Hamilton convinced Washington to use a 1,200-man military force against the rebels. Washington led the force into western Pennsylvania, but found no real organized opposition. Although some twenty men were arrested, only two were tried and convicted, and both were pardoned by Washington. Yet, the significance of the action was clear. The federal government was prepared to use military force, if necessary, to enforce its will and prove its superiority over the states.

3.   Examine President Jefferson's war with the judiciary.

Answer: Jefferson's war with the judicial branch of the federal government was rooted in one major factor—his opposition to Federalist principles and the fact that the federal judiciary was controlled by Federalists. Federalist judges, such as Josh Pickering and Supreme Court Justice Samuel Chase, regularly used their positions on the Court to attack Jeffersonian ideals and practices. The House of Representatives, led by Jeffersonians, impeached and removed Pickering (who, judging by his actions, was clearly insane) from office. However, when the House attempted to go after Chase, many doubted the wisdom of this move, since Chase, although openly partisan, had not broken any legal standards. He was not removed from office.

The most important court battle, however, lay in the *Marbury v. Madison* case. The grounds of the case, the failure of Jefferson to deliver posts to certain Federalist appointees, were insignificant compared to the actual repercussions of the case. John Marshall's Supreme Court, a formidable foe of Jeffersonian republicanism, challenged Jefferson. Although the court ruled in favor of Jefferson (actually Madison, the secretary of state), it also asserted the right of "judicial review," the power to examine acts of Congress as to their constitutionality.

4.   Explore the U.S. attempt to remain neutral during the protracted struggle between France and Great Britain.

Answer: Since the mid-seventeenth century, France and England had engaged in a protracted war for the empire. This continued into the early nineteenth century, although the wars at this time (with Napoleon in power in France) took on a different texture. Both nations, France and England, attempted to injure the commercial capabilities of the other by seizing ships and cargo headed for enemy shores. The United States, claiming the right of a neutral nation to trade with both sides in a conflict, thus found itself caught in the middle of this struggle, with its ships and sailors regularly seized. Jefferson, seeing England as the greater culprit, first passed a nonimportation act in 1806 in an attempt to decrease the reliance on English goods. This proved unsuccessful.

In 1807, viewing few changes in the position of either belligerent, Jefferson proposed, and Congress passed, the Embargo Act calling for a complete cessation of American exportation. If the United States could not prevent the seizure of its ships, Jefferson argued, then no ships would leave port. The repercussions were profound. U.S. commerce was devastated—shippers and overseas merchants, port laborers, northeastern farmers, and southern planters, all of whom relied heavily on overseas trade, were severely hurt. Only one area, domestic manufacturing, remained untouched and, in fact, prospered under the embargo since it faced no foreign competition. When Jefferson left office, the failure of the endeavor was obvious, and the embargo was repealed.

5.   What was the "undeclared war with France"? Why was it fought and how was it resolved?

Answer: In 1778, when France recognized the independence of the United States, a U.S. treaty gave France most-favored-nation status in the area of diplomatic and commercial relations. In practical terms, this was always somewhat doubtful, since the United States clearly was reliant on the tremendous commercial and economic power of Great Britain. Indeed, throughout the early nineteenth century, over 90 percent of U.S. imports (and with it some 90 percent of federal tariff income) came from Great Britain. France, although angered at this situation, really had little recourse. The relationship between France and the United States grew worse, however, following the revolution in France. The Federalists in office, particularly Hamilton and Adams, viewed the French Revolution as an attack on organized hierarchy, culminating with the execution of the king in 1793.

　　　Following Jay's Treaty with Great Britain (1795), which gave Great Britain most-favored-nation status, France broke off relations with the United States and began seizing U.S. shipping, particularly in the Caribbean. When diplomatic attempts to resolve the crisis failed, President Adams asked Congress to prepare for war, and an undeclared naval war in the Caribbean ensued from 1798–1800. In 1800, feeling that the High Federalists had pushed the United States to war, Adams began peace negotiations with the French. Ultimately, the dispute on the high seas concluded, all financial obligations of both nations to each other were canceled, and peace was restored. This happened, however, only at the expense of Adams' bid for reelection, since he lost support within his own party in the process.

6.   Examine James Madison's role in establishing a sound foundation for the new government of 1789.

Answer: In 1789, James Madison was elected to the House of Representatives by the state of Virginia. He played a leading part in that first Congress and completed his role as "Father of the Constitution" by drawing up proposals for the Bill of Rights. Madison suggested nineteen amendments to protect the liberties of the people and the states. Congress reduced Madison's proposals to ten amendments, which were sent out to the states for ratification. The public's fear of an oppressive central government was assuaged by the establishment of constitutional guarantees of freedom of religion, speech, and press; the right to bear arms; protection against peacetime quartering of troops and abusive legal procedures; and denial of unlisted rights. The Tenth Amendment provided that states and citizens retained all powers that were not specifically given to the federal government by the Constitution. The Bill of Rights protected the citizens from possible federal abuse without changing the structure or interfering with the basic powers of the central government.

　　Madison was a nationalist who worked to augment the strength of the new government. Under his leadership, the legislature provided financing for the national government in the form of an import tariff. The executive branch of the government was organized around the newly established Departments of War, State, and Treasury with department heads who were chosen by the president. The Constitution provided that Congress would establish the federal courts and determine how many federal judges there would be. The Judiciary Act of 1789 set up a six-justice Supreme Court, thirteen district courts, and three circuit appeals courts. The law also provided that some cases from state courts could be appealed to the federal system and that members of the Supreme Court would serve as traveling circuit court judges.

7.   Discuss the Louisiana Purchase and examine its impact on American society.

Answer: One of the most monumental events in American history occurred during the presidency of Thomas Jefferson—the Louisiana Purchase. Jefferson and his Republican party represented the interests of the South and the West; therefore, they viewed westward expansion as a renewal of the democratic spirit. When Jefferson assumed the presidency in 1801, approximately 500,000 Americans lived in the territories beyond the Appalachian Mountains. These westerners relied on the internal river system that flowed into the Mississippi River to carry their goods to market at New Orleans. In Pinckney's Treaty, the Spanish had given the United States free use of the Mississippi River and the port of New Orleans. In 1800, however, Napoleon Bonaparte secretly acquired the Louisiana Territory, including the city of New Orleans, for France. He dreamed of re-creating a French empire in the Americas that would include not only Louisiana but also Saint Dominique and other Caribbean islands. When the Spanish announced the closing of the river to American commerce and the possible transfer of New Orleans to French authorities, Jefferson decided to buy the city.

Napoleon's plans were disrupted by a slave rebellion in Saint Dominique and by the possibility of another war with Britain; therefore, he offered to sell all of Louisiana to the United States for only $15 million. Even though the Constitution did not specifically authorize the executive to purchase territory, Jefferson agreed to the price and Congress ratified the deal. The Louisiana Purchase doubled the size of the nation, established American control of the entire Mississippi River system and the port of New Orleans, removed the danger of a powerful French presence in the West, and inspired and thrilled the public.

LONG ESSAYS

1. Examine the Hamiltonian system. What were its goals? How successful was it in achieving those goals?

Answer: Essay should address several key points:

A. Hamilton's plan for economic growth
   1. Report on Public Credit
      a. Funding the debt
      b. Paying the entire debt
   2. Bank of the United States
      a. Public/private institution
      b. Issuance of currency
B. Hamilton's plan for manufacturing
   1. Report on Manufactures
      a. Tariffs to promote domestic manufacture
      b. Tax incentives to help fledgling manufacturing
C. Hamilton's plan for raising revenue
   1. Tariffs
      a. Promote domestic manufacture
      b. Supply revenue to federal government
   2. Excise taxes
      a. Raise money for paying interest on debt
      b. Enforcement would reveal authority of federal government to implement its power

2. Explore the significance of the War of 1812 in American history.

Answer: Essay should address several key points:

A. Causes of War of 1812
   1. United States and ship seizures
      a. United States and rights as neutrals
      b. Orders in Council and Berlin Decrees
   2. Embargo Act of 1807
      a. Repeal of Embargo Act
      b. Non-Intercourse Act
   3. Macon's Bill #2
B. Military aspects of war
   1. Naval engagements
      a. Blockade of Atlantic coast
      b. Battles for Great Lakes
   2. Failure of land engagements
      a. Invasions of Canada
      b. Destruction of Washington
      c. Victory at New Orleans
C. Significance
   1. Political and social

        a.   United States gains greater diplomatic respect
        b.   Heightened patriotism in nation
        c.   Emergence of Andrew Jackson
   2.   Economic
        a.   United States free from naval seizures/impressments
        b.   U.S. domestic industrialization sparked

3.   Describe the political warfare between the Federalists and their opponents, the Jeffersonians, during the 1790s.

Answer: Essay should address several key points:

A.   Background to political differences
      1.   Washington and reliance on Hamilton
          a.   Opposition to Hamiltonian system
          b.   No open animosity while Washington is president
      2.   Hamilton versus Jefferson
          a.   Opposition to ideas on economic growth and democracy
B.   Growth of political parties
      1.   Election of 1796
          a.   First contested election
          b.   Federalists versus Jeffersonians
             i)   Slim Adams victory
             ii)   Implications
      2.   Opposition to Adams
          a.   Jeffersonian attack on Adams's policies
             i)   Some opposition within party as well
             ii)   Implications
          b.   Alien and Sedition Acts
             i)   Clear attempt to control political opposition
             ii)   Used primarily against Jeffersonians
          c.   Election of 1800
             i)   Jeffersonian revolution
             ii)   Implications

4.   Discuss the presidency of George Washington and include examples of both his domestic and foreign policies.

Answer: Essay should address certain key points:

A.   Domestic policy
      1.   The First Congress
          a.   A title chosen for the executive
          b.   Bill of Rights created
          c.   Cabinet set up
          d.   Judiciary organized
      2.   Hamilton's economic plan
          a.   The national debt funded
          b.   Assumption of state debts
          c.   Bank of United States set up
          d.   Excise tax on whiskey passed
          e.   Whiskey Rebellion put down
B.   Foreign policy
      1.   The French Revolution
          a.   Attitudes toward the revolution
          b.   U.S. neutrality declared

    c. Citizen Edmond Genêt makes trouble

  2. Problems with England and Spain

    a. Jay's Treaty

    b. Pinckney's Treaty

C. Legacy

  1. Rise of political parties

    a. Disputes over Hamilton's plan

    b. Agrarians versus commercial interests

  2. Farewell address

    a. Two-term tradition set

    b. "Entangling alliances" renounced

    c. Dangers of party factionalism exposed

CHAPTER 9
THE MARKET REVOLUTION, 1815–1860

CHAPTER OUTLINE

I. Government and Markets
    A. The American System: The Bank of the United States
    B. The American System: Tariffs and Internal Improvements
    C. Markets and the Law
II. The Transportation Revolution
    A. Transportation in 1815
    B. Improvements: Roads and Rivers
    C. Improvements: Canals and Railroads
    D. Time and Money
    E. Markets and Regions
III. From Yeoman to Businessman: The Rural North and West
    A. Shaping the Northern Landscape
    B. The Transformation of Rural Outwork
    C. Farmers as Consumers
    D. The Northwest: Southern Migrants
    E. The Northwest: Northern Migrants
    F. Households
    G. Neighborhoods: The Landscape of Privacy
IV. The Industrial Revolution
    A. Factory Towns: The Rhode Island System
    B. Factory Towns: The Waltham System
    C. Urban Businessman
    D. Metropolitan Industrialization
V. The Market Revolution in the South
    A. The Organization of Slave Labor
    B. Paternalism
    C. Yeoman and Planters
    D. Yeoman and the Market
    E. A Balance Sheet: The Plantation and Southern Development
VI. Conclusion

CHRONOLOGY

1790	Samuel Slater constructs Arkwright spinning mill at Pawtucket, Rhode Island.
1801	John Marshall is made Chief Justice of Supreme Court.
1807	Robert Fulton launches the *Clermont* on its maiden trip.
1813	Boston Associates build the first mill in Waltham, Massachusetts.
1815	End of the War of 1812.
1816	Congress charters Second Bank of the United States.
	Dartmouth College v. Woodward.
	McCulloch v. Maryland.
	Revised protective tariff passed by Congress.
1818	National Road completed as far west as Wheeling, Virginia.
1819–1825	New York builds Erie Canal between the Hudson River and Buffalo.
1822	President Monroe vetoes National Road reparations bill.
1824	*Gibbons v. Ogden.*
1828	Baltimore and Ohio Railroad begins full operation.
1835	Main Line Canal connects Philadelphia and Pittsburgh.

THEMATIC TOPICS FOR ENRICHMENT

1. What was Henry Clay's "American System"?

2. Explain the specific legal results of the three Marshall decisions handed down between 1816 and 1824.

3. What was so important about the invention of steamboats for American transportation in the early republic?

4. Why was the transportation revolution so important to the opening of a market economy in early America?

5. Was any one region of the country mostly excluded from the burgeoning national market system?

6. Evaluate the role of the plantation on the economic development of the South.

7. In what ways were New England farmers adversely affected by the market revolution?

SUGGESTED ESSAY TOPICS

1. In what ways did the market revolution shatter Jefferson's vision of an agrarian republic?

2. What was the transportation revolution? Discuss the main features of its development between 1815 and 1860.

3. How did the decisions of the Marshall Court demonstrate Marshall's conviction that "a natural and beneficial link exists between federal power and market society"?

LECTURE OUTLINE

1. The party of Jefferson changed dramatically in the years after his retirement. Republicans increasingly agreed that **government and markets** must work closely together to foster economic expansion.

   a. Henry Clay's **"American System"** included the recharter of the formerly dreaded **Bank of the United States** in 1816.

   b. **"The American System"** incorporated an elaborate system of **tariffs and internal improvements** that expressed Clay's belief that the government must be used for progressive purposes.

   c. Politicians and lawyers sought to assure the effective interaction of **markets and the law,** as reflected in a series of important Marshall court decisions.

2. The **transportation revolution** proved critical to national economic development because the price of many commodities depended more on the costs associated with transporting them to market than to that of production.

   a. The means of **transportation** had not changed very dramatically for many years; a rudimentary system of roads barely supplemented river travel.

      i. Technology and changes in law resulted in dramatic improvements in **roads and rivers** as means of transportation.

ii. Improvements in **canals and railroads** augured a wholesale change in the means of transport in the United States, despite their high cost.

(SHOW TRANSPARENCY 53: RIVERS, ROADS, AND CANALS, 1825–1860; AND TRANSPARENCY 54: THE GROWTH OF RAILROADS)

b. The transportation revolution resulted in a dramatic reduction in the **time and money** it took to transport bulk commodities.

c. Improved transportation also meant the growth of specific **markets and regions** in an economy of scale.

3. The advent of cash markets ushered in the transformation from **yeoman to businessman,** particularly in the rural North and West.

a. Cash-oriented farms proved instrumental in shaping the **northern landscape** as farmers sought to exploit urban demand for perishable crops.

b. The **transformation of rural outwork** toward more market-oriented production had consequences for both the economy and for society in general.

c. With the shift to specialized market agriculture, much of the North and West witnessed the growth of **farmers as consumers.**

d. The Northwest became home to many **southern migrants** who rejected slavery but maintained strong ties to southern cultural traditions.

e. The Northwest was also the destination of myriad **northern migrants** who rapidly embraced agricultural improvements in order to maximize their cash-crop harvests.

f. No institution changed more dramatically than **households,** which shifted from economic production to raising fewer children and preparing them for a career outside the home.

g. New neighborhoods designed as a **landscape of privacy** ushered out the old practices and forms of neighborliness characteristic of communities where everyone knew one another.

4. The **Industrial Revolution** commenced in New England in the 1830s and 1840s.

a. Factory towns under the **Rhode Island system** emerged initially as a result of the espionage of Richard Arkwright, who stole English plans.

b. Factory towns under the **Waltham system** employed young women in their mills, exploiting this readily available source of cheap labor.

c. Cities featured the growth of a class of **urban businessmen** who used their wealth and position to dominate much of urban society.

d. **Metropolitan industrialization** sparked the development of a new middle class that made the old distinction between proprietor and dependent obsolete.

5. Proponents of the **market revolution in the South** centered their appeal around westward expansion and the world's seemingly insatiable demand for cotton.

(SHOW TRANSPARENCY 55: COTTON PRODUCTION, 1801 AND 1859)

a.   The huge profits from cotton planting necessitated the **organization of slave labor,** including the use of women in the fields and the encouragement of slave families.

b.   Planters used a system of **paternalism**—caring for slaves as more than commodities—to ensure that the supply of slaves would not wane and to discourage the most vicious treatment of blacks.

c.   With the economies of scale brought about by cotton production, southern society was increasingly differentiated into **yeomen and planters.**

d.   Planters generally mediated the relationship of **yeomen and the market,** functioning as factors, lenders of labor, and advisors.

e.   **Plantations and southern development went hand in hand;** the southern economy grew rapidly, albeit narrowly, as planters churned profits back into land and slave labor.

American Album: The Making of Rural Respectability

Conclusion: Despite the fact that the Jeffersonians attempted to foster an agrarian republic of yeomen farmers, the War of 1812 and the strength of the American economy forced the Republican Party to adapt. Under Jefferson and Madison, Republicans endorsed many of the programs and initiatives that they had condemned under their Federalist predecessors. The nation was undergoing a transformation that signaled a burgeoning capitalistic market revolution.

TEACHING RESOURCES

Remaking Society in the New Nation examines the struggles of two men who make their way in the early years of the American republic. Filmic Archives (21 minutes).

The Louisiana Purchase: Moving West of the Mississippi highlights the politics and culture of the newest settlements of turn-of-the-nineteenth-century America. Filmic Archives (16 minutes).

Settling the Old Northwest depicts the conflicts that arose between aggressive western settlers and the Native American tribes between the Ohio and Mississippi Rivers. Filmic Archives (18 minutes).

Gone West exposes the harsh realities of life on the western frontier in the eras of Jefferson and Jackson. BBC\Time–Life Video (52 minutes).

MULTIPLE CHOICE

1.   Which of the following was not part of the American System?
    a. a national bank
    b. a uniform currency
    c. a protective tariff
    d. a national system of canals and turnpikes
    e. the creation of a market-driven system

ANS: B   **TYPE: M**   **KEY 1: F**   **KEY 2: 2**   **PAGE: 296-97**

2. The "author" of the American System was
   a. John C. Calhoun.
   b. Henry Clay.
   c. John Qunicy Adams.
   d. Thomas Jefferson.
   e. Alexander Hamilton.

ANS: B   **TYPE: M**   **KEY 1: F**   **KEY 2: 1**   **PAGE: 296**

3. In 1816, Congress chartered the _____ Bank of the United States for a twenty-year term.
   a. First
   b. Second
   c. Third
   d. Fourth
   e. Fifth

ANS: B   **TYPE: M**   **KEY 1: F**   **KEY 2: 1**   **PAGE: 296**

4. The federal government agreed to do each of the following in relation to the Bank of the United States except
   a. to deposit its funds in the bank.
   b. to accept the bank's notes as payment for taxes.
   c. to give it a tax-free exemption.
   d. to buy one-fifth of the bank's stock.
   e. to allow the Bank to regulate state banks.

ANS: C   **TYPE: M**   **KEY 1: F**   **KEY 2: 1**   **PAGE: 296**

5. The Tariff of 1816 was enacted primarily to
   a. raise revenue.
   b. hurt domestic textile manufacturers.
   c. protect U.S. industry.
   d. discourage exports.
   e. create a new political party.

ANS: C   **TYPE: M**   **KEY 1: F**   **KEY 2: 2**   **PAGE: 297**

6. Most canals built before 1830 were built and financed by
   a. state governments.
   b. private corporations.
   c. foreign investors.
   d. the federal government.
   e. Wall Street bankers.

ANS: A   **TYPE: M**   **KEY 1: F**   **KEY 2: 2**   **PAGE: 297**

7. Which of the following resulted from the Supreme Court case *Dartmouth College v. Woodward* (1816)?
   a. State governments could not tax turnpikes.
   b. Indian lands were protected.
   c. The state of Maryland could not tax the Bank of the United States.
   d. Steamship monopolies could not exist in New Hampshire.
   e. Corporate charters acquired the legal status of contracts.

ANS: E   **TYPE: M**   **KEY 1: F**   **KEY 2: 3**   **PAGE: 298**

8. In *McCulloch v. Maryland*, the Supreme Court ruled that the state of Maryland
   a. had no right to alter the corporate charter of Johns Hopkins University.
   b. had no right to tax the Second Bank of the United States.
   c. had no right to grant a steamship monopoly in crossing the Chesapeake Bay.
   d. could not tax turnpikes.
   e. could not cast its electoral ballots for president.

ANS: B   TYPE: M   KEY 1: F   KEY 2: 2   PAGE: 298

9. Which of the following first made commercial agriculture feasible in the Northwest?
   a. the railroad
   b. the steamboat
   c. turnpikes
   d. the horse and buggy
   e. the telegraph

ANS: B   TYPE: M   KEY 1: F   KEY 2: 1   PAGE: 300

10. Which of the following statements is incorrect?
    a. After 1815, the United States developed a self-sustaining internal market.
    b. After 1815, the northern United States intensified its industrial development.
    c. After 1815, the United States decreased its imports from Europe.
    d. After 1815, the United States increased its exports to Europe.
    e. After 1815, the southern economy was not integrated into the domestic market economy.

ANS: C   TYPE: M   KEY 1: A   KEY 2: 3   PAGE: 302

11. By the 1830s, northeastern farmers' relationship to the market
    a. strengthened.
    b. weakened.
    c. remained unchanged.
    d. became dependent on the international market
    e. none of the above

ANS: A   TYPE: M   KEY 1: A   KEY 2: 2   PAGE: 304-05

12. Thousands of southern yeomen left slave states and moved to the free states north of the Ohio because they felt
    a. that slavery was morally evil.
    b. that slavery blocked opportunities for poor whites.
    c. that the land was better.
    d. uncomfortable living among so many slaves.
    e. that slaves would rise up and kill all of the whites.

ANS: B   TYPE: M   KEY 1: A   KEY 2: 2   PAGE: 306

13. During the early nineteenth century, the birthrates of married northern white women
    a. increased significantly.
    b. decreased significantly.
    c. remained unchanged.
    d. increased marginally.
    e. cannot be determined based on existing records.

ANS: B   TYPE: M   KEY 1: F   KEY 2: 2   PAGE: 308

14. Which of the following political groups argued that the United States must always remain a rural, agricultural nation?
    a. Federalists
    b. Whigs
    c. Jeffersonians
    d. Know-Nothings
    e. none of the above

ANS: C   TYPE: M   KEY 1: F   KEY 2: 1   PAGE: 310

15. The first power-driven spinning mill in the United States was built by_____ in Pawtucket, Rhode Island.
    a. Richard Arkwright
    b. Nathaniel Appleton
    c. Francis Cabot Lowell
    d. Samuel Slater
    e. Thomas Edison

ANS: D   TYPE: M   KEY 1: F   KEY 2: 1   PAGE: 310

16. The factory villages where entire families labored for mill owners in the process of cloth production was known as
    a. the Lowell system.
    b. the Waltham system.
    c. the Rhode Island system.
    d. the Massachusetts system.
    e. the Carnegie system.

ANS: C   TYPE: M   KEY 1: F   KEY 2: 2   PAGE: 311

17. The Waltham, or Lowell, system of textile manufacturing primarily employed
    a. entire families.
    b. immigrants.
    c. young men.
    d. skilled artisans.
    e. young women.

ANS: E   TYPE: M   KEY 1: F   KEY 2: 1   PAGE: 311

18. Young women employed in the New England textile mills
    a. grew more dependent upon their families because of their experience.
    b. grew increasingly independent from their families because of their experience.
    c. remained relatively unchanged because of their experience.
    d. tended to keep their jobs for many years, and in some cases for life.
    e. joined labor unions and led violent strikes against the factories.

ANS: B   TYPE: M   KEY 1: A   KEY 2: 2   PAGE: 313

19. The primary cash crop of the South in the nineteenth century was
    a. tobacco.
    b. rice.
    c. cotton.
    d. wheat.
    e. potatoes.

ANS: C   **TYPE: M**   **KEY 1: F**   **KEY 2: 1**   **PAGE: 316**

20. The system of master-slave relations that developed in the nineteenth-century United States is best described as
    a. paternalism.
    b. mutual dependence.
    c. maternalism.
    d. Dionysian.
    e. socialism.

ANS: A   **TYPE: M**   **KEY 1: F**   **KEY 2: 1**   **PAGE: 317**

21. The inventor of the cotton gin was
    a. James Henry Hammond.
    b. Eli Whitney.
    c. Samuel Slater.
    d. Richard Arkwright.
    e. Thomas Edison.

ANS: B   **TYPE: M**   **KEY 1: F**   **KEY 2: 1**   **PAGE: 320**

22. After the War of 1812, the Republican Party
    a. continued to favor agrarian- and export-oriented policies.
    b. was destroyed because of its association with the unpopular peace treaty.
    c. adopted Federalist policies such as the national bank and protective tariff that it had opposed in the past.
    d. rejected demands for federal support of commerce and manufacturing.
    e. died out.

ANS: C   **TYPE: M**   **KEY 1: A**   **KEY 2: 3**   **PAGE: 296**

23. In the years after the War of 1812, the Supreme Court
    a. played no significant role in American politics.
    b. denied the sanctity of contracts.
    c. discouraged commercial ventures and business use of private property.
    d. limited the power of the national government and increased the power of state governments.
    e. increased the power of the national government and limited the power of state governments

ANS: E   **TYPE: M**   **KEY 1: F**   **KEY 2: 2**   **PAGE: 298-99**

24. The Erie Canal
    a. bankrupted the state of New York.
    b. replaced the New York Central railroad as the major means of transportation in the Northeast.
    c. opened up the interior of New York and transformed the frontier into a prosperous commercial area.
    d. had little impact on the economy of the Northeast.
    e. was built by corrupt politicians who made fortunes off the venture without the state's deriving any real benefit.

ANS: C   TYPE: M   KEY 1: F   KEY 2: 2   PAGE: 300

25. The national market that developed after 1840
    a. did not include the South.
    b. created interdependencies among the Atlantic, western, and southern states.
    c. involved an exchange of manufactured goods only.
    d. was primarily a trade in which northern raw materials were exchanged for western finished goods.
    e. depended primarily on foreign trade.

ANS: A   TYPE: M   KEY 1: F   KEY 2: 3   PAGE: 302-03

26. Mid-nineteenth century New England farmers
    a. produced most of the food crops for the entire country.
    b. relied on beef and dairy products as cash crops.
    c. increased the amount of land set aside for cultivation.
    d. used the most inefficient and soil-depleting techniques in the United States.
    e. were not integrated into the domestic market economy.

ANS: B   TYPE: M   KEY 1: A   KEY 2: 2   PAGE: 305

27. In the 1830s, most rural outworkers
    a. worked part-time at home producing goods from local raw materials.
    b. were all men.
    c. became more dependent upon merchants who provided imported raw materials and set the pace of the work.
    d. were respected skilled craftsmen who determined the price and quality of the goods they made.
    e. cleaned outhouses for a living.

ANS: C   TYPE: M   KEY 1: A   KEY 2: 3   PAGE: 305

28. The development of the northeastern market economy
    a. raised prices of most necessities.
    b. lowered the quality of finished goods.
    c. made farmers more independent and self-sufficient.
    d. made farmers more vulnerable to fluctuations in the national economy.
    e. depended on southern cotton.

ANS: D   TYPE: M   KEY 1: A   KEY 2: 3   PAGE: 306

29. Southern folkways transplanted to the Northwest included
    a. dependence on slave labor for most farm work.
    b. the belief that pork products were poisonous and should not be eaten.
    c. a lending and debt repayment tradition based on family and neighbor relationships.
    d. a maternalistic structure within the family.
    e. the most advanced technology in the region.

ANS: C   TYPE: M   KEY 1: A   KEY 2: 3   PAGE: 306-07

30. Which of the following was not an agricultural improvement of the mid-1800s?
    a. horse-powered threshing machines
    b. cast-iron plows
    c. the windmill
    d. hand-cranked fanning machines
    e. the grain cradle

ANS: C   TYPE: M   KEY 1: F   KEY 2: 1   PAGE: 307

31. The market economy induced which of the following changes in American farm households?
    a. Farmers improved the appearance of their houses by painting and planting flowers.
    b. Men took over previously female jobs such as dairying and poultry raising.
    c. People were more concerned with maintaining personal and household cleanliness.
    d. Farmers adopted improved farm techniques and technology.
    e. all of the above

ANS: E   TYPE: M   KEY 1: F   KEY 2: 3   PAGE: 308-09

32. In the mid-nineteenth century, new female housework responsibilities included
    a. spinning yarn and weaving textiles for the family's clothing.
    b. less time spent in child supervision and individualized care.
    c. cash-producing activities such as candle making and cheese production.
    d. less time spent on planting flower beds and cleaning furniture.
    e. more time spent washing, sewing, and ironing.

ANS: E   TYPE: M   KEY 1: F   KEY 2: 2   PAGE: 308

33. Under the Rhode Island system,
    a. textile workers bought their own looms and bargained with merchants to establish prices.
    b. mill owners created factory towns that included farmland that was rented to the families of textile workers.
    c. factories were located in major seaport cities in order to have access to international markets.
    d. Rhode Island banks financed industrial development in other states but charged extremely high interest rates.
    e. the factories were government owned.

ANS: B   TYPE: M   KEY 1: F   KEY 2: 2   PAGE: 311

34. The young, single women who worked under the Waltham system
    a. formed a permanent, professional workforce.
    b. drank, kept late hours, and generally had bad reputations.
    c. supported their parents and paid for the college educations of their brothers.
    d. organized unions that violently resisted their exploitation.
    e. saved some of their money for dowries and spent some on clothes and books.

ANS: E   TYPE: M   KEY 1: A   KEY 2: 2   PAGE: 311-12

35. In the seaport cities, the market revolution
    a. had little or no impact.
    b. led to a decline of the handicraft industries such as shoemaking and tailoring.
    c. stimulated a rise in real estate prices for waterfront property.
    d. created a new class of "white-collar" workers that included lawyers, wholesale and retail manufacturers, bookkeepers, and clerks.
    e. none of the above

ANS: D   TYPE: M   KEY 1: F   KEY 2: 3   PAGE: 316

36. The 14th Congress was composed overwhelmingly of
    a. Jeffersonian Republicans.
    b. Federalists.
    c. Whigs.
    d. Democrats.
    e. Socialists.

ANS: A   TYPE: M   KEY 1: F   KEY 2: 2   PAGE: 316

37. Which of the following states did not establish a canal system?
    a. New York
    b. Pennsylvania
    c. South Carolina
    d. Ohio
    e. Massachusetts

ANS: C   TYPE: M   KEY 1: A   KEY 2: 2   PAGE: 300-01

38. By 1860, the Northwest was exporting _____ percent of its wheat.
    a. 60
    b. 65
    c. 70
    d. 75
    e. 12

ANS: C   TYPE: M   KEY 1: F   KEY 2: 1   PAGE: 307

39. All of the following statements are true except
    a. cotton requires a long growing season.
    b. cotton ripens evenly.
    c. cotton requires lots of attention.
    d. cotton has a long harvest season.
    e. cotton was well suited to slave labor.

ANS: B   TYPE: M   KEY 1: A   KEY 2: 3   PAGE: 316-17

40. Eastbound traffic on the National Road consisted largely of
    a. cattle and pigs.
    b. wheat and corn.
    c. lumber.
    d. whiskey.
    e. cotton.

ANS: A   TYPE: M   KEY 1: F   KEY 2: 2   PAGE: 300

41. The national market that developed after the 1840s included all of the following except
    a. western farmers.
    b. southern planters.
    c. northeastern businessmen.
    d. northeastern manufacturers.
    e. northeastern livestock producers.

ANS: B　　　**TYPE: M**　　　**KEY 1: F**　　　**KEY 2: 1**　　　**PAGE: 303-04**

42. Which of the following did not become a key, profitable agricultural product of New England?
    a. chickens
    b. sheep
    c. dairy cows
    d. grain
    e. wood

ANS: D　　　**TYPE: M**　　　**KEY 1: A**　　　**KEY 2: 2**　　　**PAGE: 304-05**

43. Which of the following statements is true?
    a. Northwestern farmers from the east allowed their hogs to run free.
    b. Southern-born farmers in the northwest learned many of their farming techniques from books and magazines.
    c. Southern farmers in the northwest were not dependent on their families or neighbors.
    d. Southern farmers in the northwest were the first to adopt improved farm techniques and technology.
    e. Eastern farmers who settled in the Northwest retained the intensive, market-oriented farming they had known at home.

ANS: E　　　**TYPE: M**　　　**KEY 1: A**　　　**KEY 2: 3**　　　**PAGE: 307**

44. The market revolution meant all of the following for American women except
    a. more intensive mothering of their children.
    b. continued work in dairying and poultry raising.
    c. more attention to baking cakes, pies, and other fancy foods.
    d. more time spent sewing, washing, and ironing.
    e. more attention to fashion.

ANS: B　　　**TYPE: M**　　　**KEY 1: A**　　　**KEY 2: 2**　　　**PAGE: 308**

45. When Congress chartered the second Bank of the United States, it
    a. did not debate its constitutionality.
    b. limited its ability to do business to the Northeast.
    c. almost defeated the bill as unconstitutional.
    d. had no power over state banks.
    e. did not accept its notes as payment for taxes.

ANS: A　　　**TYPE: M**　　　**KEY 1: F**　　　**KEY 2: 2**　　　**PAGE: 296**

46. President Monroe
    a. supported building and repairing the National Road.
    b. urged Congress to finance canal building.
    c. did not make his position on road building publicly known.
    d. believed that the Constitution authorized Congress to build roads and canals.
    e. vetoed a bill providing for repairs on the National Road.

ANS: E　　　**TYPE: M**　　　**KEY 1: F**　　　**KEY 2: 3**　　　**PAGE: 297**

47. As Chief Justice, John Marshall's Supreme Court
    a. encouraged state regulation of business.
    b. protected business from state and community interference.
    c. overturned national laws that regulated business.
    d. opposed the "implied powers" doctrine.
    e. accepted bribes from industrialists.

ANS: B   **TYPE: M**   **KEY 1: A**   **KEY 2: 3**   **PAGE: 298-99**

48. In *Gibbons v. Ogden*, the Supreme Court
    a. ruled against a state-granted monopoly.
    b. upheld principles of strict interpretation of the Constitution.
    c. destroyed the Bank of the United States.
    d. struck a blow against the market economy.
    e. ruled in favor of racial equality.

ANS: A   **TYPE: M**   **KEY 1: F**   **KEY 2: 3**   **PAGE: 299**

49. The National Road linked
    a. the Potomac River with the Ohio River.
    b. the Mississippi River with the Great Lakes.
    c. New York City with Boston.
    d. The Ohio River with the Mississippi.
    e. Boston with Charleston.

ANS: A   **TYPE: M**   **KEY 1: F**   **KEY 2: 3**   **PAGE: 299**

50. During the 1820s New England storekeepers
    a. shipped their goods to England and Europe.
    b. depended almost entirely on locally produced goods for their retail sales.
    c. depended on a barter exchange of goods and services, rather than cash sales.
    d. saw their business decline significantly.
    e. increased their stock of consumer goods significantly

ANS: E   **TYPE: M**   **KEY 1: A**   **KEY 2: 3**   **PAGE: 305**

TRUE/FALSE

_____ 1.   The American System attempted to strengthen America's economic ties with western Europe.

ANS: F   **TYPE: T**   **KEY 1: A**   **KEY 2: 2**   **PAGE: 296**

_____ 2.   State governments took a more or less "laissez-faire" approach to the building of canals in the early nineteenth century.

ANS: F   **TYPE: T**   **KEY 1: A**   **KEY 2: 3**   **PAGE: 297**

_____ 3.   In the *Gibbons v. Ogden* case (1824), the Supreme Court ruled that the state of New York could not grant monopolies to steamship companies.

ANS: T   **TYPE: T**   **KEY 1: F**   **KEY 2: 2**   **PAGE: 299**

_____ 4. The building of the Erie Canal raised the cost of transporting western wheat in the early nineteenth century.

ANS: F   TYPE: T   KEY 1: F   KEY 2: 2   PAGE: 300

_____ 5. The Erie Canal connected the rich fertile soil of New England with the New York City market.

ANS: F   TYPE: T   KEY 1: F   KEY 2: 1   PAGE: 300

_____ 6. In general, material standards of living improved for slaves in the decades before the Civil War.

ANS: T   TYPE: T   KEY 1: F   KEY 2: 2   PAGE: 318

_____ 7. The size of the average family continued to grow between 1790 and 1850.

ANS: F   TYPE: T   KEY 1: F   KEY 2: 3   PAGE: 308

_____ 8. Most middle-class and poor southern farmers stayed outside the market almost entirely.

ANS: T   TYPE: T   KEY 1: F   KEY 2: 1   PAGE: 319

_____ 9. The National Road ran from the Great Lakes to the Gulf of Mexico and linked the nation along its North–South axis.

ANS: F   TYPE: T   KEY 1: F   KEY 2: 2   PAGE: 299

_____ 10. By the 1860s, the railroads had replaced canals and rivers as the major transportation avenues in the Northeast.

ANS: T   TYPE: T   KEY 1: F   KEY 2: 1   PAGE: 301

_____ 11. Railroads reduced the price but increased the time of transporting goods.

ANS: F   TYPE: T   KEY 1: A   KEY 2: 2   PAGE: 301

_____ 12. By the 1830s, some farmers were using mass-produced farm machines such as the McCormick reaper.

ANS: T   TYPE: T   KEY 1: F   KEY 2: 2   PAGE: 307

_____ 13. "Johnny Appleseed" was a fictional character created by Walt Disney.

ANS: F   TYPE: T   KEY 1: A   KEY 2: 1   PAGE: 307

_____ 14. The major technological improvements in early American industrial development were stolen from English inventors.

ANS: T   TYPE: T   KEY 1: F   KEY 2: 1   PAGE: 310

_____ 15. The market revolution occurred only in the North

ANS: F   TYPE: T   KEY 1: A   KEY 2: 2   PAGE: 295

_____ 16.   Railroads never replaced canals because canal transportation was much cheaper.

ANS: F   TYPE: T   KEY 1: A   KEY 2: 2   PAGE: 301

_____ 17.   After 1820, planters tried (often unsuccessfully) to substitute gang labor for the task system.

ANS: T   TYPE: T   KEY 1: A   KEY 2: 3   PAGE: 317-18

_____ 18.   The market revolution in the North began in the 1850s.

ANS: F   TYPE: T   KEY 1: F   KEY 2: 1   PAGE: 295

_____ 19.   The policies enacted by the 14th Congress were consistent with the ideology of Thomas Jefferson.

ANS: F   TYPE: T   KEY 1: A   KEY 2: 3   PAGE: 295

_____ 20.   Winning congressional approval of a program of internal improvements was easier than winning approval of the tariff.

ANS: F   TYPE: T   KEY 1: A   KEY 2: 3   PAGE: 297

_____ 21.   During his term as chief justice of the Supreme Court, John Marshall handed down decisions that weakened the federal government.

ANS: F   TYPE: T   KEY 1: A   KEY 2: 2   PAGE: 298

_____ 22.   Until about 1830, most western settlers were southerners who settled near the tributaries of the Ohio-Mississippi River system.

ANS: T   TYPE: T   KEY 1: F   KEY 2: 1   PAGE: 299

_____ 23.   Between 1815 and 1830, the percentage of the U.S. total national product accounted for by exports increased.

ANS: F   TYPE: T   KEY 1: A   KEY 2: 2   PAGE: 302

_____ 24.   Until about 1840, the market revolution was more a regional than an international phenomenon.

ANS: T   TYPE: T   KEY 1: F   KEY 2: 1   PAGE: 302-303

_____ 25.   By 1860, the U.S. South produced four-fifths of the world supply of cotton.

ANS: F   TYPE: T   KEY 1: F   KEY 2: 2   PAGE: 316

_____ 26.   Members of the new middle class entertained notions of gentility based on the distinction between manual and non-manual work.

ANS: T   TYPE: T   KEY 1: A   KEY 2: 2   PAGE: 316

_____ 27.   Southern farmers were early proponents of the systematic breeding of animals.

ANS: F   TYPE: T   KEY 1: F   KEY 2: 1   PAGE: 308

_____ 28. The market revolution resulted in an increase in the size of the average American family.

ANS: F   **TYPE: T**   **KEY 1: A**   **KEY 2: 2**   **PAGE: 308**

_____ 29. The market revolution blurred the lines of farms between "male" work and "female" work.

ANS: F   **TYPE: T**   **KEY 1: A**   **KEY 2: 3**   **PAGE: 308**

_____ 30. As a result of the market revolution, old practices and old forms of neighborliness fell into disuse.

ANS: T   **TYPE: T**   **KEY 1: A**   **KEY 2: 3**   **PAGE: 310**

_____ 31. In the seaport cities, growth derived more from commerce with the hinterland than from international trade.

ANS: T   **TYPE: T**   **KEY 1: A**   **KEY 2: 2**   **PAGE: 310**

_____ 32. Samuel Slater smuggled printed copies for the water-powered spinning machine from England to
America.

ANS: F   **TYPE: T**   **KEY 1: A**   **KEY 2: 3**   **PAGE: 310**

_____ 33. The Bank of the United States had no authority to regulate state banks.

ANS: F   **TYPE: T**   **KEY 1: F**   **KEY 2: 2**   **PAGE: 297**

_____ 34. President James Monroe believed that it was unconstitutional for the federal government to build roads within the states.

ANS: T   **TYPE: T**   **KEY 1: F**   **KEY 2: 3**   **PAGE: 297**

_____ 35. The nation's transportation network was built primarily by private enterprise.

ANS: F   **TYPE: T**   **KEY 1: A**   **KEY 2: 2**   **PAGE: 297**

_____ 36. In *McCulloch v. Maryland*, the Supreme Court ruled that the states could tax the Bank of the United States.

ANS: F   **TYPE: T**   **KEY 1: F**   **KEY 2: 2**   **PAGE: 299**

_____ 37. The transportation revolution reduced both the time and the expense of moving heavy goods.

ANS: T   **TYPE: T**   **KEY 1: F**   **KEY 2: 1**   **PAGE: 301**

_____ 38. After 1820 the United States economy became more dependent than ever on foreign trade.

ANS: F   **TYPE: T**   **KEY 1: A**   **KEY 2: 3**   **PAGE: 302**

_____ 39.   In the 50 years following 1820, American cities grew at a faster rate than at any other time in history.

ANS: T   **TYPE: T**   **KEY 1: F**   **KEY 2: 2**   **PAGE: 310**

_____ 40.   The plantation economy of the South resulted in an unequal distribution of wealth.

ANS: T   **TYPE: T**   **KEY 1: F**   **KEY 2: 2**   **PAGE: 319**

FILL-INS

1.   The New York Supreme Court case _____ asserted that the right to develop property for business purposes was inherent in the ownership of property.

ANS: *Palmer V. Mulligan*   **TYPE: F**   **KEY 1: F**   **KEY 2: 3**   **PAGE: 299**

2.   The so-called _____ system attempted to develop a truly national economy.

ANS: American   **TYPE: F**   **KEY 1: F**   **KEY 2: 2**   **PAGE: 296**

3.   _____ built the first Arkwright spinning mill in the United States (in Pawtucket, Rhode Island).

ANS: Samuel Slater   **TYPE: F**   **KEY 1: F**   **KEY 2: 1**   **PAGE: 310**

4.   The slaveholding senator from South Carolina who stated that "cotton is king" was _____.

ANS: James H. Hammond   **TYPE: F**   **KEY 1: F**   **KEY 2: 3**   **PAGE: 321**

5.   The frontier pathway used by westerners returning to Kentucky and Ohio after trading in New Orleans was called _____.

ANS: The Natchez Trace   **TYPE: F**   **KEY 1: F**   **KEY 2: 1**   **PAGE: 299**

6.   The first successful American steamboat, *Clermont*, was built by _____.

ANS: Robert Fulton   **TYPE: F**   **KEY 1: F**   **KEY 2: 1**   **PAGE: 300**

7.   _____ was the eccentric Yankee who planted apple trees in the Northwest and earned himself the nickname "Johnny Appleseed."

ANS: John Chapman   **TYPE: F**   **KEY 1: F**   **KEY 2: 2**   **PAGE: 307**

8.   _____ became the great New England cash crop.

ANS: Beef   **TYPE: F**   **KEY 1: F**   **KEY 2: 1**   **PAGE: 305**

9.   In 1860, only _____ percent of slaveowners owned 20 or more slaves.

ANS: 20   **TYPE: F**   **KEY 1: F**   **KEY 2: 2**   **PAGE: 319**

10.   Congress drew up the first overtly protective tariff in U.S. history in _____.

ANS: 1816   **TYPE: F**   **KEY 1: F**   **KEY 2: 1**   **PAGE: 297**

11. The National Road linked _____ with the Ohio River at Wheeling, Virginia.

ANS: The Potomac River   **TYPE: F**   **KEY 1:**   **KEY 2: 2**   **PAGE: 299**

12. The _____ first made commercial agriculture possible in the West.

ANS: Steamboat   **TYPE: F**   **KEY 1: A**   **KEY 2: 1**   **PAGE: 300**

13. New York's governor, _____, talked the state legislature into building what became the Erie Canal.

ANS: De Witt Clinton   **TYPE: F**   **KEY 1: F**   **KEY 2: 1**   **PAGE: 300**

14. By 1860, the United States had a rail network that stretched _____ miles.

ANS: 30,000   **TYPE: F**   **KEY 1: F**   **KEY 2: 2**   **PAGE: 300**

15. By 1860, the states of the Old Northwest (Ohio, Indiana, Illinois, Michigan, and Wisconsin) held _____ percent of the nation's population.

ANS: 22   **TYPE: F**   **KEY 1: F**   **KEY 2: 2**   **PAGE: 306**

16. _____ made secret drawings of British textile factory machines during an 1811 visit and then duplicated the machines in America.

ANS: Francis Cabot Lowell   **TYPE: F**   **KEY 1: A**   **KEY 2: 3**   **PAGE: 311**

17. In 1860, the 12 wealthiest counties in the United States were in the _____.

ANS: South   **TYPE: F**   **KEY 1: F**   **KEY 2: 1**   **PAGE: 319**

18. The principal business journal of the South was _____.

ANS: *DeBow's Review*   **TYPE: F**   **KEY 1: F**   **KEY 2: 3**   **PAGE: 320**

19. The Supreme Court broke up a state-granted monopoly with its decision in _____.

ANS: *Gibbons V. Ogden*   **TYPE: F**   **KEY 1: F**   **KEY 2: 2**   **PAGE: 299**

20. The canal that linked the Hudson River with Lake Erie was the _____.

ANS: Erie Canal   **TYPE: F**   **KEY 1: F**   **KEY 2: 2**   **PAGE: 300**

21. _____ accounted for most exports from the United States.

ANS: Cotton   **TYPE: F**   **KEY 1: F**   **KEY 2: 2**   **PAGE: 316**

22. The city that became the center of the garment industry was _____.

ANS: New York   **TYPE: F**   **KEY 1: F**   **KEY 2: 3**   **PAGE: 314**

23. The manufacturing system that relied on heavily capitalized and fully mechanized mills was known as the _____ system.

ANS: Waltham   **TYPE: F**   **KEY 1: F**   **KEY 2: 3**   **PAGE: 311**

24. The railroad that paralleled the Erie Canal, making it obsolete was the _____.

ANS: New York Central   **TYPE: F**   **KEY 1: F**   **KEY 2: 3**   **PAGE: 301**

25. In the Supreme Court decision _____, John Marshall stated "The power to tax involves the power to destroy."

ANS: *Mcculloch V. Maryland*   **TYPE: F**   **KEY 1: F**   **KEY 2: 3**   **PAGE: 299**

26. The lawyer who argued Dartmouth College case before the Supreme Court in *Dartmouth College v. Woodward* was _____.

ANS: Daniel Webster   **TYPE: F**   **KEY 1: F**   **KEY 2: 3**   **PAGE: 298**

27. By making a run from New Orleans to Louisville, the steamboat _____ demonstrated that two-way river trade was possible.

ANS: *Washington*   **TYPE: F**   **KEY 1: F**   **KEY 2: 3**   **PAGE: 300**

28. Most canals were built in the _____ and _____.

ANS: Northeast and Northwest   **TYPE: F**   **KEY 1: F**   **KEY 2: 3**   **PAGE: 300-01**

29. After 1830 most migrants to the Northwest came from the _____.

ANS: Northeast   **TYPE: F**   **KEY 1: F**   **KEY 2: 3**   **PAGE: 307**

30. In the 1830s the women workers in the textile factories at _____ went on strike.

ANS: Lowell   **TYPE: F**   **KEY 1: F`**   **KEY 2: 3**   **PAGE: 313**

IDENTIFICATIONS

1. **Henry Clay**: Kentucky senator and formulator of the American System, a plan advocating a truly national and independent (from foreign control) economic system.

2. **Samuel Slater**: English textile engineer who left his homeland illegally. Built first Arkwright spinning mill in the United States.

3. **Boston Associates**: group of wealthy New England merchants turned manufacturers who put New England on the road to industrialization. Organized by Francis Lowell.

4. **Rhode Island system**: textile manufacturing system (developed by Samuel Slater and others) that employed entire families in the production of textiles.

5. **Eli Whitney**: Northern inventor of the cotton-engine (or gin) that revolutionized the production of cotton and, consequently, the southern economy.

6. **Francis Cabot Lowell**: wealthy Bostonian who secretly copied English textile machine designs. Organized the Boston Associates to finance mills that used unskilled female workers who lived in company-owned and supervised boarding houses.

7. **"sweated" trade**: a subcontracting system that developed first in clothing manufacturing. A few skilled male tailors made pattern pieces and did custom work while large numbers of underpaid females sewed the clothing pieces together. The unskilled females worked longer hours for lower wages than did the skilled males.

8. **John Marshall**: chief justice of the Supreme Court between 1801 and 1835. After 1816 his decisions encouraged business and strengthened the national government at the expense of the states. His most important decisions protected the sanctity of contracts and corporate charters against state legislatures. Among his key decisions were *Dartmouth College v. Woodward* (1816), *McCulloch v. Maryland* (1816), and *Gibbons v. Ogden* (1824).

9. **Waltham system**: labor system employed by the Boston Associates. Utilized young, single women from the farms of northern New England. The workers lived in carefully supervised boardinghouses and followed a strict set of conduct rules, both on and off the job. The workers were well known as sober, dignified, and self-respecting, unlike workers in other places. They became, in the end, a self-respecting sisterhood of independent, wage-earning women.

10. **gang system**: form of slave labor organization employed on cotton plantations. Jobs were performed by sex-segregated groups of slaves. Hoeing, for example, was a female task while men were responsible for the plowing. The gang system involved close supervision of slaves' work and a high degree of planter paternalism.

11. **up-country**: eastern slopes of the Appalachians from the Chesapeake through Georgia, the western slopes of the mountains in Kentucky and Tennessee, the pine-covered hill country of northern Mississippi and Alabama, parts of Texas and Louisiana, most of the Ozark Plateau in Missouri and Arkansas. Home to most of the small farms in the South, these lands were too high, cold, isolated, and wooded to support plantation crops.

12. **"subsistence plus" agriculture**: practiced by a majority of southern yeomen and involved mixing farming for household subsistence and neighborhood exchange with a small surplus or cash crop sent to market. Farmers would put most of their land into subsistence crops and livestock, cultivating only a few acres of cotton. With the income generated from their small cotton crops, they could pay their debts and taxes and buy coffee, tea, sugar, tobacco, cloth, and shoes. This system allowed farmers to enter the market when they wished; it kept them from ever being dominated by it.

SHORT ESSAYS

1.   Examine the purposes and goals of the American System.

Answer: The American System was the first truly national attempt to create a self-sufficient and invigorated national economy. Primarily the work of Kentucky senator Henry Clay, the "system" was actually a series of plans for strengthening the infrastructure as well as the financial institutions of the United States. One of the first goals of the system was to create a strong national banking institution that would make loans available to prospective businessmen, give the government a safe place to invest its funds, and issue currency. The second part of the American System called for a vastly improved, government-built system of internal transportation (at this early stage, turnpikes and canals). The third part included high protective tariffs to help fledgling American industries.

Northeastern states clearly benefited from the American System—manufacturing was developing there, and good transport routes were needed. The American System offered much less to the South, where good river systems supplied ample transportation to farmers and planters and where a lack of industrial pursuits made tariffs unpopular and, possibly, destructive. The American System represented an attempt to break away from western European economic control and also to commercialize the U.S. economy.

2.   Explore changes in the local rural economies of the United States in the early nineteenth century.

Answer: The nineteenth-century market revolution helped to usher in dramatic changes in the social and economic life of farmers in rural America. Before the nineteenth century (even several decades into it), most of rural America was relatively isolated from markets and, thus, from market control. Most farmers produced enough goods for home use and more for local exchange with neighbors or local storekeepers.

Little of this produce was exchanged outside of each community, a form of exchange that cemented the bonds of community—central to the survival of pre-industrial households.

Little cash exchanged hands, and storekeeper accounts usually were settled in goods and services. Most farmers exchanged not only goods with each other but capital equipment and services as well. This process was known in some areas as "neighboring." The market revolution of the early nineteenth century forever changed these precommercial local communities, giving farmers opportunities to purchase factory-made textiles and other domestic items. In order to purchase goods, farmers needed cash, and the only way to obtain cash was by increasing agricultural production and adopting commercial patterns. The new transportation systems allowed farmers the opportunity to do just that. With increased production came increased ties to the market and, eventually, the decline of the old community-oriented way of life.

3.   Describe Samuel Slater's importance to industrialization in the United States.

Answer: Before the arrival of Samuel Slater in the United States, the nation was, at best, backward as an industrial center. England was the major industrial power, the nation that Alexander Hamilton argued that the United States should emulate. Through the first several decades of the new republic, however, the nation seemed to be heeding Jefferson's warnings against industrialization. Samuel Slater, among others, helped to alter the nation's economic direction. Slater left England illegally. (As a skilled textile engineer, he was supposed to remain in England, by English law.) He arrived in the United States with the plans to Arkwright's spinning mill memorized in detail.

Once in the United States, Slater, with financial support from Moses Brown, built the first fully contained (all processes of operation included) spinning mill in the United States (in Pawtucket, Rhode Island). In this way, Slater revolutionized the textile industry. Textiles no longer had to be constructed primarily in the home. In the mill, entire families were employed by the new textile manufacturers. Children would work the machinery inside (the new technology replaced the need for skilled artisans to work the wheels), and their parents would farm small plots and participate in various types of outwork. Although this system soon was replaced by larger, more heavily capitalized factory enterprises, Slater's mill marked an important turning point in the economic history of America.

4.   Examine the transportation revolution in the period from 1800 to 1840.

Answer: The transportation revolution of the nineteenth century had many stages, beginning with pretechnical aspects and culminating in the railroads of mid-century. Two things were central to the revolution: first, technological advances in the area of transportation vehicles and second, significant advances in transportation systems. Even in the late eighteenth century, the federal government and the states already were debating whether turnpikes would allow for speedier transportation of goods and, therefore, would increase commerce. By 1810, the debate shifted to the funding of canals. Canals, the most important of which was the Erie, were especially important since they allowed for the rapid movement of ships and boats at a far reduced cost for the shipper.

Canals connected areas that were not served by rivers but that were especially rich in agricultural production. For example, the Erie Canal linked the Genesee Valley and the "Old Northwest" to the New York City market, revolutionizing grain production (and more) in the United States. Equally important to these transportation systems were developments in transportation vehicles, such as the steamboat, which made commercial agriculture feasible in the West.

One example of the impact of the steamboat is the dramatic increase in market-bound produce after steamboat travel was introduced. In 1810, only 60,000 tons of produce was shipped from western areas. By 1840, this number increased to 500,000 tons.

5.   Describe the market revolution. What were its causes and repercussions?

Answer: In the period before the War of 1812, the United States was primarily a rural, agrarian-based economy. Although Alexander Hamilton exhorted his fellow Americans to engage more fully in commercial enterprises (and called on the federal government to do the same), little movement had taken place in this direction. The 1812 war, as well as the end of the Napoleonic conflicts in Europe, convinced many American merchants and financiers to devote more attention to internal trade and commerce and less to overseas trade. Beginning in the last years of the eighteenth century, but not developing in earnest until after 1815, merchants began to increase their investments in both internal trade networks (canals and turnpikes) as well as in fledgling industries.

Western rural communities were brought into commercial exchange systems because of dramatic developments in transportation and marketing. This introduction of previously unused farmland (in western New York and the "Old Northwest") all but destroyed agricultural production in New England, preparing that region for industrial development (textile mills and outwork production). As transportation systems developed further (with the Erie Canal, for example), the cost and time that it took to market items decreased substantially, further accelerating market development.

6.   Examine the impact of slavery and the cotton culture on southern economic development.

Answer: The southern economy in the mid-nineteenth century was based on commercialized plantations, which produced approximately three-fourths of the world's cotton crop. Many cotton producers were extremely wealthy. The richest counties in the nation in 1860 were in the southern states. The members of the planter aristocracy accounted for only 2 to 3 percent of the white male population, yet they owned half of the slaves and influenced the entire social, financial, and political structure of the region. There was a wide disparity between the wealthy elite, the self-sufficient yeoman, and the "dirt poor" white farmers. Although only one family in four owned slaves, the institution of slavery shaped the culture and limited the opportunities for non-slave-owning lower-class whites.

Most southerners did not really participate in the market economy. Rural southerners made what they needed or did without. The only southern technological innovations were those, such as the cotton gin, that directly affected cotton production. Reliance on slave labor retarded agricultural innovations and kept the South from implementing new, more efficient farming techniques. Even the transportation system and urban development of the region were tied to the cotton culture. Railroads, canals, and roads in the South existed for the sole purpose of transporting cotton to the nearest river for shipment to seaport cities. In fact, the only real cities in the South were coastal ports that provided cotton producers with access to national and international markets. The South depended on the North for banking, insurance, and manufactured goods. Overall, slavery and the cotton culture restricted the economic development of the area.

7.   Describe the home life of Americans in the nineteenth century.

Answer: The development of a market economy changed the lifestyle of those families most directly involved in the new trends. One noticeable change occurred in the size of families: The average number of children was reduced from 6.4 in 1800 to 4.9 by 1849. The change was most common in the North where new farming techniques and the expansion of livestock production lessened labor requirements. In poor southern communities, which continued production of traditional labor-intensive crops, large families were still the rule.

For many Americans, the concept of housework and gender distinctions between "man's work" and "woman's work" also changed. Previously female duties such as dairy farming, vegetable gardening, and poultry production were taken over by men when these activities became more profitable than field work. Within the household, women's roles altered as the number of children declined and as outside responsibilities were reduced. The market economy offered women better stoves, a variety of food products, manufactured cloth and clothing, and cleaning utensils. Women could devote more time to nurturing and instructing their children, baking pies and cakes, and decorating and cleaning their homes. They dressed their families in clean, pressed clothing, and improved the appearance and comfort of their surroundings. More families painted their houses and fences, planted flowers and shade trees, added on extra bedrooms, lighted their homes with oil lamps, and dined on tables set with table cloths and china dishes. The privacy, comfort, and attractiveness of prosperous American households improved as the nation became more market oriented.

LONG ESSAYS

1.   Explore the beginnings of textile manufacturing in New England in the period 1790 to 1830.

Answer: Essay should address several key points:

A.   Background to industrialization
     1.   Samuel Slater
          a.   Moses Brown and Pawtucket, Rhode Island
          b.   Importance
     2.   Development of the Rhode Island system
          a.   Entire families engaged in production
          b.   Small-scale operations
B.   Industrialization grows
     1.   Francis Cabot Lowell
          a.   Boston Associates
          b.   Lowell mills
     2.   Lowell (or Waltham) system
          a.   Young women operators
          b.   Implications
C.   Repercussions
     1.   Development of wage labor
          a.   Independent artisans undermined
          b.   Rise of unskilled workforce
          c.   Early work conditions generally good

2.   Describe the developing economy of the South in the years from 1800 to 1850.

Answer: Essay should address several key points:

A.   Importance of the plantation
     1.   Plantations: self-sufficient worlds
          a.   Heavily dependent upon the market
          b.   Not truly capitalist
     2.   Rise of King Cotton
          a.   Heavy demand in Europe and North
          b.   Great wealth of southern elite
B.   Middling and poor farmers
     1.   Uneven distribution of slave ownership
          a.   90 percent of southern whites were not wealthy planters
          b.   Three-fourths of southerners owned no slaves in 1861
     2.   Most southern farmers avoided commercial markets
          a.   Retained precommercial exchange systems
          b.   Local community and idea of "neighboring" dominated
C.   Slavery
     1.   Great wealth of the South dependent upon slave labor
          a.   Only 3 percent of white southerners part of plantation aristocracy
          b.   Master-slave relationship characterized by paternalism
     2.   After 1820—slavery both more systematic and humane
          a.   Slave labor increasingly rationalized
          b.   Further development of "paternalism"

3.   Describe the importance of John Marshall's Supreme Court to the commercialization of the United States in the years from 1800 to 1830.

Answer: Essay should address several key points:

A.   Major court decisions
     1.   *Dartmouth College v. Woodward* (1816)
          a.   Charter of college protected against attempt by state legislature to change it
          b.   Corporate charters acquired the legal status of contracts
     2.   *Gibbons v. Ogden* (1824)

    a.   New York denied the right to impose steamboat monopoly

    b.   Further empowered the national government over that of the states

   3. *McCulloch v. Maryland* (1816)

    a.   State of Maryland denied the right to tax branch of the Bank of the United States

    b.   Federal government not to be dependent upon the states

B. Implications

   1. Power of the federal government over that of the state asserted in each case

   2. Corporations granted significant protections under their charters from attempts to subvert them

   3. Commercial enterprises and competition promoted by these decisions

4. Discuss the role of the transportation revolution in creating the market economy of the nineteenth century.

Answer: Essay should address certain key points:

A. Rural transportation problems in 1815

   1. East of Appalachians

    a.   Primitive to nonexistent facilities

    b.   Cost of transporting goods

   2. West of Appalachians

    a.   Undeveloped resources

    b.   Utilization of Ohio–Mississippi River system

    c.   Time frame for transporting goods

B. Improvements in transportation

   1. Roads

    a.   National Road built by Congress

    b.   Lancaster Turnpike built by Pennsylvania

   2. Steamboats

    a.   *Clermont* launched by Robert Fulton

    b.   Impact on trade

   3. Canals

    a.   Erie Canal built by New York

    b.   Canal boom in the Northwest and Northeast

   4. Railroads

    a.   Rivers and canals linked by rails

    b.   Impact of railroads on other transportation systems

C. Repercussions

   1. Time and money

    a.   Turnpikes, canals, and steamboats reduce costs

    b.   Railroads and steamboats increase speed

    c.   Foreign trade expands

   2. Markets and regions—North and South

CHAPTER 10
TOWARD AN AMERICAN CULTURE

CHAPTER OUTLINE

I.   The Northern Middle Class
II. The Evangelical Base
     A. Domesticity
     B. Sentimentality
     C. Fine Arts
     D. Nature and Art
     E. Scenic Tourism: Niagara Falls
III. The Plain People of the North
     A. Religion and the Common Folk
     B. Popular Millennialism
     C. Family and Society
     D. The Prophet Joseph Smith
IV. The Rise of Popular Culture
     A. Blood Sports
     B. Boxing
     C. An American Theater
     D. Minstrelsy
     E. Novels and the Penny Press
V.   Family, Church, and Neighborhood: The White South
     A. Southern Families
     B. Southern Entertainments
     C. The Camp Meeting Becomes Respectable
     D. Religious Conservatism
     E. Proslavery Christianity
VI. The Private Lives of Slaves
     A. The Slave Family
     B. White Missions
     C. Slave Christians
     D. Religion and Revolt
     E. Nat Turner
VII. Conclusion

CHRONOLOGY

1822	Denmark Vesey slave revolt plans exposed in Charleston, South Carolina.
1828	Alexander Campbell debates Robert Owen on religious piety in Cincinnati, Ohio.
1830	Charles G. Finney leads religious revival in Rochester, New York.
	Joseph Smith publishes the *Book of Mormon* and founds the Church of Jesus Christ of Latter-Day Saints.
1831	Mount Auburn Cemetery opens in Boston.
	First minstrel show is presented.
	Nat Turner's slave revolt breaks out in Virginia.
1835	Landscape artist Thomas Cole publishes "Essay on American Scenery."
1836	Emerson begins writing career with publication of *Nature*.
1837	Hawthorne publishes his first collection of stories, *Twice-Told Tales*.
1843–1844	William Miller converts thousands to the belief that the world is about to end.
1845	George Lippard's lurid novel *Quaker City* becomes a huge bestseller.
1849	Theater riot in New York City leaves twenty dead.

1851	Melville publishes *Moby-Dick.*
1852	Harriet Beecher Stowe's antislavery novel *Uncle Tom's Cabin* is published to great popularity and controversy.
1853	Henry David Thoreau's *Walden* appears.
1856	Whitman publishes first editions of *Leaves of Grass.*

THEMATIC TOPICS FOR ENRICHMENT

1. How did the northern middle class's perceptions of Christianity differ from those of the "plain people"?

2. Explain the rise of domesticity and sentimentalism. How did women benefit from the new definition of their roles?

3. Discuss the changes in Americans' appreciation of the fine arts. How did their view of nature change?

4. Define the "popular culture" that arose among unmarried, urban males in the early decades of the century. What role did immigrants play in this transformation?

5. Discuss the religious beliefs and social philosophy of southern plantation owners and their families.

6. Discuss how southerners used Christianity to justify the enslavement of blacks.

SUGGESTED ESSAY TOPICS

1. Define the term *middle class* and discuss the factors that led to its growth in the early nineteenth century.

2. What is a religious revival? In what ways did religion figure into the lives of Americans?

3. What were the key features in the development of American literary culture in the decades before the Civil War?

4. Compare and contrast the cultures of the North and the South.

5. Explain the slave interpretation of religion and family. Did Christianity help or hamper slaves in dealing with their condition?

LECTURE OUTLINE

1. A great development of the first part of the nineteenth century was the advent of a distinct **northern middle class** of Protestant business-oriented folk who came to dominate northern culture.

   a. Members of the middle class not only attended church regularly but also emerged from a solid **evangelical base** of Christian revivalism.

   b. The **cult of domesticity** resulted from the middle-class distinction between home and work, with the latter the exclusive provenance of men.

   c. The popular literature of the class, such as *Godley's Ladies Book,* featured effusive **sentimentality** directed primarily at women.

   d. Americans slowly came to view the **fine arts** as something that could take on a non-European, indigenous character.

e.   American artists' unique contribution to fine arts was the incorporation of **nature and art,** especially in the work of the Hudson River School of painting.

2.   The **plain people of the North** rejected much of the sentimentality and evangelicalism of middle-class values, pursuing their own distinct forms of culture.

     a.   The **religion of the common folk** proved far less sentimental and far more participatory than that of the well-heeled and the middle class.

     b.   **Popular millennialism,** particularly that of William Miller and the Millerites, looked forward to God's imminent arrival to redeem the saved.

     c.   Some religious ideologies appealed to the notions that **family and society** must be counterpoised against encroaching and immoral market forces.

     d.   The **prophet Joseph Smith,** after the angel Moroni appeared to him in a vision in 1827, articulated a version of American Protestantism known as Mormonism.

3.   Coterminous with the profusion of religious institutions came the **rise of popular culture.**

     a.   **Blood sports** such as cockfighting, ratting, and dogfights proved highly popular with the urban working class.

     b.   Prizefighting, or **boxing,** grew out of subterranean culture to become a highly popular form of entertainment throughout society.

     c.   Americans of all stripes overcame the old Puritan squeamishness and began to patronize an **American theater** which featured everything from Shakespeare to amateur spectacles.

     d.   The most popular form of theater was the **minstrelsy,** which demonstrated the blatant racism of most of America.

     e.   Among the many commodities the market revolution made available, few were more ubiquitous than **novels and the penny press,** which included sales of millions of cheap books and magazines.

4.   The leading elements of southern whites self-consciously built their society around the three pillars of **family, church, and neighborhood.**

     a.   The individualism of northern culture proved secondary to the place of **southern families** and southern honor in the values of the South.

     b.   **Southern entertainments,** including horse racing, hunting, fishing, and other outdoor activities reflected the essentially rural character of the South.

     c.   As more southerners found religion a form of entertainment as well as a source of spiritual nourishment, the **camp meeting** became respectable.

     d.   Southerners embraced **religious conservatism** together with a conviction that fundamental political and social traditionalism was vital to its culture.

     e.   In time, the union of plantation economic interests and Protestantism resulted in a distinctly **proslavery Christianity.**

5.   Determined to shield themselves from their masters in some measure, slaves sought to maintain distinctly **private lives,** often at great personal risk.

      a.   The **slave family,** a vital element in the difficult rigor of slave life, emerged as a crucial institution separate from white oversight, at least to some extent.

      b.   In spite of events like Nat Turner's Rebellion, **white missions** resulted from southern evangelical preachers' abandonment of their hostility toward slave religiosity.

      c.   **Slave Christians** embraced the evangelism but ignored much of the secular teachings of the white missionaries who sought to use religion as a means of assuring slave submissiveness.

      d.   Invariably, **religion and revolt** came together in the violent insurrections of Denmark Vesey in South Carolina and Nat Turner in Virginia.

      e.   **Nat Turner** led a rebellion in 1831 that forced Virginians to reconsider the institution of slavery in the Old Dominion.

Conclusion: In the wake of the changes that accompanied the market revolution, a distinct set of American cultural values emerged, although with distinct differences north and south of the Mason–Dixon Line. Adherence to republican values and a wholesale embrace of market capitalism characterized the new culture of the northern middle class while southerners were more reticent about embracing market forces.

TEACHING RESOURCES

Harriet Beecher Stowe: Uncle Tom's Cabin offers an abridged version of the George Aiken dramatization. Films for the Humanities & Sciences (45 minutes, color).

The West, episode two, examines the early, yet steady expansion of Americans into the West. PBS Video (55 minutes).

Working for the Lord discusses the impact of religion on the lives of eighteenth- and nineteenth-century Americans. Republic Pictures Home Video (52 minutes).

MULTIPLE CHOICE

1.   The new, northern middle class of the early nineteenth century would best be described as
    a. country merchants, master craftsmen, and market-oriented farmers.
    b. mill workers, journeymen, and wage-laborers.
    c. tenant farmers, day laborers, and outworkers.
    d. factory workers and small farmers.
    e. plantation owners.

ANS: A   **TYPE: M**   **KEY 1: A**   **KEY 2: 2**   **PAGE: 324**

2.   The large revivals in the northern United States most affected the values and beliefs of the
    a. working class.
    b. middle class.
    c. upper class.
    d. poverty stricken.
    e. African Americans

ANS: B   **TYPE: M**   **KEY 1: F**   **KEY 2: 1**   **PAGE: 324**

3. Which of the following would be an accurate description of a nineteenth-century revivalist's message to a northern religious revival?
   a. Men and women had no power over their own salvation.
   b. Most men and women were destined to everlasting eternal life.
   c. Most men and women were damned to eternal hell.
   d. The end of the world was nigh.
   e. Men and women were moral free agents.

ANS: E   TYPE: M   KEY 1: A   KEY 2: 3   PAGE: 324-25

4. By the 1830s, most of the responsibility for child-rearing in northern homes rested with
   a. fathers.
   b. mothers.
   c. the school.
   d. the church.
   e. the servants.

ANS: B   TYPE: M   KEY 1: F   KEY 2: 1   PAGE: 325

5. During the early nineteenth century, the birthrate among northern middle-class mothers
   a. increased.
   b. decreased.
   c. remained the same.
   d. is impossible to determine because few accurate records survive.
   e. none of the above

ANS: B   TYPE: M   KEY 1: F   KEY 2: 2   PAGE: 325

6. The first mass-circulation magazine for women was
   a. *Woman's Day*.
   b. *Good Housekeeping*.
   c. *Godey's Ladies Book*.
   d. *Family Circle*.
   e. *New Yorker*.

ANS: C   TYPE: M   KEY 1: F   KEY 2: 1   PAGE: 326

7. The most widely read novelist in the United States before the publication of *Uncle Tom's Cabin* was
   a. Nathaniel Hawthorne.
   b. Herman Melville.
   c. Harriet Beecher Stowe.
   d. Susan Warner.
   e. Walt Whitman.

ANS: D   TYPE: M   KEY 1: F   KEY 2: 2   PAGE: 326

8. The author of *Uncle Tom's Cabin* was
   a. Harriet Beecher Stowe.
   b. Lydia Maria Child.
   c. Catherine Beecher.
   d. Sarah Josepha Hale.
   e. Nathaniel Hawthorne.

ANS: A   TYPE: M   KEY 1: F   KEY 2: 1   PAGE: 327

9. For the most part, the domesticity novels written by women during the mid-nineteenth century were
    a. frivolous fairy tales.
    b. subversive attacks on the power relations in society.
    c. sentimental pastimes of little import.
    d. political calls for revolution.
    e. stories that supported the power structure.

ANS: B   **TYPE: M**   **KEY 1: A**   **KEY 2: 2**   **PAGE: 327**

10. The leading artists of mid-nineteenth-century America were
    a. portrait painters.
    b. landscape painters.
    c. surrealists.
    d. sculptors.
    e. political activists.

ANS: B   **TYPE: M**   **KEY 1: F**   **KEY 2: 2**   **PAGE: 328**

11. The religious leader who believed that the Earth would be destroyed in 1844 was
    a. Brigham Young.
    b. Joseph Smith.
    c. William Miller.
    d. Mathias.
    e. John Noyes.

ANS: C   **TYPE: M**   **KEY 1: F**   **KEY 2: 2**   **PAGE: 331**

12. The founder of Mormonism, born in upstate New York in the early nineteenth century, was
    a. Brigham Young.
    b. William Miller.
    c. Mathias.
    d. Joseph Smith.
    e. Sylvester Graham.

ANS: D   **TYPE: M**   **KEY 1: F**   **KEY 2: 1**   **PAGE: 332**

13. Each of the following was popular among the northern working class in the mid-nineteenth century except
    a. cock fighting.
    b. prize fighting.
    c. dog fighting.
    d. opera.
    e. minstrel shows.

ANS: D   **TYPE: M**   **KEY 1: F**   **KEY 2: 1**   **PAGE: 332-33**

14. The most popular form of theater among nineteenth-century Americans was
    a. Shakespearean dramas.
    b. Sir Walter Scott romances.
    c. minstrel shows.
    d. burlesque shows.
    e. opera.

ANS: C   **TYPE: M**   **KEY 1: F**   **KEY 2: 2**   **PAGE: 334**

15. For the most part, the white family in the South was committed to
    a. egalitarian family relations.
    b. almost equal sharing of authority between mothers and fathers.
    c. promiscuous family relationships.
    d. a maternalistic familial organization.
    e. traditional, paternalistic control.

ANS: C   **TYPE: M**   **KEY 1: A**   **KEY 2: 2**   **PAGE: 338**

16. Although camp meetings continued to be held in the South, for the most part they were held by
    a. Methodists.
    b. Baptists.
    c. Anglicans.
    d. Lutherans.
    e. Blacks

ANS: A   **TYPE: M**   **KEY 1: F**   **KEY 2: 2**   **PAGE: 340**

17. White southerners justified the institution of slavery with each of the following religious arguments except
    a. Jesus never criticized slavery.
    b. slaves were the descendants of Ham and deserved enslavement.
    c. slavery had given African Americans Christianity.
    d. the Epistles of Paul urged slaves to obey their masters.
    e. slavery was a gift to God.

ANS: E   **TYPE: M**   **KEY 1: A**   **KEY 2: 2**   **PAGE: 340-41**

18. For the most part, owners _____ slave marriages.
    a. encouraged
    b. discouraged
    c. gave little thought to
    d. did not sanction
    e. forced

ANS: A   **TYPE: M**   **KEY 1: F**   **KEY 2: 1**   **PAGE: 342**

19. At their own religious meetings, slaves practiced a faith that was
    a. similar to that of their masters.
    b. at variance with that of their masters.
    c. exactly the same as that of their masters.
    d. none of the above—slaves were not allowed to run their own slave meetings.
    e. a call for violent revolution to bring on the end of the world.

ANS: B   **TYPE: M**   **KEY 1: A**   **KEY 2: 2**   **PAGE: 344-45**

20. The leader of the aborted slave rebellion in South Carolina in 1822 was
    a. Nat Turner.
    b. Gabriel.
    c. Denmark Vesey.
    d. Frederick Douglass.
    e. none of the above

ANS: C   **TYPE: M**   **KEY 1: F**   **KEY 2: 1**   **PAGE: 346-47**

21. The large slave rebellion that began in Southampton, Virginia, in 1831 under the leadership of a Baptist lay minister was known as the
    a. Nat Turner Revolt.
    b. Denmark Vesey Revolt.
    c. Swamplands Revolt.
    d. Gullah Revolt.
    e. Southampton Revolt.

ANS: A   TYPE: M   KEY 1: F   KEY 2: 1   PAGE: 346-47

22. Which of the following were most likely to be postmillennialists?
    a. evangelicals
    b. Baptists
    c. Methodists
    d. Disciples of Christ
    e. Anglicans

ANS: A   TYPE: M   KEY 1: A   KEY 2: 2   PAGE: 330

23. The national culture that developed after the 1830s included all of the following elements except
    a. republicanism.
    b. capitalism.
    c. abolitionism.
    d. Protestantism.
    e. paternalism

ANS: C   TYPE: M   KEY 1: A   KEY 2: 1   PAGE: 324

24. Slave rebellions had little chance of success in the southern United States because
    a. the slaves generally were content with their situation.
    b. slaves were far outnumbered by whites.
    c. slaves were more interested in freedom in the next world.
    d. slaves feared punishment if they were caught.
    e. whites gave in to most slave demands.

ANS: B   TYPE: M   KEY 1: F   KEY 2: 3   PAGE: 346

25. After 1830, American national culture
    a. did not really exist.
    b. was predominantly elitist and Roman Catholic.
    c. was based on slavery and inequality.
    d. was heavily influenced by immigration from eastern and southern Europe.
    e. included numerous regional, economic, and racial subcultures.

ANS: C   TYPE: M   KEY 1: A   KEY 2: 3   PAGE: 348

26. Which of the following was not a characteristic of the emerging middle class of the 1830s?
    a. The Southwest was its center.
    b. Its domestic life was mother-centered and very private.
    c. It was individualistic rather than communalistic.
    d. It followed the basic moral precepts of reformed Protestantism.
    e. It benefited from the market economy.

ANS: A   TYPE: M   KEY 1: A   KEY 2: 3   PAGE: 324

27. Traditional Yankee Calvinists believed
    a. that Christians should redistribute the wealth of the nation in order to help the poor.
    b. that human beings were basically good, moral, and selfless.
    c. in a revolutionary philosophy that constantly challenged the existing class system.
    d. that slavery must be abolished.
    e. that it was sinful to try to change the nation's social order.

ANS: E   **TYPE: M**   **KEY 1: A**   **KEY 2: 2**   **PAGE: 324**

28. The popular literature of the 1830s
    a. was primarily written by women for women.
    b. characterized women as weak, helpless, and fragile.
    c. first introduced the male dominated action-adventure story to the public.
    d. consisted of newspapers and magazines.
    e. was not widely circulated.

ANS: A   **TYPE: M**   **KEY 1: F**   **KEY 2: 2**   **PAGE: 326**

29. The popularity of *Uncle Tom's Cabin* was a result of its
    a. portrayal of the redemptive spiritual power of submissive Christians.
    b. indictment of all southern whites as evil, abusive slave drivers.
    c. uplifting, happy ending.
    d. attack on the dangerous, subversive power of a female-dominated society.
    e. attack on the corruption of American politics.

ANS: A   **TYPE: M**   **KEY 1: A**   **KEY 2: 3**   **PAGE: 327**

30. In the 1820s and 1830s, American attitudes toward the fine arts were shaped by all of the following except
    a. the rejection of traditional Calvinistic suspicion of—and distrust for—aesthetic expression.
    b. the acceptance of a romantic and sentimental approach to literature and painting.
    c. the triumph of civilization over the wilderness.
    d. an appreciation of nature.
    e. immigration to the United States from Europe.

ANS: E   **TYPE: M**   **KEY 1: A**   **KEY 2: 3**   **PAGE: 327-28**

31. In the 1820s and 1830s, the American public viewed nature as
    a. an evil wilderness controlled by the devil.
    b. an orderly, beautiful example of God's creative plan.
    c. a dangerous and terrifying threat to the survival of mankind.
    d. boring and uninteresting when compared to the thrills of city life.
    e. a haven for the savage Indians.

ANS: B   **TYPE: M**   **KEY 1: A**   **KEY 2: 2**   **PAGE: 327-28**

32. Protestant postmillennialists
    a. were mostly Southern Baptists and Methodists.
    b. believed that the world would be destroyed by fire.
    c. believed that there would be a thousand years of perfect social order followed by the return of Christ.
    d. predicted the destruction of the world in 1837.
    e. hoped to unite all Protestant faiths into one.

ANS: C   **TYPE: M**   **KEY 1: F**   **KEY 2: 2**   **PAGE: 330**

33. Members of the Church of Jesus Christ of Latter-Day Saints (the Mormons) believed that
    a. descendants of the ancient Hebrews had been living in the Americas for many generations before Columbus' 1492 voyage.
    b. merchants and lawyers were the best spiritual leaders for the church.
    c. the church leadership should be equally divided between women and men.
    d. angels were mythological pagan fantasies.
    e. all races were created equal.

ANS: A   TYPE: M   KEY 1: F   KEY 2: 2   PAGE: 332

34. Which of the following is true of early boxing matches?
    a. Most of the fighters were native-born Americans of German descent.
    b. The bare-knuckled fights were so brutal that the participants were sometimes severely injured or killed.
    c. There were no rules and "no holds barred" in the contests.
    d. The audiences were usually from the middle and upper classes.
    e. No one was ever actually hurt.

ANS: B   TYPE: M   KEY 1: F   KEY 2: 2   PAGE: 333-34

35. The American theater in the mid-nineteenth century
    a. produced plays and musicals written and performed by American citizens, not by Europeans.
    b. was considered a low-class, vulgar form of entertainment.
    c. inspired heated class loyalties and debates that sometimes led to violence.
    d. was so expensive that only the wealthy could afford to buy tickets.
    e. none of the above

ANS: C   TYPE: M   KEY 1: F   KEY 2: 2   PAGE: 334

36. Nineteenth-century minstrel shows
    a. were traveling productions in which white men in "black face" imitated African-American songs and dances.
    b. were most popular with female audiences.
    c. were the first theatrical entertainments to include black performers as regular troupe members.
    d. were popular only in the large seaport cities of the Northeast.
    e. were popular only in the South.

ANS: A   TYPE: M   KEY 1: F   KEY 2: 2   PAGE: 334

37. The "yellow backed" fiction and penny press publications
    a. portrayed a benign world in which good always triumphed over evil.
    b. were popular with women readers because of the strong, morally superior female characters in the stories.
    c. used graphic violence and sexual perversion to attract customers.
    d. were designed to appeal to well-educated, sophisticated, upper-class readers.
    e. appealed only to immigrants.

ANS: C   TYPE: M   KEY 1: F   KEY 2: 3   PAGE: 337

38. In the southern code of behavior,
    a. people were encouraged to think of themselves as independent, free-thinking individuals.
    b. wealth was the primary factor in determining social status.
    c. peaceful and friendly relations between whites and blacks were promoted.
    d. religion played the most important role in shaping behavior.
    e. personal reputation and family honor were the basis of community respect.

ANS: E   **TYPE: M**   **KEY 1: F**   **KEY 2: 3**   **PAGE: 338**

39. Successful slave owners found that the easiest way to control their slaves was through
    a. terror and draconian discipline (whippings and even murder).
    b. treating slaves like little children.
    c. educating and training slaves to encourage feelings of self-worth.
    d. giving slaves their freedom and paying them wages.
    e. offering slaves limited independence and privileges in return for their labor and obedience.

ANS: E   **TYPE: M**   **KEY 1: A**   **KEY 2: 3**   **PAGE: 341**

40. Southern slaves
    a. had no noticeable culture.
    b. simply imitated white behavior.
    c. created their own culture, which included religious piety and African-style songs and folk magic.
    d. were brutalized to the extent that they became irresponsible and childlike.
    e. never resisted slavery.

ANS: C   **TYPE: M**   **KEY 1: F**   **KEY 2: 3**   **PAGE: 341-43**

41. The most popular religions among plain folk after the 1830s shared all of the following except
    a. a rejection of middle-class optimism and reformism.
    b. the belief that churchly authority was more important than individual experience.
    c. a distrust of religious professionalism.
    d. a preference for local control of religious life.
    e. a belief in God's vast and unknowable plan.

ANS: B   **TYPE: M**   **KEY 1: A**   **KEY 2: 3**   **PAGE: 329-30**

42. All of the following were significant components of the Millerite movement except
    a. Congregationalists.
    b. Methodists.
    c. Baptists.
    d. Disciples of Christ.
    e. poor people from New York, Ohio and Michigan.

ANS: A   **TYPE: M**   **KEY 1: F**   **KEY 2: 2**   **PAGE: 331**

43. The first center of factory production was
    a. the Midwest.
    b. the Southeast.
    c. New England.
    d. New York.
    e. the Great Lakes region.

ANS: C   **TYPE: M**   **KEY 1: F**   **KEY 2: 1**   **PAGE: 324**

44. With the rise of middle class culture, child rearing practices changed in all of the following ways except
    a. Mothers assumed the primary child rearing responsibilities.
    b. Children were reared with love and reason, rather than fear.
    c. Fewer children meant that each child received more attention.
    d. Harsher discipline became necessary to instill the values of a market-driven society.
    e. Sunday schools became training grounds for moral free agency.

ANS: C   **TYPE: M**   **KEY 1: A**   **KEY 2: 2**   **PAGE: 325-26**

45. After 1825, middleclass Americans' favorite tourist destination was
    a. Washington, D.C.
    b. New York City.
    c. Niagara Falls.
    d. Charleston, South Carolina.
    e. Lake Michigan.

ANS: C   **TYPE: M**   **KEY 1: F**   **KEY 2: 2**   **PAGE: 328**

46. Most Protestant denominations in America
    a. emphasized the importance of a hierarchy of authority in the church.
    b. favored local control in their churches.
    c. rejected evangelicalism
    d. believed that human society was perfectible.
    e. taught racial equality.

ANS: B   **TYPE: M**   **KEY 1: A**   **KEY 2: 3**   **PAGE: 329-30**

47. When working class American audiences found theater productions too sophisticated for their tastes,
    a. they walked out of the theater.
    b. they began producing their own plays.
    c. they resorted to mob violence.
    d. they refused to attend the productions.
    e. the theatres were closed.

ANS: C   **TYPE: M**   **KEY 1: A**   **KEY 2: 2**   **PAGE: 334**

48. Minstrel shows included
    a. political satire.
    b. sexual jokes.
    c. ridicule of the elite.
    d. racial humor
    e. all of the above.

ANS: D   **TYPE: M**   **KEY 1: F**   **KEY 2: 3**   **PAGE: 334**

49. The Biblical figure most revered in white Southern churches was
    a. Abraham.
    b. Adam.
    c. Moses.
    d. Noah.
    e. Isaac.

ANS: A   **TYPE: M**   **KEY 1: F**   **KEY 2: 3**   **PAGE: 340**

50. Slave marriages
    a. were not recognized by the law.
    b. were discouraged by slave owners.
    c. were legally binding.
    d. were not recognized or respected within the slave community.
    e. did not exist.

ANS: A   TYPE: M   KEY 1: F   KEY 2: 2   PAGE: 342

TRUE/FALSE

____1.   Slave revolts in nineteenth-century North America were regular and violent.

ANS: F   TYPE: T   KEY 1: F   KEY 2: 2   PAGE: 346

____2.   For the most part, religion and the position of pro-slavery advocates were compatible in the South.

ANS: T   TYPE: T   KEY 1: A   KEY 2: 2   PAGE: 343

____3.   Most southern whites regarded themselves less as individuals and more as representatives of families.

ANS: T   TYPE: T   KEY 1: F   KEY 2: 2   PAGE: 338

____4.   For the most part, the evangelical middle class and poorer, conservative evangelists both shared similar positive views of the developing market economy.

ANS: F   TYPE: T   KEY 1: A   KEY 2: 2   PAGE: 324-25

____5.   Millerites were a religious group that believed the world would end in the year following March 1843.

ANS: T   TYPE: T   KEY 1: F   KEY 2: 1   PAGE: 331

____6.   Gullah Jack helped to spread word of plans for Denmark Vesey's revolt.

ANS: T   TYPE: T   KEY 1: F   KEY 2: 1   PAGE: 346

____7.   The best-selling author of the antebellum period (before Harriet Beecher Stowe) was Susan Warner.

ANS: T   TYPE: T   KEY 1: F   KEY 2: 2   PAGE: 326

____8.   The religious revivalist who preached to, and converted, thousands was Nat Turner.

ANS: F   TYPE: T   KEY 1: F   KEY 2: 1   PAGE: 346

____9.   For the most part, slave marriages were legally recognized and respected by white society.

ANS: F   TYPE: T   KEY 1: F   KEY 2: 2   PAGE: 341-42

____10.   In their daily lives, middle-class Christians carefully abided by the strict Puritan beliefs.

ANS: F   TYPE: T   KEY 1: A   KEY 2: 2   PAGE: 324

_____ 11.   Prosperous Americans in the 1830s believed in progress and in human ability to control and improve society.

ANS: T   TYPE: T   KEY 1: A   KEY 2: 2   PAGE: 324

_____ 12.   Most of the members of Denmark Vesey's African Methodist Congregation were free blacks.

ANS: F   TYPE: T   KEY 1: F   KEY 2: 2   PAGE: 346

_____ 13.   Educated Americans before the 1820s viewed the fine arts as extravagant, artificial products of European monarchial society.

ANS: T   TYPE: T   KEY 1: A   KEY 2: 2   PAGE: 327-28

_____ 14.   An 1849 dispute over the acting styles of two Shakespearians led to a riot in which twenty people were killed.

ANS: T   TYPE: T   KEY 1: F   KEY 2: 2   PAGE: 334

_____ 15.   The southern literary market was the largest specialized constituency in the nation.

ANS: F   TYPE: T   KEY 1: F   KEY 2:2   PAGE: 339

_____ 16.   The United States experienced a single wave of social and cultural change after 1815.

ANS: F   TYPE: T   KEY 1: A   KEY 2: 1   PAGE: 324

_____ 17.   Market-oriented farmers were part of the newly emerging middle class.

ANS: T   TYPE: T   KEY 1: A   KEY 2: 2   PAGE: 324

_____ 18.   Northern lay people uniformly accepted the leadership of the middle-class evangelicals.

ANS: F   TYPE: T   KEY 1: A   KEY 2: 2   PAGE: 329

_____ 19.   Slave girls were often named after their mother.

ANS: F   TYPE: T   KEY 1: F   KEY 2: 1   PAGE: 343

_____ 20.   Evangelicals often criticized market society.

ANS: T   TYPE: T   KEY 1: F   KEY 2: 1   PAGE: 329-30

_____ 21.   The Baptist millenarian William Miller condemned greed and the city of New York.

ANS: T   TYPE: T   KEY 1: F   KEY 2: 1   PAGE: 331

_____ 22.   Joseph Smith set himself up as the first patriarch of the Mormon Church.

ANS: F   TYPE: T   KEY 1: F   KEY 2: 1   PAGE: 332

_____ 23.   Early prizefights had a firm time limit.

ANS: F   TYPE: T   KEY 1: F   KEY 2: 2   PAGE: 334

_____ 24.   Audience participation was discouraged at minstrel shows.

ANS: F   **TYPE: T**   **KEY 1: F**   **KEY 2: 1**   **PAGE: 335**

_____ 25.   Southern life was all about freedom, individual fulfillment, and social progress.

ANS: F   **TYPE: T**   **KEY 1: A**   **KEY 2: 1**   **PAGE: 338**

_____ 26.   Southern camp meetings were usually limited to a single denomination.

ANS: T   **TYPE: T**   **KEY 1: A**   **KEY 2: 1**   **PAGE: 339-40**

_____ 27.   Like southern whites, slaves often married a first cousin.

ANS: F   **TYPE: T**   **KEY 1: A**   **KEY 2: 3**   **PAGE: 343**

_____ 28.   Southern laws after 1830 outlawing black preachers were rigidly enforced.

ANS: F   **TYPE: T**   **KEY 1: A**   **KEY 2: 2**   **PAGE: 344**

_____ 29.   Slaves often took the surname of their current owner.

ANS: F   **TYPE: T**   **KEY 1: F**   **KEY 2: 1**   **PAGE: 342**

_____ 30.   The Yankee middle class made crucial distinctions between the home and the world.

ANS: T   **TYPE: T**   **KEY 1: A**   **KEY 2: 2**   **PAGE: 325-26**

_____ 31.   Child rearing became an increasingly female task in the antebellum period.

ANS: T   **TYPE: T**   **KEY 1: A**   **KEY 2: 1**   **PAGE: 325**

_____ 32.   Sunday schools after the 1820s and 1830s focused on having students copy long passages from the Bible.

ANS: F   **TYPE: T**   **KEY 1: A**   **KEY 2: 2**   **PAGE: 326**

_____ 33.   The action in sentimental novels normally took place outdoors.

ANS: F   **TYPE: T**   **KEY 1: A**   **KEY 2: 1**   **PAGE: 326**

_____ 34.   The most successful sentimental novel in the antebellum period was *The Wide, Wide World*.

ANS: F   **TYPE: T**   **KEY 1: F**   **KEY 2: 1**   **PAGE: 326**

_____ 35.   In 1831, wealthy New Yorkers put up the money to build Mount Auburn Cemetery.

ANS: F   **TYPE: T**   **KEY 1: F**   **KEY 2: 1**   **PAGE: 328**

_____ 36.   The plain folk of the North were culturally conservative.

ANS: T   **TYPE: T**   **KEY 1: F**   **KEY 2: 1**   **PAGE: 329**

_____ 37.   Northern plain folk believed that all events were willed or allowed by God.

ANS: T   TYPE: T   KEY 1: A   KEY 2: 2   PAGE: 330

_____ 38.   Northern parents displayed tremendous grief at the death of a child.

ANS: F   TYPE: T   KEY 1: A   KEY 2: 2   PAGE: 330

_____ 39.   Plain folk in the North built elaborate local cemeteries.

ANS: F   TYPE: T   KEY 1: A   KEY 2: 2   PAGE: 330

_____ 40.   The plain Protestants of the North talked often of the millennium.

ANS: F   TYPE: T   KEY 1: A   KEY 2: 2   PAGE: 330

FILL-INS

1.   The religious evangelical who led a middle-class revival in Rochester, New York was
_____.

ANS: Charles Finney   TYPE: F   KEY 1: F   KEY 2: 3   PAGE: 324

2.   The free black who organized a slave rebellion in 1822 South Carolina was _____.

ANS: Denmark Vesey   TYPE: F   KEY 1: F   KEY 2: 2   PAGE: 346

3.   The author of _Uncle Tom's Cabin_ was _____.

ANS: Harriet B. Stowe   TYPE: F   KEY 1: F   KEY 2: 1   PAGE: 326

4.   The first mass-circulation magazine for women was _____.

ANS: _Godey's Ladies Book_   TYPE: F   KEY 1: F   KEY 2: 2   PAGE: 326

5.   Cheap "story papers," "yellow-back" fiction, and dime novels found their first and largest audience among _____.

ANS: city workers   TYPE: F   KEY 1: F   KEY 2: 2   PAGE: 337

6.   The Southern Presbyterian minister who wrote "how to preach to slaves" manuals and encouraged slaves to be obedient was _____.

ANS: Charles Colcock Jones   TYPE: F   KEY 1: F   KEY 2: 2   PAGE: 343

7.   Middle-class culture was most profoundly shaped by the _____ section of the country.

ANS: northeastern   TYPE: F   KEY 1: A   KEY 2: 2   PAGE: 324

8.   After the 1830s, Baptists and Methodists came to contain _____ of the nation's professing Protestants, North and South.

ANS: two-thirds   TYPE: F   KEY 1: F   KEY 2: 1   PAGE: 329

9. The Mormon Church was organized along _____ lines.

ANS: patriarchal   **TYPE: F**   **KEY 1: F**   **KEY 2: 1**   **PAGE: 332**

10. Some of the best early American prizefighters were _____ from New York City.

ANS: butchers   **TYPE: F**   **KEY 1: F**   **KEY 2: 2**   **PAGE: 333**

11. The most popular author among wealthy southerners was _____.

ANS: Shakespeare   **TYPE: F**   **KEY 1: F**   **KEY 2: 1**   **PAGE: 339**

12. The horse racing capital of the United States during the decades before the Civil War was _____.

ANS: New Orleans   **TYPE: F**   **KEY 1: F**   **KEY 2: 1**   **PAGE: 339**

13. Nat Turner's revolt occurred in the state of _____.

ANS: Virginia   **TYPE: F**   **KEY 1: F**   **KEY 2: 1**   **PAGE: 346**

14. The most likely converts at evangelical gatherings were seated on the _____.

ANS: anxious bench   **TYPE: F**   **KEY 1: F**   **KEY 2: 2**   **PAGE: 325**

15. The leading artists of the antebellum period were _____.

ANS: landscape painters   **TYPE: F**   **KEY 1: F**   **KEY 2: 2**   **PAGE: 328**

16. According to Thomas Cole, America's most distinctive feature was its _____.

ANS: wilderness   **TYPE: F**   **KEY 1: F**   **KEY 2: 2**   **PAGE: 328**

17. _____ ran New York City's Sportsman Hall, a saloon that became a frequent venue for blood sports.

ANS: Kit Burns   **TYPE: F**   **KEY 1: F**   **KEY 2: 3**   **PAGE: 333**

18. Prize fighting was imported into the United States from _____.

ANS: Britain   **TYPE: F**   **KEY 1: F**   **KEY 2: 2**   **PAGE: 333**

19. The section of the nation where middleclass culture was most pervasive was _____.

ANS: New England   **TYPE: F**   **KEY 1: F**   **KEY 2: 2**   **PAGE: 324**

20. In New England _____ served the purpose of developing children's moral sensibilities without harsh discipline.

ANS: Sunday schools   **TYPE: F**   **KEY 1: A**   **KEY 2: 3**   **PAGE: 326**

21. The best selling novel printed in the years before the Civil War was _____.

ANS: *Uncle Tom's Cabin*   **TYPE: F**   **KEY 1: F**   **KEY 2: 2**   **PAGE: 326**

22. A cemetery that became a public park celebrating nature's renewal was _____.

ANS: Mount Auburn   **TYPE: F**   **KEY 1: F**   **KEY 2: 2**   **PAGE: 328**

23. An American author who wrote about living a deliberately simple life in the woods was _____.

ANS: Henry David Thoreau   **TYPE: F**   **KEY 1: F**   **KEY 2: 2**   **PAGE: 328**

24. Followers of the William Miller, a New York Baptist who predicted that God would destroy the world in 1843, founded the _____ church.

ANS: Seventh-Day Adventist   **TYPE: F**   **KEY 1: F**   **KEY 2: 3**   **PAGE: 331**

25. Joseph Smith labeled the centuries of greed and error of the Christian churches the _____.

ANS: Apostasy   **TYPE: F**   **KEY 1: F**   **KEY 2: 3**   **PAGE: 332**

26. _____ was a Shakespearean actor targeted by a mob because of his refined and restrained style.

ANS: William Charles Macready   **TYPE: F**   **KEY 1: F**   **KEY 2: 2**   **PAGE: 334**

27. The Shakespeare play preferred by working-class audiences was _____.

ANS: Richard III   **TYPE: F**   **KEY 1: F**   **KEY 2: 2**   **PAGE: 334**

28. African American song and dance was introduced to American audiences in the _____ shows.

ANS: minstrel   **TYPE: F**   **KEY 1: F**   **KEY 2: 1**   **PAGE: 334-35**

29. The author of *Quaker City,* a novel attacking the hypocrisy of the Christian elite, was _____.

ANS: George Lippard   **TYPE: F**   **KEY 1: F**   **KEY 2: 2**   **PAGE: 336-37**

30. Southerners held jousting tournaments and other medieval events inspired by the works of _____.

ANS: Sir Walter Scott   **TYPE: F**   **KEY 1: F**   **KEY 2: 2**   **PAGE: 339**

IDENTIFICATIONS

1. **Nat Turner**: slave rebellion leader in 1831 Virginia. Experienced visions, which he understood to foretell a successful rebellion against the white master. Large-scale rebellion eventually was crushed, but only after the death of about one hundred whites and blacks.

2. *Uncle Tom's Cabin:* best-selling novel in nineteenth-century America, written by Harriet Beecher Stowe. Although primarily seen as an attack on slavery, also written as an attack on the market-dominated society in America at the time.

3. **Susan Warner**: nineteenth-century domestic author. Very popular; the themes of her books tended to emphasize the importance of a well-ordered home life as a necessary antidote to the market-oriented society. Wrote the best-selling novel *The Wide, Wide World.*

4. **Joseph Smith**: upstate New Yorker who claimed to receive visions from angels that led him to the golden plates that he translated into the *Book of Mormon*. With several thousand followers, he began the Church of Jesus Christ of Latter-Day Saints.

5. **minstrel shows**: popular form of entertainment in the North that first appeared in 1831. White actors, dressed in blackface, parodied racial stereotypes for white audiences. Although these shows promoted the idea of black racial inferiority, they also introduced mainstream society to certain aspects of black culture that otherwise would not have been acknowledged.

6. **William Miller**: Baptist evangelical preacher from New York who predicted that the destruction of the world would occur after March 1843. Thousands of his followers, called Millerites, gathered together, prayed, and attended meetings waiting for the end of the world. The movement faded after March 1844 but in the 1860s former Millerites established the Seventh-Day Adventist Church.

7. **Denmark Vesey**: free black Methodist from Charleston, South Carolina who plotted a complicated slave rebellion. In 1822 he and his followers planned to seize an arsenal, arm slaves, kill whites, take over Charleston and sail to Haiti. The plan was betrayed by slaves and Vesey and thirty-three co-conspirators were hanged.

8. **blood sports**: popular among urban working men. Included cockfighting, ratting, and dog fighting. They became very popular during the 1850s, when they came to be staged by saloonkeepers, despite laws banning such activities in many states.

9. **Sunday schools**: shifted to an emphasis on preparing children's souls for conversion after the revivals of the 1820s and 1830s. Middle-class children were now included in classes, corporal punishment was forbidden, and teachers tried to develop the moral sensibilities of their charges. Sunday schools became training grounds for free agency and moral accountability.

10. **rural cemeteries**: pioneered in Boston in 1831 and soon copied in Brooklyn, Rochester, and other northern cities. Incorporated rolling ground, footpaths that followed the contours of the land, natural vegetation supplemented with wildflowers, and small dignified headstones. They embodied the faith that nature could teach moral lessons, particularly if nature was shaped and made available to humankind through art.

SHORT ESSAYS

1. Explore the value and belief structures of the Northern middle class.

Answer: The Northern middle class came together consciously as a class during the first several decades of the nineteenth century. The rise of this group was the direct consequence of the market and transportation revolutions that had occurred during the period from 1790 to 1840. A middle class, of course, always had existed in some form, but this group of merchants, master craftsmen, manufacturers, and commercially driven farmers and other entrepreneurs created the new emerging market economy.

For the most part, these values emphasized the principles of capitalist acquisitivism. The idea of progress directed this group, a progress that rested firmly with material goals. Competitive, profit oriented, and individualistic, this new middle class turned its back on the emphasis on community, reciprocity, and group-oriented goals most evident in the seventeenth and eighteenth centuries. The new middle class was not consciously opposed to these ideas and, much like their forebears, hoped for the material growth of the entire community. A cardinal tenet of the new middle-class ideology, however, was that, ultimately, the individual was responsible for himself—opportunities existed only for those who worked hard.

2. Examine the antebellum home-life-oriented, or domestic, literature of the United States.

Answer: With important developments in the areas of printing and education, the early nineteenth century became a fertile time for literature and literary developments. The most famous writers of the nineteenth century—authors like Hawthorne, Poe, and Melville—were not necessarily the most widely read. Indeed, an author like Hawthorne complained about the lagging sales of his books as compared to those of popular sentimental writers like Lydia Maria Child and Susan Warner. Women authors controlled the literary market in the early nineteenth century, selling several hundred thousand copies of books during these years. Their novels were both a reflection of, and a catalyst for, the emerging middle-class culture of the North. Emphasizing sentimentality and domesticity, these novels juxtaposed the sanctity of the home to the vagaries and dangers of the marketplace. Indeed, in novels like Warner's *The Wide, Wide World* and Harriet Beecher Stowe's *Uncle Tom's Cabin,* it is the family that is seen as the last bastion of republican virtue—the family under the moral direction of the virtuous and domestic mother figure. In many ways, these novels were a subversive depiction of a world unrelated to the one dominated by the economic market, a market that, to many, seemed to threaten the republic itself.

3.   Describe the various types of popular entertainment that appealed to northern Americans in the nineteenth century.

Answer: With the various market developments that characterized northern society in the period from 1820 to 1840, new forms of entertainment, and new-found leisure time to enjoy this entertainment, were emerging. Although originating in working-class urban areas, these forms of entertainment also permeated rural parts of the North, although usually textured with a local flavor. While many of these amusements were violent—such as cockfighting and ratting—others simply were action-packed, such as exuberant dramatizations of Shakespeare's plays. One of the most popular was *Richard III,* although a very broadly played version to be sure.

        Quite possibly the most popular nineteenth-century amusement was prizefighting, or boxing. The appeal of the participants was their courage, strength, and masculinity, but ethnic, national, and class pride was tied to the success of this sport as well. Although most of the audience was working-class, a good deal of society's older aristocracy made their way to these events. Conspicuously absent, however, was the emerging middle class; their values and beliefs looked with suspicion on the so-called blood sports. Indeed, during the course of the nineteenth century, middle-class reformers and lawmakers attempted to decrease the growing appetite for these activities, though usually with little success.

4.   Explore the various slave rebellions of the early nineteenth century.

Answer: Although minor slave disturbances occurred throughout colonial and Revolutionary America, rebellions were rarely a threat to the system of slavery itself. When compared to other plantation societies around the globe, there was a relatively small number of such rebellions in the United States. The limited number of rebellions not only had to do with the small size of the plantations but also with the distance between plantations. Whites outnumbered slaves, making large-scale rebellions unlikely and, if they occurred, unsuccessful. Two rebellions of some size, however, the Denmark Vesey and the Nat Turner Revolts, shocked the white South and spread fear throughout the nation.

        The Vesey Revolt was begun by a free black from Charleston, a leading member of the African Methodist congregation there. His plot was an ambitious one that included seizing the state armory, arming rural slaves, and murdering white slaveholders. The plan was betrayed by slaves before it ever began, and Vesey and others were executed by fearful white authorities. The Turner Revolt, in 1831 Virginia, involved far more carnage and the loss of over one hundred white and black lives. It was doomed because of overwhelming odds. Ultimately, the result of these two revolts, aside from the relatively small material and human loss, was to spread fear among whites and reveal a powerful, latent slave militancy that existed despite benign daily appearances.

5.   Examine the millennialist religions that emerged in the nineteenth-century Northeast.

Answer: While the market revolution of the early nineteenth century promised material progress and rewards to the new middle class, it also engendered resentment and tension from other groups in society. Market development sparked a significant increase in new religious groups, particularly those that emphasized millennialism. Market society brought with it uncertainty and insecurity, as well as more tangible problems, such as poverty, vice, and crime. Many were appalled by these developments and could not necessarily blame commercial development directly, but recognized that their world was significantly different and was less certain than that of their parents.

Contrary to the uncertainty of the market was the security of religious dogma. The Mormons were founded by Joseph Smith, an upstate New York farmer who claimed to have received visions from angels. Millerites, on the other hand, were the most dramatic example of the new millennial trends (the belief that the second coming of Christ would occur at the end of a thousand years of social perfection). Founded by William Miller, a New York Baptist, the Millerites believed that the Earth would end in the year following 1843. Of course, the failure of this prediction to occur led to the decline of the church, but the uncertainty that plagued nineteenth-century Americans still existed.

6.   Examine the feminization of middle-class American domestic life in the nineteenth century.

Answer: During the nineteenth century the traditional patriarchal home life of middle-class Americans gave way to a new paradigm. Urban men worked in the world outside the home, while women and children remained within the household. Thus the concept developed that there were separate masculine and feminine spheres. Men went into the public sphere of business and politics; women stayed secluded in the private sphere of child care and housework. The creation of these realms of influence lessened the authority of the male breadwinner within the home and increased the role of the female homemakers. Women were accorded new responsibilities for maintaining the spiritual life of the family and for instructing children in proper behavior. The harsh discipline that had characterized the old male-dominated households gave way to gentle childrearing techniques based on love. Mothers reasoned with their children and tried to instill in them the desire to live a life of self-discipline and righteousness.
　　　By the 1830s, middle-class women were having fewer children and were spacing them further apart than had previous generations. The average woman in Utica, New York, for example, gave birth to 3.6 children at intervals of five years apiece. Homes were no longer noisy and overcrowded, and mothers could devote quality time to the care and instruction of individual children. In general, the feminization of middle-class domestic life created a positive and trusting atmosphere within the home.

7.   Examine the changing American attitudes toward nature and art.

Answer: Traditional American attitudes toward nature and art were shaped by the frontier experience and by the influence of Calvinism. For over two hundred years, Americans struggled to overcome the wilderness and to transform it into a safe and hospitable environment. The world of nature was perceived as a dangerous and hostile place where human beings battled for survival against demonic forces. By the early nineteenth century, nature had been subdued and Americans saw beauty and God's creative powers where once they had seen only death and destruction. Intellectuals and artists found religious inspiration in the wilderness. Thomas Cole and other artists looked to nature for the subject matter of their paintings and celebrated the wonders of America's wild places. Landscape painting was the most distinctive and popular art form of the era. Homeowners cultivated wildflowers, and even cemeteries were designed as public parks to reflect the natural cycles of birth and death. Henry David Thoreau and Ralph Waldo Emerson believed that men could learn moral lessons and experience God's power in the forests. Prosperous Americans took vacation trips to view wonders of nature such as Niagara Falls. In the presence of the awesome beauty of nature, tourists enjoyed an emotional epiphany and felt that they were in the presence of the Creator.

LONG ESSAYS

1.   Compare the cultures of the northern and southern United States in the period from 1820 to 1850.

Answer: Essay should address several key points:

A.   Northern middle-class culture
　　1.   Origins
　　　　a.   Market and transportation revolutions
　　　　b.   Developments in commerce and production
　　2.   World view
　　　　a.   Values, beliefs, and attitudes
　　　　b.   Religious developments
　　3.   Amusements

            a.   Literary and artistic developments
            b.   Popular amusements, sports, and so forth
B.   Southern elite culture
        1.   Origins
                a.   Seventeenth-century origins
                b.   Impact of market revolution
        2.   World view
                a.   Values, beliefs, and attitudes
                b.   Religious developments
        3.   Amusements
        4.   Significance of slavery
                a.   Defense of slavery
                b.   Slavery and the South

2.   Examine the slave culture that flourished in the nineteenth-century United States.

Answer: Essay should address several key points:

A.   Background to slave culture
        1.   African origins
                a.   Cultural developments
                b.   Religious beliefs
        2.   North American innovations
                a.   Naming patterns
                b.   Marriage practices
B.   Slave culture in nineteenth-century South
        1.   Importance of extended family
                a.   Limitations placed on traditional family
                b.   Coping strategies developed by slaves
        2.   Significance of religion
                a.   Christianization (1780–1820)
                b.   Evangelical basis

3.   Examine the rise of new religious denominations in the United States in the nineteenth century.

Answer: Essay should address several key points:

A.   Background to religious developments
        1.   Market and commercial developments
                a.   Transportation and market revolutions
                b.   Uncertainty of the market
B.   Evangelical developments
        1.   Millerites and Millennialism
                a.   Belief in the end of the world
                b.   Popularity skewed to certain geographical areas
        2.   Joseph Smith and Mormonism
                a.   Return to patriarchy
                b.   Relationship to society in general
C.   Religion and the South
        1.   Significance of camp meetings
                a.   Articulation of community
                b.   Evangelical orientation
        2.   Effects on denominational orientation

4.   Examine the role and influence of women in the development of nineteenth-century American culture.

Answer: Essay should address several key points:

A.   Feminization of domestic life
    1.   Male sphere
        a.   Politics and economics
        b.   Traditional disciplinarians
    2.   Female sphere
        a.   Moral influence within home
        b.   Child rearing
        c.   Sunday schools

B.   Popular literature
    1.   Magazines and novels
        a.   *Godey's Ladies Book*
        b.   *Uncle Tom's Cabin*
    2.   Sentimentality
        a.   Middle-class ideals upheld
        b.   Religious message
        c.   Critics of male writers

C.   Romantic cult of nature
    1.   Religious purposes
    2.   Scenic tourism
    3.   The sublime experience

D.   Southern traditions
    1.   Male roles
        a.   Defending family honor
        b.   Protecting reputations
    2.   Female roles
        a.   Subordinate status
        b.   Fulfilling prescribed expectations

CHAPTER 11
SOCIETY, CULTURE, AND POLITICS, 1820s–1840s

CHAPTER OUTLINE

I. Constituencies
    A. The North and West
    B. The South

II. The Politics of Economic Development
    A. Government and Its Limits
    B. Banks
    C. Internal Improvements

III. The Politics of Social Reform
    A. Public Schools
    B. Ethnicity, Religion, and the Schools
    C. Prisons
    D. Asylums
    E. The South and Social Reform

IV. Excursus: The Politics of Alcohol
    A. Ardent Spirits
    B. The Origins of Prohibition
    C. The Democratization of Temperance
    D. Temperance Schisms
    E. Ethnicity and Alcohol

V. The Politics of Race
    A. Free Blacks
    B. Discrimination
    C. Democratic Racism
    D. Conceptions of Racial Difference
    E. The Beginnings of Antislavery
    F. Abolitionists
    G. Agitation

VI. The Politics of Gender and Sex
    A. Appetites
    B. Moral Reform
    C. Women's Rights

VII. Conclusion

CHRONOLOGY

1816	African Methodist Episcopal Church forms in Philadelphia.
	American Colonization Society created to send blacks to Africa.
1819	Prison reform system implemented at Auburn, New York.
1826	Reformers set up American Society for the Promotion of Temperance.
	Lyman Beecher publishes sermons against alcohol.
1828	New York Magdalen Society founded.
1829	New York Safety Fund law passed.
1830	Alexis de Tocqueville tours the United States.
1831	William Lloyd Garrison's *The Liberator* begins publication in Boston.
	New York Magdalen Society's report on prostitution shocks the city and launches the moral reform crusade.
1833	Abolitionists found the American Anti-Slavery Society.
1834	Antiabolition mob sacks the house of abolitionist Lewis Tappan in New York.
	First major race riot breaks out in Philadelphia.

1835	American Anti-Slavery Society commences postal campaign agitation.
1838	Massachusetts legislature passes Fifteen-Gallon Law.
1840	Washington Temperance Society forms as an organization for reformed drunkards.
1844	Native American Party wins New York City elections.
1848	First Women's Rights Convention held in Seneca Falls, New York.
1851	Maine becomes the first of 17 states to enact statewide prohibition.
1860	New York State passes Married Women's Property Act.

THEMATIC TOPICS FOR ENRICHMENT

1. What issues united southern and northern Whigs? What issues divided them?

2. Discuss the banking situation in the United States after the destruction of the Second Bank of the United States.

3. What were the differences between Whigs and Democrats in their plans for public education?

4. Why were Catholic parents upset with public schools and determined to establish church-controlled schools?

5. Discuss the differences between the Philadelphia System and the Auburn System for prison reform.

6. Which social reform of the era did the South support most enthusiastically? Why?

7. Describe the different ways that temperance reformers tried to curtail the consumption of alcohol.

8. What was the response of free blacks to declining economic, political, and social conditions in the 1830s and 1840s?

9. What caused the race riots of the 1830s in Philadelphia and New York?

10. How did abolitionists during this period differ from antislavery advocates that had come before them?

11. Describe the reform efforts of the Female Moral Reform Society.

12. What was the link between abolitionism and the women's rights movement?

SUGGESTED ESSAY TOPICS

1. Contrast the Whig and Democratic parties of the 1830s and 1840s. Who were their respective leaders and constituents, and what were their ideologies?

2. Compare the first party system of Federalists and Republicans with the second party system of Whigs and Democrats.

3. Define "social reform" and discuss its many goals in the 1830s and 1840s.

4. Explain the relationship of religion and politics in the second party system.

5. Characterize the life and struggles of free blacks in antebellum America.

1.   As politics became more institutionalized, politicians had to compete for specific **constituencies** largely based on region and class.

    a.   The **North and West**, dominated by commercial farmers and enterprising immigrants, became the key locus of support for the emerging Whig Party**.**

    b.   Both Whigs and Democrats held constituencies in the **South**, but party preference was based mostly on economics and not region.

2.   The **politics of economic development** were played out in the two-party rivalry of Democrats and Whigs, with the differences between the parties often proving more rhetorical than real.

    a.   No issue was more central to the parties than that of the nature of **government and its limits**, with the Whigs arguing for more forceful and imaginative use of the central power.

    b.   Like Jefferson's Republicans, Jackson's Democrats believed **banks** were of dubious morality.

    c.   The Whigs, and Henry Clay in particular, contended that **internal improvements** fostered economic growth and therefore should be funded by the federal government.

3.   Members of both major parties, as well as the many lesser ones, fought vociferously over **social reform,** especially as it became clear that reform issues proved critical in elections.

    a.   Far from being universally acclaimed, **public schools** became a prominent feature, and a large public expenditure, solely in the North and Northwest.

    b.   For many locally minded citizens, the mixture of **ethnicity, religion, and the schools** was so volatile that party affiliation became a passionate issue even in small towns.

    c.   State investment in **prisons** grew dramatically in the period, with some states following the Pennsylvania system and others following the Auburn system.

    d.   States also funded the construction of **asylums** to house orphans, the insane, the dependent poor, and criminals.

    e.   Cultural and political conservatism inhibited the South from taking similar positive steps on **social reform** as had the North.

4.   The **politics of alcohol** was so great an issue that in many regions the temperance question constituted the difference between Whig and Democrat.

    a.   The fight to prohibit **ardent spirits** became the obsession of many Americans, who started temperance organizations such as the American Temperance Society.

    b.   The **origins of prohibition** were rooted in New England, where Massachusetts passed a "Fifteen-Gallon Law" in 1838.

    c.   The **democratization of temperance** stemmed from the increasing willingness of citizens to vote according to their views on ardent spirits.

    d.   Whig disapproval of the Washingtonians' tactics led to a series of **temperance schisms** in the 1840s.

e. By the 1850s with the immigration of many **Irish and Germans** whose culture included drinking, ethnicity and alcohol became the focus of political and social discord.

5. When it had become clear that slavery was not about to disappear of its own accord, the **politics of race** became increasingly contentious, threatening to divide almost all institutions along the Mason–Dixon line.

(SHOW TRANSPARENCY 56: PERCENTAGE OF POPULATION ENSLAVED, 1820 AND 1840)

a. One peculiar result of slavery and racism was the anomalous condition of the increasing numbers of **free blacks** in both the North and South.

b. Rampant **discrimination** against blacks and immigrants was endemic in the United States before the Civil War.

c. While discrimination was ubiquitous in antebellum America, **democratic racism** served to encourage a systematic attempt to equate American citizenship solely with white Protestantism.

d. Antebellum America featured an entire community of pseudoscience that espoused a number of pernicious **conceptions of racial difference.**

e. The **beginnings of antislavery** dated to years prior to the American Revolution, but most antislavery advocates believed that the end of slavery would necessitate the colonization of blacks.

f. **Abolitionists** believed that slavery was a sin, and as such it had to be removed immediately, not gradually.

g. Copying other reformers, abolitionists began to use various active forms of **agitation** to raise consciousness of the treatment of slaves.

6. With the discussions of racial slavery came similar debate over women's rights, which resulted in a new **politics of gender and sex,** culminating in the Seneca Falls Convention of 1848.

a. Numbers of different reform groups sought to curb dangerous and **licentious appetites.**

b. **Moral reform,** through organizations such as the New York Magdalen Society, was proposed as a means to improve society through nonpolitical avenues.

c. From the 1820s onward, middle-class women began the century-long struggle toward **women's rights** and the American woman suffrage movement.

Conclusion: The society, culture, and politics of the decades of the 1820s, 1830s, and 1840s incorporated changing attitudes toward family, religion, race, class, ethnicity, and more. As the United States became an increasingly democratic, aggressive nation, America's cultural institutions adapted to serve the ideological needs of a people on the move.

TEACHING RESOURCES

"Harriet Tubman" and "Sojourner Truth" are video biographies in the twelve-part *The Black Americans of Achievement* video collection. Filmic Archives (30 minutes).

The Freedom Station is a drama about the Underground Railroad that is set in a "safe house" in 1850. It explores the concept of freedom versus the reality of being free. Filmic Archives (30 minutes).

Mr. Lincoln of Illinois re-creates the era and the man in this documentary about Lincoln during his prairie years. Films for the Humanities & Sciences (30 minutes, color).

Elizabeth Cady Stanton and Susan B. Anthony examines the lives of the women's rights pioneers. Films for the Humanities & Sciences (24 minutes, color).

Roots of Resistance details the story of the Underground Railroad in graphic, compelling terms. PBS Video (60 minutes).

Not for Ourselves Alone: The Story of Elizabeth Cady Stanton and Susan B. Anthony – PBS documentary by Ken Burns. Part 1 examines the early women's rights movement in the nineteenth century through the lives of Elizabeth Cady Stanton and Susan B. Anthony. PBS Video (1 hour 30 minutes).

MULTIPLE CHOICE

1. Which political party was most supportive of government involvement in the market developments of the period from 1820 to 1840?
    a. Republican
    b. Democratic
    c. Whig
    d. Know-Nothing
    e. Federalist

ANS: C   **TYPE: M**   **KEY 1: F**   **KEY 2: 2**   **PAGE: 352**

2. Who was most interested in creating a public school system?
    a. William Lloyd Garrison
    b. Lydia Maria Child
    c. Dorothea Dix
    d. Horace Mann
    e. Alexander Hamilton

ANS: D   **TYPE: M**   **KEY 1: F**   **KEY 2: 2**   **PAGE: 357**

3. Many Catholic parents refused to send their children to public school because
    a. they felt that the education received there was inadequate.
    b. the teachers were not qualified.
    c. students were forced to recite Protestant prayers and read the Protestant Bible.
    d. they believed their children would be persecuted.
    e. they were too poor to buy their supplies.

ANS: C   **TYPE: M**   **KEY 1: A**   **KEY 2: 2**   **PAGE: 359**

4. The leading advocate of humane treatment of the insane was
    a. Dorothea Dix.
    b. Lydia Maria Child.
    c. Sarah Josepha Hale.
    d. Caroline Kirkland.
    e. Andrew Jackson.

ANS: A   **TYPE: M**   **KEY 1: F**   **KEY 2: 1**   **PAGE: 360**

5. Which of the following was not true of the Auburn System of prisons?
   a. Prisoners were forbidden to speak to one another at any time.
   b. Prisoners were required to work to provide their own keep.
   c. Prisoners were kept in solitary confinement to contemplate their misdeeds.
   d. Prisoners were regimented in military-type formation.
   e. The system was designed to reform prisoners and to save money.

ANS: C   TYPE: M   KEY 1: F   KEY 2: 2   PAGE: 360

6. One of the leading crusaders against the use of alcohol was
   a. Horace Mann.
   b. Lyman Beecher.
   c. Stephen Douglas.
   d. Lydia Maria Child.
   e. Andrew Jackson.

ANS: B   TYPE: M   KEY 1: F   KEY 2: 1   PAGE: 361

7. The annual consumption of alcohol, which had reached an all-time high during the 1820s,
   a. was no longer perceived as a problem by the 1830s.
   b. remained roughly the same during the 1830s.
   c. doubled during the 1830s.
   d. quadrupled during the 1830s.
   e. dropped by more than one-half during the 1830s.

ANS: E   TYPE: M   KEY 1: F   KEY 2: 3   PAGE: 362

8. The abolitionists of the 1830s
   a. were all members of the Quaker faith.
   b. advocated a bloody civil war to punish slave owners.
   c. encouraged the admission of the free state of Texas to the union.
   d. persuaded the majority of northern citizens to oppose slavery.
   e. were an active and influential minority within the reform movements of the era.

ANS: E   TYPE: M   KEY 1: F   KEY 2: 2   PAGE: 371

9. By the 1830s, slavery in the northern states was
   a. fairly healthy—about 100,000 people remained enslaved.
   b. much the same as it was in the early decades of the nineteenth century.
   c. virtually extinct, only a handful remained.
   d. increasing at a rapid pace.
   e. still strong but coming under increasing attack from abolitionists.

ANS: C   TYPE: M   KEY 1: A   KEY 2: 1   PAGE: 365

10. Which is true of the Democratic Party of the 1840s regarding the issue of race?
    a. Many Democrats considered blacks unfit to be citizens.
    b. Many Democrats wanted to end slavery.
    c. Many Democrats wanted to grant equal opportunity to free blacks.
    d. Many Democrats wanted to expand slavery.
    e. Many Democrats thought that slavery should not be based on race but that it should extend to poor whites as well as blacks.

ANS: A   TYPE: M   KEY 1: A   KEY 2: 2   PAGE: 369

11. The major antislavery society before the 1830s was the
    a. American Anti-Slavery Society.
    b. William Lloyd Garrison Society.
    c. New England Anti-Slavery Society.
    d. American Colonization Society.
    e. Free Labor Society.

ANS: D   TYPE: M   KEY 1: F   KEY 2: 1   PAGE: 369

12. Few people agreed with the American Colonization Society's attempt to transport blacks to Africa because
    a. it was illegal.
    b. most slaveowners had already freed their slaves.
    c. few free blacks were interested in moving to Africa.
    d. no land was available in Africa.
    e. all of the above

ANS: C   TYPE: M   KEY 1: F   KEY 2: 2   PAGE: 369

13. The leader of the slave uprising in Haiti that led to that nation's independence in 1804 was
    a. Toussaint L'Ouverture.
    b. Gabriel.
    c. Denmark Vesey.
    d. Simon Bolivar.
    e. Stono

ANS: A   TYPE: M   KEY 1: F   KEY 2: 1   PAGE: 369

14. The most prominent abolitionist in antebellum United States was
    a. Charles Finney.
    b. Horace Mann.
    c. William Lloyd Garrison.
    d. Lyman Beecher.
    e. Dorothea Dix

ANS: C   TYPE: M   KEY 1: F   KEY 2: 1   PAGE: 369-70

15. Support for abolitionists came from which of the following regions?
    a. western New York
    b. southern New England
    c. northern Ohio
    d. northeastern cities.
    e. all of the above

ANS: D   TYPE: M   KEY 1: F   KEY 2: 2   PAGE: 370

16. The primary goal of the American Anti-Slavery Society was
    a. the gradual abolition of slavery.
    b. the immediate emancipation of the slaves.
    c. the recolonization of slaves to Africa.
    d. the emancipation of some slaves, for appearances.
    e. reconciliation between North and South.

ANS: B   TYPE: M   KEY 1: F   KEY 2: 2   PAGE: 371

17. Most women became advocates of women's rights through
    a. temperance.
    b. abolitionism.
    c. sabbatarianism.
    d. public school reform.
    e. prison reform.

ANS: B   TYPE: M   KEY 1: F   KEY 2: 2   PAGE: 373

18. Which of the following was not a demand of women's rights reformers in the 1840s?
    a. better access for women to property
    b. more restrictive divorce laws
    c. wages for their own labor
    d. custody of their children in cases of divorce
    e. the right to vote.

ANS: B   TYPE: M   KEY 1: F   KEY 2: 2   PAGE: 375

19. The first Women's Rights Convention (1848) was held in
    a. Philadelphia.
    b. Seneca Falls.
    c. Boston.
    d. Charleston.
    e. New York City.

ANS: B   TYPE: M   KEY 1: F   KEY 2: 1   PAGE: 375

20. The Declaration of Sentiments was modeled most closely on the
    a. Declaration of Rights and Grievances.
    b. Rights of Man.
    c. Declaration of Independence.
    d. Declaration of Man and the Citizen.
    e. the Bible.

ANS: C   TYPE: M   KEY 1: F   KEY 2: 1   PAGE: 375

21. Members of the Democratic Party were not suspicious of
    a. banks.
    b. inequality for African Americans.
    c. temperance.
    d. evangelical revivals.
    e. the working classes.

ANS: B   TYPE: M   KEY 1: A   KEY 2: 2   PAGE: 366

22. Which of the following political parties was most suspicious of federal attempts to promote internal improvements (canals and turnpikes)?
    a. Federalist
    b. Whig
    c. Democratic
    d. Republican Party of the 1850s
    e. Know Nothing

ANS: C   TYPE: M   KEY 1: F   KEY 2: 2   PAGE: 356

23. The group most likely to be denied political power in the Northeast was the
    a. Irish.
    b. African Americans.
    c. Italians.
    d. Poles.
    e. farmers.

ANS: B   TYPE: M   KEY 1: F   KEY 2: 1   PAGE: 366

24. The Whig party supported all of the following except
    a. public suspicion and mistrust of the influence of privileged economic groups on federal policies.
    b. moral legislation regulating alcohol consumption.
    c. government-supported internal improvements.
    d. an active government role in encouraging the expansion of the market economy.
    e. public schools.

ANS: A   TYPE: M   KEY 1: A   KEY 2: 3   PAGE: 354, 357, 362

25. The Democratic Party was supported by
    a. Irish Catholic immigrants.
    b. evangelical Protestants.
    c. wage earners
    d. independent yeoman farmers.
    e. all of the above.

ANS: E   TYPE: M   KEY 1: F   KEY 2: 3   PAGE: 353

26. During the 1820s through the 1840s, the Democrats
    a. trusted the government to do what was best for the country.
    b. favored limitations on government power.
    c. called for immigration restrictions in order to protect the jobs of native-born workers.
    d. believed the government should legislate to encourage "correct" religious behavior.
    e. called for religious training in public schools.

ANS: B   TYPE: M   KEY 1: F   KEY 2: 2   PAGE: 355

27. In the U.S. banking system of the 1830s and 1840s,
    a. the federal government issued paper money and controlled interest rates.
    b. paper money was eliminated and specie was the only currency in circulation.
    c. only gold and silver circulated as money.
    d. Democrats in Congress passed laws increasing the amount of paper money and expanding credit for speculators.
    e. state-chartered and state-owned banks controlled the amount of money in circulation

ANS: E   TYPE: M   KEY 1: F   KEY 2: 3   PAGE: 355-56

28. On the issue of internal improvements, the Democrats
    a. opposed funding projects that would raise taxes and increase state debts.
    b. favored increased spending as a means of helping isolated manufacturers reach bigger markets.
    c. believed that "good roads and good morals" were interrelated.
    d. encouraged "partial" policies that aided certain areas and were paid for by other areas.
    e. did not take a stand on the issue.

ANS: A   TYPE: M   KEY 1: F   KEY 2: 3   PAGE: 357

29. The "common" schools of the 1820s and 1830s
    a. were private, tuition-based church schools.
    b. were tax-supported public schools that promoted citizenship and moral standards.
    c. were popular with immigrant Irish Catholics who had positive memories of similar institutions set up by the English in Ireland.
    d. carefully followed the concept of separation of church and state.
    e. caused no controversy, as they enjoyed near unanimous support from both political parties.

ANS: B   TYPE: M   KEY 1: A   KEY 2: 2   PAGE: 357

30. Many nineteenth-century northern social reformers believed that criminals, the mentally ill, and poor people
    a. were lazy, sinful, devil worshippers.
    b. could not be helped by government policies or institutions.
    c. should either be drafted into the army or employed in federal work camps.
    d. should be deported.
    e. had been mistreated as children and could be rehabilitated as adults.

ANS: E   TYPE: M   KEY 1: A   KEY 2: 3   PAGE: 359

31. The temperance crusade of the mid-nineteenth century
    a. was primarily a middle-class movement that was strongest in the Northeast.
    b. was ignored by the U.S. Army, which continued to issue each soldier a weekly liquor ration.
    c. targeted Catholics because they used "real wine" in their services.
    d. was promoted by the Democratic Party, which called for a constitutional prohibition amendment.
    e. led to more widespread drinking.

ANS: A   TYPE: M   KEY 1: A   KEY 2: 3   PAGE: 361

32. The Washington Temperance Society was different from other reform groups in that it
    a. was a working-class organization.
    b. was not affiliated with any religious institutions.
    c. opposed prohibition legislation.
    d. supported male authority
    e. all of the above

ANS: E   TYPE: M   KEY 1: F   KEY 2: 3   PAGE: 363

33. After 1820, free black workers in the North
    a. held most of the skilled labor jobs in the seaport cities.
    b. were displaced by Irish immigrants who worked for low wages and used violence to intimidate competitors.
    c. enjoyed integrated schools, churches, and social clubs.
    d. were included equally in the political and voting reforms of the era.
    e. outnumbered whites in all the major cities.

ANS: B   TYPE: M   KEY 1: A   KEY 2: 3   PAGE: 366

34. Which of the following is not true about the Washington Temperance Society?
    a. Its members identified themselves as members of the laboring classes.
    b. It only accepted short-term drinkers and rejected "hopeless drunks."
    c. It was avowedly nonreligious.
    d. It rejected politics and legislation.
    e. It called for restoring male authority within the family.

ANS: B   TYPE: M   KEY 1: A   KEY 2:32   PAGE: 363

35. In the nineteenth century supposedly "scientific" theories on racial differences indicated that
    a. blacks and whites were intellectually and morally equal.
    b. blacks were less likely than whites to become drunkards and thieves.
    c. whites and blacks were actually two separate species.
    d. it was impossible to determine the causes of the physical and mental variations among human beings.
    e. All races are equal.

ANS: C   TYPE: M   KEY 1: F   KEY 2: 3   PAGE: 368

36. *The Advocate of Moral Reform* was the newsletter of the
    a. American Temperance Society.
    b. Magdalen Society.
    c. American Anti-Slavery Society.
    d. Female Moral Reform Society.
    e. the Whig party.

ANS: D   TYPE: M   KEY 1: F   KEY 2: 1   PAGE: 373

37. Sylvester Graham
    a. was a temperance lecturer who warned that dietary and sexual indulgence was unhealthy.
    b. was the inventor of the telegram.
    c. admired flamboyant, decadent political leaders like Andrew Jackson.
    d. founded the first women's college in the United States.
    e. called for public school reform.

ANS: A   TYPE: M   KEY 1: F   KEY 2: 2   PAGE: 372

38. The New York Magdalen Society
    a. was a Roman Catholic School for girls.
    b. set up missions to save and reform prostitutes.
    c. blamed social ills on the innate sinfulness of women.
    d. encouraged women to set up female-owned and controlled factories and businesses.
    e. started orphanages.

ANS: B   TYPE: M   KEY 1: F   KEY 2: 2   PAGE: 373

39. In general, the wealthiest men in cities were
    a. Republicans.
    b. Democrats.
    c. Whigs.
    d. Know-Nothings.
    e. apolitical.

ANS: C   TYPE: M   KEY 1: A   KEY 2: 1   PAGE: 352

40. The most overwhelmingly Democratic group in the country were
    a. northern free blacks.
    b. immigrant Chinese.
    c. native Protestant wage earners.
    d. native-born farmers.
    e. immigrant Irish Catholics

ANS: E   TYPE: M   KEY 1: A   KEY 2: 2   PAGE: 353

41. Which of the following had a wholly state-owned bank?
    a. Massachusetts
    b. Ohio
    c. Georgia
    d. Pennsylvania
    e. New York

ANS: C   TYPE: M   KEY 1: F   KEY 2: 3   PAGE: 355

42. The New York Magdalen Society sought to eliminate
    a. prostitution.
    b. alcohol use.
    c. poverty.
    d. childhood disease.
    e. capitalism.

ANS: A   TYPE: M   KEY 1: F   KEY 2: 2   PAGE: 373

43. Those who were atheists or who were least concerned about religion tended to be
    a. Democrats.
    b. Whigs.
    c. Federalists.
    d. Know-Nothings.
    e. apolitical.

ANS: A   TYPE: M   KEY 1: A   KEY 2: 2   PAGE: 353

44. In the South wealthy planters tended to vote for the _____ Party.
    a. Democratic
    b. Republican
    c. Whig
    d. Green
    e. Know Nothing

ANS: C   TYPE: M   KEY 1: A   KEY 2: 2   PAGE: 354

45. Democrats feared that government would
    a. fail to control the rising crime rates.
    b. concentrate power and wealth in the hands of a few.
    c. admit too many immigrants.
    d. discourage the growth of the market economy.
    e. abolish the national bank.

ANS: B   TYPE: M   KEY 1: A   KEY 2: 2   PAGE: 355

46. "Hard Money" Democrats
    a. support Whig candidates for president.
    b. wanted the banks to inflate the currency.
    c. lost their jobs in the Panic of 1837.
    d. opposed paper money.
    e. hated Andrew Jackson.

ANS: D　　　**TYPE: M**　　　**KEY 1: F**　　　**KEY 2: 3**　　　**PAGE: 356**

47. The Whig Party believed that government
    a. was an agency of moral reform.
    b. was a necessary evil.
    c. was a corrupting influence on political leaders.
    d. offered the most the most effective means of ending slavery.
    e. should strengthen the military and embark on overseas expansion.

ANS: A　　　**TYPE: M**　　　**KEY 1: A**　　　**KEY 2: 2**　　　**PAGE: 354**

48. Whigs differed from Democrats in their approach to public schools in that Whigs believed
    a. religious instruction should not be included in public schools.
    b. schools should be centralized and controlled by state boards of education.
    c. schools should be locally controlled.
    d. women should not be allowed to teach in the public schools.
    e. schools should be integrated.

ANS: B　　　**TYPE: M**　　　**KEY 1: A**　　　**KEY 2: 3**　　　**PAGE: 358**

49. Most southern voters
    a. supported extending the right to vote to free blacks.
    b. supported social improvement legislation.
    c. believed in government support for religion.
    d. supported higher taxes.
    e. opposed social improvement legislation

ANS: E　　　**TYPE: M**　　　**KEY 1: A**　　　**KEY 2: 2**　　　**PAGE: 354**

50. Beer was introduced into America by
    a. the English.
    b. the Germans.
    c. the Irish.
    d. the Africans.
    e. the Italians.

ANS: B　　　**TYPE: M**　　　**KEY 1: F**　　　**KEY 2: 2**　　　**PAGE: 364**

TRUE/FALSE

_____ 1.　　The primary goal of the American Colonization Society was the immediate abolition of slavery in the United States.

ANS: F　　　**TYPE: T**　　　**KEY 1: F**　　　**KEY 2: 2**　　　**PAGE: 369**

_____ 2.   The Female Moral Reform Society attempted to teach prostitutes morality and household skills.

ANS: T   TYPE: T   KEY 1: F   KEY 2: 2   PAGE: 373

_____ 3.   The reformer Sylvester Graham (creator of the graham cracker) lectured that sex was a dangerous activity that led to bodily weakness and disease.

ANS: T   TYPE: T   KEY 1: F   KEY 2: 3   PAGE: 372

_____ 4.   The abolitionist newspaper edited by William Lloyd Garrison was *The North Star*.

ANS: F   TYPE: T   KEY 1: F   KEY 2: 1   PAGE: 369

_____ 5.   Of the two major political parties between 1820 and 1840, the Whigs and Democrats, the Democrats were far more likely to promote racism.

ANS: T   TYPE: T   KEY 1: A   KEY 2: 2   PAGE: 366

_____ 6.   After the 1820s, free blacks in the North found increasing opportunity in business and education.

ANS: F   TYPE: T   KEY 1: A   KEY 2: 1   PAGE: 366

_____ 7.   Many new public schools of the early nineteenth century attempted to inculcate students with the individualistic values of the developing market economy.

ANS: T   TYPE: T   KEY 1: F   KEY 2: 3   PAGE: 357

_____ 8.   In the 1830s and 1840s, the Whig Party argued that the government should support economic growth and social progress.

ANS: T   TYPE: T   KEY 1: A   KEY 2: 2   PAGE: 354

_____ 9.   Most Democrats in the period from 1820 to 1840 were suspicious of any type of paper currency.

ANS: T   TYPE: T   KEY 1: F   KEY 2: 2   PAGE: 356

_____ 10.   For the most part, in the 1830s and 1840s, the strongest support for the Whig Party was in the North and the strongest support for the Democratic Party was in the South.

ANS: F   TYPE: T   KEY 1: F   KEY 2: 3   PAGE: 353

_____ 11.   In the 1830s, most atheists and free thinkers voted for the Whig Party.

ANS: F   TYPE: T   KEY 1: F   KEY 2: 2   PAGE: 353

_____ 12.   Democrats in the mid-nineteenth century saw the government as a potentially dangerous concentration of power in the hands of selfish and greedy businessmen.

ANS: T   TYPE: T   KEY 1: A   KEY 2: 2   PAGE: 355

_____ 13.   Democrats often doubted the value of commerce.

ANS: F   **TYPE: T**   **KEY 1: A**   **KEY 2: 3**   **PAGE: 376**

_____ 14.   Dorothea Dix advocated the use of flogging and cold showers in the treatment of the insane.

ANS: F   **TYPE: T**   **KEY 1: F**   **KEY 2: 2**   **PAGE: 360**

_____ 15.   Irish and German immigrants strongly supported the temperance movement.

ANS: F   **TYPE: T**   **KEY 1: F**   **KEY 2: 1**   **PAGE: 364**

_____ 16.   Democrats believed in a limited government.

ANS: T   **TYPE: T**   **KEY 1: F**   **KEY 2: 2**   **PAGE: 352**

_____ 17.   Support for the Democratic or Whig Party was a matter of personal identity as much as of political preference.

ANS: T   **TYPE: T**   **KEY 1: A**   **KEY 2: 2**   **PAGE: 352**

_____ 18.   The New York Magdalen Society blamed prostitution on the brutality and lust of men.

ANS: T   **TYPE: T**   **KEY 1: F**   **KEY 2: 2**   **PAGE: 373**

_____ 19.   Throughout the 1830s and 1840s, the southern states as a whole voted overwhelmingly Whig.

ANS: F   **TYPE: T**   **KEY 1: A**   **KEY 2: 1**   **PAGE: 353**

_____ 20.   Southern political divisions had little to do with religion.

ANS: T   **TYPE: T**   **KEY 1: A**   **KEY 2: 1**   **PAGE: 354**

_____ 21.   Democrats often praised market society outright.

ANS: F   **TYPE: T**   **KEY 1: A**   **KEY 2: 3**   **PAGE: 355**

_____ 22.   Democrats saw government as a tool of progress.

ANS: F   **TYPE: T**   **KEY 1: A**   **KEY 2: 2**   **PAGE: 355**

_____ 23.   "Hard-money" Democrats trusted and supported banks.

ANS: F   **TYPE: T**   **KEY 1: A**   **KEY 2: 2**   **PAGE: 356**

_____ 24.   Whig education reformers cared more about character building than about traditional academic subjects.

ANS: T   **TYPE: T**   **KEY 1: A**   **KEY 2: 2**   **PAGE: 358**

_____ 25.   Whig educators taught that social questions could be reduced to questions of individual character.

ANS: T   **TYPE: T**   **KEY 1: A**   **KEY 2: 2**   **PAGE: 358**

_____ 26.   A majority of middle-class evangelicals supported abolition.

ANS: F   **TYPE: T**   **KEY 1: A**   **KEY 2: 1**   **PAGE: 370**

_____ 27.   The Democrats' approach to prisons emphasized rehabilitation.

ANS: F   **TYPE: T**   **KEY 1: A**   **KEY 2: 2**   **PAGE: 359**

_____ 28.   Democrats were more likely than Whigs to approve appropriations for the more expensive and humane moral treatment centers.

ANS: F   **TYPE: T**   **KEY 1: A**   **KEY 2: 3**   **PAGE: 359**

_____ 29.   The first temperance organization was originally called the American Society for the Promotion of Temperance.

ANS: T   **TYPE: T**   **KEY 1: F**   **KEY 2: 1**   **PAGE: 361**

_____ 30.   The American Colonization Society posed a serious threat to slavery.

ANS: F   **TYPE: T**   **KEY 1: A**   **KEY 2: 2**   **PAGE: 369**

_____ 31.   Washingtonians openly identified themselves as members of the working class.

ANS: T   **TYPE: T**   **KEY 1: A**   **KEY 2: 2**   **PAGE: 364**

_____ 32.   The Washington Temperance Society remained strong throughout the 1850s.

ANS: F   **TYPE: T**   **KEY 1: F**   **KEY 2: 2**   **PAGE: 364**

_____ 33.   By 1804, most northern states had taken some sort of action against slavery.

ANS: F   **TYPE: T**   **KEY 1: F**   **KEY 2: 3**   **PAGE: 365**

_____ 34.   Whigs and Democrats encouraged the aspirations of slaves and free blacks.

ANS: F   **TYPE: T**   **KEY 1: A**   **KEY 2: 2**   **PAGE: 366**

_____ 35.   Herman Melville, a lifelong Democrat, wrote a novel about slave violence and treachery.

ANS: T   **TYPE: T**   **KEY 1: F**   **KEY 2: 2**   **PAGE: 369**

_____ 36.   The American Anti-Slavery Society demanded gradual emancipation of slaves.

ANS: F   **TYPE: T**   **KEY 1: A**   **KEY 2: 3**   **PAGE: 369**

_____ 37.   Lyman Beecher and Charles Finney supported the abolitionists in the 1830s.

ANS: F   **TYPE: T**   **KEY 1: A**   **KEY 2: 2**   **PAGE: 370**

_____ 38.   Many of the reforms urged by Whig evangelicals had to do with domestic and personal life rather than with politics.

ANS: T   **TYPE: T**   **KEY 1: A**   **KEY 2: 2**   **PAGE: 372**

_____ 39.   Democrats believed that because government rested in the hands of imperfect individuals, it had to be limited.

ANS: T   **TYPE: T**   **KEY 1: A**   **KEY 2: 3**   **PAGE: 355**

_____ 40.   Whigs based their argument for internal improvements on as assumed connection between market society and moral progress.

ANS: T   **TYPE: T**   **KEY A: A**   **KEY 2: 3**   **PAGE: 357**

FILL-INS

1.   Horace Mann was most interested in the establishment of _____.

ANS: public schools   **TYPE: F**   **KEY 1: F**   **KEY 2: 2**   **PAGE: 357**

2.   The _____ Temperance Society was primarily a working-class organization opposed to the abuse of alcohol.

ANS: Washington   **TYPE: F**   **KEY 1: F**   **KEY 2: 3**   **PAGE: 363**

3.   The first major race riot broke out in the United States in _____ in 1834.

ANS: Philadelphia   **TYPE: F**   **KEY 1: F**   **KEY 2: 2**   **PAGE: 367**

4.   The vice president under Martin Van Buren was _____.

ANS: Richard Johnson   **TYPE: F**   **KEY 1: F**   **KEY 2: 3**   **PAGE: 372**

5.   One of the most prominent forms of prison reform, attempting to both reform and reduce expenses, was the _____.

ANS: Auburn System   **TYPE: F**   **KEY 1: F**   **KEY 2: 1**   **PAGE: 360**

6.   Rural Democrats in the Northwest were called _____ because of the vegetable dye used to color their clothing.

ANS: Butternuts   **TYPE: F**   **KEY 1: F**   **KEY 2: 2**   **PAGE: 353**

7.   Tax-supported public schools were known as _____.

ANS: common schools   **TYPE: F**   **KEY 1: F**   **KEY 2: 1**   **PAGE: 357**

8.   Most northern states freed their slaves through a lengthy process of _____.

ANS: gradual emancipation   **TYPE: F**   **KEY 1: F**   **KEY 2: 3**   **PAGE: 365**

9.   The more cosmopolitan southern communities tended to support the _____.

ANS: Whigs   **TYPE: F**   **KEY 1: A**   **KEY 2: 1**   **PAGE: 354**

10.	Evangelicals in the _____ were most likely to push for moral legislation on such issues as Sabbath observance or temperance.

ANS: North	**TYPE: F**	**KEY 1: A**	**KEY 2: 2**	**PAGE: 354**

11.	In the North, the churchgoing middle class were the core of the _____ Party.

ANS: Whig	**TYPE: F**	**KEY 1: A**	**KEY 2: 1**	**PAGE: 357**

12.	The leading advocate of humane treatment for the insane was _____.

ANS: Dorothea Dix	**TYPE: F**	**KEY 1: F**	**KEY 2: 1**	**PAGE: 360**

13.	By 1860, the legislatures of _____ of the 33 states had established state-run insane asylums.

ANS: 28	**TYPE: F**	**KEY 1: F**	**KEY 2: 2**	**PAGE: 360**

14.	The U.S. Army put an end to the liquor ration in _____.

ANS: 1832	**TYPE: F**	**KEY 1: F**	**KEY 2: 2**	**PAGE: 362**

15.	The first major American race riot occurred in _____ in 1834.

ANS: Philadelphia	**TYPE: F**	**KEY 1: F**	**KEY 2: 1**	**PAGE: 367**

16.	The British outlawed the Atlantic slave trade in _____.

ANS: 1808	**TYPE: F**	**KEY 1: F**	**KEY 2: 1**	**PAGE: 369**

17.	New York's Married Women's Property Act was passed in _____.

ANS: 1860	**TYPE: F**	**KEY 1: F**	**KEY 2: 2**	**PAGE: 375**

18.	_____ political divisions had little to do with religion.

ANS: Southern	**TYPE: F**	**KEY 1: A**	**KEY 2: 1**	**PAGE: 354**

19.	_____ argued for the primacy of citizenship.

ANS: Democrats	**TYPE: F**	**KEY 1: A**	**KEY 2: 2**	**PAGE: 355**

20.	_____ believed that alcohol was an addictive drug that could turn even moderate drinkers into hopeless drunkards.

ANS: Lyman Beecher	**TYPE: F**	**KEY 1: F**	**KEY 2: 2**	**PAGE: 361**

21.	_____ became the first state to limit the sale of alcohol through passage in 1838 of the Fifteen Gallon Law.

ANS: Massachusetts	**TYPE: F**	**KEY 1: F**	**KEY 2: 2**	**PAGE: 362-63**

22.	The first independent black church was the African Church of _____.

ANS: Philadelphia	**TYPE: F**	**KEY 1: F**	**KEY 2: 2**	**PAGE: 366**

23. Oberlin College was established in _____.

ANS: 1832   **TYPE: F**   **KEY 1: F**   **KEY 2: 3**   **PAGE: 372**

24. _____ wrote *Appeal to the Colored Citizens of the World* urging blacks to revolt against slavery.

ANS: David Walker   **TYPE: F**   **KEY 1: F**   **KEY 2: 2**   **PAGE: 366**

25. The abolitionists launched the _____ Campaign to flood the mails with their antislavery material.

ANS: postal   **TYPE: F**   **KEY 1: F**   **KEY 2: 3**   **PAGE: 371**

26. An organization that blamed prostitution on the brutality of men and sought to reform prostitutes was the _____ Society.

ANS: Magdalen   **TYPE: F**   **KEY 1: F**   **KEY 2: 2**   **PAGE: 373**

27. The only male delegate to the first Woman's Rights Convention at Seneca Falls was _____.

ANS: Frederick Douglass   **TYPE: F**   **KEY 1: F**   **KEY 2: 3**   **PAGE: 375**

28. In the North the Whig party was grounded in the _____ revolution.

ANS: market   **TYPE: F**   **KEY 1: A**   **KEY 2: 1**   **PAGE: 352**

29. The political party that advocated separation of church and state was the _____ Party.

ANS: Democratic   **TYPE: F**   **KEY 1: A**   **KEY 2: 1**   **PAGE: 353**

30. The political party most likely to support prohibition of alcohol was the _____ Party.

ANS: Whig   **TYPE: F**   **KEY 1: A**   **KEY 2: 1**   **PAGE: 362**

IDENTIFICATIONS

1. **William Lloyd Garrison**: leading abolitionist of the mid-nineteenth century. Editor of the *Liberator* and leading advocate for immediate abolition of slavery. Was a major participant in the American Anti-Slavery Society.

2. **American Colonization Society**: leading antislavery society through the early 1830s. Advocated transportation of freed slaves to Africa. Was replaced in the mid-1830s by more radical abolitionist societies.

3. **Dorothea Dix**: leading advocate for the humane treatment of the insane in early national America. She wanted asylums to be clean, safe, nurturing places where the insane would receive gentle care.

4. **Declaration of Sentiments**: statement of the women's rights advocates at Seneca Falls (1848) that called for equal wages, better access to property, and, most importantly, the right to vote.

5. **Horace Mann**: superintendent of Massachusetts school system in the early nineteenth century. One of the leading supporters for a system of public education, or common schools.

6. **Washington Temperance Society**: a working-class organization that tried to persuade drinkers to reform. Hoped to preserve the self-respect and authority of laboring men. Not an evangelical religious movement. Promoted popular entertainment and speeches by reformed alcoholics.

7. **gradual emancipation**: the process used by most of the northern states to free the slaves. Pennsylvania's 1780 law was the first to do this, providing that all slaves who were born after 1780 would be set free on their twenty-eighth birthday. Those born prior to 1780 would not be freed.

8. **Sylvester Graham**: evangelical minister and temperance lecturer who preached that excessive indulgence in rich food and sexual excitement was unhealthy. He advocated bland food, vegetarianism, and dull marital sex. The graham cracker was named for him.

9. **Lyman Beecher**: leader of the temperance movement who wrote *Six Sermons on the Nature, Occasions, Signs, Evils and Remedy of Intemperance* declaring alcohol an addictive drug and warning of the dangers of drinking any alcohol.

10. **Auburn system**: prison system that used military discipline and the rule of silence in an effort to reform criminals.

SHORT ESSAYS

1. What was the temperance movement? How did it affect American society in the early national period?

Answer: The temperance movement of the early national period was a reaction to the growth in the use (and abuse) of alcohol that characterized early nineteenth-century society. The early national period was a time of profound change: market development, industrial growth, and political splintering. These factors exacerbated the dramatic growth in alcoholism. The social repercussions of alcohol abuse—domestic violence, poor work habits, and crime—were compounded by the medical repercussions—mental illness, physical ailments, and even death. Many believed that men addicted to alcohol could not be good republican citizens. Hence, the advocates of temperance believed that abstinence from the use of alcohol altogether would uphold republican values and would make possible the practices necessary to uphold a virtuous society.

Very influential in the temperance movement were religious evangelists, like Lyman Beecher and Charles Finney, who argued that alcohol was a master controlling a slave (the drinker), and preventing him from attaining salvation. By 1835, the American Temperance Society, a mixture of Whigs and evangelists, claimed over 1.5 million members. In addition, working-class organizations such as the Washington Temperance Society joined the attack on alcohol (although they never allied themselves with their more conservative middle-class compatriots), arguing that drink undermined the important role that the worker played in American politics. These combined movements were successful, since the annual consumption of alcohol dropped by more than one-half in the 1840s.

2. Describe the various approaches to prison reform during the period from 1820 to 1840. What were the goals and successes of those who wished to reform America's prisons?

Answer: Before the 1820s and the market revolution, many Americans saw crime, vice, and poverty as a sign of God's retribution on sinful people. In the period following the dramatic social changes of these years, however, many Americans increasingly saw crime as a product of circumstance, the result of abusive parents, poor schooling and upbringing, and limited opportunities. Reformers hoped to place criminals in a controlled and regimented setting in order to teach them the good middle-class values of discipline and work, and make them better citizens.

The "Auburn System" stands out as the culmination of reformist ideas regarding convicted criminals. This system was designed to reform criminals as well as reduce expenses, since prisons were involved in various types of outwork production. Prisoners slept in solitary cells and, when together, were forbidden to speak to one another at any time. Democrats tended to favor a harsher, more profitable system, the best example being Sing Sing (Ossining). Punishment, not reward (as put forward by the Auburn System) was favored. Whether either system was successful is unclear, since there was no noticeable reduction in crime (although neither system claimed to act as a deterrent) in the years following their introduction.

3.   Examine the movement for public-school reform in the United States.

Answer: Before the early nineteenth century, common schools, or public schools, were entirely matters of the local community. Few states mandated that children had to receive an education—Massachusetts being one of the most significant exceptions. Even in Massachusetts, though, the matter of education was a local concern—a community could choose to supply a school for at least some months of the year, or it had the option of paying a fine. Not until the 1830s did both major political parties, Democrats and Whigs, concede that a public education was a proper function of government, since an educated citizenry was also a more virtuous and healthy one. How the citizen was to be educated, however, still led to disagreement.

       Horace Mann and many Whig school reformers felt that students should be educated to respect authority, in addition to learning to read and write. Of special importance to school reformers was teaching the values and beliefs of the new emerging market society. Because of this, there was a middle-class bias to the school curriculum. Often, books that were read and lessons that were studied emphasized the prevailing Protestant middle-class ideology of mid-nineteenth-century America. The public school system, at least in the minds of the middle class, was not to be a democratizing experience, but an elevating one, for the increasingly Catholic working class.

4.   Explore the condition of free African Americans in northern society during the early national period.

Answer: Before the American Revolution, many northern cities (and some rural areas for that matter), had large numbers of black slaves. Following the Revolution, because of both ideological and economic changes, the North began to move away from slavery. The earliest manumission societies evolved during the Revolution itself and, by the 1820s, only a few hundred African Americans were still enslaved. During this period, although racism existed, African Americans occupied an important position in the social and economic sphere of many northern cities. They were craftsmen and skilled artisans, as well as day laborers, dock workers, and cartmen.

       From the 1820s onward, however, significant changes began to take place in the urban economies of the Northeast. First, the movement toward a market economy spurred interest in commercial development, creating opportunities in port cities (New York, Boston, and Philadelphia). Second, an increasing number of white wage-workers began to edge black workers out of jobs because of discrimination in hiring practices and, finally, the use of violence. 1834 was the date of the first major race riot in American history, and the issue was jobs. Free blacks also saw the franchise, their political voice, being taken away from them during the 1830s, as the Democratic Party became the party of race-baiting. Black children were excluded from public schools, and blacks were excluded from many white churches.

5.   Analyze the antislavery movement in the United States in the years following the 1830s.

Answer: Before the 1830s, the antislavery movement in the United States was limited to very few organizations and individuals. The two most significant antislavery groups were the Quaker Church and the American Colonization Society. The Colonization Society was a somewhat awkward organization whose goal was to transport freed slaves back to Africa. Neither organization was very successful in opposing slavery. During the 1820s and 1830s, however, at the height of the market transformation of American society, a new and far more significant challenge to the institution of slavery developed—the American Anti-Slavery Society with William Lloyd Garrison at its helm.

       Garrison and others were clear about their desires. Dismissing the feeble call for "gradual emancipation," Garrison demanded full and immediate abolition of slavery, or "immediatism." Immediatism was a new and radical demand and dramatically altered the landscape of the antislavery movement. Within a few years, several hundred thousand middle-class artisans, businessmen, factory workers, and commercial farmers from the Northeast and Northwest joined the antislavery crusade. This upswell of support for abolitionism was directly related to the rise of commercial capitalism and the possibilities of "free labor."

6.   Examine the development of the Women's Rights Movement in post-1820 America.

Answer: In the early nineteenth century, the role of women in American society changed significantly. More lower-class women and girls were entering the workforce and experiencing wage and job discrimination. Women could not own property, vote, control their pay, or obtain fair divorce decrees. In middle-class families, women were viewed as moral arbiters, nurturers, and homemakers. Their religious sentiments encouraged them to participate in the major reform movements of the era. Women were active in combating prostitution, alcoholism, and slavery. As they fought to improve the lives of others, many women activists realized that their own rights were being violated. The abolitionist movement especially served as a training ground for feminists. The inequalities of slavery were similar in many ways to the inequalities of gender. The official beginning of the Women's Rights Movement was the Seneca Falls Woman's Rights Convention of 1848. The members of the convention issued a paraphrased version of the Declaration of Independence titled "Declaration of Sentiments and Resolutions." They asserted their unalienable rights of life, liberty, property, and happiness and maintained that "all men and women were created equal." Elizabeth Cady Stanton and other activists organized and worked steadily from 1848 on to obtain recognition of the citizenship rights of American women. The franchise was the most controversial of the feminists issues and many men responded by ridiculing and insulting the "unsexual women" who made such outrageous demands.

7. Describe the southern reaction to the middle-class social reforms of the early nineteenth century.

Answer: Southern society was patriarchal, agricultural, and conservative. The white-male-dominated southern culture rebuffed outside influences, ideas, and interference. Southerners were proud of their traditions and suspicious of expensive social-improvement concepts. Unlike the North, the South had a homogeneous population united by common bonds of ideology and family ties. Even when state legislatures promoted plans for public schools, local authorities limited course offerings and attendance requirements. Schools were not deemed necessary for economic success in the rural cotton culture of the southern states.

Southern prisons, though patterned after the Auburn system, emphasized economy and punishment not rehabilitation. Old Testament visions of corporal punishments such as branding, beating, and execution were favored by southern law-enforcement officials and the general public. The prisoner-leasing system was widely used as a means of making prisons cost effective.

The temperance movement did make some inroads in southern society. Methodist and Baptist preachers warned against the evils of alcohol, gambling, and dancing. Many men cut back on—or abstained from—the consumption of alcohol. The Washington Temperance Society was influential in many areas of the South. Temperance, however, did not become a matter of public policy in the South as it did in the North. Southerners regarded legislative prohibition as an unwarranted intrusion by the state into a purely private and personal matter. In general, southerners opposed any change that undermined the prevailing power structure. Most of the reform movements originated in the North and therefore seemed to be an attempt to remake southern society according to a Yankee model.

LONG ESSAYS

1. Explore the movement for reform in American society during the market revolution of the early nineteenth century.

Answer: Essay should address several key points:

A. Background to reform
    1. Wide-scale commercial development
        a. Transportation and market revolutions
        b. Industrialization
    2. Social ills in need of reforming
        a. Abuse of alcohol
        b. Crime and vice
        c. Education
B. Representative nineteenth-century reforms

1. Temperance
   a. American Temperance Society
   b. Importance
2. Prison reform
   a. Auburn System
   b. Implications
3. Education
   a. Horace Mann
   b. Importance
C. Dominant reform movements
   1. Slavery
      a. American Anti-Slavery Society
      b. William Lloyd Garrison
   2. Women's rights
      a. Seneca Falls
      b. Declaration of Sentiments

2. Examine the demand for women's rights in the years between 1820 and 1850.

Answer: Essay should address several key points:

A. Background to women's rights
   1. Subordinate position of women in American society
   2. Implications of market revolution for women
      a. Rise of middle-class ideal
      b. Mill and factory girls
B. Path to women's rights
   1. Abolitionism and antislavery
      a. Women take leading role in antislavery movement
      b. Implications
   2. Problems of inequality
      a. Unequal divorce and custody laws
      b. Poor access to property control
      c. No public political voice
C. Seneca Falls (1848)
   1. First women's rights convention
   2. Demands of Declaration of Sentiments
      a. Right to vote
      b. Right to divorce
      c. Right to property

3. Describe the differences between the two major political parties, the Democrats and the Whigs, between 1820 and 1840.

Answer: Essay should address several key points:

A. General principles of both parties
   1. Democratic Party
      a. Limited federal government
      b. Opposed to active intrusion in the economy
         i) internal improvements
         ii) banks
         iii) tariffs
   2. Whig Party
      a. Call for active federal intervention
      b. Strong supporter of federal role in the economy

          i)   internal improvements
          ii)   banks
          iii)   tariffs

B.   Base support of both parties
       1.   Democratic Party
           a.   Working-class, small farmers
           b.   Groups suspicious of market development
       2.   Whig Party
           a.   Emerging middle class: farmers, merchants, financiers
           b.   Groups supportive of commercial development

4.   Discuss American views on slavery and racial differences in the years from 1820 to 1840.

Answer: Essay should address several key points:

A.   Free blacks
       1.   Northern abolition of slavery
           a.   Influence of revolutionary ideals
           b.   Gradual emancipation
       2.   Urban life
           a.   Job opportunities
           b.   Discrimination
           c.   African-American institutions

B.   Racism in politics and philosophy
       1.   Democratic Party promotes racism
           a.   Stereotypes of African Americans
           b.   Race riots
       2.   Biological determinism
           a.   Early views of black character
           b.   Post-1820 views of black character
           c.   Unfit for citizenship

C.   Antislavery movement
       1.   Early abolitionists
           a.   Quakers
           b.   American Colonization Society
       2.   American Anti-Slavery Society
           a.   William Lloyd Garrison
           b.   Postal Campaign of 1835

CHAPTER 12
JACKSONIAN DEMOCRACY

CHAPTER OUTLINE

I. Prologue: 1819
    A. The West: 1803-1840s
    B. The Argument over Missouri
    C. The Missouri Compromise
    D. The Panic of 1819

II. Republican Revival
    A. Martin Van Buren Leads the Way
    B. The Election of 1824
    C. "A Corrupt Bargain"
    D. Jacksonian Melodrama

III. Adams versus Jackson
    A. Nationalism in an International Arena
    B. Nationalism at Home
    C. The Birth of the Democratic Party
    D. Election of 1828
    E. A People's Inauguration
    F. The Spoils System

IV. Jacksonian Democracy and the South
    A. Southerners and Indians
    B. Indian Removal
    C. Southerners and the Tariff
    D. Nullification
    E. The "Petticoat Wars"
    F. The Fall of Calhoun
    G. Petitions, the Gag Rule, and the Southern Mails

V. Jacksonian Democracy and the Market Revolution
    A. The Second Bank of the United States
    B. The Bank War
    C. The Beginnings of the Whig Party
    D. A Balanced Budget

VI. The Second American Party System
    A. "Martin Van Ruin"
    B. The Election of 1840
    C. Two Parties

VII. Conclusion

CHRONOLOGY

1804–1806	Lewis and Clark expedition explores upper Louisiana and crosses the Continental Divide.
1816	Congress charters Second Bank of the United States.
1819	Panic of 1819 marks first failure of the national market economy.
	Crisis arises over Missouri's admission to the Union.
	Adams–Onís Treaty extends American border to the Pacific Ocean.
1820	Missouri Compromise adopted.
	Maine becomes the twenty-third state.
1821	Missouri becomes the twenty-fourth state.
1822	Denmark Vesey conspiracy uncovered in South Carolina.
1823	Monroe Doctrine written by John Quincy Adams.

1824–1825	Adams wins presidency over Andrew Jackson.
	Adams appoints Henry Clay Secretary of State.
	Jacksonians charge "corrupt bargain" between Adams and Clay.
1827	Cherokees in Georgia declare themselves a republic.
1828	Jackson defeats Adams for presidency.
	"Tariff of Abominations" passed by Congress.
	John C. Calhoun's Exposition and Protest presents nullification doctrine.
1830	Congress passes Indian Removal Act.
	Marshall hands down verdict in case of *Cherokee Nation v. Georgia.*
1831	Nat Turner's rebellion extinguished in Virginia.
1832	"Bank War" erupts in Washington politics.
	Jackson reelected over Henry Clay.
	Worcester v. Georgia favors Cherokees in jurisdiction dispute.
	Jackson vetoes bill to recharter the Bank of the United States.
1833	Force Bill and Tariff of 1833 end the nullification crisis.
1834	Whig Party formed.
1836	House of Representatives adopts "gag rule" to table abolitionists' petitions.
	Martin Van Buren elected president.
1837	A severe economic depression begins with the Panic.
1838	"Trail of Tears" begins as army force-marches Cherokees to the Indian Territory.
1840	Whig William Henry Harrison defeats Van Buren for the presidency.
	Congress passes Independent Treasury Bill.

THEMATIC TOPICS FOR ENRICHMENT

1. How did the North and the South react to Missouri's petition to enter the Union?

2. Discuss the causes of the Panic of 1819. What role did banks play in this recession?

3. Who were the presidential candidates in 1824? What did each have to offer to the voters?

4. Discuss Andrew Jackson's background, character, and political philosophy.

5. How did John Quincy Adams differ from Jackson in regard to background and political philosophy?

6. Discuss the 1828 election in terms of the issues and the propaganda that each put forth.

7. Describe the Indian-removal issue from either the point of view of the Georgia government or from the point of view of the Cherokees.

8. Explain John C. Calhoun's nullification doctrine and why it was opposed by Andrew Jackson.

9. Discuss the Bank War from the viewpoints of Andrew Jackson and Nicholas Biddle.

SUGGESTED ESSAY TOPICS

1. Compare Andrew Jackson's political career and his views on government with those of Thomas Jefferson.

2. Explain the impact of the Missouri debates on the politics of the Jacksonian era. Why did Thomas Jefferson call the controversy "a fire-bell in the night"?

3. Define the term *nationalism.* In what ways is nationalism a positive characteristic for a people? In what ways is it a negative one?

1.   The year **1819** was a volatile one in the United States as debates over Missouri statehood and the bank panic set the stage for tumultuous events in the subsequent two decades.

        a.   The **West** from 1803 to the 1840s was a land of bold exploration and methodical settlement, opened up by the Lewis and Clark expedition.

(SHOW TRANSPARENCY 57: WESTERN EXPLORATION, 1803-1807)

        b.   Congress was almost paralyzed by sectional arguments over **Missouri statehood** and the fate of slavery in the West.

        c.   Congress averted disaster with the passage of the **Missouri Compromise,** which made Missouri a slave state and Maine a free state, as well as established a northern boundary for the expansion of slavery in the Louisiana Purchase territory.

(SHOW TRANSPARENCY 58: THE MISSOURI COMPROMISE)

        d.   The **Panic of 1819** caused the collapse of many banks and brought economic depression to many regions of the nation.

2.   Events of 1819 and 1820 led to a **Republican revival,** with virtually all national political figures seeming to call for small government, sectional peace, and government noninterference in slavery.

        a.   New Yorker **Martin Van Buren** led the way toward the construction of a new, more modern political party, known as the Jacksonian Democratic Party.

        b.   The **election of 1824** proved a fiasco with none of the four candidates garnering an electoral majority, thus throwing the election into the House of Representatives.

        c.   Henry Clay's support of John Quincy Adams and his subsequent appointment to the post of Secretary of State led to widescale accusations that a **"corrupt bargain"** had been struck between Clay and Adams.

        d.   Between 1825 and the next election, a veritable **Jacksonian melodrama** ensued, in which Jackson's men publicly lamented their candidate's unfair denial of the nation's highest office.

3.   The nation found itself in the midst of the **rebirth of sectionalism** under the guise of two highly contentious personalities, Jackson and Adams.

        a.   The **Adams–Onís Treaty** and the promulgation of the **Monroe Doctrine** moved American nationalism to a much larger international arena.

        b.   **Nationalism at home**, while getting a big boost from Adams's educational and scientific initiatives, failed to take root in a Congress and public that remained wary of central power.

        c.   The **birth of the Democratic Party** stemmed directly from the public persona of Andrew Jackson and the behind-the-scenes machinations of Martin Van Buren.

        d.   Jackson's victory in the **election of 1828** vindicated the general and demonstrated the power of Van Buren's emerging party machine.

e.   Sympathetic contemporaries called Jackson's March 4, 1828, inauguration a **people's inauguration** while skeptics viewed it as a display of the debauchery of the common folk.

f.   Contemporaries termed Jackson's open replacement of government appointees with his own political operatives the **spoils system.**

4.   Elections from the 1820s to the Civil War demonstrate the crucial ties of **Jacksonian Democracy and the South.**

a.   Simmering tensions between **southerners and Indians**, whose land claims proved anathema to expansionists, turned to open conflict in large measure with Jackson's explicit approval and his public disavowal of the Supreme Court's decision in the case of *Worcester v. Georgia.*

b.   The official government policy known as **Indian Removal** was predicated upon the almost reflexive assumption that white and red could not live in harmony.

(SHOW TRANSPARENCY 60: THE REMOVAL OF THE AMERICAN INDIANS)

c.   One constant from Jefferson to Jackson proved to be **Southern opposition to the tariff.**

d.   Ostensibly in response to artificially high tariff rates, South Carolinian John C. Calhoun promulgated the doctrine of state **nullification** of national law.

e.   The dispute over the reputation of Secretary Eaton's wife, Peggy, among the wives of Jackson's Cabinet resulted in the **"petticoat wars"** that split the administration between Peggy's attackers and defenders.

f.   The Eaton affair and the publication of the vice president's criticism of Jackson's actions during the Seminole War led to the **fall of Calhoun.**

g.   The sectional dispute over slavery erupted around Congress's debate over **petitions, the gag rule, and the southern mails**.

5.   **Jacksonian democracy and the market revolution** ultimately went hand in hand, as aggressive nabobs and the nouveaux riches sought political power to displace entrenched elites.

a.   Supporters of rechartering the **Second Bank of the United States** faced growing popular and presidential opposition in the 1830s.

b.   When the president vetoed the Second Bank's rechartering bill, a **bank war** ensued as the "monster bank" became the central issue of the 1832 presidential campaign.

c.   The **beginnings of the Whig Party** date from the bank war and Jackson's heavy-handed and highly personal style of governance.

d.   Jackson's supporters enthusiastically endorsed a **balanced budget** as a means to ensure that the government remained relatively small and unobtrusive.

6.   The birth of the Whigs and the consolidation of the Jacksonian Democrats brought about the **second American party system.**

a.   Jackson's inflationary bank policies led to the Panic of 1837 and made the reelection of **"Martin Van Ruin"** a virtual impossibility.

b.   The patently crude political machinations of both Whigs and Democrats in the **election of 1840,** such as dispensing of massive quantities of hard cider, were caricatured throughout the emerging popular press of the day.

c.   Despite the shenanigans, the election of 1840 ensured the success of an American electoral system driven by **two parties.**

American Album: Log Cabins and Hard Cider

Conclusion: Despite Jacksonian nostrums about minimal government, the economic growth, territorial expansion, and remarkable immigration of the 1830s and 1840s forced both political parties to actively pursue control of the national government to accomplish their highly political ends. Echoing the sentiments of the Jeffersonians, the Democratic Party proved far more adept at winning national office than their Whig opponents.

TEACHING RESOURCES

When the White Man Came briefly describes life among the major tribes across the United States at the time of European arrival. Films for the Humanities & Sciences (13 minutes, color).

The Trail of Tears focuses on white expansion and the impact on Native-American cultures. Films for the Humanities & Sciences (13 minutes, color).

Journals of Lewis & Clark re-creates with live action scenes of the journey along the Missouri River. Filmic Archives (60 minutes).

Gone West examines the myths and realities of nineteenth-century life on the frontier. BBC /Time–Life Video (52 minutes).

Andrew Jackson: A Man for the People is the best portrait of the American president, Indian fighter, and symbol for an age. Arts and Entertainment Video (50 minutes).

Lewis and Clark: The Journey of the Corps of Discovery is Ken Burns's rendition of the most famous American expedition of the nineteenth century. PBS Video (120 minutes each).

The West – Episodes 1 and 2 trace the development of the American West from pre-1800s through the 1840s. PBS Video (60 minutes each).

MULTIPLE CHOICE

1. Lewis and Clark explored
   a. northeastern Mexico.
   b. Canada.
   c. the Louisiana Purchase.
   d. the Oregon Territory.
   e. Florida.

ANS: C   **TYPE: M**   **KEY 1: F**   **KEY 2: 1**   **PAGE: 380**

2. Senator _____ proposed an amendment to Missouri's application for statehood that forbade slavery in the state.
   a. Martin Van Buren
   b. David Wilmot
   c. Henry Clay
   d. Stephen Douglas
   e. James Tallmadge

ANS: E   TYPE: M   KEY 1: F   KEY 2: 2   PAGE: 381

3. The so-called Thomas Proviso stated that
   a. slavery would be forever forbidden in the state of Missouri.
   b. each slave would count as three-fifths of a white person for purposes of representation.
   c. slavery would be outlawed in territories north of a line extending from the southern border of Missouri to Spanish territory.
   d. citizens of a territory could decide for themselves whether to permit slavery.
   e. slavery would be forbidden throughout the Louisiana Territory.

ANS: C   TYPE: M   KEY 1: A   KEY 2: 2   PAGE: 381

4. Which of the following was not a cause of the Panic of 1819?
   a. recovery of European agriculture in the early nineteenth century
   b. overexpansion of credit by American bankers
   c. underproduction by American farmers
   d. the hoarding of available specie by European nations
   e. revolution and war had cut off the supply of precious metals from Peru and Mexico.

ANS: C   TYPE: M   KEY 1: A   KEY 2: 2   PAGE: 382

5. The winner of the crowded presidential election of 1824 was
   a. Henry Clay.
   b. Andrew Jackson.
   c. John Quincy Adams.
   d. William Crawford.
   e. James Monroe.

ANS: C   TYPE: M   KEY 1: F   KEY 2: 1   PAGE: 384

6. The winner of the popular vote in the election of 1824, though not the victor in the election, was
   a. Henry Clay.
   b. Andrew Jackson.
   c. John Quincy Adams.
   d. William Crawford.
   e. James Monroe

ANS: B   TYPE: M   KEY 1: F   KEY 2: 1   PAGE: 384

7. The "corrupt bargain" of 1824 refers to the deal made between which two statesmen?
   a. Andrew Jackson and Martin Van Buren
   b. John Quincy Adams and Andrew Jackson
   c. John Quincy Adams and Henry Clay
   d. Henry Clay and Martin Van Buren
   e. James Monroe and John Quincy Adams

ANS: C   TYPE: M   KEY 1: F   KEY 2: 2   PAGE: 384

8. The Monroe Doctrine stated that
   a. the United States opposed the independence of the new Latin American republics.
   b. the United States was opposed to any further European attempt at colonization in the Americas.
   c. the United States could not colonize or annex new territory.
   d. the United States would take control of the new Latin American republics.
   e. Europe was opposed to any further U.S. expansion in Latin America.

ANS: B   **TYPE: M**   **KEY 1: A**   **KEY 2: 2**   **PAGE: 386**

9. The author of the Monroe Doctrine was
   a. James Monroe.
   b. John Quincy Adams.
   c. Martin Van Buren.
   d. Henry Clay.
   e. Andrew Jackson.

ANS: B   **TYPE: M**   **KEY 1: F**   **KEY 2: 2**   **PAGE: 386**

10. John Quincy Adams's ambitious program for national development called for which of the following?
   a. federal money for roads and canals
   b. federal money for a national university
   c. a high tariff
   d. a national astronomical observatory
   e. all of the above

ANS: E   **TYPE: M**   **KEY 1: F**   **KEY 2: 2**   **PAGE: 386**

11. The Indian Removal Act of 1830 stated that Native Americans
   a. needed to be removed to west of the Mississippi River.
   b. needed to be removed, but with no clear destination.
   c. needed to be removed to reservations in Canada.
   d. needed to be removed to California.
   e. were entitled to remain on their ancestral lands.

ANS: A   **TYPE: M**   **KEY 1: F**   **KEY 2: 1**   **PAGE: 391**

12. In _____, the Supreme Court argued that Georgia state law had no authority over the Indian nations within the state's boundaries.
   a. *Cherokee Nation v. Georgia*
   b. *Gibbons v. Ogden*
   c. *Worcester v. Georgia*
   d. *Jackson v. Georgia*
   e. *Marbury v. Madison*

ANS: C   **TYPE: M**   **KEY 1: F**   **KEY 2: 2**   **PAGE: 391**

13. The Tariff of 1828 was known throughout the South as the
   a. horrible tariff.
   b. tariff of subordination.
   c. tariff of abominations.
   d. tariff of dependence.
   e. tariff of plantations.

ANS: C   **TYPE: M**   **KEY 1: F**   **KEY 2: 1**   **PAGE: 393**

14. The primary defender of the right of "nullification" was
    a. Henry Clay.
    b. Daniel Webster.
    c. Martin Van Buren.
    d. John C. Calhoun.
    e. Andrew Jackson.

ANS: D   **TYPE: M**   **KEY 1: F**   **KEY 2: 1**   **PAGE: 393**

15. The "Force Bill" refers to Andrew Jackson's attempt to
    a. remove the Cherokee Indians.
    b. reorganize his cabinet.
    c. destroy the Second Bank of the United States.
    d. impose martial law whenever he desired.
    e. prevent South Carolina from nullifying the tariff

ANS: E   **TYPE: M**   **KEY 1: F**   **KEY 2: 2**   **PAGE: 395**

16. The "Gag Rule" refers to the congressional attempt to avoid discussing which issue?
    a. Indian removal
    b. nullification
    c. tariffs
    d. slavery
    e. Sunday mail deliveries

ANS: D   **TYPE: M**   **KEY 1: F**   **KEY 2: 1**   **PAGE: 397**

17. Which of the following did Andrew Jackson hate most?
    a. the Second Bank of the United States
    b. the House of Representatives
    c. the Senate
    d. the Supreme Court
    e. the Democratic party

ANS: A   **TYPE: M**   **KEY 1: F**   **KEY 2: 1**   **PAGE: 398**

18. The president of the Second Bank of the United States was
    a. Nicholas Biddle.
    b. Amos Kendall.
    c. Frank Blair, Jr.
    d. Daniel Webster.
    e. Henry Clay.

ANS: A   **TYPE: M**   **KEY 1: F**   **KEY 2: 1**   **PAGE: 398**

19. The political party that emerged in the 1830s to oppose Andrew Jackson was the
    _____ Party.
    a. Republican
    b. Federalist
    c. Whig
    d. Know-Nothing
    e. Socialist

ANS: C   **TYPE: M**   **KEY 1: F**   **KEY 2: 1**   **PAGE: 400**

20. The issue that led to the final and complete break between Andrew Jackson and John C. Calhoun was
    a. the tariff of 1830.
    b. "nullification."
    c. the Peggy Eaton affair.
    d. Indian removal.
    e. the Bank of the U.S.

ANS: C   TYPE: M   KEY 1: F   KEY 2: 2   PAGE: 396

21. The treaty that acquired Florida for the United States was the
    a. Rush–Bagot Treaty.
    b. British–American Convention.
    c. Adams–Onis Treaty.
    d. Treaty of Paris.
    e. Treaty of Florida.

ANS: C   TYPE: M   KEY 1: F   KEY 2: 2   PAGE: 386

22. Jacksonian Democrats viewed the "American System" as
    a. the most efficient approach to solving the nation's economic and political problems.
    b. an unconstitutional violation of local, state, and citizen rights.
    c. a means of reducing sectional tensions and calming the fears of southern slave owners.
    d. a tax-reform policy that would benefit honest citizens and impoverished politicians.
    e. socialism.

ANS: B   TYPE: M   KEY 1: A   KEY 2: 3   PAGE: 379

23. In the Missouri Compromise,
    a. slavery was outlawed in and west of the Louisiana territory.
    b. the issue of slavery was not addressed.
    c. Missouri was admitted to the union as a free state.
    d. citizens could decide for themselves whether to permit slavery.
    e. Maine was admitted to the union as a free state.

ANS: B   TYPE: M   KEY 1: F   KEY 2: 2   PAGE: 381

24. Andrew Jackson's popularity was
    a. confined to remote areas of the South.
    b. a result of his reputation for calm and peaceful resolution of problems.
    c. based in part on his image as a forceful and exciting military hero.
    d. dependent upon his avoidance of partisan political disputes.
    e. destroyed when he vetoed the Bank.

ANS: C   TYPE: M   KEY 1: F   KEY 2: 2   PAGE: 383

25. Which of the following was not true of John Quincy Adams?
    a. He was the son of Federalist President John Adams.
    b. He served with distinction as secretary of state for James Monroe.
    c. He negotiated the treaty by which the United States acquired Florida.
    d. He opposed federal support for internal improvements.
    e. He supported a strong national government.

ANS: D   TYPE: M   KEY 1: F   KEY 2: 3   PAGE: 386

26. The Democratic Party
   a. supported both agrarian democratic principles and the continuation of southern slavery.
   b. favored strict limitations on voting rights.
   c. was similar in policy and constituencies to the Federalist Party.
   d. was almost destroyed by the election of 1828.
   e. was organized to oppose Andrew Jackson.

ANS: A   TYPE: M   KEY 1: F   KEY 2: 2   PAGE: 388

27. The election of 1828 was
   a. one of the dullest and most uninteresting campaigns in U.S. history.
   b. noteworthy because of the civility and lofty intellectual tone of its political debates.
   c. the first election that included a popular vote for presidential electors.
   d. decided by the House of Representatives.
   e. marred by a smear campaign that turned Andrew Jackson's private life into a public issue.

ANS: E   TYPE: M   KEY 1: A   KEY 2: 3   PAGE: 388

28. The phrase "the spoils system" referred to
   a. corrupt politicians who spoiled the public image of national office holders.
   b. the government agency set up to regulate garbage collection and disposal.
   c. Andrew Jackson's use of presidential appointive powers to reward his supporters with government jobs.
   d. Martin Van Buren's efforts to ruin the relationship between Jackson and John C. Calhoun.
   e. the bargain made between Clay and Adams in the election of 1824.

ANS: C   TYPE: M   KEY I: F   KEY 2: 2   PAGE: 390

29. Andrew Jackson's Indian policy
   a. protected the sovereign rights of Indian nations within their own territories.
   b. openly violated Supreme Court rulings by allowing state governments to encroach on Indian land.
   c. increased the size of Indian reservations as a reward for tribal support in the War of 1812.
   d. terminated the reservations and assimilated Indians into white society.
   e. was based on the assumption that all Indians would ultimately have to be killed.

ANS: B   TYPE: M   KEY I: F   KEY 2: 3   PAGE: 391-92

30. Southern states opposed the tariff of 1828 because it
   a. unfairly taxed southern agricultural products.
   b. lowered the price of most manufactured goods.
   c. violated the states' constitutional right to control intrastate trade.
   d. benefited northern and western farmers at the expense of export-driven southern producers.
   e. benefited British merchants at their expense.

ANS: D   TYPE: M   KEY 1: F   KEY 2: 3   PAGE: 393

31. In response to the nullification crisis, Andrew Jackson
   a. asserted the inviolability of the union and of federal control of tariffs and other matters of foreign policy.
   b. defended the states' rights position that states were the ultimate judges of constitutional principles.
   c. challenged John C. Calhoun to a duel.
   d. demanded that Congress enact an even higher new tariff.
   e. became best friends with Calhoun.

ANS: A   TYPE: M   KEY 1: F   KEY 2: 2   PAGE: 395

32. The relationship between Andrew Jackson and John C. Calhoun was ruined by all except which of the following?
    a. Calhoun's support of the concepts of nullification and secession
    b. a letter revealing that Calhoun had criticized Jackson's invasion of Florida in 1818
    c. Calhoun's participation in the dirty political campaign of 1818
    d. Floride Calhoun's rude treatment of the Eatons
    e. Calhoun's vote against Van Buren's diplomatic appointment.

ANS: C   TYPE: M   KEY 1: F   KEY 2: 3   PAGE: 394-97

33. Andrew Jackson criticized the Bank because he believed that it
    a. benefited northern and foreign investors at the expense of southern and western farmers.
    b. was too liberal with its loan policies.
    c. did not exercise enough centralized control over the monetary system.
    d. charged excessive interest rates.
    e. benefited plantation owners more than small farmers.

ANS: A   TYPE: M   KEY 1: A   KEY 2: 3   PAGE: 398-99

34. The political party system that emerged in 1840 included
    a. a regional alignment in which the South voted for the Democrats and the North voted for the Whigs.
    b. the destruction of the two-party system and the emergence of numerous independent parties.
    c. increased public interest in politics as indicated by extremely high voter turnout.
    d. increasingly unstable, unpredictable, and violent political contests.
    e. no national political party.

ANS: C   TYPE: M   KEY 1: A   KEY 2: 3   PAGE: 404

35. Which of the following was not among the Civilized Tribes?
    a. Creeks
    b. Iroquois
    c. Seminoles
    d. Cherokees
    e. Choctaw

ANS: B   TYPE: M   KEY 1: F   KEY 2: 3   PAGE: 391

36. The great depression of 1837 occurred during the presidency of
    a. Andrew Jackson.
    b. Martin Van Buren.
    c. William Henry Harrison.
    d. Henry Clay.
    e. John Quincy Adams.

ANS: B   TYPE: M   KEY 1: F   KEY 2: 2   PAGE: 402

37. Martin Van Buren's plan to develop an independent financial system to avoid the federal government's dependence on banks was known as
    a. the Third Bank of the United States.
    b. the "subtreasury."
    c. the Federal Reserve system.
    d. the "minitreasury."
    e. pet banks.

ANS: B   **TYPE: M**   **KEY 1: F**   **KEY 2: 2**   **PAGE: 403**

38. The election of 1840 pitted which two candidates against each other?
    a. Andrew Jackson and Henry Clay
    b. Martin Van Buren and Henry Clay
    c. Martin Van Buren and William Henry Harrison
    d. Henry Clay and John Tyler
    e. Andrew Jackson and John Quincy Adams

ANS: C   **TYPE: M**   **KEY 1: F**   **KEY 2: 2**   **PAGE: 403**

39. Who of the following was not a Whig candidate for president in 1836?
    a. Henry Clay
    b. Daniel Webster
    c. Hugh Lawson White
    d. William Henry Harrison
    e. none of the above

ANS: A   **TYPE: M**   **KEY 1: F**   **KEY 2: 1**   **PAGE: 402**

40. The Lewis and Clark Expedition went through lands inhabited by all of the following peoples except
    a. Oto.
    b. Crow.
    c. Sioux.
    d. Mandan.
    e. Creek

ANS: E   **TYPE: M**   **KEY 1: F**   **KEY 2: 2**   **PAGE: 380**

41. Andrew Jackson carried all of the following states in the presidential election of 1824 except
    a. Indiana.
    b. New Jersey.
    c. Pennsylvania.
    d. New York.
    e. Illinois.

ANS: D   **TYPE: M**   **KEY 1: F**   **KEY 2: 2**   **PAGE: 384**

42. Andrew Jackson's inaugural address proposed all of the following except
    a. civil service reform.
    b. retiring the national debt.
    c. removal of Indians from eastern states to western reservations.
    d. respect for states' rights.
    e. caution with regard to the tariff.

ANS: C   **TYPE: M**   **KEY 1: F**   **KEY 2: 2**   **PAGE: 389**

43. Which of the following occurred in 1819?
    a. Adams-Onis Treaty
    b. Rush-Bagot Treaty
    c. Monroe Doctrine
    d. British-American Convention
    e. none of the above

ANS: A   **TYPE: M**   **KEY 1: F**   **KEY 2: 3**   **PAGE: 386**

44. John Quincy Adams's nationalistic program included all of the following except
    a. a national university.
    b. a national astronomical observatory.
    c. a national language.
    d. nationally financed roads and canals.
    e. a protective tariff.

ANS: C   **TYPE: M**   **KEY 1: A**   **KEY 2: 3**   **PAGE: 386**

45. Voter turnout in the election of 1828 was _____ that of 1824.
    a. one-quarter
    b. one-half
    c. triple
    d. double
    e. ten times

ANS: D   **TYPE: M**   **KEY 1: F**   **KEY 2: 3**   **PAGE: 389**

46. Voter turnout in the election of 1840 was _____ percent of the eligible voters.
    a. 78
    b. 69
    c. 81
    d. 75
    e. 50

ANS: A   **TYPE: M**   **KEY 1: F**   **KEY 2: 1**   **PAGE: 404**

47. Newspaper estimates put the number of citizens who came to Washington to witness Andrew Jackson's inauguration at
    a. 10,000 to 15,000.
    b. 1,000 to 2,000.
    c. 20,000 to 25,000.
    d. 25,000 to 30,000.
    e. 15,000 to 20,000

ANS: B   **TYPE: M**   **KEY 1: F**   **KEY 2: 2**   **PAGE: 389**

48. Which of the following states did not extend its control over Indian lands and deny federal jurisdiction?
    a. Florida
    b. Georgia
    c. Alabama
    d. Mississippi
    e. none of the above

ANS: A   **TYPE: M**   **KEY 1: F**   **KEY 2: 2**   **PAGE: 391**

49. Which of the following did not occur during Andrew Jackson's first term as president?
    a. the controversy over the spoils system
    b. the nullification crisis
    c. the struggle over Indian removal
    d. the veto of the Bank bill
    e. the creation of the Whig Party

ANS: E   TYPE: M   KEY 1: F   KEY 2: 3   PAGE: 391

50. The free state admitted to the Union as part of the Missouri Compromise was
    a. Illinois.
    b. Iowa.
    c. Maine.
    d. Ohio.
    e. Missouri.

ANS: C   TYPE: M   KEY 1: F   KEY 2: 2   PAGE: 381

TRUE/FALSE

_____ 1.   Jacksonian democracy can best be understood as the inheritance of the old Hamiltonian emphasis on federal power.

ANS: F   TYPE: T   KEY 1: A   KEY 2: 1   PAGE: 379

_____ 2.   The victor of the 1828 presidential election was John Quincy Adams.

ANS: F   TYPE: T   KEY 1: F   KEY 2: 3   PAGE: 389

_____ 3.   The "Trail of Tears" refers to the removal of the Cherokee Indians to the Indian Territory (Oklahoma).

ANS: T   TYPE: T   KEY 1: F   KEY 2: 1   PAGE: 393

_____ 4.   The postal campaign was halted by a federal censorship law.

ANS: F   TYPE: T   KEY 1: F   KEY 2: 1   PAGE: 397

_____ 5.   The man most responsible for resolving the "nullification" crisis of 1830 was John C. Calhoun.

ANS: F   TYPE: T   KEY 1: F   KEY 2: 3   PAGE: 394-95

_____ 6.   An important component of Andrew Jackson's vision for America was to use federal money to build large transportation systems throughout the United States.

ANS: F   TYPE: T   KEY 1: A   KEY 2: 2   PAGE: 398

_____ 7.   The Missouri Compromise allowed Missouri to enter the union, but forbade slavery in any state carved out of the Louisiana Territory north of Missouri.

ANS: F   TYPE: T   KEY 1: F   KEY 2: 2   PAGE: 381

_____ 8.	Andrew Jackson supported evangelicals' efforts in 1828 and 1829 to stop movement of the mail on Sundays.

**ANS: F	TYPE: T	KEY 1: F	KEY 2: 3	PAGE: 381**

_____ 9.	Many northerners opposed the admission of Missouri to the Union because they feared it would increase the power of the slave states in Congress.

**ANS: T	TYPE: T	KEY 1: F	KEY 2: 2	PAGE: 381**

_____ 10.	The Panic of 1819 was the first nationwide failure of the market economy.

**ANS: T	TYPE: T	KEY 1: F	KEY 2: 2	PAGE: 382**

_____ 11.	In the election of 1824, Martin Van Buren was the only candidate for the vice presidency.

**ANS: F	TYPE: T	KEY 1: F	KEY 2: 2	PAGE: 383**

_____ 12.	Andrew Jackson believed that his wife's death was caused by the campaign tactics of his political opponents.

**ANS: T	TYPE: T	KEY 1: F	KEY 2: 2	PAGE: 389**

_____ 13.	John C. Calhoun's last exercise of national power was blocking Martin Van Buren's appointment as minister to Great Britain.

**ANS: T	TYPE: T	KEY 1: F	KEY 2: 2	PAGE: 397**

_____ 14.	The first presidential election in which national, not sectional, alignments determined the outcome was the election of 1840.

**ANS: T	TYPE: T	KEY 1: F	KEY 2: 3	PAGE: 404**

_____ 15.	Democrats feared that an activist federal government might threaten the slaveholding South.

**ANS: T	TYPE: T	KEY 1: F	KEY 2: 2	PAGE: 379**

_____ 16.	Smallpox proved very deadly to the Sioux.

**ANS: F	TYPE: T	KEY 1: F	KEY 2: 2	PAGE: 381**

_____ 17.	Congressional debates on the Missouri question were primarily absent about the morality of slavery.

**ANS: F	TYPE: T	KEY 1:A	KEY 2: 2	PAGE: 381**

_____ 18.	Voting on the Tallmadge amendments was starkly sectional.

**ANS: T	TYPE: T	KEY 1: F	KEY 2: 1	PAGE: 381**

_____ 19.	Congress admitted Missouri as a slave state with little debate.

**ANS: F	TYPE: T	KEY 1: F	KEY 2: 2	PAGE: 381**

_____ 20.   Thomas Jefferson was deeply concerned about the implications of the Missouri Compromise.

ANS: T   **TYPE: T**   **KEY 1: A**   **KEY 2: 3**   **PAGE: 382**

_____ 21.   European demand for American foodstuffs increased after the Napoleonic wars.

ANS: F   **TYPE: T**   **KEY 1: A**   **KEY 2:2**   **PAGE: 382**

_____ 22.   South Carolina opposed the Tariffs of 1828 and 1832 but never attempted to nullify them.

ANS: F   **TYPE: T**   **KEY 1: F**   **KEY 2: 3**   **PAGE: 395**

_____ 23.   By 1820, many Republicans were calling for a Jeffersonian revival that would limit governmental power and guarantee southern rights within the Union.

ANS: T   **TYPE: T**   **KEY 1: A**   **KEY 2: 3**   **PAGE: 382**

_____ 24.   Andrew Jackson believed that the republic was safe only when governed by the will of the majority.

ANS: T   **TYPE: T**   **KEY 1: A**   **KEY 2: 1**   **PAGE: 385**

_____ 25.   Indian removal announced Andrew Jackson's commitment to federal authority and limited state power.

ANS: F   **TYPE: T**   **KEY 1: A**   **KEY 2: 3**   **PAGE: 393**

_____ 26.   The Democratic Party linked popular democracy with the defense of southern slavery.

ANS: T   **TYPE: T**   **KEY 1: A**   **KEY 2: 1**   **PAGE: 388**

_____ 27.   John C. Calhoun did not wish to stay on as vice president as the election of 1828 approached.

ANS: F   **TYPE: T**   **KEY 1: F**   **KEY 2: 3**   **PAGE: 391**

_____ 28.   John Quincy Adams did a lot of preparing for the election of 1828.

ANS: F   **TYPE: T**   **KEY 1: F**   **KEY 2: 2**   **PAGE: 386**

_____ 29.   The presidential campaign of 1828 was run cleanly and was free of dirty tricks or slanderous accusations.

ANS: F   **TYPE: T**   **KEY 1: F**   **KEY 2: 2**   **PAGE: 388**

_____ 30.   Vice President John C. Calhoun and Secretary of State Martin Van Buren had the same position on the right of states to secede.

ANS: F   **TYPE: T**   **KEY 1: A**   **KEY 2: 3**   **PAGE: 391**

_____ 31.   Andrew Jackson supported the Civilized Tribes against state governments that wanted to seize control of their lands.

ANS: F   **TYPE: T**   **KEY 1: A**   **KEY 2: 2**   **PAGE: 391**

_____ 32. The tariff of 1828 was primarily designed as a revenue-raising measure.

ANS: F   TYPE: T   KEY 1: A   KEY 2:3   PAGE: 393

_____ 33. Jackson's veto message surprised the Bank of the United States' supporters.

ANS: F   TYPE: T   KEY 1: F   KEY 2: 1   PAGE: 399

_____ 34. The Bank and Jackson's veto message were the principal issues in the election of 1832.

ANS: T   TYPE: T   KEY 1: F   KEY 2: 2   PAGE: 399

_____ 35. Slaveholding Missouri was the first new state to be carved out of the Louisiana Purchase.

ANS: T   TYPE: T   KEY 1: F   KEY 2: 2   PAGE: 381

_____ 36. In 1819, the North held a majority in the House of Representatives.

ANS: T   TYPE: T   KEY 1: F   KEY 2: 1   PAGE: 381

_____ 37. It was not clear until the last minute that the election of 1828 would be between John Quincy Adams and Andrew Jackson.

ANS: F   TYPE: T   KEY 1: F   KEY 2: 1   PAGE: 386

_____ 38. President Jackson supported South Carolina's attempt to nullify the tariff.

ANS: F   TYPE: T   KEY 1: F   KEY 2: 1   PAGE: 395

_____ 39. The Panic of 1819 had no impact on Philadelphia.

ANS: F   TYPE: T   KEY 1: A   KEY 2: 2   PAGE: 382

_____ 40. Many Americans were grateful to the Bank of the United States for its assertive and positive response to the Panic of 1819 that mitigated the damage of the economic downturn.

ANS: F   TYPE: T   KEY 1: A   KEY 2: 2   PAGE: 382

FILL-INS

1. Andrew Jackson is considered responsible for instituting the so-called _____, which allowed the winners of elections to promote loyal supporters to high office.

ANS: spoils system   TYPE: F   KEY 1: F   KEY 2: 2   PAGE: 390

2. The author of the pro-nullification tract _Exposition and Protest_ was _____.

ANS: John C. Calhoun   TYPE: F   KEY 1: F   KEY 2: 3   PAGE: 394

3. The man who received the most popular votes in the election of 1824 was _____.

ANS: Andrew Jackson   TYPE: F   KEY 1: F   KEY 2: 2   PAGE: 384

4.   The attempt to silence anti-slavery petitions in Congress was known as the _____ rule.

ANS: gag   TYPE: F   KEY 1: F   KEY 2: 1   PAGE: 397

5.   _____ was the Shoshone Indian woman who acted as a guide and interpreter for the Lewis and Clark Expedition.

ANS: Sacajawea   TYPE: F   KEY 1: F   KEY 2: 1   PAGE: 380

6.   _____ scored huge gains in the midterm elections of 1838.

ANS: Whigs   TYPE: F   KEY 1: F   KEY 2: 2   PAGE: 403

7.   The marriage of _____ to Jackson's secretary of war caused a national scandal that disrupted the administration.

ANS: Peggy (O'Neal Timberlake) Eaton   TYPE: F   KEY 1: F   KEY 2:2   PAGE: 395

8.   The crucial year for the formation of Jacksonian democracy was _____.

ANS: 1819   TYPE: F   KEY 1: F   KEY 2: 1   PAGE: 380

9.   _____ applied in 1819 to become the first new state to be carved out of the Louisiana Purchase.

ANS: Missouri   TYPE: F   KEY 1: F   KEY 2: 2   PAGE: 381

10.   The Thomas Proviso opened _____ Territory to slavery.

ANS: Arkansas   TYPE: F   KEY 1: F   KEY 2: 1   PAGE: 381

11.   Unemployment in Philadelphia during the Panic of 1819 hit _____ percent

ANS: 75   TYPE: F   KEY 1: F   KEY 2: 2   PAGE: 382

12.   _____ was the driving force behind the creation of the Democratic Party.

ANS: Martin Van Buren   TYPE: F   KEY 1: A   KEY 2: 2   PAGE: 383

13.   Martin Van Buren supported _____ in the election of 1824.

ANS: William H. Crawford   TYPE: F   KEY 1: F   KEY 2: 2   PAGE: 383

14.   In 1828, Andrew Jackson ran strongly in every region but _____.

ANS: New England   TYPE: F   KEY 1: F   KEY 2: 1   PAGE: 389

15.   Jackson won _____ percent of southern votes in 1828.

ANS: 80   TYPE: F   KEY 1: F   KEY 2: 2   PAGE: 389

16.   Resistance to federal authority to formulate Indian policy within individual states centered in

_____.

ANS: Georgia   TYPE: F   KEY 1: F   KEY 2: 1   PAGE: 391

17. The creation of the second party system was complete in the election of _____.

ANS: 1840   TYPE: F   KEY 1: 1   KEY 2: 2   PAGE: 404

18. _____ was president during the Trail of Tears.

ANS: Martin Van Buren   TYPE: F   KEY 1: F   KEY 2: 2   PAGE: 393

19. Georgia's dispute over state power over Indian groups focused on the _____.

ANS: Cherokees   TYPE: F   KEY 1: F   KEY 2: 1   PAGE: 391

20. The Chief Justice of the Supreme Court during the *Worcester v. Georgia* decision was _____.

ANS: John Marshall   TYPE: F   KEY 1: F   KEY 2: 2   PAGE: 391

21. _____ was the strongest card held by southern extremists.

ANS: Nullification   TYPE: F   KEY 1: A   KEY 2: 2   PAGE: 394-95

22. The secretary of the treasury who ordered the removal of federal deposits from the Bank of the United States was _____.

ANS: Roger B. Taney   TYPE: F   KEY 1: F   KEY 2: 2   PAGE: 399

23. _____ led the campaign in the Senate to censure Andrew Jackson.

ANS: Henry Clay   TYPE: F   KEY 1: F   KEY 2: 2   PAGE: 400

24. When Henry Clay used his influence as Speaker of the House to win the presidential election for John Quincy Adams in 1824, Andrew Jackson's supporters labeled their alliance a _____.

ANS: corrupt bargain   TYPE: F   KEY 1: F   KEY 2: 2   PAGE: 384

25. The Treaty that acquired Florida for the United States was the _____ Treaty.

ANS: Adams-Onis   TYPE: F   KEY 1: F   KEY 2: 3   PAGE: 386

26. Author of the Monroe Doctrine was _____.

ANS: John Quincy Adams   TYPE: F   KEY 1: F   KEY 2: 3   PAGE: 386

27. John Quincy Adams was elected president by the _____.

ANS: House of Representatives   TYPE: F   KEY 1: F   KEY 2: 1   PAGE: 384

28. President Van Buren's plan for the divorce of government from the banking system was known as the _____.

ANS: Sub-Treasury or Independent Treasury   TYPE: F   KEY 1: F   KEY 2: 2   PAGE: 403

29.   The man who ran for President on the Log Cabin campaign was _____.

ANS: William Henry Harrison   TYPE: F   KEY 1: F   KEY 2: 1   PAGE: 404

30.   _____, vice presidential candidate in 1840, had joined the Whig Party because of his opposition to Jackson.

ANS: John Tyler   TYPE: F   KEY 1: F   KEY 2: 2   PAGE: 403

IDENTIFICATIONS

1.   **Trail of Tears**: the forced march of the Cherokee Indians off their homeland to the Indian Territory (Oklahoma). Some four thousand Cherokees (one-fourth of those who embarked) died on the march.

2.   **nullification:** political theory proposed by John C. Calhoun that argued a state convention had the right to "nullify" (declare null and void) a federal law within its borders.

3.   **Martin Van Buren**: eighth president of the United States. Most memorable, however, for his expert organization of the Democratic Party in the years of Jackson's presidency.

4.   **force bill**: bill passed by Congress allowing President Jackson to use military force, if necessary, to force South Carolina not to nullify various tariffs.

5.   **John Quincy Adams**: sixth president of the United States. Won the election of 1824 even though he did not win the popular vote. Generally unsuccessful term. Defeated by Andrew Jackson in 1828.

6.   **Lewis and Clark Expedition**: In 1804 Thomas Jefferson sent this expedition to explore the Louisiana territory. Meriwether Lewis and William Clark led forty-one men from St. Louis, Missouri, to the Pacific coast of Oregon. They kept detailed records of plants, animals, and Indians in the area; made maps; and returned with volumes of information.

7.   **Peggy Timberlake Eaton**: pretty, flirtatious daughter of a Washington tavern owner. Gossips linked her with Jackson's friend Henry Eaton. When Peggy's first husband committed suicide and Peggy quickly married John Eaton, the rumors seemed to be confirmed. Cabinet wives snubbed Peggy, and Jackson split his administration by defending her.

8.   **corrupt bargain**: alleged to have been struck between John Quincy Adams and Henry Clay in the election of 1824. In exchange for Clay's support once the election had gone to the House of Representatives, Adams supposedly promised to appoint Clay secretary of state. After Adams won and did make Clay secretary of state, his opponents, led by Andrew Jackson (who had won the popular vote), denounced the "corrupt bargain" that had stolen the election for Adams.

9.   **kitchen cabinet**: unofficial group of advisers to Andrew Jackson that emerged in the wake of the cabinet shake up that followed the Peggy Eaton controversy. Included journalists Amos Kendall and Francis Preston Blair, along with Martin Van Buren and a few others.

10. **gag rule**: procedure employed between 1836 and 1844 in Congress to avoid discussing the slavery issue. Involved tabling antislavery petitions sent by the general public without even reading them. Passed by southerners with the help of most northern Democrats.

1. Examine the war between President Andrew Jackson and the Second Bank of the United States.

Answer: From Jackson's time as a backwoods speculator and soldier, he always had a profound distrust of banks and banking institutions. He had significant reservations about the mammoth Second Bank of the United States. This bank, a quasi-federal institution (in the sense that it was federally chartered, though still a private bank), wielded enormous power over the nation's economy—a power that was wielded under the tutelage of Nicholas Biddle, the bank's president. The Second Bank was not only a repository for government money, but also acted as a check on the overly speculative interests of the various state banks and private banks.

Jackson made clear that he would attempt to deny the rechartering of the Second Bank before the expiration of its 1836 charter. Proponents of the bank—including Biddle and the Whig candidate for president, Henry Clay—proposed making rechartering the paramount issue of the 1832 election. They did, and Jackson won by a landslide. Whether or not the American people gave Jackson a mandate with this action, he certainly saw this as the case and began withdrawing federal monies from the bank, depositing them in the so-called pet banks. This action, in conjunction with Biddle's attempt to call in state loans, led directly to the Panic of 1837. But the "monster" bank was in the end destroyed and, in popular tradition, if not fully in fact, a major democratic victory occurred.

2. Explore the Indian Removal of the 1830s—what were the reasons for the removal? What were the repercussions?

Answer: Following the War of 1812 and the general defeat of the Woodland Indians that occurred at that time, many white Americans believed that general removal of eastern Indians across the Mississippi would occur. Judging from his actions before becoming president, it is clear that Andrew Jackson was a firm believer in this idea as well. With his election to office in 1818, Jackson made it clear that the removal of the Creek and Cherokee Nations, among other civilized tribes, was one of his primary goals. This plan of removal was made law in the Indian Removal Act of 1830, which, in essence, called for the removal of Indians to reservations in Indian Territory (present-day Oklahoma).

In the state of Georgia, the process of removal began before the federal government could act. There, the discovery of gold led Georgians to expel Indians from the land. Although the Supreme Court argued that Georgia had no jurisdiction over the matter, President Jackson refused to interfere. This set the removal process into action. Ultimately, it was Martin Van Buren who oversaw the final removal of Indians from the Southeast. Of particular note was the "Trail of Tears," the forced march of 18,000 Cherokees from Georgia. One-fourth of those who marched (men, women, and children) died en route.

3. What was the American System? Describe opponents and proponents of this system of national development.

Answer: The American System was primarily a plan of national economic development that owed much to the Hamiltonian plan of the 1790s. Essentially, the system argued for an activist federal government, one that aggressively promoted economic and commercial development. The major proposals of this system, of which Henry Clay was the leading spokesperson, were high tariffs to protect developing industry and to generate revenue, money allocated for internal improvements (roads, turnpikes, and canals), and the continued support of a strong national banking system that would be receptive to business interests. Quite possibly, the most important action taken by President John Quincy Adams during his one term in office was the strong executive support he gave to this system.

At this time, however, much of the nation was opposed to this type of development. The opposition, centered around Jackson, occurred for several reasons. First, on a theoretical level, many Americans, only one generation removed from the Revolution, were steeped in republican theory, which had grave reservations about unrestrained commercial development, national debts, and the type of greedy, ant republican society that might emerge with a bigger government. On a more practical level, most of the nation was still overwhelmingly agrarian and had little interest in promoting the development of industrial-financial institutions of which they were already suspicious.

4.   Describe the election of 1824. Why was it so controversial?

Answer: The 1824 election was unique in American history for a variety of reasons. First, four major candidates ran for the presidency: Andrew Jackson, John Quincy Adams, Henry Clay, and William Crawford. Each had significant sectional support—only Crawford had a more national background. The results of the popular vote were clear. Andrew Jackson had won the election handily. But because there were four candidates, the electoral vote was divided several different ways, and Jackson was over thirty electoral votes short of an electoral majority. Having won over 40 percent of the popular vote, many thought Jackson deserved to win the election. As prescribed in the Constitution, the House of Representatives was to decide the outcome of the election.

Once in the House, all previous calculations were thrown out. Crawford, who had suffered a stroke, and Clay, who had come in third, both were eliminated. Clay, however, had enough support in the House to throw the election to Adams, which he did. Even though he only had won 33 percent of the popular vote, Adams was appointed president by the House of Representatives. Jackson and his supporters were outraged. Their belief that a dirty deal had been worked out between Adams and Clay was all but confirmed when Adams, in one of his first official acts, appointed Clay secretary of state. These actions motivated Jacksonians—they resolved never to let an election slip away again.

5.   Examine the emergence of the second American Party system.

Answer: The years 1828 through 1840 were, at the level of national politics, more or less controlled by Andrew Jackson and his supporters, although a lively opposition existed. Throughout these years, however, elections revealed significant changes in voter constituencies and regional support. In 1828, when Jackson was elected, his support clearly came from the South and West. His opponents were strongest in the mid-Atlantic states and in the Northeast. Over the course of the Jackson years (including the presidency of Van Buren), new alignments emerged and offered new possibilities for political coalitions.

During the 1830s, Jackson's support in the Northeast grew, but, because of his various southern policies (most notably his stance during the nullification crisis), he lost support in the South. The 1836 election between Martin Van Buren and three opposition candidates revealed the extent of the realignment, since support for the two opposing parties was general throughout. It was the election of 1840, however, that revealed the emergence of two national, opposing political parties. William Henry Harrison and Van Buren contested the election in every state and received equal support in both the slave and the free states. A national, two-party system emerged.

6.   What were the "Petticoat Wars" of Jackson's presidency? What were the results of these disputes?

Answer: The atmosphere of slander and character assassination that permeated the election of 1828 continued into the presidency of Andrew Jackson. Jackson's close friend, John Henry Eaton, was linked in rumor with a young married woman named Peggy O'Neal Timberlake. When Peggy's husband committed suicide, Washington gossips blamed John Eaton. Suspicions appeared confirmed by the unseemly haste with which Peggy and John married. Jackson gave his blessing to the union and named John Eaton secretary of war. Thus Peggy Eaton became a cabinet wife. Washington socialites, led by Vice President John C. Calhoun's wife Floride, refused to associate with a fallen woman like Peggy and attempted to ostracize the Eatons. Many cabinet members and even Jackson's nephew Andrew Jackson Donelson and his family snubbed the secretary of war and his wife. Jackson bitterly remembered the false accusations and distortions leveled at his beloved Rachel in 1828 and vowed to protect Peggy Eaton from similar mudslinging. The petticoat war helped split Jackson's administration into warring factions. Secretary of State Martin Van Buren, a widower, used the Eaton controversy to discredit Calhoun and to solidify a close relationship with the president. Eventually most of Jackson's cabinet resigned; Jackson's "White House Family" was sent back to Tennessee; Van Buren replaced Calhoun as vice president in 1932; and Peggy Eaton became the hostess at official presidential social functions.

7. Describe the origin of the spoils system. Were the criticisms of Jackson's appointment policies justified?

Answer: When Jackson was elected president, he rewarded his friends and supporters by giving them government jobs. Some of his appointees, such as Secretary of War Martin Van Buren, were competent and experienced, but others were merely political opportunists. Jackson was determined to reform the civil service and to remove those office holders he considered competitionists. He also used his appointment powers to punish those who sided with John Quincy Adams in the election of 1828 and who were, in Jackson's opinion, partially responsible for the death of Rachel Jackson. Unfortunately some of the president's replacements were themselves incompetent grafters.

Jackson considered his patronage policy a reform measure that would eliminate lazy bureaucrats who expected lifetime jobs. Nine out of ten officeholders remained in their positions, thus complaints about executive excesses were exaggerated. The president clearly surrounded himself with loyal Democratic supporters. When critics complained that Jackson had turned the civil service into a branch of the Democratic Party, one of the president's appointees replied "to the victor belong the spoils."

LONG ESSAYS

1. Examine the Missouri Compromise. What were the issues at stake, and how were they resolved?

Answer: Essay should address several key points:

A. Missouri's application for statehood
    1. Existence of slavery in Missouri Territory
        a. Northern fear of a new southern-voting state
        b. Tallmadge amendment to Missouri's application
    2. Application of Maine as a free state
        a. Constructed from Massachusetts
        b. Maine and Missouri would keep relative balance in Senate
B. Thomas Proviso
    1. North would admit Missouri as a slave state
    2. South would agree to outlaw slavery in the territories north of 36° 30'
    3. Both parts of the package would be voted on together
C. Congressional vote
    1. Two parts of Thomas Proviso divided
        a. Vote in Congress close
        b. Slavery outlawed north of 36° 30' with large majority
        c. Fourteen northern congressmen support Missouri's admission
    2. Not truly a debate on slavery
        a. Vote reveals tension over South's power in federal government
        b. Harbinger of future conflicts

2. Analyze the "nullification" controversy of 1830. Who were the primary figures involved, and how did this controversy represent significantly different viewpoints on the power of the federal government?

Answer: Essay should address several key points:

A. Tariff of 1828
    1. Tariff of abominations
        a. Southern anger over high tariff
        b. Threat to avoid enforcement
B. Calhoun and nullification
    1. Idea of nullification
        a. Based on Jefferson and Madison's Virginia and Kentucky Resolutions

       b.   John C. Calhoun's *Exposition and Protest*
    2.   Nullification crisis
        a.   South Carolina nullifies tariff
        b.   Clear assertion of states' rights theory
C.   Jackson and Force Bill
    1.   Jackson prepared to use military to protect federal power
        a.   Exertion of federal authority
        b.   No other southern state aids South Carolina
    2.   Henry Clay and compromise
        a.   South Carolina rescinds ordinance of nullification
        b.   Tariff revised downward

3.   What was "Jacksonian democracy"? Explore the ideals of this movement in their political, social, and economic realms.

Answer: Essay should address several key points:

A.   Political aspects of Jacksonian democracy
    1.   Changes in politics
        a.   Rise of caucus system
        b.   Increase in the franchise
        c.   Spoils system
    2.   Second American Party system
        a.   Competitive politics on national scale
        b.   Two national competitive parties
B.   Social aspects of Jacksonian democracy
    1.   Rise of middle class
        a.   New economic possibilities
        b.   New value and belief systems
    2.   Return to ideals of Jeffersonian democracy
        a.   Emphasis on republicanism
        b.   Opposed to powerful state-commercial relationship
C.   Economic aspects of Jacksonian democracy
    1.   Bank war
        a.   Assault on privilege
        b.   Impetus to middle-class development
    2.   Opposed to government aid for special privilege
        a.   Maysville Road veto
        b.   Downward-revised tariffs

4.   Examine the ideals, policies, and consequences of the Bank War.

Answer: Essay should address several key points:

A.   Philosophy
    1.   Agrarian republicanism
        a.   Paper economy versus real work
        b.   Opposition to American system
    2.   Market economists
        a.   Activist government policies
        b.   Federally supported improvements
B.   The Second Bank of the United States
    1.   Origin
        a.   Chartered by Congress in 1816
        b.   Repository of federal revenues
        c.   Control of interest rates and currency

       2.   Debate over recharter of the bank
             a.   Clay's, Webster's, and Biddle's views
             b.   Jackson's criticism

C.   The Bank War
       1.   Jackson's attack
             a.   Veto of the Bank Bill
             b.   Withdrawal of deposits
             c.   Establishment of pet banks
       2.   Response of supporters
             a.   Creation of Whig party
             b.   Biddle demands loan repayment
             c.   Deposit Act of 1836
       3.   Consequences
             a.   Specie Circular of 1836
             b.   Collapse of inflationary boom
             c.   Panic and depression in 1837
             d.   "Martin Van Ruin"

CHAPTER 13
MANIFEST DESTINY: AN EMPIRE FOR LIBERTY OR SLAVERY?

CHAPTER OUTLINE

I. Growth as the American Way
    A. Manifest Destiny and Slavery
    B. The Westering Impulse
    C. The Hispanic Southwest
    D. The Oregon and California Trails
    E. The Mormon Migration
    F. The Republic of Texas
    G. The Annexation Controversy
    H. Acquisition of Texas and Oregon

II. The Mexican War
    A. Military Campaigns of 1846
    B. Military Campaigns of 1847
    C. Antiwar Sentiment
    D. The Wilmot Proviso

III. The Election of 1848
    A. The Free Soil Party
    B. The Gold Rush and California Statehood

IV. The Compromise of 1850
    A. The Senate Debates
    B. Passage of the Compromise
    C. The Fugitive Slave Law
    D. The Slave-Catchers
    E. Uncle Tom's Cabin

V. Filibustering
    A. The Gray-Eyed Man of Destiny

VI. Conclusion

CHRONOLOGY

1836	Mexican army captures the Alamo.
	Texans defeat the Mexican army at San Jacinto.
1840	Richard Henry Dana publishes *Two Years before the Mast*.
1840s	"Young America" movement defines the nation's Manifest Destiny.
1842	*Prigg v. Pennsylvania* declares the state's ant kidnapping law unconstitutional.
1842–1843	"Oregon fever" impels thousands to move to the Oregon Country.
1844	Anti-Mormon mob kills Joseph Smith in Illinois.
	James K. Polk elected president.
1845	United States annexes Texas.
1846	Mexican War begins.
	U.S. and Britain settle Oregon boundary dispute.
	Wilmot Proviso causes great controversy over slavery's expansion.
1847	Brigham Young leads the Mormons west to the Great Basin.
	Mexico City falls to the United States Army.
1848	Treaty of Guadalupe Hidalgo ends the Mexican War.
	Popular sovereignty proposed by Lewis Cass.
	Free Soil Party forms.
	Gold discovered in California.
	Zachary Taylor wins the presidency.
1849	California gold rush begins.

1850	Henry Clay and Stephen A. Douglas craft the Compromise.
	John C. Calhoun and Zachary Taylor die.
	Millard Fillmore sworn in as president.
	California admitted as a free state.
1851	Fugitive slave laws enacted.
1852	*Uncle Tom's Cabin* is published.
	Franklin Pierce elected president.
1854	Ostend Manifesto causes uproar over Cuba.
	William Walker leads filibustering expedition to Nicaragua.

THEMATIC TOPICS FOR ENRICHMENT

1. Describe what Manifest Destiny meant for white laborers and farmers in the 1840s. What did it mean for slave owners?

2. Discuss what Manifest Destiny held in store for western Native Americans. What did Manifest Destiny mean for black Americans?

3. Discuss the various reasons Americans went west in the 1840s.

4. Why did Texans seek independence from Mexico in the 1830s? Why did they want the United States to annex Texas?

5. Discuss how California and the actions of President Taylor led to a sectional crisis at the end of 1849.

6. What were the provisions of the Fugitive Slave Act that upset northerners? Describe how northerners reacted to the act's enforcement.

SUGGESTED ESSAY TOPICS

1. Define the concept of Manifest Destiny and assess its impact upon American politics in the 1840s.

2. Assess the causes and consequence of the U.S. war with Mexico. Why did many Americans oppose the war?

3. Contrast the platforms of the Liberty Party, the Free Soil Party, and the Conscience Whigs. What views did all three share?

4. What issues did the Compromise of 1850 resolve? Which ones did it not?

LECTURE OUTLINE

1. Citizens of almost all regions of the country in the 1840s instinctively viewed **territorial growth** as the American way, as the country's right-of-way. Indians and Mexicans could not stop this juggernaut.

   a. Many northerners understood that **Manifest Destiny and slavery** were intimately tied together, as new lands in the South spelled the expansion of the "peculiar institution."

   (SHOW TRANSPARENCY 62: FREE AND SLAVE STATES AND TERRITORIES, 1848)

   b. As old as the first seventeenth-century settlers, Americans' **westering impulse** proved as much a northern as a southern phenomenon.

c.   Spanish descendents populated the **Hispanic Southwest** which had strong economic ties to the United States.

d.   The **Oregon and California Trails** served as routes for literally hundreds of thousands to make their way, often at great peril, into the alluring lands of the West as "Oregon fever" swept the country.

(SHOW TRANSPARENCY 63: TRAILS TO THE WEST)

e.   Joseph Smith gave his life in leading the remarkable **Mormon migration** which culminated in Brigham Young's settlement of the Utah Territory in 1847.

f.   American expansionists, led by Sam Houston, founded the **Republic of Texas** in March of 1836.

g.   Texans' desire to join the United States precipitated the **Annexation Controversy** in Congress during the administration of John Tyler.

h.   Dark-horse candidate James Knox Polk made the **acquisition of Texas and Oregon** the key planks of his successful campaign for the presidency in 1844.

2.   Deliberate American provocations resulted in a two-year land grab called the **Mexican War**.

(SHOW TRANSPARENCY 65: THE WAR WITH MEXICO, 1846-1847)

a.   The **military campaigns of 1846** proved highly successful, particularly in California, but created a formidable Whig presidential prospect in Zachary Taylor, "Old Rough and Ready," who led his forces to successive victories in Texas.

b.   The **military campaigns of 1847** proved even more successful with the rather meager army of Winfield Scott performing an amphibious landing at Vera Cruz, decimating a larger Mexican force, and capturing Mexico City.

c.   Northerners, ever skeptical of southern motives, publicly and vociferously expressed their heart-felt **anti-war sentiment.**

d.   Reservations about war aims led the House to pass the **Wilmot Proviso** which sought the exclusion of slavery from all territory acquired in the war.

3.   The overlapping issues of territorial expansion and slavery dominated the politics of the **election of 1848** and promised to plague the short-lived presidency of Louisianan Zachary Taylor.

a.   Northern antislavery activists founded the **Free Soil Party** upon the same principals as those of the Wilmot Proviso.

b.   The year 1849 marked the start of the **gold rush** and the subsequent movement for **California statehood.**

(SHOW TRANSPARENCY 66: THE GOLD RUSH IN CALIFORNIA)

4.   While hailed by many as the savior of the Union, the **Compromise of 1850** in its final form only delayed the ultimate breakdown of the party system.

a.   The **Senate debates** over the 1850 Compromise revolved around the efforts of Clay and Webster, who supported compromise, and Calhoun, who opposed it.

b. The **passage of the Compromise** as an omnibus bill proved impossible but succeeded under the clever direction of freshman Senator Stephen A. Douglas of Illinois.

c. Northerners found anathema the **Fugitive Slave Law**.

d. Southern representatives condemned **fugitive slave escapes** such as that of Anthony Burns, while many antislavery advocates materially supported the Underground Railroad.

e. No one event contributed more to antislavery sentiment than Harriet Beecher Stowe's ***Uncle Tom's Cabin***, published in 1852 and reprinted many times subsequently.

5. Southern expansionists sought through **filibustering** expeditions to acquire more lands for the expansion of slavery.

a. Filibusterers, like the supporters of the Ostend Manifesto, believed that Manifest Destiny included American slave colonies in the Caribbean and Central America.

b. The most remarkable of the filibusteros was William Walker, the **gray-eyed man of destiny,** who—after naming himself president of Nicaragua—was later executed by a firing squad in Honduras while attempting another coup.

American Album: The California Gold Rush

Conclusion: Americans termed "Manifest Destiny" the notion that North America ought to be the sole domain of white Americans and their institutions. Manifest Destiny justified the acquisition through war and treachery of over 1.1 million square miles of territory at the end of the 1840s. While few disavowed the acquisition of new territory, many northerners suspected that expansion westward was a vehicle for the expansion of the South's "peculiar institution."

TEACHING RESOURCES

Frederick Douglass: When the Lion Wrote History is a documentary on the "most influential black man" of the nineteenth century. PBS Video (90 minutes).

The Donner Party gives the tragic history of the ill-fated group trying to reach California in 1846. PBS Video (90 minutes).

The Oregon Trail is a four-part documentary of the 1840s land rush to Oregon. Films for the Humanities & Sciences (25 minutes each, color).

"The Golden Land," in *The West of the Imagination* series, documents the West in the 1830s and 1840s. Films for the Humanities & Sciences (52 minutes, color).

Texas and the Mexican Cession is the history of Texas's quest for independence. Filmic Archives (14 minutes).

Gold Rush and the Settlement of California provides an account of the developments in 1848–1849 in the West. Filmic Archives (16 minutes).

The West, episodes two and three, discusses the American westward expansion often called Manifest Destiny. PBS Video (60 minutes each).

Mexican-American War is the PBS series detailing the history of the conflict from both the U.S. and Mexican perspectives. PBS Video.

1. The term *manifest destiny* refers to
   a. the belief that Providence had destined the American continent to be dominated by the United States.
   b. the belief that war between the United States and Mexico was inevitable.
   c. the belief that American Indians were to be driven from the continent.
   d. the belief that the U.S. would defeat the British and become the leading world power.
   e. all of the above.

   ANS: A   **TYPE: M**   **KEY 1: A**   **KEY 2: 2**   **PAGE: 408**

2. The religious prophet and founder of the Mormons was
   a. Joseph Smith.
   b. John O'Sullivan.
   c. Robert Walker.
   d. Jonathan Edwards.
   e. William Miller

   ANS: A   **TYPE: M**   **KEY 1: F**   **KEY 2: 2**   **PAGE: 412**

3. The Mexican commander who granted Texas independence from Mexico was
   a. Santa Anna.
   b. Narciso Lopez.
   c. William Walker.
   d. General Huerta.
   e. General Lopez.

   ANS: A   **TYPE: M**   **KEY 1: F**   **KEY 2: 1**   **PAGE: 413**

4. The primary goal of President John Tyler was to
   a. establish a strong national bank.
   b. impose higher tariffs on English textiles.
   c. abolish slavery.
   d. build a transcontinental railroad.
   e. annex Texas.

   ANS: C   **TYPE: M**   **KEY 1: F**   **KEY 2: 1**   **PAGE: 413**

5. The Mexican War was least popular in which of the following regions?
   a. Southwest
   b. New England
   c. Southeast
   d. Midwest
   e. Great Lakes region

   ANS: B   **TYPE: M**   **KEY 1: F**   **KEY 2: 2**   **PAGE: 416-17**

6. The congressional act that opposed the extension of slavery into any territory ceded by Mexico was the
   a. Ostend Manifesto.
   b. Popular Sovereignty Act.
   c. Crittenden Compromise.
   d. Treaty of Guadalupe Hidalgo.
   e. Wilmot Proviso

ANS: E   TYPE: M   KEY 1: F   KEY 2: 1   PAGE: 419-20

7. The Treaty of Guadalupe Hidalgo
   a. authorized the United States to pay $15 million to Mexico.
   b. fixed the Texas border at the Rio Grande.
   c. ended the United States' war with Mexico.
   d. ceded the Northwestern section of Mexico to the U.S.
   e. all of the above

ANS: E   TYPE: M   KEY 1: F   KEY 2: 2   PAGE: 420

8. "Popular sovereignty" was the belief that
   a. the United States was destined to control the entire continent.
   b. the American Indian was the ward of the U.S. government.
   c. settlers to a territory should decide for themselves whether or not to permit slavery.
   d. the federal government had the final authority on slavery in the territories.
   e. citizens should be free to choose their own reading material.

ANS: C   TYPE: M   KEY 1: A   KEY 2: 2   PAGE: 422

9. In response to the Whig Party nomination of Zachary Taylor in 1848, many "conscience Whigs" fled the party, joined with antislavery Democrats, and formed the
   a. Liberty Party.
   b. Republican Party.
   c. Free Soil Party.
   d. Know-Nothing Party.
   e. Socialist Party.

ANS: C   TYPE: M   KEY L: F   KEY 2: 2   PAGE: 422

10. California's population increased dramatically in the late 1840s due to the
    a. discovery of lush, fertile farm land.
    b. discovery of gold.
    c. excellent trade opportunities afforded by San Francisco.
    d. building of the Union Pacific Railroad.
    e. discovery of oil.

ANS: B   TYPE: M   KEY 1: A   KEY 2: 1   PAGE: 422

11. In 1850, southerners were most upset by
    a. the admission of California as a free state.
    b. the presidency of Zachary Taylor.
    c. the power of the abolitionists.
    d. the failure to annex Cuba.
    e. the settlement of the Texas boundary with New Mexico.

ANS: A   TYPE: M   KEY 1: F   KEY 2: 2   PAGE: 425

12. Which of the following was not part of the Compromise of 1850?
    a. repeal of all existing fugitive slave laws
    b. abolition of the slave trade in the District of Columbia
    c. guarantee of slavery in the District of Columbia
    d. admission of California as a free state
    e. settlement of the Texas-New Mexico boundary.

ANS: A   TYPE: M   KEY 1: A   KEY 2: 2   PAGE: 425

13. The Supreme Court case *Prigg v. Pennsylvania* (1842) involved
    a. the kidnapping of fugitive slaves.
    b. territorial control of the slavery issue.
    c. unfair labor practices in Pennsylvania mines.
    d. aid for parochial schools in Pennsylvania.
    e. removal of Indians to the lands west of the Mississippi.

ANS: A   TYPE: M   KEY 1: F   KEY 2: 3   PAGE: 425

14. The one issue in the Compromise of 1850 that clearly favored the South was
    a. resolution of the Texas–New Mexico boundary dispute.
    b. the Fugitive Slave Act.
    c. the abolition of slavery in the District of Columbia.
    d. the settlement of Texas war debt.
    e. the admission of California.

ANS: B   TYPE: M   KEY 1: A   KEY 2: 2   PAGE: 425

15. Anthony Burns
    a. was a three-time invader of Nicaragua.
    b. attempted to mediate the slavery dispute in the Senate.
    c. was a runaway slave arrested under the Fugitive Slave Act.
    d. ran for president in 1848.
    e. introduced the Compromise of 1850.

ANS: C   TYPE: M   KEY 1: F   KEY 2: 2   PAGE: 427

16. The central theme of *Uncle Tom's Cabin* is
    a. the decadence of southern society.
    b. the tragedy of the breakup of families by slavery.
    c. the wanton cruelty of slave owners.
    d. the complicity of northerners in the continuance of slavery.
    e. the cruelty of the African slave trade.

ANS: B   TYPE: M   KEY 1: A   KEY 2: 1   PAGE: 428

17. The four-time invader of Central America and the self-proclaimed president of Nicaragua was
    a. William Walker.
    b. Narciso Lopez.
    c. William Crittenden.
    d. Franklin Pierce.
    e. James Buchanan.

ANS: A   TYPE: M   KEY 1: F   KEY 2: 1   PAGE: 430

18. The man most responsible for passing the Compromise of 1850 was
    a. Daniel Webster.
    b. William Seward.
    c. John C. Calhoun.
    d. Stephen Douglas.
    e. Frederick Douglass.

ANS: D   **TYPE: M**   **KEY 1: F**   **KEY 2: 2**   **PAGE: 425**

19. The author of *Uncle Tom's Cabin* was
    a. Sarah Josepha Hale.
    b. Harriet Beecher Stowe.
    c. Catherine Beecher.
    d. Lydia Maria Child.
    e. Nathaniel Hawthorne.

ANS: B   **TYPE: M**   **KEY 1: F**   **KEY 2: 1**   **PAGE: 428**

20. Who of the following did not earn an impressive military reputation in the War with Mexico?
    a. Winfield Scott
    b. Abraham Lincoln
    c. Jefferson Davis
    d. Zachary Taylor
    e. Stephen Kearny

ANS: B   **TYPE: M**   **KEY 1: F**   **KEY 2: 2**   **PAGE: 417-18**

21. The term *Oregon fever* refers to
    a. a deadly disease that killed thousands of northwestern Indians.
    b. the mass migration of thousands of farm families to the Northwest.
    c. the call for war with Great Britain in 1846 for control of "all of Oregon."
    d. a cattle sickness that bankrupted many ranchers.
    e. the demand for western lands that led to war with Mexico.

ANS: B   **TYPE: M**   **KEY 1: F**   **KEY 2: 1**   **PAGE: 410**

22. In the 1840s, the westward expansion of the United States
    a. did not extend beyond the Mississippi River.
    b. included the 2000-mile-long Oregon trail to the Pacific coast.
    c. was prohibited by the territorial government of Mexico.
    d. halted at the Rocky Mountains.
    e. included Canada.

ANS: B   **TYPE: M**   **KEY 1: F**   **KEY 2: 2**   **PAGE: 410**

23. Women in the migration westward
    a. outnumbered men by three to one.
    b. achieved economic and political status equal to that of men.
    c. seldom survived long enough to reach their destinations.
    d. fulfilled the same roles as homemakers and care givers as they did in the East.
    e. none of the above

ANS: D   **TYPE: M**   **KEY 1: F**   **KEY 2: 2**   **PAGE: 411-12**

24. Which of the following is not true about Brigham Young?
   a. He was married to fifty-five women.
   b. He led the Mormons to Utah and created a prosperous community there.
   c. He was the founder of the Church of Jesus Christ of Latter-Day Saints.
   d. He was the governor of the Utah territory for seven years.
   e. He selected the site for the Mormon settlement.

ANS: C   **TYPE: M**   **KEY 1: F**   **KEY 2: 3**   **PAGE: 412-13**

25. Which of the following was true of the Texas Revolution?
   a. Many Mexican *tejanos* joined with the Anglo-Americans to fight for independence.
   b. It lasted seven years.
   c. Both Andrew Jackson and Martin Van Buren offered statehood to Texas.
   d. The government of Mexico recognized the independence of Texas in return for a payment of $20 million.
   e. Mexican soldiers refused to fight against the Texans.

ANS: A   **TYPE: M**   **KEY 1: F**   **KEY 2: 3**   **PAGE: 413**

26. In the election of 1844, James K. Polk
   a. advocated legislation prohibiting the admission of any more slave states to the union.
   b. threatened to declare war on England.
   c. promised to acquire Texas and Oregon.
   d. lost the presidency to Henry Clay.
   e. opposed slavery.

ANS: C   **TYPE: M**   **KEY 1: F**   **KEY 2: 2**   **PAGE: 415**

27. In the 1840s, the United States acquired all of the following states except
   a. California.
   b. Alaska.
   c. Oregon.
   d. New Mexico.
   e. Utah.

ANS: B   **TYPE: M**   **KEY 1: F**   **KEY 2: 3**   **PAGE: 419-20**

28. In the Mexican War,
   a. U.S. soldiers outnumbered the Mexicans in every battle.
   b. the United States won every battle due to its superior leadership and weapons.
   c. General Zachary Taylor arrested and executed the president of Mexico.
   d. U.S. troops were humiliated by their failure to take Mexico City.
   e. Texans refused to fight.

ANS: B   **TYPE: M**   **KEY 1: F**   **KEY 2: 2**   **PAGE: 417-18**

29. On the issue of slavery in the territories, John C. Calhoun asserted that
   a. Congress could and should prohibit slavery there.
   b. the Missouri Compromise line should be extended to the Pacific Ocean.
   c. the Constitution protected the right of citizens to move from place to place and to take their property with them.
   d. the topic should be ignored for a few years in order to let congressional tempers cool down.
   e. the South should secede and take the western territories with them.

ANS: C   **TYPE: M**   **KEY L: F**   **KEY 2: 3**   **PAGE: 421**

30. The Ostend Manifesto was
    a. a document in which the United States threatened to seize control of Cuba.
    b. the treaty that gave Cuba its independence.
    c. an attempted Spanish invasion of Louisiana.
    d. the antislavery newspaper that published *Uncle Tom's Cabin.*
    e. the U.S. demand for Texas.

ANS: A   **TYPE: M**   **KEY 1: F**   **KEY 2: 2**   **PAGE: 429**

31. The filibusters of the 1840s and 1850s
    a. explored the New Mexico territory.
    b. attempted to acquire new territories in which to extend slavery.
    c. were Spanish pirates who attacked American seaports.
    d. were heated congressional debates over slavery.
    e. opposed slavery in all national territories.

ANS: B   **TYPE: M**   **KEY 1: F**   **KEY 2: 3**   **PAGE: 428**

32. Opponents of the Mexican War
    a. were mostly merchants who feared the war would disrupt their profitable trade with Mexico.
    b. were arrested and tried for treason.
    c. claimed the war was a plot to expand slavery into new territories.
    d. convinced the public that the war was a terrible mistake.
    e. came primarily from the southern states.

ANS: C   **TYPE: M**   **KEY 1: A**   **KEY 2: 2**   **PAGE: 416-17**

33. President Polk provoked a war with Mexico
    a. in order to acquire New Mexico and California.
    b. by sending General Zachary Taylor and four thousand soldiers to patrol the Rio Grande.
    c. by encouraging settlers in Monterey, California to dream of U.S. annexation.
    d. by attempting to buy New Mexico and California.
    e. all of the above

ANS: E   **TYPE: M**   **KEY 1: F**   **KEY 2: 3**   **PAGE: 416**

34. The United States increased its size by _____ percent between 1845 and 1848.
    a. 25
    b. 40
    c. 50
    d. 45
    e. no

ANS: C   **TYPE: M**   **KEY 1: F**   **KEY 2: 2**   **PAGE: 407**

35. *Two Years before the Mast*, which helped to encourage westward expansion, was written by
    a. Richard Henry Dana.
    b. Mark Twain.
    c. Horace Greeley.
    d. William Walker.
    e. Nathaniel Hawthorne.

ANS: A   **TYPE: M**   **KEY 1: F**   **KEY 2: 2**   **PAGE: 409**

36. All of the following fought for Texas's independence from Mexico except
    a. Andrew Jackson.
    b. Sam Houston.
    c. Jim Bowie.
    d. Davey Crockett.
    c. William Travis.

ANS: A   TYPE: M   KEY 1: F   KEY 2: 2   PAGE: 413

37. Which of the following statements is not true?
    a. The United States went to war against Mexico with a regular army of fewer than 8,000 men.
    b. American soldiers had higher morale than Mexican soldiers during the Mexican War.
    c. Most Whigs opposed the Mexican War.
    d. U.S. forces won every battle of the Mexican War.
    e. American soldiers outnumbered Mexican soldiers in most of the battles of the Mexican War.

ANS: E   TYPE: M   KEY 1: A   KEY 2: 2   PAGE: 417

38. General Winfield Scott's nickname was
    a. "Blood and Guts."
    b. "Old Fuss and Feathers."
    c. "Grizzly."
    d. "Rough and Ready."
    e. "Fat and Saucy."

ANS: B   TYPE: M   KEY 1: F   KEY 2: 2   PAGE: 418

39. Which of the following was not involved in supporting the Ostend Manifesto?
    a. the U.S. minister to Spain
    b. the U.S. minister to Great Britain
    c. the U.S. minister to France
    d. the U.S. minister to Cuba
    e. the Democratic party

ANS: D   TYPE: M   KEY 1: F   KEY 2: 1   PAGE: 429-30

40. In the election of 1848, the idea of "popular sovereignty" was most closely identified with
    a. James K. Polk.
    b. John C. Calhoun.
    c. Lewis Cass.
    d. John P. Hale.
    e. William Lloyd Garrison.

ANS: C   TYPE: M   KEY 1: F   KEY 2: 2   PAGE: 422

41. Which of the following is not true about the "Conscience Whigs"?
    a. They were antislavery.
    b. They hoped to convince their party to renounce the expansion of slavery.
    c. They condemned their party's decision to nominate Zachary Taylor for president.
    d. They eventually forged a coalition with the Liberty Party and antislavery Democrats.
    e. They formed the basis of the Free Soil Party.

ANS: B   TYPE: M   KEY 1: A   KEY 2: 3   PAGE: 422

42. The idea of "one big reservation" for Native Americans in the West was replaced in the 1850s with a policy calling for
    a. exterminating of all Indian tribes.
    b. electing Indians to public office.
    c. expelling all Indians to California.
    d. recognizing the independence of Indian nations.
    e. forcing Indians onto small reservations.

ANS: E   TYPE: M   KEY 1: A   KEY 2: 2   PAGE: 408

43. Most Hispanics in the West lived in
    a. Oregon.
    b. California.
    c. Rio Grande Valley of New Mexico.
    d. Utah.
    e. Idaho.

ANS: C   TYPE: M   KEY 1: F   KEY 2: 3   PAGE: 410

44. Relations between the Mormon settlement in Utah and the U.S. government became strained, especially when
    a. the Mormons attacked and killed peaceful Plains Indians.
    b. the Mormons sided with Mexico in the Mexican War.
    c. the settlement authorized polygamy.
    d. gold was discovered in Utah.
    e. the Mormons opposed the admission of California.

ANS: C   TYPE: M   KEY 1: F   KEY 2: 3   PAGE: 413

45. American settlers who migrated to Texas defied Mexican law by
    a. abolishing slavery.
    b. adopting polygamy.
    c. attacking the Indians.
    d. bringing slaves.
    e. becoming Mormons.

ANS: D   TYPE: M   KEY 1: F   KEY 2: 2   PAGE: 413

46. Anglo settlers in Texas declared their independence when
    a. a conservative Mexican government attempted to consolidate authority over their settlements.
    b. the Mexican government abolished slavery.
    c. the Catholic Church attempted to abolish their Protestant churches.
    d. the Mexican government refused to protect them from Indian raids.
    e. Texans were executed for opposed the Mexican government.

ANS: A   TYPE: M   KEY 1: A   KEY 2: 2   PAGE: 413

47. Henry Clay's position on the annexation of Texas in the campaign of 1844 is best described by which of the following statements?
    a. Texas should be annexed immediately regardless of the consequences.
    b. Texas should be annexed only when New Mexico was ready for annexation.
    c. Texas should be annexed under no circumstances.
    d. Slavery should be abolished in Texas prior to annexation.
    e. Texas should be annexed if it could be accomplished without starting a war with Mexico.

ANS: B   TYPE: M   KEY 1: A   KEY 2: 3   PAGE: 415

48. President Polk's compromise with the British on the Oregon Treaty
    a. united the Democratic Party.
    b. angered Southern Democrats.
    c. angered Democrats from the Old Northwest.
    d. alienated Whigs.
    e. started war with Mexico.

ANS: C   **TYPE: M**   **KEY 1: A**   **KEY 2: 3**   **PAGE: 416**

49. The Wilmot Proviso
    a. was passed by the House of Representatives, but failed in the Senate.
    b. won the support of southern Whigs.
    c. was passed in the Senate, but failed in the House of Representatives.
    d. was passed by Congress, but vetoed by the President.
    e. none of the above

ANS: A   **TYPE: M**   **KEY 1: F**   **KEY 2: 2**   **PAGE: 419-20**

50. In the election of 1848, Zachary Taylor carried southern states primarily because
    a. he had opposed the Mexican War.
    b. he was a slaveholder.
    c. he opposed the admission of any free states to the Union.
    d. he supported popular sovereignty.
    e. he supported the acquisition of Oregon.

ANS: B   **TYPE: M**   **KEY 1: A**   **KEY 2: 3**   **PAGE: 422**

TRUE/FALSE

_____ 1.   The Ostend Manifesto claimed that Cuba should be part of the United States.

ANS: T   **TYPE: T**   **KEY 1: F**   **KEY 2: 2**   **PAGE: 429**

_____ 2.   Democrats dropped the idea of annexing Cuba after the Ostend Manifesto.

ANS: F   **TYPE: T**   **KEY 1: F**   **KEY 2: 2**   **PAGE: 430**

_____ 3.   "Mr. Polk's War" refers to the war between Great Britain and the United States over Oregon.

ANS: F   **TYPE: T**   **KEY 1: F**   **KEY 2: 1**   **PAGE: 417**

_____ 4.   President James Polk was prepared to declare war against Mexico even before news of hostilities arrived in Washington.

ANS: T   **TYPE: T**   **KEY 1: F**   **KEY 2: 2**   **PAGE: 416**

_____ 5.   The Wilmot Proviso stated that African Americans were not allowed to enter any territory ceded by Mexico to the United States because of the Mexican War.

ANS: F   **TYPE: T**   **KEY 1: F**   **KEY 2: 3**   **PAGE: 419-20**

_____ 6.   The United States won virtually every battle during the Mexican War.

ANS: T   **TYPE: T**   **KEY 1: F**   **KEY 2: 1**   **PAGE: 417-18**

_____ 7.   Attempts to enact the new Fugitive Slave Act of 1850 made little or no impression on northerners.

ANS: F   TYPE: T   KEY 1: F   KEY 2: 3   PAGE: 424-26

_____ 8.   Southern Democrats were unhappy about the nomination of Franklin Pierce as their party's presidential candidate in 1852.

ANS: F   TYPE: T   KEY 1: F   KEY 2: 3   PAGE: 429

_____ 9.   "Conscience Whigs" refers to those members of the party that most vigorously opposed the war with Mexico.

ANS: F   TYPE: T   KEY 1: F   KEY 2: 2   PAGE: 422

_____ 10.   President William Henry Harrison caught pneumonia on his inauguration day and died one month later.

ANS: T   TYPE: T   KEY 1: F   KEY 2: 1   PAGE: 407

_____ 11.   General Zachary Taylor established the "bear flag republic" in California in 1846.

ANS: F   TYPE: T   KEY 1: F   KEY 2: 2   PAGE: 417

_____ 12.   The Constitution makes no provision for the return of escaped slaves.

ANS: F   TYPE: T   KEY 1: F   KEY 2: 1   PAGE: 425

_____ 13.   William Henry Harrison delivered the shortest inaugural address in U.S. history.

ANS: F   TYPE: T   KEY 1: F   KEY 2: 1   PAGE: 407

_____ 14.   John Tyler supported the creation of a new national bank.

ANS: T   TYPE: T   KEY 1: F   KEY 2: 2   PAGE: 407

_____ 15.   The Whigs lost control of the House of Representatives in the midterm elections of 1842.

ANS: T   TYPE: T   KEY 1: F   KEY 2: 1   PAGE: 407

_____ 16.   Manifest Destiny was universally popular throughout the United States.

ANS: F   TYPE: T   KEY 1: A   KEY 2: 2   PAGE: 408

_____ 17.   By 1821, 80,000 Mexicans lived in New Mexico and California.

ANS: T   TYPE: T   KEY 1: F   KEY 2: 2   PAGE: 410

_____ 18.   During the California gold rush, men migrating westward outnumbered women by 8 to 1.

ANS: F   TYPE: T   KEY 1: F   KEY 2: 3   PAGE: 411

_____19.   Although the territorial legislatures of Utah and New Mexico legalized slavery, few slaves were brought there.

ANS: T   **TYPE: T**   **KEY 1: F**   **KEY 2: 3**   **PAGE: 425**

_____20.   Henry Clay remained steadfastly opposed to the annexation of Texas throughout the presidential campaign of 1844.

ANS: F   **TYPE: T**   **KEY 1: A**   **KEY 2: 3**   **PAGE: 415**

_____21.   Most Whigs supported war with Mexico.

ANS: F   **TYPE: T**   **KEY 1: A**   **KEY 2: 2**   **PAGE: 416**

_____22.   The first battle of the Mexican War occurred two weeks after Congress had declared war.

ANS: F   **TYPE: T**   **KEY 1: F**   **KEY 2: 2**   **PAGE: 417**

_____23.   Stephen Kearny's campaign to occupy Santa Fe was long and bloody.

ANS: F   **TYPE: T**   **KEY 1: T**   **KEY 2: 1**   **PAGE: 417**

_____24.   President James K. Polk supported a rivers and harbors bill to provide federal aid for transportation improvements in the Old Northwest.

ANS: F   **TYPE: T**   **KEY 1: A**   **KEY 2: 2**   **PAGE: 420**

_____25.   James K. Polk opposed efforts to acquire "all Mexico."

ANS: T   **TYPE: F**   **KEY 1: A**   **KEY 2: 2**   **PAGE: 420**

_____26.   The Treaty of Guadalupe Hidalgo settled the question of slavery in the new territories acquired by the United States.

ANS: F   **TYPE: T**   **KEY 1: A**   **KEY 2: 2**   **PAGE: 420**

_____27.   The Liberty Party supported the Wilmot Proviso.

ANS: T   **TYPE: T**   **KEY 1: F**   **KEY 2: 1**   **PAGE: 421**

_____28.   The Democratic Party took an extreme states'-rights stance in the election of 1848.

ANS: F   **TYPE: T**   **KEY 1: F**   **KEY 2: 2**   **PAGE: 422**

_____29.   With regard to the idea of "popular sovereignty," northerners believed that the decision on slavery should come earlier in a territory's history than southerners did.

ANS: T   **TYPE: T**   **KEY 1: A**   **KEY 2: 3**   **PAGE: 422**

_____30.   The Whigs in 1848 had no party platform.

ANS: T   **TYPE: T**   **KEY 1: F**   **KEY 2: 2**   **PAGE: 422**

_____ 31.   In late 1848, the Democrats controlled the House of Representatives and the Whigs controlled the Senate.

ANS: F   TYPE: T   KEY 1: F   KEY 2: 3   PAGE: 423

_____ 32.   Most of the forty-niners who rushed to California in search of gold were pro-slavery.

ANS: F   TYPE: T   KEY 1: F   KEY 2: 2   PAGE: 423

_____ 33.   Once California became a state, its senators turned out to be conservative Democrats who voted with the South on most issues.

ANS: T   TYPE: T   KEY 1: A   KEY 2: 3   PAGE: 425

_____ 34.   In pushing for strict compliance with the Fugitive Slave Act, southerners were motivated primarily by financial concerns.

ANS: F   TYPE: T   KEY 1: A   KEY 2: 2   PAGE: 426-27

_____ 35.   Statistics show that the Fugitive Slave Act was rigged in favor of slave owners.

ANS: T   TYPE: T   KEY 1: A   KEY 2: 3   PAGE: 426

_____ 36.   Personal liberty laws passed by several northern states made it impossible to recover escaped slaves.

ANS: F   TYPE: T   KEY 1: A   KEY 2: 2   PAGE: 427

_____ 37.   _Uncle Tom's Cabin_ was not read in the South.

ANS: F   TYPE: T   KEY 1: F   KEY 2: 2   PAGE: 428

_____ 38.   John Tyler was a firm believer in the Whig Party's philosophy and planned to complete the construction of Clay's American System.

ANS: F   TYPE: T   KEY 1: A   KEY 2: 3   PAGE: 407

_____ 39.   Half of westward migrants were mothers and children.

ANS: T   TYPE: T   KEY 1: F   KEY 2: 1   PAGE: 411

_____ 40.   The Democrats scored a resounding victory in the election of 1844.

ANS: F   TYPE: T   KEY 1: F   KEY 2: 2   PAGE: 415

FILL-INS

1.   The diplomat who negotiated the Treaty of Guadalupe Hidalgo was _____.

ANS: Nicholas Trist   TYPE: F   KEY 1: F   KEY 2: 3   PAGE: 420

2.   The religious sect from western New York that settled in the Great Salt Lake basin was the _____.

ANS: Mormons   TYPE: F   KEY 1: F   KEY 2: 1   PAGE: 412

3.   The president who completed the annexation of Texas to the United States was
_____.

ANS: John Tyler   **TYPE: F**   **KEY 1: F**   **KEY 2: 2**   **PAGE: 416**

4.   The popular leader of American forces in Mexico, who later was elected to the presidency, was
_____.

ANS: Zachary Taylor   **TYPE: F**   **KEY 1: F**   **KEY 2: 2**   **PAGE: 417**

5.   The congressional attempt to resolve the controversy over California's statehood was the
_____.

ANS: Compromise of 1850   **TYPE: F**   **KEY 1: F**   **KEY 2: 1**   **PAGE: 424**

6.   The newspaper man who urged Americans to "Go West young man" was _____.

ANS: Horace Greeley   **TYPE: F**   **KEY 1: F**   **KEY 2: 2**   **PAGE: 409**

7.   In the 1830s and 1840s the arid plains of the west were known as _____.

ANS: the Great American Desert   **TYPE: F**   **KEY 1: F**   **KEY 2: 2**   **PAGE: 410**

8.   The Missouri businessman who brought the first three hundred families into Texas from the United States was _____.

ANS: Stephen F. Austin   **TYPE: F**   **KEY 1: F**   **KEY 2: 2**   **PAGE: 413**

9.   John Tyler became a Whig because of his hatred for _____.

ANS: Andrew Jackson   **TYPE: F**   **KEY 1: F**   **KEY 2: 2**   **PAGE: 407**

10.   Between 1803 and _____, the population of the United States quadrupled.

ANS: 1850   **TYPE: F**   **KEY 1: F**   **KEY 2: 3**   **PAGE: 408**

11.   The only free state admitted as a result of territorial acquisition between 1803 and 1846 was
_____.

ANS: Iowa   **TYPE: F**   **KEY 1: F**   **KEY 2: 2**   **PAGE: 408**

12.   Patriarchal rule on the frontier was strongest among those migrants with the most nearly equal sex ration--the _____.

ANS: Mormons   **TYPE: F**   **KEY 1: F**   **KEY 2: 2**   **PAGE: 412**

13.   After winning their independence from Mexico, Texans elected _____ president of their new republic.

ANS: Sam Houston   **TYPE: F**   **KEY 1: F**   **KEY 2: 2**   **PAGE: 413**

14.   The most respected member of the U.S. Senate during the antebellum period was
_____.

ANS: Henry Clay   **TYPE: F**   **KEY 1: F**   **KEY 2: 2**   **PAGE: 424**

15. The first Whig president was _____.

ANS: William Henry Harrison   TYPE: F   KEY 1: F   KEY 2: 1   PAGE: 407

16. The Mormons were settled in _____ when their founder, Joseph Smith, received a revelation sanctioning the practice of polygamy.

ANS: Illinois (or Nauvoo, Illinois)   TYPE: F   KEY 1: F   KEY 2: 3   PAGE: 412

17. It took the Texans less than _____ months to win and consolidate their independence from Mexico.

ANS: seven   TYPE: F   KEY 1: F   KEY 2: 2   PAGE: 413

18. _____ raised the flag of an independent California after capturing Sonoma.

ANS: Captain John C. Frémont   TYPE: F   KEY 1: F   KEY 2: 2   PAGE: 417

19. The Free Soil Party received _____ percent of the popular vote in the North in 1848.

ANS: 14   TYPE: F   KEY 1: F   KEY 2: 3   PAGE: 422

20. *Prigg v. Pennsylvania* ruled that enforcement of the Constitution's fugitive slave clause was a _____ responsibility.

ANS: federal   TYPE: F   KEY 1: F   KEY 2: 2   PAGE: 424

21. _____ led a revolt in Cuba in 1849.

ANS: Narciso Lopez   TYPE: F   KEY 1: F   KEY 2: 3   PAGE: 428

22. Franklin Pierce came from the state of _____.

ANS: New Hampshire   TYPE: F   KEY 1: F   KEY 2: 3   PAGE: 429

23. Men who attempted to take Cuba and other lands for the U.S. were known as _____.

ANS: filibusters   TYPE: F   KEY 1: F   KEY 2: 1   PAGE: 428

24. The candidate of the Liberty Party who may have cost Henry Clay the election in 1844 was _____.

ANS: James G. Birney   TYPE: F   KEY 1: F   KEY 2: 3   PAGE: 415

25. The political party that supported westward expansion most strongly was the _____ Party.

ANS: Democratic   TYPE: F   KEY 1: F   KEY 2: 1   PAGE: 414

26. The slogan "Fifty-four forty or fight!" rose out of the demand for _____.

ANS: Oregon   TYPE: F   KEY 1: F   KEY 2: 2   PAGE: 416

27. The U.S. commander who took Mexico City in the Mexican War was _____.

ANS: Winfield Scott **TYPE: F** **KEY 1: F** **KEY 2: 2** **PAGE: 418**

28. The Free Soil Party candidate for President in 1848 was _____.

ANS: Martin Van Buren **TYPE: F** **KEY 1: F** **KEY 2: 3** **PAGE: 422**

29. The Senator who opposed slavery as being contrary to a "higher law" was _____.

ANS: William Seward **TYPE: F** **KEY 1: F** **KEY 2: 3** **PAGE: 425**

30. The Senator who deliver the "seventh of March" speech supporting the Compromise of 1850 was _____.

ANS: Daniel Webster **TYPE: F** **KEY 1: F** **KEY 2: 3** **PAGE: 424**

IDENTIFICATIONS

1. **Anthony Burns**: one of the most famous runaway slaves to be returned under the Fugitive Slave Act enacted by the Compromise of 1850. This action generated much antisouthern anger in the North.

2. **Wilmot Proviso**: congressional proposal of David Wilmot of Pennsylvania that forbade the expansion of slavery into any territory annexed from Mexico. First introduced in August 1846, it was supported by a majority in the House of Representatives but defeated in the Senate.

3. **William Walker**: American filibustero who invaded Nicaragua three times. Took over the country and declared himself president in 1856. Reinstated slavery in order to win the support of the southern states. Ousted in 1857. Executed in Honduras in 1860 after a failed attempt to invade that country.

4. **popular sovereignty**: theory of Lewis Cass that stated that settlers should decide for themselves whether to permit slavery. Introduced during the presidential campaign of 1848, the idea was incorporated into the Kansas-Nebraska Act of 1854.

5. *Uncle Tom's Cabin:* Harriet Beecher Stowe's best-selling novel of the early 1850s. This novel, though sentimental and exaggerated, generated indignation and support for the antislavery cause in the North. It resulted in anger and book-bannings in the South.

6. **Joseph Smith**: founder of the Mormon faith. Claimed God spoke directly to him; organized a private army, the Nauvoo Legion. Sanctioned polygamy. Was arrested by a sheriff in Illinois and killed by a mob that attacked the jail.

7. **Stephen Watts Kearny**: U.S. general in Mexican War who took Santa Fe, New Mexico, without violence. He then divided his forces, sent one group of eight hundred men to attack Chihuahua, Mexico and personally led the rest to California. He arrived in California in time to assist Captain John C. Frémont with the last stages of establishing U.S. control there.

8. **Young America movement**: group of expansionists affiliated with the Democratic Party. During the 1840s they helped to popularize the idea of Manifest Destiny, claiming that the nation was charged by Providence with occupying the entire North American continent.

9. **Ostend Manifesto**: agreed to in 1854 by the American ministers to Spain, Britain, and France. Maintained that if Spain continued to refuse to sell Cuba to the United States, the U.S. government would be justified in taking the island by force. Denounced by President Franklin Pierce and opposed by antislavery Americans.

10. **Free Soil Party**: resulted from union of the Conscience Whigs with the Liberty Party and antislavery Democrats. Stood for "no more Slave States and no more Slave Territories." Nominated Martin Van Buren for president and Charles Francis Adams for vice president in 1848. Ensured that the slavery question was part of the campaign's debate. Won no electoral votes but captured 14 percent of the popular vote in the North.

SHORT ESSAYS

1. What was manifest destiny? In what ways did it shape American history during the 1840s?

Answer: The idea of manifest destiny, though not really new, came to prominence during the 1840s. Essentially, manifest destiny argued that the entire American continent had been destined by God to fall under white European dominance. White Americans, believing themselves to be more civilized than Indians to the west or Mexicans to the south, argued that they (white America) would bring the ideals of democracy, freedom, and Protestant Christianity to lesser peoples.

Proponents of manifest destiny (which enjoyed equal popularity throughout the United States) argued that, if need be, force should be used to wrest control of western lands. Ultimately, of course, force was used, first in Texas, then against Mexico in the war of 1846–1848. In some ways, manifest destiny revealed the brashness of the United States in its early years. In fact, it revealed an ugly, racist attitude among white Americans—many of whom cared less about creating an "empire of liberty" than about securing wealth and profits for themselves.

2. Describe the western movement of the 1830s and 1840s. What were the experiences of men and women in this movement?

Answer: For many Americans in the early nineteenth century, the future was to be found in the West. The decline of available, arable farmland in the Northeast, and with it the decline in opportunities, led many Americans to believe that their only hope for advancement existed in such exotic places as California and Oregon. Many became infected with the so-called Oregon fever upon hearing reports of the fertile land and soil available there.

In the early 1840s, thousands of farm families left their homes in the Mississippi Valley to make the 2,000-mile trip to the Northwest. Although most of those who journeyed west were men (by a ratio of 2 to 1), entire families made the trek as well. Records reveal that most of the women who went were reluctant migrants. For many, however, the journey was well worth the trouble, since they helped in the process of turning their isolated family homes into thriving communities. By the 1860s, some half-million men and women had made the journey and had successfully created thriving communities in the West—transporting the "old East" to the "new West."

3. Examine the impact of the Fugitive Slave Act in the 1850 Compromise.

Answer: The impact of the Fugitive Slave Act was dramatic. In the eyes of northerners, the federal government's resolve to return runaway slaves seemed to defend the interests of southern slaveholders beyond reasonable bounds. A $1,000 fine became the punishment for the criminal offense of refusing to assist in the capture and return of a fugitive.

The case of Anthony Burns reveals the change in attitudes of northerners toward slavery after the act. Few northern whites were abolitionists at that time, and even fewer believed blacks to be equal to whites. But the sight of slave catchers in the streets of Boston, there to capture the runaway Burns, and the use of the army to protect these slave catchers shocked and angered northerners. Until that time, few had an interest in slavery or in abolitionism. Although it would be inaccurate to describe the attitude of these politicized whites as antislavery, their attitudes were becoming antisouthern. The failure of northern whites to enforce the slave codes and, at times, the outright interference of northern crowds in slave-catching efforts, angered southern states. In 1860, southerners would claim the failure of the North to enforce the act was an important reason for their secession.

4. Describe the growing impact of the antislavery movement on American politics.

Answer: Never a force before the 1840s, the politicization of the antislavery movement had widespread ramifications for American politics in the years before the Civil War. The first real party devoted to the abolition of slavery (or, more precisely, to preventing the extension of slavery) was the Liberty Party. Centered in the Northeast, primarily in New York, the party ran James G. Birney for the presidency in 1840, but fared miserably. In 1844, however, with the issue of the annexation of Texas ruffling political feathers, the Liberty Party had far greater impact. This time, candidate Birney successfully undermined Whig candidate Henry Clay's election in New York, costing him that state and, with it, the election.

In 1844, antislavery forces, few in number, helped to determine the outcome of an election. Many of them combined in 1848 with the so-called conscience Whigs (Whigs opposed to the extension of slavery) and formed the Free Soil Party, aiming to stop the spread of slavery into the territories. It would be incorrect to view the Free Soilers as progressive on the race issue because many opposed the extension of slavery simply because it threatened white settlers moving west. This group, though not in favor of racial equality, began to see the South, with its different traditions and culture, as the enemy—ultimately devoted to the protection of slavery.

5.   Explore the significance of the Wilmot Proviso. In what ways did it shape American politics over the next decade?

Answer: The Wilmot Proviso, advocated in Congress by Pennsylvania Democrat David Wilmot, quite possibly set the parameters of the slavery and sectional debate for the crucial decade of the 1850s. In 1848 (before the Treaty of Guadalupe Hidalgo), the proviso argued that "slavery or involuntary servitude" would not be permitted in any territory ceded by Mexico as a result of the war. Strongly supported by both Whigs and Democrats in the North, the proviso passed in the House of Representatives although it was opposed vehemently by southerners of both parties. In the Senate, however, where a rough equality still existed between slaveholding and non-slaveholding states, the proviso failed. Several more times the proviso passed the House only to fail in the Senate.

The impact of the Wilmot Proviso cannot be overestimated. Many southerners were shocked by such legislation because the issue of slavery and its extension was so rarely a part of national political debate. But the issue was a timely one, since the addition of new territories (California and New Mexico) was imminent. It is incorrect, however, to see in the proviso an explicit attack on the South because this was not primarily its intention. It also is incorrect to see in it an attack on slavery. The proviso was an attempt to protect white settlers and "free soilers" in the new territories, and many, like David Wilmot, saw slavery as a direct threat to settlers.

6.   Examine the causes and results of Mormon migration to Utah.

Answer: The (Mormon) Church of Jesus Christ of Latter-Day Saints was founded by Joseph Smith in New York. Wherever they settled, the Mormons were persecuted. Smith's assertion that he communicated directly with God, his autocratic rule, the exclusivity of his teachings on election, and his control of a private army all inspired fear and hostility among outsiders. In June of 1844, Smith was killed by a mob in Illinois and his followers moved further west.

Brigham Young, who succeeded Smith, carefully planned the long migration to what was then the Mexican territory of Utah. The Mormons built a garden in the desert in the Great Salt Lake Basin. When the United States asserted its authority over Utah and other territories gained in the Mexican War, Young served as territorial governor. Officials in Washington were disturbed by Young's 1852 order legalizing polygamy. Young had fifty-five wives but most Mormon men could only support one. In 1857, violence between the U.S. Army and the Mormons caused Young's resignation from the civil government. He continued his spiritual leadership of the church, and the Kingdom of the Saints in Utah flourished.

7.   Discuss *Uncle Tom's Cabin* and examine its impact on the debate over slavery.

Answer: *Uncle Tom's Cabin* was a sentimental novel written by Harriet Beecher Stowe. Stowe was the daughter and sister of two of the most influential Calvinist theologians of the pre-Civil War era. She grew up in a household where Christian ideals guided personal actions and where runaway slaves and abolitionists visited and sought refuge. Though she had virtually no personal contact with slavery, Stowe acquired a wealth of secondhand knowledge regarding the South's peculiar institution.

In 1851 she responded to the Fugitive Slave law of 1850 by writing *Uncle Tom's Cabin,* which was published in installments in an abolitionist newspaper. In 1852, the series was compiled in book form and immediately became a best seller. In *Uncle Tom's Cabin,* Stowe personalized the institution of slavery and created memorable characters. White people--who had never given much thought to the slavery issue before--read the book, sympathized with the suffering slaves, and awakened to the evils of slavery. The book was banned in many southern states and proslavery authors cranked out novels that were designed to counteract the impact of *Uncle Tom's Cabin.* Millions of people all over the world responded to the novel's powerful portrayal of families torn apart by slavery. During the Civil War, Abraham Lincoln credited Harriet Beecher Stowe with starting "this great war."

LONG ESSAYS

1.   Explore the movement for, and the eventual conclusion of, the U.S. annexation of Texas in 1845.

Answer: Essay should address several key points:

A.   Background to annexation
        1.   Manifest destiny
        2.   Texas Revolution
B.   President Tyler's demand for Texas
        1.   Senate's rejection of annexation
        2.   Polk and Democratic platform for annexation
                a.   Polk's victory seen as mandate
                b.   Sectional motives
C.   Tyler's lame-duck move for annexation
        1.   Joint resolution for annexation
                a.   Simple majority required
                b.   Circumvent northern opposition
        2.   Texas annexed in March 1845

2.   Examine the importance of the Mexican War in American politics from 1848 to 1850.

Answer: Essay should address several key points:

A.   War with Mexico
        1.   Northeastern antiwar sentiment
                a.   Whig opposition to war
                b.   War's tangible effects
        2.   Treaty of Guadalupe Hidalgo
                a.   Annexation of California and New Mexico
                b.   All Mexico movement
B.   Wilmot Proviso
        1.   Stance of northeastern political interests
        2.   Argument of the proviso
                a.   Forbids slavery in any territory ceded by Mexico
                b.   Support for homesteaders
        3.   Bitter congressional fight over proviso
                a.   Passes House of Representatives three times
                b.   Fails in Senate
                c.   Sectional ramifications
C.   California's application for statehood
        1.   1849 gold rush and "free" California
        2.   Southern opposition to California

3.   Analyze the Compromise of 1850. What were its major goals and conclusions? Was the compromise a success?

Answer: Essay should address several key points:

A.   Background to the compromise
     1.   War with Mexico
         a.   Wilmot Proviso
         b.   Southern concerns
     2.   Annexation of California and New Mexico
         a.   California applies as a "free state"
         b.   Southern concerns

B.   Henry Clay and the "Omnibus Bill"
     1.   California as free state; New Mexico with no restrictions on slavery
     2.   Fugitive Slave Act
     3.   End of slave trade in Washington, DC
     4.   Rejection of Omnibus Bill
         a.   Sectional vote
         b.   Southern states and Mississippi convention

C.   Stephen Douglas and passage of compromise
     1.   Omnibus Bill divided into several separate bills
     2.   Compromise measures are passed; vote is still sectional

D.   Compromise as temporary success
     1.   No real solution to slavery and western territories
     2.   Permanent solution still sought

4.   Discuss the concept of manifest destiny and its impact on U.S. foreign policy in the 1840s and 1850s.

Answer: Essay should address several key points.

A.   Manifest Destiny
     1.   Early expansion of United States
         a.   Louisiana Purchase
         b.   Population growth
     2.   God's Plan
         a.   Impact on Indian population
         b.   Extension of slavery

B.   "Go West Young Man"
     1.   Oregon
         a.   The Oregon trail
         b.   "Fifty-four forty or fight"
         c.   Oregon Treaty of 1846
     2.   Migrations
         a.   Mormons to Utah
         b.   California gold rush
     3.   Texas
         a.   Anglo settlement
         b.   Revolution
         c.   Republic of Texas d. Annexation

C.   Mexican War
     1.   Disputes with Mexico
         a.   Annexation of Texas
         b.   Border dispute

     2.   Mr. Polk's War
         a.   Military victory
         b.   Territorial acquisitions

CHAPTER 14
THE GATHERING TEMPEST, 1853–1860

CHAPTER OUTLINE

I. Kansas and the Rise of the Republican Party
    A. The Kansas-Nebraska Act
    B. The Death of the Whig Party
II. Immigration and Nativism
    A. Immigrants in Politics
    B. The Rise of the "Know-Nothings"
    C. The Decline of Nativism
III. Bleeding Kansas
    A. The Caning of Sumner
IV. The Election of 1856
    A. The Dred Scott Case
    B. The Lecompton Constitution
V. The Economy in the 1850's
    A. "The American System of Manufacturers"
    B. The Southern Economy
    C. The Sovereignty of King Cotton
    D. Labor Conditions in the North
    E. The Panic of 1857
    F. Sectionalisim and the Panic
    G. The Free-Labor Ideology
    H. *The Impending Crisis*
    I. Southern Nonslaveholders
VI. The Lincoln – Douglas Debates
    A. The Freeport Doctrine
    B. John Brown at Harpers Ferry
VII. Conclusion

CHRONOLOGY

1846	*DeBow's Review* first published in New Orleans.
1851	Crystal Palace exhibit in London draws great attention.
1853	The American (Know-Nothing) Party becomes significant political factor.
1854	Congress passes the Kansas–Nebraska Act.
	Republican Party forms in Wisconsin.
	"Know-Nothings" gain strength on nativist agenda.
1854–1856	Crimean War rocks Europe.
1855	"Bleeding Kansas" develops as free-soil settlers refuse to accept proslavery election fraud.
1856	Lawrence, Kansas, sacked by proslavery mob.
	John Brown murders proslavery defenders at Pottawatomie Creek.
	Preston Brooks canes Charles Sumner in Senate chamber.
	James Buchanan defeats Republican John C. Frémont and nativist Millard Fillmore for the presidency.
1857	Dred Scott decision rendered by the Supreme Court.
	Economic recession begins with the Panic.
	George Fitzhugh publishes *Cannibals All.*
	Hinton R. Helper issues *The Impending Crisis of the South.*
	Lecompton Constitution written by Kansas proslavery forces.

1858	Lincoln delivers his "house divided" speech.
	Great Debates between Illinoisans Lincoln and Douglas foreshadow upcoming presidential race.
1859	John Brown raids Harpers Ferry; Brown hanged after conviction.

THEMATIC TOPICS FOR ENRICHMENT

1. Discuss the motivations in 1854 for repealing the Missouri Compromise and organizing Kansas and Nebraska on the basis of popular sovereignty.

2. What was the "black belt,' and why was it so named?

3. Why did "nativism" reemerge in the 1850s in the form of the "Know-Nothing" political movement? Who were the nativists' targets? Why?

4. Why did Kansas become "Bleeding Kansas" in the mid-1850s? Explain why Missourians believed that they had to interfere in Kansas politics.

5. Discuss the issues behind the Dred Scott decision. Why did the Court rule the way it did? Why did many ignore its ruling?

6. Explain why the national economy expanded so greatly in the 1850s and how this expansion played a role in sectional politics.

7. Contrast George Fitzhugh's concept of slavery with that of Hinton R. Helper.

8. Compare the northern reaction to John Brown in 1859 with the southern reaction.

9. What were the differences between "free-labor ideology" and the southern version of herrenvolk democracy?

SUGGESTED ESSAY TOPICS

1. What was Stephen Douglas's rationale for the 1854 Kansas–Nebraska Act? Why did the passages of the act lead to "Bleeding Kansas" and so much discord in American politics?

2. What was the "free labor" ideology of the Republican Party?

3. Explain the Dred Scott case and Taney's decision and their impact on sectional strife.

4. Contrast the economies of the North and South. Why had they diverged so greatly in the preceding three decades?

LECTURE OUTLINE

1. Nothing contributed more to the sense of sectional crisis than the fight over slavery in **Kansas.** The rise of the **Republican Party** in opposition to the spread of slavery and to slaveholders' interests anywhere guaranteed that slavery would dominate the political debates of the remainder of the 1850s.

   a. The brainchild of Stephan A. Douglas of Illinois, the **Kansas–Nebraska Act of 1854** repealed the Missouri Compromise line that had marked the northern border of slave expansion in the Louisiana Purchase.

b.   The sectional fighting over slavery and related issues led directly to the **death of the Whig Party,** as northern Whigs joined the Republican Party.

2.   Concerns over immigration and **nativism** proved important political issues that in other times might have overshadowed the growing crisis over slavery.

(SHOW TRANSPARENCY 67: FOREIGN BORN POPULATONS, 1840-1860)

a.   A visceral fear of **immigrants in politics** among many Protestants resulted in the formation of the American, or Know-Nothing, Party.

b.   The rise of the **"Know-Nothings"** culminated in the candidacy of Millard Fillmore for president in 1856 on a platform of immigrant restriction and delay of full political rights to newcomers.

c.   The furor over slavery was coterminous with the **decline of nativism,** itself critical to any chance of Republican success in national politics.

3.   A virtual civil war known as **Bleeding Kansas** broke out in that territory as competing pro- and antislavery factions battled for supremacy.

(SHOW TRANSPARENCY 68: KANSAS–NEBRASKA AND THE SLAVERY ISSUE)

a.   Charles Sumner's **"Crime against Kansas"** speech so inflamed South Carolina Representative Preston Brooks that he beat Sumner nearly to death. Brooks's caning of the Massachusetts senator was as hailed in the South as it was condemned in the North.

4.   The Republican's first presidential candidate, John C. Frémont, ran well in the **election of 1856** but failed to win enough border states to defeat Democrat James Buchanan.

a.   In the **Dred Scott case,** Supreme Court Chief Justice Roger B. Taney ruled that the Missouri Compromise constituted an illegal denial of the property rights of slaveholders and that slaves were not citizens and, therefore, could not sue in court.

b.   President Buchanan endorsed Kansas's blatantly proslavery **Lecompton Constitution,** despite the vehement opposition of Stephen Douglas and other northern Democrats.

5.   The **economy in the 1850s** hummed along as economic production outstripped even the prodigious rate of population increase.

a.   Contemporaries heaped praise on "Yankee ingenuity" and the so-called **"American system of manufactures,"** which incorporated the widescale use of interchangeable parts and other technical innovations.

b.   The **southern economy** grew rapidly in the 1850s, largely on the basis of growing worldwide demand for cotton.

c.   The inherent dangers of the **sovereignty of king cotton** were noted by James D. B. De Bow and other Southerners who favored diversification and modernization of techniques.

(SHOW TRANSPARENCY 69: SLAVERY AND STAPLE CROPS IN THE SOUTH, 1860)

d.   While northern leaders espoused the glories of free labor, **labor conditions in the North** were often miserable, as wages were low and urban life unhealthy in the extreme.

e. While the **Panic of 1857** hit hardest in the industrial areas of the North, the Republican Party actually gained strength due to southern opposition to economic reform bills.

f. **Sectionalism and the Panic** went hand in hand, as northern interests exploited southern politicians' intransigence on economic reform measures.

g. The **free labor ideology** of "free soil, free labor, free men" was at the heart of the Republican Party's sectional message in the 1850s.

h. Republicans skillfully exploited the publication of North Carolinian Hinton Rowan Helper's *The Impending Crisis* to demonstrate how slavery negatively affected the material conditions of non-slaveholders.

i. While few **southern non-slaveholders** seemed to be aware of the negative impact of slavery on their economic fortunes, most understood that their white skin made them part of the "ruling race" of their region.

6. The **Lincoln–Douglas debates** of 1858 served to highlight the deep divide over the morality of slavery in Illinois, and the North generally, and quickly came to be regarded as perhaps the finest example of stump speech eloquence from the era.

(SHOW TRANSPARENCY 70: THE PATH OF THE LINCOLN – DOUGLAS DEBATES)

a. Abraham Lincoln stirred great controversy when, upon accepting the Senate nomination, he declared that the Union could not forever remain "a house divided."

b. Douglas lost any chance of southern extremist support for his 1860 presidential campaign when he espoused in his **"Freeport doctrine"** that citizens could effectively exclude slavery from the territories.

7. The capture of abolitionist **John Brown at Harpers Ferry** and his subsequent execution stirred the conscience of northerners who previously had considered abolitionists to be nothing less than dangerous disunionists.

Conclusion: Despite the efforts of many politicians, who feared for the Union, the events of the 1850s reinforced the growing schism between slavery and freedom. The birth of the Republican Party and the election of Lincoln inexorably led southerners to reconsider the value of remaining within the United States, while John Brown's raid at Harpers Ferry proved true the South's greatest fears.

TEACHING RESOURCES

America Grows Up (1850–1900s) offers an overview of the nation's economic development. Filmic Archives (53 minutes).

On a Clear Day You Can See Boston describes the Irish immigration to the nation in the 1850s. Films for the Humanities & Sciences (52 minutes, color).

Go West, Young Man covers the Norwegian movement to the Midwest. Films for the Humanities & Sciences (52 minutes, color).

Out of Ireland focuses on Irish immigrants who arrived in the mid-nineteenth century. PBS Video (111 minutes).

Lincoln: Making of a President describes his formative years and his rise to national prominence during the Lincoln–Douglas debates. Movies Unlimited (60 minutes).

The Civil War: Union at Risk presents the prewar differences between North and South and emphasizes Constitutional interpretation. Filmic Archives (25 minutes, color).

The Civil War-episode one — by Ken Burns offers an award-winning account of the war's beginning. PBS Video (99 minutes).

The West episode four examines the events of the 1850s and the Civil War. PBS Video (60 minutes).

MULTIPLE CHOICE

1. Under the Missouri Compromise
    a. slavery would be excluded in the new territory of Nebraska.
    b. the issue of slavery would be determined by the territorial legislature in Nebraska.
    c. slavery in Nebraska was not affected since the compromise referred to lands ceded from Mexico during the Mexican War.
    d. Nebraska's residents would decide whether to permit slavery.
    e. slavery was not excluded from any territory in the west.

ANS: A   TYPE: M   KEY 1: F   KEY 2: 2   PAGE: 434

2. The leading advocate for southern rights in the dispute over Kansas was
    a. Stephen Douglas.
    b. David Atchison.
    c. Franklin B. Pierce.
    d. Jefferson Davis.
    e. Abraham Lincoln.

ANS: B   TYPE: M   KEY 1: F   KEY 2: 2   PAGE: 434

3. The Kansas-Nebraska Act
    a. divided the Nebraska Territory into two territories.
    b. repealed the Missouri Compromise.
    c. represented the interests of the southern faction of the Democratic Party.
    d. was supported by Stephen Douglas.
    e. all of the above

ANS: E   TYPE: M   KEY 1: F   KEY 2: 2   PAGE: 434

4. The final act that destroyed the Whigs as a national political party was the
    a. passage of the Missouri Compromise.
    b. passage of the Kansas-Nebraska Act.
    c. passage of the Compromise of 1850.
    d. passage of the Lecompton Constitution.
    e. the Fugitive Slave Act.

ANS: B   TYPE: M   KEY 1: F   KEY 2: 2   PAGE: 436

5. The destruction of the Whig Party led to the formation of the
    a. liberal Democrats.
    b. Liberty Party.
    c. Republican Party.
    d. Free Soil Party.
    e. the Socialist Party.

ANS: C   TYPE: M   KEY 1: F   KEY 2: 1   PAGE: 436

6. Most immigrants between 1800 and 1830 were
    a. Irish, Catholic, and unskilled laborers.
    b. British, Protestant, and skilled workers.
    c. German, Protestant, and unskilled laborers.
    d. Italian, Catholic, and skilled workers.
    e. Russian, Jewish, and unskilled workers.

ANS: B   TYPE: M   KEY 1: A   KEY 2: 3   PAGE: 437

7. Most immigrants in the 1840s and 1850s were
    a. Irish, Catholic, and unskilled laborers.
    b. British, Protestant, and skilled workers.
    c. German, Protestant, and unskilled laborers.
    d. Italian, Catholic, and skilled workers.
    e. Russian, Jewish, and unskilled workers.

ANS: A   TYPE: M   KEY 1: A   KEY 2: 3   PAGE: 437

8. Most immigrants in the 1850s joined the
    a. Know-Nothing Party.
    b. Republican Party.
    c. Liberty Party.
    d. Democratic Party.
    e. Socialist Party.

ANS: D   TYPE: M   KEY 1: F   KEY 2: 2   PAGE: 437

9. The major issue for the Know-Nothing Party was
    a. abolition of slavery.
    b. development of business.
    c. nativism.
    d. women's rights.
    e. westward expansion.

ANS: C   TYPE: M   KEY 1: F   KEY 2: 1   PAGE: 438

10. Most northerners left the Know-Nothings and became Republicans because of
    a. the slavery issue.
    b. the immigration issue.
    c. the temperance issue.
    d. economic concerns.
    e. concern for public education.

ANS: A   TYPE: M   KEY 1: F   KEY 2: 2   PAGE: 439-40

11. The subject of Charles Sumner's speech that led to his beating on the floor of Congress was
    a. the hanging of John Brown.
    b. the Dred Scott Decision.
    c. the Compromise of 1850
    d. the Fugitive Slave Act
    e. "Bleeding Kansas."

ANS: E   TYPE: M   KEY 1: F   KEY 2: 1   PAGE: 442

12. The winner of the 1856 presidential election was
    a. Millard Fillmore.
    b. James Buchanan.
    c. Stephen Douglas.
    d. Franklin Pierce.
    e. Abraham Lincoln.

ANS: B   TYPE: M   KEY 1: F   KEY 2: 1   PAGE: 443-44

13. The *Dred Scott* decision of the U.S. Supreme Court involved
    a. a slave who had been taken to live in Kansas.
    b. a slave who was suing for his freedom because his master had taken him into free territory.
    c. a former slave who sued for his wife's freedom on the grounds that she had been married to a free black.
    d. a slave who had been freed by his master and who challenged the Fugitive Slave Act of 1850.
    e. a slave who wished to exercise his right to vote.

ANS: B   TYPE: M   KEY 1: F   KEY 2: 2   PAGE: 445

14. One feature of industry pioneered by the United States was
    a. production of prestige products by skilled artisans.
    b. mass production of interchangeable parts.
    c. production of railroads and locomotives.
    d. arms and ammunition.
    e. a unionized labor force.

ANS: B   TYPE: M   KEY 1: F   KEY 2: 1   PAGE: 449

15. One of the problems of the southern economy on the eve of the Civil War was
    a. lack of productivity in the agricultural sector.
    b. over-reliance on industrial growth.
    c. a developing commercial attitude.
    d. the decline of the cotton industry.
    e. a lack of diversification

ANS: E   TYPE: M   KEY 1: F   KEY 2: 1   PAGE: 451

16. _____ asserted that southern slaves enjoyed a higher standard of living than northern laborers.
    a. Hinton R. Helper
    b. George Fitzhugh
    c. William Seward
    d. James D. B. De Bow
    e. Abraham Lincoln

ANS: B   TYPE: M   KEY 1: F   KEY 2: 1   PAGE: 453

17. At the core of free-labor ideology was the belief that
    a. social mobility awaited those industrious laborers who worked hard and efficiently.
    b. laborers who worked for free earned merits and future promotion from employers.
    c. independent yeoman farmers formed the backbone of society.
    d. commerce bred greed and selfishness and should be avoided.
    e. all industries should be publicly owned.

ANS: A   TYPE: M   KEY 1: A   KEY 2: 2   PAGE: 456

18. The great enemy of a free-labor society was
    a. commerce.
    b. slavery.
    c. agriculture.
    d. merchants.
    e. the government.

ANS: B   TYPE: M   KEY 1: F   KEY 2: 2   PAGE: 457

19. Which political party endorsed the ideas of "free labor"?
    a. American Party
    b. Democratic Party
    c. Socialist Party
    d. Liberty Party
    e. Republican Party

ANS: E   TYPE: M   KEY 1: F   KEY 2: 1   PAGE: 456-57

20. Who of the following would have argued that "freedom is not possible without slavery"?
    a. Stephen Douglas
    b. John C. Calhoun
    c. Abraham Lincoln
    d. Henry Clay
    e. Nathaniel Hawthorne

ANS: B   TYPE: M   KEY 1: F   KEY 2: 1   PAGE: 458

21. The central issue in the Lincoln-Douglas debates of 1858 was
    a. the transcontinental railroad.
    b. secession.
    c. slavery.
    d. states' rights.
    e. westward expansion.

ANS: C   TYPE: M   KEY 1: F   KEY 2: 1   PAGE: 458-59

22. The result of John Brown's raid on Harpers Ferry was
    a. northern anger at his actions.
    b. northern rejection of the Republican Party.
    c. slave unrest in the South.
    d. dramatic growth for the northern Democratic Party.
    e. revulsion and fear throughout the South.

ANS: B   TYPE: M   KEY 1: F   KEY 2: 2   PAGE: 461-62

23. The violence in "Bleeding Kansas" involved clashes between
    a. white settlers and American Indians.
    b. blacks and whites.
    c. proslavery and antislavery groups.
    d. residents of Nebraska who invaded Kansas and the settlers there.
    e. Mexican invaders and the settlers of Kansas.

ANS: C   TYPE: M   KEY 1: F   KEY 2: 1   PAGE: 440-42

24. Which of the following was Abraham Lincoln's view on the extension of slavery into the territories?
    a. Slavery was unconstitutional in the states and in the territories.
    b. Slavery was constitutional in the slave states but it should not be allowed to extend into the territories.
    c. Congress did not have the authority to prohibit the expansion of slavery.
    d. He had no opinion on the subject.
    e. Congress must support the expansion of slavery into the territories.

ANS: B   TYPE: M   KEY 1: A   KEY 2: 3   PAGE: 435-36

25. Members of the Know-Nothing Party were all of the following except
    a. American-born Protestants.
    b. middle-aged and elderly professional men.
    c. supporters of the temperance movement.
    d. advocates of legislation increasing the naturalization period.
    e. pledged to maintain secrecy about their order.

ANS: B   TYPE: M   KEY 1: F   KEY 2: 2   PAGE: 438

26. In the Kansas territorial election of 1855,
    a. approximately five thousand Missourians illegally voted.
    b. a free-soil legislature was elected.
    c. women were allowed to vote.
    d. slavery was abolished in the area.
    e. blacks were allowed to vote.

ANS: A   TYPE: M   KEY 1: F   KEY 2: 2   PAGE: 441

27. In the mid-nineteenth-century American system of education,
    a. most lower-class students worked as apprentices and did not attend school.
    b. 95 percent of white southerners and 20 percent of the slaves could read and write.
    c. was stronger in the North than in the South.
    d. most public school teachers were men.
    e. literacy was more common in the United States than in Europe.

ANS: E   TYPE: M   KEY 1: A   KEY 2: 2   PAGE: 450

28. The southern economy was "colonial" in that
    a. foreign investors owned over 50 percent of the land in the South.
    b. southern financial institutions loaned money to European colonial powers.
    c. it depended upon exportation of agricultural goods and importation of manufactured products.
    d. it employed slaves.
    e. it exported no products.

ANS: C   TYPE: M   KEY 1: A   KEY 2: 2   PAGE: 451

29. Defenders of slavery claimed all of the following except
    a. elderly slaves were automatically freed when they reached retirement age.
    b. slaves never had to worry about losing their jobs.
    c. slaves received free medical care.
    d. in general, slaves were better off than white wage earners in the North.
    e. slaves did not have to worry about having their wages cut.

ANS: A   TYPE: M   KEY 1: A   KEY 2: 3   PAGE: 453-54

30. The Panic of 1857
    a. caused bloody riots in which dozens of people were killed.
    b. increased hostility between northerners and southerners who disagreed over the tariff issue.
    c. lasted longer than any other nineteenth-century depression.
    d. caused millions of workers to join labor unions.
    e. all of the above

ANS: B   **TYPE: M**   **KEY 1: A**   **KEY 2: 3**   **PAGE: 455-56**

31. Advocates of the free labor ideology viewed labor strikes as
    a. dangerous, subversive plots.
    b. unfortunate misunderstandings that could be solved by prayer.
    c. evidence of the increased influence of foreign immigrants.
    d. justification for forming a new political party.
    e. positive events that helped free workers improve their working conditions.

ANS: E   **TYPE: M**   **KEY 1: A**   **KEY 2: 3**   **PAGE: 457**

32. In *The Impending Crisis of the South*, Hinton Rowan Helper
    a. described southern society as bustling, prosperous, and progressive.
    b. blamed South Carolina for the violence in "Bleeding Kansas."
    c. said that slavery caused economic retardation, illiteracy, and poverty in the South.
    d. defended the states' rights position on secession.
    e. insisted that slavery must expand to al of the territories.

ANS: C   **TYPE: M**   **KEY 1: A**   **KEY 2: 3**   **PAGE: 457**

33. The belief in white supremacy was
    a. confined to the southern United States.
    b. less important than economic class in determining social status in the South.
    c. only characteristic of the wealthy plantation owners.
    d. rejected prior to the Civil War.
    e. attractive to poor southern whites and northern immigrant laborers and poor farmers because it gave them status.

ANS: D   **TYPE: M**   **KEY 1: A**   **KEY 2: 3**   **PAGE: 457-58**

34. In the "Freeport Doctrine,"
    a. the Supreme Court ruled that residence in Freeport, Illinois, did not automatically free runaways.
    b. Stephen Douglas suggested that the territories could maintain popular sovereignty by refusing to protect slavery there.
    c. Abraham Lincoln agreed that there was no means of preventing the extension of slavery.
    d. Stephen Douglas insisted that slavery was legal in all the free states and territories.
    e. slaves who escaped to the North were declared free.

ANS: B   **TYPE: M**   **KEY 1: A**   **KEY 2: 2**   **PAGE: 461**

35. John Brown was noted for all of the following except
    a. killing unarmed proslavery farmers in the civil war in "Bleeding Kansas."
    b. attempting to incite a slave rebellion in Virginia.
    c. coining the phrase "the irrepressible conflict" to explain the coming of the Civil War.
    d. dying as a "martyr to freedom."
    e. attacking Harpers Ferry.

ANS: C   **TYPE: M**   **KEY 1: F**   **KEY 2: 3**   **PAGE: 442, 461-62**

36. As a result of the Lincoln-Douglas debates,
    a. the state of Illinois passed legislation making slavery a punishment for crime.
    b. Stephen Douglas was re-elected to the U.S. Senate.
    c. Abraham Lincoln was almost kicked out of the Republican Party.
    d. both Lincoln and Douglas were defeated by Know-Nothing candidate Nathaniel Banks.
    e. the Kansas-Nebraska Act was repealed.

ANS: B   TYPE: M   KEY 1: F   KEY 2: 2   PAGE: 460-61

37. Stephen A. Douglas was chair of the Senate Committee on
    a. Westward Expansion.
    b. Kansas and Nebraska.
    c. Territories.
    d. New States.
    e. the Economy.

ANS: C   TYPE: M   KEY 1: F   KEY 2: 2   PAGE: 434

38. Members of the Order, which eventually evolved into the Know-Nothings, supported all of the following except
    a. temperance.
    b. restricting public office to native born men.
    c. lengthening the naturalization period before immigrants could become citizens.
    d. keeping their Order secret.
    e. tax support for parochial schools.

ANS: E   TYPE: M   KEY 1: F   KEY 2: 1   PAGE: 438

39. Which of the following did not run a presidential candidate in 1856?
    a. Republican Party
    b. Democratic Party
    c. Whig Party
    d. American Party
    e. none of the above.

ANS: C   TYPE: M   KEY 1: F   KEY 2: 2   PAGE: 443

40. James Buchanan won all of the following states in 1856 except
    a. Maryland.
    b. California.
    c. Pennsylvania.
    d. New Jersey.
    e. Pennsylvania.

ANS: A   TYPE: M   KEY 1: F   KEY 2: 3   PAGE: 444

41. The value of American exports and imports increased by _____ percent between 1844 and 1856.
    a. 75
    b. 100
    c. 200
    d. 250
    e. no

ANS: C   TYPE: M   KEY 1: F   KEY 2: 3   PAGE: 447

42. Which of the following was not among the nation's four leading industries measured by value added in manufacturing by 1860?
    a. cotton textiles
    b. floor milling
    c. lumber products
    d. boots and shoes
    e. steel

ANS: E   TYPE: M   KEY 1: F   KEY 2: 3   PAGE: 449

43. By 1855, cotton provided more than _____ of total U.S. exports.
    a. one-quarter
    b. one-third
    c. one-half
    d. two-thirds
    e. one-tenth

ANS: C   TYPE: M   KEY 1: A   KEY 2: 2   PAGE: 451

44. The 3 million immigrants that entered the United States in the decade after 1845 represented _____ percent of the total America population in 1845.
    a. 5
    b. 10
    c. 15
    d. 20
    e. 50

ANS: C   TYPE: M   KEY 1: F   KEY 2: 2   PAGE: 437

45. During the Kansas-Nebraska debate, Missouri's David Atchison held the position of
    a. speaker of the House of Representatives.
    b. vice president.
    c. president pro tem of the Senate.
    d. secretary of state.
    e. secretary of war.

ANS: C   TYPE: M   KEY 1: F   KEY 2: 3   PAGE: 434

46. After serving four terms in the Illinois legislature and one term in Congress, Abraham Lincoln was propelled back into politics by the shock of
    a. the Kansas-Nebraska bill
    b. the Dred Scott decision.
    c. John Brown's raid on Harpers Ferry.
    d. Bleeding Kansas.
    e. the Fugitive Slave Law.

ANS: A   TYPE: M   KEY 1: F   KEY 2: 2   PAGE: 435

47. Organization of the Nebraska territory was necessary in order to
    a. expand slavery in the West.
    b. stop the Republican Party.
    c. establish reservations for Native Americans.
    d. get Lincoln elected President.
    e. build a railroad across the area.

ANS: E   TYPE: M   KEY 1: A   KEY 2: 2   PAGE: 434

48. The American or Know Nothing Party failed to become the leading opposition party in the 1850s primarily because
    a. large numbers of immigrants joined the party.
    b. the slavery issue divided northern and southern supporters of the party.
    c. the Democratic Party picked up its anti-immigrant platforms.
    d. the Whig Party was revived, diluting its strength.
    e. the business community strongly supported increased immigration.

ANS: B   TYPE: M   KEY 1: A   KEY 2: 3   PAGE: 439-40

49. Most former northern members of the American Party became
    a. dropped out of politics.
    b. Democrats.
    c. Whigs.
    d. Free Soilers.
    e. Republicans.

ANS: E   TYPE: M   KEY 1: F   KEY 2: 2   PAGE: 440

50. With regard to the Kansas issue, President Franklin Pierce
    a. endorsed John Brown's abolitionist campaign.
    b. recognized the antislavery legislature.
    c. recognized the proslavery legislature.
    d. refused to get involved in the conflict.
    e. asked Kansas to secede from the Union.

ANS: C   TYPE: M   KEY 1: F   KEY 2: 2   PAGE: 441

TRUE/FALSE

_____ 1.   The leading advocate for southern economic diversification was James D. B. De Bow.

ANS: T   TYPE: T   KEY 1: F   KEY 2: 1   PAGE: 451

_____ 2.   On average, wages and opportunities for workers were greater in the North than anywhere else.

ANS: T   TYPE: T   KEY 1: A   KEY 2: 2   PAGE: 455

_____ 3.   John Brown's raid on Harpers Ferry lasted for thee days.

ANS: F   TYPE: T   KEY 1: F   KEY 2: 2   PAGE: 461

_____ 4.   The Panic of 1857 virtually destroyed the southern cotton economy.

ANS: F   TYPE: T   KEY 1: F   KEY 2: 3   PAGE: 456

_____ 5.   The single greatest enemy of the American Party was Irish immigrants.

ANS: T   TYPE: T   KEY 1: F   KEY 2: 2   PAGE: 437-38

_____ 6.   The leading southern advocate of free labor ideology was Jefferson Davis.

ANS: F   TYPE: T   KEY 1: F   KEY 2: 3   PAGE: 456

_____ 7.   The Lecompton Constitution was invalid because it was written by the antislavery
              minority in the proslavery territory of Kansas.

ANS: F   TYPE: T   KEY 1: A   KEY 2: 2   PAGE: 446

_____ 8.   The first year that the Republican Party ran a presidential candidate was 1854.

ANS: F   TYPE: T   KEY 1: F   KEY 2: 2   PAGE: 443

_____ 9.   Abraham Lincoln believed that slavery and freedom were incompatible.

ANS: T   TYPE: T   KEY 1: F   KEY 2: 1   PAGE: 457

_____ 10.   Most of the foreign-born voters in the 1830s and 1840s joined the Democratic Party.

ANS: T   TYPE: T   KEY 1: F   KEY 2: 2   PAGE: 437

_____ 11.   The Know-Nothing Party was so named because its members were ignorant and
              uneducated.

ANS: F   TYPE: T   KEY 1: F   KEY 2: 2   PAGE: 436

_____ 12.   Many of the abolitionists advocated depriving white immigrants and Catholics of equal
              rights.

ANS: T   TYPE: T   KEY 1: F   KEY 2: 2   PAGE: 438

_____ 13.   _The Impending Crisis of the_ South exaggerated the disaffection of most non-slaveholders
              in the South.

ANS: T   TYPE: T   KEY 1: F   KEY 2: 2   PAGE: 457

_____ 14.   Many southerners read _The Impending Crisis of the South_.

ANS: F   TYPE: T   KEY 1: F   KEY 2: 2   PAGE: 457

_____ 15.   Some northern industrial workers volunteered to become slaves in order to get free food
              and medical care.

ANS: F   TYPE: T   KEY 1: F   KEY 2: 2   PAGE: 455

_____ 16.   The Kansas-Nebraska Act destroyed the Whig Party.

ANS: F   TYPE: T   KEY 1: F   KEY 2: 1   PAGE: 436

_____ 1 7.   Application of popular sovereignty to the Nebraska Territory was the brainchild of
              Stephen A. Douglas.

ANS: T   TYPE: T   KEY 1: F   KEY 2: 2   PAGE: 434

_____ 18.   It was David R. Atchison who insisted that the Missouri Compromise had to be explicitly
              repealed in order for the South to accept the organization of the Nebraska Territory.

ANS: T   TYPE: T   KEY 1: F   KEY 2: 2   PAGE: 434

_____ 19.   The Panic of 1857 stemmed entirely from domestic causes.

ANS: F   TYPE: T   KEY 1: F   KEY 2: 2   PAGE: 455

_____ 20.   Abraham Lincoln saw the prevention of the expansion of slavery into the territories as the first step to its eventual extinction.

ANS: T   TYPE: T   KEY 1: A   KEY 2: 2   PAGE: 435-36

_____ 21.   The Kansas-Nebraska bill passed easily in the House of Representatives.

ANS: F   TYPE: T   KEY 1: A   KEY 2: 2   PAGE: 436

_____ 22.   Franklin Pierce was president during the debate over the Kansas-Nebraska bill.

ANS: T   TYPE: T   KEY 1: F   KEY 2: 1   PAGE: 434

_____ 23.   The elections of 1854 were disastrous for northern Democrats.

ANS: T   TYPE: T   KEY 1: F   KEY 2: 2   PAGE: 436

_____ 24.   Franklin Pierce supported southern efforts to legalize slavery in Kansas.

ANS: T   TYPE: T   KEY 1: F   KEY 2: 2   PAGE: 441

_____ 25.   When two competing legislatures emerged in Kansas, the House of Representatives recognized the one that supported slavery.

ANS: F   TYPE: T   KEY 1: F   KEY 2: 3   PAGE: 441

_____ 26.   The Republicans were the first truly sectional party in American history.

ANS: T   TYPE: T   KEY 1: F   KEY 2: 1   PAGE: 443

_____ 27.   The Republican Party advocated racial equality in the election of 1856.

ANS: F   TYPE: T   KEY 1: F   KEY 2: 3   PAGE: 443

_____ 28.   No southern justices supported the Dred Scott decision.

ANS: F   TYPE: T   KEY 1: F   KEY 2: 3   PAGE: 444-45

_____ 29.   The Dred Scott decision finally settled the slavery question.

ANS: F   TYPE: T   KEY 1: F   KEY 2: 1   PAGE: 446

_____ 30.   The Lecompton debate seriously split the Democratic Party.

ANS: T   TYPE: T   KEY 1: A   KEY 2: 2   PAGE: 446

_____ 31.   Between 1844 and 1856, the distance between rich and poor was narrowing.

ANS: F   TYPE: T   KEY 1: A   KEY 2: 3   PAGE: 449

_____ 32.   By the late 1850s, the United States was the second-leading industrial producer in the world.

ANS: T   TYPE: T   KEY 1: A   KEY 2: 2   PAGE: 449

_____ 33.   The South did not share in the economy's rapid growth following recovery from the depression of 1837-1843.

ANS: F   TYPE: T   KEY 1: A   KEY 2: 3   PAGE: 451

_____ 34.   The cover of _De Bow's_ Review proclaimed that "Cotton is King."

ANS: F   TYPE: T   KEY 1: F   KEY 2: 3   PAGE: 451

_____ 35.   Economic diversification made no headway in the South during the 1850s.

ANS: F   TYPE: T   KEY 1: A   KEY 2: 2   PAGE: 451

_____ 36.   Southerners had a larger percentage of their capital invested in lands and slaves in 1860 than they had had ten years earlier.

ANS: T   TYPE: T   KEY 1: A   KEY 2: 2   PAGE: 451

_____ 37.   Virginians in the late 1850s supported the reopening of the international slave trade.

ANS: F   TYPE: T   KEY 1: A   KEY 2: 3   PAGE: 451

_____ 38.   George Fitzhugh supported the free-market capitalist system.

ANS: F   TYPE: T   KEY 1: A   KEY 2: 2   PAGE: 453

_____ 39.   Four million immigrants came to the United States between 1845 and 1860.

ANS: T   TYPE: T   KEY 1: F   KEY 2: 2   PAGE: 455

_____ 40.   The widespread use of the sewing machine in the 1850s made life easier for seamstresses.

ANS: F   TYPE: T   KEY 1: A   KEY 2: 2   PAGE: 454

FILL-INS

1.   The first Republican presidential candidate (1856) was _____.

ANS: John C. Frémont   TYPE: F   KEY 1: F   KEY 2: 3   PAGE: 443

2.   The Supreme Court chief justice who was motivated more by "Southern life and values" than the law in the Dred Scott case was _____.

ANS: Roger Taney   TYPE: F   KEY 1: F   KEY 2: 1   PAGE: 445-46

3.   Stephen Douglas introduced the idea of _____, which states that the people of a territory should decide whether they want the institution of slavery, into the debate over the Kansas territory.

ANS: popular sovereignty   TYPE: F   KEY 1: A   KEY 2: 2   PAGE: 434

4. Although officially called the American Party, the more popular name for this political group was the
    _____.

ANS: Know-Nothings   **TYPE: F**   **KEY 1: F**   **KEY 2: 2**   **PAGE: 438**

5. The abolitionist zealot who massacred five proslavery advocates at Pottawatomie Creek was
    _____.

ANS: John Brown   **TYPE: F**   **KEY 1: F**   **KEY 2: 1**   **PAGE: 442**

6. After his Kansas speech, _____ was attacked in the Senate by a U.S. representative from South Carolina.

ANS: Charles Sumner   **TYPE: F**   **KEY 1: F**   **KEY 2: 1**   **PAGE: 442**

7. _____ was the North Carolinian who wrote *The Impending Crisis of the South*.

ANS: Hinton Rowan Helper   **TYPE: F**   **KEY 1: F**   **KEY 2: 1**   **PAGE: 457**

8. Southern society was based on the concept of _____ democracy in the idea that all members of the superior white race are equal.

ANS: herrenvolk   **TYPE: F**   **KEY 1: F**   **KEY 2: 3**   **PAGE: 458**

9. The dispute over Kansas and Nebraska gave rise to the _____ Party.

ANS: Republican   **TYPE: F**   **KEY 1: A**   **KEY 2: 1**   **PAGE: 436**

10. The Dred Scott decision denied the power of _____ to restrict slavery in the territories.

ANS: Congress   **TYPE: F**   **KEY 1: A**   **KEY 2: 2**   **PAGE: 446**

11. The Senate effort to ensure that slavery would not be kept out of Nebraska was led by
    _____.

ANS: David R. Atchison   **TYPE: F**   **KEY 1: F**   **KEY 2: 3**   **PAGE: 434**

12. The Whig candidate for president in 1852 was _____.

ANS: Winfield Scott   **TYPE: F**   **KEY 1: F**   **KEY 2: 2**   **PAGE: 436**

13. _____ was the first state to enact a prohibition law.

ANS: Maine   **TYPE: F**   **KEY 1: F**   **KEY 2: 2**   **PAGE: 438**

14. By 1856, the _____ had become the largest party in the North.

ANS: Republicans   **TYPE: F**   **KEY 1: F**   **KEY 2: 2**   **PAGE: 443**

15. By the late 1850s, the United States was behind only _____ in total industrial production.

ANS: Britain   **TYPE: F**   **KEY 1: F**   **KEY 2: 2**   **PAGE: 449**

16. The argument that slaves were better off than northern factory workers reached its fullest development in the writings of _____.

ANS: George Fitzhugh TYPE: F   KEY 1: F   KEY 2: 2   PAGE: 453

17. Less than _____ percent of the U.S. labor force was unionized in 1860.

ANS: 1   TYPE: F   KEY 1: F   KEY 2: 3   PAGE: 456

18. The most important social distinction in the antebellum South was _____.

ANS: race   TYPE: F   KEY 1: A   KEY 2: 2   PAGE: 458

19. _____led the drive for passage of a federal slave code for all territories.

ANS: Jefferson Davis TYPE: F   KEY 1: F   KEY 2: 3   PAGE: 461

20. _____ lost control of the House of Representatives in 1854.

ANS: Democrats   TYPE: F   KEY 1: F   KEY 2: 3   PAGE: 436

21. _____ of foreign-born workers settled in free states.

ANS: Seven-eighths   TYPE: F   KEY 1: F   KEY 2: 3   PAGE: 437

22. By 1856, most northern Know-Nothings had become _____.

ANS: Republicans   TYPE: F   KEY 1: F   KEY 2: 3   PAGE: 439-40

23. About _____ "border ruffians" from Missouri voted illegally in the spring of 1855 to elect a proslavery territorial legislature in Kansas.

ANS: five thousand   TYPE: F   KEY 1: F   KEY 2: 2   PAGE: 441

24. The first use of the term "Republican" to describe the new political party in the 1850s was at _____.

ANS: Ripon, Wisconsin TYPE: F   KEY 1: F   KEY 2: 3   PAGE: 436

25. The leading Catholic prelate who attacked abolitionists and boasted of the decline of Protestantism was _____.

ANS: John Hughes   TYPE: F   KEY 1: F   KEY 2: 2   PAGE: 438

26. The Supreme Court decision that declared the Missouri Compromise unconstitutional was the _____ decision.

ANS: Dred Scott   TYPE: F   KEY 1: F   KEY 2: 1   PAGE: 446

27. A constitution designed to impose slavery on Kansas was the _____ constitution.

ANS: Lecomptin   TYPE: F   KEY 1: F   KEY 2: 2   PAGE: 446

28. A feature of modern industry that utilizes machines to cut identical parts that fit together with other parts produced in the same way is mass production of _____.

ANS: Interchangeable Parts   TYPE: F   KEY 1: F   KEY 2: 2   PAGE: 449

29. The end of the _____ War in Europe caused a decline in grain exports contributing to the onset of the Panic of 1857.

ANS: Crimean   TYPE: F   KEY 1: F   KEY 2: 3   PAGE: 455

30. _____ declared, "A house divided against itself cannot stand."

ANS: Abraham Lincoln   TYPE: F   KEY 1; F   KEY 2: 3   PAGE: 458

IDENTIFICATIONS

1. **John Brown**: antislavery zealot whose violent raids frightened and enraged southerners. Attacked proslavery forces in Kansas, then launched an unsuccessful raid on the federal arsenal in Harpers Ferry, Virginia in hopes of starting a slave insurrection. Arrested along with several of his supporters and ultimately executed. Became a hero for abolitionists.

2. **George Fitzhugh**: a farmer-lawyer from Virginia who defended slavery as a paternalistic system that took care of the slaves. Published *Sociology for the South* and *Cannibals All*. Insisted that capitalism mistreated and exploited free workers.

3. **Know-Nothing Party**: nativist, anti-Catholic, political party that grew to great strength in the northeastern United States. Formally known as the American Party, it won big in the elections of 1854, mostly by cutting into the Whig constituency. Shortly thereafter, though, it was overtaken by Republicans who focused on the issue of slavery. Disappeared after 1856.

4. **Republican Party**: northern political party that emerged following the Kansas controversy. Primary platform was "no extension of slavery." First wholly sectional party in American history.

5. **Kansas-Nebraska Act**: 1854 congressional act that repealed the Missouri Compromise and effectively destroyed the two-party system in the United States.

6. **Hinton Rowan Helper**: North Carolinian who wrote *The Impending Crisis of the South*. Spokesperson for white non-slaveowners who blamed the backwardness of southern economy, the illiteracy of whites and slaves, and the widespread poverty of the South on the institution of slavery. His book was banned in the South.

7. **Lincoln-Douglas debates**: a series of seven debates between Stephen Douglas and Abraham Lincoln during the Illinois senatorial race in 1858. These debates focused on the issue of slavery, made Lincoln a national figure, and lost support for Douglas among southern Democrats.

8. **James D. B. De Bow**: Southern publisher of *De Bow's Review*. Championed economic diversification in the South. Organized annual commercial conventions in various southern cities during the 1850s. Encouraged southerners to invest in shipping lines, railroads, textile mills, and other enterprises.

9. **Homestead Act:** a bill supported by the Republican Party that would grant 160 acres of public land to farmers who settled the land.

10. **Freeport Doctrine:** Stephen Douglas' attempt to reconcile the Dred Scott Decision with his popular sovereignty approach to the issue of slavery in the territories. He contended that even if slavery were legal in the territories its enforcement would still depend on the people who lived there.

1.   Examine the controversy involving the Kansas-Nebraska Act. What were the issues involved and how were they resolved?

Answer: The Kansas-Nebraska Act (1854) was the result of the belief on the part of both regions of the nation (the capitalist North and the proslavery South) that their own expansion was absolutely essential for the survival of the nation. The issue at hand was whether slavery would exist in the Nebraska Territory. Stephen Douglas's attempt to build a railroad ignited great controversy. When southern leaders demanded that Nebraska be split into two territories, Douglas responded by proposing that slavery exist in at least one of the territories. His Kansas-Nebraska Act not only split the region in two, but officially overturned the Missouri Compromise by allowing slavery to exist north of the Missouri Compromise line. The bill caused an outrage in the North, particularly among northern Whigs who refused to vote in favor of the bill. Southerners of both parties strongly supported the bill, especially its provision allowing for the renewed expansion of slavery. Northern Democrats split on this issue; about half voted with the Whigs against the act, but the other half (for the sake of national unity and the belief that slavery would never take hold in Kansas in any case) joined with the South and passed the bill. The passage of the Kansas-Nebraska Act destroyed the Whig Party as well as the two-party system and set the national stage for renewed sectional struggle.

2.   Explore the importance of nativism to U.S. politics in the 1850s.

Answer: Political and social nativism were central to northeastern politics in the 1840s and 1850s. Massive immigration introduced a huge variety of ethnic backgrounds to those already populating the United States. Primarily Irish and German, usually Catholic, most often unskilled, the cultural and social values of these groups varied tremendously. Native-born Americans saw immigrants as outsiders, as threats to native skilled labor and to the social order. Many native-born northeasterners also saw the religious beliefs of immigrants (mainly Catholicism) as a despotic, backward, and repressive institution that they equated with slavery.

       These beliefs and fears led to one of the most powerful anti-immigrant movements in American history: the American Party, or the Know-Nothings. The Know-Nothings were essentially localist in nature and were most concerned with temperance and parochial schools at the state and local levels. They were a secretive party—hence their name—and they won several important state elections, primarily in the North. The movement eventually declined for two reasons: first, the increasing attention to the issue of slavery, and, second, the decline in immigration.

3.   Describe the issues surrounding the *Dred Scott* Supreme Court case of 1857. What was the effect of this decision on the nation?

Answer: Dred Scott was a slave from Missouri who sued for his freedom because his owner had taken him into free territories. After working its way through Missouri courts, the case reached the Supreme Court in 1856–57. The case tested whether Congress had the power to control slavery in the territories. The court, under the control of southerner Roger Taney, ruled that Congress did not have the power to keep slavery out of the territories, because slaves were property and therefore were protected by the Fifth Amendment to the Constitution.

       This decision had wide-ranging effects on American politics. It uplifted the South, which saw the decision as a triumph for slavery and the southern way of life. It angered northerners—even those who had little concern about slavery. It confirmed the northern belief that the government was controlled by a "slaveocracy," thus increasing their support for the Republican Party.

4.   Examine the important repercussions of John Brown's raid on Harpers Ferry.

Answer: Brown was an antislavery zealot. In 1856, he and several followers attacked and killed five proslavery advocates at Pottawatomie River during the fighting in "Bleeding Kansas." In October 1859,

Brown, hoping to foment slave rebellions throughout the South, led a raid on the arsenal town of Harpers Ferry, Virginia. Brown's plan was to gather guns and materials, move through the mountain ranges of the South, and bring about the collapse of southern slavery.

Brown and his followers were surrounded and captured at the arsenal, and they were soon hanged by the state of Virginia. The long-term repercussions of the failed plot were significant, however. In the South, the raid seemed to confirm widely held suspicions about the motives and desires of northerners, leading to the rise of southern militia units throughout southern states. In the North, Brown's actions were condemned, although he himself gained the stature of a martyr for the antislavery cause. This outpouring of northern sympathy enraged the people of the South, further deepening the sectional crisis.

5.   Describe the issues and events involved in "Bleeding Kansas."

Answer: In 1854 the Kansas-Nebraska Act organized and provided for popular sovereignty in the two territories. Kansas became a symbol for both pro- and antislavery advocates. A majority of the settlers who moved to Kansas came from northern states. Neighboring slaveowners from Missouri crossed into Kansas to vote for a proslavery government in the territorial election. Approximately five thousand illegal votes were cast, but President Franklin Pierce ignored the fraud and recognized the proslavery government. Free-soil settlers rejected the "bogus legislature" and elected an antislavery government that actually reflected the popular sovereignty of Kansas.

The national government was split over the issue with the president and Senate siding with the proslavery group and the House of Representatives supporting the free-soil government. The dispute turned violent when Senator Charles Sumner was attacked in the Senate by Representative Preston Brooks. Northerners declared Sumner a martyr and southerners hailed Brooks as a hero. A bloody civil war erupted in Kansas after a group of proslavery Missourians sacked the antislavery town of Lawrence, Kansas. In retaliation for the Lawrence raid, the grim abolitionist John Brown led an attack on a proslavery settlement and murdered five men. Acts of murder and vengeance were repeated over and over until President Pierce appointed a new territorial governor with 1,300 soldiers to quell the hostilities.

6.   Describe the free-labor ideology and the southern response to it.

Answer: Republican abolitionists believed in the nobility of work and created what historians call the "free-labor ideology." Antislavery advocates asserted that slavery demeaned honest labor. Slaves were forced to toil without compensation and they, therefore, took no pride in their work. In a free-labor system, independent laborers were motivated by ambition and therefore, worked efficiently and determinedly. Economic opportunities and upward mobility stimulated the Protestant virtues of hard work, frugality, and sobriety. Free workers achieved success and profited from their labors. This view was not necessarily an accurate description of the possibilities available to wage earners in the North, but it did reflect the commonly held ideals of northern society.

Southerners responded by pointing to free workers' complaints of low wages and mistreatment. They noted that strikes and violence were often a part of the labor movement in the North. Slaveowners contended that slaves were "taken care of" by their masters. George Fitzhugh, for example, claimed that slaves were better fed, housed, clothed, and had better medical care than northern industrial workers.

LONG ESSAYS

1.   Compare northern and southern images of each other and their own regions during the turbulent 1850s.

Answer: Essay should address several key points:

A.   The relationship between economic conditions and realities with ideologies, or world views, in each region by the 1850s
B.   Northern idea of "free labor" and its relationship to the antislavery position
    1.   Belief in capitalism, industry, individual initiative
    2.   Slavery as a threat to free, white laborers, as well as dehumanizing to blacks
    3.   Expansive northern economy depends on free labor

4. Slavery must be kept out of territories to allow free labor to expand

C. Southern proslavery argument (or slavery as a positive commodity)
    1. Description of paternalistic aspects of slavery
    2. Comparison of slavery to free labor
    3. Criticism of irregularities of northern economy

D. How these two world views (free labor versus proslavery) were related to the politics of the 1850s, and became motivating factors for behavior and argumentation between the two regions
    1. Southern attack on northern institutions:
        a. George Fitzhugh
        b. James Henry Hammond
    2. Northern attack on slaveholding South
        a. Abraham Lincoln
        b. William Seward
    3. Instances of conflict
        a. "Bleeding Kansas"
        b. *Dred Scott* decision
        c. Harpers Ferry

2. Examine the political crisis of the 1850s. What were the origins of this crisis, the central issues involved, and the repercussions for the United States?

Answer: Essay should address several key points:

A. Kansas-Nebraska Act (1854)
    1. Southern fear of being surrounded by free states
    2. Role of Stephen Douglas
    3. Repeal of Missouri Compromise
    4. Breakdown of Whig Party and national politics

B. Rise of alternative political parties
    1. Know-Nothing Party
    2. Republican Party and Free Soilers

C. Political breakdown in the mid-1850s
    1. "Bleeding Kansas"
    2. Lecompton Constitution
    3. *Dred Scott* decision
    4. Harpers Ferry

D. Repercussions
    1. Development of sectional parties
    2. Regional mistrust and threats of secession (1856)

3. Examine the Lincoln-Douglas debates. What were the issues examined and the two opponents' views on these issues? What effects did this have on politics in the late 1850s?

Answer: Essay should address several key points:

A. Setting for the debates
    1. Illinois senatorial election of 1858
    2. Backgrounds of Lincoln and Douglas

B. Issues debated
    1. Douglas's views on slavery—morally neutral
    2. Douglas as defender of the Constitution and popular sovereignty
    3. Lincoln on "free soil" and inhumanity of slavery
    4. Lincoln's "house divided" speech

C. Outcome
    1. National attention on debates
    2. Douglas wins election, but alienates southern wing of Democratic Party

3.   Lincoln emerges as major political figure

4.   Examine the Kansas-Nebraska Act and describe its role in pushing the nation closer to Civil War.

Answer: Essay should address several key points:

A.   Kansas-Nebraska Act
      1.   Provisions
            a.   Organization of the territories
            b.   Repeal of Missouri Compromise
            c.   Popular sovereignty
      2.   Douglas's motives
            a.   Southern support for presidency
            b.   Real estate holdings
            c.   Belief in expansion
      3.   Political consequences
            a.   Destruction of Whig Party
            b.   Creation of Republican Party
B.   "Bleeding Kansas"
      1.   Migration to Kansas
            a.   Proslavery settlers
            b.   Antislavery settlers
      2.   Territorial elections
            a.   Fraudulent proslavery election
            b.   Free-soil election
      3.   Violence
            a.   Caning of Sumner
            b.   Sacking of Lawrence
            c.   John Brown's raid on Pottawatomie
            d.   Military rule
C.   Lecompton Constitution
      1.   Proslavery constitutional convention
            a.   Rigged elections
            b.   "Fair" referendum
      2.   Free-Soil Constitution
            a.   Fair election
            b.   Voters reject both constitutions
      3.   Congressional debate
            a.   Senate votes yes
            b.   House votes no
            c.   Southerners and Douglas at odds

CHAPTER 15
SECESSION AND CIVIL WAR, 1860–1862

CHAPTER OUTLINE

I. The Election of 1860
   - A. The Republicans Nominate Lincoln
   - B. Southern Fears

II. The Lower South Secedes
   - A. Northerners Affirm the Union
   - B. Compromise Proposals
   - C. Establishment of the Confederacy
   - D. The Fort Sumter Issue

III. Choosing Sides
   - A. The Border States
   - B. The Creation of West Virginia
   - C. Indian Territory and the Southwest

IV. The Balance Sheet of War
   - A. Strategy and Morale
   - B. Mobilizing for War
   - C. Weapons and Tactics
   - D. Logistics
   - E. Financing the War

V. Navies, the Blockade, and Foreign Relations
   - A. King Cotton Diplomacy
   - B. The *Trent* Affair
   - C. The Confederate Navy
   - D. The *Monitor* and the *Virginia*

VI. Campaigns and Battles, 1861-1862
   - A. The Battle of Bull Run
   - B. Naval Operations
   - C. Fort Henry and Fort Donelson
   - D. The Battle of Shiloh
   - E. The Virginia Theater
   - F. The Seven Days' Battles

VII. Confederate Counteroffensives
   - A. The Second Battle of Bull Run

VIII. Conclusion

CHRONOLOGY

1858	William Seward delivers his "Irrepressible Conflict" speech.
1860	Democratic Party splits.
	Lincoln elected president.
	South Carolina secedes.
	United States Army occupies Fort Sumter.
1861	Crittenden Compromise fails to keep the Union together.
	Kansas becomes the thirty-fourth state.
	Ten states eventually join South Carolina to create the Confederate States of America.
	Jefferson Davis named president of the Confederacy.
	Fort Sumter falls and the Civil War begins.
	Union Navy blockades southern ports.
	Trent affair almost causes war between United States and Great Britain.

	Battle of Bull Run (July 21).
	George McClellan assumes command of the Army of the Potomac.
1862	Ulysses S. Grant's forces take Forts Henry and Donelson (February 6 and February 16).
	Battle of the *Virginia* and the *Monitor* marks a major change in naval warfare.
	Battle of Shiloh (April 6–7).
	Union Navy captures New Orleans.
	McClellan's peninsula campaign ends with the Seven Days' battles.
	Robert E. Lee assumes command of the Army of Northern Virginia.
	Second Battle of Bull Run (August 29–30).
1863	West Virginia becomes the thirty-fifth state.

THEMATIC TOPICS FOR ENRICHMENT

1. What economic stands did the Republicans take in 1860 that attracted northern voters?

2. Give the details of the Crittenden Compromise and explain why both Lincoln and the secessionists rejected the Compromise.

3. In what ways did the Confederate Constitution differ from the U.S. Constitution?

4. Discuss how Fort Sumter developed into a dilemma for both the Union and the Confederacy.

5. Discuss how each side in the Civil War attempted to finance its participation in the conflict. Why did the Confederacy fail in this regard?

6. Discuss military innovations in the Civil War and how they affected how battles were fought and wars were planned.

7. Explain why Union fortunes were better in western areas in 1862 than they were in the Virginia theater.

SUGGESTED ESSAY TOPICS

1. Why did both national political parties, the Whigs and the Democrats, ultimately split up on the years leading up to the Civil War?

2. Considering that Lincoln explicitly stated that he was not an abolitionist, why did South Carolina secede from the Union upon his election in 1860?

3. Assess the great difficulty in choosing sides as the Civil War broke out in 1861, particularly for residents of the border states.

4. Contrast Union and Confederate relative advantages in preparing to fight a protracted civil war. What did the Union have to do to win the war? What did the Confederacy need to do to gain its independence?

LECTURE OUTLINE

1. Although Lincoln won a clear electoral majority, the **election of 1860** was in many ways extraordinary; four candidates, Lincoln and Douglas of Illinois, Breckinridge of Kentucky, and Bell of Tennessee, representing three parties, vied for the presidency in what amounted to two separate elections.

a. Disaffection with the perceived radicalism of the major candidates led the Republicans to nominate **Abraham Lincoln,** the favorite son of the Chicago convention.

b. The nomination of Lincoln and the Republican platform did nothing to quell **southern fears** of the dangers posed by a Republican victory in the upcoming election.

2. Following the Electoral College's confirmation of Lincoln's victory, South Carolina led the **Lower South's secession** from the Union.

(SHOW TRANSPARENCY 71: ELECTION OF 1860 AND SOUTHERN SECESSION)

a. **Northerners affirmed the Union** by publicly supporting Lincoln and declaring secession unconstitutional.

b. Northerners and Southerners floated a number of compromise proposals, most notably that of **John J. Crittenden** of Kentucky, in a desperate effort to avert war in the first months of 1861.

3. Establishment of the **Confederacy** fell to a convention of seceded states that met in Montgomery, Alabama, in the beginning of February.

4. Lincoln brilliantly forced the hand of the Confederacy into firing the first shot of the Civil War at **Fort Sumter** on the morning of April 12, 1861.

5. For both states and individuals, **choosing sides** proved an agonizing dilemma with far-ranging consequences.

(SHOW TRANSPARENCY 72: PRINCIPAL MILITARY CAMPAIGNS OF THE CIVIL WAR)

a. In the aftermath of the firing on Fort Sumter, the **border states** were forced to choose sides, with Delaware, Kentucky, and Missouri choosing to remain in the Union.

b. The Unionist western counties of Virginia seceded from their state in the creation of **West Virginia.**

6. From men to money to material, the **balance sheet of war** seemed to favor the Union.

a. The Union's material advantages would not guarantee victory without **strategy and morale** equal to the daunting task at hand.

b. The prodigious numbers of volunteers on both sides made initial **mobilization for war** far less difficult than after the fighting had started in earnest.

c. The bloody engagements of the first years of the Civil War led to a revolution in the **weapons and tactics,** particularly as increasingly lethal weapons necessitated new battlefield tactics.

d. Many contemporaries called the Civil War the first "modern war" because of the incredibly complicated **logistics** involved in amassing, transporting, feeding, arming, and supplying the forces that fought on both sides.

e. **Financing the war** proved a struggle for both sides, with the North relying on printing paper money and the National Banking Act, and the Confederacy on anything and everything.

7.	The Civil War was not fought exclusively on land but with **navies and blockades and through foreign relations,** all of which ultimately proved advantageous for the Union.

    a.	The Confederacy mistakenly believed that **King Cotton diplomacy** would be its trump card, forcing the English into recognition of the Confederate States of America.

    b.	In the *Trent* **Affair** of October 1861, the Union almost so gravely insulted the English so as to lead them into assisting the Confederacy.

    c.	The **Confederate Navy** was composed largely of two purchased British vessels, the *Alabama* and the *Florida,* which captured or sank over 250 Union merchant vessels.

    d.	The *Monitor* and *Virginia,* both ironclads, dueled to a draw in their famed March 9, 1862, encounter.

8.	The **campaigns and battles of 1861–1862** proved that the war would not end quickly and that only great bloodshed and loss of life would bring the conflict to a conclusion.

    a.	With all the appearances of a smashing Union victory, the **Battle of Bull Run** on July 21, 1861, turned into a Confederate triumph when Thomas Jackson's Virginia brigade held its line, and General Johnston arrived from the Shenandoah Valley with reinforcements.

(SHOW TRANSPARENCY 73: BATTLE OF BULL RUN [MANASSAS], JULY 21, 1861)

    b.	Union **naval operations** resulted in a series of victories over Confederate coastal fortifications and the forced surrender of New Orleans to Admiral David G. Farragut.

    c.	Led by Ulysses S. Grant, combined Union forces won key victories at **Fort Henry and Fort Donelson** on the Tennessee and Cumberland rivers.

(SHOW TRANSPARENCY 74: KENTUCKY–TENNESSEE THEATER, WINTER–SPRING 1862)

    d.	Despite losses of some thirteen thousand men in two days of bloody fighting, the Union and Grant defeated Confederate forces at the **Battle of Shiloh** on April 6–7.

(SHOW TRANSPARENCY 75: BATTLE OF SHILOH, APRIL 6–7, 1862)

    e.	The Union's fortunes reversed dramatically in the spring of 1862 in the **Virginia theater,** as Johnston's army put McClellan's Army of the Potomac on the defensive and Jackson's "foot cavalry" wreaked havoc in the Shenandoah Valley.

    f.	In the **Seven Days' Battle** at the end of June 1862, Robert E. Lee's Army of Northern Virginia turned the momentum of the war in favor of the Confederacy by driving McClellan's larger force from the outskirts of Richmond back toward the James River.

(SHOW TRANSPARENCY 76: PENINSULA CAMPAIGN, APRIL–MAY 1862, AND SEVEN DAYS' BATTLE, JUNE 25–JULY 1, 1862)

9.	For the remainder of 1862, **Confederate counteroffensives** were designed to break the Union's will to fight, and at the **Second Battle of Bull Run,** the Confederates again demonstrated that Union victory, if it ever were to come, was a far way off.

(SHOW TRANSPARENCY 77: MAP, SECOND BATTLE OF MANASSAS [BULL RUN], AUGUST 29–30, 1862)

American Album: Confederate Dead on the Battlefield

Conclusion: The election of Lincoln and the subsequent secession of eleven southern states culminated in Civil War. Neither Lincoln nor any party—North or South—could have predicted in 1860 that within two years the country would be mired in a brutal war without any foreseeable end. Perhaps only a few abolitionists sensed that the war would spell the end of slavery in the United States.

TEACHING RESOURCES

The Civil War-episodes one, two, and three—by Ken Burns offers an award-winning account of the war's beginning and its first two years. PBS Video (99 minutes, 69 minutes, and 76 minutes, respectively).

The Divided Union: The American Civil War is a five-part history of the conflict. Filmic Archives (55 minutes each).

Civil War Journal, Volumes I and II, offers the history of the war using diary and letter excerpt to tell a more personal point of view of the conflict. Topics covered include social, military, political, and racial issues related to the war. (200 minutes total for each volume).

Ironclads: The Monitor *and the* Merrimac covers a turning point in naval history. Filmic Archives (30 minutes).

The Battle of Glorietta Pass: Gettysburg of the West recounts this battle in the West in 1862. Films for the Humanities & Sciences (28 minutes, black and white).

The Massachusetts 54th Colored Infantry illustrates the compelling story of African Americans' devotion to the Union as well as remarkable heroism. PBS Video (60 minutes).

MULTIPLE CHOICE

1. Who of the following did not run for the presidency in 1860?
    a. John C. Breckinridge
    b. Stephen Douglas
    c. William Seward
    d. John Bell
    e. Abraham Lincoln

ANS: C   TYPE: M   KEY 1: F   KEY 2: 1   PAGE: 466-67

2. The main plank of the Republican Party's 1860 platform called for
    a. a higher tariff.
    b. federal aid for railroad construction.
    c. a homestead act.
    d. abolishing the slave trade in Washington, D.C.
    e. exclusion of slavery from the territories.

ANS: E   TYPE: M   KEY 1: F   KEY 2: 2   PAGE: 467

3. Which of the following statements is not true about Abraham Lincoln's election in 1860?
    a. He was elected with southern support.
    b. He received less than 40 percent of the popular vote.
    c. He won every free state.
    d. He won by a substantial margin in the electoral college.
    e. He received more popular votes than Breckinridge.

ANS: A   TYPE: M   KEY 1: A   KEY 2: 1   PAGE: 470

4. According to the theory of secession,
   a. each state gave away its fundamental sovereignty and therefore was permanently subject to the Constitution.
   b. no state could withdraw from the union.
   c. no state had given away its fundamental sovereignty and therefore each could withdraw from the union.
   d. no state had ever given away its fundamental sovereignty, but each had to recognize the final authority of the federal government.
   e. secession could only be accomplished if a popular vote were held on the issue.

ANS: C   TYPE: M   KEY 1: A   KEY 2: 2   PAGE: 470

5. The Crittenden Compromise
   a. promised to protect slavery in all territories south of 36° 30'.
   b. guaranteed more representation to southern states in the House of Representatives.
   c. denied the right of slaveholders to be compensated for runaway slaves.
   d. argued for popular sovereignty on the slavery question.
   e. received strong support in the South.

ANS: A   TYPE: M   KEY 1: A   KEY 2: 2   PAGE: 471

6. The president of the Confederacy was
   a. Robert E. Lee.
   b. Alexander Stephens.
   c. Jefferson Davis.
   d. John C. Calhoun.
   e. Stonewall Jackson.

ANS: C   TYPE: M   KEY 1: F   KEY 2: 1   PAGE: 473

7. The Constitution of the Confederate States of America
   a. argued for the sovereignty of the Confederate government over that of the states.
   b. specifically denied the right of secession.
   c. guaranteed slavery in both the states and the territories.
   d. was significantly different from the U.S. Constitution.
   e. provided for the gradual abolition of slavery.

ANS: C   TYPE: M   KEY 1: A   KEY 2: 2   PAGE: 472-73

8. The Civil War began on April 12, 1861, at
   a. Bull Run.
   b. Fort Sumter.
   c. Fort Wagner.
   d. Lawrence, Kansas.
   e. Gettysburg.

ANS: B   TYPE: M   KEY 1: F   KEY 2: 1   PAGE: 474-75

9. Which of the following slave states did not secede from the United States?
   a. Kansas
   b. Kentucky
   c. Arkansas
   d. Tennessee
   e. Texas

ANS: B   TYPE: M   KEY 1: F   KEY 2: 2   PAGE: 475

10. Which of the following states entered the Union during the Civil War?
    a. Utah
    b. Oklahoma
    c. West Virginia
    d. Colorado
    e. Maine

ANS: C   TYPE: M   KEY 1: F   KEY 2: 2   PAGE: 477

11. Which was not a Northern military advantage over the South?
    a. large manpower advantages
    b. better commanding officers in the field
    c. industrial advantages
    d. transportation and communications advantages
    e. greater bank capital and wealth

ANS: B   TYPE: M   KEY 1: F   KEY 2: 1   PAGE: 477-78

12. To achieve victory, the Confederacy felt it had to
    a. "bring" the war to the North in order to dampen morale there.
    b. capture Washington, DC.
    c. defend the South from Northern armies.
    d. enlist aid from foreign governments.
    e. mobilize the Indians to fight the Union.

ANS: C   TYPE: M   KEY 1: A   KEY 2: 1   PAGE: 479

13. The Confederate war effort was financed primarily by
    a. war bonds.
    b. income taxes.
    c. tariffs.
    d. treasury notes.
    e. charitable contributions.

ANS: D   TYPE: M   KEY 1: F   KEY 2: 2   PAGE: 482

14. The Union war effort was financed primarily by
    a. war bonds.
    b. "greenbacks."
    c. tariffs.
    d. income taxes.
    e. charitable contributions.

ANS: A   TYPE: M   KEY 1: F   KEY 2: 2   PAGE: 483

15. The essence of "King Cotton Diplomacy" was
    a. to cut off the supply of cotton to the North (where it was essential to production) and to force Lincoln to the bargaining table.
    b. to cut off the supply of cotton to England (where it was essential to production) and gain British recognition of the Confederacy.
    c. to sell Southern cotton abroad and use it for collateral for loans to purchase war materials.
    d. to use the lure of cotton exports to win support from France.
    e. to reopen the African slave trade and increase cotton production.

ANS: B   TYPE: M   KEY 1: A   KEY 2: 3   PAGE: 483-84

16. The *Trent* Affair
    a. almost ended the Civil War before it began.
    b. was as close as the South came to winning the war.
    c. almost ruptured British–American relations.
    d. broke off relations between the South and Britain.
    e. prevented the South from shipping cotton to South America.

ANS: C   **TYPE: M**   **KEY 1: F**   **KEY 2: 2**   **PAGE: 484-85**

17. The first significant battle of the Civil War took place at
    a. Bull Run.
    b. Harpers Ferry.
    c. Shiloh.
    d. Seven Pines.
    e. Gettysburg.

ANS: A   **TYPE: M**   **KEY 1: F**   **KEY 2: 2**   **PAGE: 487**

18. One of the major problems faced by Union armies during the campaigns of 1862 was
    a. poor training and inexperience of the troops.
    b. inadequate supplies and war materials.
    c. resistance to the draft.
    d. Lincoln's hesitancy in pressing the war effort.
    e. McClellan's reluctance to fight.

ANS: E   **TYPE: M**   **KEY 1: F**   **KEY 2: 2**   **PAGE: 489**

19. The reputation of General Ulysses S. Grant was established in 1862
    a. because of his brilliant service under McClellan in Virginia.
    b. with his stirring victories at Forts Donelson and Henry in Tennessee.
    c. with his important victory at Perryville.
    d. in defeat, at Bull Run.
    e. with his victory at Gettysburg.

ANS: B   **TYPE: M**   **KEY 1: A**   **KEY 2: 2**   **PAGE: 489-90**

20. The appointment of _____ to command Confederate armies in Virginia marked a turning point in the Civil War.
    a. Thomas "Stonewall" Jackson
    b. J. E. B. Stuart
    c. Robert E. Lee
    d. Joseph Johnston
    e. Jefferson Davis

ANS: C   **TYPE: M**   **KEY 1: F**   **KEY 2: 1**   **PAGE: 492**

21. At the Battle of the Seven Days, Confederate armies prevented George McClellan from capturing which vital Southern city?
    a. Atlanta
    b. Charleston
    c. Richmond
    d. New Orleans
    e. Memphis

ANS: C   **TYPE: M**   **KEY 1: F**   **KEY 2: 2**   **PAGE: 492-93**

22. The Northern ship, *Monitor,* faced what Southern ironclad ship in the famous naval battle of 1861?
    a. the *Virginia*
    b. the *Alabama*
    c. the *Carolina*
    d. the *Georgia*
    e. the *Confederate*

ANS: A   TYPE: M   KEY 1: F   KEY 2: 1   PAGE: 486-87

23. One of the most feared Southern raiding ships was
    a. the *Alabama.*
    b. the *Virginia.*
    c. the *Merrimac.*
    d. the *Carolina.*
    e. the *Rebel*

ANS: A   TYPE: M   KEY 1: F   KEY 2: 1   PAGE: 486

24. Abraham Lincoln's rival for the Republican nomination in 1860 was
    a. Salmon Chase.
    b. William Seward.
    c. Henry Stanton.
    d. Charles Sumner.
    e. John Brown.

ANS: B   TYPE: M   KEY 1: F   KEY 2: 2   PAGE: 467

25. By the fall of 1860, all of the following national organizations had split into Northern and Southern factions except
    a. the Republican Party.
    b. the Democratic Party.
    c. the Baptist Church.
    d. the Methodist Church.
    e. several voluntary associations.

ANS: A   TYPE: M   KEY 1: F   KEY 2: 3   PAGE: 465

26. Abraham Lincoln was nominated for the presidency by the Republican Party in 1860 because
    a. he had a reputation as a radical opponent of slavery.
    b. his wealthy family funded an expensive grassroots campaign for the nomination.
    c. he had the support of southern Republicans.
    d. his strong public stand on immigration restrictions would attract nativist voters to the Republican Party.
    e. he was a moderate whose career symbolized the economic opportunities possible in a free-labor system.

ANS: E   TYPE: M   KEY 1: A   KEY 2: 2   PAGE: 467

27. On the issue of secession, most Northerners agreed that
    a. the union was a voluntary association and therefore could be dissolved.
    b. the Southern states were an economic drain on the nation and so the North would actually profit from secession.
    c. secession was unconstitutional, treasonable, and impossible.
    d. the issue should be decided by the Supreme Court, not by the president.
    e. the issue should be decided by a nationwide referendum.

ANS: C   TYPE: M   KEY 1: F   KEY 2: 2   PAGE: 470

28. Jefferson Davis was chosen president of the Confederacy because he was
    a. the most outspoken of the radical secessionists.
    b. a nephew of George Washington and would therefore make the Confederacy seem more respectable.
    c. a moderate who had extensive military and political experience.
    d. the only person who wanted to assume the office.
    e. from the North.

ANS: C   TYPE: M   KEY 1: F   KEY 2: 2   PAGE: 473

29. South Carolina attacked Fort Sumter when
    a. the Union navy blockaded Charleston Harbor.
    b. Lincoln announced his plan to peacefully resupply the fort.
    c. soldiers from the fort fired on local fishermen.
    d. Secretary of War Edwin Stanton declared the seceded state "in rebellion."
    e. southern sympathizers were executed in the North.

ANS: B   TYPE: M   KEY 1: F   KEY 2: 2   PAGE: 474-75

30. Robert E. Lee joined the Confederacy because he
    a. was offered more money by the Confederacy than he was making in the Union military.
    b. owned over two hundred slaves and feared that he would be bankrupted if they were freed.
    c. believed the Southern states had a constitutional right to secede from the Union.
    d. was anxious to help weaken the North.
    e. loved his home state of Virginia and could not fight against it.

ANS: E   TYPE: M   KEY 1: A   KEY 2: 2   PAGE: 475

31. During the Civil War, the state of Missouri
    a. seceded and joined the Confederacy.
    b. was invaded by Confederate troops and remained under their military control.
    c. was torn by a vicious guerrilla war between Confederate bushwhackers and Union jayhawkers.
    d. contributed more men to the Union Army than any other state.
    e. attempted to create a western confederacy.

ANS: C   TYPE: M   KEY 1: F   KEY 2: 3   PAGE: 476-77

32. Many of the civilized Native Americans in Indian Territory (Oklahoma)
    a. owned slaves and thus sided with the Confederacy.
    b. ignored the Civil War completely.
    c. took advantage of the Civil War by killing all the white people in the area.
    d. moved further west to avoid being drawn into the conflict.
    e. sued for the right to fight in the Union army.

ANS: A   TYPE: M   KEY 1: F   KEY 2: 2   PAGE: 477

33. At the beginning of the war, the Confederacy benefited from its
    a. loyal slaves, many of whom were recruited as soldiers.
    b. friendly relations with European countries that gave money and supplies to the "new nation."
    c. calm and reasonable leaders who created sympathy for "the cause" among Northern conservatives.
    d. rural traditions of hunting and riding that prepared its population for military activities.
    e. large numbers of factories.

ANS: D   **TYPE: M**   **KEY 1: F**   **KEY 2: 3**   **PAGE: 479**

34. The Civil War is considered the first modern war because
    a. it was the first internal rebellion in a major nation.
    b. modern weapons such as machine guns and hand grenades were introduced.
    c. new forms of communication and transportation (railroads, telegraph, and steamships) played an important role.
    d. it affected all segments of society.
    e. of the relative lack of bloodship.

ANS: C   **TYPE: M**   **KEY 1: F**   **KEY 2: 3**   **PAGE: 481**

35. The first battle of the "ironclads" at Hampton Roads was significant because
    a. the Confederate navy lost its only metal-plated ship and never built another.
    b. it proved that steam-powered ships were too dangerous to use in coastal waters.
    c. it was the biggest Union naval victory of the war.
    d. it demonstrated that the age of wooden ships was over, and a new era of naval technology had begun.
    e. it proved the effectiveness of submarine warfare.

ANS: D   **TYPE: M**   **KEY 1: A**   **KEY 2: 3**   **PAGE: 487**

36. The Anaconda Plan was
    a. Secretary of State William Seward's program for ensuring the loyalty of the Anaconda Indians during the war.
    b. General Winfield Scott's strategy for encircling and squeezing the South into submission.
    c. a congressional design for building dams and flood controls on the Anaconda River.
    d. the Confederate battle plan for the attack at Bull Run.
    e. a Union plan for financing the war effort.

ANS: B   **TYPE: M**   **KEY 1: F**   **KEY 2: 2**   **PAGE: 487**

37. Which of the following was true of Ulysses S. Grant?
    a. He was known as "the young Napoleon" because he was short but successful.
    b. He was such a perfectionist that he was hesitant to commit his troops to battle.
    c. He lost fewer men in battle than any other Union general.
    d. He secretly supported the South.
    e. His determination and willingness to take risks brought him victories at Forts Henry and Donelson in Tennessee.

ANS: E   **TYPE: M**   **KEY 1: F**   **KEY 2: 2**   **PAGE: 489-90**

38. About _____ of the Union's wartime revenue came from selling war bonds.
    a. two-thirds
    b. one-half
    c. three-quarters
    d. four-fifths
    e. nine-tenths

ANS: A   **TYPE: M**   **KEY 1: F**   **KEY 2: 3**   **PAGE: 483**

39. The 1860 Republican Party platform called for all of the following except
    a. a higher tariff.
    b. a homestead act.
    c. abolition.
    d. federal aid for a transcontinental railroad.
    e. federal program to improve river transportation.

ANS: E   **TYPE: M**   **KEY 1: A**   **KEY 2: 2**   **PAGE: 467**

40. John Bell won all of the following states in the election of 1860 except
    a. Missouri.
    b. Kentucky.
    c. Virginia.
    d. Tennessee.
    e. none of the above

ANS: A   **TYPE: M**   **KEY 1: F**   **KEY 2: 3**   **PAGE: 470**

41. The Constitution of the Confederate States of America was drawn up in
    a. Atlanta, Georgia.
    b. Montgomery, Alabama.
    c. Richmond, Virginia.
    d. Charleston, South Carolina.
    e. Austin, Texas

ANS: B   **TYPE: M**   **KEY 1: F**   **KEY 2: 3**   **PAGE: 472**

42. _____ of the white population in the border states (Delaware, Maryland, Kentucky, and Missouri) favored the Union.
    a. one-quarter
    b. one-half
    c. two-thirds
    d. three-quarters
    e. nine-tenths

ANS: C   **TYPE: M**   **KEY 1: FA**   **KEY 2: 3**   **PAGE: 477**

43. The total Confederate population of 9 million included _____ slaves.
    a. 1.6 million
    b. 2.1 million
    c. 2.9 million
    d. 1 million
    e. 3.7 million

ANS: E   **TYPE: M**   **KEY 1: F**   **KEY 2: 2**   **PAGE: 477**

44. George B. McClellan commanded the Army of the Potomac for
    a. six months.
    b. one year.
    c. two years.
    d. three years.
    e. nine years

ANS: B   TYPE: M   KEY 1: F   KEY 2: 3   PAGE: 489

45. William L. Yancey and Edmund Ruffin
    a. were prominent secessionists who founded the League of United Southerners.
    b. were the first two volunteers from South Carolina when the war started.
    c. tried to arrange a compromise Democratic candidate in 1860 who would bridge sectional differences.
    d. were early backers of Abraham Lincoln for president in 1860.
    e. were members of Lincoln's cabinet.

ANS: A   TYPE: M   KEY 1: F   KEY 2: 3   PAGE: 467

46. John C. Breckinridge ran for president in 1860 under the banner of the _____ Party.
    a. Whig
    b. Southern Rights Democratic
    c. Democratic
    d. Republican
    e. American

ANS: B   TYPE: M   KEY 1: F   KEY 2: 2   PAGE: 467

47. Before 1860 southerners had
    a. controlled the presidency most of the time.
    b. been a majority on the Supreme Court.
    c. provided the leadership of both the House.
    d. provided the leadership of the Senate.
    e. all of the above.

ANS: E   TYPE: M   KEY 1: A   KEY 2: 2   PAGE: 468

48. Lincoln opposed the Crittenden Compromise because he feared that it would
    a. lead to southern filibustering to take Cuba and other southern lands.
    b. bring the British into the war.
    c. surrender all of the western territories to the South.
    d. reunite the Democratic Party.
    e. cause war with Mexico.

ANS: A   TYPE: M   KEY 1: A   KEY 2: 3   PAGE: 471

49. Under the National Banking Act of 1863, national banks issued bank notes based on
    a. the amount of gold that they held on deposit.
    b. the level of federal taxation.
    c. the amount of state bank notes that they held.
    d. the foreign exchange rate.
    e. the value of U.S. bonds that they held.

ANS: E   TYPE: M   KEY 1: A   KEY 2: 3   PAGE: 483

50. The Confederate economy suffered from
    a. extremely high rates of inflation.
    b. severe deflation.
    c. exorbitant income taxes.
    d. overproduction.
    e. high import duties

ANS: A   **TYPE: M**   **KEY 1: A**   **KEY 2: 2**   **PAGE: 483**

TRUE/FALSE

_____ 1.   The Republican platform of 1860 called for the abolition of slavery.

ANS: F   **TYPE: T**   **KEY 1: F**   **KEY 2: 1**   **PAGE: 467**

_____ 2.   The president who immediately preceded Abraham Lincoln in office was Millard Fillmore.

ANS: F   **TYPE: T**   **KEY 1: F**   **KEY 2: 3**   **PAGE: 470**

_____ 3.   South Carolina seceded from the union in 1860 because the state viewed Lincoln as an enemy to slavery.

ANS: T   **TYPE: T**   **KEY 1: A**   **KEY 2: 1**   **PAGE: 468-71**

_____ 4.   All states with slaves seceded from the union between 1860 and 1861.

ANS: F   **TYPE: T**   **KEY 1: F**   **KEY 2: 2**   **PAGE: 475**

_____ 5.   Leaders of the Union and the Confederacy both foresaw a long, bloody struggle as war began in 1861.

ANS: F   **TYPE: T**   **KEY 1: A**   **KEY 2: 2**   **PAGE: 475**

_____ 6.   The Democratic Party split into two factions before the election of 1860.

ANS: T   **TYPE: T**   **KEY 1: F**   **KEY 2: 1**   **PAGE: 467**

_____ 7.   The Civil War began when Abraham Lincoln attempted to reinforce Fort Sumter with more Union troops, which was viewed as an act of war by the South.

ANS: F   **TYPE: T**   **KEY 1: F**   **KEY 2: 2**   **PAGE: 474-75**

_____ 8.   Maryland and Missouri were the only two slave states that did not secede.

ANS: F   **TYPE: T**   **KEY 1: F**   **KEY 2: 2**   **PAGE: 475**

_____ 9.   The Crittenden Compromise essentially repudiated the Republican platform of 1860.

ANS: T   **TYPE: T**   **KEY 1: A**   **KEY 2: 3**   **PAGE: 471-72**

_____ 10.   The Battle of Seven Pines was a Union victory.

ANS: F   **TYPE: T**   **KEY 1: F**   **KEY 2: 3**   **PAGE: 492**

_____ 11.   The Battle of Shiloh hurt Ulysses S. Grant's image.

ANS: T   TYPE: T   KEY 1: A   KEY 2: 3   PAGE: 491-92

_____ 12.   The delegates at the Southern secession conventions voted unanimously in favor of withdrawing from the Union.

ANS: F   TYPE: T   KEY 1: F   KEY 2: 2   PAGE: 470

_____ 13.   Southerners defended their withdrawal from the Union by asserting that the leaders of the American Revolution were also secessionists.

ANS: T   TYPE: T   KEY 1: A   KEY 2: 2   PAGE: 471

_____ 14.   Members of the postwar James/Younger gang were Confederate bushwhackers during the Civil War.

ANS: T   TYPE: T   KEY 1: F   KEY 2: 2   PAGE: 477

_____ 15.   Citizens of both the Union and the Confederacy believed they were defending their nation, flag, Constitution, and liberty.

ANS: T   TYPE: T   KEY 1: F   KEY 2: 2   PAGE: 475

_____ 16.   The Battle of Shiloh began as a likely Union victory.

ANS: F   TYPE: T   KEY 1: A   KEY 2: 2   PAGE: 491-92

_____ 17.   The 1860 Democratic platform endorsed popular sovereignty.

ANS: T   TYPE: T   KEY 1: F   KEY 2: 2   PAGE: 467

_____ 18.   Constitutional Union Party presidential candidate John Bell had no chance of winning the election of 1860.

ANS: T   TYPE: T   KEY 1: F   KEY 2: 1   PAGE: 467

_____ 19.   The South's voluntary embargo of cotton exports suggested to British and French diplomats that the Union blockade was at least partly effective.

ANS: T   TYPE: T   KEY 1: A   KEY 2: 1   PAGE: 484

_____ 20.   Southerners considered the Republican pledge not to interfere with slavery in the states meaningless.

ANS: T   TYPE: T   KEY 1: F   KEY 2: 2   PAGE: 468

_____ 21.   Although Stephen Douglas came in second in the popular vote in 1860, he carried only one state.

ANS: T   TYPE: T   KEY 1: A   KEY 2: 2   PAGE: 470

_____ 22.   James Buchanan was president when the first state seceded.

ANS: T   TYPE: T   KEY 1: F   KEY 2: 2   PAGE: 470

_____ 23.   The crisis at Fort Sumter began while Abraham Lincoln was president.

ANS: F   **TYPE: T**   **KEY 1: F**   **KEY 2: 3**   **PAGE: 473**

_____ 24.   The Confederacy reaped great profits from the sale of the 1861 cotton crop.

ANS: F   **TYPE: T**   **KEY 1: A**   **KEY 2: 3**   **PAGE: 484**

_____ 25.   Over the course of the Civil War, a larger proportion of the North's male population of
                 military age served in the military than did in the South.

ANS: F   **TYPE: T**   **KEY 1: A**   **KEY 2: 3**   **PAGE: 478**

_____ 26.   Had the Confederacy lost the war in the spring of 1862, the South might have returned to
                 the Union with slavery intact.

ANS: T   **TYPE: T**   **KEY 1: A**   **KEY 2: 3**   **PAGE: 496**

_____ 27.   Democratic Party rules in effect gave Southerners veto power over the selection of the
                 party's presidential nominee.

ANS: T   **TYPE: T**   **KEY 1: F**   **KEY 2: 3**   **PAGE: 466**

_____ 28.   Southern Democrats embraced Stephen A. Douglas as a possible presidential nominee in
                 1860.

ANS: F   **TYPE: T**   **KEY 1: A**   **KEY 2: 3**   **PAGE: 466**

_____ 29.   Stephen A. Douglas supported a federal slave code for the territories.

ANS: F   **TYPE: T**   **KEY 1: A**   **KEY 2: 2**   **PAGE: 466**

_____ 30.   The 1860 Republican platform was designed to appeal to many groups in the North.

ANS: T   **TYPE: T**   **KEY 1: A**   **KEY 2: 2**   **PAGE: 467**

_____ 31.   The Republican platform in 1860 proved especially attractive to young people.

ANS: T   **TYPE: T**   **KEY 1: A**   **KEY 2: 2**   **PAGE: 467**

_____ 32.   Southern moderates were convinced that secession was not inevitable if Abraham
                 Lincoln was elected president in 1860.

ANS: F   **TYPE: T**   **KEY 1: A**   **KEY 2: 3**   **PAGE: 468**

_____ 33.   European monarchists and conservatives were distressed at the idea of Southern
                 secession leading to the breakup of the United States.

ANS: F   **TYPE: T**   **KEY 1: A**   **KEY 2: 1**   **PAGE: 471**

_____ 34.   All Republicans insisted that slavery be kept out of all future territories, even if doing so
                 destroyed the Union.

ANS: F   **TYPE: T**   **KEY 1: A**   **KEY 2: 3**   **PAGE: 471-72**

_____ 35.   The Crittenden Compromise never had a chance of winning congressional passage.

ANS: F   TYPE: T   KEY 1: A   KEY 2: 2   PAGE: 471-72

_____ 36.   Lincoln instituted a Union blockade of Confederate ports three months after the surrender of Fort Sumter.

ANS: F   TYPE: T   KEY 1: A   KEY 2: 3   PAGE: 475, 483

_____ 37.   Seceded states did not seize federal property within their borders.

ANS: F   TYPE: T   KEY 1: F   KEY 2: 1   PAGE: 473

_____ 38.   Lincoln's cabinet advised him not to withdraw the federal troops from Fort Sumter.

ANS: F   TYPE: T   KEY 1: F   KEY 2: 2   PAGE: 474

_____ 39.   The siege at Fort Sumter lasted for ten days.

ANS: F   TYPE: T   KEY 1: F   KEY 2: 1   PAGE: 475

_____ 40.   Lincoln's initial call for military volunteers yielded only half the number of recruits he had requested.

ANS: F   TYPE: T   KEY 1: F   KEY 2: 2   PAGE: 475

FILL-INS

1.   The vice president of the Confederacy was _____.

ANS: Alexander Stephens   TYPE: F   KEY 1: F   KEY 2: 3   PAGE: 473

2.   The first state to secede from the union was _____.

ANS: South Carolina   TYPE: F   KEY 1: F   KEY 2: 2   PAGE: 470

3.   The young, heralded commander-in-chief of the Army of the Potomac in 1861 was

_____.

ANS: George B. McClellan   TYPE: F   KEY 1: F   KEY 2: 2   PAGE: 487

4.   The victorious forces at the Second Battle of Bull Run were _____.

ANS: Confederates   TYPE: F   KEY 1: F   KEY 2: 2   PAGE: 494

5.   The government measure that modernized the American monetary system was the

_____.

ANS: National Banking Act   TYPE: F   KEY 1: A   KEY 2: 3   PAGE: 483

6.   A total of _____ states passed secession ordinances and joined the Confederate States of America.

ANS: eleven   TYPE: F   KEY 1: F   KEY 2: 3   PAGE: 475

7. The _____ was a series of five proposed constitutional amendments that would have protected slavery in the states and in the territories south of 36°30'.

ANS: Crittenden Compromise   **TYPE: F**   **KEY 1: F**   **KEY 2: 2**   **PAGE: 471-72**

8. The slave states that sided with the Union in the Civil War were called the _____.

ANS: border states   **TYPE: F**   **KEY 1: F**   **KEY 2: 1**   **PAGE: 475**

9. As 1860 began, the _____ Party was one of the few national institutions left in the United States.

ANS: Democratic   **TYPE: F**   **KEY 1: F**   **KEY 2: 2**   **PAGE: 465**

10. William L. Yancey and Edmund Ruffin founded the _____ .

ANS: League of United Southerners   **TYPE: F**   **KEY 1: F**   **KEY 2: 3**   **PAGE: 466**

11. As the election of 1860 approached, the Republicans' leading presidential prospect was _____.

ANS: William H. Seward   **TYPE: F**   **KEY 1: F**   **KEY 2: 2**   **PAGE: 467**

12. The only state that Stephen Douglas carried in 1860 was _____.

ANS: Missouri   **TYPE: F**   **KEY 1: F**   **KEY 2: 3**   **PAGE: 470**

13. _____ refused Southern requests to withdraw federal troops from Fort Sumter.

ANS: James Buchanan   **TYPE: F**   **KEY 1: F**   **KEY 2: 3**   **PAGE: 473**

14. The most lethal weapon of Civil War battles was the _____.

ANS: infantry rifle   **TYPE: F**   **KEY 1: F**   **KEY 2: 2**   **PAGE: 481**

15. General-in-Chief of the United States Army Winfield Scott was from _____.

ANS: Virginia   **TYPE: F**   **KEY 1: F**   **KEY 2: 3**   **PAGE: 487**

16. In May 1861 the Confederacy moved its capital to _____.

ANS: Richmond, Virginia   **TYPE: F**   **KEY 1: F**   **KEY 2: 1**   **PAGE: 487**

17. Stonewall Jackson earned his nickname at the Battle of _____.

ANS: Bull Run (or Manassas)   **TYPE: F**   **KEY 1: F**   **KEY 2: 2**   **PAGE: 487**

18. _____ captured New Orleans for the Union in April 1862.

ANS: David G. Farragut   **TYPE: F**   **KEY 1: F**   **KEY 2: 2**   **PAGE: 489**

19. Most whites in the South voted for _____ in 1860.

ANS: John C. Breckinridge   **TYPE: F**   **KEY 1: F**   **KEY 2: 2**   **PAGE: 470**

20. Major _____ commanded the federal garrison at Fort Sumter.

ANS: Robert Anderson   **TYPE: F**   **KEY 1: F**   **KEY 2: 2**   **PAGE: 473**

21. _____ was the highest-ranking general on either side to be killed during the Civil War.

ANS: Albert Sidney Johnston   **TYPE: F**   **KEY 1: F**   **KEY 2: 3**   **PAGE: 491**

22. The appointment of _____ as commander of what came to be called the Army of Northern Virginia marked a turning point in the Shenandoah campaign.

ANS: Robert E. Lee   **TYPE: F**   **KEY 1: A**   **KEY 2: 3**   **PAGE: 492**

23. In the election of 1860, John Bell was nominated by the _____ Party.

ANS: Constitutional Union   **TYPE: F**   **KEY 1: F**   **KEY 2: 2**   **PAGE: 467**

24. The conflict at Fort Sumter resulted in victory for the _____.

ANS: Confederacy   **TYPE: F**   **KEY 1: F**   **KEY 2: 2**   **PAGE: 475**

25. During the Civil War, the Confederate forces that pushed into New Mexico were made up primarily of men from _____.

ANS: Texas   **TYPE: F**   **KEY 1: F**   **KEY 2: 3**   **PAGE: 477**

26. A new kind of tax authorized by the U.S. Congress during the Civil War was the _____ tax.

ANS: income   **TYPE: F**   **KEY 1: F**   **KEY 2: 3**   **PAGE: 483**

27. The U.S. Secretary of State during the Civil War was _____.

ANS: William Seward   **TYPE: F**   **KEY 1: F**   **KEY 2: 3**   **PAGE: 484**

28. The Union Commander who prevailed at the Battle of Shiloh was _____.

ANS: U.S. Grant   **TYPE: F`**   **KEY 1: F**   **KEY 2: 2**   **PAGE: 491-92**

29. The President when the southern states began seceding was _____.

ANS: James Buchanan   **TYPE: F**   **KEY 1: F**   **KEY 2:2**   **PAGE: 470**

30. John J. Crittenden, the man who led the compromise efforts before the Civil War came from the state of _____.

ANS: Kentucky   **TYPE: F**   **KEY 1: F**   **KEY 2: 3**   **PAGE: 471**

IDENTIFICATIONS

1. **Jefferson Davis**: moderate secessionist from Mississippi. West Point graduate. Officer in U.S. Army in the Mexican War. Secretary of war for President Franklin Pierce. President of the Confederacy.

2. **National Banking Act**: part of the Republican economic program, rationalized and modernized the American monetary system by issuing stable currency and controlling inflationary state banks.

3. **George B. McClellan**: Union commander, superb organizer and trainer of Army of the Potomac. Reluctant to take risks in the field. Replaced in the fall of 1862 because of his caution and inaction.

4. **border states**: originally four in number. Kentucky, Delaware, Maryland, and Missouri were joined in 1863 by the new state of West Virginia. These states remained loyal to the Union but allowed slavery and were sharply divided at the outbreak of the war.

5. **Crittenden Compromise**: compromise proposal put forward by Senator John Crittenden to resolve the secession crisis. Proposed amendments guaranteed that the federal government would not interfere with slavery in the states and protected slavery in the territories south of 36°30'.

6. **Battle of Glorieta Pass**: took place in March 1862 in New Mexico. Confederates from Texas invaded New Mexico but were stopped by Colorado miners who marched through the Rockies to save the region. The battle was inconclusive, but the Confederates lost their supplies and had to abandon New Mexico.

7. **King Cotton diplomacy**: Confederate foreign policy based on idea that Britain and other European nations needed Southern cotton so badly that they would intervene to keep Southern ports open. Poor planning and bad judgment doomed it to failure.

8. **Anaconda Plan**: Union General Winfield Scott's strategy for defeating the South by blockading the Southern ports and taking control of the Mississippi River. Named after the South American snake that encircles its prey and squeezes it to death.

9. *Trent* **Affair**: diplomatic tussle in the fall of 1861. Occurred when two Confederate diplomats, James Mason and John Slidell, were forcibly removed from a British mail steamer, arrested, and taken to Boston. The incident sparked outrage in England and demands for an apology and the release of Mason and Slidell. Although calls for war were heard on both sides of the Atlantic, calm was restored when the Lincoln administration distanced itself from the seizures and released the two Confederates.

10. **Robert E. Lee.** Confederate commander of the Army of Northern Virginia who brilliantly defended Richmond and won the loyalty of his men.

SHORT ESSAYS

1. Examine the election of 1860. What were the issues that divided the two parties? How were these issues resolved?

Answer: The major issue was slavery. The Republican Party adopted a platform demanding exclusion of slavery from the territories. The Democratic Party was split: the southern wing demanded a federal slave code for the territories; the northern and western wings rejected this and endorsed popular sovereignty. The party broke up and two different Democratic candidates came forward: Stephen Douglas (representing the North and West) and John C. Breckinridge (representing the South).

The election turned into a four-way race. Besides the two Democrats, the Republicans endorsed Abraham Lincoln (considered a moderate on race issues), and John Bell, who ran for the Constitutional Union Party (a coalition of former Whigs who found the Republicans too radical). Lincoln won the election with less than 40 percent of the popular vote but a landslide in the electoral college. His election, of course, led directly to the secession of seven southern states.

2. Explore the diplomatic efforts of both the Confederacy and the Union to enlist foreign support. Which side was more successful?

Answer: Both North and South felt they needed strong foreign support if their cause was to be successful. The Union simply wanted Great Britain and France to refuse diplomatic recognition of the Confederacy, and also to refuse military aid and loans to them. Very important here was the role played by Minister to Great Britain Charles F. Adams. Adams was particularly important during the *Trent* Affair, when relations between the United States and Great Britain reached their lowest point since the War of 1812. The Confederacy was less successful in foreign affairs. It needed the support of England (money and material), and attempted to force the issue through "King Cotton diplomacy," hoping to deprive Britain of cotton and force it to aid the Confederate cause, a policy that failed. The Union was more successful, particularly after the Emancipation Proclamation, which appealed to humanitarian sentiments in western Europe.

3.   Examine the various attempts on the part of the Union and the Confederacy to finance their war efforts.

Answer: The Union and the Confederacy used similar measures to finance their military efforts, but in varying degrees and with different results. The North had a far more powerful and diverse economy, enabling that region to muster greater financial strength. Both used some combination of war bonds (loans), taxation, and paper money. Paper money, the most dangerous because of its inflationary potential, was the primary method employed by the Confederacy (financing 60 percent of its war effort), mainly because it had no choice. This led to a 9,000 percent inflation rate and fiscal chaos. Confederate attempts to finance the war were utter failures.

The Union, on the other hand, raised most of its revenue by selling war bonds (66 percent of its finances were raised this way). Taxation and paper money were used in far smaller measures and, as a result, inflation over the war years was "only" 80 percent. In addition, the Union passed the National Banking Act, which helped to rationalize and modernize the American monetary system.

4.   Naval strategies formed an integral part of the early war effort. Describe the goals and strategies of the North and then discuss the Southern response.

Answer: The major naval strategy of the North was to blockade Southern ports and prevent the export of cotton in return for military supplies as well as prevent the import of other goods. The task was daunting: The Southern coastline covered over 3,500 miles. In 1861, nine of ten vessels carrying Southern exports or foreign imports eluded capture. By 1862, however, the blockade was fairly successful, helping the North to squeeze the Southern economy further, causing shortages and runaway price growth.

The South's response to the blockade was limited by several factors (specifically money and ships necessary to run the blockade). The South, however, was able to purchase two vessels from England, (the *Alabama* being the most feared by the North). These raiding ships inflicted severe damage on Union merchant vessels. But this was ineffectual in lifting the blockade, a factor in the slow destruction of the Confederacy.

5.   Examine the establishment of the Confederacy in 1860. Compare and contrast the new government with that of the Union.

Answer: At first, the Confederacy consisted of seven Southern states that seceded from the Union following Lincoln's election. The constitution of the new government was a virtual copy of the original U.S. Constitution except for several important distinctions. First, it contained clauses that guaranteed slavery in the territories and in the states. Second, it championed and reaffirmed the idea of states' rights. Third, it prohibited the government from implementing a protective tariff. The presidency was extended to six years, but was limited to a single term.

The new government attempted to appeal to moderate influences by electing moderate secessionists, like Jefferson Davis and Alexander Stephens, to its highest offices. One of the primary problems the new government faced was apparent immediately: the tension between some sort of central control and state sovereignty. Ultimately, this was one of the Confederacy's overwhelming flaws.

6.   Examine the Crittenden Compromise. Why was it rejected by the Republicans?

Answer: In December 1860, Senator John J. Crittenden proposed a series of compromises that he hoped would halt the secessionist movement. The Crittenden Compromise included amendments protecting slavery in the states, forbidding the prohibition of slavery on federal property, eliminating federal authority over the interstate slave trade, paying slaveowners for their runaway slaves, and protecting slavery in the territories south of the old Missouri Compromise line. The last of the proposals would permit southern slave culture to expand southward into Central America and the Caribbean. Many Republicans considered the compromise an acceptable means of preserving the union. But Lincoln—who had been elected on a free-soil platform—sent word to Republican congressmen to reject any compromise on the extension of slavery into the territories. The compromise therefore failed to pass Congress. In February 1861, a peace convention held in Washington drew up proposals similar to the Crittenden Compromise, but they were also rejected by Congress. The time for compromise had passed.

7.   Describe the first battle of the ironclads and assess its significance.

Answer: The Union navy was mostly superior to the Confederate, but the Southerners challenged the North in innovation and experimentation. Confederates were pioneers in the effective use of metal-plated ships. The first ironclad was the C.S.S. *Virginia*, usually referred to as the *Merrimac*. It was a badly damaged Union vessel that was salvaged, covered with armor, and renamed. The Confederates hoped the *Merrimac/Virginia* would break open the Northern blockade at Hampton Roads. On the first two days of battle, the ironclad sank two Union ships and ran several aground. The armor plating was impervious to Union shot and shell.

The North soon had an ironclad of its own, the U.S.S. *Monitor*. The Union vessel had a revolving turret and was in better condition than its Confederate counterpart. The *Virginia* and the *Monitor* met in a lengthy battle that ended in a draw. Both sides continued building ironclads, thus ushering in a new period of naval technology.

LONG ESSAYS

1.   Examine the secession crisis and the various attempts at compromise to avert the dissolution of the Union. Do you believe that secession could have been avoided in 1860? Why or why not?

Answer: Essay should address several key points:

A.   Slavery and the territories
         1.   Role of federal government in legislating slavery
         2.   Sectional debate on slavery in territories
B.   Election of 1860
         1.   Republican platform and territorial slavery
         2.   Southern fear of Republican victory
C.   Secession crisis
         1.   Role of South Carolina
         2.   Political theory of secession (John C. Calhoun)
         3.   North's unfavorable view of secession
D.   Attempts to avert crisis
         1.   Crittenden Compromise
         2.   Washington Peace Convention
E.   Fort Sumter
         1.   Buchanan and compromise
         2.   Lincoln and resupplying
         3.   Confederate attack

2.   Compare Northern and Southern advantages and disadvantages at the beginning of the Civil War.

Answer: Essay should address several key points:

A.   Northern advantages
1.   Industrial strength
2.   Transportation capabilities
        a.   Twice as many railroad miles
        b.   Economic and military consequences
3.   Population advantage
        a.   Three times as many soldiers
        b.   Larger pool of potential workers
4.   Financial power

B.   Northern disadvantages
1.   Large-scale offensive war
2.   Vague motivation
3.   Divisions within North

C.   Southern advantages
1.   Defensive military strategy
        a.   Fighting to protect home
        b.   Home front conditions
2.   Patriotic motivation
        a.   Clear cause and purpose
        b.   Sense of nationhood
3.   Superior military commanders

D.   Southern disadvantages
1.   Limited industrial capabilities
2.   Small number of troop reinforcements
3.   Problems in financing war effort

3.   Explore the early campaigns and strategies of 1861 and 1862. What were the goals of both the Union and the Confederacy? Could the war have ended at this early point?

Answer: Essay should address several key points:

A.   Southern military goals
1.   Defensive strategy
2.   Wear Union down
3.   Occasional forays into Northern territory

B.   Northern goals
1.   Early end to the war
2.   Capture Richmond
3.   Defeat Southern armies in the field

C.   Early campaigns
1.   Southern victory at Bull Run
        a.   Northern disbelief
        b.   Reassessment of war strategy
2.   McClellan and command of Union forces
        a.   Superb training of Union troops
        b.   McClellan's reluctance to deploy army
3.   Grant and western theaters
        a.   Control of Tennessee
        b.   Shiloh
4.   Robert E. Lee and Army of Northern Virginia

CHAPTER 16
A NEW BIRTH OF FREEDOM, 1862–1865

CHAPTER OUTLINE

CHRONOLOGY

1862	Confederacy enacts conscription (April 16).
	Battle of Antietam (September 17).
	Lincoln issues the preliminary Emancipation Proclamation (September 22).
	Battle of Fredericksburg (December 13).
	Homestead Act and Morrill Act pass.
	Battle of Stones River (December 31–January 2).
1863	Lincoln signs the final Emancipation Proclamation (January 1).

Union enacts conscription (March 3).
Food riots break out in the Confederacy (April).
Battle of Chancellorsville (May 1–5).
Battle of Gettysburg (July 1–3).
Vicksburg falls to Grant's besieging army (July 4).
Port Hudson surrenders (July 9).
Draft riots erupt in New York City (July 13–16).
Battle of Chickamauga (September 19–20).
Battle of Chattanooga (November 24–25).

1864   Grant becomes the Union's general in chief.
Battle of the Wilderness (May 5–6).
Battle of Spotsylvania (May 8–19).
Siege of Petersburg begins (June).

1864   Atlanta falls to William T. Sherman's army (September 1).
Philip Sheridan's forces rout Confederates from the Shenandoah Valley (October).
Lincoln wins reelection (November).
Sherman begins his march to the sea.
Battles of Franklin (November 30) and Nashville (December 15–16) cripple the Confederates.

1865   Lee surrenders to Grant at Appomattox (April 9).
Lincoln is assassinated (April 14).
Last Confederate army surrenders (June 23).
Thirteenth Amendment is ratified (December).

THEMATIC TOPICS FOR ENRICHMENT

1. Explain the writ of *habeas corpus* and why the Lincoln administration suspended it on occasion during the war.

2. Discuss the Clement L. Vallandigham affair and how it became an issue of treason versus freedom of speech.

3. Why are the battle of Gettysburg and the fall of Vicksburg often considered the turning point of the Civil War?

4. Discuss how black men became involved in the Union war effort and how they fared.

5. Describe how each side handled prisoners of war and how treatment of prisoners became a major controversy.

6. Why did General Sherman march across Georgia, and what were the results of his campaign?

SUGGESTED ESSAY TOPICS

1. Trace the course of the military campaign in the eastern theater from Antietam to Appomattox, noting key battles and Union command changes as you go.

2. Discuss the impact of the war on the Union and Confederate "home fronts." Note economic issues, draft policy, and the roles of women.

3. Explain the considerations that led Lincoln to issue the Emancipation Proclamation. Discuss its overall impact on the war effort.

1.   Lincoln's decision to issue an emancipation proclamation led directly to a **new birth of freedom** while it radically enlarged the scope and purpose of the war and raised difficult questions concerning the future of the Union.

2.   Both sides initially tried to sidestep the **issue of slavery,** but as time passed many northerners came to see a strike against it as a means of defeating the South.

    a.   Slaves themselves helped force the issue by fleeing to Union lines where they were allowed to remain on grounds that they were **"contraband"** of war.

    b.   Lincoln's efforts to persuade border-state leaders to accept **"compensated emancipation"** met with abstinence and failure.

    c.   Slave-owner recalcitrance and calls from various advisors for tougher action led Lincoln to make a decision **for full emancipation.**

        i.   Lincoln further reasoned that emancipation would enhance northern resolve and be well received by foreign nations.

        ii.   Lincoln made his decision in July 1862 but was advised to **wait until** his armies had scored a **military success,** lest the policy look like a move of desperation.

    d.   Lincoln called for 300,000 **new federal troops** and 300,000 more militiamen in the summer of 1862.

    e.   General Lee, following upon his victory at Second Bull Run, came north in September in a campaign that climaxed at the **Battle of Antietam.**

(SHOW TRANSPARENCY 78: LEE'S INVASION OF MARYLAND 1862; AND BATTLE OF ANTIETAM, SEPTEMBER 17, 1862)

        i.   Numerous things went wrong for the Confederates; most notably, a copy of **Lee's orders** was found and given to General McClellan.

        ii.   Twenty-three thousand combined casualties made September 17, 1862, the **bloodiest single day of the war.**

    f.   Though in many ways a draw, Lee's forces had retreated. The Union claimed victory, and Lincoln issued the **Emancipation Proclamation.**

3.   Several developments made 1862–1863 a **winter of discontent.**

    a.   Antietam encouraged Lincoln to remove McClellan. His replacement, Ambrose Burnside, launched a frontal assault on the heights of **Fredericksburg** that was repulsed with heavy casualties.

    b.   The **Copperheads,** antiwar northern Democrats, called for the cessation of hostilities and recognition of southern independence.

    c.   While the North struggled with low morale, southerners faced chronic food shortages which at times exploded into **food riots.**

d. In both the South (1862) and North (1863), wartime drafts were met with contempt by poorer elements, who resented exemptions afforded the wealthy.

    i. Southern **plantation owners were often excused** so as to keep watch over the slaves and prevent uprisings.

    ii. **Wealthy northerners could avoid the draft** by simply paying $300.00 as a commutation fee.

e. Closer historical examination reveals that the war was **not exclusively a poor man's fight,** however.

4. The Thirty-seventh Congress enacted three laws which provided what historians have called a **blueprint for modern America.**

a. The **Homestead Act** granted farmers 160-acre homesteads, virtually free, provided they lived thereupon and made efforts to improve the land.

b. The **Morrill Act** gave states thousands of acres of land with which to establish colleges.

c. The **Pacific Railroad Ac**t granted land and loans to railroad companies so as to spur the growth of transcontinental lines.

5. The war also offered many **opportunities to women,** which bolstered the fledgling women's rights movement.

a. Their most notable achievement was likely the formation of the **United States Sanitary Commission,** which supplied nurses to army hospitals.

b. Some women served in war industries, others joined the civil service, still more served as spies, and **some actually enlisted** (posing as men).

6. The summer of 1863 is often considered the **high tide of the Confederacy.**

a. Lee's defeat of Joseph Hooker at **Chancellorsville** that May owed to Lee's bold, aggressive reaction and Hooker's loss of nerve.

(SHOW TRANSPARENCY 79: BATTLE OF CHANCELLORSVILLE, MAY 2–6,1863)

b. Another Confederate invasion of the North climaxed from July 1 to 3, 1863, when Lee's army clashed with that of Hooker's replacement, George Meade, at **Gettysburg,** one of the greatest battles of American history.

(SHOW TRANSPARENCY 80: BATTLE OF GETTYSBURG, JULY 1–3,1863)

    i. Three times Lee attempted to dislodge Union forces from a series of hills east of the town, first attacking the northern and southern ends of the line, before assaulting the center in the quixotic **Pickett's charge.**

    ii. In three days of fighting, fifty thousand men perished. Lee's army limped back to Virginia.

c. Grant's successful conclusion of the **Vicksburg campaign** coincided with Lee's retreat from Gettysburg.

(SHOW TRANSPARENCY 81: VICKSBURG CAMPAIGN, APRIL–JULY, 1863)

d.   Just a few months later, in September, Union forces under William Rosecrans captured **Chattanooga.**

    i.   With reinforcements from the Army of Northern Virginia, Braxton Bragg was able to spring a trap on Rosecrans at **Chickamauga.**

(SHOW TRANSPARENCY 82: ROAD TO CHICKAMAUGA, JUNE–SEPTEMBER, 1863)

    ii.   Lincoln reinforced Chattanooga with troops from Virginia and the Vicksburg campaign and **brought in Grant,** who drove Confederate forces off the surrounding heights in November.

7.   The Emancipation Proclamation had reinforced calls for the enlistment of **black men in the Union armies.**

(SHOW TRANSPARENCY 83: BLACK SOLDIERS IN THE UNION ARMY)

a.   Initially envisioned as garrison and supply forces, black regiments would themselves **push for the opportunity of combat.**

    i.   In May and June 1863, black troops fought well in the campaign for **Port Hudson.**

    ii.   The **54th Massachusetts** gallantly assaulted Fort Wagner (South Carolina) that July, suffering fifty percent casualties in a failed effort.

b.   Continued military victories were the principal factors in **confirming emancipation policy,** leading to Congressional approval of the 13th Amendment by the end of 1864.

8.   Many southerners succumbed to defeatism during the trying winter of 1863–1864. More would do so in the following **"year of decision."**

a.   Confederate armies continued to resist, hoping that a **war of attrition** could tap antiwar sentiments, weaken northern wills, and prompt voters to oust Lincoln in the 1864 election in favor of a "peace Democrat."

b.   Grant, now general in chief, struck southward from Washington in early May. In two days of hellish fighting, the Confederates inflicted severe casualties on Grant's forces in the **"Wilderness."**

(SHOW TRANSPARENCY 84: BATTLES OF THE WILDERNESS AND SPOTSYLVANIA, MAY 5–12, 1864)

c.   **Grant did not retreat,** unlike earlier commanders. Instead, he regrouped and again attempted to outflank Lee.

    i.   In mid-May, assaults against Confederate entrenchments at **Spotsylvania** again produced high Union casualties.

    ii.   On June 3, an ill-advised assault at **Cold Harbor** led to Union casualties reminiscent of Gettysburg.

d.   Grant eventually settled into what would become a nine-month siege of Petersburg, having suffered **sixty-five thousand total casualties** since May.

e.	In the West, **William Tecumsah Sherman** gradually pushed Joseph Johnston's forces back toward Atlanta.

    i.	An impatient Jefferson Davis replaced Johnston with **John Bell Hood,** who launched three futile offensives, severely weakening his forces.

    ii.	Sherman placed **Atlanta under siege.**

(SHOW TRANSPARENCY 85: CAMPAIGN FOR ATLANTA, MAY–SEPTEMBER, 1864)

f.	The Confederate attrition strategy seemed to be working, evidenced not only by Democratic opposition but also by **growing dissent** among the Republicans.

    i.	The **Democrats nominated George McClellan,** who called for an immediate cessation of hostilities.

    ii.	**Lincoln himself despaired** that he would be badly beaten in his attempt at reelection, unless something drastic changed.

g.	Controversy over **prisoners of war** was further complicating matters for Lincoln.

    i.	The most ghastly example of their suffering came at **Andersonville,** a "hellhole" in which nearly thirteen thousand soldiers died.

    ii.	Lincoln resisted southern offers of **prisoner exchanges** until early 1865, however, largely because the South refused to include black troops in the proposals.

h.	A desperate Confederacy decided upon **recruiting slaves to fight,** but the war ended before any such regiments were organized.

9.	An improved military situation eventually ensured the **reelection of Lincoln and the end of the Confederacy.**

(SHOW TRANSPARENCY 86: ELECTION OF 1864)

a.	Sherman's **capture of Atlanta** from Hood's depleted forces in September was both a symbolic and substantive victory.

b.	Further Union success came in the **Shenandoah Valley.**

    i.	Philip Sheridan sought not only to drive Jubal Early's forces from the valley but also to **deprive the Confederacy of the area's resources.**

    ii.	Sheridan's men thoroughly destroyed the region and routed Early in a series of battles climaxing at **Cedar Creek** in October.

c.	**The Confederate leadership resolved to keep fighting.** Sherman, who had long pondered the nature of war, resolved to convince them otherwise.

d.	**Sherman marched southward** 280 miles from Atlanta to Savannah, his sixty thousand men wrecking almost everything in their path.

e.	Hood marched his forces northward, where he sacrificed the bulk of his men in attacks at **Franklin and Nashville.**

f.   The capture of **Fort Fisher** in January 1865 closed the Confederacy's last open port (Wilmington, North Carolina).

(SHOW TRANSPARENCY 87: HOOD'S TENNESSEE CAMPAIGN, OCTOBER–NOVEMBER 1864; NASHVILLE, DECEMBER 15–16, 1864)

g.   Sherman's forces headed **northward through the Carolinas,** inflicting even more destruction than they had wrought upon Georgia.

h.   Grant, meanwhile, finally pressured Lee out of Richmond and Petersburg. Lee fled westward, only to have his remnant force cornered near **Appomattox.** On April 9, 1865, Lee surrendered.

i.   Northern celebrations soon turned to mourning, however, following the **assassination of Lincoln** on April 14.

Conclusion: The Civil War resolved two fundamental questions. The first involved the elimination of slavery. The second involved the superiority of federal authority to that of the states. Such resolution came at a cost of over 600,000 lives.

TEACHING RESOURCES

The Civil War—episodes four through nine—by Ken Burns offers an award-winning account of the war's middle and closing years. PBS Video (62 minutes, 95 minutes, 70 minutes, 72 minutes, 69 minutes, and 68 minutes, respectively).

The Red Badge of Courage is a feature film of Stephen Crane's classic novel, directed by John Huston and starring Audie Murphy. Filmic Archives (69 minutes).

Smithsonian's *Great Battles of the Civil War* is a six-part series that offers narration by James M. McPherson and documentation of each major battle of the war. Filmic Archives.

Royal Federal Blues provides the most comprehensive account of African-American participation in the Civil War. Filmic Archives (30 minutes).

Glory is a feature film, starring Denzel Washington, about the 54th Massachusetts Infantry. Filmic Archives (120 minutes).

Lincoln is a four-part series about the president. Filmic Archives (240 minutes total).

Great Generals of the South focuses on Robert E. Lee and Stonewall Jackson. Filmic Archives (60 minutes).

Civil War Journal – Volume 2 has episode on women in the Civil War

MULTIPLE CHOICE

1.   The prisoner-of-war issue became a serious problem
     a. after the Union began organizing regiments of former slaves.
     b. during the election of 1864.
     c. after the original prison compounds filled up.
     d. because of both sides' plans for mass executions of prisoners.
     e. when the Union began deporting prisoners to Mexico.

ANS: A   **TYPE: M**   **KEY 1: A**   **KEY 2: 2**   **PAGE: 525-26**

2. Contraband of war referred to
   a. military equipment captured by the Confederacy.
   b. escaped slaves.
   c. shipments of war material from abroad.
   d. stolen food.
   e. a secret code.

ANS: B   TYPE: M   KEY 1: F   KEY 2: 2   PAGE: 500

3. The single bloodiest day in American history took place at what Maryland battlefield?
   a. Shiloh
   b. Wilderness
   c. Antietam
   d. Chancellorsville
   e. Fort Sumter

ANS: C   TYPE: M   KEY 1: F   KEY 2: 1   PAGE: 504

4. Which of the following was not accomplished by the Union victory at Antietam?
   a. It convinced England to withhold recognition of the Confederacy.
   b. Northern Democrats failed to gain control of the House.
   c. The Confederates retreated across the Potomac.
   d. It led Lincoln to issue the Emancipation Proclamation.
   e. It led to the elevation of Robert E. Lee as commander of Confederate forces.

ANS: E   TYPE: M   KEY 1: A   KEY 2: 3   PAGE: 505

5. The Emancipation Proclamation
   a. ended slavery in the border states.
   b. officially ended slavery in the United States.
   c. ended slavery in areas in rebellion.
   d. ended slavery in Confederate states under Union occupation.
   e. ended slavery only in national territories.

ANS: C   TYPE: M   KEY 1: F   KEY 2: 2   PAGE: 505-06

6. The foremost Peace Democrat in the United States (eventually banished to the Confederacy) was
   a. Clement Vallandigham.
   b. Edward Everett.
   c. Ben Butler.
   d. Horatio Seymour.
   e. William Lloyd Garrison.

ANS: A   TYPE: M   KEY 1: F   KEY 2: 2   PAGE: 507

7. The main problem faced by the Confederacy during the war was
   a. poor military and governmental leadership.
   b. low morale.
   c. threat of slave revolts.
   d. food shortages and hyperinflation.
   e. inability to dispatch troops to fight the north directly.

ANS: D   TYPE: M   KEY 1: F   KEY 2: 2   PAGE: 508

8. One of the most common denunciations of the Union draft of 1863 was
    a. that it made the war a fight to end slavery.
    b. that it was a "rich man's war and a poor man's fight."
    c. that blacks would be forced to fight to save white lives.
    d. that it was illegal.
    e. it was too expensive.

ANS: B   TYPE: M   KEY 1: F   KEY 2: 2   PAGE: 509

9. The race riots of the summer of 1863 were a result of
    a. the Emancipation Proclamation.
    b. the draft.
    c. Confederate victories at Chancellorsville.
    d. decreasing support for Lincoln.
    e. black migration from the South.

ANS: B   TYPE: M   KEY 1: F   KEY 2: 1   PAGE: 509-10

10. In what area did women make the most visible impact during the war?
    a. war industries
    b. taking control of plantations
    c. clerical roles
    d. medicine
    e. the arts

ANS: D   TYPE: M   KEY 1: F   KEY 2: 2   PAGE: 510-11

11. Initially, black troops were recruited in the North in order to
    a. make it clear that this was a war about equal rights.
    b. show the ability of black troops.
    c. inspire slave insurrections in the South.
    d. free up white men for domestic jobs.
    e. answer the need for more troops.

ANS: E   TYPE: M   KEY 1: A   KEY 2: 1   PAGE: 518

12. The most celebrated black regiment in the Union army was the
    a. 10th Maine.
    b. 54th Massachusetts.
    c. 7th New York.
    d. 39th Illinois.
    e. Texas 5th.

ANS: B   TYPE: M   KEY 1: F   KEY 2: 1   PAGE: 518

13. The Thirteenth Amendment
    a. finally gave African Americans the right to vote.
    b. ended slavery.
    c. took the vote away from Confederate officials.
    d. outlawed segregation.
    e. gave women the vote.

ANS: B   TYPE: M   KEY 1: F   KEY 2: 1   PAGE: 520

14. By 1863, Confederate President Jefferson Davis
    a. had become a very popular and heroic figure.
    b. had the complete support of Confederate governors.
    c. was an able commander-in-chief.
    d. had been executed.
    e. was losing respect and support throughout the South.

ANS: E   **TYPE: M**   **KEY 1: A**   **KEY 2: 2**   **PAGE: 520**

15. Grant's strategy as general-in-chief was
    a. to make occasional probes against the enemy and then quickly retreat.
    b. to take Richmond.
    c. to make constant attacks against Confederate forces on all fronts.
    d. to avoid an all-out military showdown.
    e. to wait the Confederacy out.

ANS: C   **TYPE: M**   **KEY 1: A**   **KEY 2: 2**   **PAGE: 520-21**

16. Through 1864, Northerners were _____ about the war effort.
    a. frustrated
    b. suspicious
    c. confident
    d. confused
    e. angry

ANS: A   **TYPE: M**   **KEY 1: A**   **KEY 2: 2**   **PAGE: 520**

17. Which of the following battles was not a Union victory?
    a. Vicksburg
    b. Chickamauga
    c. Gettysburg
    d. Antietam
    e. Chattanooga

ANS: B   **TYPE: M**   **KEY 1: F**   **KEY 2: 3**   **PAGE: 504, 513, 514**

18. The Democratic candidate for president in 1864 was
    a. Abraham Lincoln.
    b. Ulysses Grant.
    c. Stephen Douglas.
    d. George McClellan.
    e. James Buchanan.

ANS: D   **TYPE: M**   **KEY 1: F**   **KEY 2: 1**   **PAGE: 524-25**

19. The Southern prison camp where 13,000 Union soldiers died was
    a. Shiloh.
    b. Andersonville.
    c. Franklin.
    d. Shenandoah.
    e. Chickamauga

ANS: B   **TYPE: M**   **KEY 1: F**   **KEY 2: 1**   **PAGE: 525**

20. The man most often associated with the "total war" is
    a. William T. Sherman.
    b. Ulysses S. Grant.
    c. Robert E. Lee.
    d. Thomas "Stonewall" Jackson.
    e. George McClellan.

ANS: A   **TYPE: M**   **KEY 1: F**   **KEY 2: 2**   **PAGE: 527**

21. Robert E. Lee surrendered his Army of Northern Virginia in
    a. Petersburg.
    b. Richmond.
    c. Appomattox.
    d. Manassas.
    e. Atlanta.

ANS: C   **TYPE: M**   **KEY 1: F**   **KEY 2: 1**   **PAGE: 529-30**

22. At the beginning of the Civil War most Northerners
    a. hoped to add Mexican territory to the Union.
    b. were indifferent to the issues and avoided the draft.
    c. were determined to free the slaves.
    d. felt that the South should be allowed to secede.
    e. agreed they were fighting to preserve the Union.

ANS: A   **TYPE: M**   **KEY 1: A**   **KEY 2: 2**   **PAGE: 500**

23. The Civil War was a "total war" in that
    a. the entire citizenry of both the North and the South were totally dedicated to victory.
    b. the entire Southern male population aged 18 to 25 was either killed or wounded.
    c. the North mobilized all its resources in order to destroy all the Southern resources.
    d. the motives of the Union were totally noble.
    e. it marked the first use of bombs to destroy cities.

ANS: C   **TYPE: M**   **KEY 1: F**   **KEY 2: 2**   **PAGE: 499**

24. Lincoln issued the Emancipation Proclamation for all of the following reasons except
    a. to quiet abolitionists who were pressuring him to make a strong statement on the subject.
    b. because the border states rejected his plan for compensation and gradual emancipation.
    c. because he truly believed that the "monstrous" institution of slavery should be outlawed.
    d. as a means to save the Union
    e. in order to win British support for the Union.

ANS: E   **TYPE: M**   **KEY 1: F**   **KEY 2: 3**   **PAGE: 501-02**

25. The Twenty Negro Law
    a. replaced the three-fifths rule as the method of counting slaves for representation purposes.
    b. gave a draft exemption for one white man on each plantation that owned at least twenty slaves.
    c. provided that no more than twenty Negroes per week could be liberated by the Union Army.
    d. assigned free blacks and fugitive slaves to white military units in groups of twenty or more.
    e. required each plantation to sent twenty Negroes to help the army.

ANS: B   **TYPE: M**   **KEY 1: F**   **KEY 2: 2**   **PAGE: 508**

26. All except which of the following were true of the draft in both the North and the South?
    a. It caused protests, violence, and class conflicts.
    b. Those who could afford it could hire a replacement and thereby avoid service.
    c. The age limit was set at 45.
    d. Only poor men were subject to conscription.
    e. Both sides resorted to the draft because of a shortage of available troops.

ANS: D   TYPE: M   KEY 1: F   KEY 2: 3   PAGE: 508-10

27. During the Civil War, Congress created a "blueprint for modern America" with
    a. the Homestead Act, which provided 160 acres of free land to those who lived on it for five years.
    b. Civil Rights Acts that protected the voting rights of free black Americans.
    c. the passage of the Emancipation Proclamation.
    d. plans for aid to business.
    e. plans for building skyscrapers in northern cities.

ANS: A   TYPE: M   KEY 1: F   KEY 2: 2   PAGE: 510

28. Northern women contributed to the war effort by
    a. sitting at home patiently waiting for their men to return.
    b. donating money to establish retirement homes for veterans.
    c. picketing the White House and demanding that Congress stop the war.
    d. working in factories, offices and hospitals.
    e. providing entertainment for the troops.

ANS: D   TYPE: M   KEY 1: F   KEY 2: 2   PAGE: 510-11

29. At Gettysburg, General Robert E. Lee
    a. ordered the complete destruction of the town in retaliation for the townspeople's disloyalty.
    b. lost fewer men than the Union did.
    c. deserted his troops.
    d. was drunk in his tent during the battle.
    e. believed his army was invincible and therefore ordered the disastrous Pickett's charge.

ANS: C   TYPE: M   KEY 1: A   KEY 2: 2   PAGE: 513-14

30. The 54th Massachusetts Infantry was
    a. a black regiment that fought bravely and suffered heavy casualties at Fort Wagner.
    b. the only black battalion in the Union Army.
    c. the honor guard for President Lincoln.
    d. commanded by William Tecumseh Sherman at Vicksburg.
    e. responsible for the Union victory at Gettysburg.

ANS: A   TYPE: M   KEY 1: F   KEY 2: 2   PAGE: 518

31. The Confederate strategy for winning the war in 1864 included
    a. a full-scale invasion of the North in order to take control of the border states.
    b. besieging Washington, DC and capturing Abraham Lincoln and his cabinet.
    c. the assassination of Lincoln and the leading Union Generals Grant and Sherman.
    d. continuing the war until the presidential election in the North and exhausting the North's will to fight.
    e. mobilizing their European allies to fight.

ANS: D   TYPE: M   KEY 1: F   KEY 2: 2   PAGE: 520

32. The peace initiatives of 1864 failed because
    a. by this time neither side was willing to compromise on the issues of secession and slavery.
    b. the South believed Ulysses S. Grant was an incompetent drunk who could not possibly defeat Robert E. Lee.
    c. Lincoln was bitter over the rising Union casualty rate and wanted to kill as many Confederates as possible.
    d. the Northern press and public totally opposed any attempt to reconcile with the South.
    e. Lincoln was too anxious to compromise with the South.

ANS: A   **TYPE: M**   **KEY 1: A**   **KEY 2: 3**   **PAGE: 522-25**

33. Which of the following represents the Confederacy's position on the possibility of recruiting slaves for the Southern armies?
    a. The Confederate government never even considered such a ridiculous idea.
    b. Throughout the war, each Confederate battalion included one regiment of noncombat black troops to do menial labor jobs.
    c. A few weeks before the end of the war, the Confederate Congress authorized the recruitment of black soldiers.
    d. Jefferson Davis vetoed a bill that offered slaves freedom in return for military service.
    e. slaves were recruited to fight for the Confederacy from the beginning of the war.

ANS: C   **TYPE: M**   **KEY 1: F**   **KEY 2: 3**   **PAGE: 526**

34. In both Northern and Southern prisoner of war camps,
    a. prisoners were held for an average of five months and then exchanged or released.
    b. thousands died from exposure, overcrowding, and malnutrition.
    c. at least half of the prisoners were executed for trying to escape.
    d. the International Red Cross assured that prisoners were treated humanely.
    e. few prisoners were taken and so the camps were unnecessary.

ANS: B   **TYPE: M**   **KEY 1: F**   **KEY 2: 3**   **PAGE: 525-26**

35. General William T. Sherman's tactics included
    a. hit-and-run guerrilla attacks to harass Southern armies.
    b. terrorist bombings and assassinations.
    c. destruction of both military and nonmilitary facilities in order to crush the spirit of the civilians.
    d. murdering civilians.
    e. waiting until the Confederates attack and then fighting back aggressively.

ANS: C   **TYPE: M**   **KEY 1: F**   **KEY 2: 3**   **PAGE: 527**

36. All except which of the following were results of the Civil War?
    a. Slavery was abolished.
    b. The concept of secession was discredited.
    c. Power in national politics was transferred from the South to the North.
    d. The states' rights philosophy was upheld.
    e. The South was left impoverished.

ANS: D   **TYPE: M**   **KEY 1: A**   **KEY 2: 3**   **PAGE: 531**

37. Early in the war, Frederick Douglass argued that
    a. the South should be allowed to secede so that the North could become a nation truly dedicated to equality.
    b. foreign aid would be necessary to win the war.
    c. Union commanders must return slaves to their masters until a decision was made for emancipation.
    d. Lincoln should be impeached for his refusal to issue an emancipation proclamation.
    e. the North must fight a war against slavery as well as against slaveholders.

ANS: E   TYPE: M   KEY 1: A   KEY 2: 2   PAGE: 500

38. "Copperheads" were
    a. fugitive slaves who came into Union army camps.
    b. Republicans who opposed Lincoln because he refused to emancipate the slaves.
    c. Peace Democrats.
    d. Union army commanders who adopted the tactic of total war the South.
    e. abolitionists.

ANS: C   TYPE: M   KEY 1: F   KEY 2: 2   PAGE: 507

39. Once President Lincoln had decided to issue the Emancipation Proclamation, he delayed
    a. hoping for a military victory.
    b. expecting the South to surrender.
    c. until a new Union commander could be found who would support his decision.
    d. until after the election of 1864.
    e. until the British entered the war.

ANS: A   TYPE: M   KEY 1: F   KEY 2: 3   PAGE: 502

40. Lincoln suspended the writ of habeas corpus in order to
    a. arrest deserters from the Union army.
    b. hold fugitive slaves without bail.
    c. arrest rioters and antiwar activists.
    d. execute Confederate commanders.
    e. arrest his political opponents.

ANS: C   TYPE: M   KEY 1: A   KEY 2: 3   PAGE: 502

41. Lincoln removed General McClellan from his command because
    a. he failed to move aggressively against the Confederate forces.
    b. he was corrupt.
    c. he was a Democrat.
    d. he was a slave owner himself.
    e. he was a drunk.

ANS: A   TYPE: M   KEY 1: A   KEY 2: 2   PAGE: 506

42. Once the Emancipation Proclamation had been issued Democrats
    a. gave it their full support.
    b. demanded its retraction.
    c. did not attempt to use it as a political issue.
    d. insisted that blacks be given full equality in the North as well as in the South.
    e. tried to use it to get the British involved in the war effort.

ANS: B   TYPE: M   KEY 1: A   KEY 2: 2   PAGE: 507

43. In the North Democrats generally
    a. supported the draft.
    b. did not take a stand on the draft.
    c. pushed for a provision that allowed wealthy men to buy their way out of the draft.
    d. supported the draft for blacks but not for whites.
    e. opposed the draft.

ANS: E   TYPE: M   KEY 1: F   KEY 2: 2   PAGE: 507

44. Bounty jumpers were men who
    a. changed political parties for a bribe.
    b. deserted the Confederacy and joined the Union army.
    c. enlisted for the bounty and then deserted.
    d. were slaves who left the plantations to join the Union army.
    e. supported the abolition of slavery.

ANS: C   TYPE: M   KEY 1: F   KEY 2: 3   PAGE: 509

45. The Morrill Land-Grant College Act
    a. established colleges for the freed slaves.
    b. created a national university.
    c. provided scholarships for poor students.
    d. created technical colleges in the North.
    d. gave states land to fund colleges.

ANS: E   TYPE: M   KEY 1: F   KEY 2: 2   PAGE: 510

46. As a result of the Confederate victory at Chancellorsville
    a. opposition to Lincoln grew in the North.
    b. efforts were renewed to gain British recognition of the Confederacy.
    c. Lee decided to invade the North.
    d. Stonewall Jackson was accidentally shot by his own men.
    e. all of the above.

ANS: E   TYPE: M   KEY 1: A   KEY 2: 3   PAGE: 512

47. At the Battle of Gettysburg, Pickett's charge
    a. resulted in failure and defeat for Lee's army.
    b. succeeded temporarily in breaking through the Union defenses.
    c. won great acclaim for Lee's battle strategy.
    d. stopped Lee's retreat to Virginia.
    e. secured an important victory for the Confederacy.

ANS: A   TYPE: M   KEY 1: F   KEY 2: 2   PAGE: 514

48. The victory at Vicksburg was significant because
    a. it finally convinced Lincoln to issue the Emancipation Proclamation.
    b. it gave the Union control of the Mississippi and divided the Confederacy.
    c. it stopped Lee's invasion of the North.
    d. it opened the way for the Union to take Richmond.
    e. it stopped the Indian raids in the West.

ANS: B   TYPE: M   KEY 1: F   KEY 2: 2   PAGE: 514

49. In 1863 peace candidates in the Confederacy
    a. were overwhelmingly defeated.
    b. won both houses of Congress.
    c. made significant gains.
    d. were all arrested for treason.
    e. joined the Republican party.

ANS: C   **TYPE: M**   **KEY 1: F**   **KEY 2: 3**   **PAGE: 520**

50. With regard to prisoner of war exchanges, Lincoln
    a. agreed that black Union prisoners would not be exchanged for Confederate prisoners.
    b. insisted that black prisoners of war be accorded equal treatment with white prisoners of war.
    c. refused to negotiate any exchanges because he knew that the shortage of manpower hurt the South more than the North.
    d. succeeded in negotiating a satisfactory agreement with the South concerning these exchanges.
    e. insisted that prisoners of war be tried for war crimes.

ANS: B   **TYPE: M**   **KEY 1: F**   **KEY 2: 2**   **PAGE: 525-26**

TRUE/FALSE

_____ 1.   Tennessee was one of only four slave states not to secede from the union.

ANS: F   **TYPE: T**   **KEY 1: F**   **KEY 2: 2**   **PAGE: 501**

_____ 2.   The Emancipation Proclamation ended slavery.

ANS: F   **TYPE: T**   **KEY 1: A**   **KEY 2: 1**   **PAGE: 506**

_____ 3.   Abraham Lincoln was assassinated by an unstable Confederate supporter.

ANS: T   **TYPE: T**   **KEY 1: F**   **KEY 2: 1**   **PAGE: 531**

_____ 4.   Many Southerners succumbed to defeatism in the winter of 1863-64.

ANS: T   **TYPE: T**   **KEY 1: F**   **KEY 2: 2**   **PAGE: 520**

_____ 5.   The Confederate government passed a bill that recruited slaves to fight for the South.

ANS: T   **TYPE: T**   **KEY 1: F**   **KEY 2: 2**   **PAGE: 526**

_____ 6.   Throughout 1861, both Southern and Northern leaders attempted to keep the issue of slavery out of the war.

ANS: T   **TYPE: T**   **KEY 1: F**   **KEY 2: 2**   **PAGE: 500**

_____ 7.   It was pragmatism more than principle that pushed the North toward black recruitment.

ANS: T   **TYPE: T**   **KEY 1: A**   **KEY 2: 2**   **PAGE: 517**

_____ 8.   Northerners rallied behind Lincoln's Emancipation Proclamation.

ANS: F   **TYPE: T**   **KEY 1: A**   **KEY 2: 2**   **PAGE: 506**

_____ 9.   The Democratic Party's 1864 platform called for an immediate cessation of hostilities.

ANS: T   TYPE: T   KEY 1: F   KEY 2: 2   PAGE: 525

_____ 10.   The planter class was underrepresented in the Confederate army.

ANS: F   TYPE: T   KEY 1: A   KEY 2: 2   PAGE: 510

_____ 11.   During the Civil War, Lincoln violated the civil rights of antiwar activists by having them arrested and held without trial.

ANS: T   TYPE: T   KEY 1: F   KEY 2: 2   PAGE: 502

_____ 12.   Andersonville was a notorious Confederate prisoner of war camp in which 13,000 Union soldiers died.

ANS: T   TYPE: T   KEY 1: F   KEY 2: 1   PAGE: 525

_____ 13.   Before the Civil War, two-thirds of the time U.S. presidents were from southern states.

ANS: T   TYPE: T   KEY 1: F   KEY 2: 1   PAGE: 531

_____ 14.   In both the North and the South, thousands of draft age men patriotically demonstrated in favor of the conscription laws.

ANS: F   TYPE: T   KEY 1: F   KEY 2: 2   PAGE: 508-09

_____ 15.   In the North, the issue of slavery was deeply divisive.

ANS: T   TYPE: T   KEY 1: F   KEY 2: 2   PAGE: 500

_____ 16.   As Union forces penetrated the South, a growing number of slaves came over to Union lines.

ANS: T   TYPE: T   KEY 1: F   KEY 2: 2   PAGE: 500-01

_____ 17.   Lincoln supported the order of Major General John C. Frémont freeing the slaves of all Confederate sympathizers in Missouri.

ANS: F   TYPE: T   KEY 1: A   KEY 2: 3   PAGE: 501

_____ 18.   Lincoln believed that issuing an emancipation proclamation was a military necessity.

ANS: T   TYPE: T   KEY 1: A   KEY 2: 3   PAGE: 501-02

_____ 19.   Lincoln's preliminary emancipation proclamation came as a total surprise.

ANS: F   TYPE: T   KEY 1: A   KEY 2: 2   PAGE: 502

_____ 20.   The Union's conscription law was designed more to encourage volunteers to come forward than it was to draft men directly.

ANS: T   TYPE: T   KEY 1: A   KEY 2: 3   PAGE: 509

_____ 21.   The Copperheads had no effect at all on Northern morale.

ANS: F   **TYPE: T**   **KEY 1: A**   **KEY 2: 2**   **PAGE: 507**

_____ 22.   Lincoln endorsed the swift arrest and trial of Clement Vallandigham for treason.

ANS: F   **TYPE: T**   **KEY 1: A**   **KEY 2: 2**   **PAGE: 507**

_____ 23.   The North instituted conscription before the South.

ANS: F   **TYPE: T**   **KEY 1: F**   **KEY 2: 2**   **PAGE: 508**

_____ 24.   The South's many problems during the Civil War did not include food shortages.

ANS: F   **TYPE: T**   **KEY 1: A**   **KEY 2: 2**   **PAGE: 508**

_____ 25.   Democrats in Congress supported conscription.

ANS: F   **TYPE: T**   **KEY 1: A**   **KEY 2: 2**   **PAGE: 509**

_____ 26.   Northerners greeted the Emancipation Proclamation with great enthusiasm.

ANS: F   **TYPE: T**   **KEY 1: A**   **KEY 2: 2**   **PAGE: 520**

_____ 27.   The state elections in the fall of 1863 were a powerful endorsement of the administration's emancipation policy.

ANS: T   **TYPE: T**   **KEY 1: A**   **KEY 2: 3**   **PAGE: 520**

_____ 28.   Partisan rivalry between the Democrats and the Whigs continued throughout the entire Civil War.

ANS: F   **TYPE: T**   **KEY 1: A**   **KEY 2: 1**   **PAGE: 520**

_____ 29.   Jefferson Davis experienced little public criticism in the South.

ANS: F   **TYPE: T**   **KEY 1: A**   **KEY 2: 3**   **PAGE: 520**

_____ 30.   Several Southern black regiments fought during the Civil War.

ANS: F   **TYPE: T**   **KEY 1: A**   **KEY 2: 3**   **PAGE: 526**

_____ 31.   Lincoln won a higher proportion of the soldier vote than he civilian vote in 1864.

ANS: T   **TYPE: T**   **KEY 1: F**   **KEY 2: 2**   **PAGE: 527**

_____ 32.   The peace terms that Ulysses S. Grant dictated to Robert E. Lee at Appomattox were harsh.

ANS: F   **TYPE: T**   **KEY 1: F**   **KEY 2: 1**   **PAGE: 530**

_____ 33.   Lincoln decided in July 1862 to issue an emancipation proclamation.

ANS: T   **TYPE: T**   **KEY 1: F**   **KEY 2: 3**   **PAGE: 502**

_____ 34.   The Confederate incursion into Maryland in September 1862 went well from the start.

ANS: F   TYPE: T   KEY 1: A   KEY 2: 2   PAGE: 503

_____ 35.   The divisions between the two political parties in the South prevented the Confederacy from uniting behind the war effort.

ANS: F   TYPE: T   KEY 1: F   KEY 2: 2   PAGE: 520

_____ 36.   Northern Democrats supported enlisting black troops to serve in the Union army.

ANS: F   TYPE: T   KEY 1: F   KEY 2: 2   PAGE: 517

_____ 37.   The Union victory at Atlanta improved Lincoln's prospects for victory in 1864.

ANS: T   TYPE: T   KEY 1: A   KEY 2: 2   PAGE: 526

_____ 38.   Lincoln won the election of 1864 by a narrow electoral margin.

ANS: F   TYPE: T   KEY 1: A   KEY 2: 2   PAGE: 527

_____ 39.   With Lincoln's reelection to the presidency, Confederate President Jefferson Davis began supporting surrender.

ANS: F   TYPE: T   KEY 1: F   KEY 2: 3   PAGE: 527

_____ 40.   Sherman's march through Georgia encountered little resistence.

ANS: T   TYPE: T   KEY 1: F   KEY 2: 1   PAGE: 527

FILL-INS

1.   The president of the Confederacy was _____.

ANS: Jefferson Davis   TYPE: F   KEY 1: F   KEY 2: 1   PAGE: 520

2.   The _____ Act granted a farmer 160 acres of land after he had lived on it for five years.

ANS: Homestead   TYPE: F   KEY 1: F   KEY 2: 3   PAGE: 510

3.   The commander of the Union Army who "marched to the sea" was _____.

ANS: William Sherman TYPE: F   KEY 1: F   KEY 2: 2   PAGE: 527

4.   Those Northerners who favored peace with the South at almost any cost were referred to as _____.

ANS: Copperheads   TYPE: F   KEY 1: F   KEY 2: 3   PAGE: 507

5.   An order issued by a judge to law enforcement officers requiring them to bring an arrested person before the court to be charged with a crime is called a writ of _____.

ANS: habeas corpus   TYPE: F   KEY 1: F   KEY 2: 2   PAGE: 502

6. Northern men who joined the army to collect the enlistment fee and then deserted were called

    _____.

ANS: bounty jumpers   **TYPE: F**   **KEY 1: F**   **KEY 2: 2**   **PAGE: 509**

7. _____ applied the term "contraband of war" to slaves who came within Union lines.

ANS: Benjamin Bulter   **TYPE: F**   **KEY 1: F**   **KEY 2: 3**   **PAGE: 500**

8. The Battle of Antietam was referred to as _____ by the Confederates.

ANS: Sharpsburg   **TYPE: F**   **KEY 1: F**   **KEY 2: 2**   **PAGE: 503-04**

9. _____ replaced George B. McClellan as commander of the Army of the Potomac.

ANS: Ambrose E. Burnside   **TYPE: F**   **KEY 1: F**   **KEY 2: 2**   **PAGE: 506**

10. _____ was the Democratic presidential nominee in 1864.

ANS: George B. McClellan   **TYPE: F**   **KEY 1: F**   **KEY 2: 2**   **PAGE: 524**

11. The Battle of Stones River was a victory for the _____.

ANS: Union (or North)   **TYPE: F**   **KEY 1: F**   **KEY 2: 2**   **PAGE: 507**

12. The case of _____ raised questions about martial law and the use of military courts in areas where civil courts were functioning.

ANS: Clement L. Vallandigham **TYPE: F**   **KEY 1: A**   **KEY 2: 2**   **PAGE: 507**

13. The New York draft riots were led mostly by _____.

ANS: Irish Americans   **TYPE: F**   **KEY 1: F**   **KEY 2: 2**   **PAGE: 509**

14. Copperhead opposition to the Lincoln administration intensified after the Union defeat at

    _____.

ANS: Chancellorsville   **TYPE: F**   **KEY 1: F**   **KEY 2: 2**   **PAGE: 512**

15. _____ advised Robert E. Lee against attacking the Union forces at Gettysburg.

ANS: James Longstreet   **TYPE: F**   **KEY 1: F**   **KEY 2: 3**   **PAGE: 513**

16. _____ was a black abolitionist whose sons fought for the Union in the Civil War.

ANS: Frederick Douglass   **TYPE: F**   **KEY 1: F**   **KEY 2: 2**   **PAGE: 500**

17. _____ issued an order freeing the slaves of Missouri in 1861.

ANS: John C. Fremont   **TYPE: F**   **KEY 1: F**   **KEY 2: 3**   **PAGE: 501**

18. Lincoln's decision to issue the Emancipation Proclamation came after the battle of

    _____.

ANS: Antietam   **TYPE: F**   **KEY 1: F**   **KEY 2: 3**   **PAGE: 505**

19. Lincoln replaced General Burnside as commander of the Army of the Potomac with _____.

ANS: Joseph Hooker   TYPE: F   KEY 1: F   KEY 2: 2   **PAGE: 507**

20. _____ led the siege that ultimately defeated Vicksburg.

ANS: U. S. Grant   TYPE: F   KEY 1: F   KEY 2: 2   **PAGE: 514**

21. The most serious economic problem for the South was_____.

ANS: inflation   TYPE: F   KEY 1: A   KEY 2: 3   **PAGE: 508**

22. In the North the conscription law required that all men between the ages of _____ and _____ had to enroll for the draft.

ANS: 20 to 45   TYPE: F   KEY 1: F   KEY 2: 3   **PAGE: 509**

23. The _____ Act granted land and loans to build a transcontinental railroad.

ANS: Pacific Railroad   TYPE: F   KEY 1: F   KEY 2: 3   **PAGE: 510**

24. The founder of the American Red Cross was _____.

ANS: Clara Barton   TYPE: F   KEY 1: F   KEY 2: 3   **PAGE: 510**

25. The most important voluntary association of the Civil War that provided nursing care for soldiers and that became an adjunct of the Union army's medical bureau was _____.

ANS: United States Sanitary Commission   TYPE: F   KEY 1: F   KEY 2: 2   **PAGE: 511**

26. The Confederate hero of Chancellorsville who died from pneumonia after being accidentally wounded by his own men was _____.

ANS: Stonewall Jackson   TYPE: F   KEY 1: F   KEY 2: 2   **PAGE: 512**

27. Commander of the 54th Massachusetts Infantry, the first black regiment, was _____.

ANS: Robert Gould Shaw   TYPE: F   KEY 1: F   KEY 2: 3   **PAGE: 518**

28. Black Union soldiers were murdered as they tried to surrender at _____.

ANS: Fort Pillow   TYPE: F   KEY 1: F   KEY 2: 3   **PAGE: 525**

29. The Union commander who took Atlanta was _____.

ANS: William T. Sherman   TYPE: F   KEY 1: F   KEY 2: 1   **PAGE: 526**

30. The man who assassinated President Lincoln was _____.

ANS: John Wilkes Booth   TYPE: F   KEY 1: F   KEY 2: 1   **PAGE: 531**

IDENTIFICATIONS

1. **Emancipation Proclamation**: executive order that freed all slaves in the states in rebellion, but not those that remained loyal to the Union. Issued by Abraham Lincoln in 1862. It went into effect at the beginning of 1863.

2. **greenbacks:** paper money issued by the federal government to help finance the war.

3. **Battle of Gettysburg**: Lee's second major unsuccessful attempt to invade the North, generally considered the turning point of the war. Occurred in 1863.

4. **Robert E. Lee**: celebrated commander of the Army of Northern Virginia. Noted for his aggressive leadership and the devotion of his men.

5. **conscription:** drafting men for fighting in the armies. Conscription acts were passed in the South (1862) and in the North (1863). Widely seen as unfair, these acts led to riots in several Northern cities.

6. **54th Massachusetts Infantry**: first black Union regiment; commanding officer was abolitionist Colonel Robert Gould Shaw. Two of Frederick Douglass's sons were in the regiment. It suffered 50 percent casualties in the Battle of Fort Wagner.

7. **Ulysses S. Grant**: Union general who achieved success in taking Forts Henry and Donelson in Tennessee and Vicksburg in Mississippi. Quiet, determined, bold, willing to take risks. Outflanked Lee in Virginia and accepted Lee's surrender at Appomattox.

8. **Twenty Negro Law**: enacted by the Confederate Congress in October 1862. Exempted one white man from the draft on every plantation with twenty or more slaves. Designed to keep up agricultural production and prevent slave uprisings. Generated opposition from nonslaveholders and led to widespread draft-dodging and desertion.

9. **United States Sanitary Commission**: established by the Women's Central Association for Relief and became the most powerful voluntary association of the Civil War. Focused its efforts on providing more efficient, humane care for sick and wounded soldiers. Most of its volunteers were women.

10. **"blueprint for modern America"**: phrase used to describe three measures passed by the 37th Congress. The Homestead Act granted 160 acres of land to farmers who lived on and improved it for five years. The Morrill Land-Grant College Act gave each state land for the establishment of colleges. And the Pacific Railroad Act granted land and loans to railroad companies to spur the building of a transcontinental railroad from Omaha to Sacramento.

SHORT ESSAYS

1. What was the purpose of Lincoln's Emancipation Proclamation? In what ways was the proclamation both important and successful?

Answer: The proclamation had several purposes. First, in a practical sense, by ending slavery in the rebellious states, Lincoln undermined the wealth and labor of the South. Slaves were a capital investment for planters and were an important labor resource. Their work fueled the Southern economy. In addition, the proclamation led to increased runaways in the South and black troop enlistments in the North.

Second, and more symbolically, the proclamation changed the goal of the war. What had been a fight to restore the old union was abandoned and was replaced with a war to create a new, different nation: a nation without slavery. The importance of the proclamation lay in several areas. Although not universally popular in the North, it changed the very meaning of the war for those who fought it. Some saw it as mere revenge against the old plantation aristocracy. By 1862, however, others began to see the war in much the way Lincoln did, as a war against the "monstrous injustice" of slavery.

2.   Describe the Northern military strategy after Ulysses S. Grant became general-in-chief. How was the strategy different from that of previous Union commanders?

Answer: Union military strategy before Grant tended to be disjointed and disorganized. The main goal of Union military commanders had been to capture Richmond, but they rarely used auxiliary forces in any concerted way to help in this endeavor. Historically, once Union campaigns against Richmond failed, the army would retreat and allow Confederate forces to regroup and resupply.

In contrast, Grant's strategy was different. His reputation in the West was based on "unconditional surrender," and this concept shaped his thinking in the eastern theater as well. His main plan coordinated strong Union armies to prevent the Confederacy from moving supplies and troops from one front to another. In addition, Grant believed in "total war": continued military assaults (even if this meant heavy casualties) that destroyed the Southern countryside that supplied Lee's army.

3.   Describe the reasons for, and the general reaction to, the enlistment of black troops into the Union armies.

Answer: Clearly, one goal of enlisting black troops in the Union effort was symbolic: Fighting for the Union would advance blacks in the move toward equal rights with whites. This was one reason that some whites protested black enlistment. Other goals were far more pragmatic, however. The Emancipation Proclamation deprived the South of black labor, leaving an untapped workforce in its wake (runaway slaves). Enlisting those slaves either for labor support for Union armies or as soldiers themselves was an obvious way to utilize that workforce. This was especially popular as white enlistments began to decline in 1862. Black troops had been used in some war zones before 1862 (primarily as support troops or garrison duty), and the Emancipation Proclamation simply legitimized this use.

Reaction to black troops was varied, much like the reaction to emancipation itself. The Confederacy asserted that it would execute all captured black troops as if they were participants in a slave insurrection. The border states also were resistant to the idea, since slavery still flourished within their borders. The greatest criticism, however, came from the Democratic Party in the North, which argued that the idea was a plot to establish equality between the races. Many white Union soldiers bristled at the idea that they now would be serving with black troops.

4.   Examine the outbreak of class tensions in both Northern and Southern society during the Civil War.

Answer: Class tensions, always present in the United States, were exacerbated during the Civil War. Wartime deprivations suffered by both regions, particularly in the South, were most severe among the poorest sectors of society. This led to a belief among these groups that they were bearing the largest brunt of the war. Tensions increased with the implementation of the draft in both the North and the South. Although men from every social stratum could be drafted equally, a drafted man could hire a substitute, but at a price that the ordinary farmer or worker could not afford. This led to the argument that the conflict was a "rich man's war and a poor man's fight."

These tensions were not just rhetorical, however, since they led to some of the worst urban violence in American history—the draft riots of summer 1863. Over a hundred people were killed (most were black and many were lynched) in the worst of the riots in New York City. This violence also spilled over into labor strife, such as in the Pennsylvania coal industries. Federal troops were used in both areas to quell the violence.

The South also witnessed class riots—usually less violent and without the racial or ethnic overtones. These were the food and bread riots, usually led by women, that occurred in several Southern cities. The most notable was in Richmond in 1863 in which President Davis made a personal appeal to the rioters to disperse. Overall, although the violence that broke out was very real, what stands out in both regions is unity in purpose among social and class divisions.

5.   Examine the military importance of the year 1863. In what ways was this a "turning point" in the war?

Answer: 1863 began well for the Confederacy; it still held portions of the Mississippi River, and its armies won important engagements over Union troops in the eastern theater, particularly at Chancellorsville. Lee decided to use his recent victories on the field to his advantage and ordered a second military invasion of the North, feeling that a victory there would disillusion Northerners and, perhaps, persuade foreign governments to recognize the Confederacy. Lee was stopped at Gettysburg, however, in the most important battle of the war, effectively ending any chance the South had for military aggression.

In addition, on the same day as the military defeat at Gettysburg, the Confederacy lost control of the Mississippi River with the fall of Vicksburg to Ulysses S. Grant, a second crushing blow. The reputation of Grant soared, leading to his transfer to the eastern theater—changing the Northern military strategy to one of "total war."

6.   Examine the role of women in the Civil War.

Answer: During the Civil War women stepped in to fill the factory and farm jobs left vacant when the men joined the military. More and more females were hired as teachers, civil servants, and clerks. The success of women in government positions opened opportunities in the private sector as well. In the years following the war, many office jobs such as bookkeeping and typing were available for females.

Women also helped organize and administer volunteer groups such as hospitals and Soldiers' Aid Societies. The United States Sanitary Commission was organized by Dr. Elizabeth Blackwell, the first female M. D. in the United States. This volunteer group set up thousands of local auxiliaries that provided nurses for army hospitals. Clara Barton served as a Union Army nurse and later founded the American Red Cross. Many husbands, fathers, and traditionalist army surgeons opposed the inclusion of women in the battlefield medical profession. The prejudicial attitudes of the pre-Civil War era rated nursing as an "unsuitable job for a woman." The dedication and hard work of the volunteer nurses raised the respectability level of the nursing profession. The momentum gained from the activities of working women in the war carried over into the women's rights movement and contributed to the founding of the National Woman Suffrage Association in 1869. Elizabeth Cady Stanton, Susan B. Anthony, and others reasoned that females who made sacrifices and successfully shouldered responsibilities in wartime should also participate in the political process in peacetime.

7.   Describe the conditions in the prisoner-of-war camps and examine the prisoner exchange controversy.

Answer: At the beginning of the war, the Union and the Confederacy readily exchanged prisoners. Large prison camps were not necessary because the exchanges took place fairly quickly. Once the Union organized black regiments that contained not only free blacks but also ex-slaves, however, the South declared that it would not treat those soldiers as prisoners of war. Instead, the Confederacy announced its intention to execute the captured black troops and their white officers. There were some incidents such as the notorious Fort Pillow maneuver in which surrendering Union soldiers were murdered. Lincoln stopped the prisoner exchanges in 1863 and refused to resume the process without Southern assurances that whites and blacks would be treated equally.

By 1864, the number of prisoners held by both sides was in the thousands and the prison camps were inadequate to meet the needs of the inmates. Captured soldiers lived and died in crowded, unsanitary facilities. They were underfed, deprived of good medical care, and exposed to the elements. More Union soldiers died in Confederate camps than Confederates in Union camps. The South lacked the resources necessary to provide food, shelter, and medical care for the prisoners. Despite the loss of life and the horrendous conditions, the ban on exchanges continued because the North continued to demand and the Confederacy continued to refuse equal treatment for black soldiers.

LONG ESSAYS

1.   Compare and contrast the economic effects of the Civil War on both Northern and Southern societies.

Answer: Essay should address several key points:

A. Northern and Southern economies in 1860
    1. Northern economy
        a. Industrial and commercial
        b. Poised for economic expansion
    2. Southern economy
        a. Agricultural and staple crops
        b. Centrality of slavery
B. Economic mobilization for the war
    1. Northern advantages
        a. Labor
        b. Industry
        c. Capital investment
    2. Southern disadvantages
        a. Food shortages
        b. Blocked ports
        c. Hyperinflation
C. Conclusion
    1. Northern economy grew dramatically during the war
        a. Significant production of materials and supplies
        b. Growth in capital investments (railroads and factories)
    2. South remained behind

2. Compare and contrast the military strategies of the Union and the Confederacy. Begin with plans at the start of the war and show how these strategies changed over time.

Answer: Essay should address several key points:

A. Strategies of both regions at war's commencement
    1. Southern strategy
        a. Defensive war, fought in South
            i) Extend Union supply lines
            ii) Protect Richmond
        b. Hoped to wear down Union and make war lengthy
    2. Northern strategy
        a. Use overwhelming strength to push back Confederate forces in Virginia
            i) Take Richmond
            ii) Split the Confederacy in half
        b. Northern forces rarely were used in massive numbers nor were they used very aggressively (for example, McClellan)
B. Changing strategies, 1862–63
    1. Southern strategy
        a. The Confederacy now attempted advances into the North (Antietam, Gettysburg)
        b. Hoped to affect Northern sentiments on the war
    2. Northern strategy
        a. By late 1863, Union strategy (now under the command of Grant) changed as well
        b. "Total war" (in both East and West)
            i) Massive numbers of Union troops were to be used to destroy Confederate armies
            ii) Supply areas (Shenandoah), and Richmond

3. Examine both Northern and Southern politics from 1861 to 1865. In what ways did the internal political opposition faced by each government help or hinder the war effort?

Answer: Essay should address several key points:

A.   Northern political situation in 1861
      1.   Analysis of Lincoln's plans for fighting the war
            a.   Opposition to these plans within Congress
            b.   Role of Democratic Party ("Copperhead faction")
                  i)   Role of Supreme Court
                  ii)   Role of border states
      2.   Reluctance of many in Republican Party to support Lincoln's initiatives
            a.   Emancipation Proclamation
            b.   Conscription Act
            c.   black recruitment
      3.   Heated election of 1864 with McClellan
            a.   General consensus behind Lincoln in late 1864–1865
B.   Southern political situation in 1861
      1.   General consensus behind war effort and Jefferson Davis during the first years of the war
            a.   Military successes were plentiful and economic problems were small
            b.   After military reversals—serious economic and financial difficulties
      2.   Anti-administration party emerged and made significant gains in 1863 elections
            a.   In some states (for example, North Carolina) a strong peace group emerged
C.   Effects of opposition had on various administrations
      1.   Lincoln and the Democratic Party
            a.   Dealt effectively with opposition
            b.   Enjoyed great wartime powers and regularly employed them
      2.   Davis and the anti-administration faction
            a.   Had virtually no powers in a government system that favored states' rights
            b.   Had great trouble quieting critics

4.   Discuss the major military aspects of the war from 1862 to 1865.

Answer: Essay should address several key points:

A.   The war in 1862
      1.   Antietam
            a.   Lee invades Maryland
            b.   McClellan moves cautiously
            c.   Bloodiest day in U.S. history
            d.   Confederates retreat
      2.   Vicksburg and Murfreesboro
            a.   Confederates fortify Vicksburg
            b.   Grant launches a two-prong attack
            c.   Rosecrans defeats Bragg at Murfreesboro
B.   The war in 1863
      1.   Chancellorsville
            a.   Stonewall Jackson surprises Union troops
            b.   Lee drives Union across the Rappahannock
            c.   Jackson dies from battle-wound complications
      2.   Gettysburg
            a.   Lee invades Pennsylvania
            b.   Union settles in at Gettysburg
            c.   Pickett's charge
            d.   Lee "limps back to Virginia"

      3.   Vicksburg
            a.   Grant's troops ferry across Mississippi River
            b.   Nine-week siege
            c.   Vicksburg surrenders

C. The war in 1864
    1. The Atlanta campaign
        a. Sherman besieges Atlanta
        b. Hood abandons the city
        c. Sherman's march to the sea
    2. The Virginia campaign
        a. Spotsylvania stalemate
        b. Grant loses seven thousand men in one hour

CHAPTER 17
RECONSTRUCTION, 1863–1877

CHAPTER OUTLINE

I. Wartime Reconstruction
    A. Radical Republicans and Reconstruction
II. Andrew Johnson and Reconstruction
    A. Johnson's Policy
    B. Southern Defiance
    C. The Black Codes
    D. Land and Labor in the Postwar South
    E. The Freedman's Bureau
    F. Land for the Landless
    G. Education
III. The Advent of Congressional Reconstruction
    A. Schism between President and Congress
    B. The Fourteenth Amendment
    C. The 1866 Elections
    D. The Reconstruction Acts of 1867
IV. The Impeachment of Andrew Johnson
    A. The Completion of Formal Reconstruction
    B. The Fifteenth Amendment
    C. The Election of 1868
V. The Grant Administration
    A. Civil Service Reform
    B. Foreign Policy Issues
    C. Reconstruction in the South
    D. Blacks in Office
    E. "Carpetbaggers"
    F. "Scalawags"
    G. The Ku Klux Klan
    H. The Election of 1872
    I. The Panic of 1873
VI. The Retreat from Reconstruction
    A. The Mississippi Election of 1875
    B. The Supreme Court and Reconstruction
    C. The Election of 1876
    D. Disputed Results
    E. The Compromise of 1877
    F. The End of Reconstruction
VII. Conclusion

CHRONOLOGY

1863	Lincoln announces his Reconstruction plan.
1864	Louisiana, Arkansas, and Tennessee follow Lincoln's Reconstruction plan for readmittance to the Union.
	Wade–Davis Bill passed by Congress; Lincoln kills it through pocket veto.
1865	Freedmen's Bureau established by Congress.
	Andrew Johnson becomes president.
	Johnson issues his Reconstruction plan and readmits the rest of the former Confederate states to the Union.
	Southern states enact the Black Codes.

	Congress refuses to seat southern Congressmen elected under Johnson's Reconstruction plan.
1866	Freedmen's Bureau is extended and given more power.
	Congress approves the Fourteenth Amendment.
	Race riots break out in Memphis and New Orleans.
	Republicans increase their majority in congressional elections.
1867	Congressional Reconstruction plan is passed over Johnson's veto.
	Tenure of Office Act is enacted to trim Johnson's power to interfere in Reconstruction.
1868	Most southern states are readmitted to Congress under the congressional plan.
	Andrew Johnson is impeached but not convicted.
	Fourteenth Amendment is ratified.
	Ulysses S. Grant wins election as president.
1869	Congress passes the Fifteenth Amendment, ratified in 1870.
1871	Ku Klux Klan Act is enacted and enforced in part of South Carolina.
1872	Liberal Republicans defect from the party. Grant wins reelection.
1873	Economic depression begins with the Panic.
1875	"Whiskey Ring" and other scandals befoul the Grant administration.
	Congress passes Civil Rights Act.
1877	Rutherford B. Hayes becomes president after a disputed election.
	Compromise of 1877 removes last federal soldiers from the South.
1883	Supreme Court declares Civil Rights Act of 1875 unconstitutional.

THEMATIC TOPICS FOR ENRICHMENT

1. How did Andrew Johnson's background, especially his experiences as a prewar politician, affect his Reconstruction position?

2. Discuss the Black Codes and why Republicans found them so objectionable.

3. Explain the role of the Freedmen's Bureau in the South and discuss the labor and racial problems with which it tried to deal.

4. Why did Congress and Andrew Johnson part ways on Reconstruction policies? What events in early 1866 worsened relations between the two?

5. Discuss the provisions of the Fourteenth Amendment and explain why the amendment became such an important guarantor of civil rights.

6. Discuss the events leading to the impeachment of Andrew Johnson. Why did the Senate fail to remove him from office?

7. Discuss the role of the Ku Klux Klan and other terrorist groups during Reconstruction.

8. Discuss the Compromise of 1877 and why it marked the end of Reconstruction.

SUGGESTED ESSAY TOPICS

1. Compare and contrast the Reconstruction policies (noting attitudes toward both former slaves and ex-Confederates) of Abraham Lincoln, Andrew Johnson, and the Radical Republicans.

2. Explain what was meant by the terms *carpetbagger, scalawag,* and *Negro rule.* How true was the propaganda against Republican-controlled state governments in the South?

3. Assess U.S. Grant's two terms as president. What did he accomplish? What were his failures?

1.   From the beginning of the Civil War, the North fought with **Reconstruction** in mind. The precise meaning of that word, however, varied among individuals and changed as the war continued.

2.   Lincoln's **Proclamation of Amnesty and Reconstruction** seemed, to many Republicans, both too lenient toward former Confederates and insufficient in guaranteeing the rights and liberties of former slaves.

        a.   When certain Confederate state governments reorganized under this plan, they denied blacks the vote and enacted restrictive labor laws that **seemed a veritable return to slavery.**

        b.   Radical Republicans came to support tougher policies epitomized in the **Wade–Davis Bill.**

3.   **Andrew Johnson** became president upon Lincoln's assassination.

        a.   Johnson expressed no love for the planter class but was a **white supremacist** who aimed to deny blacks the fruits of Reconstruction.

            i.   Under Johnson's plans, the southern states defiantly **elected prominent Confederate officials** to office.

            ii.   Johnson also granted **special pardons** to many of those "aristocrats" whom he had earlier vowed to punish.

        b.   Even more alarming to Radical Republicans was the establishment of the **Black Codes,** which relegated blacks to second-class citizenship.

        c.   The war had left the **southern** economy in chaos. Planters had no labor, and ex-slaves often had neither land nor work.

        d.   The **Freedmen's Bureau** sought to establish labor contracts between landowners and the former slaves.

            i.   Proposals to provide **land for the landless** through confiscation of plantations failed to reach fruition.

            ii.   Eventually, a new system of **sharecropping** emerged.

        e.   The Freedmen's Bureau was more successful in providing **educational opportunities for blacks.**

4.   By the time Congress met in 1865, the Republican majority had resolved to challenge Johnson with **new Reconstruction policies.**

        a.   **Johnson showed contempt** for Congressional initiatives.

        b.   Congress passed a civil rights bill and another expanding the Freedmen's Bureau's powers, **overriding presidential vetoes.**

        c.   More dramatically, Congress sent to the states the **Fourteenth Amendment,** which vastly expanded federal powers to prevent state violations of civil rights.

d. Johnson's obstinacy and courting of disgraced Democrats were pivotal factors in a sweeping radical Republican victory in the **1866 congressional elections.**

e. Given a three-to-one majority, the Republican Congress passed the **Reconstruction Acts of 1867**.

    i. They enfranchised black males, disfranchised certain ex-Confederates, and sent the army south for **enforcement.**

    ii. Some **735,000 enfranchised black voters** became the backbone of the Republican Party in the South, which took control of southern state governments.

5. Johnson did everything he could to stop Congressional Reconstruction, provoking considerable ire. His firing of the secretary of war was the final straw, which convinced the House to vote for **impeachment.**

a. A few Republicans were persuaded to **acquit** the president, sparing him from removal **by one vote.** Johnson was left politically impotent, however.

b. **Majority Republican state conventions** enacted universal male suffrage and mandated statewide public schools for both races.

c. With ratification of the **Fifteenth Amendment** in 1870, the Constitution became color blind for the first time in history.

d. Ulysses S. Grant, who had openly broken with Johnson, won the **1868 election.**

6. The **Grant administration** is usually branded a failure, owing to widespread corruption among presidential subordinates.

a. In reality, several government agencies made real progress in establishing a more professional and qualified **civil service.**

b. The administration also achieved some **foreign policy** success by ameliorating tensions with Great Britain and Canada.

c. Blacks comprised eighty percent of southern Republican voters yet held only fifteen to twenty percent of elected positions. The **myth of "ignorant" black politicians** is patently false.

d. **Carpetbaggers** (northern whites who moved to the South) did occupy a disproportionate number of political offices, but most were not unscrupulous as southern myths would have it.

e. **Scalawags** (southern native white Republicans) came largely from areas with traditional hostility to the southern planter aristocracy.

f. While the Fifteenth Amendment seemed to many a victory for Reconstruction, there was **no peace in the South.**

(SHOW TRANSPARENCY 88: RECONSTRUCTION IN THE SOUTH)

g. The most potent weapon of the Democrat arsenal was violence, epitomized by the **Ku Klux Klan.**

i. One Klan goal was to keep blacks consigned to second-class citizenship. The **burning of schools** represents but one example of this intention.

ii. The Klan also strove to destroy the Republican Party by **terrorizing voters.**

h. Grant staved off the challenge of "Liberal Republican" Horace Greeley to win **reelection in 1872,** but Greeley's calls to abandon Reconstruction struck a responsive chord with many northerners.

(SHOW TRANSPARENCY 89: THE ELECTION OF 1872)

i. To make matters worse, **panic on Wall Street in 1873** plunged the economy into a five-year recession.

7. Economic anguish and a growing weariness with the seemingly endless turmoil of southern politics turned many northern voters against the Republican party and prompted **retreat from Reconstruction.**

a. Democratic tactics of coercing white Republicans and intimidating black voters threw the **Mississippi election of 1875.**

b. The **Supreme Court,** meanwhile, ruled against many aspects of civil rights legislation, even challenging the Fourteenth and Fifteenth Amendments via narrow interpretation.

c. The **election of 1876** between Samuel Tilden and Rutherford Hayes was held amidst Democratic attempts to "bulldoze" black voters into submission.

(SHOW TRANSPARENCY 90: THE ELECTION OF 1876)

d. The candidates polled nearly an equal number of votes. But three southern states experienced **disputed returns** owing to widespread "bulldozing."

e. Congress had to appoint a special committee to break the deadlock by hammering out the **Compromise of 1877.**

i. To avert crisis, the Republicans agreed to provide economic help to the South and to end **"bayonet rule."**

ii. The Democrats agreed to accept **Hayes as president.**

f. Without federal troop support, the southern Republican Party collapsed. Thus the Compromise marks the **end of Reconstruction.**

Conclusion: Reconstruction had both reincorporated former Confederate states into the Union and destroyed slavery. But continued inequities relegated the newly freed slaves into second-class citizenship, wherein most would remain for nearly another century.

TEACHING RESOURCES

Opening of the West is a documentary on the Reconstruction and westward expansion. Filmic Archives (53 minutes).

America Grows Up covers the period from 1850 to about 1900, focusing on manufacturing, foreign policy, and the shift from a rural to an urban society. Filmic Archives (53 minutes).

The Klan: A Legacy of Hate in America provides an overview of the first 120 years of the organization. Filmic Archives (30 minutes).

The Iron Road details the building and completion of the transcontinental railroad. PBS Video (60 minutes).

MULTIPLE CHOICE

1. The "black codes"
   a. restricted emigration of freedmen to the North.
   b. provided political and social opportunities unknown under slavery.
   c. reduced freedmen to a condition close to slavery.
   d. were passed by the northern states.
   e. prevented blacks from migrating to the West.

   ANS: C   TYPE: M   KEY 1: F   KEY 2: 1   PAGE: 540

2. The main purpose of the Freedmen's Bureau was to
   a. oversee relations between former masters and slaves.
   b. implement the process of land redistribution.
   c. deny access to legal redress for white southerners.
   d. punish former slave holders.
   e. get the Fourteenth Amendment passed.

   ANS: A   TYPE: M   KEY 1: A   KEY 2: 1   PAGE: 540

3. Which of the following is not part of the Fourteenth Amendment?
   a. It gave all citizens equal protection of the law.
   b. It funded the Confederate war debt.
   c. It created a constitutional definition of citizenship.
   d. It gave Congress broad powers to enforce the amendment.
   e. It provided for equal protection under the law.

   ANS: B   TYPE: M   KEY 1: F   KEY 2: 2   PAGE: 544

4. The election of 1866 revealed
   a. strong support for Andrew Johnson's reconstruction plans.
   b. the emergence of white "backlash" in the South.
   c. the increasing popularity of the Republican Party among southern whites.
   d. the increasing popularity of the Democratic Party.
   e. the belief among northerners that much more needed to be done to reconstruct the South.

   ANS: E   TYPE: M   KEY 1: A   KEY 2: 2   PAGE: 544

5. The Tenure of Office Act
   a. angered congressmen by limiting their terms to two years.
   b. stated that a president could only hold office while in good standing.
   c. required Senate approval before the president could remove a cabinet member.
   d. was designed to implement the spoils system.
   e. limited the president to two terms in office.

   ANS: C   TYPE: M   KEY 1: F   KEY 2: 2   PAGE: 545-46

6. The impeachment of Andrew Johnson was
    a. because of crimes and misdemeanors committed while he was president.
    b. the first time a president was forced to resign.
    c. in retaliation for his opposition to congressional reconstruction.
    d. because of his failure to appoint a vice president.
    e. because of his affair with an office worker.

ANS: C   TYPE: M   KEY 1: A   KEY 2: 2   PAGE: 546

7. Which of the following is not true regarding the Fifteenth Amendment?
    a. It prohibited states from denying the right to vote on grounds of race or color.
    b. It was very popular throughout the North.
    c. It encountered much resistance in the white South.
    d. It was part of the congressional reconstruction plan.
    e. Congress required southern states to ratify it.

ANS: B   TYPE: M   KEY 1: F   KEY 2: 1   PAGE: 547

8. The election of 1868
    a. witnessed a referendum on the reconstruction policy of the Republicans.
    b. saw the re-emergence of a powerful Democratic Party in the North.
    c. brought about the "end of Reconstruction."
    d. witnessed the election of southerners to important congressional positions.
    e. proved that black suffrage made no difference in the outcome of elections.

ANS: A   TYPE: M   KEY 1: A   KEY 2: 2   PAGE: 547-49

9. Ulysses S. Grant depended on this group for his presidential victory in 1868.
    a. northern Democrats
    b. southern Democrats
    c. African Americans
    d. National Union Party members
    e. immigrants from Europe.

ANS: C   TYPE: M   KEY 1: F   KEY 2: 2   PAGE: 549

10. One of the major political scandals of the Grant presidency involved
    a. the Compromise of 1877.
    b. the black codes.
    c. the Central Pacific Railroad.
    d. the Specie Resumption Act.
    e. Credit Mobilier.

ANS: E   TYPE: M   KEY 1: F   KEY 2: 2   PAGE: 549

11. The 1871 Treaty of Washington
    a. resolved border disputes between the United States and Canada.
    b. was a diplomatic solution to the unsuccessful attempt to annex Santo Domingo.
    c. settled U.S. claims against Britain for destruction of American shipping.
    d. resolved differences between the Confederacy and the Union.
    e. secured title to western lands from Native Americans.

ANS: C   TYPE: M   KEY 1: F   KEY 2: 3   PAGE: 550

12. Southern whites regarded "Carpetbaggers" as
    a. traitors to their home region.
    b. noble and idealistic "modernizers" to the region's social structure.
    c. agents of an army of occupation.
    d. incorruptible in political affairs.
    e. supporters of white supremacy.

ANS: C **TYPE: M** **KEY 1: A** **KEY 2: 1** **PAGE: 551**

13. The main purpose of the Ku Klux Klan during Reconstruction was to
    a. destroy the Republican Party in the South.
    b. deny freedmen equal protection under the law.
    c. return black Americans to slavery.
    d. dismantle the Democratic Party.
    e. take the South out of the Union.

ANS: A **TYPE: M** **KEY 1: A** **KEY 2: 2** **PAGE: 553**

14. Ulysses S. Grant was guilty of
    a. standing in the way of congressional Reconstruction.
    b. participation in the "Whiskey Ring."
    c. unwise appointments of public officials.
    d. lying to Congress.
    e. treason.

ANS: C **TYPE: M** **KEY 1: A** **KEY 2: 2** **PAGE: 549**

15. _____ was the presidential candidate nominated by both the Liberal Republicans and the Democratic Party in the election of 1872.
    a. Horatio Seymour
    b. Samuel B. Tilden
    c. Ulysses S. Grant
    d. Horace Greeley
    e. Rutherford Hayes.

ANS: D **TYPE: M** **KEY 1: F** **KEY 2: 2** **PAGE: 554**

16. By the mid-1870s, northern Americans had grown
    a. increasingly supportive of the government's efforts to restructure the South.
    b. stronger in the belief that black Americans needed further protection from racist southern governments.
    c. increasingly weary of the turmoil of southern politics.
    d. increasingly weary of the federal government's failure to restructure the South.
    e. increasingly supportive of black immigration to the North to meet their labor needs and to stop the upheaval in the South.

ANS: C **TYPE: M** **KEY 1: A** **KEY 2: 3** **PAGE: 555**

17. The strategy known as the "Mississippi Plan" aimed to do all of the following except
    a. intimidate black voters.
    b. force all southern whites to join the Democratic Party.
    c. end Republican rule in the South.
    d. return confiscated land to former owners.
    e. use economic coercion to control election outcomes.

ANS: D   TYPE: M   KEY 1: A   KEY 2: 2   PAGE: 555-56

18. Which of the following was not a part of the Compromise of 1877?
    a. removal of federal troops from southern states
    b. appointment of a southern vice president
    c. federal aid for a southern railroad
    d. federal appropriations to rebuild war-destroyed levees.
    e. appointment of a southern postmaster general.

ANS: B   TYPE: M   KEY 1: F   KEY 2: 2   PAGE: 559-60

19. The idea of redistributing plantation land to freedmen was tried first by
    a. Jefferson Davis.
    b. Benjamin Wade.
    c. William T. Sherman.
    d. Andrew Johnson.
    e. Abraham Lincoln

ANS: C   TYPE: M   KEY 1: F   KEY 2: 3   PAGE: 541-42

20. Scalawags were
    a. northerners who attempted to finance economic enterprises in the postwar South.
    b. southern blacks attempting to exert their newly acquired political power.
    c. white, southern-born Republicans.
    d. white southerners who opposed reconstruction policies.
    e. criminals who stole public funds during Reconstruction.

ANS: C   TYPE: M   KEY 1: F   KEY 2: 2   PAGE: 552

21. Radical Republicans objected to Lincoln's initial Reconstruction plan because it
    a. offered a presidential pardon to former Confederate political and military leaders.
    b. did not require the establishment of educational opportunities for freed people.
    c. restored the political rights of white men who had fought against the Union.
    d. was too difficult to enforce.
    e. gave too many rights to freedmen.

ANS: C   TYPE: M   KEY 1: A   KEY 2: 2   PAGE: 537-38

22. Andrew Johnson was all of the following except
    a. a southern Democrat.
    b. the only senator from a Confederate state who did not support the Confederacy.
    c. a supporter of yeoman farmers
    d. a white supremacist.
    e. a strong supporter of the planter aristocracy.

ANS: E   TYPE: M   KEY 1: F   KEY 2: 1   PAGE: 538

23. Northern Republicans rejected the southern state governments set up under the Johnson Plan because they
   a. elected ex-Confederate leaders to political office.
   b. jeopardized Republican control of Congress.
   c. did not offer full citizenship rights to freedmen.
   d. did not control the violence.
   e. all of the above

ANS: E   TYPE: M   KEY 1: A   KEY 2: 3   PAGE: 538-40

24. Which of the following is characteristic of the post-Civil War southern labor system?
   a. Black workers preferred working in gangs as they had done under slavery.
   b. The new system of sharecropping evolved.
   c. Foreign immigrants were brought in to replace slave laborers.
   d. Most ex-slaves purchased land and often employed their former masters.
   e. The economy quickly recovered from the ravishes of war.

ANS: B   TYPE: M   KEY 1: A   KEY 2: 2   PAGE: 541

25. During the Reconstruction period
   a. thousands of ex-Confederate leaders were tried, imprisoned, and executed for war crimes.
   b. each adult freedman was given "forty acres and a mule."
   c. three-fourths of the ex-slaves moved north to take advantage of higher wages there.
   d. the illiteracy rate among southern blacks was reduced significantly.
   e. most of the ex-slaves moved west.

ANS: D   TYPE: M   KEY 1: A   KEY 2: 2   PAGE: 542

26. In regard to civil rights, the Fourteenth Amendment
   a. greatly expanded the federal government's powers and limited the authority of state governments.
   b. extended citizenship to Native Americans (Indians).
   c. reduced constitutional protection of minority rights.
   d. limited the power of the federal government and expanded the authority of state governments.
   e. gave blacks the right to vote.

ANS: A   TYPE: M   KEY 1: A   KEY 2: 2   PAGE: 544

27. Which of the following is true of Andrew Johnson's impeachment trial?
   a. The Senate sat as a court to try Johnson on charges drawn up by the House.
   b. All the Republican senators voted for conviction.
   c. A three-fourths majority in both Houses was required to remove Johnson from office.
   d. The vote against him was unanimous.
   e. Johnson voluntarily resigned before he could be removed.

ANS: A   TYPE: M   KEY 1: F   KEY 2: 1   PAGE: 545-46

28. The new state constitutions drawn up in the South from 1867 to 1868
   a. specifically prohibited segregated public schools.
   b. were created in conventions dominated by northern black delegates.
   c. included universal male suffrage.
   d. were too conservative for liberal southern voters.
   e. were not influenced by Republicans.

ANS: C   TYPE: M   KEY 1: F   KEY 2: 2   PAGE: 547

29. Ulysses S. Grant's presidency is known as an era of
    a. honesty and integrity of both state and federal officeholders.
    b. military efficiency and discipline in the executive branch of the government.
    c. mutual understanding between North and South, Democrats and Republicans, whites and blacks.
    d. renewal of civil war.
    e. scandal and corruption at all levels of government.

ANS: E   **TYPE: M**   **KEY 1: A**   **KEY 2: 2**   **PAGE: 549**

30. The Republican Party in the South
    a. was a new party that was not established there before the Civil War.
    b. represented the wealthiest, most powerful elements of society.
    c. was supported primarily by poor and middle-class whites.
    d. created the most corrupt and inefficient governments in southern history.
    e. did not attract the support of the former slaves.

ANS: A   **TYPE: M**   **KEY 1: A**   **KEY 2: 3**   **PAGE: 551**

31. Which of the following is not true of black political activity during Reconstruction?
    a. Most black voters were illiterate ex-slaves.
    b. More than 50 percent of high state and federal offices were held by blacks.
    c. Prominent black leaders were educated and most had been free prior to the Civil War.
    d. A majority of black voters were members of the Republican Party.
    e. Blacks served in both the US House of Representatives and the Senate.

ANS: B   **TYPE: M**   **KEY 1: F**   **KEY 2: 3**   **PAGE: 551**

32. In the 1870s and 1880s the U.S. Supreme Court
    a. strengthened the authority of federal officials in prosecuting individuals who violated the civil rights of blacks.
    b. declared the military occupation of the South unconstitutional.
    c. banned racial discrimination in public transportation and accommodations.
    d. ordered the desegregation of public schools in the South.
    e. declared the Civil Rights Act of 1875 unconstitutional.

ANS: E   **TYPE: M**   **KEY 1: F**   **KEY 2: 2**   **PAGE: 556-57**

33. Which of the following describes the southern political power structure during Reconstruction?
    a. Power shifted from the Democratic Party to the Republican Party then back to the Democratic Party again.
    b. By the end of the period, poor whites and blacks held most local and state offices.
    c. The southern planter aristocracy remained in power throughout the period.
    d. Northern Republicans and southern blacks dominated southern politics from 1865 to 1900.
    e. No southern whites supported the Republican Party.

ANS: A   **TYPE: M**   **KEY 1: A**   **KEY 2: 3**   **PAGE: 542-55**

34. The term "bayonet rule" refers to
    a. the use of threats and intimidation to prevent blacks from voting.
    b. a requirement that all U.S. Army officers carry a bayonet while on guard duty.
    c. the use of federal troops to support Republican state governments and black rights in the South.
    d. civil rights leaders' call for mass arrests of Ku Klux Klan members.
    e. the methods used by white southerners to regain control of their state governments.

ANS: C   **TYPE: M**   **KEY 1: F**   **KEY 2: 2**   **PAGE: 556**

35. The Compromise of 1877 signified
    a. a renewal of federal support for the civil rights of all Americans.
    b. the end of Reconstruction.
    c. the beginning of the Industrial Revolution in the United States.
    d. the decline of Democratic Party control of Congress.
    e. the end of the spoils system.

ANS: B   TYPE: M   KEY 1: A   KEY 2: 1   PAGE: 559-60

36. Members of Abraham Lincoln's own party opposed his Proclamation of Amnesty and Reconstruction because
    a. it promised too much financial compensation to former Confederates.
    b. it didn't go far enough to force the Confederacy to pay its debts.
    c. it granted too much land to freed people
    d. it left the door open to restrictive Southern measures to control former slaves.
    e. it punished former Confederates too harshly.

ANS: D   TYPE: M   KEY 1: A   KEY 2: 3   PAGE: 537-38

37. In 1864, Republicans adopted the name
    a. Union Party.
    b. Victory Party.
    c. Reconstruction Party.
    d. Peace Party.
    e. Federalist

ANS: A   TYPE: M   KEY 1: FA   KEY 2: 13   PAGE: 538

38. The four southern states remaining under Republican control in 1875 were South Carolina, Florida, Mississippi, and
    a. Georgia.
    b. Louisiana.
    c. South Carolina.
    d. Virginia.
    e. Texas

ANS: B   TYPE: M   KEY 1: F   KEY 2: 2   PAGE: 555

39. The Fourteenth Amendment did all of the following except
    a. define blacks as American citizens.
    b. grant equal protection of the laws.
    c. guarantee the Confederate debt.
    d. disqualify a significant number of ex-Confederates from holding federal or state office.
    e. grant due process under the law.

ANS: C   TYPE: M   KEY 1: A   KEY 2: 3   PAGE: 544

40. Andrew Johnson's National Union Party included all of the following except
    a. border state Unionists.
    b. freedmen.
    c. Democrats.
    d. conservative Republicans.
    e. white supremacists

ANS: B   TYPE: M   KEY 1: F   KEY 2: 1   PAGE: 544

41. Ulysses S. Grant struck a responsive chord with many in the North when, in accepting the presidential nomination, he declared
    a. "We are all Americans."
    b. "Let us reunite."
    c. "Come together as one nation."
    d. "Save the nation."
    e. "Let us have peace."

ANS: E   TYPE: M   KEY 1: F   KEY 2: 2   PAGE: 550

42. At the height of Reconstruction, blacks held _____ percent of public offices.
    a. 15-20
    b. 25-30
    c. 35-40
    d. 45-50
    e. 90-95

ANS: A   TYPE: M   KEY 1: F   KEY 2: 3   PAGE: 551

43. Which of the following statements is not true?
    a. Carpetbaggers often brought considerable capital with them in hopes of investing in a New South.
    b. Most Carpetbaggers were Union Army officers.
    c. Few Carpetbaggers were college graduates.
    d. Carpetbaggers sought to modernize the South's social structure and democratize its politics.
    e. Carpetbaggers hoped to establish the Republican Party in the South.

ANS: C   TYPE: M   KEY 1: A   KEY 2: 3   PAGE: 551-52

44. Congressional laws in 1870 and 1871 did all of the following except
    a. empower the president to send in federal troops to suppress armed resistance to federal law.
    b. declare that any attempt to deprive another person of civil or political rights became a felony.
    c. classify interference with voting rights a federal offense.
    d. authorize martial law to guarantee racial harmony.
    e. give the president the power to suspend the writ of habeas corpus.

ANS: D   TYPE: M   KEY 1: A   KEY 2: 3   PAGE: 554

45. The majority of southern Republican voters were
    a. wealthy planters.
    b. poor whites.
    c. blacks.
    d. women.
    e. Native Americans

ANS: C   TYPE: M   KEY 1: F   KEY 2: 2   PAGE: 551

46. Almost all of the blacks elected to the United States House and Senate during Reconstruction
    a. were illiterate.
    b. had attended secondary school.
    c. were college graduates.
    d. were Democrats.
    e. had fought for the Confederacy.

ANS: B   TYPE: M   KEY 1: F   KEY 2: 2   PAGE: 551

47. During Reconstruction most of the Republican governors of southern states
    a. were blacks.
    b. were northerners.
    c. had been southern Whigs before the Civil War.
    d. had been Confederate officer holders during the Civil War.
    e. were European immigrants.

ANS: B　　　**TYPE: M**　　　**KEY 1: F**　　　**KEY 2: 3**　　　**PAGE: 551**

48. Before the Civil War many of the Scalawags had belonged to
    a. the Whig Party.
    b. the Ku Klux Klan.
    c. the Democratic Party.
    d. the Republican Party.
    e. the American Party.

ANS: A　　　**TYPE: M**　　　**KEY 1: F**　　　**KEY 2: 2**　　　**PAGE: 552**

49. An act that gave the President the power to use federal troops to suppress resistance to federal law was
    a. the Tenure of Office Act.
    b. the Civil Rights Act.
    c. the Voting Rights Act.
    d. the Force Act
    e. the Ku Klux Klan Act.

ANS: E　　　**TYPE: M**　　　**KEY 1: F**　　　**KEY 2: 3**　　　**PAGE: 554**

50. In response to the Hamburg Massacre, President Grant
    a. sent in federal troops.
    b. withdrew troops from the South.
    c. decided not to run for a third term.
    d. encouraged the southern states to create their own militia units.
    e. organized black militia units.

ANS: A　　　**TYPE: M**　　　**KEY 1: F**　　　**KEY 2: 3**　　　**PAGE: 558**

TRUE/FALSE

_____ 1.　　　Samuel Tilden was probably the real victor in the disputed election of 1876.

ANS: T　　　**TYPE: T**　　　**KEY 1: A**　　　**KEY 2: 1**　　　**PAGE: 558**

_____ 2.　　　The Wade–Davis Bill granted the franchise to black Americans.

ANS: F　　　**TYPE: T**　　　**KEY 1: F**　　　**KEY 2: 3**　　　**PAGE: 537**

_____ 3.　　　The Fourteenth Amendment to the Constitution gave states the option of enfranchising black males or losing seats in Congress.

ANS: T　　　**TYPE: T**　　　**KEY 1: F**　　　**KEY 2: 2**　　　**PAGE: 544**

_____ 4.　　　The Democratic Party was distrusted in the early years of Reconstruction because it was seen as sympathetic to the South.

ANS: T　　　**TYPE: T**　　　**KEY 1: A**　　　**KEY 2: 1**　　　**PAGE: 544**

_____ 5.   The Reconstruction Act of 1867 divided the South into an occupied territory under military command.

ANS: T   TYPE: T   KEY 1: F   KEY 2: 1   PAGE: 544

_____ 6.   Bulldozing in several parts of the South during the presidential election of 1876 hurt Republican candidate Rutherford B. Hayes.

ANS: T   TYPE: T   KEY 1: A   KEY 2: 3   PAGE: 558

_____ 7.   Carpetbaggers were southerners who served Republican Reconstruction governments.

ANS: F   TYPE: T   KEY 1: F   KEY 2: 3   PAGE: 551

_____ 8.   Blacks held a majority of public political offices in several southern states during Reconstruction.

ANS: F   TYPE: T   KEY 1: F   KEY 2: 2   PAGE: 551

_____ 9.   The Ku Klux Klan was created by former Confederate soldiers.

ANS: T   TYPE: T   KEY 1: F   KEY 2: 1   PAGE: 553

_____ 10.   Under the Johnson Reconstruction Plan, no ex-Confederate state gave blacks the right to vote.

ANS: T   TYPE: T   KEY 1: F   KEY 2: 1   PAGE: 539

_____ 11.   White southerners' main complaint against the Freedmen's Bureau was that it was inefficient.

ANS: F   TYPE: T   KEY 1: A   KEY 2: 2   PAGE: 541

_____ 12.   The Fourteenth Amendment encouraged southern states to enfranchise blacks but did not force them to do so.

ANS: T   TYPE: T   KEY 1: A   KEY 2: 2   PAGE: 544

_____ 13.   Tennessee was the first ex-Confederate state to ratify the Fourteenth Amendment in order to be "readmitted" to the union.

ANS: T   TYPE: T   KEY 1: F   KEY 2: 1   PAGE: 544

_____ 14.   Under the U.S. Constitution, impeachment by the House removes an official from office.

ANS: F   TYPE: T   KEY 1: F   KEY 2: 3   PAGE: 546

_____ 15.   The border between the United States and Canada is the longest hostile border in the world.

ANS: F   TYPE: T   KEY 1: F   KEY 2: 2   PAGE: 550

_____ 16.   The need to "reconstruct" the South became obvious once the abolition of slavery became a Northern war aim.

ANS: T   **TYPE: T**   **KEY 1: A**   **KEY 2: 1**   **PAGE: 536**

_____ 17.   Abraham Lincoln never encouraged freed people to emigrate to all-black countries like Haiti.

ANS: F   **TYPE: T**   **KEY 1: A**   **KEY 2: 3**   **PAGE: 536**

_____ 18.   A majority in Congress in 1864 believed that freed slaves should be given the right to vote.

ANS: F   **TYPE: T**   **KEY 1: A**   **KEY 2: 2**   **PAGE: 537**

_____ 19.   The Wade-Davis bill proposed lenient loyalty requirements for Southern whites.

ANS: F   **TYPE: T**   **KEY 1: A**   **KEY 2: 3**   **PAGE: 537-38**

_____ 20.   Abraham Lincoln vetoed the Wade-Davis bill after he had won reelection.

ANS: F   **TYPE: T**   **KEY 1: F**   **KEY 2: 2**   **PAGE: 538**

_____ 21.   Radical Republicans in Congress initially believed that Andrew Johnson would support their program.

ANS: T   **TYPE: T**   **KEY 1: A**   **KEY 2: 3**   **PAGE: 538**

_____ 22.   Both major political party presidential candidates in 1876 were reformist governors.

ANS: T   **TYPE: T**   **KEY 1: F**   **KEY 2: 2**   **PAGE: 558**

_____ 23.   None of the postwar Southern state governments opposed the abolition of slavery.

ANS: F   **TYPE: T**   **KEY 1: A**   **KEY 2: 2**   **PAGE: 539**

_____ 24.   Most freed slaves continued to work for their former owners after the war.

ANS: F   **TYPE: T**   **KEY 1: A**   **KEY 2: 2**   **PAGE: 540**

_____ 25.   The Southern black illiteracy rate was reduced from 70 percent in 1880 to 48 percent in 1900.

ANS: T   **TYPE: T**   **KEY 1: F**   **KEY 2: 3**   **PAGE: 542**

_____ 26.   Republicans in Congress refused to admit the representatives and senators from the former Confederate states elected under Andrew Johnson's reconstruction plan.

ANS: T   **TYPE: T**   **KEY 1: F**   **KEY 2: 2**   **PAGE: 542**

_____ 27.   The Fourteenth Amendment dealt only with awarding the franchise to African Americans.

ANS: F   **TYPE: T**   **KEY 1: F**   **KEY 2: 1**   **PAGE: 544**

_____ 28.   Republicans had a bare majority in both houses of Congress in late 1865.

ANS: F   **TYPE: T**   **KEY 1: F**   **KEY 2: 2**   **PAGE: 543-44**

_____ 29.   Andrew Johnson advised Southern legislatures to accept the Fourteenth Amendment.

ANS: F   **TYPE: T**   **KEY 1: A**   **KEY 2: 2**   **PAGE: 544**

_____ 30.   The Reconstruction Acts of 1867 embodied a true revolution.

ANS: T   **TYPE: T**   **KEY 1: A**   **KEY 2: 3**   **PAGE: 544-45**

_____ 31.   By September 1867, blacks registered to vote outnumbered whites in the ten states covered by Reconstruction.

ANS: T   **TYPE: T**   **KEY 1: F**   **KEY 2: 2**   **PAGE: 545**

_____ 32.   Andrew Johnson removed Edwin M. Stanton from office because he supported congressional Reconstruction policy.

ANS: T   **TYPE: T**   **KEY 1: F**   **KEY 2: 1**   **PAGE: 545**

_____ 33.   The new southern state constitutions written during the winter and spring of 1867-68 were among the most progressive in the nation.

ANS: T   **TYPE: T**   **KEY 1: F**   **KEY 2: 2**   **PAGE: 547**

_____ 34.   During the 1866 congressional election campaign, Republicans made clear that any ex-Confederate state that ratified the Fourteenth Amendment would be considered "reconstructed" and that its representatives and senators would be seated in Congress.

ANS: T   **TYPE: T**   **KEY 1: A**   **KEY 2: 3**   **PAGE: 544**

_____ 35.   Without black enfranchisement, Ulysses S. Grant would have had a minority of the popular vote in 1868.

ANS: T   **TYPE: T**   **KEY 1: F**   **KEY 2: 3**   **PAGE: 549**

_____ 36.   Politicians at all levels universally embraced civil service reform.

ANS: F   **TYPE: T**   **KEY 1: A**   **KEY 2: 2**   **PAGE: 550**

_____ 37.   The "Southern Question" was the most intractable issue during Grant's two administrations.

ANS: T   **TYPE: T**   **KEY 1: A**   **KEY 2: 2**   **PAGE: 550**

_____ 38.   Most Southern Republicans were poor, illiterate, and property less; most Northern Republicans represented the most prosperous, educated, and influential elements of society.

ANS: T   **TYPE: T**   **KEY 1: A**   **KEY 2: 3**   **PAGE: 551**

_____ 39. Blacks held office in many states throughout the South in numbers far exceeding their proportion of the population.

ANS: F   **TYPE: T**   **KEY 1: A**   **KEY 2: 3**   **PAGE: 551**

_____ 40. Carpetbaggers held a disproportionate number of high political offices in southern state governments during Reconstruction.

ANS: T   **TYPE: T**   **KEY 1: F**   **KEY 2: 2**   **PAGE: 551**

FILL-INS

1. Disputed election returns in the 1876 presidential election came from Louisiana, South Carolina, and _____.

ANS: Florida   **TYPE: F**   **KEY 1: F**   **KEY 2: 3**   **PAGE: 558**

2. The Democratic Party policy of intimidating black voters to keep them away from the polls was called _____.

ANS: bulldozing   **TYPE: F**   **KEY 1: F**   **KEY 2: 2**   **PAGE: 558**

3. Ulysses S. Grant's opponent in the election of 1868 was _____.

ANS: Horatio Seymour   **TYPE: F**   **KEY 1: F**   **KEY 2: 3**   **PAGE: 547**

4. White southerners who joined the Republican Party were called _____.

ANS: Scalawags   **TYPE: F**   **KEY 1: F**   **KEY 2: 1**   **PAGE: 552**

5. The notorious massacre of black militiamen in Louisiana in 1873 was known as the _____.

ANS: Colfax Massacre   **TYPE: F**   **KEY 1: F**   **KEY 2: 2**   **PAGE: 553**

6. The agricultural system under which workers farmed land they did not own in return for part of the crop they produced was called _____.

ANS: sharecropping   **TYPE: F**   **KEY 1: F**   **KEY 2: 1**   **PAGE: 541**

7. The removal of _____ from the post of secretary of war triggered the impeachment of Andrew Johnson.

ANS: Edwin M. Stanton   **TYPE: F**   **KEY 1: F**   **KEY 2: 1**   **PAGE: 545**

8. _____ was the first state to reorganize under Abraham Lincoln's moderate reconstruction request.

ANS: Louisiana   **TYPE: F**   **KEY 1: F**   **KEY 2: 2**   **PAGE: 537**

9. The _____ Act established the modern structure of the civil service.

ANS: Pendelton   **TYPE: F**   **KEY 1: F**   **KEY 2: 1**   **PAGE: 550**

10. Ulysses S. Grant suffered public criticism for its efforts to acquire _____ _____.

ANS: Santo Domingo   **TYPE: F**   **KEY 1: F**   **KEY 2: 2**   **PAGE: 550**

11. About _____ percent of southern Republican voters were black.

ANS: 80   **TYPE: F**   **KEY 1: F**   **KEY 2: 2**   **PAGE: 551**

12. The _____ Party won control of the House of Representatives in 1874 for the first time in 14 years.

ANS: Democratic   **TYPE: F**   **KEY 1: F**   **KEY 2: 2**   **PAGE: 555**

13. Congress passed the _____ imposing loyalty requirements on southern whites that were intended to disenfranchise them, but it was vetoed by President Lincoln.

ANS: Wade-Davis Bill   **TYPE: F**   **KEY 1: F**   **KEY 2: 1**   **PAGE: 537-38**

14. President Johnson's Reconstruction policies were intended to empower _____ in the South.

ANS: yeoman whites   **TYPE: F**   **KEY 1: A**   **KEY 2: 2**   **PAGE: 538**

15. The _____ Amendment gave blacks the right to vote.

ANS: Fifteenth   **TYPE: F**   **KEY 1: F**   **KEY 2: 1**   **PAGE: 547**

16. Johnson restored political and property rights to former Confederate leaders by granting them _____.

ANS: pardons   **TYPE: F**   **KEY 1: F**   **KEY 2: 2**   **PAGE: 540**

17. The agency created to oversee relations between former slaves and their former masters during Reconstruction was the _____.

ANS: Freedman's Bureau   **TYPE: F**   **KEY 1: F**   **KEY 2: 1**   **PAGE: 540**

18. In the northern Congressional elections of 1866 the _____ Party won sweeping victories.

ANS: Republican   **TYPE: F**   **KEY 1: F**   **KEY 2: 1**   **PAGE: 544**

19. The congressional acts that divided the former Confederate states (except Tennessee) into five military districts, enfranchised black men, disenfranchised some Confederates, and called for new constitutional conventions were the _____.

ANS: Reconstruction Acts of 1867   **TYPE: F**   **KEY 1: F**   **KEY 2: 1**   **PAGE: 544**

20. In order for a Southern state to be declared reconstructed and its delegates seated in Congress, the state had to ratify the _____ Amendment.

ANS: Fourteenth   **TYPE: F**   **KEY 1: F**   **KEY 2: 2**   **PAGE: 544**

21. Women suffrage leaders who opposed the Fifteenth Amendment were _____ and
     _____.

ANS: Elizabeth Cady Stanton; Susan B. Anthony   TYPE: F   KEY 1: F   KEY 2: 2   PAGE: 547

22. _____ was a construction company for the Union Pacific Railroad that gave
     congressmen stock in return for land grants and loans from the government.

ANS: Credit Mobilier   TYPE: F   KEY 1: F   KEY 2: 2   PAGE: 549

23. The _____ Brotherhood was a secret society of Irish Americans who conducted raids
     across the U.S. border into Canada.

ANS: Fenian   TYPE: F   KEY 1: F   KEY 2: 3   PAGE: 550

24. A terrorist organization that attacked blacks and set out to destroy the Republican Party in the South
     was the _____.

ANS: Ku Klux Klan   TYPE: F   KEY 1: A   KEY 2: 1   PAGE: 553

25. Republicans dissatisfied with Grant's administration who nominated Horace Greeley for President in
     1872 called themselves the _____ Republicans.

ANS: Liberal   TYPE: F   KEY 1: F   KEY 2: 2   PAGE: 554

26. The financier whose pyramid schemes collapsed in 1873 and helped touch off an economic collapse
     was _____.

ANS: Jay Cooke   TYPE: F   KEY 1: F   KEY 2: 2   PAGE: 555

27. The Republican governor of Mississippi who asked Grant to send troops to control whites' violent
     intimidation of black voters in that state during the election of 1875 was _____.

ANS: Adelbert Ames   TYPE: F   KEY 1: F   KEY 2: 2   PAGE: 555

28. In _____, South Carolina, a battle between a black militia and the white Red Shirts led
     to the murder of several militiamen.

ANS: Hamburg   TYPE: F   KEY 1: F   KEY 2: 3   PAGE: 558

29. In the 1876 presidential election the Democrat _____ appeared to have won the election
     when the results were first in.

ANS: Samuel Tilden   TYPE: F   KEY 1: F   KEY 2: 1   PAGE: 558

30. After the election of 1876 the Reconstruction Republican governments collapsed in the last two
     southern states, _____ and _____.

ANS: Louisiana; South Carolina TYPE: F   KEY 1: F   KEY 2: 2   PAGE: 559

IDENTIFICATIONS

1.   **Credit Mobilier**: railroad construction company that inflated building costs and bribed congressmen.
     Reflective of corrupt business activities of the Gilded Age.

2. **Andrew Johnson**: seventeenth president; opposed Radical Republicans on various Reconstruction issues. Impeached by the House of Representatives but ultimately acquitted by the Senate.

3. **Jay Cooke**: northern businessman who helped finance the Union war effort; his financial collapse precipitated the Panic of 1873.

4. **Whiskey Ring**: network of collusion among distillers and revenue agents that deprived the government of millions of tax dollars. Active during the presidential administration of Ulysses S. Grant. Contributed to the perception that the administration was corrupt when Grant's private secretary was alleged to have ties to the ring.

5. **universal male suffrage**: a system where all adult males have the right to vote. Became a feature of the new state constitutions written in the South during 1867 and 1868. Amounted to a true political revolution.

6. **Carpetbaggers:** northerners who moved to the South to live and/or to participate in Reconstruction governments. Most were Union Army officers who stayed on after the war as Freedmen's Bureau agents, teachers in black schools, or business investors. Many brought investment capital to the South in a sincere effort to rebuild and modernize it.

7. **Black Codes**: a series of post-Civil War laws that established second-class status for freed people. Passed by southern state governments beginning in the fall of 1865, these laws excluded blacks from juries and the ballot box, prevented blacks from testifying against whites in court, banned interracial marriage, and punished blacks more severely than whites for certain crimes.

8. **Freedmen's Bureau**: officially called the Bureau of Refugees, Freedmen, and Abandoned Lands. Created by Congress in 1865 to supervise black-white relations in the South. Sought to ensure that blacks were paid for their labor, distributed food to the poor, and established schools throughout the South for freed slaves. Southern whites opposed the Bureau, for obvious reasons.

9. **Liberal Republicans**: emerged to challenge Ulysses S. Grant in the election of 1872. Believed that conciliation of Southern whites rather than continued military intervention was the only way to achieve peace in the South. Nominated Horace Greeley for president. He urged his fellow northerners to put the issues of the Civil War behind them. (Greeley was also nominated by the Democrats.)

10. **Compromise of 1877**: agreement that settled the disputed election of 1876 by giving the Republican Rutherford Hayes the presidency in return for Hayes' agreement to support federal aid for economic development in the South, his support of a southern postmaster general, and his commitment to withdraw the last of the federal troops from the South. Marked the end of Reconstruction.

SHORT ESSAYS

1. Compare and contrast the Lincoln Reconstruction plan with the Wade–Davis Bill.

Answer: The Lincoln plan, a fairly lenient attempt to reconstruct southern society, called for 10 percent oath of allegiance to the Union from the white male population; the acceptance of all wartime acts of Congress; the right of some black males to vote; and abolition of slavery.

The Wade–Davis Bill went further in attempting to punish certain groups in southern society. Although it did not call for black enfranchisement, it did impose such stringent loyalty requirements on southern whites that few of them could take the required oath. Essentially, this bill was suspicious of white southerners' interest in restructuring their society. Lincoln killed the bill with a pocket veto, angering many northern Republicans, hastening action on more radical plans for dealing with the South.

2.   Examine the attempt to impeach President Andrew Johnson. Explore the various reasons that Congress wanted to impeach him (both implied and expressed) and the reasons for their ultimate success or failure.

Answer: Congress, controlled by Radical Republicans, had been at odds with the president over the proper method of reconstructing southern society. Andrew Johnson had vetoed several important parts of congressional Reconstruction plans, but these vetoes were overturned. Although Johnson was ineffectual in office, he was still responsible for implementing acts of Congress.

Johnson was impeached by the House on eleven counts, most connected to his violation of the Tenure of Office Act. The real reason he was impeached was his defiance of Congress. The proceedings failed in the Senate—one vote short of the necessary two-thirds majority. Many senators voted not to convict Johnson because of their fear of his successor, Radical Republican Benjamin Wade.

3.   Examine the attempts to help the recently freed former slaves. What were the goals of the federal government for these freed men and women? How successful was the government in achieving those goals?

Answer: The Freedmen's Bureau, created by the federal government, had as its primary goal to oversee relations between former slaves and masters. This agency also issued food to 150,000 whites and blacks during 1865. Freedmen's aid societies established schools for former slaves and thereby reduced illiteracy dramatically. In addition, Congress, through the Fourteenth Amendment, began to protect the civil rights and liberties of black Americans. The Fifteenth Amendment granted black males the franchise. Other measures included disenfranchising segments of the white population, passage of laws (for example, the Ku Klux Klan Act) to stop racist attacks against blacks, and the use of federal troops to maintain order in the South.

Ultimately, many of the government's attempts to help freedmen were unsuccessful. Southern white racism toward black Americans and resistance to the presence of federal troops undermined much of the government's agenda for Reconstruction. In addition, northern racism and lack of concern for southern blacks further weakened the government's hand. Finally, the inability to attend to economic concerns adequately (redistribution of property) and political concerns (violation of Fifteenth Amendment) left the government's goals virtually unfulfilled.

4.   Examine both the achievements and failures of the Grant administration. Keeping his two terms in context with the larger political and social backdrop that was Reconstruction America, would you assert that his administration was a failure?

Answer: Although personally honest, President Ulysses Grant and his administration were plagued by scandals: the "Whiskey Ring," Credit Mobilier, and a variety of lesser, though important, scandals. Grant tended to be a supporter of radical Reconstruction, but he used his powers with restraint. He was, however, successful in breaking the power of the Klan in the Deep South. The successes of the Grant administration tended to be in two areas: foreign policy and fiscal affairs. Grant's able secretary of state, Hamilton Fish, negotiated the Washington Treaty, finally settling the Alabama claims. Also, relations with Britain over the status of Canada were resolved.

In financial issues, Grant steered the nation toward a "sound money" footing. He strongly supported the Specie Resumption Act and opposed western paper money supporters, but the long-term results of these actions have caused much debate. All in all, Grant probably was not completely up to the job of being president, and he certainly showed lapses in judgment when appointing important government officials. But his administration should be viewed within the context of the times, the so-called Gilded Age. Corruption in government and business was widespread, having much to do with the expansion of government contracts and bureaucracy during the Civil War. Even a stronger president than Grant would have found conditions formidable.

5.   Examine the election of 1876. Who were the candidates? What were the issues? What were the results?

Answer: In many ways, there was little choice between New York Democrat Samuel Tilden and Ohio Republican Rutherford B. Hayes. Both were honest politicians who strongly supported civil service reform, and both held similar views on economic and financial issues. What was striking about the election was the real potential for a Democratic victory—the first in twenty years. The election results seemed to support a Tilden victory, except for disputed returns in three southern states (the last three under federal military supervision). The votes in these states were disputed at several levels. For example, in many counties, black Republicans were prevented from voting by southern officials. In addition, Republican government officials in these states sent in returns that gave the election to Hayes. State officials sent in returns that gave the election to Tilden.

Congress was faced with determining the winner, but found that the Constitution offered no clear solution to the problem. Eventually, a fifteen-person committee (drawn from Congress and the Supreme Court), controlled by Republicans, determined Hayes to be the winner. Hayes was inaugurated, however, only after a series of compromises were worked out between northern and southern interests in 1877.

6.   Discuss the southern Democrats' attempts to limit opportunities and to control the activities of the freedmen during the Reconstruction period.

Answer: Beginning in 1865, southern state governments followed the lead of white supremacist President Andrew Johnson in establishing a Reconstruction process that excluded freedmen from the political system. None of the ex-Confederate states enfranchised blacks and all passed laws that established second-class citizenship for the freedmen. These so-called Black Codes limited job opportunities, freedom of movement, and political activities of black southerners. African Americans could not serve on juries, vote, marry outside their race, or lease land. Vigilante groups such as the Ku Klux Klan were organized to intimidate Republican Party organizers and black voters. The Klan and other similar groups terrorized freedmen who sought economic advancement or who tried to exercise the rights of citizenship. The congressionally controlled military Reconstruction system was designed to counteract ex-Confederate resistance to the Radical Republican vision of an integrated southern society.

7.   Why is the period from 1863 to 1877 called the "Reconstruction" era? Describe the conditions that existed in the post-Civil War South that necessitated a reconstruction process.

Answer: The designation of the postwar era as a period of Reconstruction is literally accurate. During the Civil War property was destroyed, traditional agricultural production was disrupted, and hundreds of thousands of people were killed or injured. The South was devastated and had to be rebuilt physically, politically, economically, and socially. Ex-Confederate state governments had to be reorganized; political ties with the union had to be re-established; and the status of approximately four million southerners (the freedmen) had to be determined. Since the antebellum southern economy was based on slave labor, emancipation necessitated the restructuring of the entire system and the establishment of a free labor workforce. Social relationships between whites and blacks also could not remain static. Southern state governments were faced with the difficult tasks of rebuilding what the war had destroyed and of creating new policies that addressed the legal and social changes that resulted from losing the war.

LONG ESSAYS

1.   One recent historian has called America's Reconstruction a "splendid failure." What do you think was meant by this statement? Evaluate the goals, successes, and failures of those who attempted to reconstruct southern society. Do you think that the historian's statement is an accurate assessment of the postwar years?

Answer: Essay should address several key points:

A.   Overview of various Reconstruction plans
     1.   Lincoln-Johnson plan
     2.   Wade-Davis plan
B.   Goals of congressional Reconstruction
     1.   Defense of civil rights of freedmen
          a.   Fourteenth Amendment
          b.   Fifteenth Amendment
     2.   Reconstruction Acts of 1867
          a.   Ten southern states under control of Congress
          b.   Impact on nation as a whole
     3.   Humanitarian goals
          a.   Freedmen's Bureau
          b.   Education
          c.   Limited attempts at property distribution
C.   Success or failure of Reconstruction
     1.   Return of white Democratic control
     2.   Mississippi Plan
          a.   Bulldozing of black vote
          b.   White control
     3.   Removal of federal troops
     4.   Election of 1876

2.   Explore the Compromise of 1877. Explain the participants in the agreement, the goals of each group, and the details of the final compromise.

Answer: Essay should address several key points:

A.   Election of 1876
     1.   Presidential candidates
     2.   Sectional support
     3.   Rebirth of the Democratic Party
     4.   Disputed election
B.   Compromise of 1877
     1.   Bipartisan commission
     2.   Demands of "Whig" South
          a.   Federal money for internal improvements
          b.   Removal of federal troops
          c.   Cabinet post
     3.   Republican Party concessions
     4.   Southern congressmen do not block Rutherford B. Hayes's election
     5.   Election of Hayes

3.   Compare southern society in 1860 with that of 1877. Describe the similarities and differences, as well as adaptations and changes that took place during the Civil War and Reconstruction years. Was the "New South" a very different place after Reconstruction than it had been before the war?

Answer: Essay should address several key points:

A.   Southern society before the war
     1.   States' rights
     2.   Social relations (slavery, plantations)
     3.   Economy: agriculture, cotton
B.   Changes in southern society: 1860–1877
     1.   Rise of racist Democratic Party
     2.   Rise of "New South"
C.   The South after Reconstruction

1.   Decline of states' rights and reintegration (political) of the South into the nation
2.   Social relations (racism, segregation)
3.   Economy
        a.   Crop lien system
        b.   Beginnings of industrialization and internal improvements

4.   The Reconstruction period is one of the eras most often portrayed in literature and films. Analyze and evaluate the accuracy of the popular conceptions of the character of southern society between 1865 and 1877 and contrast the myths with the realities of that time period.

Answer: Essay should address several key points:

A.   Myths
     1.   "Bones and banjoes conventions"
     2.   White Republicans; carpetbaggers
     3.   Africanized governments
     4.   Incompetent, abusive, corrupt policies
B.   Realities
     1.   State constitutional conventions, racial and political characteristics
     2.   Northern and southern white officeholders
     3.   Freedmen, voters and officials
     4.   Educational and political reforms, economic policies
C.   Evaluation
     1.   Negative aspects of Reconstruction
     2.   Positive aspects of Reconstruction